BOTSFORD and ROBINSON'S

HELLENIC
HISTORY FIFTH EDITION

REVISED BY

DONALD KAGAN

PROFESSOR OF HISTORY, CORNELL UNIVERSITY

THE MACMILLAN COMPANY

COLLIER-MACMILLAN LIMITED, LONDON

Earlier editions entitled *Hellenic History*, by George
Willis Botsford, copyright 1922 by The Macmillan Com-
pany; *Hellenic History*, Revised Edition, by George Willis
Botsford and Charles Alexander Robinson, Jr., copyright
1939 by The Macmillan Company. *George Willis Botsford's
Hellenic History*, Third Edition, by Charles Alexander
Robinson, Jr., copyright 1948 by The Macmillan Company.
Botsford (George Willis) and Robinson's Hellenic History,
Fourth Edition, by Charles Alexander Robinson, Jr., ©
1956 by The Macmillan Company. Copyright renewed 1949
by Athena M. Poisson. Copyright renewed 1967 by Celia
S. Robinson, Charles A. Robinson, III, Samuel S. Robin-
son, and Franklin W. Robinson.

Library of Congress catalog card number: 69–15096

THE MACMILLAN COMPANY
866 THIRD AVENUE, NEW YORK, NEW YORK 10022
Collier-Macmillan Canada, Ltd., Toronto, Ontario

Printed in the United States of America

PRINTING   5678910   YEAR   3456789

BOTSFORD and ROBINSON'S

HELLENIC
HISTORY

PREFACE TO THE FIFTH EDITION

I T is a sad privilege to undertake the revision of Botsford and Robinson's *Hellenic History:* a privilege because of the book's fine reputation and because of my respect for my teacher, C. A. Robinson, Jr., sad because of his death in 1965. The fundamental character of the book remains very much the work of Botsford and Robinson. The most significant changes may be found in the chapter on the Bronze Age (where note has been taken of the new theories evolved by Professor Leonard Palmer); in the sections on the politics of fifth-century Athens; and especially in the chapter on the origins of the

Peloponnesian War, where I have allowed my own ideas to appear. I have tampered little with the interpretation of the career of Alexander the Great, but Professor Ernst Badian's view of the Philotas affair was too persuasive to ignore.

New photographs have been introduced. New endpaper maps have also been incorporated. The entire bibliography has been revised, with a prominent place given to scholarly works written since World War II.

D. K.

Ithaca, New York

PREFACE TO
THE FOURTH EDITION

WHEN the third edition (1948) was reprinted in 1950, various changes were made in the text; a two-page map and a photograph were added. Further changes have been made throughout the text of this edition, nine new photographs have been added, and several substitutions for older photographs have been made. There are now one hundred and fourteen plates (some of these have necessarily been lettered rather than numbered separately) containing one hundred and twenty-four photographs. The photographs are intended to elucidate the text and carry an understanding of it further. I have tried to present a rounded picture of Greece, not only through photographs of the major arts of architecture and sculpture, but also by means of photographs showing fortifications, scenery, public and private antiquities, fifteen vases, sixty-three coins, and so on. There are sixty-three maps and diagrams, a few of them being substitutions for those previously reproduced. The chief textural change is the chapter on the Bronze Age, which has been rewritten.

The main reason for a new edition at this time is, of course, the discovery of inscribed tablets of the Bronze Age at Pylos and Mycenae by, respectively, Carl W. Blegen of the University of Cincinnati and Alan J. B. Wace of Cambridge University and the Institute for Advanced Study at Princeton, together with Michael Ventris' extraordinary accomplishment in deciphering them and proving them to be written in an early form of Greek. These achievements, coupled with recent research on the Bronze Age in general, have made our knowledge of the period clearer and in many fundamentals different from what we had previously supposed.

I find it impossible to thank Professor Wace adequately for the help he has generously given me, both by correspondence and in conference. He kindly sent me an advance copy of his manuscript on "The Coming of the Greeks," which was subsequently published in *Classical Weekly* for March 22, 1954; and a copy of his article, "The History of Greece in the Third and Second Millenniums B.C.," *Historia,* 1953 (with an excellent bibliography). I have drawn freely on both, as well as on his great *Mycenae,* Princeton, 1949. Professor Wace has also given me the detailed photograph, by T. Leslie Shear, Jr., of the Lion Gate at Mycenae. Both Professor and Mrs. Wace have read the manuscript of my new chapter and have made many valuable suggestions; I extend to them my warmest thanks. It is also a duty and privilege to thank Professor Blegen for much kind help, for copies of his articles on Pylos in *Archaeology,* 1952, and *American Journal of Archaelogy,* 1953 and 1954. I have also drawn on his great *Troy,* which is being published by Princeton University Press. I thank Professor Sterling Dow, Harvard University, for his help, especially for his article, "Minoan Writing," in *American Journal of Archaeology,* 1954. I owe much to M. Ventris' and J. Chadwick's crucial article, "Evidence for Greek Dialect in the Mycenaean Archives," *Journal of Hellenic Studies,* 1953; M. Ventris' "King Nestor's Four-Handled Cups," *Archaeology,* 1954; J. D. S. Pendlebury's fundamental *The Archaeology of Crete,* London, 1939; E. J. Forsdyke's charming "Minoan Art," *Proceedings of the British Academy,* XV; E. Bell's *Prehellenic Architecture in the Aegean,* London, 1926; M. P. Nilsson's *Homer and Mycenae,* London, 1933; H. J. Kantor's *The Aegean and the Orient in the Second Millennium B. C.,* Bloomington, 1947; E. L. Bennett, Jr.'s *The Pylos Tablets,* Princeton, 1951; and, of course, to Sir Arthur Evans' monumental *The Palace of Minos at Knossos,* 4 vols., London, 1921–35.

The completion of large-scale excavation in Athens, by the American School of Classical Studies, makes it appropriate at this time to devote extended remarks to the Agora, but I have placed them in an Appendix, in order not to interrupt the text unduly. I am under the heaviest obligations to the Field Director of the excavations, Professor Homer A. Thompson of the Institute for Advanced Study at Princeton. He gave me an advance copy of the manuscript of *The Athenian Agora: A Guide to the Excavations* by Mabel Lang and C. W. J. Eliot (now published; Athens, 1954). I have drawn freely on it. Professor Thompson has also very kindly read the manuscript of my Appendix and provided me with the new plan of the Agora, which he has now published in *Hesperia,* 1955. . . . Miss Lucy T. Shoe, Institute for Advanced Study, has kindly helped me on several occasions. The American

School of Classical Studies at Athens, through its office in Princeton, New Jersey, continues to publish specialized articles in its journal, *Hesperia,* but it is now also issuing definitive volumes on the Agora. Though further information is given in the Bibliography, I may add that the Archaeological Institute of America now publishes, in addition to the *American Journal of Archaeology,* the popular magazine, *Archaeology.* . . . I thank very especially Professor Rhys Carpenter of Bryn Mawr College for his encouragement and help. I also gratefully acknowledge help from Professors D. A. Amyx, University of California, M. Bieber, Columbia University, M. Cary, University of London, Jotham Johnson, New York University, J. A. O. Larsen, University of Chicago, T. Means, Bowdoin College, G. E. Mylonas, Washington University, A. D. Nock, Harvard University, L. A. Post, Haverford College, W. T. Radius, Calvin College, J. R. Workman, Brown University, and, above all, from Celia Robinson, my wife.

C. A. ROBINSON, JR.

Providence, Rhode Island

PREFACE TO
THE THIRD EDITION

I N THE reprinted edition of 1946 various changes were made in the body of the text. A good many more have been made in this edition, several chapters have been enlarged, and the chapters on the Persian Wars, the Peloponnesian War, and Alexander the Great have been rewritten. The bibliography has been brought up to date, a chronological table, a glossary, and a list of recommended reading in Greek literature have been added. I have included all the former illustrations, although a new plan has been substituted for the Athenian Agora and corrections have been made on certain maps. Of the thirty-eight maps and insets, fifteen are new; of the nineteen figures in the text, ten are new; and of the one hundred and seven plates (eight of which are lettered as well as numbered, because at the last moment it was possible to give a full page to each of the subjects), thirty-five are new. I am grateful to The Macmillan Company for its co-operation and help.

It is a pleasure, as well as a duty, to express my thanks to many friends for their help in connection with this edition, and in particular to Alfred R. Bellinger, Oscar Broneer, Howard Comfort, William B. Dinsmoor, Sterling Dow, Charles Edson, Clark Hopkins, A. G. M. Little, Louis E. Lord, Stephen B. Luce, Benjamin D. Meritt, L. A. Post, Oscar W. Reinmuth, Gisela M. A. Richter, David M. Robinson, Lucy Talcott, W. W. Tarn, Homer A. Thompson; and I desire also to acknowledge my general obligation to the reviewers of the 1939 edition. . . . Dr. Erwin Raisz of the Institute of Geographical Exploration, Harvard University, has drawn or redrawn the new maps and the plans of temples and orders of architecture; Mr. John Alcott of the Rhode Island School of Design has redrawn the remaining figures in the text. To both these gentlemen I express my hearty thanks. Professor Henry B. Van Hoesen, Librarian of Brown University, has helped me in many ways. The chapter on Alexander is based in part on my *Alexander the Great* (New York, 1947), by permission of E. P. Dutton and Company. Without the encouragement of my wife I would not have undertaken this revision at this time. Finally, I would mention the great kindness and skill of Mrs. James J. Fine, who once again has typed my manuscript and helped with the proofs.

C. A. ROBINSON, JR.

Providence, Rhode Island

PREFACE TO
THE REVISED EDITION

THE *Hellenic History* was first published in 1922 after Professor
Botsford's death, having been seen through the press by his son,
the late Professor Jay Barrett Botsford of Brown University.
The present edition was decided upon in 1936. Several chapters are
entirely new; in each of the remaining chapters some passages are new,
while many other passages are the same as in the first edition, except
for such revision or rearrangement as seemed necessary.

It is impossible in a work of this kind to make detailed acknowledg-
ments, but it will be obvious to any one familiar with the subject that
I have drawn upon the researches of others. Some of the books which I
have found most useful are mentioned in the bibliography, but to the
list should be added articles, reviews, and reports. It is a duty, then, as
well as a pleasure, to record my debt here. Certain specific acknowl-
edgments, however, I may make. I am very grateful to my friend and
colleague, Professor B. C. Clough, for reading the manuscript and for
much else besides. I am also grateful to Professor B. D. Meritt of the
Institute for Advanced Study, who has read the manuscript; to Professor C. W. Blegen of the University of Cincinnati, who has read the
chapter on the Bronze Age; and to Professor W. S. Ferguson of Harvard University, who has read the chapter on Alexander.

Professor Edward Capps and Professor T. L. Shear of Princeton
University have given me permission to use material in *Hesperia*. Specific acknowledgment is made in the list of illustrations to various
presses for permission to reproduce material. The maps have been
drawn by Dr. Erwin Raisz of the Institute of Geographical Exploration, Harvard University. All the coins that are illustrated are in the
Museum of the American Numismatic Society. I am very grateful to

the President of the Society, Dr. E. T. Newell, and to the Secretary, Mr. S. P. Noe, for help in the selection of the coins. Mr. G. P. Stevens, Director-elect of the American School of Classical Studies at Athens, has given me prints of his study of the Periclean entrance court of the Acropolis and of his new study of the Parthenon. From the Hellenic Society of London I have received photographs of the cup-bearer fresco, the Mycenaean daggers, and the temple at Sunium; from Miss G. M. A. Richter, Curator of Classical Art in the Metropolitan Museum, the photograph of the Dipylon amphora; from Professor Richard Stillwell of Princeton University the photograph of the palace of Minos; from Mr. P. B. Cott, Associate Curator of the Worcester Art Museum, the photograph of the Antioch mosaic; from Professor Blegen the photograph of the Parthenon; from Professor Meritt the photograph of the list of Athenian tributaries; and from Professor Shear the photographs of the excavations in the Athenian Agora and of the ostraca from the Agora. For all the remaining photographs I owe a debt of gratitude to Professor P. J. Sachs, Director, and to Miss E. L. Lucas, Librarian, of the Fogg Art Museum, Harvard University. Professor H. B. Van Hoesen, Librarian of Brown University, has helped me in many ways. The Index has been prepared by my colleague, Mr. J. H. Monroe. My deepest debt of all, to Celia Sachs Robinson, must remain, save for this brief mention, unexpressed.

The gold coin of Syracuse on the cover is enlarged two and a half diameters and is from the dies cut by the famous engravers Cimon and Euaenetus (413 B.C.); it depicts Heracles struggling with the lion and symbolizes the triumph of Greek genius over brute force. The system of transliteration of the Greek words in the text is that suggested by the Council of the Hellenic Society.

C. A. ROBINSON, JR.

Providence, Rhode Island

CONTENTS

MAPS AND DIAGRAMS

Chapter I

INTRODUCTION

G REECE is a small mountainous peninsula (some 45,000 square miles in area) with a long seacoast, formed by countless inlets and bays and provided, especially on the east, with many harbors adequate for the boats of antiquity. Everywhere there are plains, some of considerable size, but these are hemmed in by ranges of mountains, which generally do not come to a peak. Mountain ·passes, as we understand them, are not common, and to go from one plain or valley to the next is difficult. These mountains are part of the great Pindus range, thrust southward by the Balkan mountains of eastern Europe. The Greeks were of course profoundly influenced, as any people must be, by the land in which they lived, and these barriers to travel and communication were destined to play a leading role in Greek life. It is easy to understand, for example, that a nation or empire will not at once develop naturally in such a land, but that a smaller political unit (the *polis* or city-state), centering in the chief town of each valley, will be characteristic. The beautiful manifestation of the human spirit known as Hellenism, or Greek civilization, developed, through many centuries, in just such small states.

The historian must ask how far geography helps to explain Greek history: its particularism and local rivalries. The geography of the country tends to divide rather than unite and, thus, goes far toward explaining why the Greeks, unlike the Romans, could not bring unity to their peninsula. Both geography and past experience gave to the Greek character an unyielding quality that made it difficult for the city-states to combine into larger and more stable units of government. Intense local patriotism, responsibility, and love of liberty engendered a fearlessness which in time of war produced good fighters and in time of peace produced a restless, inquisitive spirit willing to experiment. This was not universally true, for mountain ranges and a minimum of harbors in Aetolia, Epirus, and the northwest, generally, made progress there slow, whereas in Thebes and Sparta special conditions were responsible for conservatism. Strictly speaking, then, there was no typical Greek.

Certain characteristics, however, do seem typical. Moderation, self-restraint, and an eagerness to know oneself, all of which were ideals of the Greek, may explain why it was that the scientific spirit first emerged in Greece. Love of truth for its own sake and a passionate devotion to reason constitute our closest link with the Greeks. They bequeathed to posterity profound and sensible thought, noble poetry, and beautiful art. Perhaps it is well for us to be reminded of the fact that these great achievements of the mind and spirit were the work of a people who had none of our scientific instruments and few of our comforts. These particular achievements are a delight to the mind and eye; they are timeless and must be constantly relived, so that through a study of them one is in a better position not only to understand and to correct his own civilization, but to get his bearings for the future as well. The Greeks were also the first people in Europe to evolve the ideal of free democracy, and they still have valuable lessons for us in the field of government.

We have many things in common, then, with the ancient Greeks; but this is not surprising, because our civilization, through the medium of Rome, is founded on theirs. It is also a fact, however, that there are many differences between their civilization and ours and that these may teach even more than the point of similarity, just as their failures may have a greater lesson for us than their successes. It has been truly remarked that in a sense the *polis* is simply our own civilization in

GREECE

Landforms

Miles
0 — 80

- Karst
- High complex mountains
- Crystalline uplands
- Alluvium

IONIAN SEA

AEGEAN SEA

CANDAVIAN MTS.
L. Lychnites
MT. TOMARUS
Aous R.
MT. BORA
MT. BERMIUS
MT. TYMPHE
MT. BARNUS
Haliacmon
Axius R.
Strymon
MT. ORBELUS
Nestus R.
MT. PANGAEUS
MT. ATHOS
MT. OLYMPUS
Peneus
MT. OSSA
MT. PELION
PINDUS MTS.
TZOUMERKA
OTHRYS MTS.
MT. DIRPHYS
PARNASSOS MT.
MT. HELICON
MT. PARNES
MT. AENUS
MT. CYLLENE
Alpheus
PARNON MT.
Eurotas
TAYGETUS MT.
MT. LEUCA
MT. IDA

Map 2

3

miniature, that Greek history portrays the birth, growth, and decay of a civilized society which we are able to understand; yet in many ways their civilization was wholly different from our own. Our broad general problem is to study these people who were of mixed origin and speech, and who were full of contradictions and paradoxes. We shall do well to look further at their homeland.

To describe the Balkan peninsula, as we have done, as mountainous and as washed everywhere by the sea does it scant justice, for Greece is a beautiful and a varied country. Oranges grow in the subtropical south. Olive groves and vineyards cover the countryside. In the spring, blood-red anemones, pale hyacinths, and a profusion of other wild flowers are a riot of color, softened by the blossoms of the almond trees. In summer it is hot; in winter, during the prolonged rainy season, cold and wet. The changes in the seasons make for activity, though in general the mild, subtropical climate, although not enervating, renders life far easier than in the temperate zones. On the Mediterranean shores men need less food, clothing, and shelter. They live more in the open air in social contact with one another. Thus their struggle for existence is not all-absorbing; they have more leisure to devote to thought and to the creation of the adornments of life and more opportunity for discussion, for the interchange and clarification of ideas. The simplicity of modern Greece (not unlike that of ancient days) strikes the Westerner most, perhaps, when he visits the country. Instead of a busy industrial civilization he finds a quiet agricultural life. Directness and naturalness have taken the place of specialization and professionalism. Most of the people are peasants, living in villages, in small houses often built of sun-dried brick. The day is hard, spent among the fields or tending the sheep and goats, for the soil is not fertile enough to support large herds of cows. Meat is rarely eaten, though fish is popular. Travel, until recently, was by mule-pack. The charm of the country lies in the simplicity of the life, in the peacock-blue sea (the wine-dark sea as Homer calls it), and in the mountains which change in color, with the brilliance of the sun, from russet to violet. Stunted firs grow on the mountains; otherwise they are apt to be bare of timber, and the rocks glare in the sun. The sharp clear outlines of these mountains undoubtedly influenced the Greek sculptors of antiquity. On the other hand, the poverty of animal and vegetable products and the scarcity of minerals forced the ancient Greeks to colonization and commerce, which still further stimulated their intelligence and enterprise, but tended even more to decentralization.

This beautiful and storied land consists of various districts. In the north are Thrace, Macedonia, and Epirus, bounded today by Turkey,

Bulgaria, Yugoslavia, and Albania. Macedonia is large and compact. Mt. Olympus, the home of the gods, rising to a height of almost 10,000 feet, separates Macedonia from the broad fertile plains of Thessaly. Here is one of the largest rivers in Greece, the Peneus, though it is hardly navigable beyond its mouth. Greek rivers are small and frequently dry, except after a sudden rain when they become rushing torrents. Central Greece includes Boetia, with its great city of Thebes, and Phocis, where the oracle of Delphi, perched high on Mt. Parnassus, the dwelling place of the Muses, looks down on the Corinthian Gulf and across to the Peloponnesus. Attica is divided from Boeotia by Cithaeron and Parnes, though the ring of mountains continues to the east and south in Pentelicus, famed for its marble, and Hymettus, equally famous for its honey. The wonderful clay fields here made possible the potter's trade. Amid the olive groves and vineyards of the Attic plain rises the broad flat rock known as the citadel or acropolis of Athens, and four miles beyond are the ancient harbors of Phaleron and Piraeus. Here, of course, lived the most brilliant of all the Greeks, the Athenians, nimble-witted, radical and inventive, and yet in some matters strangely conservative. The Peloponnesus, to the south, is connected with central Greece by the Isthmus of Corinth, now cut by a canal. In earliest times the most famous section was the Argolid, in the northeast, where Mycenae and Tiryns produced a mighty civilization. Land-locked Arcadia, where strawberry and oak trees grow in the lowlands and firs on the higher slopes of the mountains, is particularly isolated. To the south is Laconia, home of Athens' rival Sparta, located in the pleasant valley of the Eurotas and separated from Messenia by Taÿgetus, which, like so many mountains in Greece, is snow-covered except in the hottest months. To the northwest is Olympia, in Elis, where the famous games were held.

This country, hill and plain, northern and subtropical, is not so much a part of Europe as of the Mediterranean basin. Connected with Europe, it was destined of course to receive waves of invaders from the north, though, be it added, Greece has generally succeeded in moulding newcomers to her ways. Some remains of Palaeolithic man have been discovered in Greece, but we can understand that when the Neolithic or New Stone Age, with its discovery of agriculture and breeding, pottery and textiles, dawned throughout Europe, mankind was ready for significant progress. Man develops most rapidly, however, under the stimulus of new ideas, and because northern and western Europe were relatively isolated and long retained their Neolithic culture, we find that Greece outstrips the rest of Europe. This was due, as intimated above, to the fact that southern Greece juts far into the Mediterranean, in the direction of the ancient civilizations of Asia and Egypt. Inevitably the island of Crete, the large island which blocks off the Aegean Sea from the Mediterranean, fell under important influences, which led to the brilliant Bronze Age of Greece. This civilization was shared not only by Crete and the mainland, but also by the islands of the Aegean Sea, especially those known as the Cyclades, encircling the sacred island of Delos, and to a lesser extent by the opposite coast of Asia Minor, in the northwest corner of which lay Troy. In speaking of the physical characteristics of the mainland, we noted the extraordinary division of the country into littoral and hinterland and the difficulty of communication by land. This was largely compensated for, however, by the sea and its many islands, which always invited sailors to explore beyond the horizon. The Aegean area, then, was a natural unit and in later times the Ionian islands, off the west coast of Greece, were in their turn to expedite trade and travel to Sicily, Italy, and the West.

Our knowledge of ancient Greece comes principally from written records. Those that have come down to us represent, of course, but a small fraction of the original total. Their preservation is due in part to the fact that the Roman Empire largely adopted Greek culture, and in part to the labors of monks, who through the Middle Ages kept learning alive. A problem of the historian is properly to evaluate these ancient writings, just as it is the reader's duty to be on his guard against conclusions drawn by the historian. The fragmentary character and restricted scope of the available evidence are part of the charm of studying Greek history, but caution must ever be the watchword. In recent years, however, our knowledge has been immeasurably increased by the archaeologist's spade. Documents, buildings, statues, utensils, stones inscribed with decrees, treaties and the like, are multiplied yearly by many excavations in various lands. Not only do they add to our knowledge, but they also unsettle previous opinions which we had considered to be true and they open up new and unsuspected vistas as well. Archaeology's chief contribution is an enrichment of our knowledge of the social life of the ancients, but when all is said and done it cannot hope to do more than supplement the written records. This is true, however, only of classical Greece. Within recent years a new and great Bronze Age civilization in Greece has come to light. Though documents have been discovered in excavataions and are being deciphered, the chief things we have to go by are the objects made by the hand of man, and consequently for the preclassical period archaeology is history.

It had previously been thought that the history of Greece, and with it the history of Europe, began about 1100 B.C., when rude iron-possessing Greeks invaded and settled in the Aegean area. The moving epics of

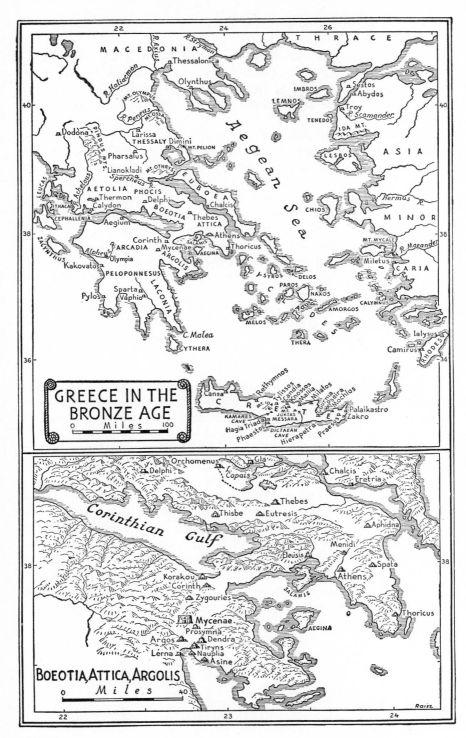

GREECE IN THE BRONZE AGE
0 Miles 100

BOEOTIA, ATTICA, ARGOLIS
0 Miles 40

Map 4

7

Homer, to be sure, echoed an earlier period, but they were regarded as legends. History began with the Iron Age and the Greeks. In 1870, however, a merchant prince of Germany, named Schliemann, realized a childhood ambition by excavating at Troy. Though he made many mistakes, for archaeology was then in its infancy, Schliemann showed by his excavations at Troy and later on the Greek mainland at Mycenae and elsewhere that he had discovered a new and wholly unsuspected civilization. The work was continued at Knossos in Crete by Sir Arthur Evans, whose explorations began in 1900; others now conduct them. This is among the most important of all excavations in Greek lands, not simply because of its chronological significance, but because of the amazing beauty and the quantity of the finds. A richer civilization than even Homer dreamed of had been found. This was a civilization where bronze was the chief metal, and it existed for 2,000 years before the beginning of the Iron Age; as we now know, the Bronze Age itself was preceded by a lengthy period of Neolithic culture. Although it is thrilling to contemplate our discovery of this Bronze Age, so wonderful in itself and so important for the contributions it made to classical Greece, it is a little disturbing to reflect that all knowledge of it had passed from man's mind for some 3,000 years.

Finally, it should be remarked here that man, in ancient times, as generally now in the Near East, built his house of sun-dried brick on a foundation of field stones. With the passage of time these bricks disintegrated into earth again, and instead of the debris being carried away, the old house was leveled off and a new one built on top of the debris. Thus a mound might rise, and in the various layers houses, palaces, jewelry, and other objects might be buried. Pottery in great quantities, because baked clay pots were an ordinary household article, is always found on ancient sites, generally in broken fragments called potsherds, which enable us to give relative dates to all the other objects. By a careful study of the pottery, the fabric and decoration, and the strata in which it is found, as well as by comparison with ·other sites, a relative and fairly accurate dating has been worked out for it and thus for all the objects found with it. The presence of Egyptian objects in Crete, and vice versa, enables us, with the help of the Egyptian calendar, to speak approximately in terms of years B.C.

Chapter II # THE
BRONZE AGE

THE Bronze Age of Greece is one of the most fascinating episodes in the history of man. The fascination doubtless lies partly in its very antiquity, partly in its legendary and romantic setting, partly, too, in its dramatic discovery. Heinrich Schliemann was an amateur, of course, a successful businessman turned archaeologist, but as the father of the science of excavation he had the great good fortune to uncover a remarkable civilization. Ever since his day, scholars in many lands, through study and further excavation, have labored to bring this civilization into sharper focus.

As we observed in the previous chapter, one of these scholars was Sir Arthur Evans, whose professional career was spent in Crete. At the end of the nineteenth century he bought a tract of land—grain and olive groves were growing on it then—at a spot near the north coast of Crete called Knossos (Cnossus). According to legend King Minos kept a monster—half bull and half man—the Minotaur, in a vast stable or labyrinth there. Evans found in his excavations, instead of a labyrinth, a tremendous palace. It is interesting to note in passing, because it shows how legend can preserve a kernel of truth, that the Palace of Minos is decorated in various places with signs depicting a double axe. The Greek word for *double axe* is *labrys,* a word of non-Greek origin adopted from earlier inhabitants. We can see that this word, used to describe a common sign on a huge building, might in time, as in fact it did, take on its present meaning. Another kernel of historical truth may be preserved in the famous legend that each year the people of Athens had to send seven youths and seven maids to Crete to be devoured by the Minotaur, until finally the Athenian hero, Theseus, brought the shameful business to an end. The story may indicate that once upon a time Athens (and much of mainland Greece) was under strong Cretan influence. It also serves to remind us that myths and legends can occasionally be of limited use to the historian.

Whether King Minos ever actually lived we may never know, but Evans took the adjectival form of his name, Minoan, to describe Cretan civilization of the Bronze Age. The civilization of contemporary mainland Greece, even though it fell under the influence of Knossos, was in many ways different from the Cretan, and the word *Helladic* (derived from Hellas, Greece) has been invented for its designation. When, therefore, we speak of the Bronze Age, we are able to be quite specific and use the word *Minoan* for the Cretan phase, and the word *Helladic* for the mainland phase. Those islands of the Aegean Sea which make a circle around the sacred isle of Delos, and consequently are known as the Cyclades, had certain characteristics of their own during the Bronze Age, and as a result their remains are referred to as Cycladic. Other islands of the Aegean, such as Rhodes, the coasts of Asia Minor (in the northwest corner of which was located Troy), Syria, Palestine, and Egypt came with varying degrees of intensity into the orbit of our Bronze Age civilization, as indeed did the western Mediterranean, especially Sicily and southern Italy.

We shall probably never know the extent and intimacy of the relations between the various states of the ancient Near East, at any rate not until further excavations have been conducted in Hither Asia. Not so long ago the Hittite records were made to yield their secrets, and although some philologists do not yet agree, it seems certain that the Trojans, Achaeans, and Atreus are mentioned in them. Recent excavations, however, at Ras Shamra (the ancient Ugarit) on the Syrian coast reveal strong Mycenaean influences mingling with the Sumerian. Late in 1954 English excavators discovered the long-lost Arzawa Empire in

Asia Minor and found that Aegean influence was particularly strong there. The Near East in the second millennium before Christ was an exciting world, full of powerful states whose rulers made war upon one another, corresponded with each other, intermarried, drew up treaties, and occasionally enjoyed long periods of peace. The reaction of various cultures upon one another is almost as thrilling to watch as the state of our knowledge is exasperating.

Obviously it has been a tremendous undertaking to recover and interpret the civilization of the Bronze Age of Greece, and the task is not nearly finished. For example, when Schliemann completed his excavations on the mainland—especially at Mycenae and Tiryns—other scholars continued at the same sites and elsewhere. Notable among these may be mentioned the Greek scholar Chr. Tsountas, the English archaeologist Alan J. B. Wace of Cambridge University, and the American Carl W. Blegen of the University of Cincinnati. Mycenae has taken on new and significant meaning through the recent excavations of Wace, as have Troy and Pylos through those of Blegen.

We should also say that until very recently archaeology has provided our sole evidence for the period. In other words, no inscribed tablets could be referred to the mainland—the oldest written record of any kind was supposed to be the Greek inscription on a vase from the cemetery at Athens. Its date is about 750 B.C., and it says, "The dancer who performs best shall receive this." Accordingly, the mainland civilization of the Bronze Age was known as prehistoric. The Minoan civilization was also called prehistoric, for although Evans had found about 2,000 inscribed tablets at Knossos, they could not be read and understood. It is exciting to observe, first, that Blegen has now discovered at Pylos about a thousand tablets written in a script derived from Crete (Figure 1), and Wace has found others at Mycenae; and, next, as the twentieth century passed into its second half, that an English architect—another amateur like Schliemann—succeeded in breaking the secret of the mainland tablets. This is Michael Ventris, and his work must be compared with that of the other pioneers of decipherment, Champollion, Rawlinson, Grotefend, Sayce, and George Smith. That is to say, when the third edition of this book was published in 1948, this particular chapter was out of date, and in some respects incorrect, practically on the day of publication. It is now certain, for example, that the Greeks entered their historic mainland home about 1900 B.C., some eight centuries earlier than we had previously known; they spoke and wrote an early form of Greek, as Ventris and his fellow workers have discovered; the great civilization of Mycenae, therefore, was Greek—not "pre-Greek"—the first manifestation of the Greek genius; finally, the Mycenaean Greeks for a time at least actually controlled Knossos, an important and until recently wholly unsuspected fact.

It is a little cumbersome, however, to speak of the "Mycenaean" Greeks; it can be inexact, too, because "Mycenaean" tends to limit the people to Mycenae, whereas in fact the Greeks were spread throughout the mainland after 1900 B.C. Just the same, it is essential—because labels do help—to differentiate these very early Greeks from their descendants of classical times. As a rule, therefore, when we speak in general terms of the early Greeks we shall not call them Mycenaean Greeks, but Achaeans. There is some evidence, in fact, that this is what they were actually called; at any rate, it is a name applied by Homer to the mainland invaders of Troy.

But if the Bronze Age represents one of the most fascinating and romantic episodes in man's history, it was also of great length (some 2,000 years) and, at certain moments, of startling sophistication and a high degree of exquisite taste. In a word, it is of the first importance, both in its own right and as a forerunner to classical Greece.

A moment's reflection will convince the reader that any period lasting as long as the Bronze Age must have gone through various phases of evolution, to which we in our turn must attach convenient labels of identification. That is why we speak of the Early, Middle, and Late Bronze Age or, as already explained, of its chief phases such as Early or Middle Helladic, Early or Middle Minoan, and so on. The cultures of all these phases in the main areas of the Aegean—Helladic, Minoan, Cycladic, Trojan—are akin to one another and taken together form, of course, the Bronze Age. The individual phases, or sequences, are clear, but the points of contact of one sequence with another are not always clear. For example, it is not possible to say certainly that the beginning of Middle Minoan is contemporary with the beginning of Middle Helladic; indeed, Middle Minoan itself begins at different dates in east, central, and south Crete. Obviously, early communities did not enter a new stage of development everywhere simultaneously. For absolute dates, the chronological equations must ultimately be derived from Egyptian and Babylonian chronology (which have their own difficulties); Cappadocian tablets and Hittite records provide some help.[1]

---

[1] The Early, Middle, and Late Bronze Age—in its chief phases, the Minoan and Helladic—can be broken down into many subdivisions. The approximate dates, which must of course be regarded as provisional, of the main subdivisions are as follows:

Early Minoan, 2900–2100.   Early Helladic, 2900–1900.
Middle Minoan I, 2100–1900.   Middle Helladic, 1900–1580.

THE NEOLITHIC AGE

People lived in what we call Greece long before the Bronze Age. Though some remains have been found of the Paleolithic or Old Stone Age, very considerable remains of the Neolithic or New Stone Age exist. We do not know the origin of the Neolithic people on the mainland—there is no apparent connection between them and those of Crete—and must content ourselves by saying that they were about as indigenous as any people can be. At all events, they reached their new homes some centuries before 4000 B.C.

It used to be thought that the Neolithic population came to the mainland from the north, but there is no evidence for this. Instead, it is clear that the Neolithic culture of the mainland actually spread northward from Dimini and other Thessalian sites to Macedonia, Moesia, and Thrace (modern Yugoslavia and Bulgaria); in general, into the areas south of the main Balkan ranges, but apparently not north of the Danube.

The Neolithic Age marked a new epoch in the development of man-

---

Middle Minoan II, 1900–1750.
Middle Minoan III, 1750–1600.
Late Minoan I, 1600–1500.   Late Helladic I, 1580–1500.
Late Minoan II, 1500–1400.   Late Helladic II, 1500–1425.
Late Minoan III, 1400–1150.   Late Helladic III, 1425–1150.

The civilization of Crete reached its height at Knossos in Middle Minoan III and Late Minoan I; on the mainland the peak was reached in the Late Helladic Period at Mycenae, which thereafter dominated the eastern Mediterranean. The table above represents only two real breaks in cultural development. The first occurred at the opening of the Early Helladic Period soon after 3000 B.C. with the arrival of non-Indo-Europeans in the Neolithic mainland; the second, at the opening of the Middle Helladic Period in 1900 B.C. This latter break marks the entrance of the first Greeks to arrive in what we call mainland Greece; it was the last time in antiquity that a new racial factor entered Greece. Though the people of the mainland from the opening of the Middle Helladic Period were Greeks— we use Homer's term, Achaeans, to differentiate them from the Greeks of the period after 1100 B.C.—it was the lot of another branch of the Greek people, the Dorians, to bring the Bronze Age to an end about 1100 B.C. Modern historians have invented the phrase, "Dorian Invasion," to describe this episode, and perhaps it is a convenient label, but the classical Greeks spoke of it as the "Return of the Heracleidae," certain Greeks who came with their Dorian supporters to reclaim their heritage. At all events, it produced a political upheaval in Greece, but no violent break in the cultural development. It also coincided with the beginning of the Iron Age, in which presumably we still live; the three and a half centuries immediately after 1100 B.C. form a bridge—a so-called Middle Age—between the Bronze Age and the great classical.

kind. Hitherto, in the Paleolithic Age, man had been more or less at the mercy of nature. The old-time flint-axe, for example, was too brittle to chop much wood; now, in the new Age, the axes, knives, hammers, chisels, and hoes were ground and polished on a whetstone, and the ground stone axe led to carpentry. The significant new fact about the Neolithic Age, however, does not consist of the different treatment of the stone tools—the terminology would suggest this, for it is a long-established, conventional one—but of the discovery of agriculture and herding. It took man hundreds of thousands of years to learn to produce his food, so we must be careful not to minimize the importance of this discovery. Once you had learned to plant seeds, however, you naturally wished a harvest, and this meant that you had to abandon a nomadic life and remain in the same place. This inevitably led to the concept of property—at least to family or community holdings—and at the same time there arose the need of rules to regulate conflicting claims and interests. Someone had to settle disputes and administer things in general, and because a fertile community was eyed enviously by others, it was only natural to select one person, probably the smartest, as the leader.

In a word, the development of agriculture made life more complex. Man learned to cultivate not only wheat and barley, but also oats, rye, millet, lentils, fruit trees, olives, and grapes. The domestication of the ox, sheep, goat, pig, and other animals provided people with meat, clothing, and fat for fuel. At the same time, the plow was invented. The more certain and larger food supply caused a great and sudden increase in population and permitted men to pursue different careers. Though Neolithic communities were able to get on with very little specialization, not everyone needed to be a farmer. Some men made tools, others became shepherds or hunters of deer and wild boars. Still others made pottery. Textiles represent another major discovery of the Neolithic Age; the ability to spin and weave flax and wool meant better clothing, baskets, and fish nets.

The many mounds in the plains of the mainland suggest a large population for Neolithic Greece, and this is confirmed by excavations at Dimini, Lianokladi, Orchomenos, and other sites. Intellectual life was, of course, not far advanced, but the marble, stone, and clay statuettes prove that there was some kind of primitive religion. Most of the statuettes are female and probably represent the cult of a Great Mother. A very considerable trade by sea also grew up, for knives of obsidian are frequently found, and we know that this volcanic stone came from the island of Melos.

The architecture of the small houses is not impressive, though they do display a feeling for a definite plan. On the other hand, much of the pottery is beautiful. At first, of course, it was crude, and during the entire age it was shaped by hand, for the invention of the potter's wheel was to occur in the succeeding Bronze Age. Gradually, however, finer shapes and texture were obtained, especially after it was learned that it was better to bake a pot in an oven than in an open fire. Because clay is plastic, it can be modeled in any form and gives us an idea of the potter's sense of shape and line, just as the decorations reveal his imagination and feeling for color; incidentally, a variety of shapes testifies to the varied needs of the day and the ability to satisfy them. Some of the earliest Thessalian pottery consists of a beautiful, polished red monochrome of excellent fabric, while other Thessalian pots, made red by firing, had white linear ornaments added. Or, again, the pot might be given a white slip as a ground for red designs. So much for the First Neolithic period of Greece. In the Second Neolithic period, which was much shorter, the pottery is ornamented with a mixture of spiral and linear patterns in deep brown on a pale buff ground (popularly known as chocolate on cream ware). This style is called Dimini Ware after the Thessalian site where it was first discovered. Sometimes the patterns are in three colors, black-brown, red, and white. Frequently the patterns are incised and filled with a white substance.

Neolithic finds on the Cyclades are as yet rare, but in Crete they are abundant. For example, the Neolithic deposit is 25 feet thick beneath the floors of the Palace of Minos at Knossos. Other remains have been found in the eastern end of the island as well as at Phaestus and in the neighboring plain of Messara. The settlements resemble rather scattered farms and are at a distance from the coast. Apparently the people feared pirates, and yet the presence of Egyptian artifacts testifies to trade by sea. A few houses have been found at Knossos, Phaestus, and elsewhere, but many of the people lived in caves. The whole culture seems to have been much more primitive than on the mainland. The hand-made pottery is thick and generally undecorated, though there may be incised and rippled patterns. Not infrequently incised geometrical decorations were employed, and at a later period the lines were filled with powdered gypsum. As we have already said, there is no likeness whatever between the culture of the mainland and that of Crete. The Neolithic remains of Crete are far from clear, but the people seem to have had cultural connections with southwestern Asia Minor.

THE EARLY BRONZE AGE

In speaking of the Paleolithic and Neolithic Ages, we remarked that we must use a conventional terminology that emphasizes the difference in treatment of stone tools. What really mattered, we said, was the domestication of plants and animals, or their absence. Similarly, in the case of the Bronze Age, the significant point is not the presence of metal. What counts is the presence of towns, or at least large villages. An established community needs cooperative effort and organization. This is the explanation, in part at least, for early monarchies.

It was in the Bronze Age, then, that man finally became civilized. Actually, man did not go directly from the use of stone to bronze. First he learned to beat copper out of its ore. The copper, with its natural alloy, was hardened by hammering it cold; this caused crystallization and gave a better cutting edge. Still, it was relatively soft for general use, and accordingly stone tools continued to be popular. This transitional period, when both copper and stone were used side by side, is spoken of as the Chalcolithic Age. The Bronze Age started when people learned to mix tin with copper, thus obtaining bronze, a metal far superior to stone.

The Early Bronze Age of Greece began soon after 3000 B.C. It was introduced by a non-Indo-European people who moved from southwestern Asia Minor into mainland Greece and was akin to the contemporary populations of Crete and the Cyclades. Doubtless these are the people whom we must credit with using words that survived the centuries and are to be found in classical Greek: especially non-Greek place and plant [2] names such as those ending in *-inthos* (*Korinthos*), *-ssos* (*Parnassos*), *-ttos* (*Hymettos*), *-ene* (*Mykene*). Southwestern Asia Minor preserves the same linguistic phenomena, and it is probably there that the ultimate origin of the Early Bronze Age culture must be sought.[3] It goes without saying that the newcomers mixed with the

[2] The name *terebinth,* for instance, which we still use, is one of them.

[3] Professor Leonard R. Palmer in his *Mycenaeans and Minoans,* (2nd, ed., New York, 1965) argues that the words and names with such endings come from Luvian, an Indo-European language spoken in southwestern Asia Minor as well as in Greece between 2000 and 1500 B.C. He believes that the pre-Indo-European place names in Greece are of the type *Thebai, Athenai.* In his view, Greece in the Early Bronze Age was occupied by peoples speaking a "Mediterranean" language. About 2000 B.C., Indo-Europeans speaking the Luvian language swept into Greece and introduced the Middle Bronze Age. About 1500 B.C., new Indo-Europeans speaking Greek came along and dominated the Late Bronze Age. Because their culture was similar or inferior to the Luvian, they left no evidence

descendants of the Neolithic population; in Crete, the Early Minoan people evolved from the Neolithic population, but there was a different evolution on the mainland.[4]

One reason why we know that a new people moved into the mainland soon after 3000 B.C.—at the opening of the Early Helladic phase of the Early Bronze Age—is that the cultural development shows such a sharp break with the past. The pottery found in the Peloponnesus, for example, is coarse, handmade, polished, and occasionally incised with decorations. Later, white geometrical patterns were painted on a black-glaze ground and black patterns on a light ground. Some of this pottery became very beautiful; there are good characteristic examples from Hagia Marina in Phocis, Hagios Kosmas in Attica, and Tiryns and Lerna in Argolis.

Some idea of the diet in these days, as well as of sanitation, is given by the First Settlement of Troy (*ca.* 2900 B.C.). Here, at the bottom of the famous mound, where nine successive settlements were built, there has been found on the floors of the houses a great quantity of animal bones, oysters, cockles, and other edible mussels.[5] If a pot was broken, it too was allowed to remain on the floor. Floors were often relaid, equivalent to a modern recarpeting or spring cleaning. Under the floor of a house has been discovered an infant burial. So much rubbish collected in the narrow lanes which served as streets that their levels were raised, and eventually houses had to be torn down and rebuilt in order to give the owner free access. This settlement, though surrounded by a circuit wall, was not really a city, but a citadel or royal stronghold, and was able, because of its location near the Hellespont, to take toll of traffic crossing between Europe and Asia, and between the Aegean and Black Seas.

The control of trade routes and the proximity to silver mines helped

---

in the archaeological record. As of 1969, this reconstruction has not won general support and remains a minority opinion.

[4] Enough has already been said to suggest the interrelation of various lands in the Near East. Europe's debt, racially and culturally, to Asia and Africa is very great. Not only did civilization begin early in lower Mesopotamia and Egypt, but those and neighboring countries continued to contribute to European civilization. We think at once of Babylonian astronomy, of Egyptian art, and of the imperial achievements of Persia in the sixth and fifth centuries B.C. Oswald Spengler remarked in his *The Decline of the West* that the word *Europe* should be stricken from our books, lest we forget the role played by Hither Asia and North Africa in our developing civilization. (Cf. the rear endpaper map.)

[5] Similar remains of food indicating the same animals (sheep, deer, pig, ox) and shell fish have been found in practically all the sites of this period excavated on the Greek mainland.

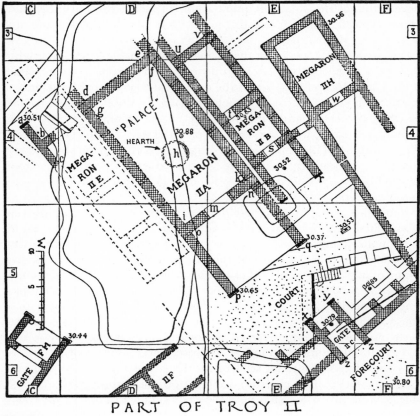

PART OF TROY II

Map 5

the Second Settlement at Troy develop into a place of importance. A lively traffic in metals grew up. Troy II, also, was more a citadel than a city, for its circuit was only about a quarter of a mile, and the people lived outside the walls. The walls, however, were massive and were strengthened by angle bastions and towers, one of which was 60 feet square. A paved ramp led through a gateway. Within the walls lived the king and his chief retainers. The largest house, approximately 66 feet long and 33 feet wide, was probably the palace; the ends of its brick side-walls (*antae*) were faced with wood for protection. Schliemann mistakenly thought that this was the Homeric Troy and with his typical enthusiasm called the vast hoard of gold and silver pins, earrings, vases and weapons the Treasure of Priam (Map 5).

The opening of the Early Minoan phase of the Early Bronze Age saw a marked increase in the population of Crete. Those who had recently arrived came from southwestern Asia Minor and hence were akin to the Neolithic population; it is possible, however, that people also came from Libya in North Africa, and settled in the plain of southern Crete known as Messara. The island does not yet present a unified cultural appearance, but seems to have consisted of three groupings, in east, central, and south Crete. Apparently the eastern end of the island was the most prosperous.

A significant fact at this time is the growth of urban life. Towns such as Palaikastro, Mochlos, Pseira, and Gournia were founded on the coast. The Cretans engaged in agriculture, pasturing flocks, hunting, fishing, and overseas trade with the Cyclades, Asia, the Levant, Egypt, Libya, and perhaps the Greek mainland. A cylinder seal hints at connections with Mesopotamia. Cretan art was influenced, of course, by these foreign relations, but we must emphasize the independence and originality of the art from the beginning. Though they occasionally copied Egyptian objects deliberately, the Cretan artists as a rule molded their works according to their own taste. The free spirit of Minoan art, consequently, came to influence other areas and in this period dominated the Cyclades. The most important town in the Cyclades, Phylakopi on the island of Melos, grew rich from the export of obsidian, whereas from Amorgos and other islands curious marble idols found their way abroad. The earliest ones are fiddle-shaped, but even later they present an odd appearance with their long heads and flattened limbs; almost all of them are female and no doubt represent a Great Mother.

The pleasant houses of the Cretans, such as those at Vasilike, were wide, shallow, and rectangular, with flat roofs. In time, the houses were several stories high, the lower part being built of rubble and pierced by a door, the upper of sun-dried bricks, with windows. The frame was of wood, and the whole was covered with plaster. As rooms were added to Minoan houses in haphazard fashion, courts and light wells became necessary for air and light, and these became striking features of the later palaces. When the inhabitants of the houses died, they were buried in round ossuaries, as in the case of the Messara plain,[6] which were used from one generation to the next. (The Glossary explains technical terms.)

It was the growth of towns that accounted for the tremendous advance in Cretan art and made possible such specialized activities as those of the potter and engraver. We have, for instance, seals of marble and ivory, on some of which are pictographs, the first example of writing

---

[6] These are often incorrectly called *tholoi,* domed tombs.

in Europe. From the little island of Mochlos, which was originally a peninsula, come beautiful vases of colored stone and steatite. What is more surprising is the quantity of gold—necklaces, bracelets, diadems, pins in the shape of flowers—indicating taste and comparative luxury at the very beginning.

THE MIDDLE BRONZE AGE

With the Middle Minoan period the potter's wheel was introduced. The manufacture of pottery was easier now, and it was possible to obtain better shapes. The patterns were taken from stone and weaving, from metal and leather work, and especially from nature, a field in which Minoan painters were to become great masters. The pots were frequently given a brilliant black glaze with geometric devices in color; at other times, bands of varnish were painted on the natural buff color of the clay. There were two chief styles of decoration: first, dark on light decoration, and then white paint on a dark background, which held the stage for eight centuries.

The unity of Cretan culture [7] is an outstanding change that marks the opening of the Middle Minoan period. It is proved by the similarity of building methods, uniform pottery styles, and a common type of burial (in large jars known as *pithoi*). Another outstanding change is the rise of palaces. Indeed, the Palace of Minos at Knossos, the labyrinth of legend, represents the greatest achievement of Minoan civilization. About 1800 B.C. isolated buildings, which had stood around a public square, were probably consolidated to form a palace. Later, the palace was damaged by an earthquake and rebuilt. When Knossos was captured by the Achaeans, various mainland features were introduced.

In other words, the palace of Minos, as it has been revealed through excavation, represents various periods. It covers more than six acres and, being built on the slope of a hill, is in parts several stories high. A tower and bastion at the north are practically the only signs of defense, from which we infer that the priest-kings of Knossos feared neither domestic nor foreign foe. This is confirmed by the legend that speaks of a Cretan thalassocracy. There was a small entrance to the palace at the north, and a stepped portico entrance decorated with horns of consecration at the south. Here a great road, from the south coast near Phaestus, terminated in a viaduct and bridge over a ravine. Weary travelers in the Late Minoan Period—arriving by horse and chariot or

[7] The population had not changed and was still non-Indo-European.

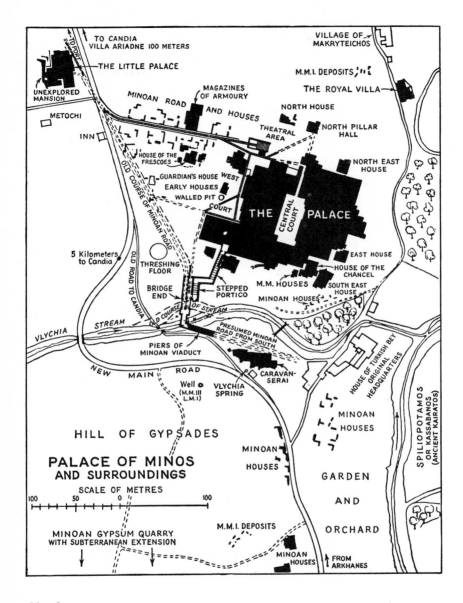

TO CANDIA
VILLA ARIADNE 100 METERS

VILLAGE OF
MAKRYTEICHOS

THE LITTLE PALACE

M.M.I. DEPOSITS

UNEXPLORED
MANSION

THE ROYAL VILLA

MINOAN ROAD

MAGAZINES
OF ARMOURY

METOCHI

AND HOUSES

NORTH HOUSE

INN

THEATRAL
AREA

NORTH PILLAR
HALL

HOUSE OF THE
FRESCOES

NORTH EAST
HOUSE

GUARDIAN'S HOUSE

WEST

EARLY HOUSES

WALLED PIT

COURT

CENTRAL
COURT

THE   PALACE

5 Kilometers
to Candia

THRESHING
FLOOR

EAST HOUSE

HOUSE OF THE
CHANCEL

M.M. HOUSES

SOUTH EAST
HOUSE

BRIDGE
END

STEPPED
PORTICO

MINOAN HOUSES

PIERS OF
MINOAN VIADUCT

PRESUMED MINOAN
ROAD FROM SOUTH

VLYCHIA   STREAM

NEW   MAIN   ROAD

CARAVAN-
SERAI

Well
(M.M.III
L.M.I)

VLYCHIA
SPRING

HOUSE OF TURKISH BEY
ORIGINAL
HEADQUARTERS

SPILIOPOTAMOS
OR KASSABANOS
(ANCIENT KAIRATOS)

HILL   OF   GYPSADES

MINOAN
HOUSES

PALACE OF MINOS
AND SURROUNDINGS

MINOAN
HOUSES

GARDEN

SCALE OF METRES

100   50   0   100

AND

ORCHARD

MINOAN GYPSUM QUARRY
WITH SUBTERRANEAN EXTENSION

M.M.I. DEPOSITS

MINOAN
HOUSES

FROM
ARKHANES

Map 6

21

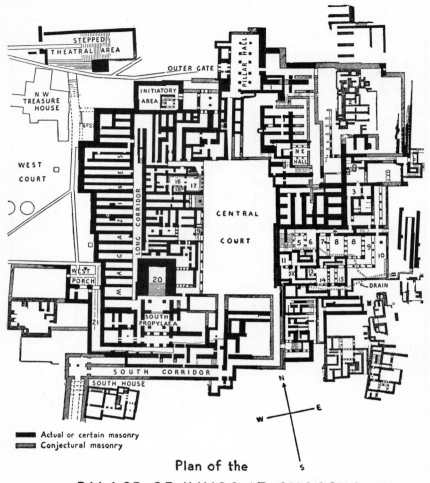

Plan of the

PALACE OF MINOS AT CNOSSUS

Meters
0 ——————————— 50

1. Guard room	12. w. c.
2. Royal pottery stores	13. Bath
3. School room	14. Queen's Megaron
4. Lower east-west corridor	15. Light area
5. Light area	16. Room of the Throne
6. Hall of the Colonnades	17. Ante-room
7. Light area	18. Lustral basin
8. Hall of the Double Axes	19. Shrine
9. Portico	20. Grand Staircase up to Piano Nobile
10. Light area	21. Corridor of the Procession
11. Court of the Distaffs	

Map 7

22

in a four-wheeled cart (earlier, if they could afford it, in a litter)—found awaiting them at this point a caravanserai, or hostel, with a foot bath and marvelous frescoes of partridges and hoopoes. The entrance led into the central court, approximately 200 feet long and 85 feet wide, around which the palace was built.

The palace, with its olive press, arsenal, school room, workshops, and storerooms, was almost a self-contained village, and the long corridors with their vivid frescoes, the stately rooms, the staircases, bathrooms, latrines, and various appointments were the last word in comfort and good taste. The main rooms were in an upper story, but on the west side of the court were certain official state rooms. Here was located, in the Late Minoan period (during the time of the mainland supremacy) the throne room, decorated with striking frescoes of griffins against a deep red background. The simple throne was flanked by benches, on which, no doubt, the king's advisers sat; the benches were covered with red and white plaster. Connected with this room is another with a lustral basin, so perhaps we should think of the throne room as concerned with religious rites, where acts of purification were performed. In that case, the king might also have been a priest representing the Great Mother Goddess. Behind the throne room and opening on a long corridor were a score of magazines where immense jars stood, filled with olive oil, wine, and cereals; perhaps they represented taxes paid in kind to the king, who used them in the export trade.

Facing the court, not far from the throne room, was the palace shrine. On the opposite side, at a lower level, were the private dwelling rooms—the Domestic Quarter—of the royal family. At night the rooms were lighted by beautiful oil lamps of porphyry and other colored stone; winter's dampness was dissipated by low tripod hearths of painted stucco. Perhaps it was during the long winter evenings that indoor games were especially popular; at any rate, an extraordinarily beautiful gaming table had been found, made of ivory, crystal, blue paste, silver, and gold.

It will be observed from the plan how the stately Hall of the Double Axes was approached through a series of columns and piers, thus giving the maximum of light and air, which was further increased by a light well and window at the rear. Outside rooms were avoided because of the heat and the cold winds that Crete enjoys at different seasons; rain water that collected in the light wells was carried off by an elaborate drainage system. It will also be observed from the plan that near the Hall of the Double Axes was the so-called Queen's Megaron (Hall of State), which had its own bathroom, including a painted terra-cotta bath tub, and a water closet. A private staircase enabled the queen to come and go as she pleased, without disturbing the men in the Hall of the Double Axes. North of this Hall a long east-west corridor led to the Hall of the Colonnades. Here is the impressive Grand Staircase, a marvel of antiquity; five flights, with broad shallow treads, still stand. The columns, rather typical of Minoan architecture, were of wood and tapered downward, in order, presumably, to protect them as much as possible from the rain water. They stood on stone bases or in sockets; their capitals were crowned with rectangular blocks with convex and concave moldings below, and thus suggest the origin of the classical Doric capital. The palace itself was built of unburnt brick or rubble, in a timber frame, though the lower courses generally were a dado of gypsum or limestone blocks. The walls were stuccoed.

In the immediate neighborhood of the palace stood the private homes of princes, officials, and wealthy individuals. Particularly imposing are the "Little Palace" and the smaller "Royal Villa," with their reception rooms, lavatories, halls, light wells, and flights of stairs. This solid evidence of peace and prosperity was not limited to Knossos. It may be discovered, on a smaller scale, at the towns we have already mentioned and at Zakro, Tylissos, and elsewhere. There was a striking palace at Mallia, but the greatest of all the palaces, second only to Knossos, was the one at Phaestus. Here the Italian excavators have uncovered a truly regal Minoan palace, reminiscent of Knossos in every way. So wealthy was the ruler of Phaestus that in summer he had a small, informal residence at nearby Hagia Triada. It seems reasonable to suppose that the ruler of Phaestus was independent, but the extended period of peace, implicit in all these extraordinary remains, suggests that one ruler, the King of Knossos, exercised the chief political power. The paved roads, bridges, aqueducts, the sea wall of the Harbor Town of Knossos, and the far-flung trade [8] are some of the other things which indicate not only an ability in engineering and organization but a powerful hegemony as well. A society such as this needed writing for at least its commerce and inventories. A syllabic script, called by us Linear A for want of a better name, was substituted for the old hieroglyphic writing. More will be said of it again, but we may note here that it reveals a knowledge of arithmetic.

To judge from the available evidence, the life of the people was exceptionally gay and carefree. Exquisitely cut gems and seal-stones emphasize the Minoan love of nature. Games of various kinds, boxing, wrestling, and bull baiting were popular. It used to be thought that

[8] The Aegean Sea was dotted with trading stations called Minoa.

the theatral area near the Palace of Minos was used for the latter sport, but it seems better suited to ceremonial dances. The men wore simple loin cloths with an apron; the women, long flounced skirts and bodices open in the front and high collars at the back. Rings were rarely worn, but both sexes wore seals around the neck or wrist. The life of the children was much the same as in most days, as we can imagine from their pullcarts and other toys.

Great religious temples were unknown to Minoan Crete. Sanctuaries on mountain peaks were common, such as the one on Mt. Juktas (where the classical Greeks thought Zeus was buried), at the Kamares cave on Mt. Ida, and the Dictaean cave at Psychro. The Minoans apparently believed that the divinities of nature lived in pillars and stones, and that one called them forth by dancing and other ceremonies. Private houses, therefore, had their own pillar rooms. With the rise of the palaces, the pillar rooms, like the sacred caves, lost popularity and were replaced by shrines. The principal cult was that of the Great Mother Goddess, whose symbol was the double axe, which was sacrificial in its origin and presumably placed a building or object under a higher protection. Associated with the goddess was a young male divinity. The small house chapels had in the center a circular three-legged table with offerings, and against the wall at the back was a bench on which might be placed bell-shaped idols and a double axe between horns of consecration. In the Palace of Minos was discovered a shrine with a beautiful faience Snake Goddess showing the priestess with snakes in her hands and surrounded by models of garments, painted sea shells, doves, a marble cross (in its origin a star), a lustral basin, and faience plaques of a goat and cow with their young. The snake was probably regarded as the protector of the household, something that brought good luck. It appears from evidence such as this, as well as from frescoes showing ceremonial dances and an extraordinary painted sarcophagus from Hagia Triada, that the women played an important role in Minoan religion.

The sculpture, it will have been noted, was usually small. The most extraordinary of all the Snake Goddesses is a figure about 6½ inches high, carved in ivory, with gold snakes in her hands and gold ornamentation on her dress. The statuette represents a goddess of austerity and breeding and shows a long tradition in sculpture. It comes from the Late Minoan period and is now in Boston (Figure 2). We also have other small figures in ivory, such as the leaping youths from Knossos, and terra-cotta from Petsofa and elsewhere.

The artistic genius of the Minoans can probably be appreciated most vividly in the palace frescoes, full of bright colors and action and imagination. The artist executed his design with a brush on the wall while the plaster was still wet and thus his work was of necessity rapid. Animals, fish, and flowers (a wonderful love of nature, though the artist never hesitated to make plants grow upside down or to change red roses to green, if it helped the effect) characterize this art. One of the loveliest examples shows saffron being gathered in a meadow filled with crocuses. In another fresco we see a simple blue bird amid rocks and roses, and from Hagia Triada comes the famous fresco of a lifelike cat creeping amid the rushes toward an unsuspecting pheasant. In stucco relief was painted the priest-king himself. The grand fresco of a cup-bearer shows a tall handsome youth, with decorated dress and an engraved signet on his wrist, marching in solemn procession (Figure 3). His features are refined, his complexion and hair dark. By an artistic convention the men are generally painted red or dark, the women white or yellow. Perhaps their waists were artificially restricted. The artist could also give the impression of crowds of people when he wished. A very beautiful fresco shows flying fish; it comes from the palace at Phylakopi in Melos and was probably executed by a Cretan artist.

It was to be expected that the major art of mural decoration should influence the pottery. The manufacture of some Middle Minoan pottery is so fine that it is called egg shell. Rarely are men or animals painted, for the artist understood that the shape of a pot is ill suited to this design.[9] The emphasis, rather, is on an exciting polychromy, with abstract patterns in various colors. In time naturalistic designs were used almost exclusively. One of the most beautiful vases, Late Minoan in date, is from Gournia and shows two dark brown octopuses floating across the light surface of the vase (Figure 4). It was the tendency toward flamboyance, imitation, and stylization—the death always of human endeavor—that caused this great art to degenerate. Thus far, Crete.

The opening of the Middle Helladic phase of the Middle Bronze Age, on the Greek mainland, was introduced about 1900 B.C. by a wave of Indo-European invaders—whence they came is not clear, but we now know that they were Greeks. Excavated sites on the mainland, such as those at Lianokladi, Hagia Marina, Korakou, and Lerna, show a definite division in the stratification between Early and Middle Helladic strata; and, very especially, the material remains of the two periods are quite different, as can be seen in the tombs, pottery, and house plans. After the people of the Middle Helladic period came into Grece, there is no apparent archaeological interruption to the steady and gradual evolution of civilization in Greece. Nor is there ever again in ancient Greek history a sign of the intrusion of any new racial factor. The new

[9] A brilliant exception is the Harvester's Vase, Late Minoan in date, from Hagia Triada, but this is carved steatite; it shows vivid movement and life.

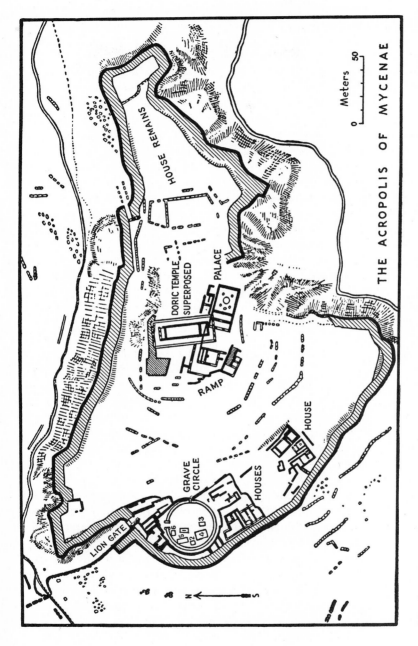

THE ACROPOLIS OF MYCENAE

HOUSE REMAINS

DORIC TEMPLE
SUPERPOSED

PALACE

RAMP

GRAVE
CIRCLE

HOUSES

HOUSE

LION GATE

Meters

0   50

Map 8

27

Indo-European invaders of the Middle Helladic period were the first members of the Hellenic race ever to come to Greece; we call them Achaeans to differentiate them from the Greeks of classical times, as already explained. They mingled with the earlier population, a non-Indo-European people who in their turn, it will be remembered, had already mixed with the Neolithic population of unknown origin.

The significant new cultural elements in Greece at this time consist of the houses, whose plan anticipates the megaron type of the Late Bronze Age; the tombs, often of a "cist" type, which are noticeable for their lack of funerary offerings; and a mysterious pottery called Minyan. Minyan pottery, a distinctive creation of the Achaeans, has a soapy feeling; at first it was gray in color and then changed to yellow. The technique is fine, the fabric thin, the surface highly polished, and often the shape of metal vases is imitated. Cretan influences became strong and doubtless did as much as anything to civilize the Achaeans and prepare them for their great moment in history, which lay just ahead. Meanwhile the Achaean kings nurtured their states at Orchomenos and Thebes and Athens in Central Greece; at Mycenae and Tiryns, at Mideia (Dendra), Prosymna (the later Argive Heraeum), Asine, Pylos and elsewhere in the Peloponnesus; on Aegina and other islands.

THE LATE BRONZE AGE

The opening of the Late Helladic period, about 1580 B.C., represented a steady evolution of culture, not a break with the past. The Achaeans in general—and their most important representatives, the Mycenaeans, in particular—were now in possession of great prosperity and power. The hill on which the Mycenaean citadel was built had the advantage of dominating the broad Argive plain and the trade routes to Corinth and the western sea. The source of Mycenae's wealth has been a mystery, but recently the attractive suggestion has been made that there were copper mines in the mountains back of Mycenae, which would of course help resolve the mystery.

At the end of the Middle Helladic period we find a family of rulers at Mycenae whom we call the Shaft Grave Dynasty from their method of burial. Where the Lion Gate now stands was once an extensive cemetery. A stone circle enclosing a number of graves of a royal family has recently been discovered and excavated outside the walls, northwest of the Lion Gates, close to the so-called Tomb of Clytemnestra. The graves within this circle are of the Shaft Grave type and belong to the close of the Middle Helladic period and the transition to the succeeding Late Helladic period. Many fine vases have been found in them, along with many gold and electrum ornaments, including a mask, bronze swords and daggers with pommels of gold and ivory, objects made of rock crystal, faience, and other valued materials.

The citadel, on the side of which the cemetery was located, later underwent a reconstruction, and few of the graves survived. Here, just inside the Lion Gate, is the famous stone Grave Circle found by Schliemann in 1876, whose graves were part of this large cemetery. The graves were cut vertically, like rectangular shafts, into the rock; the floors at the bottom were pebbled, and above the graves were placed sculptured tomb stones (*stelae*). The contents of the graves—one dates to the end of the Middle Helladic period and the rest to the Late Helladic—constitute one of the greatest gold treasures from any Bronze Age site in the world, and it is easy to imagine Schliemann's excitement at their discovery. With the nineteen skeletons were unearthed quantities of thin gold disks, which probably were sewn to the dresses of the women, and gold bracelets, signets, diadems, breastplates, beads, swords, and cups. Of particular beauty are gold death masks and bronze daggers with inlays in dark and light gold, niello, and silver, showing scenes from life, such as lion hunts (Figure 6). When the Cyclopean citadel was constructed about 1350 B.C., the cemetery was built over inside the walls, part of it remaining outside but disused. The royal graves were inside and were made into a sacred area: six graves were enclosed by a double row of stone slabs forming a concentric circle (the Grave Circle, that is), with an impressive entrance altogether worthy of these royal Shaft Graves.

Just before 1500 B.C. there occurred at Mycenae an important change in the burial customs. It appears that a new dynasty had come into power, and once again, accordingly, we designate it by its tombs, the Tholos Tomb Dynasty. A tholos tomb was approached by an unroofed passage (*dromos*) cut horizontally into the side of a hill (Figure 7). At the end of the dromos, which was lined with blocks, was a doorway leading into the circular chamber (*tholos*). This had been excavated from above and had then been lined with blocks, each course projecting slightly beyond the one immediately below, until finally the whole was arched over (Diagrams 10, 11, and 12). We call this method of construction a corbel arch; and the resulting dome strangely resembles a beehive in appearance. In such tombs—nine have been found at Mycenae—the immediate members of the royal family were buried, and the nobility were laid away in tombs only slightly less impressive. Two hundred at least of these tombs have been discovered at Mycenae, and

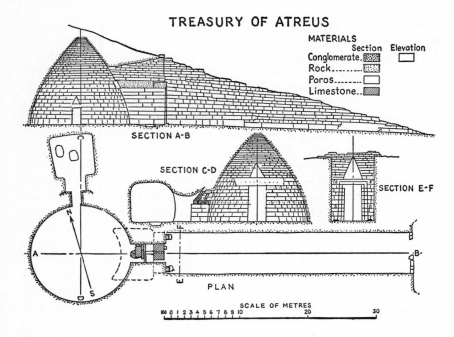

Diagrams 10, 11, 12

many others elsewhere. They are called rock-cut chamber tombs. The dromos, in the beginning at least, was short and unfaced with blocks, whereas the chamber itself was cut out in the native rock (which was left exposed), instead of being excavated from above. A chamber tomb is really an artificial cave cut out of the soft rock of a hillside.

The royal family, with its retainers, lived within the citadel of Mycenae, whereas the civilian population was scattered in settlements along the nearby hills; the location of springs would be a decisive factor in choosing a home. The typical house of the day is known as a megaron; the palaces, quite naturally, incorporated its plan. (See Plan of Palace at Tiryns, Map 9.). A fine example of a characteristic simple megaron—deep, narrow, and rectangular—has been found by Blegen at Korakou, near Corinth. It had three compartments. In front was the porch, with wooden columns on stone bases. The main room was entered directly from the porch and had columns down its axis to hold up the ceiling. Here, around the hearth, the family held its gatherings. A small room in the rear was probably used for storage. The roof of the house was probably flat.

As the power and wealth of Achaean Greece increased, Cretan motives became more prominent in its art, the florid and the

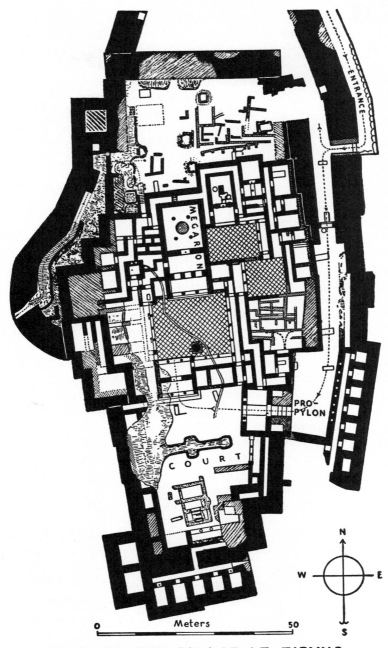

MEGARON

ENTRANCE

PRO-
PYLON

COURT

N

W   E

S

0   Meters   50

PLAN OF THE PALACE AT TIRYNS

Map 9

31

flamboyant being especially popular in the fifteenth century B.C. When, therefore, the Mycenaeans and other Achaeans felt the need of keeping records, it was only natural that they should borrow their script also from Crete. As we have already said, the script then being used in Crete was a syllabic one, which we call Linear A. It had been devised for the Cretan language, which was non–Indo-European. Even though it was not very well suited to Greek, the Indo-European language of the Achaeans, the Achaeans nevertheless took it over with some changes. We call this script of the Achaeans Linear B, and it is this that Ventris has deciphered (Figure 1). It is preserved on about a thousand tablets from the palace at Pylos; on tablets (written in various hands) from private houses at Mycenae; on vases from Orchomenos, Thebes, Eleusis, Tiryns, and Mycenae. The conclusion is inescapable that writing was not limited to the learned few in Achaean Greece.

While Achaean Greece, paced by Mycenae, grew in political and economic power, the people of Knossos were the unfortunate victims of an earthquake, which severely damaged their palace and perhaps wiped out their fleet. In the period of weakness that followed, the Achaeans, doubtless under the leadership of Mycenae, descended upon Crete and captured Knossos. Two different kinds of evidence support this interpretation. On the archaeological side, we know that Knossos (but no other place in Crete) now incorporated many mainland features into its so-called Palace Style of art in the fifteenth century B.C. Beehive tombs, fluted columns, throne rooms, a new military spirit in the frescoes, alabaster vases, characteristic features of the mainland, now occur at Knossos. The linguistic evidence, however, is conclusive. Knossos is the only place in Crete where we find tablets written in Linear B script. The significant point about this script, of course, is that it was employed for the Greek language. Therefore, Knossos was now occupied by Greeks—Achaeans—from the mainland.

For the remainder of the Late Bronze Age (The Late Helladic III period, 1425–1150 B.C.), Mycenae was at the zenith of its power, the great state of the Aegean world, enjoying diplomatic relations with Egypt and other ancient lands, and extending her economic and cultural influence throughout the Mediterranean. For example, large quantities of Mycenaean pottery have been found at Tell el-Amarna in Egypt, which was the capital of the "heretic" King Akhnaton (1375–1358 B.C.). Mycenaean boats, propelled by oars and sails, reached Italy. There were Mycenaean settlements in Melos, Thera, Rhodes, Miletus, and Cyprus. Certain manufacturing and trading centers, such as Rhodes and Cyprus, paid Mycenae the compliment of imitating its pottery on a tremendous scale. It is not surprising to find that the chief house at Zygouries, between Corinth and Mycenae, apparently belonged to a dealer in pottery.

About 1400 B.C. the great palace was destroyed, not by natural disaster, but by man. Some scholars hold that the destruction was the result of an attack from the Greek mainland; others, that it was caused by a rebellion of the native Cretan population against their Greek overlords. Leonard Palmer's theory, which must still be regarded as idiosyncratic, holds that the great-palace-period of Knossos was one in which Luvians, not Greeks, were in control. In his view the destruction of 1400 B.C. was the result of a Greek invasion that permanently ended Luvian domination. Present evidence is insufficient to confirm any theory.

Thus ended Mycenae's domination of Crete, but her power was otherwise unaffected. At home, about 1350 B.C., the Tholos Tomb Dynasty enlarged and reconstructed the citadel, giving it its present appearance. An immense wall, 23 feet thick and originally 60 feet high, constructed of huge blocks (Cyclopean construction), was carried around the hill. At the point of the old cemetery of the Shaft Grave Dynasty, it deviated far enough to include royal graves, as we have already explained. The wall had two gates, a postern and the famous Lion Gate (Figure 8), where a lion stands guard on either side of a column, above which appear the beams of a roof. The Lion Relief indicates divine protection of the citadel.

On the summit of the Mycenaean citadel, or Acropolis, was built a new palace, which occupied the area of the original Middle Helladic citadel. It had a spacious court with a Hall of State (megaron) and other apartments, such as a throne room, bathroom, and shrine. The walls were covered with gay frescoes, among which military scenes are prominent.

We do not know the name of the mighty king who rebuilt the citadel of Mycenae, but he constructed a tholos tomb which probably will always be called the Treasury of Atreus. The word *treasury* is easy enough to understand from the riches discovered in such tombs— although this particular one was robbed long ago—and tradition has caused this great architectural wonder to be named after the famous ruler who, in fact, lived in the next century. The tomb (Figure 7) is approached by a dromos approximately 115 feet long and 20 feet wide. The dromos is faced with well-cut conglomerate blocks set in regular courses (ashlar construction) and at its end is the impressive doorway, 18 feet high and capped by two lintel blocks, the inner one of which weighs more than 100 tons. On either side of the doorway stood green breccia columns; above the lintels the empty area—

known as the relieving triangle, for the corbel arching throws the main weight off the lintels—was originally filled by red porphyry slabs carved with spirals. Within the doorway is the great circular chamber, approximately 48 feet in diameter and crowned by a dome about 44 feet high. The stone blocks enclosing the chamber were adorned with bronze decorations. The chamber was probably used for ceremonies; the dead were buried in a small room to one side.

Over forty tholos tombs have been discovered in various parts of Greece. The one at Vaphio, near Sparta, has yielded famous gold cups, with embossed scenes showing the capture and taming of wild bulls (Figure 9). At Mideia (Dendra) in Argolis, the Swedish excavators discovered a tomb of great wealth. Four pits had been cut in the floor of the chamber, in one of which were buried the king and queen; the second pit held the bones of their young daughter. Human and animal bones, including a dog's skull, were buried in the third, and the fourth was a sacrificial pit. An exquisite gold cup with octopuses in relief, a gold-lined silver cup with bulls in relief, rings, swords, spearheads, knives, and gems had been laid away with the king. With the queen were a gold-lined silver cup decorated with bulls' heads inlaid in gold and niello, a gold box, a carnelian gem, and sixty-one gold beads of a necklace. A neighboring chamber tomb contained a slaughter table, a sacrificial table, two *poros stelae,* together with steatite lamps, boars' tusks, and beads of glass paste. In a cist under the doorway were twenty-four bronze vessels, four mirrors, knives, a six-pronged fishing spear, and other bronze objects. Apparently it was felt that the dead needed in the next world equipment reminiscent of that which they had enjoyed during life. Achaean religion had Minoan features; the chief cult was that of the Great Mother, the Goddess of the Double Axes, with whom was associated her son. Names of Greek divinities, such as Poseidon (who was particularly important at Pylos), Athena (originally the house goddess of Achaean kings), the God of War (Ares), Dionysus, and the Healer (Apollo), occur on Linear B tablets. About the tombs sacrifices in honor of the dead chieftains were performed. Gradually this worship spread downward socially, until finally hero worship developed, and ordinary men were offered hopes of immortality.

The most important city in the Argive plain, after Mycenae, was Tiryns,[10] a dependency, perhaps, of Mycenae. The best preserved of all the royal residences on the mainland is located here, for the contemporary one at Mycenae has been badly damaged by a landslide and by

[10] Tiryns was a place of equal antiquity with Mycenae; both were first inhabited in the Early Helladic period. Beneath the palace at Tiryns lies a great circular structure, estimated to be 91 feet in diameter, Early Helladic in date.

the classical temples and other buildings erected on its ruins. Of the three natural terraces on the Acropolis of Tiryns, the lowest was used as a refuge for the people, who characteristically lived in settlements nearby. The middle terrace was used by the king's retinue, and on the upper one was the palace. The whole hill was protected by an immense Cyclopean wall, in places 57 feet thick, formed of huge blocks, roughly hewn, and with small stones in the interstices. Within the walls, at two points, were corbelled galleries with several storage chambers. A symbol of the prince's wealth and power, this citadel must have seemed forbidding to raiding bands. A friendly visitor, coming up the inclined ramp and through the doorway, continued along a corridor to the entrance gates (in plan, porticoes *in antis,* ancestor of the classical Propylaea of Athens). Crossing the colonnaded court, beyond, he passed through another propylon into another court, also surrounded by columns. To the right was an altar; across the court, the Hall of State or megaron. Two columns *in antis* (above which was a flat roof) stood at the entrance to the megaron. A bench of alabaster, inlaid with blue glass paste and resembling a triglyph frieze, was the most notable decoration in this vestibule. Three doorways led into an antechamber, and beyond this a single doorway opened into the main room, with its four columns, a hearth, and dais which served for a throne. The stucco floor of the megaron consisted of red and yellow squares with scale patterns and blue squares with octopuses and dolphins. Other rooms, including a bathroom, courts, and corridors, completed the palace, which in places was two stories high. (See Glossary for technical terms.)

The walls of a palace such as this were covered with frescoes, showing epic scenes, battles, and boar hunts. The vases—for example, the Warrior Vase from Mycenae (Figure 10)—remind us that these artists, unlike the Minoan, did not hesitate to use figured representations. With the growing prosperity, art became an industry, and the designs were stereotyped and repeated: concentric circles, spirals, and wavy lines; a typical shape was the so-called stirrup vase.

The wealth and peace and urbanization of Achaean Greece seem extraordinary for almost any period in history. For example, another great city was located at Thebes, the traditional home of Cadmus, who reputedly gave Greece its writing. At nearby Orchomenos a magnificent tholos tomb, called the Treasury of Minyas, has been found; its side chamber has a stone ceiling carved with spirals, lotus flowers, and rosettes. In the center of the Copaic basin lies a mysterious island, Goulas (Gla) by name, whose palace was protected by a wall almost a mile in circuit. Recent excavations prove that Athens (Map 38) was an important place in the Late Helladic period. A necropolis has been discovered along the north slope of the Areopagus. On the summit of the Athenian Acropolis stood a palace, protected by a massive wall. The houses of the populace clustered on the north slope near the eastern gateway; this was ruined by the later classical buildings erected over it.

In southwestern Peloponnesus, as Blegen's excavations now show, stood a great city, a worthy rival of Mycenae and Tiryns (Figures 1 and 11). This is "sandy" Pylos, where, Homer tells us, Nestor lived through three generations of men and, as Agamemnon's friend and adviser, led a contingent of ninety ships against Troy. The discoveries, in the necropolis and the palace itself, reveal extraordinary wealth: much jewelry, ivories, fine frescoes, hundreds of vases, as well as the fundamentally important inscribed Linear B tablets. Ventris has pointed out that the tablets prove the differentiation of labor which the sophisticated products of Mycenaean industry indicate. They speak of smiths, physicians, cooks, carpenters, masons, bow-makers, tailors, shepherds, huntsmen, bath attendants, woodcutters, priests, kings, and landowning citizens. The palace at Pylos is exceptionally large. The main room of the megaron had a throne and a hearth about 13 feet in diameter and decorated along the side with a flame pattern; overhead there probably was a clerestory. The wooden columns have left impressions in the cement-like plaster of the floor which show that they were neatly fluted in a manner anticipating Doric channeling.

About 1210 B.C. the ruling dynasty at Mycenae—we may safely call it now the House of Atreus—ran into its own problems of succession. At any rate, some large buildings outside the citadel walls were fired, apparently deliberately, as if in civil strife. We are reminded of the legend that tells how Atreus and his brother Thyestes quarrelled, and how Atreus had to drive Thyestes from the throne ohe had usurped. Soon after this, Atreus must have died, for it was his son, Agamemnon, who led the Achaeans in the famous expedition against Troy.

Until recent times, after Schliemann's guess about Troy II had been proved wrong, it was thought that the important settlement known as Troy VI, was the "city" of the War, but Blegen has shown that the succeeding settlement, known as Troy VIIa, must have the honor. The legendary date for the fall of Troy, 1184 B.C., agrees extraordinarily well with the archaeological evidence, which proves that the whole place was gutted by fire early in the twelfth century B.C. It was in this period, probably, that great epic sagas were developing, as bards traveled from town to town, singing in the palaces of the deeds of local heroes. We should like to believe with Homer that the rape of Helen set off the

Trojan War, but it is far more likely that it was symptomatic of tribal migrations taking place at this time.[11]

Thucydides, the great fifth-century historian, tells us that "in the eightieth year after the Trojan War the Dorians, led by the Heracleidae, conquered the Peloponnesus." The Return of the Heracleidae—the dscendants of Heracles, come to regain their ancient heritage, as legend has it—coincided with the transition from the use of bronze to iron.[12] They arrived from the north and northwest. As a result of the "Dorian Invasion" (to use the convenient label invented by modern historians), the Bronze Age came to an end, towards 1100 B.C. The political organization of Greece promptly changed. Achaean kings and their chief men were killed, their palaces went up in smoke (incidentally baking and thereby preserving the inscribed tablets). Those who could, escaped to the islands of the Aegean Sea and the opposite coast of Asia Minor, but cultural life continued essentially the same as before, though on a simpler scale.

It is necessary to emphasize this, because it was formerly thought that the Dorian Invasion introduced both a new race to Greece and a violent break in the cultural development. In fact, however, the Dorians were Greeks, entering a land that had been Greek for 800 years. And the archaeological evidence proves that life continued much the same as before; for example, the pottery from the end of the Bronze Age gradually evolved into the protogeometric ware of the early Iron Age. Moreover, the archaeological evidence, such as the German excavations in the cemetery (Cerameicus) of Athens, confirms the legend that the Dorians by-passed Attica altogether.

Earlier in our own century, a famous Oxford archaeologist could say: "The chasm dividing prehistoric and historic Greece is growing wider and deeper; and those who were at first disposed to leap over it now recognize such feats are impossible." The truth is the precise opposite of this, so dramatic is the march of modern scholarship.

We are in the dark, nevertheless, about many things that happened at this time, for no early Iron Age site has yet been excavated; when this is done, we may find that we have been quite mistaken in speaking of a "simpler" cultural life. It may be that the Greeks forgot entirely how to write, which would seem odd; or excavations may ultimately prove that they continued to write in their old Linear B syllabic script

[11] For example, Aegean raiders ravaged the Egyptian Delta. The Peleset, another tribe, moved from the Aegean area through Asia Minor to Syria; settling south of Phoenicia, they became known to history as Philistines.

[12] Iron had been used in small quantities, for jewelry, during the Bronze Age. As a weapon, it was of course superior to bronze.

and the new Phoenician alphabet simultaneously. At all events, they spent the next three and a half centuries—the Middle Age, as we call it —laying the solid foundations of the great age which has inspired men ever since.

Finally, we must think of the classical Greeks as being a biologically mixed people, along the lines suggested earlier in this chapter. Nevertheless, they consisted of three main branches: the descendants of the Dorians and the two branches of the descendants of the Achaeans, known in classical times as Ionians and Aeolians (but again much mixed). The name *Achaea* passed into heroic legend, except as a minor geographical term. Nor can the culture of classical Greece be separated from the preclassical; the Treasury of Atreus and the Parthenon equally represent Greek genius.

THE
MIDDLE AGE

I T WAS inevitable that the steady arrival of Greeks from the less civilized north should ultimately affect the life of the Aegean world. We have already seen how civilization gradually became disturbed and how wars and shifts of population characterized the last century of the Bronze Age. The Greeks of a later day, to be sure, looked back upon that unhappy period as an Heroic Age, but for us its chief importance lies in the fact that the future political and racial map of Greece was now crystallizing. Classical Greece is distinguished not only by the fact that the small city-state became the normal political unit, but also that from one large area to another, social and political development, and even dialect, varied. The causes for this are to be found to a considerable extent in the Greek Migrations, as they are known (Maps 59 and 60).

About 1200 B.C., and for several generations after that, large numbers of Greeks left the Balkan peninsula and moved eastward across the Aegean Sea, settling in the islands and on the opposite Anatolian shore. This process had of course been going on from a much earlier time, but now it was accelerated, partly because of the pressure of new arrivals, as was the case particularly with the Dorians in the next century, and possibly too because of natural over-crowding. The Greeks of Thessaly and Boeotia, called Aeolians, colon-ized the large islands of Lesbos and Chios and the adjoining mainland. This area became known as Aeolis. Most of the colonists were men of new blood and fresh ideas, for they had been but slightly touched by Mycenaean culture and only in its decadent form. From central Greece, especially Attica, there was a movement to the Cyclades, which in time continued eastward till it reached and included the narrow strip of territory on the Anatolian coast afterward known as Ionia. On the sites of native villages these immigrants founded small cities. It was a motley population that came, and they made themselves more hetero-geneous by mingling with the natives. Doubtless it was partly the composite nature of the population, as well as the lovely climate, the most favorable in the world known to Herodotus, the rich soil, the highly articulated coast adapted to commerce, and the situation on the borderland between Greek and Oriental civilizations which made the Ionians for centuries the most brilliant and most versatile of Greeks, in the age of their glory the standard bearers of the world's civilization. The Ionian name applied to the section extending from Attica and Euboea to the central Asia Minor littoral.

The Aeolian and Ionian migrations were, strictly, movements extend-ing over a long period of time. The Dorian Invasion, however, was an-other matter. It was abrupt and especially violent, and affected most of Greece. It would be a mistake, however, to think of a cataclysm at this time; it is more correct to say that life now became decidedly simple, and that a new day, a new civilization, was in store for Greece. The expression *Dorian Invasion* is used to designate the incursion of those Greeks who, speaking a common dialect, moved into Greece from the northwest, a little later than the legendary date of 1104 B.C. Some of these northwestern Greeks crossed into Thessaly and Boeotia, though not in sufficient numbers to overwhelm the Aeolian dialect of these two sections. Others crossed into the Peloponnesus, where, too, they mingled with the earlier inhabitants. Thus arose historical Achaea, into which were pushed, as in the case of Achaea Phthiotis in Thessaly, many of the earlier inhabitants. Its dialect was akin to that north of the Cor-inthian Gulf, and to the more distantly related speech of the Dorians of Argolis and Laconia. From Argolis the Dorian dialect passed to Corinth and Megara, and from Laconia to Messenia. The dialect of

Chapter III THE
MIDDLE AGE

Elis likewise points to a migration from across the Gulf. Attica, it will be noted, remained untouched. So did Arcadia. Its people had once extended over the coast region to the south, but toward the end of the Bronze Age many of them had gone as colonists to Cyprus. Those who remained in Laconia were merged in the Dorian race, whereas the people of the interior highlands, under the name of Arcadians, maintained their original language and their racial character. Having adopted but little of the higher Mycenaean culture, they had little to lose by its downfall. Finally, emigrants from Argolis and Laconia, first Achaean and afterward Dorian, made their homes in Melos, Thera, and Crete. Beyond Crete the Dorians pushed on to Carpathos, to Rhodes, and ultimately to the southwestern coast of Asia Minor. Thus the Dorians spread from the Greek mainland across the Aegean to that part of Anatolia which was roughly opposite their starting point. The Aeolians and Ionians had done likewise.

The Dorians, with the Ionians, occupied the area once most thoroughly permeated with Minoan-Mycenaean culture and were its principal heirs. In material civilization, religion, government, and social structure the Dorians and Ionians were essentially alike; and it was owing chiefly to developments beginning near the close of the Greek Middle Age, above all to the brilliant growth of industry, commerce, and intellectual life among the Ionians, that in the historical period the leading Dorian and Ionian communities differed widely from each other. Though the Dorian Invasion was no catastrophe, the arrival of so many northerners and the attendant breakup of the Mycenaean federation set the stage for a new development in Greek lands, that of the great classical epoch. The Greek Middle Age (*ca.* 1100–750 B.C.) bears close analogies to the later European Middle Ages, in that both periods were characterized not only by invasions of less civilized peoples, but also by a decline and an incipient recovery of culture. The first two centuries, apart from pottery, are practically a blank. The decoration of the pottery, however, still has the familiar circles and wavy lines, and illustrates in general the steady deterioration of Bronze Age motifs (Figure 12). Not long after 1000 B.C. a new type of pottery emerges. It is geometric in its decoration, and becomes the prevailing style for a long time. Our information is now more complete and satisfactory, deriving chiefly from the *Iliad* and *Odyssey* of Homer. These epic poems purport to speak of the heroes of the Mycenaean Age, but it is generally agreed that they really describe the conditions of life in the tenth and ninth centuries B.C.

With Mycenae and other great sites destroyed, with the finer aspects of civilization a thing of the past, life in Greece had reverted to the simplicity of a much earlier day. The gradual closing of the lines of communication, too, fostered local development and variations. Conquest for the Dorians apparently had been easy. This was due in part to their superior weapons, which were often of iron [1] and could be used for cutting as well as thrusting. It was also due to their superior organization. Slowly order prevailed, life became settled, and the tribes, under their kings, built small and rudely fortified cities. Therein lived the king, in a palace of simple Mycenaean form, the nobles and wealthy with their household slaves, and the common farmers. There, too, dwelt potters, bronzesmiths, and a few merchants, who dealt in useful metals and in imported Eastern luxuries. Into the harbor sailed Phoenicians in their ships, and while they traded they kidnaped children, profitably combining commerce with robbery. Among a people of action the pirate was more esteemed than the merchant.

The monarchy appears in its simplest elements, though with some enormous pretensions. The king was a near descendant, preferably a great grandson, of Zeus or some other god. The king maintained his place chiefly by superior personal ability, as in semibarbarous life, and his power depended on the number of troops he led. Relations were personal, and no theory of government, or even idea of government in the abstract, had yet arisen. Ordinarily the kingship was hereditary, but the scepter might, for one reason or another, pass to a brother or to a new family. For support the king depended on the great estate attached to the scepter, personal or family property, gifts from his subjects, his large share of booty, and choice portions of sacrificial victims. He wore no crown or purple robe, but dressed and equipped himself little better than other nobles.

The state was a crude, undeveloped institution, with functions correspondingly few and ill-defined. The duty, clearly conceived, of protecting the population from foreign enemies made the king a general, the commander-in-chief of the army. The need of protecting the state itself from domestic foes, from treason and rebellion, gave him judicial power. It was no less incumbent upon the government to avert the anger of the gods and to secure their good will and beneficence. From this need arose the king's priestly character. Notable is the fact that the state had not yet acquired the function of protecting the lives and property of the citizens; that was a private affair. One who slew another fled from the country to escape the vengeance of the murdered man's kin, or remained on condition of paying a sum acceptable to the kinsman. With such things the government had nothing to do. Likewise it was

---

[1] Iron was known in the Bronze Age but it was not common.

incumbent on each individual to protect his own property from thieves and robbers. There were no police or officers of justice, and in time of peace no army. It often happened, however, that the disputants brought their case for arbitration to the king, queen, or councillors.

The king was absolute only on the battlefield, where he exercised the power of life and death. It is true that there was no constitutional way of checking him or of calling him to account; but in point of fact he was limited by the Council of elders and by the popular Assembly. The members of the Council had the same honors and titles as the king. They, too, were "scepter-bearing kings" and "fosterlings of Zeus." The king was himself a councillor, and merely the first among equals. Whereas the Council was an essential element of government, the king was not so considered, as his presence was unnecessary to the assembly of that body or the transaction of business by it. Individual members rebuked him sharply, denounced him as unfit to rule, and often disobeyed his command.

The right to give advice depended on the wisdom of age—hence the members were called elders—on lineage, or on success in war. The number was small. Any man of influence in the community, especially with ability to raise and command military forces, was sure to be given a place in the Council by the king; and when once a seat was established it became hereditary. Usually the councillors assembled round the table of the king, and began business after partaking of his hospitality. The discussion lasted till all agreed. The idea of majority vote was largely absent. There were no specialized functions or departments of administration; individually and collectively the councillors assisted and limited the king in all his duties, military, judicial, and religious. Though they had no legal way of coercing the king, their collective will generally prevailed. It required but a slight shift in the political balance to change the kingship into an aristocracy.

For the commons the Zeus-nurtured prince cherished supreme contempt, but in practice he sometimes had to heed their will. In war all fighters, in peace all men within or near the city attended the Assembly called by king or noble. The questions brought before them had previously been considered in the Council; they were few and usually such as affected the people, whose cooperation was required to carry them out. The chief speakers were the kings and councillors; it was unusual for commoners to speak. The commoners expressed their opinions by acclamation. Sometimes their opinion was decisive, chiefly when there was strong disagreement among the nobles. In their gathering in Assembly lay a germ of democracy, which was to grow and ripen to perfection in Greek states like Athens. The strong tendency of the time, however, was to abridge this influence in the aristocratic interest.

The economy of this period was pre-eminently agricultural, a fact that will characterize Greece for many centuries to come. Most of the people were farmers, who had their homes within or near the city and early each morning proceeded to their near-by holdings to spend the day. These farms were small, and they were worked with only the slightest specialized knowledge. Because the rotation of crops was not yet understood, the production was still further restricted through the necessity of letting the soil lie fallow in alternate years. Irrigation and the use of fertilizers, however, were known. With a plough of wood, drawn by oxen, the farmer prepared his fields for wheat, barley, and millet. Vineyards, vegetable gardens, and orchards of olive, orange, fig, and apple trees demanded his attention. Free laborers helped him at harvest time; otherwise, with the help of slaves, the owner worked the land himself. The slave's routine was not a hard one, differing little from that of his master. The lot of the small free-holder, however, became progressively worse, until finally social revolution was inevitable. The chief evil throughout early Greek history was the system which allowed a man to borrow first on his land and then on his person. Successive failures of crops meant slavery for many. The landed aristocrat as a result became wealthier and more powerful. His advantages over his less fortunate neighbor were particularly great in an economy where reserves were limited, money unknown, and barter the rule.

Although the idea of private ownership was of great antiquity, it applied generally to home and farm. Pasture land often belonged to the community. Here, under the supervision of a youth, grazed sheep, goats, cows, horses, the various animals needed by man for food, clothing, and burden. The forests of oak and evergreen, so important for houses and boats, were also probably owned by the community. In them man hunted with spear and bow and arrow for food—for boars, hares, deer— and in the sea he fished with net and hook. Bees provided him with his only sweet; the olive gave him fuel and soap.

Industry, as we understand it, was practically nonexistent. This is comprehensible when we consider the self-sufficiency of the ordinary family. Where we today must buy practically everything we use, the early Greek not only raised his food, but in the home the women turned wool into clothing and blankets, and hides into shoes. It would be more correct to say, then, that industry was limited in extent and was on a family basis. The chief exceptions were the specialized crafts of metal work and pottery manufacture. Cooperative enterprise was necessary, however, for the extraction of ore from the mountain side, for quarrying stone for public buildings, and, as communications began to be reopened, for roads and bridges. The horizon gradually widened, no doubt accelerated by trade. The Greeks exported practically nothing, to be sure, and their imports were limited largely to luxury articles, such as purple stuffs from Tyre and Sidon. Nevertheless, thanks to the Phoenician sailors, there was some communication betwen the Aegean and Egypt, Phoenicia, and Cyprus. Indirectly, the lines were kept open as far as central Africa and the Baltic, for ivory and amber. The great fifth-century historian Thucydides was not far wrong when he remarked that the people of this time had no mercantile traffic and mixed little with one another without fear, either on land or sea, and that each man tilled his own land only enough to procure a livelihood from it, having no surplus of wealth.

In similar fashion the religious beliefs of the Greeks had the humblest origin, but from fetish worship and the fear of the unseen they were able to evolve the Immortals of Olympus. Many elements of their religion, as in so many other matters, were inherited from Minoan-Mycenaean times, but the Olympic religion won out over the prehistoric. There is no question, however, about the prehistoric contribution. Certain cult places continued in use, such as Delphi, Delos, and Eleusis, which had been sacred in the Bronze Age. The Minoan house-goddess became Athena. Elements in the Greek religion that are alien to the Greek spirit, such as the Cretan myth of the birth and death of Zeus, must be Minoan in origin. The notion of Elysium, the Isles of the Blest, the Garden of the Hesperides, was inherited from the Minoans and survived by the side of the genuine Greek conception of Hades, in the far West or beneath the earth, whither souls went to lead a shadowy, joyless existence.

The Indo-European and Minoan religions, then, gradually melted into one. The northern invaders adopted Minoan Artemis and Aphrodite, apparently with little change. The immigrants to Miletus were as receptive of native cults as of native blood. The desire to secure the protection of the local deities and the good will of the Carians went hand in hand with greed for the properties of these gods. Identifying their own sky-deity Zeus with the god of the double axe, they converted the shrines and sacred domains of the Carian deity to their own service. In like manner their Artemis usurped the property and various attributes of the Great Mother, Cybele. Elsewhere Zeus was identified with the son of the Cretan Rhea. The character and attributes of the archer Apollo, especially his healings, purifications, and oracles, seem to be in considerable part Minoan. We may assume that no deity of historical Greece may safely be regarded as purely Indo-European or purely Minoan, and that the Minoans, endowed with a creative genius in religion as in art, contributed far more than the incoming northerners to Greek belief and ritual. The prevailing tendency today is to assign to the invading people the sunnier aspects of religion, while leaving to the Minoans the gloomy features, including magic, the worship of ghosts, the doctrine of sin, and its purification by washing in blood. Be that as it may, the generically new cultural influence which so tempered and altered the prehistoric religion and produced the pantheon of Olympus was due of course, as were the new (though not universal) custom of cremation and the rapid spread of hero worship, to the changed situation of the country.

The gods of the Greeks had human form, and with the exception of the lame smith Hephaestus, all were models of beauty. They differed from men only in their superior stature, strength, and physical perfection, in the character of their food and drink (ambrosia and nectar), in their dwelling place and life of ease, and in their immortality. They needed sleep, suffered pain, and were sometimes wounded by men in battle. Though Zeus was superior, all were limited in knowledge and power. They pursued their several inclinations, now in disobedience to Zeus, now winning him by persuasion or cajolery. At times his throne, like that of the mortal king, was insecure, and again his vast superiority seems to indicate a growing monotheism.

The great deities dwelt together as a family on the summit of snowy Olympus. There they spent their time in happy feasting; or schemed and quarreled; or under the presidency of Zeus, father of gods and men, they sat in council on the destinies of human kind. Their society was a reflection from that of earth, yet freer from moral restraint. They had all the evil as well as good qualities of man. In their dealings with men they were moved by caprice; they helped those whom they loved and brought misfortune upon the objects of their hate, or upon those who neglected sacrifice or the fulfilment of a vow to them. Yet in a limited measure they were the protectors of right and the avengers of wrong. They rewarded the good, but loved not evil deeds.

There was no priestly caste or hierarchy. The gods were so near to men as to demand no intermediaries. The father prayed and sacrificed for the family, the king and nobles for the state, and each individual for himself. Here and there were temples, most of them doubtless only large enough to shelter an image. Such a shrine was under the care of a priest, who, though dear to the gods, was as a rule not a noble or in any way superior to other men. Seers were classed along with craftsmen. In time, of course, the nobles monopolized religion and converted it to a political instrument.

In moral living the early Greeks derived little aid from their deities. It is true that religion taught them to pity and protect stranger suppliants, to honor parents, to refrain from overweening pride, and in a general way, by precept rather than by the example of the gods, to cultivate righteousness. But their moral progress, whatever it was, must be attributed to purely human effort. Their virtues were pre-eminently military—above all, physical strength and bravery. The bad man was the coward and weakling. Wisdom was skill in the use of arms or in the management of men, or shrewdness in daily life. Though the Greeks were proverbially deceitful, and Homer's gods and men indulge in clever lying, people such as Achilles protested against it. Patience, temperance, and self-control were admired. The spirit of justice and general good order within the state and the army is pronounced; the number of crimes is remarkably few in view of the lack of supervision on the part of the government.

Perhaps the most charming feature of life, as we see it in the pages of Homer, is the love of husband and wife, of parents and children—the affection which binds the family together in a moral unity. This bond was drawn the closer by the circumstance that, unaided by the state, the family had to protect its own property and lives and avenge its wrongs. The father was head of the family but the mother's place was equally honorable, and descent through her was highly esteemed. Her father had received for her hand a gift in oxen, which went to her as dowry; and the lady of rank chose her husband from among the suitors. Women sat with men in the great hall and went about freely in city and country. This honorable and influential place of woman was one to which Indo-European and Minoan sentiments and usages alike contributed. It is true that her pacific nature and her physical inferiority made her the prey of war, the victim of the brutal conqueror; and often her husband's lack of respect for the marriage bond subjected her to distressing humiliation; yet at least in the higher class these disadvantages were in part made good by the love and honor, the chivalrous treatment and social power accorded her alike by kin, townspeople, and guests from other states.

Much of our information about early Greece comes from Homer, who, in spite of a consistent archaism, frequently reflects contemporary life. Thus at the outset of its history, and amid the simplest surroundings, Greece was able to produce one of its greatest minds, perhaps the greatest poet who has ever lived, although some scholars still question his existence.

In fact, the Homeric question is the subject of the world's oldest scholarly debate. We cannot be sure that there really was a single poet who composed the *Iliad* and the *Odyssey,* or even all of one of them. We do not know when the poems were composed, and dates have been suggested ranging from 850 to 650 B.C. Modern scholarship has made it clear that the origins of the epics are to be found in oral poetry. For the greater part, the poems are made up of metrical formulas, used with great skill and versatility. Some time in this period, the poems were standardized somewhat in the form they have today. There is no good reason why we should not credit this achievement to Homer, as did the ancient Greeks. Conjecture has it that Homer probably worked near Chios, telling of heroes of the Trojan War, which had taken place centuries earlier.

Long before his day, long before the Trojan War indeed, rhapsodes had traveled from town to town, praising in short epics in hexameter the deeds of the local prince. Many of these sagas were brought to Asia Minor by the colonizing Greeks, and there lay at Homer's hand a mass of material to use, if he wished. Whether or not he actually wrote his poems down will never be known. All we can say is that writing was now probably known to the Greeks; that is, to priests and merchants, not to the masses. In that case it would have been available to Homer.[2] The poems themselves, however, were meant to be recited, not to be read. Their dialect is mainly Ionic, with an admixture of Aeolic, the result of the juxtaposition of those peoples on the Asia Minor coast. In addition, the vocabulary occasionally betrays the early speech of the Achaeans.

Behind Homer, then, lay great cycles of heroic legend which had originated during Mycenaean times. The cities to which the mythological cycles are attached, such as Mycenae, Argos, Troy, Athens, and Thebes, have in fact Mycenaean remains. We may say with some confidence that well before 1400 B.C. a continuous tradition in epic poetry grew up, which was passed on from generation to generation, the individual (and to us unknown) poets adding to the material, discarding other portions, until finally most of the themes, except those dealing with Troy and Thebes, were pushed into the background. At last there apparently emerged a great poet, Homer, who infused life and vigor into epic poetry, and liberated his native literature from a tradi-

---

[2] The question of the origin of the alphabet and the date of its introduction to Greece is obscure and at the present moment much debated. It seems clear that the Greek alphabet was adopted from Phoenicia. By the eighth century writing was fairly common in Greece; probably it had been used by the initiated for a long time.

tion that had lost its vitality with the passing of the world that had created it.

Although the *Iliad* deals with only a few weeks in the tenth year of the Trojan War, the poet makes us feel the whole background and environment. The theme of the *Iliad* is how Achilles' temper led him both to disaster and to moral degradation. This wrath of Achilles, thwarted by Agamemnon, leader of the Achaeans, holds the poem together and gives it its most dramatic developments. The deeds of other heroes, of Patroclus and of Hector, are also sung, but Achilles, who symbolizes the destiny of man, is the real hero. The poet sings of the tragedy of a city and of a man. The *Odyssey*, on the other hand, is an epic romance, and blends in one artistic whole a number of folklore motives and deep sea tales. The goal, though not the end of the poem, is to reunite Odysseus with his wife Penelope, who has faithfully waited for him on the island of Ithaca during his absence at Troy and his subsequent wanderings.

Throughout his poems Homer has tried to picture a bygone epoch, but actually what we have is a mingling of the traditional and the ideal with contemporary facts. It must be added, furthermore, that certain portions of the poems, such as the Catalogue of the Ships in the *Iliad*, are clear interpolations. Although the Homeric authorship of the two poems was not doubted in classical antiquity, in the seventeenth and eighteenth centuries of our era there commenced a controversy, associated with the names of d'Aubignac and Wolf, which has raised serious questions about Homer. Some students would deny his existence altogether and insist that the poems are a patchwork, put together possibly at the time of their official admission to the great Panathenaic festival at Athens in the sixth century. The Homeric question has not yet been resolved. (Figure 13).

Although Homer shines as a beacon during these early days, as indeed he might in any age, we must not imagine that the period which he illumined was otherwise wholly dark culturally. The remaining evidence consists chiefly of pottery, and concerning its artistic merits opinions differ, as is bound to be the case with anything that is purely subjective. Some consider geometric pottery primitive and crude, whereas others, with a surer eye and understanding, see in it a beautifully simple style, a little naïve perhaps, but charming and complete in itself. Between late Mycenaean and geometric pottery there is a connection, it will be recalled, through the so-called proto-geometric. By the tenth century, however, the decadent circles and wavy lines have yielded to the new style. This is not the first time that geometric art appeared in the Aegean, for we have observed its occurrence at various moments in the Bronze Age. Now, however, it holds universal sway for at least two centuries. There is no reason to look for oriental influence, from Mesopotamia for example, to explain the new style, since the invading Greeks probably brought it with them. It occurred only sporadically in the second millennium while Minoan influence was paramount, but inevitably it came to the surface with the final incursion of northerners.

The geometric style employs angular patterns, zig-zags, rows of dots, swastikas, triangles, crosses, and maeanders. These are placed in horizontal bands, row over row (Figure 14). The main zone might be divided by vertical bands into rectangular fields, metopes, which would be filled with rosettes and circles drawn with a compass, or it might be occupied by a procession. Here would be represented scenes from everyday life, battles, and funerals. The figures of men and animals, birds, horses, deer, are stylized silhouettes. The chests of men are drawn frontally, whereas the legs and heads are in profile; it is a considerable time before the heads look really human. The manufacture of the pot is splendid. Some new shapes are introduced; the profile is sharpened, the neck lengthened, due, as the composition itself, to a tectonic principle which as a matter of fact will dominate all Greek art and which seems to have been innate in the people themselves. We can see this principle illustrated by the great Dipylon amphoras, so called from their discovery in the Dipylon quarter of Athens (Figure 15). These vases are often over 6 feet tall and originally stood above graves. The best geometric pottery comes from Athens, though Rhodes, Corinth, and other sites produce fine examples. There is considerable variation from district to district, which was natural in an age where communication was difficult.

No large statues have come down to us, for, if they were carved at all, they were made of wood or some other perishable material. Many small bronzes and ivories of persons and animals, however, have survived. Some of them have considerable charm and show the beginning of truly great art. They are realist, individualist, nonformularistic, and three-dimensional in feeling. Of special interest are the bronze fibulas, for although safety pins were known in the prehistoric period, the great increase in their number at this time indicates a change of dress, brought in by the northerners, the loose-fitting chiton and *peplos*. Little need be said now of the architectural remains. The foundations of a few shrines and temples, and of miserable houses, represent practically all that is left.

The Greek Middle Age, an interesting and complete though simple chapter in man's existence, is chiefly important as the prelude to classical Greece. During this period, moreover, the fusion of population elements, discussed in the previous chapter, was modified somewhat by isolation and in-breeding. Though there was no clear-cut type, the skeletal remains recently recovered from the Athenian market place suggest a male stature of about 5 feet, 5 inches, a stocky European type of body build, and a complex of posture traits that appears to be an adaptation to the steep and rocky paths of Greece. The most striking feature of the face was an excessive breadth at the angles, emphasizing the squareness of jowl that still marks Greeks. The only important conclusion that can be drawn from the skeletal remains is that the classical Athenians were much mixed biologically, a web of diverse gene complexes woven together in a dynamic synthesis which makes the fusion of diverse cultural and ethnic elements a key to understanding the splendid flowering of classical Greek civilization.

Chapter IV THE
CITY-STATE

FROM the close of the Greek Middle Age (*ca.* 750 B.C.)
Greek civilization developed with remarkable rapidity.
No other Indo-European or Oriental people has
achieved results comparable to those of the next centuries.
The one institution more responsible for this extraordinary
achievement than any other was the city-state (*polis*). Its
origin was due to various causes, its character inevitably
combined good and bad features, and its constitution varied,
being in each case determined by special factors, for the city-
state did not function *in vacuo*. It should be noted that when
Greeks said that life not lived in a city was semibarbarous,
they did not mean that the alternative was life on an open
farm. They had in mind villages, for these lacked the centralized and highly coordinated political life so essential for
happy and rational existence.[1] The city-state, always small

[1] Mere size had nothing to do with the case, for a village might be very
large; what mattered was the presence or absence of political institutions.

but varying in area from a few square miles to a few hundred, and independent in all its affairs, was the ideal of Greek, but not even by the fifth century was it everywhere attained.

The origin of the city-state goes back to the Bronze Age, when urban settlement was an accepted way of life. The Greeks of the following period had this example before them and in some cases occupied the the old sites or new ones nearby. The new settlers were grouped in clans, or *gene,* the members of which traced their ancestry to a common hero or god. Perhaps it was this feeling for kinship which had led them to settle together in the first instance. Growth for a long time was slow, but the factors developed in the process were perhaps more important for the birth of the city-state than the mere previous existence of urban settlements. The first thing necessary was a fortified refuge, *asylum,* to which the people might flee with their flocks and belongings in time of danger. The fortified spot became, too, a convenient center where villages or clans might sacrifice or exchange goods. Because the king was needed to lead the people in war, or to conduct the sacrifices, it was natural for him to build his house at first near, and later within, the fortified area. This area was generally on a low hill-top; with the king and his retainers living there, and the commons scattered below, a settlement had been created which actually had a political center. A city such as this, which provided greater protection in time of war and in time of peace promoted trade and facilitated the performance of the king's duties, no doubt stimulated the growth of other cities.

We have noted that the inhabitants considered themselves descended from a common ancestor. In addition, each citizen was a member of a brotherhood, or phratry, an association originally of close kinsmen, who stood side by side on the field of battle. Several phratries formed a tribe, or *phyle.* These associations, as well as the family which was their base, were bound together by blood and worship. The result was a double-edged sword. Intimacy of life and intensity of effort were inevitable, but so too was a certain exclusiveness. Here we have at once the great virtue and the great failing of the city-state. Intimacy, intensity, and free opportunity are rare privileges, but if they are looked upon as the exclusive possession of the man born to them, the time will come when the system itself must fail. Birth was essential for citizenship, for only thus could one share in the necessary religious ceremonies. The Greek system suffered severely from this unwillingness to envisage a broader citizenship.

Nevertheless, the city-state made possible boundless versatility in the fields of literature, art, and philosophy. Perhaps its most precious contribution to civilization is republican government, which the Greeks devised in endless variety and which assured to the citizens a varying degree of liberty and self-government.

It was under the aristocracies, however, that the city-states developed significantly. Throughout the Greek Middle Age there had been steady pressure against the kingship, and although the details are obscure, by the eighth century the nobles had everywhere succeeded in superseding the king. This they had done either through outright usurpation or by causing the kingship to become an elective office. The kingship now became an ordinary office, generally priestly or judicial. Other offices were created, until at last the city became a complicated organism. During this process the Assembly of citizens lost what significance it had enjoyed. Although, as we shall see, most aristocracies eventually fell because of their own errors, they stimulated greatly the growth of Greece. The most important contribution which they made to the development of the city-state was the codification of law.

In the days when the laws were unwritten, it was to the obvious advantage of the nobles to twist to their own interest the laws, which, though not revealed by the gods, were under their protection and therefore deserving of great respect. In time the people protested against this custom and, because there already existed written lists of magistrates and treaties, insisted that the laws also be inscribed. The earliest codes of which we have any knowledge are not elaborate and tend to be harsh. They are associated with the names of lawgivers, persons, chosen to arbitrate between conflicting interests and entrusted with the task of ordering and writing down the laws. Something has been preserved of the code of the half-mythical Zaleucus of Locri in southern Italy. Of great importance is the fact that the penalties were determined not by the judges, but by the law itself. The provision regulating the dress of men and women reveals the typically Greek desire to educate, not simply to punish. The possibility of contract is recognized. This idea is, of course, opposed to the theory that might makes right and results from enlightened individualism. Another statute made it death by hanging to propose without success a change in an existing law. Here we can see the Greek dread of revolution—the drastic nature of the law, however, tended to freeze the *status quo*. Zaleucus' provision of "an eye for an eye and a tooth for a tooth" is probably historical. It is unique in Greek law and reflects Eastern influence. On the whole, Greek law was more humane than the Semitic. Certain traditional laws of Charondas, an early lawgiver of Catana, are also probably genuine and reveal a wide scope. They have to do with false witness, incendiarism, danger to property, buying and selling, divorce, orphans, heiresses, military service, and keeping bad company. Naturally, homicide and the dread of pollution which it involved received considerable attention in early law, but the motivating force here was not primarily religious. We can make out from the beginning a vague desire for self-help, which eventually became a determination that the will of the community should be superior to special interests, whether they belonged to individual, family, or clan. The end aimed at was to regulate the whole public and private life. Under the aristocracies, then, was created the sovereign law of the city-state, the idea that law should be supreme over men. There was, however, no written constitution—the constitution might change overnight with a change in party, but the body of civil law remained.

The Greek looked upon the city-state as normal. It afforded him liberty and generally protection; here he could trade and here he found the apparatus of government, magistrates, boards, codified law. Here, too, he could take some part in government, for, whether it was oligarchy or democracy, he might not delegate his functions. By the seventh century there were many city-states, in Thessaly, central Greece, the Peloponnesus, the Aegean islands, Asia Minor, and after the pattern of the mother cities, the newer colonies of the West. It should be emphasized that though the state was small, a city might extend its citizenship to an entire valley, the inhabitants of which would then look upon themselves not as citizens of this or that hamlet (deme), but of the chief city. This was called *synoikismos*. A federal state, however, might have a dual citizenship, in the state itself and in the local unit (*sympoliteia*). In spite of the obvious advantages of the city-state, however, many villages continued to exist in Greece.

Not infrequently a group of neighboring states combined in a league. The motive which first led to this lies far anterior to recorded history. It might have been a border market, the need of allies, the desire for frontier security, or a consciousness of kindred blood. Whatever may have been the practical impetus to friendly intercourse, such neighboring states chose the sanctuary of a deity conveniently situated. Here at stated times they met to worship or to hold a fair for the interchange of goods. A union of neighbors ostensibly for a religious object, but sometimes serving more practical ends, was termed an amphictyony. That of Delos, centering in the shrine of Apollo, reached the height of its splendor probably early in the seventh century. The Homeric *Hymn to the Delian Apollo,* composed a little later by a Chian poet, celebrates the gathering of the Ionians with their wives and children to worship this god with music, dancing, and gymnastic exercises, and to trade. From an original union of insular neighbors it had come to include all the Ionians. Without ever assuming a political character, it eventually declined. Another amphictyony comprised twelve states in the neighborhood of Thermopylae. Its earliest seat of worship was the shrine of Demeter at Anthela; but in time it acquired a second and more important center in the temple of Apollo at Delphi; [2] hence it came to be known as the Delphic Amphictyony. The object of the League was the protection of the shrines, especially of the temple and oracle of Apollo. The government lay in the hands of an amphictyonic Council, comprising forty-eight "speakers," four from each state, and twelve recorders. The speakers alone proposed and debated measures; the recorders alone voted. A resolution adopted by this Council in the immemorial past imposed an oath upon the members of the League not to destroy an amphictyonic city or to cut it off from running water in war or peace. Here was one of the earliest attempts to mitigate the primitive rigors of war. Many other decrees of the Council are known to us, including one which forbade the Greeks to levy tolls on pilgrims to the shrine, and another requiring the states of the League to keep in repair their own roads leading to Delphi. Against a state which trespassed upon any rights of the gods it had the power to declare a "sacred war." Although the Council sometimes championed the cause of Greece, as could any association or individual, it never acquired a recognized authority over all the Greeks; and notwithstanding its occasional participation in political affairs, it remained essentially a religious association (Figure 16).

A religious union tended to become political, especially when it contained a state of superior power and secular ambition. For example, the Boeotian Amphictyony, whose deities were Poseidon and Athena, was converted into a federal union by Thebes. Its constitution, which developed toward the end of the fifth century, grouped the states of the League in eleven units roughly equal in population. These units were equally represented in the federal magistracy, Council, and court, and had equal military and financial burdens. It provided further for a referendum of important matters to the states, and seems to have admitted of an initiative from the states. Theoretically the arrangement was most admirable; but in fact the Thebans, who constituted four of the eleven units of representation, dominated the federal policy.

On the whole, federation was a mark of political and intellectual backwardness and was popular with people such as the Aetolians and

[2] This happened about 590 B.C., when Thessaly, dominating the Amphictyony and hoping to become influential in central Greece, declared a Sacred War against Crisa and wrested Delphi from its control. Thessaly was then a strong military state, ruled by aristocrats who had made the masses serfs, called penestae.

Acarnanians. The intense particularism of the city-state was mitigated in part, however, by the amphictyony. Other factors, such as a common language, art, and literature, and general meeting places such as Olympia and Delphi, tended further to remind the Greeks that they were one people. The city-state, then, was the driving force in the development of Greece. Not least among its achievements was the period of colonization which it inaugurated shortly after 750 B.C.

Chapter V COLONIAL EXPANSION AND THE RISE OF TYRANNY

THE two centuries after 750 B.C. are among the most interesting in the world's history. Our information concerning this period approaches reasonable adequacy, so that, in spite of many problems, Greece for the first time takes on real flesh and blood. The Greek world, it will be recalled, was now ruled by aristocracies. Permanency was in the air. Yet in another century the aristocracies have gone and tyrants rule in their stead. Another century will witness the beginning of democracy. Meanwhile the Greek people have embarked on a second phase of colonial expansion, and dot the Mediterranean and Black Seas with their new settlements. The invention of coinage, the rise of industry, stimulating ideas from the East alter the scene. A veritable renaissance in literature and art occurs, but violence, class hatred, and poverty are not absent.

The fascination of a rapidly changing era is further enhanced by the number of problems. Did industry and trade cause colonization, or was it simply the need for more land that sent Greeks across the seas? Was tyranny due to the development of industry, or was it just a coincidence that tyranny flourished along the trade routes from Asia Minor to the West? It will not always be easy to separate cause and effect, and the further we proceed in point of time from the beginning of colonization the more likely will it be that various forces are involved, including the power of example. Indeed, different factors were always present.

We may start with the proposition that as a rule men do not willingly leave home, and if the land for which they are headed is unknown, perhaps a wilderness or inhabited by unfriendly natives, then it becomes clear that the motivating force must have been especially strong. Discontent of some sort is present. We have already noted that there was much poverty during the Greek Middle Age. The nobles succeeded to the king's power, and the rich became richer, the poor poorer, and many of the small farmers were reduced to slavery or serfdom. Besides this, in many communities the descendants of the pre-Dorians had been forced into serfdom. Hesiod of Ascra, the Boeotian poet who probably lived about 750 B.C., has left us a picture of contemporary conditions. In his *Works and Days* he complains bitterly against the greedy nobles who have seized the best land, whereas the poor farmers must be content with a stony and barren soil. He tells how one may increase the productiveness of the land and lessen somewhat the rigors of hard work and the heat and cold of the seasons. The first thing a man must do is to get a house, a woman, an ox for ploughing, and a dog. Work and save should be one's motto. The rising of certain stars and other phenomena of nature should be observed. Because peasant estates, divided equally among sons, soon became too small to support a family, Hesiod said it were better to bring up but a single son, especially as heirs often waste the estate in litigation, and the judges are ready to give the verdict to the one who brings the largest bribe. Packed though the poem is with good advice, Hesiod is essentially a prophet of justice, many of his ideas being borrowed from Ionia. Unlike Homer, he is already a poet of the *polis,* for his concept of justice is one that presumes the society of the city-state. He had a lasting influence on the next centuries.

By 750 B.C. the condition in many areas was even worse—not only had many farmers lost their freedom, but other farms were heavily mortgaged. As wealth accumulated in the hands of the nobles, there arose a demand for better wares than could be supplied by unskilled hands. To meet this need some of the poor who felt cramped on their little farms, or were made homeless by economic oppression, began

WESTERN ASIA MINOR

Miles
0   100

Map 13

60

manufacturing on a small scale. Those who had skill and thrift grew wealthy. Occasionally nobles joined in the new enterprise. Hand in hand with skilled industry developed slavery. A man who could buy a single slave for his shop became a capitalist on a small scale, until finally, as his business grew, he rivaled the old noble in wealth and could contend with him for political supremacy. The growth of industry was accordingly interwoven with the political and constitutional development of Greece.

The industries of the new age had their principal origin in Ionia and her neighbor Lydia, a country of diverse natural resources. The great plateau of Asia Minor was especially adapted to raising sheep, so that the textile industry quickly developed in the cities of the coast. Miletus won fame for her finely woven woollens of rich violet, saffron, purple, and scarlet colors, and her rare embroideries for the decoration of hats and robes. Pottery and wine formed other exports. Though the number of small factories gradually increased in the cities, the economy of the surrounding district remained agricultural. But as the cities grew in size, the problem of food arose, and also the need of markets. Second only to Miletus were other cities of Ionia, and Mytilene on the island of Lesbos.

Naturally the extension of skilled industry was from Asia Minor to the Greek mainland. Aegina, whose scant soil forced the people to industry and commerce, produced bronze work—such as cauldrons, tripods, and sculptured figures and groups—in addition to small wares of various kinds. In Euboea, on the strait of Euripus, Chalcis became a thriving industrial city. With metals, obtained in part from neighboring mines, and with the purple mollusc caught from the strait, she manufactured wares for war and peace and costly dyes for the wealthy.

In industry and commerce Chalcis had eventually to yield to Corinth, from early time renowned for her wealth. Its citadel was Acrocorinth, a steep and lofty peak commanding a view of the Isthmus below and of a wide expanse of country all about. The two harbors, one on the Saronic Gulf, the other on the Corinthian, afforded easy commerce with east and west. To avoid the hazardous doubling of Cape Malea, ships often unloaded their freight here, which was hauled across the Isthmus. Eventually a "drag-way" for pulling small ships across was constructed. The city was not only a mart but also a thriving center of industry, which produced wonderful vases, under a new strong influence from the East, bronze wares for utensils and arms, well-woven and beautifully dyed woollen fabrics for clothing and tapestries. Even the Ionians, not content with their rich native fabrics, welcomed the Corinthian robes of purple, sea-green, hyacinth, violet, and brilliant

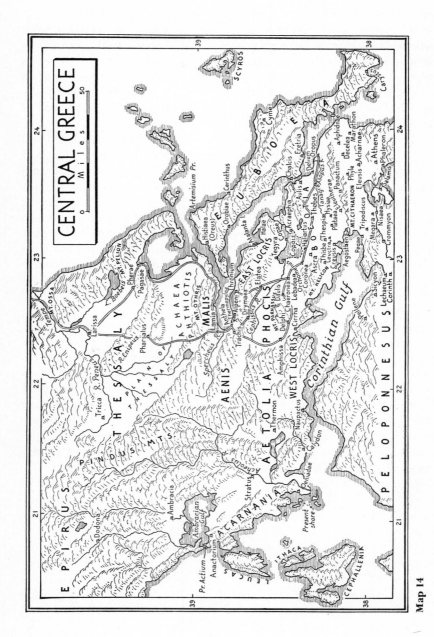

CENTRAL GREECE

Miles
0   5   50

62

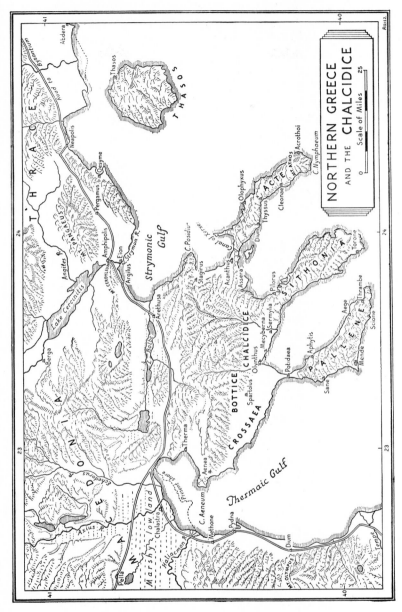

NORTHERN GREECE
AND THE CHALCIDICE

Scale of Miles

Map 15

63

red. In the vases were exported wines, olive oil, and toilet ointments. Under the leadership of the Bacchiadae, the ruling aristocracy,
Corinth began a momentous career and, often in friendly cooperation with Chalcis, extended its line of commerce in various directions.

Immediately to the north of Corinth was Megara, a little city-state
with a narrow territory extending across the Isthmus. The soil was
stony, scarcely fit for anything but grazing. This condition compelled
the Megarians to manufacture, with their scant means, coarse woollens
and heavy potteries, and from both their narrow coasts to traffic with
east and west. Attica remained essentially agricultural, though she
exported oil and wine in beautifully decorated vases. Her great industrial and commercial development belongs to the future, but even now
the growth of the city and the preponderance of the vine and olive over
grain raised a problem.

By the middle of the eighth century, then, the Aegean world presented
a complex and contradictory picture. The rise of industry, which
brought with it wealth and luxury, promoted slavery. Extremes of
wealth and poverty existed side by side. A proletarian class had come
into existence. The growth of trade gave birth to a new middle class,
the merchants. Thriving cities demanded not only an increased food
supply but also an importation of raw materials from distant countries, and markets for manufactured products. Even on the farms
slavery had increased, and many men had lost their land if not their
freedom. The land problem was further aggravated by a rapidly
growing population. The Greeks desired to live well. This was denied
to many, and the nobles made matters worse by denying them political
rights. Class consciousness and class hatred developed. In some places,
especially around the Corinthian Isthmus, there was bitter racial feeling between the Dorian lords and the non-Dorian serfs. We find in one
district, for example, that the non-Dorians were called by such humiliat-
ing names as *Dustyfoots, Sheepskins,* and *Club-bearers.* It is little
wonder that, when revolution finally came, the non-Dorians of Sicyon
should have named their tribe the *Rulers,* and designated the Dorian
tribes as *Pigmen, Swinemen,* and *Assmen.* The pages of the poet
Theognis show how bitter a noble might be. Not all these forces, it
will be observed, were everywhere present, nor by 750 B.C. were all of
them as active as somewhat later. The one thing uniform to the Aegean
world was discontent, varying in its cause from district to district.
Revolution might be forestalled, however, if enough people left. Ambitious nobles and the troublesome poor might in a new country satisfy
their yearnings to hold land and to rule. Being an adventurous race,

many Greeks decided on emigration as the best solution of their difficulties.

The two centuries from 750 to 550 B.C. are the period of colonial expansion. This was not the first time that people from the Aegean had traveled west, for during the Late Minoan colonies had been sent forth, and not long after 1000 B.C. mysterious refugees or pirates left the neighborhood of the Aegean and settled in central Italy where they became known to history as Etruscans. Some knowledge of this earlier expansion may have existed to encourage the new colonists in their venture. After all, they were going to the unknown. Fortunately, however, much of the Mediterranean basin enjoys the same climate and scenery, so that ordinarily the new home did not seem wholly strange. Somewhat oddly, perhaps, the natives as a rule were not hostile. As the expansion continued, more and more of the better sites being occupied, the Greeks found themselves opposed by Phoenicians, Carthaginians, and Etruscans. The advantages of colonial expansion had become obvious, and the chief powers of the Mediterranean were determined to gain as much as possible for themselves. In the beginning, some of the Greek states carved out for themselves spheres of influence, though all too frequently in the future they were to clash.

In the planting of a colony, *apoikia,* the Greeks gradually developed a body of customs, to which they felt morally bound. Generally speaking, the founding city, metropolis, after obtaining the sanction of the Delphic Apollo, appointed a noble as founder, to conduct the colonists to their new home, establish the government, and after death receive worship as a hero. Often an invitation was issued to friendly neighbors to take part. A charter of incorporation was drawn up which constituted the proposed settlement as a community, named the founder, provided for the assignment of lands and for other necessary matters, and regulated the relations between the mother and daughter cities. The tie was fundamentally one of kinship, such as binds parents and children. The strong bond of filial sentiment showed itself in the participation in common religious festivals, in the reciprocal rights and honors extended by each community to the members of the other, and in the general continuity of religious, social, and political usages and institutions of the old city in the new. A colony in the neighborhood of the mother-state usually remained politically dependent. The decentralizing tendencies were so strong, however, that distant colonies became forthwith sovereign states, yet united with the mother-state by the firmest bond of alliance known to the Greeks. The colonial movement tended to widen interest beyond the narrow limits of city-state.

Certain states were particularly active in sending out colonies. The

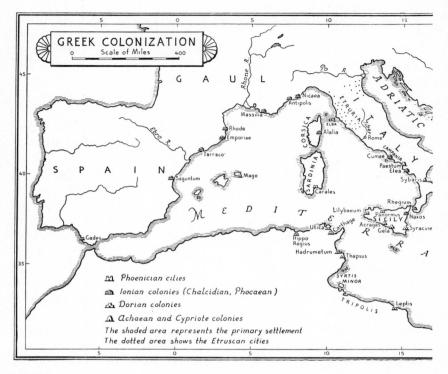

GREEK COLONIZATION
Scale of Miles

Phoenician cities
Ionian colonies (Chalcidian, Phocaean)
Dorian colonies
Achaean and Cypriote colonies
The shaded area represents the primary settlement
The dotted area shows the Etruscan cities

Map 16A

general direction taken by these new colonies was to the north Aegean, the Black Sea and its approaches, North Africa, and the West—Sicily, Italy, southern France, and Spain. Colonists from Chalcis were the first to go to Italy, and about the year 750 B.C. planted a colony near the bay of Naples, first on the island Pithecusae and then on the mainland at Cumae. Afterward, with some Athenians, the Cumaeans established Neapolis (Naples) nearby. The Cumaeans manufactured vases and metal wares for trade with the native Ausonians and with the Latins farther north. Their rich fields yielded an abundance of grain. Cumae was the first Greek center of culture with which the Romans came into touch; thence they borrowed religious ideas, especially the cult of Apollo, and the art of writing. Indeed, from the Grai, who had gone out with the Chalcidians as colonists, the Romans derived the word by which to designate the whole Greek race, though the Greeks, whenever they thought of themselves as one people, called themselves Hellenes. Other Chalcidian colonies were Himera, on the north coast of Sicily, Rhegium, on the Italian side of the Strait of Messene, and Zancle, the

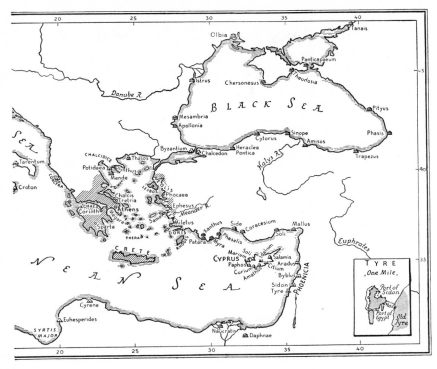

Map 16B   **Map 17**

"sickle-shaped" town, on the opposite side. In later years, when refugees fleeing before the Spartan conquest of Messenia settled there, it came to be called Messene (Messana).

Meanwhile Achaeans from the northern Peloponnesus founded Sybaris in the instep of the Italian peninsula. In the unhealthy but productive plain the people grew rich and expanded by colonization and conquest. A colony on the west coast, founded partly by them, was Posidonia (Paestum), famous for the lovely majesty of its temple to Poseidon (Figure 17). Although they were originally agricultural, the Achaeans developed a great commerce, especially as intermediaries between Ionia and Etruria. Milesian woollens, brought to Sybaris, were transported across the peninsula to her coast colonies, where Etruscan merchants eagerly bought them. Croton, another Achaean city, was famous for its athletes and warriors. Locri, a colony from Locris, remained purely agricultural, hence far inferior in wealth and population to the great Achaean cities.

The Dorians made one settlement of primary importance in Italy—

Tarentum, founded from Laconia in the time of the Messenian Wars. The acquisition of Messenia so satisfied Sparta's need for land that she sent out no further colonies. Tarentum had an excellent harbor in the instep of Italy, northeast of Sybaris. The settlers wrested from the native Iapygians a wide tract of land, where they farmed and raised sheep. Equally important were fishing and the preparation of purple dye. The Tarentines developed a great industry in weaving and dyeing fine woollens as well as in vase making. They exported their wares throughout the peninsula. So many Greeks settled in southern Italy that it was called Magna Graecia (Map 34).

One of the greatest colonizing states was Corinth, and among her foundations perhaps the greatest was Syracuse, destined to become in her day the most populous and the most strongly fortified city in Europe. Archias, a noble, sailing from Corinth, left a band of settlers under Chersicrates on Corcyra,[1] the large island off the coast of Epirus which made a convenient halting place for boats traveling to the West; and thence he proceeded to Sicily, where in 734 B.C. he founded Syracuse on the island of Ortygia. Soon the city expanded to the mainland, where the surrounding country was worked by the native population, Sicels, who had been reduced to serfdom. Great landlords, merchants, artisans, serfs, and slaves made up the city.

The most brilliant of the other Dorian colonies in Sicily was Acragas (Agrigentum). Oil and wine were exported to the marts of Carthage, and were paid for in silver. Through other colonies the Greeks nearly encircled the island, a process which brought them into conflict, in the west, with colonies of Carthage, itself the most famous of all Phoenician foundations.

As the ships of the Greeks developed from small round-bottomed boats to a somewhat longer type, with flatter bottoms, furnished with fifty oars and armed with a bronze beak for attack, navigation even further west became easy. The Samians, and more especially the Phocaeans, voyaged from Asia Minor to Spain for gold, silver, and copper. Beyond the Pillars of Heracles the distant Britain yielded tin, a metal chiefly prized as an ingredient of bronze. The Phoenicians, however, stoutly resisted Greek penetration beyond Gibraltar. But on the southern coast of Gaul the Phocaeans established a city of prime importance. Massilia (Marseilles) became the chief center of Greek culture in the western Mediterranean. She founded colonies in Gaul and Spain, and from them the natives learned to speak and write Greek. The Greeks of this region brought with them the Ionian laws and from Ephesus the

---

[1] The Eretrians found there were later driven out.

cult of Artemis, whose temples rose in every city. We must accordingly regard the Phocaeans as the forerunners of Rome in the work of civilizing southwestern Europe.

A somewhat different interest attaches to colonial movements in other directions. The founding of settlements along the northern Aegean, the Hellespont, and Propontis served merely to expand Aegean Greece to its natural limits. In the occupation of the Chalcidic peninsula the name itself suggests that Chalcis took the lead, though Eretria and Corinth participated.[2] The country was rough, but the chief occupation was agriculture, along with fishing. In later time the timber of the region proved a source of revenue, and in the neighborhood were the mines of Mt. Pangaeus. It was from these colonies that the Macedonians of the interior, a backward Greek people, slowly acquired the civilization of their progressive southern kinsmen.

Meanwhile the Ionians were sailing through the Hellespont and the Propontis and along the coasts of the Black Sea, to catch the tunny fish, to trade with the natives, and to plant settlements on all the shores. Miletus, a great colonizing state, is said to have founded eighty in this region, the most important of which were Cyzicus, Olbia, Panticapaeum, and Sinope. Although Greek settlements surrounded the Black Sea in a nearly unbroken chain, their civilization failed to penetrate far into the interior or materially to affect the natives. For such results the settlers were all too few. The Black Sea region furnished Greece with useful products, especially fish, timber, dyes, wheat, metals, cattle, and slaves. On the Bosporus, however, rose a great city, Byzantium, the most famous among the colonies of Megara. On the opposite Asiatic shore was Chalcedon, an earlier foundation by Megara. Byzantium was situated on a spacious bay in touch with migrating shoals of fish—a great source of wealth to the inhabitants. Their command of the strait enabled them to levy tolls on passing ships, while splendid opportunities for commerce, combined with a strong defensible position, further contributed to their prosperity. A thousand years after its founding, this city, under the name of Constantinople, became the capital of the Roman Empire.

In another direction Greek enterprise was to bear rich intellectual fruit. About the middle of the seventh century Psammetichus, with Ionian and Carian aid, made himself master of Egypt. Being friendly to the Greeks, he and his dynasty permitted a settlement of Ionian traders on the Canobic channel of the Nile to grow. A great trading post, Naucratis, developed, and here under the protection of the government

[2] Here the most important colonies of Chalcis were Olynthus and Torone; of Eretria, Mende, Methone, and Scione; of Corinth, Potidaea (Map 14).

various Greek cities of Asia Minor and the neighboring islands, together with Aegina, established their warehouses. The king enlisted many Greek mercenaries; the natives, whose country produced few grapes, enjoyed the wines imported from Greece, and sent in exchange the varied products of the East. Native interpreters excited the impressionable Greek tourist with wondrous tales. The importation of papyrus into Greece cheapened writing material, and the elementary facts of geometry and astronomy, brought home by inquisitive tourists, stimulated the birth of Greek science and philosophy. To the opening of Egypt, therefore, we may trace in part the great intellectual awakening of Greece.

The effects of Greek colonization were, of course, immense. Though Phoenicians and Etruscans, and in places an inhospitable shore, had prevented the Greeks from settling everywhere,[3] nevertheless their settlements were numbered by the hundred and were scattered along the coasts of the Mediterranean and of its tributary waters. Colonization meant that the surplus population of a virile race found an outlet, that the needy gained land, that trade increased. It meant, too, a broadening of the Greek horizon, the steady penetration of new ideas from other countries. And inevitably Hellenism, Greek culture, was bestowed in a varying degree upon the peoples of the Mediterranean basin. In the West, for example, the Italian and Sicilian Greeks were a mighty factor in the civilization of Italy, and through Italy of central and western Europe.

The nobles had encouraged colonization, partly as a safety valve. The safety valve, however, did not work, for in spite of the many benefits from colonization, dissatisfaction remained. By the seventh century, indeed, two other causes for discontent had been added to those that we noted as contributing to colonization. The first was the growth of the hoplite force. These heavy-armed foot soldiers now constituted the citizen army, the old aristocratic cavalry being outmoded. It was inevitable that these middle-class citizens should demand and that they should receive a voice in the government.

The second cause for discontent had to do with the invention of coinage. During the Geometric period barter had been given up in favor of iron spits, and then in the early seventh century the Lydians invented metallic coinage, at first striated pieces of electrum, a natural amalgam of gold and silver.[4] The custom quickly passed to Ionia, and

[3] Cyrene, for example, was the only important Greek colony in North Africa (Map 17).

[4] Most numismatists today believe that coinage was not invented until almost a century later, somewhere toward the end of the seventh century. The evidence

regular Ionian and Lydian issues may be dated from the early seventh century. West of the Aegean Sea the people of Aegina were the first to stamp their coins, silver staters of about 12.3 grams. They had wide currency. Corinth was not far behind Aegina in coinage. Its standard coin was a silver didrachm weighing about 8.6 grams and therefore much lighter than the Aeginetan. This standard was adopted by Chalcis and Eretria in Euboea and also by Athens and came to be known as the Euboic standard. The invention of coinage, of course, greatly promoted commerce, but at the same time its introduction into an agrarian world was destined to have profound social consequences, for a new form of wealth, independent of land, was now possible. People of humble origin might become rich merchants or manufacturers and challenge the political exclusiveness of the landed proprietors.

We may say, then, that unrest was typical of the Greek world in the seventh century before Christ, but in a world as large as this the causes of unrest necessarily varied from one area to the next. Agrarian and industrial districts had their special problems. The enslaved farmer, the landless factory worker, the hoplite class, the merchant, each had his grievance. On the Corinthian Isthmus, it will be remembered, there existed bitter racial hatred between Dorian and non-Dorian, whereas in Sicily there was the added fear of Carthage. The aristocracies were threatened on many fronts, and on most of them they went down before an upheaval of the people. Still, in every case, there was a special reason. General unrest was not enough; a specific crisis was needed. It is not surprising, for example, to find revolution in the states along the trade-route from Asia Minor to the West, for the rise of industry had created its own problem, not least of which was the knowledge of a larger world and the possibility of greater comforts. But even so, aristocracy might have survived, had it not been grossly incompetent at time of crisis. Thus, when we look at Asia Minor, we see that tyranny was immediately preceded by the inability of the nobles to resist the growth of Lydia. Similarly, at Corinth, tyranny followed the failure of the nobles, the

---

for this view is numismatic and archaeological; it seems to contradict the evidence of the ancient writers. To accept the new date would require us to rewrite important parts of the history of the seventh and sixth centuries B.C., but the arguments of the numismatists do not seem sufficiently secure to justify such radical action at this time. The fundamental case for the new date is made by E. S. G. Robinson in "The Coins from the Ephesian Artemision Reconsidered," *Journal of Hellenic Studies,* **71** (1951), 156–167; and in "The Date of the Earliest Coins," *Numismatic Chronicle,* **16,** 6th Ser., (1956), 1–8. For a criticism of his arguments see Donald Kagan, "Pheidon's Aeginetan Coinage," *Transactions of the American Philological Association,* **91** (1960), 121–136.

Bacchiadae, in foreign affairs, especially in the handling of their colony Corcyra.

The procedure which the people used in ridding themselves of the hated system was to rally round an individual, not infrequently a noble turned radical, and so to overthrow the existing aristocracy. A person who thus seized the reins of government illegally was known as a tyrant, in its origin a word imported from Lydia, where the example of tyranny had first been set by Gyges. The word *tyrant* carried in the beginning no opprobrium. Tyranny has sometimes been considered a peculiar Greek institution, a sort of interregnum between the rule of the few and the many, because it seems to interrupt the progression from the rule of one to that of the few and sometimes to that of the many. Actually, however, tyranny was a necessary, though at the moment an unconscious, step on the road to democracy, for in the days before the democratic process had been worked out, the natural thing for the masses to do was first, under a leader, to destroy the present system. Later on, as the general level of the masses was raised, it would be easy enough to get rid of the tyrant. After all, the seventh and sixth centuries, the centuries of the tyrants, were an age of questioning, and the critical faculties of the Greeks were hardly limited to literature and art.

The tyrant's power rested ultimately upon the people and therefore he ruled in their interest to some degree. There must be provided not simply work, but an access to wealth and culture, to the privileges of a full life. This frequently meant a ruthless attack upon the nobles. Aside from this, however, the tyrants often maintained the civil law as they found it. By undertaking great public works, they increased prosperity. No force in the Greek world contributed so much to cultural progress. The tyrant's patronage attracted poets, painters, sculptors, and architects, who formed in his court a brilliant and versatile society. Rhapsodists recited the Homeric poems at popular gatherings; at festivals in honor of the old god Dionysus, song and recitation—the germ of the drama—celebrated the sufferings and joys he experienced among mankind. By thus fostering literary interest among the people and by attaching them to newer cults, the tyrant freed them in a degree from the priestly influence of the old nobility and educated them for self-government.

Among the great tyrants were those of Asia Minor, Ephesus and Miletus, and the neighboring islands, Mytilene (on Lesbos), and Samos, though strictly Pittacus of Mytilene was a dictator, a magistrate appointed for a definite term (*ca.* 585–575 B.C.) to relieve the distress. The tyrant *par excellence,* Thrasybulus of Miletus, is now unfortunately an obscure figure. His rise was due to the Lydian danger. The presence of a foreign enemy helps to explain why, under certain tyrants, there was a lessening of colonization, for the people were needed at home. Among the earliest tyrannies on the Greek mainland was that of Cypselus (*ca.* 655–625 B.C.), the son of a non-Dorian father, but related on his mother's side to the Bacchiad nobles. He came to power on the threat of Argos and Megara and the mishandling of Corcyra. Under Cypselus commerce greatly increased and Corinth was able to maintain herself as the greatest sea power in Greece.

His son was the famous Periander (*ca.* 625–550 B.C.). Heartless though he was in his treatment of the nobles, Periander was in other ways a wise and moderate ruler. Under him an important city in the Chalcidice, Potidaea, was founded. By checking the importation of slaves, he assured to skilled workmen a better social standing than this class enjoyed elsewhere. As market and harbor customs sufficed for the need of government, the citizens were relieved of direct taxes. Luxury, power, and brilliance characterized Corinth. During his long reign his grasp weakened, and three years after his death the tyranny was overthrown by a band of conspirators who instituted a moderate, stable, and long-lived oligarchy.

Next in brilliance among the early Greek tyrannies was that at Sicyon, founded by the non-Dorian Orthagoras (*ca.* 656 B.C.). The city of Sicyon lay northwest of Corinth in the narrow but fertile valley of the Asopus. The district was as famous for its garden and orchard products as for bronze wares and potteries. In addition to landlords and their serfs there had developed a considerable class of artisans and traders. Of the descendants of Orthagoras it was Cleisthenes (*ca.* 600–560 B.C.) who made Sicyon one of the most magnificent cities in Greece. His first effort was to free Sicyon from the political control which Argos hitherto had exercised over it. This object he accomplished in a successful war. To free his countrymen from religious dependence on their former master, he expelled from the city the cult of Adrastus, an Argive hero. The establishment of games in honor of Adrastus later on at Nemea, and of other games at the Isthmus, gives us a hint of the waning popularity of tyrants. But the incident of Adrastus illustrates the singular importance of hero cults among the early Greeks. Another picture of Cleisthenes, drawn from Herodotus, shows how, by the transformation of Sicyon from an agricultural to an industrial and commercial state, this tyrant had given his city an international importance. From various parts of Greece came many young men of noble birth to seek the hand of his daughter Agariste. After a year's entertainment and competition, the lucky suitor was the Athenian, Megacles, a member of the illustrious Alcmaeonid family. From this union was born the famous lawgiver Cleisthenes, and among their descendants in the fifth century were Pericles and Alcibiades. The story of the wooing of Agariste sheds a pleasant light on the genial elegance of the tyrant, on his wide interstate connections, and on the social relations and intermarriage of the great nobles of Greece. Indeed, at a somewhat earlier date, the tyrant of Megara, Theagenes, had aided his son-in-law, Cylon, in an abortive attempt to set up a tyranny at Athens.

On the whole tyrannies were short-lived, though for special reasons Asia Minor was an exception; Persia, as she advanced to the seaboard, found tyranny a surer method of controlling the Greeks. But in spite of the fact that the sons and grandsons of tyrants became corrupted by wealth and power and so degenerated as to give the word *tyrant* its present meaning, tyranny had performed a great service. Aristocracy had been destroyed, the base of wealth has been broadened, an intelligent patronage had been extended to the arts. Many states were now ready for democracy, but in the never-ending struggle between the few and the many, some states returned to oligarchy, albeit a more liberally constituted oligarchy than the earlier aristocracy. In this great period of colonial expansion, of industrial development, and social change two states, Sparta and Athens, stand out. Their institutions and growth make an absorbing study, and we must therefore turn to it before considering the art and literature of archaic Greece.

Chapter VI SPARTA AND THE PELOPONNESIAN LEAGUE

IN THE development of the city-state Sparta stands apart. Her history illustrates how a rigorous training can turn a people, essentially no braver than the rest of mankind, into an invincible force; it shows, too, how conservatism can stagnate until it becomes a cruel selfishness determined to maintain a system no matter what the cost. Sparta became the most powerful state in Greece as a result, but the price exacted was high.

Sparta was pleasantly situated near the center of Laconia, beside the banks of the slowly winding Eurotas. The sea was well to the south, but not far west rose the majestic range of Taÿgetus, beyond which lay non-Dorian Messenia. When the Dorians first entered Laconia, they reduced the native Achaeans to a state of serfdom. These unhappy people were called helots. Helotry does not represent the gradual enslavement of free farmers, it is the result of deliberate action. Those natives who had fled to the mountains at the coming of the Dorians were allowed to remain there in a semi-independent condition and, together with the Dorians who had settled amongst them, perhaps as colonists, became known as perioeci, "dwellers around."

Whether it was due to the needs of a growing population or simply to the fact that appetite is insatiable we cannot know, but about 730 B.C. Sparta reached across Mt. Taÿgetus and appropriated the land of Messenia. The Spartan poet Tyrtaeus, who lived a century after the Messenian Conquest, tells us that the real motive was a desire "to plough and plant fertile Messenia." The bitter struggle centered on Mt. Ithome, but finally, after twenty years, the Spartans and King Theopompus were victorious. The land was divided amongst the Spartan citizens, and the Messenians were reduced to serfdom. The new helots, Tyrtaeus tells us, went about "like asses worn with heavy loads, forced to bring their master the half of all the soil produces."

At the conclusion of the Messenian Conquest Sparta sent a colony of malcontents to Italy to found Tarentum; otherwise her hunger for land was temporarily satisfied. The Messenian Conquest meant, then, not only that Sparta had more than doubled the number of her helots, but also that in the long run she was to be denied the broadened horizon which came from contact with the outside world through colonization. This did not mean at all, however, that Sparta had at the moment embarked upon a policy of isolation. Sparta was in some ways the cultural leader of Greece at the opening of the seventh century. Terpander came from Lesbos to play upon his lyre; Thaletas of Gortyn introduced choral song and dance; and the great Alcman, perhaps a Lydian from Sardes, sang his verses. His poems give us a glimpse of Spartan life, a life of contentment, of peace and love and pleasure. Laconian pottery in general (Figure 18), and particularly the British discoveries at the Sanctuary of Artemis Orthia, illustrates the fine taste of the early Spartans. Sparta also had commercial relations with the Asiatic Greeks.

There was no real reason, consequently, why Sparta should not develop much as other Greek states. The helot system and the withdrawal from colonization set her somewhat apart, to be sure, and would inevitably leave their mark, but each state had its own individuality. Then, in the second half of the seventh century, the whole course of Spartan history began to change. Taking advantage of internal disturbances and of the fact that the refinements of life were causing the Spartans to lose their warlike character, the Messenians revolted. They were aided by Argives, Arcadians, and Pisatans, a coalition strong enough to defeat Sparta at first. It was under these conditions that Tyrtaeus came forward to inspire and guide. He was not merely a poet but a statesman and military leader, as was Solon shortly afterward at Athens. Through his generalship the Spartans conquered Messina, and those people who had not escaped from the country resumed the yoke of serfdom.

The Spartans were quick to see the significance of the Messenian revolt. Could they hope to lead an ordinary life devoted to commerce, agriculture, and the arts, and indefinitely keep in subjection a population ten times their size? The easy life of the helot system was apparently too great a temptation. They decided to keep it, but this meant a reordering of their lives. Art and poetry, the pursuit of culture and

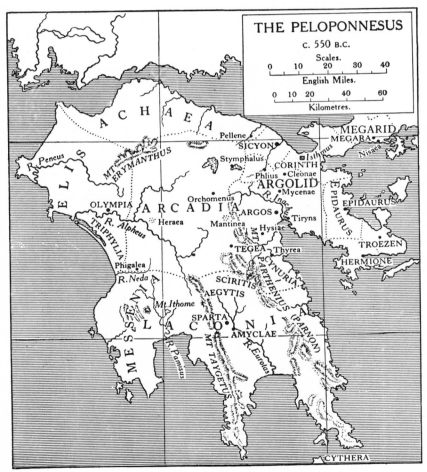

Map 18

comfort, all must go. Resolutely they turned their backs upon commerce, upon all currency except iron money. Within a few decades the old Sparta was gone. Nothing mattered now except keeping the helots in their place and making Sparta a powerful military state. The name of Lycurgus is associated with the reform of about 600 B.C. which brought the new state into being. Although Sparta must be considered an oligarchy, in view of the great masses whom she ruled, we shall note that the constitution for the citizens had a slightly democratic element, whereas a socialistic despotism governed their own lives.

The Spartans now constituted themselves as a perpetual army and transformed their city into an unwalled camp. Their whole life was occupied with training. This principle controlled marriage, the birth and education of children, economy, and occupation—in brief, every activity of life. In other countries of Greece custom gave the father the option of rearing his child or of putting it to death immediately after birth. In Sparta this function was usurped by a board, which might order the exposure of a weak child on Mt. Taÿgetus. If, however, the child was allowed to live, he was put in the care of his mother and a nurse until his seventh year. On reaching the age of seven he was taken from his mother and placed directly under the control of the state. Under youthful captains the boys were organized for athletic and military drill. They had no bedclothes, cooked their own meals, and contributed to the mess what they had stolen, for theft was encouraged as an exercise in agility and cleverness, though one caught in the act was punished. Once a year the supreme test of endurance was applied, when at the altar of Artemis Orthia the boys submitted to a flogging. The severe training resulted not only in strength, agility, and endurance, but also in a quiet, modest bearing which has no parallel in modern life.

At the age of twenty the youth became a man liable to service in the field. He was now permitted to marry, but for a long time he could see his wife only by stealth. In fact, he never had the enjoyment of a home, but passed his entire life in military drill, eating and sleeping in the barracks. He now joined a *syssition* (mess) of about fifteen members. Each member contributed his monthly share of barley, wine, cheese, figs, and meat. At thirty the Spartan became a mature man, privileged to attend the Assembly, if indeed this was not granted to him earlier, and to fill such political offices as required no advanced age qualification. Continuing their military exercises, the men passed the remainder of their time in the gymnasia and clubs or at the *syssitia*. The severity of life was mitigated in campaigns, which seemed a relief from the labors of peace.

A similar training for girls continued, however, only till marriage. The chief wedding rite was a pretended abduction of the bride by force —a relic of the primitive custom of marriage by actual capture. While their husbands lived in the barracks, the women enjoyed leisure and comparative luxury at home. They had a part in many religious festivals. Through dowries and inheritances they gradually accumulated property till, in the time of Aristotle, they owned nearly two fifths of the land. The land which each Spartan received from the state was inalienable, but other lands might be bought and sold. However, the disparities in wealth which developed made no difference, for in Sparta all lived alike in a socialistic community, which sacrificed the individual to the ideal good of the state.

The people for whom all this careful preparation was being made were the helots, the pre-Dorian population that had been reduced to serfdom. They were assigned to the lands of the citizens, who were forbidden to enfranchise them or to sell them outside the country. The idea was that they belonged to the state rather than to the individual. They lived with their families in cottages on the lots assigned them, and rendered to their masters the amount of produce fixed by law— this was rigorously insisted upon, for a member falling behind in his contribution was suspended from his *syssition*. In fruitful years the helots could save something. In addition to tilling the soil they aided in preparing their masters' meals and performed any other menial labor imposed by their individual lords or by the state. They were liable to service in time of war, when on rare occasions the brave received their freedom. Nevertheless the helots were subjected to many indignities, and were compelled to wear dogskin caps and mantles of sheepskin. As a means of spying upon them, a secret police force, called the *crypteia,* was formed. In order that a member of the *crypteia* might kill a dangerous helot without incurring the guilt of murder, the ephors were accustomed each year on entering office to proclaim war upon the helots.

Round about Laconia, it will be recalled, lived in towns of their own the perioeci, who were a mixture of pre-Dorians and Dorians, originally free, but now reduced to dependence on Sparta. They provided a defense for the land and hedged the helots in. Personally free, with their own town government, the perioeci formed the business community of Laconia. They worked the iron mines of Mt. Taÿgetus, and manufactured various iron, steel, and bronze objects. Commerce brought them wealth, nor were they without intellectual eminence. With the Spartans they constituted the "Lacedaemonians," and they were of course liable to military duty.

The Spartan army in fact consisted of five regiments, for part of the reform of Lycurgus had been to substitute for the three old Dorian tribes five new ones, based on locality rather than descent. Four of the tribes were confined to the town of Sparta, the fifth to Amyclae, and upon them the army was based. The commanders of the army, and in the earliest known constitution the chief magistrates, were the two kings—from the royal families of the Agiads and Eurypontids. The kings were priests of Zeus and certain other gods, and judges in cases concerning family law and public highways. As commanders of the army they originally had a right to declare war against whatsoever enemy they pleased; but this and other powers were gradually taken from them.

The hand of Lycurgus can also be seen in the new organization of the government. Although all the citizens, Spartiates, were called Peers (*Homoioi*), a certain dignity seemed to attach to those who had been citizens before the reform, for apparently new citizens were now admitted. Consequently it was only the citizens of the older type who were eligible for membership in an important body formed at this time. The *gerousia,* or Council of old men, was composed of twenty-eight elders, past the age of sixty, and the two kings. It considered measures to be presented to the *apella*, or Assembly, and assisted the chief magistrates in the management of public affairs. It exercised jurisdiction in cases affecting the life or civil status of the citizens and in all important criminal cases in which citizens were involved. The presidency of the body, originally belonging to the kings, was in time transferred to the ephors. Apparently the *gerousia* had the power to dismiss the *apella,* even though this was supposedly the sovereign body at Sparta. Under the presidency of the kings, afterward of the ephors, the *apella* elected magistrates, decided questions concerning the succession of kings, and accepted or rejected the measures which the magistrates and Council rarely brought before it. As at Rome, the members of the Assembly had no right to initiate measures or to join in the debate; they were strictly limited to listening and voting. Everywhere in Greece, however, the supreme political authority rested ultimately with the dominant military class; and at Sparta accordingly it was vested in the Assembly of heavy infantry. This body it was which wrested the supreme power from the kings. The Assembly did not exercise its authority directly, however, but devolved it upon a board of five ephors, elected annually from the citizens. Only in questions of war, peace, and other matters of unusual importance did it reserve the right of decision.

The ephors evidently existed from very early time, but with the lapse of centuries they superseded the kings as the heads of the state. They represented accordingly a democratic element in the constitution. The strong, independent development of the ephorate is associated with Chilon, 556 B.C. The ephors supervised the training of youths and watched over the conduct of the citizens. They presided over the *gerousia* and *apella,* tried nearly all the civil cases, and prosecuted criminals before the *gerousia.* Over helots they exercised absolute power, and in cases of political emergency they could put a perioecus to death untried. Their authority extended even over the kings. At the close of every nine-year period of a king's reign they watched the sky for an omen, which if found deposed him. Oftener by threats of prosecution for misconduct they drove him into exile. As heads of the state they carried on negotiations with other governments.

The great reform of the Spartan state was connected in antiquity with the name of Lycurgus, although it now seems probable that Lycurgus was a hero to whose protection the reform was entrusted. But whatever the name of the reformer, it is clear that he drew inspiration from the Dorian communities of Crete. The training of children, the public tables for the men, the military life, the division of the people into citizens of various social grades, perioeci, and serfs were somewhat the same. Much of our knowledge of Cretan customs and institutions comes from the great law code of Gortyn. The original kingship had given way in the cities to an aristocracy with a Council and Assembly. The chief magistrates were the ten *kosmoi,* drawn from the aristocracy, who commanded in war, exercised judicial and general administrative functions, and enforced discipline among the citizens. Perhaps it was from the *kosmoi* that the idea of the college of ephors arose.

Now that Sparta had turned her back upon commerce and the arts and had settled down to the enjoyment of the helot system and the perfection of her army, there was no reason why she should not use her army to obtain even more land. For one thing, she had a grudge to settle with Argos, who had defeated her at Hysiae. Argos had grown under king Pheidon to be a powerful state in the second half of the seventh century. First, however, Sparta directed her attention to Arcadia. The people here were mountaineers, non-Dorians, living in villages, but on the eastern border there had grown up under the cultural influence of Argos three city-states, Tegea, Orchomenus, and Mantinea. Several times during the first half of the sixth century Sparta attacked the Arcadians, and, while gaining an occasional success elsewhere, she was always defeated by Tegea. Finally, however, the Spartans won a victory over Tegea, but not such as to promise a conquest. Originally they had planned to helotize the Tegeans, but now they were content to form a permanent alliance with them (shortly before 550 B.C.). The ability of Sparta to carry this through was due to a master stroke of policy. She removed to Sparta the bones of Orestes, the son of Agamemnon. This was a significant gesture to non-Dorians, and showed them that the great Dorian state wished to live with them as an equal. Shortly afterward, the rest of Arcadia followed Tegea's example and entered into league with Sparta (Figure 19).

This was the beginning of the Peloponnesian League. Meanwhile, Sparta wrested Cynuria and Cythera from her ancient rival Argos and in 546 B.C., at the famous Battle of Champions, humbled her on the plain of Thyrea. The people of Elis were ready for a close alliance. Corinth and Sicyon, freed from tyrannies, entered the League, as did Troezen, Epidaurus, and, later, Megara and Aegina. Thus before the close of the sixth century, all the states of the Peloponnesus, except Argolis and much of Achaea, were leagued with Lacedaemon.

A separate treaty united each state with Sparta. In it both Sparta and her ally promised "to have the same friends and enemies." This usually meant that each ally followed Sparta's lead in foreign policy, but in practice there were important exceptions. Corinth and Themes, though located outside the Peloponnese, became allies of Sparta on equal terms with the other states and often conducted independent policies, sometimes even compelling Sparta to follow their lead. There was no formal constitution; custom and the realities of power determined the functioning of the Peloponnesian League. Meetings of the League were called by Sparta at her convenience. Obviously the Spartans would call such a meeting to gain the support of their allies before embarking on a war, in which the role of allied armies would be vital. On such occasions an important ally might veto the Spartan proposal and thrwart Sparta's will. Usually, however, the Spartans were strong enough to have their way; often they entered a war and called upon their allies for troops without holding a meeting. No tribute was assessed but, in wartime, financial contributions were sometimes required. In theory the allies were free to manage their internal affairs but in practice the Spartans usually insisted on oligarchic regimes with which they felt comfortable. Sparta was usually hostile to both tyrannies and democracies.

In spite of her great military power, Sparta was usually reluctant to take an army outside of the Peloponnese. In part this was caused by fear of a helot uprising, in part by fear of Argos, and to some degree by the fear that exposure to the temptations of conquest, glory, wealth, and customs of other men might corrupt the delicately balanced constitution and severe mode of life imposed by the Lycurgan reform. In

524 B.C., however, probably at the behest of Corinth, the Spartans launched a naval expedition against Polycrates, the piratical tyrant of Samos. The attempt was unsuccessful, though Polycrates was put to death shortly afterward by the Persian satrap at Sardes. The significant thing for history, however, is that Sparta's well-centralized military force was receiving its finishing touches at the very time when the danger of Oriental conquest began to threaten Greece.

Chapter VII

ATHENS AND THE TRIUMPH OF DEMOCRACY

O UR information about Athens is fuller than for any other Greek state, which is indeed fortunate, for in time Athens became the greatest of Greek democracies. Precisely why she became a democracy is of course as important a study as that of her democratic constitution. It was a long process, from monarchy to democracy, and the first step taken could not have been with any conscious knowledge of the ultimate goal. In a general way, however, we can say that the Athenians vaguely knew what they wanted and were able through the centuries finally to embody their wants in a code with the proper machinery for smooth operation. The Athenians, furthermore, did not inherit from the Migrations the curse of serfdom, with all the hatred and fear which it engendered; on the contrary, Attic tradition points to no conquest, but to a steady, even development. A tolerant habit of thought and a natural quickness and inventiveness of mind characterized the people. The road from monarchy to democracy is marked by aristocracy and then by a period of lawgivers who forestall revolution, though revolution and tyranny must still come before the final realization of democracy. There is a definite reason for each new chapter and generally the telling factor in each case is the failure of the existing regime.

Athens is but a part of Attica, a peninsula of about 1,000 square miles jutting into the Aegean Sea. Cithaeron, Parnes, and other mountains cut it off from central Greece, but this is compensated for by good harbors at Marathon and, nearer Athens, at Phaleron and Piraeus. The marble quarries on Mt. Pentelicus, the silver mines at Laurium, near the tip of the peninsula, and a wonderful clay were among Attica's chief natural assets. Wheat, olive groves, and vineyards grew in the Attic plain. The peninsula is large, as such things go in Greece, and in a general way it forms a natural unit. But in early times Attica comprised many different communities. Inhabited from the Neolithic period, Athens by the Mycenaean Age was clearly the most important settlement. Her broad flat rock, the Acropolis, was protected by a wall, attributed to the Pelasgians, and on the summit was a palace. Perhaps it was the mountains on the frontier which saved the various communities of Attica from the shock of overwhelming invasion at the end of the Bronze Age, but in any case the population of Attica, Ionian Greeks, was spared this trial. Not only does tradition attest this, but archaeology, particularly with the continuous development of pottery from Mycenaean into geometric, proves it.

The outstanding fact in the history of early Attica is the gradual growth of a community of interest among the inhabitants. In time—perhaps it took from 1000 to 700 B.C.—the people of Attica were willing to transfer their allegiance to one city, Athens. This is the great *synoikismos,* attributed to the hero Theseus. Many nobles no doubt came to live in the new capital, but most people remained in their own villages. Political sovereignty, however, was vested in Athens, and everyone considered himself an Athenian. There was no such thing as an Attican.

We are able to recover something of the structure of Athens before the *synoikismos.* Like other Greek states, early Athens had a king, an aristocratic Council, and an Assembly of the people. The people were grouped in the four Ionian tribes (*phylae*), each of which was divided into three phratries, originally brotherhoods of fighting comrades, but now small administrative units. In the autumn the phratries celebrated the Dionysiac festival of the Apaturia, which served to remind the world that Attica was the home of all Ionians. Though everyone belonged to tribe and phratry, only the nobles were privileged to belong to the *gene,* or clans. We can see in the very beginning, then, two institutions at Athens which were bound to hinder orderly progress. One was the phratry, closely connected with religion, membership in which was necessary for citizenship. Membership could be had only by birth, and although this made no difference in the days of primitive isolation, it stored up trouble for the future. The other institution was the aristocratic *genos,* whose only purpose was to serve the interest of the landed nobility, the Eupatrids. The sole Council in early Athens was an aristocratic body called the Areopagus, a development of the Homeric Council of elders. Its functions were administrative, judicial, and religious, and, after the creation of the archons, its membership was made up of these magistrates on the expiration of their year of office. At the top stood the king, and although the names of many kings are known to us, we can only be certain that the last ruling dynasty was that of the Medontidae.

The kings completed the unification of Attica, one of their last acts being the annexation of Eleusis and the Thriasian plain. By 700 B.C. the *synoikismos* of all Attica, a long process obscure to us, was ended, and henceforth all citizens were Athenians. Somewhat after this the monarchy ceased to be, and Athens entered upon a period of aristocratic rule. The king's power, in the first place, had been weakened by the creation of the office of polemarch, or commander-in-chief. In the year 683 B.C. or earlier, the office of archon [1] was instituted, and this left the kingship with such little power that it was thrown open to annual election.[2] The *archon basileus,* or king archon, now concerned himself with religion. Shortly afterward were instituted the six *thesmothetae,* who were charged with guarding public documents and recording legal decisions. Just as increasing business had necessitated the creation of new offices, which eventually led to the abolition of the kingship, so the *thesmothetae,* who in time became judges, were to contribute to the weakening of the Areopagus.

During this period of aristocratic government the Areopagus was the heart of the constitution. It passed on the fitness of the archons as they entered office, supervised their actions during its tenure and audited their accounts at the end of their terms. The retiring archons entered the Areopagus, on which they thereafter served for life. The Assembly (*ecclesia*) had few powers. It elected the archons from among men suited by both birth and wealth. Even this choice from the nobility was limited by the Areopagus' right to scrutinize candidates. The

---

[1] This was the *archon eponymos,* who gave his name to the year.

[2] Perhaps a preliminary attack upon the kingship was made in 753 B.C., when the office may have been made decennial.

Map 19

Assembly was consulted on matters of importance to the state, and it was convened to consider questions of war and peace. Initiative, however, lay with the magistrates and the Areopagus; probably we would be wrong to imagine that the ordinary citizen took part in debate, even on the rare occasions when the Assembly did meet.

One of the first acts of the newly entrenched aristocracy was to reorganize the military forces of the state. The Dorian phalanx was introduced, but because the Eupatrids were too few to constitute a phalanx, they had to recruit the heavy infantry from the common landowners whose income would enable them to equip themselves with a panoply. To determine which persons were liable for service and what their duties should be, a census was taken and the entire population divided into classes based on property. Aristocracy of birth is now yielding some of its power to wealth, and from this timocracy of the heavy infantry, as it is called, was to grow a more liberal form of government. The people were grouped, for the purpose of the new military organization, into three classes: the *hippeis,* or knights, who were the wealthiest people in the state; the *zeugitae,* the great mass of the people, who made up the phalanx; and the poorest people, called *thetes.* To facilitate the raising of troops and their maintenance by land and sea, Attica was divided into forty-eight districts or naucraries, twelve being distributed among each of the four tribes. The humble post of "joint-carvers"—*colacretae*—under the kings was now developed into the office of treasurer.

Dissatisfaction with their lot made the Athenian populace fertile soil for a tyranny, and about the year 632 B.C. a powerful noble named Cylon, with the help of his father-in-law, Theagenes, tyrant of Megara, seized the Acropolis and attempted to make himself tyrant. But the heavy infantry, gathering from the country, besieged the conspirators, until finally they took refuge at the great altar of Athena on the Acropolis. Cylon meanwhile had escaped, but the chiefs, or *prytaneis,* of the naucraries promised the suppliants their lives if they would submit to trial. They agreed; yet, not having full confidence in the promise, they tied a thread to Athena's image, we are told, and holding one end of it, went down to the tribunal. When they came near the shrine of the Furies, the cleft at the east end of the Areopagus, the thread by which the goddess gave them her protection broke; and then the archon Megacles and his supporters stoned and butchered them, permitting only a few to escape. Megacles belonged to the great Athenian family of the Alcmaeonidae, and soon all of its members were exiled. In popular belief Megacles' sacrilege had brought the curse of impiety upon the entire clan; but more important than this, he had greatly weakened popular respect for the nobles.

Some action, obviously, was called for if Athens was to escape a tyranny. Thus far Athens had been spared the problems of industrialism, for the city was small and unimportant in contemporary Greece, but the plight of the tenant farmers called for attention. The *hektemoroi,* as those were called who had to pay one sixth of their produce to the great landowners, were the problem of the moment. About 621 B.C., therefore, an attempt was made to bring stability into Athenian life. Draco was commissioned with extraordinary power to codify the criminal law, and, although almost nothing is known about his reforms, it is clear that they marked a great advance, particularly in the field of homicide. The Athenians were cursed with the blood feud and the acceptance of compensation for injury and homicide, but fortunately there existed in Attica sanctuaries to which the slayer might flee while making terms with the kinsmen of the slain. Draco made use of these sanctuaries as places of trial for the various classes of homicide. The nearest of kin, assisted by the phratry, were still permitted to prosecute, it is true, but henceforth the state alone had power over the accused, to punish or acquit. This represented a great step forward in the administration of justice and the assumption by the state of its responsibility for the public welfare. Distinction was made between willful and unpremediated murder. The cases came before the Areopagus, before a court of nobles, called the *ephetae,* which apparently traveled from one sanctuary to another, and before the court of the Prytaneum, for here in the town hall the king archon and the four "tribe kings" also held court. It remained for a later period to differentiate their functions.

A harsh code, operating in the interest of the landowners, could not forever prevent the solution of a problem that was largely economic. Not only were farms mortgaged, the *hektemoroi* discontented, and many freemen in slavery for debt, but the magistrates continued their career of embezzlement, plunder, and judicial oppression. Some attempt was made to solve these problems by war, for the next chapter in Athenian history records the conquest of the neighboring island of Salamis and of Sigeum in the Troad. The capture of Sigeum was perhaps due to the desire to protect the route by which grain was imported from the Black Sea. This would indicate, then, that Athens was already outgrowing the resources of Attica. But the domestic situation would not wait, and thus in the year 594 B.C. the Athenians gave the archonship to Solon, a moderately rich noble, a merchant, poet, and sage, under whose leadership they had wrested Salamis from Megara, and, as it turned out, one of the great forward-looking statesmen of ancient Greece.

So closely interwoven is the fabric of a state that Solon had to give his attention to economics, the constitution, and law. It was not his intention to set up a democracy, for he would not have understood the word, but rather he was appointed to reconcile conflicting interests and to make possible security and stability in the future. He succeeded to an extraordinary degree, though his failure to deal radically with certain problems postponed the final arbitrament for a century. On entering office Solon proclaimed the abolition of all securities on land and person, freed those who had fallen into slavery, and forbade any one in the future to offer his body as security for a loan. This was called the *seisachtheia,* or shaking off of burdens. To the cry of the "cancellation of debts," so often raised in ancient Greece, Solon had yielded, but he resisted the other, equally familiar cry for the "redistribution of the land." This seemed a fair compromise. The cancellation of debts, however, did not apply to ordinary commercial debts. Here, too, Solon recognized a problem, and to make it easier to pay one's debts he hit upon an ingenious device, or at any rate his revision of the coinage had that result. To facilitate trade with Corinth, Chalcis, Eretria, and their many colonies, Solon shifted from the Aeginetan standard to the Euboic. Debts contracted under the old standard might now be paid under the new which was lighter by a third. Solon also revised the Attic system of weights and measures.

Though he realized the importance of the land problem in Attica, one of Solon's most statesmanlike acts was his recognition that the future belonged to the city and that only through its development could the state achieve greatness. His revision of the coinage, and the emphasis on the silver trade, was a step in that direction. Meanwhile Athens needed grain, and because, not yet being an industrial state, the only way she could pay for its importation from the Black Sea was to export agricultural products, Solon concentrated upon the cultivation of the olive. It was forbidden to export grain or other products, for they were needed at home and could not in any case capture a foreign market. But the fine olive oil, stored in beautiful vases, might. This brought to the fore the question of industrial development, for clearly Attica could not support the growing city. In order to attract artisans from other centers, Solon promised them citizenship, if they came with their wives and children and settled permanently in Attica. Although this seems to us a rather natural action to take, the implications then were enormous, because the ancient point of view about citizenship was so different from our own. It will be recalled that birth brought citizenship and membership in a phratry, all accompanied by religious obligations. How could a non-Athenian aspire to this? Solon formed religious societies for the new citizens, so that they might join the body politic on much the same terms as the other members of the state, and, as for the rest of it, apparently most people, though shocked at first, felt that the plan would benefit the state. As soon as the state was built up and citizenship became a real prize, the Athenians, under the leadership of Pericles, reversed this liberal policy. The opening of the silver mines at Laurium was another momentous step. Solon also showed wisdom in limiting the amount of land an individual might own, and in requiring that public actions be entered in writing. The revision of the calendar, so that it consisted of alternate months of thirty and twenty-nine days, no doubt helped the business and agricultural life of the community.

Solon's law code was fairer and more definite than that of Draco. The laws of homicide were left substantially untouched, but the excessive penalties were lightened. To make amends for the harshness of previous judicial decisions, and to create a better atmosphere, he decreed an amnesty to all who were in exile excepting those condemned for homicide or attempted tyranny. Under this edict the Alcmaeonidae returned to their homes. In his reform of the civil code Solon noted that wills were unknown, and in default of children the estate passed to the nearest of kin. This left the individual too much in the grip of family, so that Solon enacted that in case a man had no children he might will his estate to whomsoever he pleased. This was often accomplished through the medium of adoption. In his reform of the code there is a persistent effort to free the individual from family and religious associations and to attach him more closely to the state.

Under Solon the journey from aristocracy to timocracy was completed, for, in his revision of the constitution, wealth became the sole qualification for office. The old property classes were kept, except that the richest men in the state were put into a special class known as the "500 bushel-men" (*pentacosiomedimni*); below them were the knights (*hippeis*), those whose estates produced annually 300 to 500 *medimni* or measures of produce; next, the *zeugitae* with 200–300 measures, and finally the *thetes*, the laborers who produced under 200 measures. The next step, and from the point of view of constitutional development it was a profound one, was to substitute drachma for *medimnus;* that is, to abandon the old land qualification for one expressed in terms of money. Probably at first Solon's reform of the property classes had little effect upon the working of the constitution, which would still remain in the hands of the landed nobility, but with increased prosperity just ahead it means that soon all but the poorest could qualify for high office. The various magistrates, the nine archons, the *colacretae* and other financial officials, were restricted to the two top property classes and were elected annually by the people. The importance of the naucraries was somewhat diminished, their functions being largely confined to the collection and disbursement of certain public funds. The *zeugitae* were now eligible for membership in the new Council (*boule*), and the *thetes,* though debarred from office, sat in the Assembly (*ecclesia*). (See Glossary for terms.)

The Council of Four Hundred was recruited from the four tribes,

100 from each. A characteristically Greek feature was its probouleutic nature; that is, it prepared the agenda for the meeting of the Assembly, which could only discuss matters so brought before it. This effectively controlled the deliberations of the Assembly, which was now more democratic with the admission of the *thetes*. The creation of the *heliaea,* courts to which men above thirty years from all four property classes were eligible, really laid the foundation of democracy. The function of the *heliaea* was to receive appeals from the judicial decisions of the archons, to permit the people themselves, that is, to be the court of last resort, to try the retiring magistrates for misconduct in office, in case any one accused them.

Although Solon created no democracy, his archonship opened a new chapter in the history of Athens. The people were relieved somewhat from the oppression of the nobles, and freed from the fear of tyranny. The future seemed secure. The establishment of the *heliaea* made the government more popular. In the absence of pay for public service, however, the citizens could rarely attend the Assembly in large numbers, and few could sit in the *heliaea*. The high property qualification of the magistrates was a strong aristocratic element; so too was the old Council of the Areopagus, which was left unimpaired by Solon, and, being made up of ex-archons who held office for life, could hardly be expected to show sympathy for the masses, in spite of their popular election. The net result was that the rich and noble were to fill the offices, the commons were to have only enough power to check them and preserve their own liberty. But Solon failed greatly in two respects. The nobles and their retainers were practically above the law. Recognizing this, Solon attached a heavy fine to idleness, hoping thereby to break up dangerous groupings, but a more radical operation was needed. His other failure related to land, for although he had freed the slaves, thereby alienating the Eupatrids, many men were still without land. The shepherds of the hills were especially oppressed. These two failures give the key to the next developments in Athenian history.

With a simple faith that all was now well, Solon left his country for ten years. But all was not yet well, and actually in 590–589 B.C. and again in 586–585 B.C. Athens came very near to revolution. The trouble lay primarily with the three parties which made up Athenian politics. The men of the coast, fishermen, city craftsmen, were inclined to abide by Solon's arrangements. In this party were many of the newer citizens, who had recently come to Athens, and in fact they served as a counterpoise to the men of the plain, the landed nobility. Democratic and oligarchic leanings were here balancing each other. The decision, the danger, now lay with the third party, the men of the hills, turbulent shepherds who had expected a redistribution of property.[3] The leadership of the men of the hills fell in time to Peisistratus, a distant relative of Solon. Smooth of speech, courteous in bearing, and master of political trickery, he had won a military reputation by his defeat of Megara and reconquest of Salamis. In the belief that his political adversaries sought his life, the Assembly voted him a personal guard, with which he seized the Acropolis in 560 B.C. and made himself tyrant. Twice a combination of the two rival factions caused his retirement into exile; but finally gaining complete supremacy, he maintained it with the aid of mercenaries.

Peisistratus is an excellent type of the statesman despot. His hand lay heavily on the nobles alone. Those nobles who were too independent in spirit or too ambitious to submit were forced into exile. The estates of such persons were confiscated and divided among the poor. Thus was solved the problem of the poor farmer. To those in need he gave seed and work animals for stocking their farms. This numerous, thriving agricultural class remained prosperous long after his family ceased to rule. His tax of one tenth, afterward reduced to a twentieth, on produce was burdensome only to the most sterile farms. The prosperity of the countryside was matched by an equal growth in the city. Attic wine and oil, for example, were now shipped in lovely vases to Etruria, Egypt, Asia Minor, and the Black Sea.

Commerce must in fact have derived great encouragement from the treaty relations which Peisistratus established with many states from Macedonia to Lacedaemon. The policy of intrigue and alliance which he had begun during his years of exile he now continued, and the peace which thus resulted from his vigorous foreign policy was an additional basis of prosperity. The colony of Sigeum on the Hellespont he recaptured, and under his patronage Miltiades, an eminent noble, conducted a colony to the Chersonese on the European side of the Hellespont. In brief, it is not too much to regard Peisistratus as the creator of Athenian diplomacy and of a place of dignity and influence for his city among the states of Greece.

At home he enforced the existing laws and constitution, taking care only to secure by his control of the political machinery the election of kinsmen or partisans to the chief offices. He sent judges on circuit about the countryside, partly as a convenience for the people, and partly too to keep the people safely on their farms, where they might not interfere with the government. The masses were attached to him by his

---

[3] It is possible that the three parties had a sectional, instead of—or as well as— social character.

benefits to them, and many of the nobles by the social attractions of his court.

When Peisistratus died of old age in 527 B.C., his sons Hippias and Hipparchus continued his policy. The former, as the elder and as a man of statesman-like character, managed political affairs, while the more cultured brother attended the erection of public works, and acted as a patron of literature and art. The City Dionysia, the cradle of Greek drama, and the great Panathenaic festival had already been founded. Under the Peisistratidae, as the dynasty is termed, much of the wonderful civilization of archaic Greece was nurtured. The extensive building of temples, the enlargement of religious festivals, the patronage of artists and poets advanced the social happiness, the taste, and intelligence of the citizens. The most useful public works of the Peisistratidae were a subterranean aqueduct, which brought a supply of fresh water to the city from the upper valley of the Ilissus, and a system of roads which radiated through Attica from the altar of the Twelve Gods in the Agora or market place.

In 527 B.C., at the very outset of his rule, Hippias showed himself a statesman by recalling the Alcmaeonidae (whom Peisistratus had expelled) from exile—a gesture of reconciliation which healed the breach between tyrants and nobles—and two years later made the Alcmaeonid leader, Cleisthenes, archon. Back in Athens, the Alcmaeonidae won the favor of the Delphic Apollo by their munificent rebuilding of the temple destroyed by fire. But the assassination of Hipparchus in 514 B.C. changed the character of the tyranny. The perpetrators of the deed were two nobles, Harmodius and Aristogeiton and the motive was purely personal. Throughout Athenian history, however, the murderers were celebrated in song as tyrannicides, and their descendants were decreed special privileges. But the attack on Hippias failed, and the assassins with several accomplices were put to death. The conspiracy served to changed good to bad, for Hippias now became suspicious and harsh, a tyrant in the unfavorable sense of the word.

The Alcmaeonidae, once again sent into exile, tried to force their return with the help of Boeotians, but were defeated at Leipsydrium in 513 B.C. The Delphic Apollo now came gratefully to their aid. Whenever the authorities at Sparta consulted the god, the answer always was, "Athens must be set free." At this time the Peloponnesian League reached the borders of Attica; and the command of Apollo was strengthened by Lacedaemonian ambition. With a force of Peloponnesians the able king of Sparta, Cleomenes, joined the Alcmaeonidae and their faction in besieging Hippias in the Acropolis. The children of the besieged were taken in an attempt to steal through the lines. To save them, Hippias surrendered on condition of retiring from the country. In this way the tyranny came to an end in 510 B.C.

The political scene was quite different from that of two generations earlier. Then the problem was the conflicting aims of the men of coast, plain, and hills. The people of the hills, however, had meanwhile won their farms; the men of the coast, city artisans and others, had grown strong and prosperous under the tyranny. These beneficiaries of tyranny were in fact ready for democracy. The question now was what the men of the plain, the nobility, would do. Solon, it will be recalled, had failed to break their power.

The downfall of Hippias was a victory for the exiled nobles, who on their return began to rule in lordly style. Revising the citizen lists, they struck off the names of a multitude whose ancestors had been enrolled by Solon and Peisistratus. Their object was not only to secure political control but also to return to aristocratic ideals. In 508 B.C. their leader, Isagoras, was elected to the archonship, but he had reckoned without the city population. Thereupon the Alcmaeonid Cleisthenes, son of Agariste of Sicyon, unwilling to submit to such constitutional forms as then existed, appealed to the disfranchised masses, and promised them a restoration of their political rights. The people responded, and in spite of the interference of Cleomenes, Isagoras was forced into exile. The problem before Cleisthenes was clear-cut. His task was to ward off a return of the defeated aristocrats, to recognize the special position of the city population, and to see to it that these people, so recently attached to tyranny, should not support it again.

Cleisthenes, the great noble, proved himself a greater statesman and democrat. He strengthened the tendencies begun by Solon in limited fashion at the start of the century and deserves to be called the founder of Athenian democracy. The task of bringing harmony to the state involved destroying the power (though not necessarily the existence) of certain associations, religious and otherwise, such as the phratry and the clan. Not only would this reduce the danger of the nobles, but it would also permit the enrollment of those recently disfranchised as the full equals of citizens of pure Athenian descent. To accomplish this difficult task Cleisthenes found it necessary to change the constitution. He abolished the four old Ionian tribes (except for ceremonial purposes) and substituted ten new ones in their place. Membership in the tribes was to be based on residence in a deme, kinship and religion now having nothing to do with it.[4] Henceforth the deme, and not the

---

[4] Oddly enough, however, once the change was made to the new system, membership in the demes became hereditary. The tribes, it should be added, had their own officials and boards.

naucrary, was the unit of local self-government. The demes were the villages or townships of Attica and sections of Athens itself. The Assemblies of the demes, with their elected demarchs, kept the lists of their citizens, registered real estate and mortgages, and conducted small judicial proceedings. Cleisthenes grouped the demes in "Thirds" (*trittyes*). The number of demes in a *trittys* varied, but three *trittyes* formed a tribe, and consequently we get a total of thirty *trittyes*. The *trittyes* of each tribe did not come from the same general area, but one *trittys*, with its various demes, represented the people of the coast, another the interior, and still another the city.[5] Each tribe, therefore, contained a good cross section of the population, and it would be impossible for any element, such as the nobles, to gain control. So it would seem on the surface, but actually the city *trittys* was more closely knit in sentiment than would be possible with the two other *trittyes*, composed as they were of rich and poor farmers. Here was a solid bloc within each tribe, and because the voting in the Assembly was done by tribes, it is easy to see how influential the city element might become. It is not clear from this, however, whether Cleisthenes so acted because of a conviction that the greatness of Attica lay in Athens or because of a desire to please his own followers, who were concentrated in the city. Either explanation recognizes the primacy of the city.

The Council of Four Hundred was abolished in favor of a new Council of Five Hundred, fifty members being chosen annually by lot from each of the ten tribes. A tribe's fifty members were distributed among the demes according to the size of the population, a scheme which obviously recognized the principle of proportional representation. With a growing city population, it was clear that the city deme or demes in a tribe would count for more and more. That this was deliberately planned cannot be stated with certainty, but it seems a reasonable explanation of the tribal arrangement, which, because of its artificiality, must have had a special purpose. The Council met in the Bouleuterion and was the deliberative and governing body in the state. In its administrative capacity it was responsible for financial and foreign affairs, and prepared the business that was to come before the Assembly. The Assembly met once every ten days on the Pnyx and passed measures into law. To facilitate its work, the Council was divided into ten committees, each committee being in charge for thirty-five or thirty-six days; that is to say, the fifty representatives from each tribe were the committee, and each tribe had its turn (by lot) at presiding for a tenth of the year. During this time the fifty presiding councillors were

[5] This may not have been universally true, for the evidence is not complete for all the tribes.

called *prytaneis,* and the group a prytany. The prytany thus came to be a measure of time. It met in the Tholos under a different chairman each day. The Areopagus remained, for a time at least, in the background.

Having given the city population so much importance, as it were, it was clearly the duty of Cleisthenes to ensure that this element, so recently attached to the Peisistratidae, should not support a restoration. He therefore devised the curious, but effective scheme known as ostracism.[6] Once a year the people came together in the agora, if the Assembly so resolved, and voted against any individual whom they judged dangerous to the state. A quorum of 6,000 votes was necessary, and the man who received the largest number went into exile for ten years.

The archons remained the executive officials. In addition to various small funds, there were two chief public treasuries; that of Athena, under the Treasurers (*tamiae*) of the Goddess, and the *Demosion* (state treasury) under the *colacretae*. Cleisthenes instituted a board of ten Receivers (*apodectae*), who under the supervision of the Council of Five Hundred received all incoming moneys and assigned them to the appropriate treasuries. It was a step toward the unification of public finances. The members of the *heliaea* were elected by the demes, though the courts were not yet elaborately divided into panels. In 501 B.C. the army was reorganized on the basis of the ten tribes, each tribe electing a commanding official for its troops of infantry (*taxiarch*) and cavalry (*hipparch*). A board of ten *strategoi,* or generals, was formed, and after 487 B.C., when the archons were chosen by lot, the *strategia* became the most powerful body in Athens. The archonship might become the prey of the democratic passion to leave everything to the gods,[7] but the Athenians saw to it that their generals were elected.

The energizing of the political and patriotic spirit of the people, in the demes, in the Council of Five Hundred, the Assembly, and the *heliaea,* produced prodigious military, artistic, and intellectual activities. Athens was indeed a democracy, though held in check by conservative balances. The absence of pay for public service kept the very poor from continuous participation in Assembly and courts. The property qualifications for magistrates, in view of the wider distribution of wealth, probably did not debar large numbers, though the people

---

[6] The voting was done on ostraca, potsherds (Figure 20A). It can be readily imagined how in time ostracism became an instrument of party warfare.

[7] In the case of the archonship, however, we may see a final democratic gesture of contempt for an office long associated with aristocracy. This is more fully discussed subsequently.

would find it hard to discard their practice of choosing leaders from among the great families. The prevalence of country life prevented the small, but generally conservative, farmer from frequent trips to the city. Those rich farmers who went would be outnumbered by the city poor. The eupatrid and tyrannist influence had been greatly lessened, but the Council of the Areopagus remained. Though we may speak of Cleisthenes as the founder of democracy, the government was far less democratic than it became in the following century.

In the government of deme, tribe, and state the ordinary citizen had a share—in fact, his opportunities for political development and education were immense. In other ways, too, Athens was setting the pace for the entire Greek world (Hellas). We have observed how large that world was, how varied its governments and its problems. Its literary and artistic achievements are among its loveliest and most important contributions to posterity.

Chapter VIII THE CIVILIZATION OF ARCHAIC GREECE

To the civilization of archaic Greece—those centuries of exuberant growth from the end of the Greek Middle Age to the conclusion of the Persian Wars (*ca.* 750–479 B.C.)—the entire Greek world, east and west, contributed. Despite disruptive forces, especially the particularism of the city-state, the Greeks were not lacking in national feeling or in a sense of unity. A common language, though marked by dialects, and a common alphabet, also marked by local peculiarities, set them off from other peoples, whom they called barbarian; that is, non-Greek. Literature, religion, art, and common sacred spots were other unifying forces in a world which, for all that, remained pre-eminently individual and personal.

It was due to Homer, more than to any one else, that Greek religion, into whose making had gone so many diverse elements, became refined and received a definite stamp. Under the Homeric inspiration the process was carried on by

Ionic poets of the eighth and seventh centuries, who composed various epics, forming a group known as the Epic Cycle. The gods of long ago had lived on earth with man, but the epic brought them to the sky. On Mt. Olympus they lived, under the presidency of Zeus, whose power was reminiscent of the strong Mycenaean monarchy. Of all the gods Zeus is the least primitive, the most godlike according to our ideas. His wife-sister was Hera. Poseidon had been a mighty god of the earth, but under the influence of a seafaring race he changed to a lesser god, concerned with the crafts of the sea. Certain of the gods had come originally from Asia, especially Apollo, who developed nevertheless into the great symbol of Hellenism, the champion of mankind. Athena and Artemis were Minoan in origin. In time the gods came to have certain special functions, Ares becoming the god of war, Aphrodite the goddess of love, Hermes the messenger of the gods, and so on (Figure 21).

Every state had special guardian deities, worshipped by all the citizens. Each of these gods enjoyed an independent existence: the Athena or Zeus of a given state was a personal being distinct from every other Athena or Zeus. But the gods became universalized, and because of this, the spread of hero worship was very rapid in post-Homeric Greece, for the heroes remained strictly local. Hero worship had begun with the cult of dead chieftains, but the custom was extended to ordinary mortals, so that eventually every association of men, clan, phratry, deme, tribe, had its name-giving hero, the real or fictitious ancestor of the group.

For their own happiness the gods required festivals. Most festivals were confined to a single locality, or at the widest to a city-state; but in a few instances games in honor of a local deity became for unknown reasons panhellenic. Such were the four national festivals celebrated at Delphi, on the Corinthian Isthmus, at Nemea, and at Olympia, in honor of Apollo, Poseidon, Nemean Zeus, and Olympian Zeus respectively. The games, though associated with religion, were secular in origin; the Greek love of athletics undoubtedly was inherited from Minoan days. The most famous of all the games was the Olympic. Here the most popular events were the footrace, wrestling, and the pentathlon, comprising running, wrestling, leaping, spear hurling, and discus throwing. The prizes were wreaths, in keeping with Greek simplicity, though by the fifth century semiprofessional athletes began to make their appearance.

The influence of the games did not limit itself to the promotion of physical excellence and the appreciation of music and poetry. The assembly of the Greeks took place under a sacred truce, during which the states ceased war. Merchants gathered, especially at the Isthmian festival, to display and sell their wares. Even more beneficial than this was the intercommunication of ideas and sentiments among the assembled representatives of the entire Greek world. This generated a spirit of racial unity and intensified the creative genius in the fields of art and intelligence. The national games influenced Greek life in manifold ways; and especially the competitive spirit penetrated and energized every constructive element of Hellenism. Not infrequently festivals acquired a momentary political influence, as we have noted in the case of the Delphic Amphictyony. We have also seen that out of these associations grew treaties which recognized the rights of humanity and laid the foundations of international law (Delphi, Map 26; Olympia, Map 28).

Among local festivals the most famous was the Panathenaea at Athens. Peisistratus ordained that every fourth year the festival was to be given, as the Greater Panathenaea, with special magnificence. Prisoners were set free, and slaves were permitted to feast with their masters. There were races, war dances in armor, athletic competitions, and a grand procession of all the free population, the priests and magistrates, the population in varied festive attire, youths and girls carrying articles and utensils needed for the sacrifice. The object of the ceremony was to bring the goddess the *peplos,* or robe, that had been woven and embroidered for her by her chosen girls. It was this procession, which passed through the streets and up the steep ascent of the Acropolis to the great altar before the temple of Athena, that the sculptured frieze of the Parthenon at a later day immortalized. Peisistratus added the recitation of Homer's poems; and this new feature bore immediate fruit in introducing epic subjects into the art of painting and in giving an epic content to the drama, then in its earliest beginnings (Figure 22).

It was natural that a people whose whole life was permeated with religion should seek means of communicating with the gods. So common a use for this purpose was made of the flight of birds, that the winged creature came to designate any kind of omen. All chance objects or occurrences were regarded as manifestations of the divine will. One form of divination found its omens in the vitals of a sacrificed animal. An oracle, on the other hand, had a fixed location and a definite method of expression. The most venerable oracle was that of Zeus at Dodona, where the god spoke through the rustling of the oak leaves. Favoring conditions, however, brought to pre-eminence the oracle of Apollo at Delphi. His prophetess, the Pythia, sitting on a tripod in the inmost shrine, received from Apollo the answers she gave to inquirers.

Often unintelligible, her mutterings were interpreted to the inquirer by the priests of the god. An occasional function of the oracle was to reveal the future. (When it made such a venture, the response was couched in ambiguous terms so as to be right in any event.) The god's advice was generally limited to questions of moral or religious conduct of individuals and states. His approval was sought for the founding of colonies and for other important enterprises. Sometimes the oracle was bribed; sometimes it showed undue favor to a particular state or political party. Notwithstanding these shortcomings, its general reputation for honesty and wisdom long retained for it the highest, though by no means absolute, authority in Greek morals and religion. Greek culture, however, was always independent of religion. From this general background the poetry, prose, vases, sculptures, and temples of the Greeks shine like individual jewels.

The literature was affected quite as much by politics as by religion. To express the complex conditions of Ionia, arising from aristocracies and tyrannies and colonial expansion, the old epic verse of calm, stately meter—the dactylic hexameter—proved inadequate. It gave way to new and varied measures, which would better exhibit the play of individual or communal thought and emotion characteristic of the new era.

The first variation from the epic verse is found in the elegiac pentameter, whose spirit may be either meditative or emotional. Accompanied by the pipe, it lent itself equally to the expression of political and social thought, religious devotion, and martial fire. The first great master of the elegy was Callinus of Ephesus. About the middle of the seventh century, when the savage Cimmerians from north of the Black Sea were ravaging the Ephesian territory, he roused his countrymen to battle with a song, which, in its patriotic ideal and martial spirit, is akin to Tyrtaeus and Solon. A greater personal intensity distinguishes the poetry of Archilochus, whose verses give us glimpses of his character. In addition to composing elegies, he was the first great master of the iambic, a measure adapted to energetic expression, giving utterance to the whole range of human passions from love to sarcasm and hate. His stormy life was typical of the age and of his social class. The son of an aristocratic father and slave mother, in youth he was forced by poverty and want to leave his native Paros and join a colony his countrymen had established in Thasos. Between exploiting the gold mines and fighting the Thracians, he abused friend and foe alike, and soon left Thasos. Hence he became a wanderer over sea and land, a poet soldier of fortune, perhaps a pirate. In love as in hate Archilochus reveals the same tempestuous spirit. Jilted by Neobule—so reads the tale—he lost no time in sad lament, but with his biting iambics drove her and her sisters to hang themselves. This man of muscle and redundant mental power wrote verses that placed him second to Homer and established him as the unequaled artist of personal song.

In Aeolis, in the sixth century, lived great lyric poets. They, rather than the sophists, were the true discoveries of individualism and skepticism. They, too, are children of their age, and reflect the general feeling about the gods and man's dependence on them. Mytilene, the chief city of Lesbos, trading with Egypt, enjoyed the imported refinements of the Orient. Less devoted than the Ionians, however, to commerce and the useful arts, the people gave themselves wholeheartedly to social enjoyment, to the lyre and song. The poems of Alcaeus, mere shreds as they now are, lead us into the midst of the island's civil strife, in which he actively participated. In addition to martial and political themes, he wrote on a great variety of subjects, including travel, nature, love, drinking, and other topics. His poems were personal lyrics sung among friends to the accompaniment of the lyre. With much of the genius, versatility, and fire of Archilochus, Alcaeus possessed a more amiable disposition. Both open to us an invaluable insight into the life and character of their times; and both exerted a determining influence on the literature of after ages.

In these great creative centuries the domain of literature was not monopolized by men. In fact, the social and intellectual development of women during the seventh and sixth centuries has a unique place in history, and though under Oriental influence the upper-class Ionians segregated their women, and though a poem of Semonides of Amorgos compares various types of women to different animals, this age was actually the most brilliant period, at least till recent times, in the intellectual history of women.[1]

One of these distinguished women of the early sixth century was Sappho, a member of an aristocratic family which stood high in the politics and society of Lesbos. She was influential enough to suffer banishment with her relations for political causes, but in time appreciation of her genius grew, till her native country honored her by stamp-

---

[1] Generally outside of Ionia women went about freely in the streets on foot or in carriages, and mingled with men in social life. Those of the wealthy class dyed their hair, rouged their faces, and wore luxurious jewelry and dresses. The Doric *peplos,* a woollen garment fastened at the shoulders with large pins, was relatively simple. At first it was worn on all the Greek mainland but later the Athenian women changed to the Ionic chiton of linen, either sewn or fastened with small pins down the arm. A himation, or mantle, would be thrown over this on going out. By combination of bright colors, costly embroideries, and sparkling jewelry, the wealthy lady produced a striking effect.

ing her image on its coins. She became the head of a school of beautiful, brilliant girls in Mytilene, a literary circle, or guild, sacred to Aphrodite. Music, dancing, and the technique of poetry were studied. The circle represents an effort to rise above the humdrum existence of drudgery and fashion to the nobler life of the mind and heart. Between Sappho and her girl companions there was the warmest attachment. Her poetry glorifies the beauty of form and the pleasures of sense. We get interesting glimpses of woman's literary life, of social relations between Lesbos and Lydia, of telepathic sympathy, as well as a delicate appreciation of natural beauty in the night, the sea, and flowers. With all her love of flowery fields, cool streams, and singing birds, her interest centers in human beings, their sorrows, joys, loves, and marriages. In the beauty of her thoughts, in melodious verse, and intensity of feeling she scarcely has an equal in literature. But the Athenians of later time, who could not appreciate freedom and high intelligence in women, gave her a bad reputation, and their judgment prevailed till modern scholarship succeeded in vindicating her character.

The poems of Sappho, like those of Alcaeus, were personal lyrics. Meanwhile other poets were engaged in composing choral lyrics which were essentially public. This kind of ode was sung by a group of persons appropriately dressed and trained, who accompanied the song with a rhythmic movement, or dance. The equipment and training of a chorus involved expense, borne by a wealthy person, or, more commonly, by the state. The ode was expected to express accordingly, not the feelings of the writer alone, but of the whole community. In Greece there was no sharp distinction, such as now exists, between society and state. The citizens were mostly known to one another; and the reunions of kinsmen, neighbors, phratries, and of the entire community in festivals, were not only social but religious and civic functions. These circumstances explain the existence of a form of poetry which was at one and the same time religious, social, and civic. Arising from unpolished folk songs, they gradually developed an artistic character in the hands of skilled composers. They were most at home in the Dorian states, especially in Lacedaemon, where the government aimed to regulate communal life, so to speak, in a harmonious rhythm. Among a people delicately sensitive to sights and sounds, the patriotic and moral appeal was made less to the intellect than to the eye and ear. The best-known among the earlier masters of choral song was Alcman, who, it will be remembered, has left us a beautiful picture of Spartan life. Alcman is most celebrated for his parthenia, choral songs for girls. There were similar odes for grown women, boys, and men respectively, presented at the religious festivals of the state. One form of ode contained the germ of the drama.

Of all the types of literature developed by the Greeks none is more beautiful than the drama. Its beginnings are obscure. Perhaps it developed from a ritual about the grave. Its patron god, Dionysus, was not merely a happy god of wine, but a year-god or vegetation-spirit. People celebrated the birth, marriage, death, and rebirth of the year-god. Hence arose comedy which dealt with the marriage, and tragedy with the death ritual. This will explain how tragedy, so noble and serious, came to be associated with the god of wine. As the worship of Dionysus developed, many festivals in honor of the dead were transferred to him. In December the villages of Attica celebrated the Rural Dionysia, in which a chorus of men, in rustic attire, sang in his honor an unpolished but joyous song, the dithyramb. There was a festival in the city, the Lenaea, in January, and another, the City Dionysia, in March. Similar festivals were held in other parts of Greece. The wild strain sung to Dionysus was transformed by poetic art into a choral ode. The singing was interspersed with recitation, which gradually developed into the dialogue. This growth of the drama was fostered by the tyrants. At the Corinthian court of Periander the Lesbian poet Arion set the dithyramb to order; and at the court of Peisistratus lived Thespis, reputed the first dramatic writer. Through the encouragement of popular cults, as distinguished from those monopolized by the nobility, the tyrant aimed to free the masses from eupatrid control, and attach them to himself. For a long time, however, the drama must have continued crude and immature. Even at the close of the archaic period it was essentially a cantata in which the singing was occasionally interrupted by dialogue.

Dionysus, conceived as a god of suffering, became important in Greece. His orgiastic cult, influenced by Anatolia, had developed in Thrace. The belief prevailed that in childhood he had been torn to pieces by the Titans, but restored to life through rebirth. The half-human, suffering, ever-youthful god, the spirit of life in nature and man, appealed directly to the emotions. Throngs of worshippers, the majority women, roamed in wild nocturnal revels over mountain tops and danced in ecstacy to the roll of drums and the clashing of cymbals. By such means they became one with their deity, partakers of his immortal life. The worship of Dionysus spread among the Greeks, as their springs of emotion dried up, for many of the ceremonies of their ancient worship had lost their meaning and sunk into dry barren formalism.

In the sixth century an effort was made to transform this unbridled worship of Dionysus into a theology. The leaders of the new movement looked back for their master to the Thracian Orpheus, a legendary singer and poet, to whose name eventually everything mystical was attached. The faith was spread by missionaries, who traveled throughout Greece initiating converts and founding societies of worshippers. They had their sacred scriptures, containing prophecies and hymns. Adopting the worship of Dionysus, they gave it a more regular form and a higher spiritual interpretation. After the emotional rites of initiation they lived ascetic lives. They were under the impression that the soul is suffering the punishment of sin (committed in a previous existence), and that the body is an enclosure or prison, in which the soul is incarcerated. By purity of living and the practice of their rituals, however, they were able not only to cleanse themselves from sin and secure eternal happiness, but even to redeem the souls of the dead from punishment in Tartarus. In no state was Orphism accepted as a part of the public worship, though the Peisistratidae were warm patrons of Onomacritus, its most distinguished prophet.

Athens, however, did not hesitate to worship Dionysus in shrines of his own and to join him with Demeter and her daughter Persephone, the great goddesses of Eleusis. Their worship, of great antiquity, had now become national, open to all Greeks who were free from religious pollution. Once a year the devotees of these goddesses, gathering at Athens, moved in procession along the Sacred Way to Eleusis. Arriving there, the initiated entered the Hall of the Mysteries, the Telesterion, where were performed the sacred rites which none dared disclose. Those who wished and were qualified were initiated. The Eleusinian mysteries seem to have consisted chiefly of a "passion play" representing the sorrows of Demeter, when her daughter was carried off by Hades, and the joy of recovering her. The ceremony probably once referred to the death of vegetation in winter and its rebirth in spring. In archaic Greece, however, it came to signify death and the resurrection of the soul to eternal happiness. In this way the joys of Elysium, in Homer's conception available to the favored few, were democratized by the progress of Athens toward popular liberty and equality.

The keen, rational mind of the Greek in time produced the scientific point of view toward all things connected with the world and man. The early Greek had believed that the gods were the causes of all things in nature and arbiters of human destiny. In the beginning the clashing of divine wills wrought chaos in heaven and earth, till the dawning consciousness of moral and physical unity and order led the poets to devise a system in which all existing things might have a due part. With their conception of the gods in human form, it was natural that they should attempt to explain the multitude of deities, as of men, and even the plurality of all natural objects by the one process of birth. A system so devised is a cosmogony. Hesiod, our earliest exponent of this line of thought, assumes the creation, he does not say how, of Chaos, then Earth. From Chaos sprang Erebos and black Night; and from Night in turn sprang bright Ether and Day. Earth gave birth to starry Heaven, and from them sprang Cronos of crooked counsels. When Zeus, the son of Cronos, grew to manhood in the rich island of Crete, he conquered the Titans and other monstrous beings, and himself reigned supreme.

In this way, the poet thought, came unity, system, and order from chaos. With the accumulation of knowledge and the growth of an inquiring spirit, however, the Greeks could not satisfy themselves with such reasoning. It was but natural that the the next step should be taken by the Ionians, the most enterprising and inventive of the Greeks. Among them were men who visited Egypt and perhaps other parts of the Orient, not only for trade, but also for sightseeing and instruction. One such was Thales of Miletus. In Egypt they learned such elementary science as the priests cultivated, especially arithmetic, geometry, and astronomy. The development of these branches of knowledge, together with the elements of architecture and civil engineering, had been made possible by the organized priesthoods of Egypt and Babylonia. This knowledge consisted purely of facts ascertained by experience and arbitrarily classified, but wanting the elements of reason and demonstration; hence it was far from science in the present sense of the word. The contribution of the Greek mind, brilliantly imaginative and untrammeled by religious or other convention, was to pierce beneath the fact to the underlying cause, and thus to create real science. The first step in this process, taken by Thales early in the sixth century before Christ, marks him as the founder, not merely of Greek science, but in the only true sense of the term, of the world's science.

Though we cannot be sure that everything ascribed to Thales was really his work, there is no doubt that he contributed greatly to mathematics and astronomy. The story that he fell into a well while stargazing is balanced by another to the effect that he speculated in olives on his foreknowledge of the weather and reaped a great profit from the transaction. It may well be that he foretold the eclipse of the sun, which occurred on May 28, 585 B.C., though it hardly seems possible that his knowledge enabled him to fix the very day and hour. However that may be, his fame rests, not upon any individual scientific discovery, but upon his new conception of cause. Accepting from the poets the idea of the unity of things and the necessity of causation, he sought for cause, not among the gods, but in nature itself. Water, he declared, was the one source and substance of all things. In his statement, too, that the "world is full of gods," he seems to mean that things contain in themselves the conscious power to create other things. Although not wholly free from the influence of mythology, and wrong in choosing a material substance as his first principle, yet in displacing the gods by natural causation he took the all-important step from mythology and theology to science and philosophy. This change has proved the most momentous revolution in the intellectual history of mankind.

The Ionian school of philosophy, thus founded by Thales, sought the first principle in matter. He left no writings; but a pupil, Anaximander, about the middle of the sixth century, published a scientific treatise, probably the first prose work in the Greek language. His principle was the "unlimited," evidently a boundless reservoir from which all things come and to which everything returns. In opposition to the poets he thought out a mechanical process for explaining the formation and ultimate destruction of the existing world—in fact, of an unending succession of worlds. Evolution it could not be called. Our present earth, he taught, is a cylinder, whose upper surface we inhabit. This idea, too, is an advance beyond the earlier conception of the world as a round flat disk. From information gathered by Ionian navigators Anaximander made the first map of the earth, and hence may be regarded as the earliest geographer.

A newer and deeper meaning was given to philosophy by Pythagoras of Samos, who in 522 B.C. migrated to Croton, Italy. Learned in the mathematics of the Ionian school, he sought in numbers the primary cause of all things, whether musical harmonies, stellar movements, the nature of the gods, or even abstract ideas. This attention to numbers gave a great impetus to the study of mathematics, hence to exactness in science; but it was marred by his attaching to numbers mystical powers alien to true science. In fact Pythagoras is distinguished as a mystic and a moral reformer even more than for his contribution to science. He believed in the transmigration of souls; their attainment to a higher condition in a future existence depended on moral conduct in this. The chief aim of Pythagoras seems to have been a life of moral purity, to which philosophy, religion, and mystic initiations were merely contributory. His school was a secret association, which gained adherents in most of the cities of southern Italy. It cultivated dietetics and medicine; it enjoined a life of moral discipline and self-restraint. Taking a political turn and acquiring the rule over many states, these societies endeavored to manage affairs according to their ethical standard. We must regard the organization as an element, both product and factor, in the deepening religious and moral sense of archaic Greece.

A further advance in these general philosophic and ethical directions was made by Xenophanes of Colophon (*ca.* 572–480 B.C.), who migrated to Elea, Italy, where he founded the so-called Eleatic School. He indignantly assails the Homeric conception of the gods as beings of human form, who lie and steal and commit such other sins as would shame the race of men. Beings of this kind are the creation of human fancy. The real God is One, like man neither in form nor thought. He is eternal, unchangeable, and spiritual. This seems to be the enunciation of a pure monotheism. It is clear, too, that Xenophanes' interest centers in moral improvement. It is the duty of sensible men, when they gather at banquets, for example, to pray God to give them power to do justice. His God therefore is a moral force; and Xenophanes was as much theologian and moral reformer as philosopher.

With Heracleitus of Ephesus, who flourished about 500 B.C., philosophy began to concern itself with the motion, change, and life of nature. Not Being, he asserted, but Becoming is the fundamental essence of things. Meditation on this subject led him to imagine a world-ruling reason—*logos*—which produces the ever-changing phenomena of the universe. This controlling principle can be apprehended only by a few sages like himself, who also possess a *logos* similar in kind to that of the universe, whereas the masses are doomed to eternal ignorance and folly. The self-assertive personality of Heracleitus, added to the evident depth of his mental vision, has influenced the thought of the world even to the present day, and his obscure, riddling, prophetic utterances, along with his doctrine of the divine and human *logos,* gave pronounced encouragement to mysticism.

From this intellectual progress arose a better conception of virtue, requiring not so much physical perfection as moral excellence. This demanded *sophrosyne,* self-restraint, a new word in the Greek vocabulary, yet one involving the most imperative of Hellenic commandments. Moral progress showed itself in a greater humanity, in the development of law-codes, in the improved condition of women, in the treatment of prisoners of war, in the practice of defining interstate relations by treaties, and in the submission of disputes to arbitration.

This extraordinary intellectual growth in the sixth century led also to the birth of the historical viewpoint. It had begun, naturally, with a pseudohistory, which traced the Greek descent from Prometheus, the great benefactor of mankind, or dealt with the problem of human creation, such as Hesiod's account of the races of man, golden, silver, heroic, and now iron. Genealogies of various kinds were written. Other writers interested themselves in the present and in human affairs. They were known as logographers, writers of prose, and often had a critical spirit. The greatest of them, Hecataeus of Miletus (*ca.* 500 B.C.), took an active part in public affairs during the Ionian Revolt. He may be regarded as the founder of the science of history. Against pseudo-history he applied a free, inquiring mind, unwilling to give any greater weight to Greek tradition, simply because he was a Greek, than to that of another race. His *Genealogies* contained myth and history and his *Description of the Earth* was for its day a geography of distinguished merit. An awakening consciousness of the distinction between myth and fact is shown by his own words: "I write what I believe to be true; for the various stories of the Greeks, are, in my opinion, ridiculous."

The fact that the entire Greek world contributed to the development of archaic Greece becomes even more obvious when we turn from literature to art. This is particularly true of the pottery, which is found in large quantities at every site. It is possible to follow in detail the general trend, as well as countless local variations, to see how different areas reacted on one another and how popular work led to imitation. Though the vases were mostly for everyday use, the greatest artists of the time did not hesitate to decorate them. Eventually, of course, the development of the major arts of architecture and sculpture attracted the best artists, but during the archaic period the pottery reveals the best in archaic art.[2]

Colonization, the growth of commerce, and the penetration of new ideas from the East were the chief stimuli for the wonderful and amazing development of Greek vases from the end of the eighth century. The geometric style, with its elaborate surface decoration, yields now to strong Oriental influence. Lotus flowers, winged lions and other animals, sphinxes, griffins, curved lines, and the contrasting of colors announce the new style. This sudden bursting upon the world of a pottery which is able to combine color and design to produce a superb decorative effect is a sheer delight to the mind and eye. Narrative, discipline, formalism are not uppermost; exuberance, rather, is what strikes us. From Rhodes come vases with processions of deer and goats, whereas in the so-called proto-Corinthian and Corinthian ware we see terrifying gorgons, mythological tales, human figures that move and have volume (Figure 23).

In the course of the seventh century arose the practice of painting figures in black, the natural color of the clay forming the background. This black-figured style held the stage throughout the sixth

---

[2] All traces of mural painting have long since perished.

century, until about 530 B.C. The figures, which are silhouettes with the inner lines formed by incision, are of Theseus and the Minotaur and other popular subjects. The emphasis is now on narrative, the exuberant is being disciplined by the formal, and a truly national style, which has absorbed the foreign influences, is emerging. A Corinthian crater (mixing bowl) depicting the departure of Amphiaraos shows how charmingly the artist can suggest his story. An excellent example of Laconian ware (*ca.* 550 B.C.) reveals the ability and taste of which the Spartans once were capable (Figure 18). We see in this cylix, or drinking cup, a humorous picture of king Arcesilas of Cyrene, in North Africa, watching the weighing of silphium, which is then put away in the hold of the ship. The birds, the monkey, and the lizard heighten the effect. By the middle of the sixth century, thanks to the far-seeing policy of Solon, Athenian vases were exported far and wide. Certain markets, notably the Etruscan, were exclusively Athenian. To understand this, we have only to look at the famous "François Vase," signed by the potter Ergotimos and the painter Klitias (Figure 24). We see grand archaic friezes portraying the wedding of Achilles' parents, Peleus and Thetis, a Caledonian boar hunt, chariot races, and other subjects, with a delicate band at the bottom showing the battle of pigmies and cranes. Of exquisite charm is the cylix by Exekias, in which Dionysus sails lazily across the sea, while dolphins leap round about Figure 25 and Figure 26). The Panathenaic amphoras form a special class (Figure 27). Filled with oil, they were given as prizes to victors in the great festival, a custom that was continued till Roman times.

About 530 B.C. a new style of vase painting became popular and held sway throughout the fifth century. This was the red-figured style, in which the figures were left in the color of the clay, and the background was painted black. The striking vases of Euphronios (Figure 28), Euthymides, Duris, Brygos, and others have combined with their archaic exuberance a discipline and vigor which create an air of wonderful, quiet simplicity. The artist is now able to draw the human form more skilfully and, though myths are still popular, his chief interest lies in subjects from everyday life (Figure 29 and Figure 30). (The Note on Greek Vases discusses technique.)

During the archaic period a preparation was made in architecture for the triumphs of the fifth century. The temple was more typical of Greek construction than any other kind of building. In floor plan it resembles the Mycenaean megaron, but it seems clear that the two descended from a common prototype, each being brought to Greece by a wave of northern invaders. The main room, or cella, in time acquired a vestibule, called the *pronaos,* formed by the projecting side walls of the cella. Between these *antae* were placed columns to carry the superstructure, and such a temple therefore was called a temple *in antis.* Another vestibule, known as the *opisthodomus,*[3] might be placed in the rear. The greatest temples, evolved of course after long experimentation, had columns in front of the *pronaos* and *opisthodomus* and along the sides, an arrangement which provided a covered walk (peristyle) around the temple between columns and cella. This temple, the external columns of which often numbered six by thirteen, was called *peripteral* (see, for example, the temples of Olympia, Map 28 and Diagram 20).

Eventually two great orders, the Doric and Ionic,[4] were evolved for the superstructure. The Doric order grew up in old Greece and the West, where the Dorians had settled, whereas, the Ionic order developed in Ionia. Ultimately temples of the two orders were found side by side, especially in Athens, where all ideas were at home. The two orders, which were quite different, developed from construction in wood, though it is possible to detect influences from Mycenae and Egypt. The Doric column, with its twenty shallow flutes separated by a sharp ridge or arris, has a capital at the top which, though of one block, consists of two parts. The purpose of the echinus, with its elastic swell, is to provide a transition (for the eye) from the vertical lines of the column to the horizontal lines of the entablature, whereas the abacus forms a broad slab for the course above to rest upon. This is the architrave, perfectly plain except for its broad band or taenia at the top, from which a cleat or regula depends at a point above each column and the center of each intercolumniation. The six little guttae, below the regulae, have no structural significance. They represent the nails of the original wooden construction, which, like so much else, are carried over into stone for the mere decorative effect. The nails, of course, originally held in place the ceiling beams just above. To protect these beams from the weather, and perhaps too for aesthetic reasons, the Greeks placed against their ends sheathings of bronze or terracotta and eventually stone, triglyphs, as they are called. The air chamber between the triglyphs was filled with a slab, called the metope. Triglyph and metope form the frieze course; often the metopes were carved with figures in relief (Figure 31 and Diagram 21; see Glossary for terms).

[3] Valuable objects were often kept in this area; eventually some temples became state depositories.

[4] The Corinthian order, except for its acanthus capital, is substantially the same as the Ionic (Diagram 21).

The Doric order has a noble majesty, the Ionic order a delicate grace. The column of the Ionic order is taller, with twenty-four deep flutes separated by broad fillets, and, unlike the Doric, rests upon a base. The charming volutes of its capital are a development, via Cyprus, of the Egyptian lily, in essence a bracket to support the architrave course. The architrave consists of three projecting bands, called fasciae, reminiscent of wooden beams originally piled up to support the roof. The frieze course, a later addition, is perfectly plain, thereby making possible a continuous cultural freize (Figure 32 and Diagram 21). In the Doric order, on account of the triglyphs, only isolated scenes were possible.

Above the frieze, in both orders, was the horizontal cornice, differing in its details, but projecting so as to throw the rain water away from the entablature below. This was necessary not only because of the sculptures, but for protection of the details of the architecture, which were often painted. As a matter of fact, there were also gutters along the roof which led to lion's-head spouts at the four corners. At the ends of the temple the horizontal cornice joined with the raking cornices to form a triangular gable, or pediment, in which great sculptures in the round were usually placed. The roof was covered with tiles, and to break its broad expanse little palmettes, or antefixes, were placed at regular intervals along its edge and along the top of the ridge pole; six larger figures, called acroteria, were placed at the four corners and at the apices of the pediments.

The Greek column did not stand absolutely vertically upon the stylobate, but leaned a little inward, and, unlike the Minoan-Mycenaean, tapered from the bottom upward, though for part of its course it swelled slightly (entasis). The result was that the long row of columns seemed neither rigid nor about to fall from the great weight resting upon it, for the swell of the entasis created the optical illusion that the column had already yielded to its load. The platform [5] upon which the temple rose was curved and crowned. The crowning may have been devised originally as a means of getting rid of rain water, but later its purpose and that of the curvature was to substitute elasticity for the inevitable impression of sagging which would otherwise have resulted. These are some of the famous refinements of Greek architecture, which were slowly perfected. They, and the perfect proportions of

[5] This consisted of three steps, the top one being called the stylobate. The foundations usually went down to bedrock. The individual blocks of the temple were carefully finished and joined to each other by iron dowels and clamps. It should be added that the columns of the best temples were not monolithic, but were made up of drums.

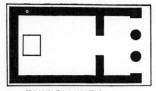

TEMPLE IN ANTIS

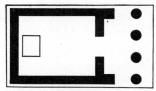

PROSTYLE TETRASTYLE TEMPLE

PROSTYLE TEMPLE IN ANTIS

AMPHIPROSTYLE TEMPLE IN ANTIS

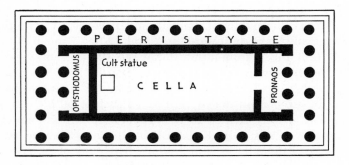

PERIPTERAL TEMPLE

Diagram 20

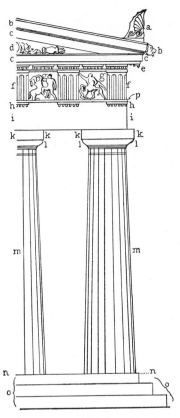

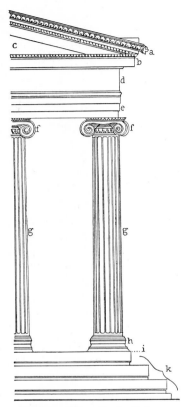

Diagram of a Doric Column
and Entablature:

a *Corner-Akroterion*
b *Sima with a lion's head as waterspout*
c *Geison (cornice)*
d *Tympanum*
e *Mutule with Guttae (drops)*
f *Triglyphs*
g *Metopes*
h *Regulae with guttae*
i *Architrave or Epistyle*
k *Abacus*
l *Echinus*
m *Shaft with 20 sharp-edged flutings*
n *Stylobate*
o *Krepis or Krepidoma*
p *Taenia*

Diagram of an Ionic Column
and Entablature

a *Sima*
b *Geison (cornice)*
c *Tympanum*
d *Frieze*
e *Architrave or Epistyle*
   (in three parts)
f *Capital with Volutes*
g *Shaft with 24 flutings*
   separated by fillets
h *Attic Base with double*
   Torus and a Trochilos
i *Stylobate*
k *Krepis or Krepidoma*

Corinthian Capital

Diagram 21

the individual members of the temple, made the difference between greatness and mediocrity.

Unfortunately, little is preserved of the archaic Ionic temples, but enough is left of the temple of Hera at Samos and of the temple of Artemis at Ephesus to justify the Ionian reputation for colossal size and magnificence. There are many examples of early Doric temples, at Thermon and Corinth, for example, but special interest lies in the early sixth-century Heraeum at Olympia. Here, in the ancient sanctuary sacred to Zeus, we have in a fair state of preservation a temple to Hera, the wife-sister of Zeus, which, together with other early temples, throws much light upon the gradual development of the Doric order. Beneath the Heraeum are the ruins of an earlier temple. Curiously enough, the best preserved temples are not in Greece itself, but in the West, silent reminders of the widespread culture of the ancient Greeks. In Sicily at Selinus and Syracuse, in Italy at Paestum (Figure 17) and elsewhere, still rise stately temples, the very embodiment of archaic beauty and aspiration. Every city-state had one or more temples, for the greater glorification of the state as well as of the gods. During the sixth century, of course, Athens was one of the great cultural leaders of the world. Peisistratus added a peristyle to the Old Temple of Athena on the Acropolis, perhaps, and later was begun the Older Parthenon—temples destined to be destroyed by the Persians. Early in the fifth century was completed the beautifully proportioned archaic temple of Aphaia on Aegina (Figure 33. Diagram 41).

Greek temples stood in an open sanctuary, or *temenos,* and generally faced the east. Except for burning lamps, the sole illumination came from the door at the east end of the cella. Opposite this, at the far end of the cella, stood the large statue of the god or goddess to whom the temple was dedicated. Sculpture was in many ways a handmaiden of architecture, though frequently statues were carved without any reference to a building. Ivories from Sparta and Ephesus show that Oriental influence spread to sculpture, as to vase painting, in the seventh century. Strong Egyptian, as well as Mesopotamian, influence is present, but it must be emphasized that, although the willingness of the Greeks to borrow ideas from any quarter redounds to their credit, these influences were quickly absorbed. Even where they are obvious, as in the stance of the early male figures,[6] they merely touch the surface, and the great qualities are essentially Greek.

[6] These standing male figures, generally nude, were formerly called Apollos, for want of a better name, though not inappropriately, because Apollo was a patron of youth and athletics, and some of the statues were actually found in sanctuaries of Apollo, in Boeotia and elsewhere. It is best to speak of them simply as

The chief characteristic of early Greek sculpture is its decorativeness, a quality which more than compensates for the sculptor's inability to carve his figures according to nature. Indeed, the early Greek sculptor was not primarily interested in men and women; his consuming interest was man. To give his impression of mankind was his object, and it delighted him to paint his statues and to stylize their features. These archaic statues have an air of aloofness, too, which is not unnatural, for the Greeks were at once devoted to goodness and to reason. Believing in goodness they created sculpture that was otherworldly, and yet, because of their devotion to reason, the sculpture became steadily more realistic. We must remember that the Greeks worshipped gods, who, for all their immortality, were human, and in their honor created temples and sculpture. Thus, worshipping gods at once divine and human, they carved statutes which are inevitably marked in the beginning by an aloofness that gradually yields to realism. This was the course of Greek sculpture, and it became doubly certain with the progress of observation and of sculptural technique. Decorativeness and simplicity are among the special delights of archaic Greek sculpture.

No large statues from before 650 B.C. have come down to us. It is possible but it does not seem probable that large statues were made at an earlier date even in wood, although such statues would have perished long ago. The sculptor worked in limestone and marble, as well as in terra-cotta and bronze. In the latter part of the sixth century the sculptor learned how to cast large figures, and henceforth bronze was the most popular material. Few big statues in bronze have survived, being too valuable to escape the melting pot,[7] but we have quantities of smaller figures (Figure 34). The artist, incidentally, did not employ clay models, in the beginning at least, though no doubt he used rough sketches and living models. The worker in stone had many tools, not unlike modern ones, to his hand. With iron chisels and abrasives he first blocked out his statue. Pointed and dentated chisels, the claw chisel, gouge, and running drill were called upon in the course of his work. He used a straight chisel and drill for folds of drapery and locks of hair, and at the end smoothed the statue's surface with soft stones and emery, though the surface remained relatively rough and was never polished.

---

kouroi (youths) and of the draped maidens, who form a large class of sculpture, as *korai*. Another type of archaic sculpture is the draped seated figure.

[7] Many marble statues went into the limekiln. We are often forced, therefore, to fill in our gaps with ancient literary descriptions and with copies made in Roman times. Fortunately, however, we are dependent for the archaic period solely upon Greek originals.

One of our earliest statues is also one of the finest. This is the colossal *kouros* from Sunium, whose broad shoulders and tapering waist, and advanced left leg, remind us of Egypt. But the spirit of it represents man and his supreme confidence. The formalized treatment of the hair, the broad sweep of the eyebrows, the arched upper eyelid, the decorative rendering of the ears, which are set too far back, the high cheek bones, and the so-called archaic smile are characteristic. So too is the frontal pose, with no twist to body or head, the arms hanging stiffly by the side. About 600 B.C., also, was made the magnificent *kouros* from Attica, now exhibited in the Metropolitan Museum of Art in New York (Figure 35). As we study this figure we begin to realize that exact faithfulness to nature is in itself no desideratum, that in other ways an artist may convey his message. The New York *kouros* strikes us first for its quiet simplicity and its fresh vigor. The necklace, the sweep of collarbones and kneecaps, the diamond-shaped abdomen, the sweeping gouges which serve for shoulder blades, these decorative touches add a unique quality to the figure which heighten its charm and tone down (if that is necessary) its deviations from nature. Certain it is that no other artist at any time could have made this statue. Perhaps that is one reason why we like it, because it is greatly Greek. When we look at the superb head from the Dipylon gate at Athens, we note how similar it and the New York and Sunium *kouroi* are.[8] There is a considerable similarity in the various examples of archaic art and in its development, for it is a period, not of eclecticism, which would hardly be possible at the threshold of history, but of common effort. Artists, like other people, availed themselves of the improved communications and traveled about, especially to the tyrants' courts. There remained, however, a difference of emphasis between the art of Asia Minor and the Peloponnesus.

Not a decade passes in archaic sculpture without improvement in the rendering of the human form. We can see this, for example, in the splendid Attic Calf-bearer (*ca*. 565 B.C.), where the stomach has become oval, with inner lines marked (Figure 36). We have here a truly grand composition, the calf sitting squarely upon the man's shoulders, the arms of man and legs of animal locked across the body, the man's drapery blocked out by a mere raised line. A Peloponnesian *kouros*

---

[8] It has been suggested that the Dipylon head and the New York *kouros* are by the same artist. The simple fillet about the head and the decorative effect of the hair, which is a series of mere punches, call for attention, as does the fact that these early statues must be viewed from one side at a time. The artist thought of each side as a complete unit.

from Tenea has more life, but the same Greek directness and assurance.

Solon's archonship had a profound effect upon the development of Attic sculpture, a field to which we must often refer, because it is so fine and because chance has preserved so much of it for us.[9] His invitation to artists to settle in Athens naturally brought to the city sculptors of differing taste. Until the middle of the sixth cenury Attic sculpure did not differ greatly from the Peloponnesian, with its emphasis on the physical, but about 550 B.C. Ionian influence became strong. Ionian sculpture tended to emphasize details such as hair and drapery, it loved the magnificent; for example, the lower drums of the temple of Artemis at Ephesus were adorned with sculpture. The Hera from Samos, which breathes the character of the material from which it is carved, shows the emphasis on drapery rather than body (Figure 37). In particular, we observe, Ionian sculpture has the diagonal himation, which is asymmetrical and presents complex areas, and beneath it is the thin long-sleeved linen chiton, whose ruffled surfaces invite decorative stylization.

Until the mid-sixth century, and even a little later, Athenian women wore the Doric *peplos*. We can see this style in one of the greatest *korai* that has come down to us, the so-called *peplos kore,* whose vivid expression and simple charm, combined with the artist's extraordinary capacity to suggest the body beneath the dress, mark it as a masterpiece. But the influx of Ionian artists, whose ways were copied by the native Athenian sculptor, changed the style of art and dress. No doubt Peisistratus' rule hastened this, for a tyrant's court would naturally prefer the splendor of Ionia. The new day can be seen in an amazing Ionic figure, whose complicated and highly stylized himation and chiton retain much of the original paint. No less stylized are the overlapping layers of hair. The face is divided into distinct areas, the eyes are slanting and almost drop from their sockets. It is an extraordinary picture of an Athenian lady of fashion, bedecked with jewelry, even though its creator was not a great artist. We get a better idea of Ionian art from the rich frieze of the Treasury of the Siphnians at Delphi (*ca.* 525 B.C.), but even here we see a persistent emphasis on detail, such as the women's drapery and the horses' tails and manes.

Great Attic art resulted in part from the happy union at Athens of Peloponnesian and Ionian influences. The problem was to combine the

---

[9] After the Persian sack of the Acropolis, the Athenians, in their hurry to level off and enlarge about the edges, filled up pits with statues, a fact that incidentally gives an *ante quem* dating for the sculpture. The statues remained there until modern times and are now preserved in the Acropolis Museum.

two with the simplicity of the early sixth century. As a matter of fact, in the decade before 500 B.C. the Athenians, without surrendering any of their recent experience, deliberately and abruptly turned to that earlier simplicity. The reason very probably was the expulsion of the tyrants and the consummation of democracy under Cleisthenes; that is to say, the Greek love of simplicity was fundamental and, when freed from the exciting influence of a tyrant's court, it naturally manifested itself. We can see that in the sculpture at both ends of the sixth century, under democracy or the promise of it. It is refreshing, then, to turn to the noble *stele* (gravestone) of Aristion (Figure 38), or, as we come into the fifth century, to the magnificent *kore* dedicated by Euthydikos (Figure 39). This is archaic art at its greatest, strong, simple, restrained, and vital. The wavy lines of the hair, the horizontal eyes, the sculpturesque face, the truly three-dimensional body hold out to us the promise of the great works which have made the fifth century so famous. The pensive Blond Boy is another pledge to the future. Thus Attic art, as well as Ionian and Peloponnesian, has its own brilliant future. From the very end of the archaic period we have great sculptures of the Peloponnesian school, the figures from the fine temple of Aphaia at Aegina (Figures 40 and 41). These are our earliest surviving examples of important pedimental sculpture. We note, incidentally, that a problem before the artist was to fill correctly the triangular area of the gable, with its sloping roof which yielded less and less standing room (cf. Diagram 42). It was aesthetically important, too, to tie the whole composition together, though the further back in time we go, the less was this done; for example, the central area of the temple at Corcyra was occupied by a horrendous limestone Medusa (early sixth century), whose body, typically twisted, and legs bent to denote running, are very naive.

The marvelous achievements of archaic Greece in literature and art were quickly leading to an era of even greater power. At the same time, however, the danger of Oriental conquest, which would have stifled further development, presented itself. A Greek victory, on the other hand, would have a tremendous effect upon the country. For some years the fate of Greece remained in the balance.

NOTE ON GREEK VASES

Put briefly, the technique of the famous black-figured style was as follows. After the vase had been shaped on the wheel and had been allowed to dry, the surface was polished in preparation for the decoration. The figure was first drawn in black outline and then filled in with a black varnish, thus presenting a black silhouette against the red background, which in reality was merely the natural color of the clay slightly tinted by a transparent wash. Other colors—white, purple, red, brown—might be added to the figure; the inner lines could be marked by incision, and so too could the outlines of figures where they crossed one another. The firing in the oven added a lustre to the black glaze. The red-figured technique, which became the style after 530 B.C. and enabled the decorator to draw the details of figures with greater ease, exhibits some of the finest free-hand drawing in the history of art. Red figures now appear against a black background. First of all, the painter sketched his figure with a dull-pointed instrument on the clay; he then painted *around* this outline and thus obtained a red silhouette, because, as in the case of the black-figured style, the vase had already received a transparent wash. The details of muscles and drapery were drawn in relief-lines, and the whole background was painted with a black varnish. Finally the pot was fired.

Chapter IX

THE PERSIAN WARS

LYDIA AND PERSIA

SCATTERED as they were around the Mediterranean and the Black Seas, the Greeks were in constant touch with other peoples. This contact greatly stimulated their development, as we have seen, but it led also to many quarrels and wars. A major conflict was inevitable, however, as soon as the expansion of a first-rate power brought it actually and actively into the orbit of the Greeks. In the West, Etruria was a potential danger, but it was too far north in Italy to be a serious one. Carthage, on the other hand, was disputing Sicily with the Greeks, and it was merely a question of time before that issue would be settled. The main struggle, however, was destined to take place in the East, the home of older and more powerful empires.

It is a strange yet characteristic fact that the growth of the brilliant Ionian culture was accompanied by continued wars among the states which produced this splendid, versatile life, and by fiercer factional struggles within the individual cities.

In some states aristocracy survived; in others democracy had gained the upper hand; but in the general internal weakness the republics were giving way, one after another, to tyranny. Civil discord and inter-state warfare, although stimulating the mind to intense productivity, rendered the Asiatic Greeks wholly unfit to defend themselves against foreign aggression.

The need for united action increased with the growth of Lydia in the interior of Asia Minor to a strong aggressive power under King Gyges (*ca.* 660 B.C.). That country was rich in gold; and the inhabitants, by manufacturing, and by overland trade with Asia, had accumulated great wealth. The delicacies of their life, however, afforded little hin-drance to the policy of conquest adopted by Gyges. It was probably in resistance to Lydian aggression that twelve cities of Ionia joined in a league, whose center was the Panionion, a shrine of Poseidon on the promontory of Mycale. In a spirit of exclusiveness they styled them-selves groundlessly the only true Ionians and would admit no other states to their union. The Aeolians and the Dorians of Asia Minor formed similar leagues, but the idea of uniting all the Asiatic Greeks under a single government seems to have occurred to no one. On critical occasions the deputies of the allied Ionian states met at the Panionion to deliberate on the common welfare; but the central government possessed no means of enforcing harmonious or efficient action.

Under these circumstances Gyges succeeded in taking Colophon, one of their cities. The conquest was completed by Croesus, a later king (*ca.* 560–546 B.C.), who incorporated the Greeks of the Asiatic coast in his realm. Miletus alone, which had taken no part in the resistance, re-mained an ally under treaty. The Greeks did not resent Croesus, for his rule ended their internecine strife, and his tribute was light. The Lydians and Greeks, moreover, were coming to possess essentially the same civilization, for as a result of their commercial and social inter-course the Lydians were becoming Hellenized. Croesus was a great patron of the arts, highly respected even on the Greek mainland. At the Halys river, however, his wealthy kingdom met the Persian Empire, and the danger in that quarter was realized more fully by Croesus than by the Greeks of the seaboard.

In spite of the Hellenization of the Lydians, there was a fundamental difference of ideals that might be said to mark East and West. It is this contrast which Herodotus [1] tried to bring out in his fabulous account

[1] Herodotus, a native of Halicarnassus in Asia Minor, was perhaps four years old at the time of the battle of Salamis, and later on at Athens he wrote his famous and delightful *History*, which is our chief source of the Persian Wars; see pp. 268 ff. for a fuller discussion. The translations here and elsewhere are those of G.

of a conversation between Solon and Croesus, in order that the reader might understand at the very outset the nature of the contestants in the forthcoming world struggle. During a visit to Croesus, late in life, Solon (after he had been shown the royal treasures) was asked who, in his opinion, was the happiest of all mortals, for the king had no doubt that Solon would name him. But when Solon mentioned first one person and then another, Croesus angrily protested, and Solon replied:

"For yourself, Croesus, I see that you are wonderfully rich, and the lord of many nations: but with respect to your question, I have no answer to give, until I hear that you have closed your life happily. For assuredly he who possesses great store of riches is no nearer happiness than he who has what suffices for his daily needs, unless luck attend upon him, and so he continue in the enjoyment of all his good things to the end of life. For many of the wealthiest men have been unfavored of fortune, and many whose means were moderate, have had excellent luck. Men of the former class excel those of the latter but in two respects; these last excel the former in many. The wealthy man is better able to content his desires, and to bear up against a sudden buffet of calamity. The other has less ability to withstand these evils (from which, however, his good luck keeps him clear), but he enjoys all these following blessings: he is whole of limb, a stranger to disease, free from misfortune, happy in his children, and comely to look upon. If, in addition to all this, he end his life well, he is of a truth the man of whom you are in search, the man who may rightly be termed happy. Call him, however, until he die, not happy but fortunate. Scarcely, indeed, can any man unite all these advantages: as there is no country which contains within it all that it needs, but each, while it possesses some things, lacks others, and the best country is that which contains the most; so no single human being is complete in every repect—something is always lacking. He who unites the greatest number of advantages, and retaining them to the day of his death, then dies peaceably, that man alone, sire, is, in my judgment, entitled to bear the name of 'happy.' But in every matter we must mark well the end; for oftentimes God gives men a gleam of happiness, and then plunges them into ruin." [2]

Such was the speech which Solon addressed to Croesus, a speech which brought him neither largess nor honor. The king saw him depart with much indifference, since he thought that a man must be

---

Rawlinson, with a few slight changes and much abbreviated. The following passage illustrates Herodotus' philosophy of history, the divine working of Nemesis (Retribution) and the transitory nature of human fortunes. In Herodotus, as in Sophocles and other writers, we catch the Greek admiration for *arete*, the "equivalent" of the Latin *virtus* and as difficult to translate, but suggesting goodness and excellence.

[2] Herodotus, I, 32–33.

an arrant fool who made no account of present good, but bade men always wait and mark the end.

Another Greek, the poet Aeschylus, who fought at both Marathon and Salamis, was also able to catch the fundamental difference between Oriental and Occidental. In the *Persians,* which is a valuable eye-witness account of the battle of Salamis, the Persian queen asks a question, to which no one has found the answer, "What is this Athens, of which all men speak?" But perhaps the answer was best spoken by the ancient playwright himself when he set the quality of Athens in the democratic spirit of her people, and let a Persian give his queen the incomprehensible response, "They bow to no man and are no man's slaves."

From about the beginning of the Greek Middle Age the great power of Asia had been Assyria. Early in the seventh century she had conquered Egypt. After this event her empire extended from above Memphis on the Nile nearly to the Caspian Sea, and from the Persian Gulf to the Black Sea. This was the first conquering state to follow a systematic policy of organization. She divided her subject territories into provinces—satrapies—each under a governor, or satrap, appointed by the Assyrian king. The functions of the satrap were military, judicial, and administrative, including a supervision of the tributes. Under him were native kings, who enjoyed far less freedom than had been possible in earlier and more loosely organized empires. It was also the policy of the central government to transplant great numbers of the newly conquered from one part of the empire to another, with a view to uprooting local patriotism and of making the subject peoples more dependent. A state so thoroughly predatory in its aims is likely ultimately to encounter a powerful enemy. Thus it happened that in 612 B.C. the Assyrian capital, Nineveh, was taken by a combination of the highly civilized Babylonians with the Medes, a fresh, virile Indo-European people.

Thence arose two empires: the Babylonian on the south of hither Asia, and the Median in the north. The latter included Persia, and by rapid conquest extended its western border to the Halys river. With this boundary the Medes might have been satisfied; but suddenly (550 B.C.) their king was overthrown by an uprising of the Persians under Cyrus. This revolution, making the Median Empire Persian, placed in control a still more vigorous, aggressive Indo-European race of mountaineers under a leader of extraordinary genius and ambition. Cyrus defeated Croesus in two battles, seized Sardes, his capital, and took the proud king captive. Lydia became a part of the Persian Empire (546 B.C.).

The Aeolians and Ionians were loth to exchange their benevolent king for the new Persian conqueror. Having treated his messengers coldly at the beginning of the war, they now sought from him the same terms of subjection as they had received from Croesus. He refused, whereupon they began to wall their towns; and calling a council at the Panionion, the Ionians resolved to ask the aid of Sparta, now the strongest power in Greece, but the Lacedaemonians would not consider so distant an enterprise. It is said, however, that they sent an embassy to warn Cyrus at his peril not harm any city of Hellas. The Persian king treated the message with contempt. Harpagus, his lieutenant entrusted with the work of conquering the Greeks, laid siege to their cities one by one and captured them. Unwilling to submit, the Phocaeans sailed away in a body to found a colony in Corsica. In like manner the people of Teos, abandoning their city, founded Abdera, in Thrace. The rest of the Ionians, with the exception of the Milesians, who had allied themselves with Cyrus, submitted; and most of the neighboring islands followed their example. Gradually all Asia Minor was conquered and incorporated in the Persian Empire. Meantime after conquering Babylon, Cyrus met death in battle with the barbarians on his northeastern frontier.

During the reign of Cambyses, son and successor of Cyrus (529–522 B.C.), the Persians made no great extension of their territory to the west, but directed themselves mainly to the acquisition of Egypt. Cambyses died by a self-inflicted wound, and after a brief interval Darius a distant relative, came to the throne. This king is famous chiefly for his organization of the Empire. Enlarging on a policy begun by Cyrus, he divided the entire area, excepting Persia, into twenty large satrapies. The Persian satrap had essentially the same functions as the Assyrian officer of that title had formerly exercised, but naturally the king interfered at will in all local affairs. A necessary element of control is to be found in the splendid system of well-kept roads which Darius built from his capital Susa to all the chief points on the frontier, the most important of which, the Royal Road, ran 1,500 miles from Susa to Sardes. The "King's Eye," a near relative of the sovereign and invested with great dignity and military power, served as a royal inspector. Not only the roads but also an excellent system of gold and silver coins favored the growth of commerce, and at the same time Darius took great pains to preserve internal peace and protect his empire from invasion. The government was less predatory in aim than that of Assyria and we find in Darius a rare benevolence toward his subjects.

All the Greeks on the Aegean coast of Asia Minor, together with some neighboring peoples, constituted the Ionian satrapy. It was placed under an officer who, from his capital Sardes, governed also the Lydian satrapy. The Asiatic Greeks paid tribute to the Persian king, as they formerly had to Croesus; and in addition they were required to perform military and naval service. The conqueror did not interfere with their religion or their habits of life or their city organizations, but everywhere set up tyrants devoted to himself. The Greeks, however, were no longer the favored people of their king; in fact, no cultural or religious sympathies existed between Hellenes and Persians, a far less civilized people whose religion knew no images or gay festivities but consisted of an eternal warfare between good and evil. Greeks, too, were humiliated by their insignificant place in a gigantic empire which embraced the east-Mediterranean countries and extended into India and central Asia. Their land forces marched with the motley army of Asiatics and their fleets were arrayed with those of Phoenicia and Egypt under officers of the king. Their new position gave them internal peace, protection from enemies, and the advantages of commerce with the Orient by land and sea, but irritated their pride and repressed their genius, which could only thrive in freedom.

The Persian Empire was predatory and seemed to set no limit to its growth, and there was now no reason why it should not spread across the Aegean to the Balkan peninsula. Booty, tribute, and the hope of excelling his predecessor in the glory of triumphant war no doubt attracted Darius. The Greeks of Asia Minor were good fighters, good mariners, civilized, virile, and strong. What should Darius' policy be toward those Greeks not within his empire? Absorption was a likely answer.

Before he could think of any invasion of Greece, it was necessary for Darius to make certain that his long line of communications would nowhere be attacked on the flank. This meant an expedition against the new Scythian Empire on the north of the Black Sea, which, as a matter of fact, was already raiding his own realm. Apparently Darius conceived the idea of attacking the Scythians in their rear, from the European side, and perhaps of conquering them in a return march through their country. If so, he must have greatly underrated the difficulties of the expedition. However that may be, he led a great army in 512 B.C. across the Bosporus on a bridge of boats and thence marched away to the Danube. This he crossed on a similar bridge made from the fleets of the Ionian tyrants who were supporting him. As the Scythians would not meet Darius in open battle, but harassed his army interminably, and as provisions and water were insufficient, a conquest of the Scythians proved impossible. Darius was forced to retreat into Asia with considerable loss. He had, however, made his might known in that part of the world, and, of greater consequence, through his lieutenant Megabazus, Thrace, from the Propontis to the Strymon river, together with the islands of Lemnos and Imbros, became a Persian province.

The Athenians, probably more than any one else, realized the approaching danger, for they had lost Sigeum and the Thracian Chersonese to Persia. They knew, too, that their exiled tyrant Hippias, now at Sigeum but hoping to be restored through Persian aid, was doing his utmost to persuade Artaphrenes, satrap of Sardes, to undertake an expedition against Athens. To counteract the influence of Hippias, the Athenians sent an embassy to Artaphrenes, but the Persian abruptly ordered them to receive Hippias back, if they wished to escape ruin. Thereupon the Athenians, who had no idea of accepting the proposal, felt that a state of war was threatening between them and Persia. The Persians, having a foothold in Europe, were certain of it.

THE IONIAN REVOLT

Darius, however, was not able to follow up his victories in Thrace immediately, because the Ionian Greeks chose this moment to revolt. Herodotus, who is our chief source here, fails to make clear the cause of the Ionian Revolt, but we may be certain that the Greeks of Asia Minor were gravely discontented under Persian rule. Not only was their great prosperity of former days declining, but they chafed under the system of tyrants which the Persians had imposed. This must have been a particularly sore point, for after the suppression of the revolt Darius permitted democratic government in most of the states. The immediate cause of the revolt, however, was Aristagoras, tyrant of Miletus, who hoped to add the island of Naxos to his rule, and, needing help, suggested to Artaphernes that here would be a good way to advance gradually upon Greece. The enterprise failed, and the tyrant, to escape the inevitable punishment, and realizing that the Greeks were ready to strike for liberty, decided on revolt. His father-in-law, Histiaeus, who was at Susa, urged it also, but Hecataeus, the historian and geographer, warned of the overwhelming superiority of Persia. The people, however, readily followed Aristagoras (499 B.C.).

Abdicating his tyranny and accepting a constitutional office, Aristagoras proceeded to overthrow the despots in the remaining Ionian cities, so that now all Ionia was free from tyranny and committed to a hopeless rebellion. Aristagoras then went to Sparta to ask for an alliance, but the Lacedaemonians could not think of so distant an expedition. Thereupon he went to Athens, where the threats of Artaphrenes and

Hippias, and the loss of territory, had produced conditions more favorable to himself. The Athenians resolved therefore to send twenty ships, which were re-enforced by five from Eretria. The crews of these vessels joined with the Ionians in an attack on Sardes, hoping that a victory at this vital point might decide the issue. They burned the city, but, failing to take the citadel, were forced to retreat. On their way to the coast they were overtaken and defeated by the Persians at Ephesus. The Athenians then returned home, and would have nothing more to do with the war. The burning of Sardes, however, encouraged the revolt, which rapidly spread to all western Asia Minor, Thrace, and Cyprus. At the same time it roused Darius to extraordinary efforts. The decisive battle was fought in 494 B.C. off Lade, near Miletus, between the Greek and Phoenician fleets, 353 against 600 ships according to Herodotus, who for obvious reasons exaggerated the size of the enemy's fleet. The Greeks might easily have won, but for the treachery of the Samians, who at the critical moment deserted. The result was disaster. Miletus, which was now besieged by land and sea, was captured and sacked, and most of the surviving population was transplanted, in Asiatic style, to the mouth of the Tigris. By 493 B.C. the entire rebellion was suppressed, and Darius, by his generally lenient treatment of the Greeks, proved himself a wise ruler.

It would be difficult to overrate the significance of these events. For centuries the Ionians had been the standard bearers of Greek civilization. Miletus, the home of commerce and industry and of the fine arts, of poetry and science, the most brilliant city in Hellas, was blotted out of existence. The effect on Athens was electric. When the poet Phrynichus produced his play *The Capture of Miletus* in 493 B.C., the Athenians were so overcome that they fined Phrynichus 1,000 drachmas for reminding them of their own misfortunes. The poet had made them see vividly the horrors which attended the Persian triumph over a city of kindred blood, and which surely impended over themselves. In this mood they elected to the archonship for 493–492 B.C. an uncompromising advocate of war for the defense of the state, a man of marvelous energy and mental resources, Themistocles. Even at this early date Themistocles seems to have understood the weak point in any effort of Persia to conquer Greece. The country was too barren to support an invading army, which consequently would be dependent on a fleet for its provisioning. It seemed obviously necessary to Themistocles to build a fleet large enough to gain the supremacy of the sea. Thus Greece would be saved and his own city raised to a towering pre-eminence. During his year of office he improved the three natural harbors of Piraeus, which would serve not only the new fleet but the merchant

ships that till now had been content with the open roadstead of Phaleron (Figure 42A).

The rise of Themistocles, a *novus homo,* illustrates the progressive
democratization of Athens. His support came largely from the industrial and commercial classes, the very element, that is, which had supported the Alcmaeonid Cleisthenes. The alignment of the political
parties at Athens at this time is not wholly clear, but it is sometimes
assumed that the Alcmaeonidae, opposing Themistocles, were necessarily pro-Persian, even though this policy would drive them into the
arms of their enemy Hippias. We understand the factional struggles
better if we imagine that hardly anyone favored the Persians or the
restoration of Hippias and the tyranny. Although some members of
the tyrannist faction must have kept faith and looked across the
Aegean hoping for a return of the good old days, their number could
not have been great. The Alcmaeonids, joined by many former supporters of the Peisistratids, had formed a powerful coalition under the
leadership of Cleisthenes. After his death, this coalition continued to
dominate Athenian politics until the rise of Themistocles, who appealed to a broad constituency and threatened the position of the
Alcmaeonid coalition, which had made many enemies in almost two
decades of leadership.

The issue was brought to a head by the sudden return to Athens of
Miltiades, nephew of the settler in the Thracian Chersonese. Miltiades
was thoroughly familiar with the Persians and their military tactics,
for he had served under Darius on the Scythian expedition, but later
had won Persia's implacable enmity by joining the Ionian Revolt. Now,
in Athens, this leader of the great Philaid clan could not be expected
to cooperate with the rival Alcmaeonidae. Indeed, these rivals might
be crushed by an alliance between Themistocles, with his popular
appeal, and Miltiades, who combined with a distinguished name a useful and timely knowledge of Persia. To prevent defeat, the Alcmaeonidae brought Miltiades to trial on a charge of tyranny in the
Chersonese. He was acquitted and elected general for the next year.
The Athenians had chosen the radicalism of Themistocles and the
special knowledge of Miltiades. Miltiades, for his part, abandoned the
naval program of Themistocles and devoted the state's whole attention
to the heavy infantry. The Ionian Revolt, then, had given the Athenians time to take their bearings. This was well, for the Persians were
already on the march.

With the crushing of the revolt, it was clearly Darius' duty to restore
his authority in Thrace, a plan which, if successful, might be extended
to Greece proper. Accordingly in 492 B.C. he sent his son-in-law Mardo-

nius across the Hellespont at the head of a large army and fleet. Thrace, Thasos, and Macedon were conquered, but the fleet was shattered in an attempt to round Mt. Athos (Map 14). As a consequence Mardonius returned home, though he had accomplished his primary purpose. The next step was to punish Athens and Eretria for their share in the Ionian Revolt. Darius began at once to gather his ships and at the same time sent heralds among the Greek states to demand "earth and water." Though his designs may have been limited to Athens and Eretria, it was essential to prevent those cities from gaining allies. Hopeless of resistance, the islanders yielded; and many on the mainland acted likewise. Among the more independent states which thus "Medized" were the Thessalian cities, Thebes—doubtless irritated by her defeat by Athens—and Argos, which could not forgive Sparta her crushing defeat at Sepeia in 494 B.C. Aegina was hostile to Athens at the moment, but the rest of the Peloponnesian League, directed by King Cleomenes, stood loyally for the cause of Greece. As usual, the Greek states were divided, but fortunately the two strongest, Sparta and Athens, maintained a consistent policy toward Persia. Sparta probably found it easier to cooperate with Athens with Themistocles at the helm instead of her old enemies, the Alcmaeonids, a fact which, no doubt, had been appreciated at Athens itself. The Athenians exerted themselves to the utmost to prepare for the impending invasion, and, as we have seen, elected Miltiades to the board of generals.

MARATHON

In the summer of 490 B.C. a Persian fleet, conveying a force of infantry and cavalry, moved westward across the Aegean Sea. It was commanded by Datis, a Mede, and Artaphernes, son of the satrap of Sardes and nephew of Darius. Most of the islanders along their route submitted. The immediate object was to subdue Eretria and Athens, and restore Hippias to the command of Athens. After a siege of six days, Eretria was betrayed by two of her people, the city was sacked and the population taken captive. From Eretria the Persians, under the guidance of the aged Hippias, crossed over to Marathon, on the coast northeast of Athens, where they hoped for support from partisans, for this had been a region of Peisistratid strength. The Athenians, who had been unwilling to send a force to Eretria and thus expose their own city, prepared to take up their position in a narrow valley (Vrana) facing the Persians in the plain by the shore, whence deployment would be easy and, should the Persians take the road to Athens, an attack could be made on their flank. Herodotus paints the picture as follows:

And first, before they left the city, the generals sent off to Sparta a herald, one Pheidippides, who was by birth an Athenian, and by profession and practice a trained runner. This man, according to the account which he gave to the Athenians on his return, when he was near Mount Parthenium, above Tegea, fell in with the god Pan, who called him by his name, and bade him ask the Athenians, "Why they neglected him so entirely, when he was kindly disposed toward them, and had often helped them in times past, and would do so again in time to come?" The Athenians, entirely believing in the truth of this report, as soon as their affairs were once more in good order, set up a temple to Pan under the Acropolis, and, in return for the message which I have recorded, established in his honor yearly sacrifices and a torch-race.

On the occasion of which we speak, when Pheidippides was sent by the Athenian generals, and, according to his own account, saw Pan on his journey, he reached Sparta on the very next day after quitting the city of Athens. Upon his arrival he went before the rulers, and said:

"Men of Lacedaemon, the Athenians beseech you to hasten to their aid, and not allow that state, which is the most ancient in all Greece, to be enslaved by the barbarians. Eretria is already carried away captive, and Greece weakened by the loss of no mean city."

Thus did Pheidippides deliver the message committed to him. And the Spartans wished to help the Athenians, but were unable to give them any present aid, as they did not like to break their established law. It was the ninth day of the month, and they could not march out of Sparta on the ninth, when the moon had not reached the full. So they waited for the full of the moon.

The Athenians, for their part, were drawn up in order of battle in a precinct belonging to Heracles when they were joined by the Plataeans, who came in full force to their aid. The Athenian generals were divided in their opinions; and some advised not to risk a battle, because they were too few to engage such a host as that of the Medes; while others were for fighting at once, and among these last was Miltiades. He therefore, seeing that opinions were thus divided, and that the less worthy counsel appeared likely to prevail, resolved to go to the polemarch, and have a conference with him. For the man on whom the lot fell to be polemarch, at Athens, was entitled to give his vote with the ten generals, since anciently the Athenians allowed him an equal right of voting with them. The polemarch at this juncture was Callimachus of Aphidnae; to him therefore Miltiades went, and said:

"With you it rests, Callimachus, either to bring Athens to slavery, or, by securing her freedom, to leave behind to all future generations a memory beyond even Harmodius and Aristogeiton. For never since the time that the

Athenians became a people were they in so great a danger as now. If they bow their necks beneath the yoke of the Medes, the woes which they will have to suffer when given into the power of Hippias are already determined on; if, on the other hand, they fight and overcome, Athens may rise to be the very first city in Greece."

Miltiades by these words gained Callimachus; and the addition of the polemarch's vote caused the decision to be in favor of fighting. Hereupon all those generals who had been desirous of hazarding a battle, when their turn came to command the army, gave up their right to Miltiades. He, however, though he accepted their offers, nevertheless waited, and would not fight, until his own day of command arrived in due course [Figure 42B].

Then at length, when his own turn was come, the Athenian battle was set in array, and this was the order of it. Callimachus the polemarch led the right wing, for it was at that time a rule with the Athenians to give the right wing to the polemarch. After this followed the tribes, according as they were numbered, in an unbroken line; while last of all came the Plataeans, forming the left wing. And ever since that day it has been a custom with the Athenians, in the sacrifices and assemblies held each fifth year at Athens, for the Athenian herald to implore the blessing of the gods on the Plataeans conjointly with the Athenians. Now as they marshalled the host upon the field of Marathon, in order that the Athenian front might be of equal length with the Median, the ranks of the center were diminished, and it became the weakest part of the line, while the wings were both made strong with a depth of many ranks.

So when the battle was set in array, and the victims showed themselves favorable, instantly the Athenians, so soon as they were let go, charged the barbarians at a run. Now the distance between the two armies was little short of a mile. The Persians, therefore, when they saw the Greeks coming on at speed, made ready to receive them, although it seemed to them that the Athenians were bereft of their senses, and bent upon their own destruction; for they saw a mere handful of men coming on at a run without either horsemen or archers. Such was the opinion of the barbarians; but the Athenians in close array fell upon them, and fought in a manner worthy of being recorded. They were the first of the Greeks, so far as I know, who introduced the custom of charging the enemy at a run, and they were likewise the first who dared to look upon the Median garb, and to face men clad in that fashion. Until this time the very name of the Medes had been a terror to the Greeks to hear.

The two armies fought together on the plain of Marathon for a length of time; and in the mid battle, where the Persians themselves and the Sacae had their place, the barbarians were victorious, and broke and pursued the Greeks into the inner country; but on the two wings the Athenians and the Plataeans defeated the enemy. Having so done, they suffered the routed barbarians to fly at their ease, and joining the two wings in one, fell upon those who had broken their own center, and fought and conquered them. These likewise fled, and now the Athenians hung upon the runaways and

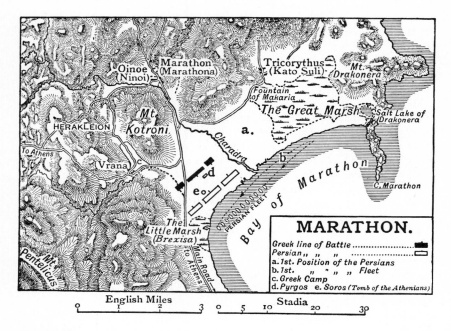

Map 22

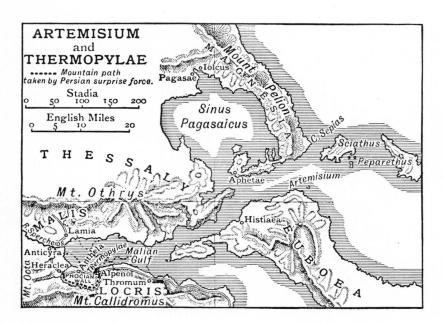

Map 23

134

cut them down, chasing them all the way to the shore, on reaching which they laid hold of the ships and called aloud for fire.

It was in the struggle here that Callimachus the polemarch, after greatly distinguishing himself, lost his life; Stesilaus too, the son of Thrasilaus, one of the generals, was slain, and Cynaegirus,[3] the son of Euphorion, having seized on a vessel of the enemy's by the ornament at the stern, had his hand cut off by the blow of an axe, and so perished; as likewise did many other Athenians of note and name.

Nevertheless the Athenians secured in this way seven of the vessels, while with the remainder the barbarians pushed off, and taking aboard their Eretrian prisoners from the island where they had left them, doubled Cape Sunium, hoping to reach Athens before the return of the Athenians. The Alcmaeonidae were accused by their countrymen of suggesting this course to them; they had, it was said, an understanding with the Persians, and made a signal to them, by raising a shield, after they were embarked in their ships.

The Persians accordingly sailed round Sunium. But the Athenians with all possible speed marched away to the defense of their city, and succeeded in reaching Athens before the appearance of the barbarians; and as their camp at Marathon had been pitched in a precinct of Heracles, so now they encamped in another precinct of the same god at Cynosarges. The barbarian fleet arrived, and lay to off Phaleron, which was at that time the harbor of Athens; but after resting awhile upon their oars, they departed and sailed away to Asia.

There fell in this battle of Marathon, on the side of the barbarians about 6,400 men; on that of the Athenians, 192. Such was the number of the slain on the one side and the other. A strange prodigy likewise happened at this fight. Epizelus, the son of Cuphagoras, an Athenian, was in the thick of the fray, and behaving himself as a brave man should, when suddenly he was stricken with blindness, without blow of sword or dart, and this blindness continued thenceforth during the whole of his after life. The following is the account which he himself, as I have heard, gave of the matter: he said that a gigantic warrior, with a huge beard, which shaded all his shield, stood over against him, but the ghostly semblance passed him by, and slew the man at his side. Such, as I understand, was the tale which Epizelus told.

After the full of the moon 2,000 Lacedaemonians came to Athens. So eager had they been to arrive in time, that they took but three days to reach Attica from Sparta. They came, however, too late for the battle; yet, as they had a longing to behold the Medes, they continued their march to Marathon and there viewed the slain. Then, after giving the Athenians all praise for their achievement, they departed and returned home.[4]

There were about 10,000 Athenians engaged in this battle, the Persian force being possibly three times as large. The moral effect of

[3] Brother of the poet Aeschylus; he and Callimachus and 190 other Athenians were buried on the battlefield, which is still marked by a great mound.

[4] Herodotus, VI, 102–120.

the victory was stupendous. Up to this time the very name of "the Medes" frightened the Greeks, but it was now demonstrated that the Greek warrior was superior to the Persian. The westward advance of the Asiatic empire was halted, and the Greeks were inspired with a fair hope of maintaining their freedom. To the Athenians, who almost singlehanded had beaten a power thought to be irresistible, this victory served as an incentive to heroism. The glory of the Marathonian warriors never faded.

The next year, 489 B.C., Miltiades, now the most popular man in Athens, persuaded the people to give him a fleet of seventy ships, saying he would lead his countrymen to a place where they could enrich themselves, but not letting them know definitely his purpose. With this armament he sailed against the Parians, on whom he levied a fine of one hundred talents for having joined the enemy in attacking Athens. On their refusal to pay he besieged the island, but failed to capture it, and returned home wounded. In their disappointment and anger, the Athenians tried Miltiades before the Assembly on the charge of having deceived the people. He was condemned to death, but because of his former services the punishment was mitigated to a fine of fifty talents. The condemned man died of his wound, and the fine was paid by his son Cimon.

POLITICAL STRIFE AT ATHENS

Miltiades had embarked on a policy of conquering the Medizing islanders in order to create a bulwark against the next Persian invasion. His failure gave his enemies their opportunity to strike at him, and so, indirectly, at Themistocles as well. The prosecutor was an Alcmaeonid by marriage, Xanthippus, husband of Cleisthenes' niece, Agariste, and father of Pericles. The conviction of Miltiades was a great victory for the Opposition, and shortly afterward a member of the Alcmaeonid party, Aristeides, was elected to the archonship. But Themistocles struck back. A man of restless energy, a statesman of great vision, he was also vain, and jealous of the fame of others; the thought of Miltiades' trophy is said to have kept him awake at night. The failure of the government to prosecute the current war with Aegina successfully and the failure to make adequate provision against the impending Persian invasion were capitalized by Themistocles, with all his cunning and popular appeal. In rapid succession his opponents were ostracized; Hipparchus, a shadowy exarchon who probably led the tyrannist forces at Athens (487 B.C.); Megacles, the leader of the Alcmaeonids, who had been unjustly suspected of flashing a treacherous signal with his shield to the Persians at Marathon (486 B.C.); Xanthippus in 484 B.C.; and two years later Aristeides. Themistocles, however, yearned for more than this; he must have power himself, a difficult matter, because re-election to the archonship was not allowed. In 487–486 B.C., through his agency, the archonship was thrown open to the lot. There was nothing startling in the proposal, for sortition was a common practice, and we can imagine Themistocles urging the people to abolish, in effect, an office so long associated with aristocracy. This represents one of the last great changes in the Athenian constitution after Cleisthenes. Henceforth the archonship lost its importance—but it was necessary to put something in its place. The board of ten generals became the new executive body at Athens. One general was elected from each of the ten tribes, and a little later provision was made that instead of one of these the tenth general might sometimes be elected from the entire citizen body. The generals were the chief officials of the state, military functions being only part of their duties, and because repeated re-election was possible, the way had been opened for continuous power for one man.

Themistocles' victory meant the abandonment of an army policy and the creation of a large navy for the war with Persia. A particularly rich vein in the silver mines at Laurium had recently been tapped, and Themistocles urged that the surplus in the treasury be used for a fleet. Two hundred ships were voted by the Assembly. The motive of Themistocles was partly patriotic—to defend the freedom of Greece and to make his own state a great power. The democratic effect, however, could have been foreseen.

To be sure, the merchants of Athens benefited from the naval policy, as did the other members of the state, through the increased security it offered. But the lower classes were the major beneficiaries. They rowed the ships and were paid for their services. As the navy came to be the bulwark of Athenian defense, the importance of the sailors grew and with it their claim to political power. The growth of the Athenian navy and Athenian democracy went hand in hand.

THERMOPYLAE

The battle of Marathon shook the military prestige of the Great King and encouraged rebellion within the Empire. The conquest of Greece became, as a consequence, even more than ever a question of practical necessity as well as of honor. Preparations for a new invasion, however, were suspended by the revolt of Egypt and the death of Darius in 486 B.C. After the reconquest of that country, Xerxes, son and successor of the deceased king, devoted himself to gathering the whole available strength of the Empire with a view to overwhelming Greece by the force of numbers. As Mardonius' route of 492 B.C. was to be followed, engineers and workmen were soon engaged in bridging the Hellespont with boats, and in cutting a canal through the isthmus of Mt. Athos. Great depots of provisions were established along the projected route. With his vast host Xerxes spent the winter of 481–480 B.C. at Sardes in the expectation of setting out early the next spring.

Thus far, outside of Athens the Greeks had made no preparation to resist the invader; and no further progress had been made toward unity. The heralds of Xerxes, as they passed to and fro throughout Greece during the winter preceding the invasion, found many states ready to purchase safety by the gift of earth and water. The patriot cause could place no reliance on Thessaly, Thebes, or Argos, or on the less progressive states of the center and west of the peninsula, or on the widely scattered islands. Gelon, tyrant of Syracuse, might have given powerful aid, but he had to face a Carthaginian attack. The brunt was to be borne by the Peloponnesian League, Athens, and a few small communities on the peninsula and the neighboring islands; and even here the prevailing sentiment was nearly akin to despair. A feeling of common nationality was, nevertheless, apparent.

Under these circumstances a congress of deputies from the loyal states was held at Corinth in 481 B.C. to discuss measures for defense. The call had been issued by Lacedaemon but at the suggestion of Athens, undoubtedly on the motion of Themistocles. One result was the reconciliation of various states, including Athens and Aegina; another was the sending of envoys to the unrepresented Greek states to invite their active support, a barren hope. Spies, sent to Xerxes' camp, were captured, shown everything, and dismissed in the expectation that their report of his immense army would induce the Greeks to yield without resistance. The congress of deputies conferred the chief command by sea as well as by land on Sparta, to whose leadership most of the states had long been accustomed. There can be no doubt that the proceedings were influenced by the mighty spirit of Themistocles and that his determination to fight out the issue on the sea was important. The strategy was to try to inflict a decisive defeat on he Persian fleet, for this would cause the army, which needed the fleet for its support, to retire, as in 492 B.C. Meanwhile, the Greek army should take up its position as far north as feasible, in order to protect as much of the country as possible, and also because all states north of that point would of necessity be pro-Persian. For this reason the Spartan suggestion that the stand be made at the Isthmus was refused. In the north, the vale of Tempe, giving access to Thessaly, was an impossible position because of other passes in the neighborhood. This left Thermopylae, the key to central Greece (Maps, 14 and 15).

Xerxes, with his vast host,[5] entered Thessaly unopposed in 480 B.C., whereupon the states of this district under the lead of Medizing oligarchs passed over to his side. In accordance with the plan of Themistocles, who was now general at Athens, the Greek fleet of 300 ships took up its station at Artemisium, off northern Euboea, to meet the Persian fleet, while a force of 10,000 Greeks, under Leonidas, king of Sparta, occupied the pass of Thermopylae to hold the enemy in check until the battle at sea had been fought (Map 23).

Such were the doings of Xerxes in Thessaly [says Herodotus]. From hence he passed on into Malis, along the shores of a bay, in which there is an ebb and flow of the tide daily. By the side of this bay lies a piece of flat land, in one part broad, but in another very narrow indeed, around which runs a range of lofty hills, impossible to climb, enclosing all Malis within them, and called the Trachinian Cliffs.

Further to the south, a river, called the Phoenix, which has no great body of water, flows from the same hills, and falls into the Asopus. Here is the narrowest place of all, for in this part there is only a causeway wide enough for a single carriage. From the river Phoenix to Thermopylae is a distance of two miles; and in this space is situated the village called Anthela, which the river Asopus passes before it reaches the sea. The space about Anthela is of some width, and contains a temple of Amphictyonian Demeter, as well as the seats of the Amphictyonic deputies, and a temple of Amphictyon himself.

King Xerxes pitched his camp in the region of Malis called Trachinia, while on their side the Greeks occupied the straits. These straits the Greeks in general call Thermopylae (the Hot Gates); but the natives and those who dwell in the neighborhood, call them Pylae (the Gates). Here then the two armies took their stand; the one master of all the region lying north of Trachis, the other of the country extending southward of that place to the verge of the continent.

The Greeks who at this spot awaited the coming of Xerxes were the following: From Sparta, 300 men-at-arms; from Arcadia, 1,000 Tegeans and Mantineans, 500 of each people; 120 Orchomenians, from the Arcadian Orchomenus; and 1,000 from other cities; from Corinth, 400 men; from Phlius, 200; and from Mycenae, eighty. Such was the number from the Peloponnesus. There were also present, from Boeotia, 700 Thespians and 400 Thebans.

---

[5] The numbers given by Herodotus, amounting to more than five millions, including noncombatants, and 1,207 warships, are an enormous exaggeration. A reasonable estimate would be 150,000 to 200,000 combatants and 700 warships.

Besides these troops, the Locrians of Opus and the Phocians had obeyed the call of their countrymen, and sent, the former all the force they had, the latter 1,000 men. For envoys had gone from the Greeks at Thermopylae among the Locrians and Phocians, to call on them for assistance, and to say, "They were themselves but the vanguard of the host, sent to precede the main body, which might every day be expected to follow them. The sea was in good keeping, watched by the Athenians, the Aeginetans, and the rest of the fleet. There was no cause why they should fear; for after all the invader was not a god but a man; and there never had been, and never would be, a man who was not liable to misfortunes from the very day of his birth, and those greater in proportion to his own greatness. The assailant therefore, being only a mortal, must needs fall from his glory." Thus urged, the Locrians and the Phocians had come with their troops to Trachis.

The various nations had each captains of their own under whom they served; but the one to whom all especially looked up, and who had the command of the entire force, was the Lacedaemonian king, Leonidas. He had now come to Thermopylae, accompanied by the 300 men which the law assigned him, whom he had himself chosen from among the citizens, and who were all of them fathers with sons living. On his way he had taken the troops from Thebes, whose number I have already mentioned, and who were under the command of Leontiades the son of Eurymachus. The reason why he made a point of taking troops from Thebes and Thebes only was that the Thebans were strongly suspected of being well inclined to the Medes. Leonidas therefore called on them to come with him to the war, wishing to see whether they would comply with his demand, or openly refuse, and disclaim the Greek alliance. They, however, though their wishes leant the other way, nevertheless sent the men.

The force with Leonidas was sent forward by the Spartans in advance of their main body, that the sight of them might encourage the allies to fight, and hinder them from going over to the Medes, as it was likely they might have done had they seen Sparta backward. They intended presently, when they had celebrated the Carneian festival, which was what now kept them at home, to leave a garrison in Sparta, and hasten in full force to join the army. The rest of the allies also intended to act similarly; for it happened that the Olympic festival fell exactly at this same period. None of them looked to see the contest at Thermopylae decided so speedily; wherefore they were content to send forward a mere advanced guard. Such accordingly were the intentions of the allies.

The Greek forces at Thermopylae, when the Persian army drew near to the entrance of the pass, were seized with fear, and a council was held to consider about a retreat. It was the wish of the Peloponnesians generally that the army should fall back upon the Peloponnesus, and there guard the Isthmus. But Leonidas, who saw with what indignation the Phocians and Locrians heard of this plan, gave his voice for remaining where they were, while they sent envoys to the several cities to ask for help, since they were too few to make a stand against an army like that of the Medes.

While this debate was going on, Xerxes sent a mounted spy to observe the Greeks, and note how many they were, and what they were doing. He had heard, before he came out of Thessaly, that a few men were assembled at this place, and that at their head were certain Lacedaemonians, under Leonidas, a descendant of Heracles. The horseman rode up to the camp, and looked about him, but did not see the whole army; for such as were on the further side of the wall (which had been rebuilt and was now carefully guarded) it was not possible for him to behold; but he observed those on the outside, who were encamped in front of the rampart. It chanced that at this time the Lacedaemonians held the outer guard, and were seen by the spy, some of them engaged in gymnastic exercises, others combing their long hair. At this the spy greatly marvelled, but he counted their number, and when he had taken accurate note of everything, he rode back quietly; for no one pursued after him, or paid any heed to his visit. So he returned, and told Xerxes all that he had seen.

Upon this, Xerxes, who had no means of surmising the truth—namely, that the Spartans were preparing to do or die manfully—but thought it laughable that they should be engaged in such employments, sent and called to his presence Demaratus the son of Ariston, who still remained with the army. When he appeared, Xerxes told him all that he had heard, and questioned him concerning the news, since he was anxious to understand the meaning of such behavior on the part of the Spartans. Then Demaratus said, "I spoke to you, O king, concerning these men long since, when we had but just begun our march upon Greece; you, however, only laughed at my words, when I told you of all this, which I saw would come to pass. Earnestly do I struggle at all times to speak truth to you, sire; and now listen to it once more. These men have come to dispute the pass with us, and it is for this that they are now making ready. It is their custom, when they are about to hazard their lives, to adorn their heads with care. Be assured, however, that if you can subdue the men who are here and the Lacedaemonians who remain in Sparta, there is no other nation in all the world which will venture to lift a hand in their defense. You have now to deal with the first kingdom and town in Greece, and with the bravest men."

Then Xerxes, to whom what Demaratus said seemed altogether to surpass belief, asked further, "How it was possible for so small an army to contend with his?"

"O king," Demaratus answered, "let me be treated as a liar, if matters fall not out as I say."

But Xerxes was not persuaded any the more. Four whole days he suffered to go by, expecting that the Greeks would run away. When, however, he found on the fifth that they were not gone, thinking that their firm stand was mere impudence and recklessness, he grew wroth, and sent against them the Medes and Cissians, with orders to take them alive and bring them into his presence. Then the Medes rushed forward and charged the Greeks, but fell in vast numbers: others however took the places of the slain, and would not be beaten off, though they suffered terrible losses. In this way it became clear to all, and especially to the king, that though he had plenty of combatants, he had but very few warriors. The struggle, however, continued during the whole day.

Then the Medes, having met so rough a reception, withdrew from the fight; and their place was taken by the band of Persians under Hydarnes, whom the king called his Immortals: they, it was thought, would soon finish the business. But when they joined battle with the Greeks, it was with no better success than the Median detachment—things went much as before—the two armies fighting in a narrow space, and the barbarians using shorter spears than the Greeks, and having no advantage from their numbers. The Lacedaemonians fought in a way worthy of note, and showed themselves far more skilful in fight than their adversaries, often turning their backs, and making as though they were all flying away, on which the barbarians would rush after them with much noise and shouting, when the Spartans at their approach would wheel round and face their pursuers, in this way destroying vast numbers of the enemy. Some Spartans likewise fell in these encounters, but only a very few. At last the Persians, finding that all their efforts to gain the pass availed nothing, and that whether they attacked by divisions or in any oher way, it was to no purpose, withdrew to their own quarters.

During these assaults, it is said that Xerxes, who was watching the battle, thrice leaped from the throne on which he sat, in terror for his army.

Next day the combat was renewed, but with no better success on the part of the barbarians. The Greeks were so few that the barbarians hoped to find them disabled, by reason of their wounds, from offering any further resistance; and so they once more attacked them. But the Greeks were drawn up in detachments according to their cities, and bore the brunt of the battle in turns, all except the Phocians, who had been stationed on the mountain to guard the pathway. So when the Persians found no difference between that day and the preceding, they again retired to their quarters.

Now, as the king was at a loss, and knew not how he should deal with the emergency, Ephialtes, the son of Eurydemus, a man of Malis, came to him and was admitted to a conference. Stirred by the hope of receiving a rich reward at the king's hands, he had come to tell him of the pathway which led across the mountain to Thermopylae; by which disclosure he brought destruction on the band of Greeks who had there withstood the barbarians. This Ephialtes afterwards, from fear of the Lacedaemonians, fled into Thessaly; and during his exile, in an assembly of the Amphictyons held at Pylae, a price was set upon his head by the Pylagorae. When some time had gone by, he returned from exile, and went to Anticyra, where he was slain by Athenades, a native of Trachis. Athenades did not slay him for his treachery, but for another reason, which I shall mention in a later part of my history: yet still the Lacedaemonians honored him none the less. Thus then did Ephialtes perish a long time afterwards.

Great was the joy of Xerxes on this occasion; and as he approved highly of the enterprise which Ephialtes undertook to accomplish, he forthwith sent upon the errand Hydarnes, and the Persians under him. The troops left the camp about the time of the lighting of the lamps. The pathway along which they went was first discovered by the Malians of these parts, who soon afterwards led the Thessalians by it to attack the Phocians, at the time when the Phocians fortified the pass with a wall, and so put themselves under covert from danger. And ever since, the path has always been put to an ill use by the Malians.

The course which it takes is the following: Beginning at the Asopus, where that stream flows through the cleft in the hills, it runs along the ridge of the mountain (which is called, like the pathway over it, Anopaea) and ends at the city of Alpenus—the first Locrian town as you come from Malis—by the stone called Black-buttock and the seats of the Cercopians. Here it is as narrow as at any other point.

The Persians took this path, and crossing the Asopus, continued their march through the whole of the night, having the mountain of Oeta on their right hand, and on their left those of Trachis. At dawn of day they found themselves close to the summit. Now the hill was guarded, as I have already said, by 1,000 Phocian men-at-arms, who were placed there to defend the pathway, and at the same time to secure their own country. They had been given the guard of the mountain path, while the other Greeks defended the pass below, because they had volunteered for the service, and had pledged themselves to Leonidas to maintain the post.

The ascent of the Persians became known to the Phocians in the following manner: During all the time that they were making their way up, the Greeks remained unconscious of it, inasmuch as the whole mountain was covered with groves of oak; but it happened that the air was very still, and the leaves which the Persians stirred with their feet made, as it was likely they would, a loud rustling, whereupon the Phocians jumped up and flew to seize their arms. In a moment the barbarians came in sight, and perceiving men arming themselves, were greatly amazed; for they had fallen in with an enemy when they expected no opposition. Hydarnes, alarmed at the sight, and fearing lest the Phocians might be Lacedaemonians, inquired of Ephialtes to what nation these troops belonged. Ephialtes told him the exact truth, whereupon he arrayed his Persians for battle. The Phocians, galled by the showers of arrows to which they were exposed, and imagining themselves the special object of the Persian attack, fled hastily to the crest of the mountain, and there made ready to meet death; but while their mistake continued, the Persians, with Ephialtes and Hydarnes, not thinking it worth their while to delay on account of Phocians, passed on and descended the mountain with all possible speed.

The Greeks at Thermopylae received the first warning of the destruction which the dawn would bring on them from the seer Megistias, who read their fate in the victims as he was sacrificing. After this deserters came in, and brought the news that the Persians were marching round by the hills: it was still night when these men arrived. Last of all, the scouts came running down from the heights, and brought in the same accounts, when the day was just beginning to break. Then the Greeks held a council to consider what they should do, and here opinions were divided: some were strong against quitting their post, while others contended to the contrary. So when the council had broken up, part of the troops departed and went their ways homeward to their several states; part however resolved to remain, and to stand by Leonidas to the last.

It is said that Leonidas himself sent away the troops who departed, because he tendered their safety, but thought it unseemly that either he or his Spartans should quit the post which they had been especially sent to guard. For my own part, I incline to think that Leonidas gave the order, because he perceived the allies to be out of heart and unwilling to encounter the danger to which his own mind was made up. He therefore commanded them to retreat, but said that he himself could not draw back with honor; knowing that, if he stayed, glory awaited him, and that Sparta in that case would not lose her prosperity. For when the Spartans, at the very beginning of the war, sent to consult the oracle concerning it, the answer which they received from the priestess was that either Sparta must be overthrown by the barbarians, or one of her kings must perish. The prophecy was delivered in hexameter verse, and ran thus:

> Oh! ye men who dwell in the streets of broad Lacedaemon,
> Either your glorious town shall be sacked by the children of Perseus,
> Or, in exchange, must all through the whole Laconian country
> Mourn for the loss of a king, descendant of great Heracles.
> He cannot be withstood by the courage of bulls or of lions,
> Strive as they may; he is mighty as Zeus; there is nought that shall
>   stay him,
> Till he have got for his prey your king, or your glorious city.

The remembrance of this answer, I think, and the wish to secure the whole glory for the Spartans, caused Leonidas to send the allies away. This is more likely than that they quarrelled with him, and took their departure in such unruly fashion.

To me it seems no small argument in favor of this view, that the seer also who accompanied the army, Megistias, the Acarnanian, said to have been of the blood of Melampus, and the same who was led by the appearance of the victims to warn the Greeks of the danger which threatened them, received orders to retire (as it is certain he did) from Leonidas, that he might escape the coming destruction. Megistias, however, though bidden to depart, refused, and stayed with the army; but he had an only son present with the expedition, whom he now sent away.

So the allies, when Leonidas ordered them to retire, obeyed him and forthwith departed. Only the Thespians and the Thebans remained with the Spartans; and of these the Thebans were kept back by Leonidas as hostages, very much against their will. The Thespians, on the contrary, stayed entirely of their own accord, refusing to retreat, and declaring that they would not forsake Leonidas and his followers. So they abode with the Spartans, and died with them. Their leader was Demophilus, the son of Diadromes.

At sunrise Xerxes made libations, after which he waited until the time when the market-place is wont to fill, and then began his advance. Ephialtes had instructed him thus, as the descent of the mountain is much quicker, and the distance much shorter, than the way round the hills, and the ascent. So the barbarians under Xerxes began to draw nigh; and the Greeks under Leonidas, as they now went forth determined to die, advanced much further than on previous days, until they reached the more open portion of the pass. Hitherto they had held their station within the wall, and from this had gone forth to fight at the point where the pass was the narrowest. Now they joined battle beyond the defile, and carried slaughter among the barbarians, who fell in heaps. Behind them the captains of the squadrons, armed with whips, urged their men forward with continual blows. Many were thrust into the sea, and there perished; a still greater number were trampled to death by their own soldiers; no one heeded the dying. For the Greeks, reckless of their own safety and desperate, since they knew that, as the mountain had been crossed their destruction was nigh at hand, exerted themselves with the most furious valor against the barbarians.

By this time the spears of the greater number were all shivered, and with their swords they hewed down the ranks of the Persians; and here, as they strove, Leonidas fell fighting bravely, together with many other famous Spartans, whose names I have taken care to learn on account of their great worthiness, as indeed I have those of all the 300. There fell too at the same time very many famous Persians: among them, two sons of Darius.

Thus two brothers of Xerxes here fought and fell. And now there arose a fierce struggle between the Persians and the Lacedaemonians over the body of Leonidas, in which the Greeks four times drove back the enemy, and at last by their great bravery succeeded in bearing off the body. This combat was scarcely ended when the Persians with Ephialtes approached; and the Greeks, informed that they drew nigh, made a change in the manner of their fighting. Drawing back into the narrowest part of the pass, and retreating even behind the cross wall, they posted themselves upon a hillock, where they stood all drawn up together in one close body, except only the Thebans. The hillock whereof I speak is at the entrance of the straits, where the stone lion stands which was set up in honor of Leonidas. Here they defended themselves to the last, such as still had swords using them, and the others resisting with their hands and teeth; till the barbarians, who in part had pulled down the wall and attacked them in front, in part had gone round and now encircled them upon every side, overwhelmed and buried the remnant left beneath showers of missile weapons.

Thus nobly did the whole body of Lacedaemonians and Thespians behave, but nevertheless one man is said to have distinguished himself above all the rest, to wit, Dieneces the Spartan. A speech which he made before the Greeks engaged the Medes, remains on record. One of the Trachinians told him, "Such was the number of the barbarians, that when they shot forth their arrows the sun would be darkened by their multitude." Dieneces, not at all frightened at these words, but making light of the Median numbers, answered,

"Our Trachinian friend brings us excellent tidings. If the Medes darken the sun, we shall have our fight in the shade." Other sayings too of a like nature are said to have been left on record by this same person.

The slain were buried where they fell; and in their honor, nor less in honor of those who died before Leonidas sent the allies away, an inscription was set up, which said:

> Here did four thousand men from Pelops' land
> Against three hundred myriads bravely stand.

This was in honor of all. Another was for the Spartans alone:

> Tell them in Lakëdaimon, passer-by,
> That here obedient to their word we lie.[6]

This was for the Lacedaemonians. The seer had the following:

> The great Megistias' tomb you here may view,
>   Whom slew the Medes, fresh from Spercheius' fords.
> Well the wise seer the coming death foreknew,
>   Yet scorned he to forsake his Spartan lords.

These inscriptions, and the pillars likewise, were all set up by the Amphictyons, except that in honor of Megistias, which was inscribed to him (on account of their sworn friendship) by Simonides, the son of Leoprepes.[7]

Meanwhile the Greeks at Artemisium were encouraged by their successful engagements with the enemy and by the damaging of the Persian fleet in a storm. When, however, they learned that Xerxes had forced the pass at Thermopylae, they felt compelled to withdraw, though they had fought no decisive battle. The total result of these conflicts by sea and land was victory to the Persians, and a strengthening of the Greek hope that under more favorable conditions the struggle might yet be successful.

SALAMIS

Xerxes was now advancing through Boeotia toward Athens, and the states of central Greece were flocking to his standard. As the Greek fleet was retiring to Salamis, Themistocles returned to his city, to find it full of gloom. The Delphic Apollo had said that they should place their

[6] Various authors, *The Oxford Book of Greek Verse in Translation.*
[7] Herodotus, VII, 198–228.

confidence in the "wooden wall," which some thought referred to the palisade around the Acropolis. They accordingly took refuge there. Themistocles, however, declared that it meant the fleet, and persuaded most of the Athenians to abandon their homes for Salamis, Aegina, and Troezen.

Herodotus represents this decision as a sudden and panicky response to the news of the Greek failure to defeat the Persians at Thermopylae and Artemisium. In 1959, however, Michael Jameson, of the University of Pennsylvania, discovered an inscription that gives quite a different picture. This inscription is the now famous Themistocles Decree, which purports to be a copy of the very decree (passed well before the battle of Artemisium) in which the Athenians planned to abandon their homeland to the wrath of the Persians and to fight a naval battle at Salamis. Although the stone we have was inscribed in the third century B.C., and the inscription is not accurate in all details, there is no good reason to doubt its fundamental authenticity (Figure 43).

The removal of the population and personal property was supervised by the Council of the Areopagus, now filled with patriots and directed by Themistocles and his associates. The Greek fleet halted in the bay of Salamis to cover the Athenian retreat, with the intention, too, of making there a further stand against the enemy. The place was well chosen, for the enemy would be compelled to fight in the strait, where superior numbers would not count. Further retreat would in fact be almost equivalent to abandoning the cause, for it would leave the enemy free to land troops on the coast of the Peloponnesus in the rear of the Isthmian line of defense then being prepared.

Xerxes laid waste the country as he advanced to Athens. From the island of Salamis, the Athenians could see their city in flames, and scouts reported the Persian fleet at anchor in the bay of Phaleron. These circumstances tended for the moment to lessen the courage of the Greeks and to suggest to the admirals the wisdom of retiring to the Isthmus, where they could cooperate with the land forces. Themistocles, however, strongly urged Eurybiades, the Spartan commander-in-chief, to remain, and even threatened in case of retreat to use his ships in conveying the Athenians to a new home in Italy. While thus pleading with the admirals, Themistocles secretly dispatched a trusty slave to Xerxes, who was encamped on the shore, and falsely informed him that the Greeks, panic-stricken, were about to sail away, and urged him to cut off their retreat.

Then the Persian captains [says Herodotus], believing all that the messenger had said, proceeded to land a large body of Persian troops on the islet of

Map 24

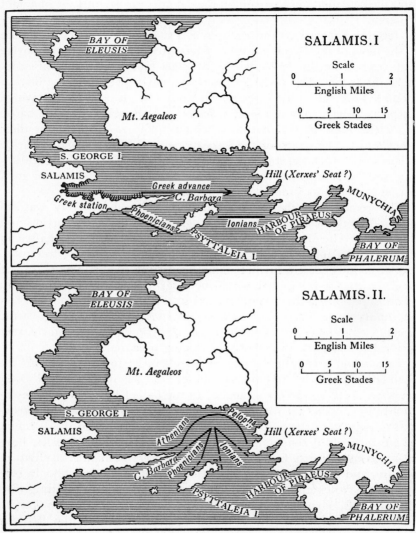

Map 25

Psyttaleia, which lies between Salamis and the mainland; after which, about the hour of midnight, they advanced their western wing towards Salamis, so as to enclose the Greeks. At the same time the force stationed about Ceos and Cynosura moved forward, and filled the whole strait as far as Munychia with their ships. This advance was made to prevent the Greeks from escaping by flight, and to block them up in Salamis, where it was thought that vengeance might be taken upon them for the battles fought near Artemisium. The Persian troops were landed on the islet of Psyttaleia, because, as soon as the battle began, the men and wrecks were likely to be drifted thither, as the isle lay in the very path of the coming fight, and they would thus be able to save their own men and destroy those of the enemy. All these movements were made in silence, that the Greeks might have no knowledge of them; and they occupied the whole night, so that the men had no time to get their sleep.

The Greeks now made ready for the coming fight. At the dawn of day, all the men-at-arms were assembled together, and speeches were made to them, of which the best was that of Themistocles; who throughout contrasted what was noble with what was base, and bade them, in all that came within the range of man's nature and constitution, always to make choice of the nobler part. Having thus wound up his discourse, he told them to go at once on board their ships, which they accordingly did; and about this time the trireme, that had been sent to Aegina for the Aeacidae, returned; whereupon the Greeks put to sea with all their fleet.

The fleet had scarce left the land when they were attacked by the barbarians. At once most of the Greeks began to back water, and were about touching the shore, when Ameinias of Pallene, one of the Athenian captains, darted forth in front of the line, and charged a ship of the enemy. The two vessels became entangled, and could not separate, whereupon the rest of the fleet came up to help Ameinias, and engaged with the Persians. Such is the account which the Athenians give of the way in which the battle began; but the Aeginetans maintain that the vessel which had been to Aegina for the Aeacidae, was the one that brought on the fight. It is also reported, that a phantom in the form of a woman appeared to the Greeks, and, in a voice that was heard from end to end of the fleet, cheered them on to the fight; first, however, rebuking them, and saying, "Strange men, how long are you going to back water?"

Against the Athenians, who held the western extremity of the line towards Eleusis, were placed the Phoenicians; against the Lacedaemonians, whose station was eastward towards the Piraeus, the Ionians. Of these last a few only followed the advice of Themistocles, to fight backwardly; the greater number did far otherwise. I could mention here the names of many captains who took vessels from the Greeks, but I shall pass over all excepting Theomestor the son of Androdamus, and Phylacus the son of Histiaeus, both Samians. I show this preference to them, inasmuch as for this service. Theomestor was made tyrant of Samos by the Persians, while Phylacus was enrolled among the king's benefactors, and presented with a large estate in land. In the Persian tongue the king's benefactors are called Orosangs.

Far the greater number of the Persian ships engaged in this battle were disabled—either by the Athenians or by the Aeginetans. For as the Greeks fought in order and kept their line, while the barbarians were in confusion and had no plan in anything that they did, the issue of the battle could scarce be other than it was. Yet the Persians fought far more bravely here than at Euboea, and indeed surpassed themselves; each did his utmost through fear of Xerxes, for each thought that the king's eye was upon himself.

There fell in this combat Ariabignes, one of the chief commanders of the fleet, who was son of Darius and brother of Xerxes, and with him perished a vast number of men of high repute, Persians, Medes, and allies. Of the Greeks there died only a few; for as they were able to swim, all those that were not slain outright by the enemy escaped from the sinking vessels and swam across to Salamis. But on the side of the barbarians more perished by drowning than in any other way, since they did not know how to swim. The great destruction took place when the ships which had been first engaged began to fly; for they who were stationed in the rear, anxious to display their valor before the eyes of the king, made every effort to force their way to the front, and thus became entangled with such of their own vessels as were retreating.

When the rout of the barbarians began, and they sought to make their escape to Phaleron, the Aeginetans, awaiting them in the channel, performed exploits worthy to be recorded. Through the whole of the confused struggle the Athenians employed themselves in destroying such ships as either made resistance or fled to shore, while the Aeginetans dealt with those which endeavored to escape down the straits; so that the Persian vessels were no sooner clear of the Athenians than straightway they fell into the hands of the Aeginetan squadron.[8]

Too thoroughly crippled to renew the fight, the Persian fleet retired to Asia. Thereupon Themistocles urged the Greeks to sail forthwith to the Hellespont and, by destroying the bridge, cut Xerxes off from his base of supplies. The advice was sound, and, if taken, would probably have ended the war; but to the other Greeks the idea seemed too venturesome, and the war continued another year. Xerxes himself returned to Asia, leaving Mardonius with the best part of the army to spend the winter in Thessaly. Mardonius' plan was to make peace with Athens and then, freed from the threat of the Athenian fleet, to crush Sparta at a blow. He sent Alexander, king of Macedonia, as his emissary, but Athens refused to desert the allied cause. There were doubts, however, and an apparent desire to hedge. Under a general amnesty decreed the year before, the exiles had returned to the city. Among them were Themistocles' opponents Xanthippus and Aristeides; the former was now placed in charge of the Athenian navy, and the latter was given command of the army.

[8] Herodotus, VII, 74–91.

PLATAEA AND MYCALE

It became clear to Sparta that speed was essential if Athens was to be kept in line. Once again Attica had been ravaged by the enemy. The Spartans therefore abandoned their insistence that the stand should be made at the Isthmus, and marched north (479 B.C.). At Plataea, just across Mt. Cithaeron in Boeotia, the allied Greek army gathered under the command of the Spartan Pausanias, who was the regent for the young son of Leonidas. The Greeks numbered 60,000 to 80,000 men, a number only slightly inferior to that of the Persian force. For almost two weeks there were maneuvers and countermaneuvers, until at last Mardonius saw his opportunity to attack the Greeks while they were in the midst of changing their position. The main attack was directed against the Peloponnesians, who patiently waited under the shower of arrows from the enemy's horsemen. But when the main body of Persians had drawn up within bowshot behind their fence of wicker shields, the order to charge was given, and the heavy Peloponnesian infantry dashed at a run upon the enemy's line. Mardonius and those about him fell. The result was decisive. The remnant of the Persian army under Artabazus hurriedly retreated to Asia. The Greek allies then besieged Thebes, and upon its fall the Boeotian League was disbanded.

The Greek ships, meanwhile, had been at Delos, keeping an eye out for the Persian fleet. Assured of help from Chios and Samos, they crossed over to the Asia Minor coast and landed at Mycale, where the Persians held a fortified position. During the battle that followed, the Asiatic Greeks in the Persian force deserted, the Persian army was destroyed, and the warships were burned. This victory, according to legend fought on the same day as Plataea (late August, 479 B.C.), pointed the way to the liberation of Asiatic Greece. Sestos, on the Hellespont, was now besieged, but as it promised to be a lengthy undertaking, the Peloponnesians, under King Leotychidas of Sparta, returned home. The Athenians, to their credit, remained. The essential difference between Athens and Sparta was here revealed, and inevitably it led to rivalry and conflict.

THE CARTHAGINIAN INVASION OF SICILY

In an earlier chapter we touched upon the Hellenic colonization of Italy and Sicily and the growth of the new settlements in that region to a high degree of economic prosperity. This success was due to the vitality, quick intelligence, and bold enterprise of the settlers, as well as to the fertility of their lands and the great extent of country open to their exploitation. The earliest settlers, dividing the lands among themselves, tended to form a closed aristocracy, but class conflicts inevitably led to tyrannies. The result was that before the close of the sixth century nearly every Greek city in Sicily had fallen under despotic rule. Those of Italy were governed by either tyrants or Pythagorean brotherhoods. In the West, as in the East, each community went its own way with little heed to the general Hellenic interest (Map 34).

This particularism, while acting as a powerful cultural stimulus, wrought little harm so long as the Hellenes had to deal merely with foreign states as small as their own. In time, however, in the West as well as in the East, they had to confront great military powers. Politically the most important people thus far in Italy were the Etruscans. In the beginning of the fifth century they held not only Etruria and parts of the Po basin farther north, but also most of Campania (around Cumae) and the coast region to the south nearly to Posidonia (Paestum) (Map 16).

While the Etruscans were developing this power within the peninsula, the Phoenicians were threatening to take possession of the islands and remaining coasts of the middle and western Mediterranean. For a time they had to yield ground to the Greeks in both Sicily and Spain. In Africa, west of Cyrenaica, however, the Phoenicians were comparatively free to work out their own destiny. On and near the African coast opposite Sicily there grew up a group of colonies, the most important of which was Carthage. Toward the end of the seventh century this city won leadership over her near neighbors and began to develop a naval power, the foundation of her future empire. Her ambition was to gather under her leadership and protection all the Phoenician colonies of the Mediterranean and to win as much new territory as possible for the race. In Sicily the Phoenicians gained ground. In Sardinia they won a footing (about 600 B.C.), though they never succeeded there in occupying more than the coasts. The Phoenician settlements in Spain acknowledged the leadership of Carthage—and the African coast became hers, from Cyrenaica to Lyxus on the Atlantic (before 500 B.C.).

Carthage had entered into close commercial relations with the Etruscans. About 550 B.C. she had begun to form treaties with the individual coast towns of Etruria for the regulation of trade and for the defense of their common interests against the Greeks. The first Hellenes to suffer from the alliance were the Phocaean colonists in Corsica. In a naval battle at Alalia between them and the combined fleets of the allies, they were overwhelmingly beaten (535 B.C.), and were forced in consequence to abandon Corsica. This was the first important loss of territory suffered by the Hellenes in the West. Shortly afterward, however, the Carthaginians were repulsed by the Greeks of Massilia, and as a consequence these two states drew up treaties which defined their spheres of influence.

At Carthage toward the end of the same century the office of general, newly instituted, fell to a certain Mago, who used his position for a thorough reorganization of the army. It was henceforth to consist largely of mercenaries, recruited from the fresh warlike native races of the western Mediterranean countries. Thereafter few citizens of Carthage served except as officers. Their immense financial resources could thus be converted into sinews of war, and a policy of conquest could be inaugurated without disturbance to the money-making pursuits of the great commercial city. The first use of the system was to be for the conquest of Sicily. Therefore, while Xerxes was preparing his stupendous expedition against Eastern Hellas, the Carthaginians, doubtless in concert with him, were recruiting a great mercenary force for the invasion of Sicily. In 480 B.C. Hamilcar, Mago's son, led forth the great armament.

It was fortunate that the Western Greeks had made progress toward political unification. Anaxilas, tyrant of Rhegium (494–476 B.C.), had seized Zancle across the strait and, recolonizing it with a mixed multitude, had named it Messene after his native land. Meanwhile in southern Sicily a succession of powerful tyrants of Gela had extended their city's sway over several neighboring states. The last and greatest of these despots was Gelon, a young cavalry officer of remarkable genius in war and statecraft. Opportunely the serfs of Syracuse had risen against the lords and had violently expelled them. Gladly espousing the cause of the exiles, Gelon made himself master of Syracuse, but instead of restoring the city to the landlords, he faithlessly held it for himself and took up his residence there. With still less moral scruple, he enlarged his new capital by transplanting to it the wealthier citizens of neighboring towns he conquered, whereas the poorer class he sold into slavery, merely remarking, "Common men are an undesirable element in a state." Thus it came about that by energy and cunning Gelon had united all southeastern Sicily under his rule.

To strengthen himself further he had married Demarete,[9] daughter of Theron, despot of the flourishing city of Acragas. Scarcely less ambitious than his son-in-law, Theron had annexed Himera to his domain,

[9] Among the most beautiful coins ever struck are the "Demareteia," issued in memory of the victory at Himera (Figure 44).

after expelling its tyrant Terillus. The combination of the powerful tyrants of Syracuse and Acragas threatened Phoenician interests in Sicily, and led to the Carthaginian invasion, wherein the exiled Terillus played the part of a Hippias, and Anaxilas, kinsman of the former, promised his cooperation. The invaders laid siege to Himera, and the great battle was fought beneath its walls, Gelon and Theron against the Carthaginians, "Hellas against Canaan." Survivors of the invading army afterward reported that all day long, as the battle raged, Hamilcar in Semitic style stood apart from his host, bent on winning aid of the gods by offering them the entire bodies of sacrificed victims on a great pyre: "And when he saw there was a rout of his own army, he being then, as it chanced, in the act of pouring a libation over the sacrifices, threw himself into the fire, and thus he was burned up and removed from sight." The details are uncertain, the results well known. A great part of the fleet went up in flames; the army was utterly overthrown; vast spoils and countless prisoners, made slaves, enriched the victors. To save her colonies, or trading posts, in Sicily, Carthage bought peace with a heavy war indemnity. The victors were proudly conscious of having done their part in freeing Hellas from the barbarian peril; and in just appreciation Pindar associated Himera on equal terms with Salamis and Plataea.

In the East and West, Hellenism had won. Not for seventy years did Carthage dare attack again, and Persia henceforth was on the defensive. The Greeks were free to work out their destiny.

Chapter X THE
DELIAN LEAGUE

THE immediate need after Plataea and Mycale was to free the Greek cities of Asia Minor and to drive the Persians from the Aegean. A fleet, supported by a daring policy, was necessary to accomplish this, for in addition to their numerous strongholds in Anatolia the Persians still kept open the route to Thrace, via the Bosporus. Sparta, by virtue of her chief command at the decisive battles, might be expected to take the lead in the new venture, but a distant expedition ill suited her temperament. At Athens, on the other hand, enthusiasm was running high, for the Athenians, and other Greeks too, considered that it was the long-view policy of the city, as well as her fleet, that had defeated Persia and prevented the barbarization of the West. Nothing now seemed impossible, and, for the liberation of the Ionians, who after all were their kinsmen, a fleet was already at hand. No one could foresee the result, but, if successful, it meant certainly the expulsion of Persia and probably the eclipse of Sparta, a circumstance that would make Athens the center of the civilized world, greater even than Ionia in its prime. Sparta's failure to seize the leadership at this moment did, indeed, allow the reins to fall to Athens. The character of the people, their very outlook on life, was such that the challenge was met. From their decision developed a confederacy, the Delian League, which in time grew into the mighty Athenian Empire.

Sparta's decision to leave the siege of Sestos to the Athenians did not mean her immediate withdrawal from the allied cause, for Leotychidas proceeded to Thessaly, a hostile neighbor. Relations between Athens and Sparta, however, were already strained. The precise details are not clear, but it seems that, with a view to centralizing the Lacedaemonian power, the ephors requested the Athenians not to rebuild their walls, but to join with the Spartans in razing the fortifications of all Greek cities outside the Peloponnesus. This would have been fatal to Athens, politically and culturally. The Spartan request was apparently more of a command, for, in the account as we have it from Thucydides, Themistocles persuaded the Athenians to send him as an envoy to Sparta where, first by delays and then by deliberate falsehoods, he concealed the truth. Meanwhile, the Athenians feverishly rebuilt their walls, and Sparta was forced to acquiesce. The next year (478 B.C.) Themistocles persuaded the people to build dockyards at Piraeus and to surround the whole promontory, known as Munychia, with a massive wall, seven miles in circuit. He pointed out to the Athenians that they should make the sea their domain, and that if they were ever hard pressed, they should go down to Piraeus and fight the world at sea. If they remained in Athens, on the other hand, it would be possible for an army to starve them out, whereas at Piraeus, with their control of the sea, they could live indefinitely. It remained for Pericles to take the obvious step and connect Athens with Piraeus by Long Walls, thus turning Athens, as it were, into a harbor.

There were other questons before Athens and Sparta which pressed for settlement, the policy toward the Asiatic Greeks being the most important. Sparta clearly did not wish to assume any burdens, and therefore proposed to expel from their homes the European Greeks who had Medized and to transplant the Asiatic Greeks to the lands thus vacated. The idea was dropped at the insistence of Athens, which once again, as in the case of Sestos, won good will by its action. In spite of this, Sparta still clung to the naval leadership. In 478 B.C. an allied fleet, under Pausanias, set sail for Cyprus, where the Greek cities were set free, though it proved impossible to wrest the Phoenician cities from the Persians. Pausanias then sailed to Byzantium, which was taken in the course of a siege. Its fall meant the reopening of the grain route to the Black Sea and the complete isolation of the Persians in Thrace. But during the siege Pausanias began to assume the airs and habits of an oriental despot, so that he was recalled to Sparta. This definitely ended Sparta's transmarine ventures, for the party in power evidently believed in Peloponnesian isolation and friendship with Athens.

In contrast to Pausanias, the Athenian commander, Aristeides, impressed the allies with his courtesy, honesty, and ability. Shortly after the fall of Byzantium, then, it was decided to form an offensive and defensive alliance against Persia (early in 477 B.C.). Representatives from the islands and the coast cast masses of iron into the sea and swore to remain faithful to their obligations till the metal should rise and float on the surface. The island of Delos, sacred to all Ionians, and its great temple of Apollo were chosen as the meeting place and treasury of the new confederacy.

Freedom for the Greeks, revenge against Persia and the hunt for booty as repayment for Persian destruction were the aims of the League. Nothing was said about withdrawal, and we have every reason to believe that the Delian League was meant to be a permanent one, just like the Peloponnesian League.

In the alliance, the states were bound by treaty, each to Athens, which from the very beginning was the dominant partner. The presidents of the synod and the commanders of the fleet were to be Athenians, and later on, when the League's financial officials were appointed, these *Hellenotamiae* were Athenian as well. Athens swore to maintain unimpaired the constitutions of the individual communities, which were to be equally free and represented in the synod and, in return for the protection given, were to make an annual payment, either in money or in ships. Naturally, the larger states such as Lesbos, Chios, Samos, Naxos, and Thasos, preferred to contribute ships to the common fleet, whereas the smaller communities found it easier to make a money payment. Aristeides was appointed to make the first assessment, which he carried through so fairly that it won for him the title of "the Just." The precise amount, unfortunately, is not known, but somewhat later, when the Delian League was larger, the tribute, or *phoros,* stood at 460 talents.

The Delian League, which might appear to be the logical conclusion of the policy of Themistocles, seems to have been shaped by others and to have made slight use of his services. We hear little of his activities in the years following the Persian War. It seems likely that the return to Athens of his former enemies Aristeides and Xanthippus had clouded his political fortunes. Together with Cimon, the son of

Miltiades, they forged a coalition which kept Themistocles from power and finally drove him from Athens. It is ironic that the final steps in the Themistoclean policy of turning Athens into a great naval state and the chief power in Greece were taken by his opponents. Xanthippus was the hero of the siege of Sestus, which won the respect of the Ionians; Aristeides was the organizer of the League; and Cimon was to be the man who expanded its extent and established Athenian dominance. For two decades this coalition was to follow a moderate, conservative policy at home and an aggressive, imperial policy in the Aegean.

The greatest figure in the early history of the Delian League was Cimon. Cimon was the son of Miltiades, and by his marriage to the granddaughter of Megacles he had allied himself with the powerful Alcmaeonidae, and his sister was married to Callias, the wealthiest man in Athens. He was elected general every year from 476 to 462 B.C., and by his brilliant victories raised Athens to great power. After the passing of Aristeides and Xanthippus, Cimon stood alone as the political leader of Athens. His position rested on the political strength of his conservative coalition, on the popularity gained by his military victories and his personal attractiveness, and, finally, on the great respect in which the Spartans held him. He was well known to be a friend of the Spartans and went so far as to name his son Lacedaemonius. His policy was to wage aggressive war against Persia and to maintain friendly relations with Sparta in foreign affairs, while holding to a policy of moderate democracy at home. As long as things went well in the Aegean and Sparta remained friendly, Cimon's position was unassailable.

In 476 B.C. Cimon set out with a fleet determined to drive the Persians from Thrace, to rid the sea of pirates, and to secure, if possible, safe communication by land and sea with the Bosporus. Without much trouble the Persian garrisons about the Strymon river, itself a region of great importance, were taken. Cimon's next step was to banish from the island of Scyros its inhabitants, who made piracy their trade. In their place was planted a cleruchy, a characteristic Athenian colony. Unlike an ordinary colony, which became a free state, an Athenian cleruchy was like a bit of Athens planted in foreign soil, all the people remaining Athenian citizens, and thus adding greatly to the might of Athens. Cimon's success, and particularly the popularity he won by bringing the bones of Theseus from Scyros to Athens, led him to take a momentous step. Thus far he had been at war with Persia or pirates, but the case of Carystus, in southern Euboea, was different. Its only offense was that it did not belong to the Delian League. Though this was originally a wholly free and voluntary alliance, it was now becoming apparent that states might not stand aloof, for Carystus was forced to join. Athens might plead that in return for a very modest levy she was giving the Greeks the command of the Aegean—an undoubted fact, but the main point was whether others wished it too, or were capable of seeing far enough ahead to understand the implications. Undoubtedly many states at the moment preferred liberty and, if necessary, poverty to Athenian aggrandizement.

On the other hand, it was plainly unfair that some states should enjoy the fruits of the labors of the Delian allies but make no contributions themselves. The Athenians, after all, had not imposed themselves upon unwilling allies but had been invited to undertake a difficult and dangerous task in leading the war against the great Persian Empire. Doubtless, the Athenians had the full support of their allies when they made war not only on Scyros but on Carystus as well.

About 470 B.C. Naxos decided to withdraw from the Delian League. This was the first great test of the League's permanence and Athens met it vigorously. Naxos was defeated, her walls dismantled, and her fleet confiscated. It is possible that the Naxians were compelled to accept a democratic constitution. It is certain that they ceased to provide ships to the League but paid tribute instead. Probably in 468 B.C., Cimon sailed with 200 triremes to Caria and Lycia and brought the coast people, both Greeks and foreigners, into the League. At the mouth of the Eurymedon river he gained a great victory over the Phoenician fleet. A subsequent victory on land over the Persian army and the capture of eighty ships which were coming from Cyprus as re-enforcements made this one of the greatest of Greek victories.

Although the Persians had suffered a serious rebuff, there was no reason to be confident that they might not return. Yet to many it must have seemed that the Persian threat was over and the need for the expenditure of effort and money no longer great enough to justify the Delian League. It is equally plain that Cimon and Athens were not ready to abandon the campaign. Were the contributions for military and naval expenses to end with the establishment of peace in Asia, or could Athens maintain the League by force on the plea of eternal vigilance? The issue was not immediately raised, but the events of 465 B.C. forced it. Flush with victory, Cimon sailed to the Thracian Chersonese, which at last was forcibly added to the League, and then continued to the Strymon. At a place of great strategic strength, known as "The Nine Ways," Cimon tried to found a colony. This was the only spot at which the Strymon could be bridged, and consequently it was an important link in the route from northern Greece to the Bosporus; it also controlled the road to the mines on Mt. Pangaeus. The 10,000 colonists, however, were badly beaten by the Thracians and the venture had to be abandoned, though some years later the site was colonized as Amphipolis. But the disappearance of the Persian danger, combined with Cimon's operations in the Chersonese and particularly about the Strymon, where they had mining interests, induced the people of Thasos, an island just off the Thracian coast, to revolt from the Delian League. It was not until 463 B.C., after a siege of two years, that Thasos surrendered to Cimon. The Thasians lost their mines, fleet, walls, liberty, and henceforth paid tribute. There could be no doubt that Athens was welding the maritime confederacy into an empire.

Among the leading statesmen of Athens there was no difference of opinion as to the treatment of the confederacy, for all classes and factions were pleased by the wealth, influence, and respect that leadership of the Delian League brought to Athens.

In domestic politics, however, important differences had begun to appear. The naval policy of Themistocles had given importance and confidence to the lower classes, but the conservative coalition led by Cimon prevented them from gaining political power. We are ill informed about Athenian politics in this period, but it is likely that Themistocles led the attack on the dominant conservatives and advocated greater democracy. In this campaign he was probably joined by the rising democratic politician Ephialtes. Themistocles had taken an anti-Spartan line in 479 B.C. and had held to it. Ephialtes, too, opposed what Cimon would have called cooperation with Sparta, something which he regarded as subordination, for Athens remained a member of the Greek league which had been organized against Persia in 481 B.C. and which was led by Sparta.

The conservatives, led by Cimon, inevitably clung close to the Peloponnesian League and looked to Sparta as an example and a moral support, whereas the democrats, understanding the rivalry of the two states, were ready to break with the Peloponnesian League. Their hands were strengthened by the fact that Sparta secretly encouraged rebellion within the Delian League and stood forth as the champion of particularism—of the complete independence and isolation of the city-states within the Athenian sphere of influence—although Sparta was unwilling to surrender her control of the Peloponnesian states. Cimon's downfall was intimately connected with his support of Sparta.

Some years after the fall of Byzantium (476 B.C.), Pausanias was brought to trial, and acquitted, for treasonable correspondence with the Persians. It was later discovered that he was also plotting for an uprising of the helots, which would enable him to seize the supreme power at Sparta. To avoid arrest, Pausanias fled to a shrine of Athena, and was there walled in by his countrymen, who brought him out only a moment or two before his death. In his fall Pausanias dragged Themistocles to ruin. About 471 B.C. Themistocles had been ostracized, owing to the great strength of Cimon, and now the correspondence of Pausanias with Persia implicated Themistocles. He was ordered back from Argos to stand trial. The prosecutor was an Alcmaeonid, and Themistocles, realizing the hatred for him, despaired of justice, and avoided arrest by flight. He tried one place of refuge after another, but finding no spot in Greece to shelter him, he finally passed over to Asia Minor and joined Artaxerxes at Susa (464 B.C. or later). A dozen years or more later Themistocles died at Magnesia on the Maeander, a puppet of the Persians. It was one of the great tragedies of history, and eminently Greek, that this brilliant and patriotic Athenian states-man, who had saved his country from the Persians and had raised it to power, should die honored by the Great King.

The plottings of Themistocles and Pausanias disturbed the domestic situation at Sparta and contributed also, no doubt, to unrest in the Peloponnesian League. About 470 B.C. Sparta had to fight a combina-tion of Argives and Tegeates at Tegea, and later a combination of all the Arcadians, except the Mantineans, at Dipaea. Sparta won and re-stored her supremacy, but in 464 B.C. she was faced with a still greater danger. A terrible earthquake leveled most of the houses at Sparta and killed thousands of the inhabitants. The helots, joined by some of the perioeci, seized this moment to revolt. As the majority of helots were Messenians, the rebellion is known as the Third Messenian War. The insurgents seized Mt. Ithome, and when the Spartans found that they could not reduce the place by assault or siege, they appealed for aid to their allies, including the Athenians.

The situation in Athens at the moment (462 B.C.) was tense. The year before, after the capture of Thasos, the democrats, in an attempt to overthrow the conservatives, had brought Cimon to trial on a charge of having accepted a bribe from Alexander of Macedonia to desist from an invasion of his country. The democrats were led by Ephialtes—the successor to Themistocles. Ephialtes inherited the policy of democratiz-ing the constitution, and the conviction that the duty of Athens to her-self was to break away from Sparta in order unhampered to make the most of her opportunity in world politics. He was aided by a young noble just entering upon his public career—Pericles, the son of Xanthippus, a grandnephew on his mother's side of the Alcmaeonid reformer, Cleisthenes. Cimon was acquitted, for the sailors enthusi-astically supported their popular admiral, and the city workers were grateful for his extensive public improvements. But when the Spartan envoy reached Athens with the request for aid, the opposition was ready, and a vehement debate ensued between Cimon and Ephialtes in the Assembly, as to whether help should be given in accordance with the existing treaty. Cimon won, and marched to the relief of Sparta with a considerable force of heavy infantry. For some reason not now wholly clear, the Spartans dismissed Cimon and the Athenian troops soon after their arrival. The Athenians were outraged at this insult and early in 461 B.C. ostracized Cimon. The triumph of the democratic party, the party of Pericles and Empire, was complete, but before we follow the Empire's development, it is necessary to view the world of which it was a part.

Chapter XI

THE GREEK WORLD AFTER PLATAEA

FTER the defeat of Persia, the Greek world tended to revolve about two states, Athens and Sparta. These two states were the most powerful at the moment, but in many ways were antipathetic; one was a maritime, liberal democracy, the other an oligarchic, reactionary land power. Before continuing our study of their development, we must consider some of the characteristic features of the Greek world in the decades after Plataea, though it will be readily seen that some of our remarks, particularly those on the economic background, may apply to the fifth century as a whole.

SICILY AND ITALY

Although it is true that most states moved in the orbit of Athens or Sparta, the West stood somewhat apart. The great success of Gelon in defeating Carthage added to the prestige and power of his city. Thus it was that under the hegemony of Syracuse there grew up a Sicilian union, for all the Greeks of Sicily now acknowledged Gelon's war leadership, with the exception of Acragas and her dependencies, whose ruler Theron remained a close friend and ally. The city of Syracuse, which long ago had outgrown the island of Ortygia, now extended even beyond the neighboring height of Achradina, thanks to Gelon's policy of bringing to Syracuse the wealthier inhabitants of nearby towns. Gelon fortified Achradina, connected Ortygia with the mainland by a mole, and established arsenals and barracks for the mercenaries who upheld his power. The sale of the vast booty from Himera furnished the means, and the victory the inspiration, for the erection of beautiful temples and other public works. The battle of Himera had brought Gelon so much glory that he was actually able to turn his tyranny into a monarchy.

Gelon was succeeded by his brother Hiero, in whose reign Sicily came into closer relations with Italy, where the Etruscans were bent upon the complete subjugation of Campania. When Cumae found herself threatened by them on land and sea, she called on Hiero for aid. His fleet inflicted a mortal blow on the Etruscan naval power in 474 B.C. Henceforth the Etruscan power, which had menaced all Italy, declined. The Latins, and especially their chief city, Rome, were friendly toward the Greeks, and were adopting from them many elements of culture. With the Sabellian peoples of the interior the Greeks were also long at peace, a condition that made possible the accumulation of wealth in the Greek states and great progress culturally as well as materially. Some of the states, such as Cumae and Rhegium, were under tyrannies like those of Sicily. Locri and Tarentum, however, were aristocratic, and most of the Achaean cities were ruled by Pythagorean fraternities.

The spirit of liberty and equality, which was working its spell upon the minds of older Hellas, lived, too, among the western Greeks. Although Syracuse became under Hiero a magnificent center of culture, neither his nor Theron's successor lasted long. By 466 B.C. all the Sicilian states were free and had adopted governments more or less democratic. Under the new regime the cities tended to political isolation, yet acknowledged the moral leadership of Syracuse. About the same time a democratic wave swept over Italy, converting tyrannies and aristocracies into more popular forms of government, though the Pythagoreans maintained themselves for some years longer. In the new republics the land question produced considerable confusion and civil war between the old citizens and those admitted by the tyrants, until finally in 461 B.C. a general Sicilian congress, meeting at Syracuse, settled the agrarian controversy. The old citizens were restored to their properties, and the others were compensated by lands to be granted them as colonists in the interior of the island. The republics were now firmly established, and though not wholly free from internal conflicts, Sicily entered upon a new and greater prosperity.

THE ECONOMIC BACKGROUND OF FIFTH-CENTURY GREECE

Trade and commerce, as well as the exchange of ideas, united East and West, but the economic basis of this world was agriculture. Certain areas naturally lent themselves better to the cultivation of various crops, whereas in other states a barren soil made necessary an almost complete reliance on industry. The climate of the Mediterranean basin, with its hot, dry summers and its damp winters punctuated by terrific cloudbursts, favored the cultivation of specific crops. Thus the great grain-growing districts (chiefly for wheat, barley, and, to some extent, millet) were Sicily, Egypt, Cyprus, Euboea, and southern Russia. Wine and oil, important staples in ancient Greece, were prized products of Attica and the Aegean islands, and the uplands of Anatolia were famous for their woolens. From the Black Sea came flax and, more particularly, dried fish, for which the Bosporus was equally famed. As more and more land was put under the plough, timber became less plentiful and had to be imported, for buildings and warships, from the Black Sea, Thrace, and Magna Graecia.

Considering the importance of agriculture, it is surprising how little the Greeks knew about it. Even in the fifth century half the land was often allowed to lie fallow in alternate years, for the value of rotating crops was but slowly recognized. The plough was simple, though made of iron, and although the farmer understood the importance of manure, he was restricted by the lack of animals. In the democracies the farms tended to be small, but the farmer took pride in being engaged in an ancient profession and in the fact that only citizens were allowed to own land. He worked the land himself, aided to a small extent by slave labor. On his farm might be seen the usual barnyard animals, and in his fields grew fruit trees, the vine, or olive, and perhaps grain. In districts near a large city, in the Megarid for example, truck-gardening was profitable. The Greek diet was simple, consisting of greens, bread, cheese, and olives. Fish and pork, though considered great delicacies, were eaten more often than other varieties of meat. Flocks of sheep and goats were kept, in summer and winter pastures, for hides, wool, milk. (See Note, p. 179.)

Although certain areas produced more than was needed locally, it was left to private initiative to arrange for export, because Greek states rarely had a commercial policy. The state was interested only in necessaries, such as grain and timber, and in harbor dues to fill its treasury. This held for industrial as well as agricultural products. There was little manufacturing in the fifth century for the export trade, though of course surpluses would be exported. The chief industrial centers were Athens, with its famous potteries; Corinth, Sicyon, Argos, and Chalcis, noted for their metal work; Miletus and Samos, with their furniture and textiles. The natural resources were varied and scattered. Marble came from the quarries of Pentelicus and Paros, silver from Laurium and Mt. Pangaeus, gold from Mt. Pangaeus and Thasos, iron from Laconia and the Black Sea, copper from Cyprus, tin from southern Gaul and Spain.

The shops were small; indeed, the largest known to us in the fourth century was owned by Cephalus, who had perhaps 120 workers making shields at Athens. Specialization there was in ancient industry, though not to the degree known today. Citizens, metics (resident alien), and slaves took part in industry on an equal basis, but the citizen's main competitor was the metic and not the slave. In the Erechtheum building inscription from the end of the fifth century, we find mentioned twenty citizens, thirty-five metics, and sixteen slaves, each of whom received a drachma as his daily wage, as did the architect. It did not cost an unmarried Athenian much more than 2 or 3 obols (half a drachma) a day to live, though of course money went much further then than now. Many manufactures, such as clothing, blankets, and the preparation of flour, were still on a home industry basis.

The exchange of goods was facilitated by the widespread use of coinage, though the many different issues and weights must have been confusing to some people (Figures 45, 46, 47). The issues of small states, however, rarely circulated beyond their frontiers, and other coins, certain one of Elis for example, were merely medals sold to tourists as souvenirs. A feeble attempt was made by the Delphic Amphictyony to bring about a unification of coinage, but in time it was the money of the great commercial states, such as the "owls" of Athens, which circulated far and wide. Most of the states of the Empire were eventually compelled to adopt Athens' coinage. In the middle of the century gold stood at 14 to 1 in relation to silver, though gold coinages were rare, and Sparta managed to get along with iron bars.

There was very little traffic by land, owing to the rough nature of the country and to the poor roads. The roads were partly economic in origin and partly religious, but they were apt to be neglected, on account of the many different governments involved and the preference for the sea. Greek ships sailed in every direction, to Thrace, to Phoenicia for dates, purple dyes, and various products from the Orient, to the Black Sea, where there was the terminus of a route from the East, and perhaps Mongolia. Silk became one of the chief imports from the East, and perhaps on the frieze of the Parthenon we can see this new material in the dresses of the Athenian ladies. Boats went to Egypt, of course, for grain, papyrus, ointments, and ivory, to Cyrene for silphium, and to Carthage for textiles. Greek sailors did not hesitate to sail across the open sea, but, if possible, they preferred to stay near land. We can thus appreciate the importance of Corcyra as a stepping-stone on the route to Italy and Sicily. Traders went to Etruria for metal work and to southern Gaul, where Massilia and other Greek colonies were located. We have slight data for Spain, but we know of trade with Tartessus at an early date and, from the sixth century, with Emporion. The boats, of about 250 tons, were propelled by oars and sail, and were able to cover more than 125 nautical miles in a twenty-four-hour run.

Piracy interfered with commerce, and although we know little about the customs of pirates, or the fate of their victims, we know that it was common for individuals, and even for states, to engage in piracy. For the first and last time between the empires of Crete and Rome the sea was cleared of pirates, however, by Athenian triremes. Warfare was another disturbing factor in ancient life, though it must be borne in mind that wars were hardly more frequent than in modern times, that arrows are less deadly than bullets, and that the barbarities to which we have become accustomed were frequently absent. Warfare in the fifth century was carried on by citizen armies, which as a rule were willing to fight only in the summer. And warfare was a very inexact science, for how else can we explain, in a country suited to light-armed troops, the use of heavy hoplites, opposed to each other in long, thin lines? Though their frontiers were easily defensible, the Greeks preferred to lock themselves up in their cities, in the knowledge that the siege engines would not suffice to knock down their walls.

To his business, as to most other things, the Greek brought much common sense. He was keen and industrious, and an air of confidence seems to have surrounded his business transactions. Various market places (agoras) were provided by the state; in the large cities the grain dealers would be found in one agora, the fish vendors in another, and so on. During the day much bargaining went on and at night the unsold articles, which had been brought out into the open to stimulate purchase, were locked in the shop. The shops were rented from the state, which in its turn provided not only the agoras and warehouses, but certain officials (*agoranomoi*) to keep order, and others, such as the *sitophylakes* for grain, to enforce a fair price and measure.

Business at Athens was largely in the hands of the metics, partly because of the citizens' prejudice against trade, which in time disappeared, but mainly because agriculture and the task of running the government attracted most citizens. The metics were aliens (Greek and barbarian) permanently domiciled in a city, and consequently had greater privileges than temporary residents. A metic in Athens was loyal to the city, paid a special tax, and, although he was free to trade as he wished, he could not own land. He was liable to military service, though without political rights, and after he had found a citizen to be his sponsor (*prostates*) he was required to register in a deme. Litigation in which he became involved was brought before the polemarch. It was proper for him to have these burdens, for the citizen carried even more. In the days of Solon, when the city needed new blood, Athens had been generous with grants of citizenship, but now it was a very rare thing for a metic to win citizenship. In view of the many privileges involved it is easy to appreciate the Athenian point of view. The Athenians could not envisage even a dual citizenship which would permit a citizen of the Empire to enjoy the citizenship of his own city and of Athens as well, or at least they did not think of it until the end of the century, when it was too late. Judging from the treaty with Phaselis, however, it was not uncommon for the Athenians to grant a quasimetic status to the entire citizen body of another city.

Some cities, such as Sparta, had state-owned slaves, helots, and in addition controlled the people of communities which were in a semi-independent condition, the perioeci. These were exceptions. Athens, to be sure, had a handful of perioecic communities, such as Plataea, and a few state slaves, but these latter were "Scythians," a few hundred in number, constituting the police force for the city and country. Little is known about the police, but prisons existed for criminals condemned to death and as a means of punishment *per se*, though exile, fines, and confiscations were the usual penalties. Most slaves in Athens, as elsewhere, were privately owned. Unquestionably they contributed to the leisure of the citizen, making it possible for him to give himself to the affairs of state, but ancient Greece was not a slave society in the accepted sense of that term. A man owned, perhaps, a half dozen slaves, and together, in house, shop, or farm, the master and slave worked. The living and working conditions were about the same for both. The slaves were mostly barbarians, and because they were allowed to work for hire, it was the usual thing for a slave to buy his freedom ultimately, if meanwhile his master had not already freed him. The freedman received metic status and frequently won a high position in the business world. The slaves we have been describing were apprentice slaves, who contributed to the material prosperity of the civilization in which they would eventually share, and yet, though it may be true that freedom is relative and that industrial slavery, for example, exists today, it is a fact that the Greek slave was not his own master. He could also be brutally treated, as was the case of the chattel slaves, who were worked like animals in the ancient quarries and mines.

Upon the citizen rested the task of governing and defending the state. He alone had political and property rights. Land was owned by the individual, rarely by the state, except in the case of forests or grazing grounds. The state claimed no rights to mineral deposits, and where it owned a mine, it leased it to an individual, taxing privately owned mines a fixed proportion of their annual production. Because the ancient Greeks took no census, it is impossible to state the size of the population of Hellas or of the various sections of it, but reasonable estimates have been made for Athens; 150,000 citizens, 35,000 metics, and 80,000 slaves (men, women, and children in each case) would be the minimum. Athens, of course, was one of the largest cities of the fifth century, and part of its size was due to the great commercial prosperity which attracted many strangers. We have no way of knowing the rate of natural increase, but infant mortality must have been very high, though infanticide was rare in the fifth century.

If we examine the finances of an imperial state such as Athens, concerning which we have much information, we shall be able to form an idea of its budget. Athens' main income was from its imperial tribute, one-sixtieth of which was dedicated to Athena. The recovery and interpretation of the quota lists enable us to trace much of the history of the Empire (Figure 20B). A property tax (*eisphora*), which was introduced soon after the beginning of the Peloponnesian War, was the only direct tax, but import and export taxes of 1 per cent (later, 2 per cent), a sales tax, and various irregular revenues, together with the income from the silver mines at Laurium, brought the annual income to perhaps, 1,000 talents. In return for this the state had to pay for temples and festivals, the army and navy, and its many officials, particularly the Council of Five Hundred, each of whom received a drachma a day, and the six thousand jurors, who received two or three obols apiece daily. The jurors were old men, as a rule, because younger persons were too active to spend much time in jury service, and we may look upon their pay, therefore, as a sort of old-age pension. The state, however, was relieved of certain large expenditures by the custom of liturgies, a capital tax on wealthy citizens. Thus a man might be expected to become a *trierarch* and pay for the equipment of a warship and the wages of its crew for a year. Among the other liturgies were the duty of equipping the chorus for dramatic and other festivals (*choregia*), of paying the expenses of torch-races at various festivals (*gymnasiarchia*), and of feasting one's tribesmen (*hestiasis*). The chief financial officials were the *colacretae*, who had charge of the internal revenue, the Treasurers of Athena, the Treasurers of the Other Gods, and, for imperial funds, the *Hellenotamiae*.

The great prosperity of Athens eclipsed that of sixth-century Ionia and put her well ahead of her rivals, Corinth and Aegina. Her industrial development was absolutely necessary to pay for the importation of 2 million bushels of grain annually, representing perhaps three quarters of her needs. This helps us to understand Athenian foreign policy in Macedonia, the Black Sea, Egypt, and Sicily. The Empire and its tribute were necessary to pay for the many local services. The citizens of Athens received, of course, a marvelous training in city and imperial government. Indeed, the most important political and criminal cases arising in the Empire were tried in Athens in the first instance or on appeal. Large commercial suits were also tried in Athens as a rule. The prosperity was shared by the cities of the Empire, who benefited greatly, for example, by various commercial treaties.

LITERATURE

The social conditions of this generation which had defended Hellas against the assaults of Persia and Carthage were at bottom similar in East and West, though outwardly they presented certain contrasts. The same poets and philosophers ministered to the intellectual needs of both regions, and the temples of Acragas and Syracuse had the same stately beauty as those of Aegina and Olympia. But in contrast with the material wealth and splendor of Sicily and Italy we may place the steadier and more substantial character of the Spartans and Athenians. And during this period we can see Athens win the leadership of the intellectual world, through the achievements of her own sons and because the congenial atmosphere of the imperial capital attracted foreigners. The spirit of the city after Plataea was high and, in spite of the reforms of Cleisthenes, Athenian society remained aristocratic.

Simonides of Ceos (*ca.* 556–469 B.C.) is an example of a great poet who chose to spend much of his time at Athens. His elegies on the victories of Marathon and Thermopylae had a simple beauty, as did his epinician hymns in honor of victors at games. Aeschylus of Eleusis (524–456 B.C.), though the most creative of Athenian dramatists, desired above all things to be considered a loyal citizen who had done good service for his country at Marathon. In his day the man of deeds was greater than the artist; and it is almost in spite of himself that we describe him as a literary man. In his hands the drama became a new and great art, casting off all traces of its primitive beginning. Tragedy, it will be recalled, had a humble origin, but was especially popular in the Peloponnesus at Corinth and Sicyon. It was Thespis of Icaria, however, who first brought order to the spring-time revels. In this small town of Attica, Thespis chose to dissociate the theme of drama from religion,[1] so that now many subjects lay to the dramatist's hand. He introduced an actor, who now might carry on a dialogue with the leader of the chorus. The members of the chorus, fifty in number, wore masks and possibly goatskins; hence they came to be called *tragoidoi*. In time, tragedy became part of the City or Greater Dionysia, the festival which Peisistratus had introduced in honor of Dionysus of Eleutherae.

Aeschylus not only cut the number of the chorus to twelve, but also reduced its share in the performance, which until now had consisted chiefly of singing. He added a second actor and made possible real conflict, with the chorus taking sides. The intense productivity of his genius, and the splendid qualities of his surviving dramas, place Aeschylus among the world's greatest poets. Though ninety plays were ascribed to him in antiquity, only seven have come down to us. The *Agamemnon,* which is the first in the trilogy called the *Oresteia,* deals with the curse that fell upon the house of the Pelopids. An ominous gloom pervades the play, but it is broken now and then by moments of joy. The characters are strongly drawn and into their mouths Aeschylus, a man of deep religious conviction, puts noble sentiments. There is room for personal responsibility, but above all hangs Zeus, who brings all things to pass (Figure 51).

Contemporary with Aeschylus lived Pindar, a Boeotian, the most famous of lyrists (*ca.* 522–441 B.C.). Like Aeschylus he was nobly born; but he was also a priest by family right. We know him chiefly through his choral songs in honor of victors at the great national games; of other poems we have a few precious fragments. For Pindar, Apollo was the most important Olympian. There were no skeptical doubts to his theol-

---

[1] About the turn of the century Pratinus of Phlius, in the Peloponnesus, introduced the satyr-play, a light bit of drama associated with the gods which served to make good this lack.

ogy, believing as he did in oracular divination. In a small class of Athenian nobles, and in wider circles within less progressive states, there survived an intensely aristocratic spirit, which found brilliant expression in Pindar. For the glory of his class he has transmuted into excellence certain blemishes of the older mythology. In the loves of gods for mortal women he sees the working of a beneficient purpose for grafting divine virtues on the human race. From such unions sprang the heroes of old, patterns of manly virtue. Their natures were the heritage of the families which they founded and which formed the nobility of every Greek state. Fortunate was the city ruled by such a stock.

A younger contemporary of Pindar was another lyric poet, Bacchylides of Ceos. The discovery, in 1897, of a papyrus containing several entire odes of this poet, in addition to fragments, makes him a useful source for the cultural history of the period. Bacchylides was the last great lyrist of Greece; after him the decline of the chorus went hand in hand with the dissolution of the rhythmic life of the city-state. Interest in public affairs waned; the market place thronged with idle gossipers while the dwindling company of patriots attended the Assembly. Among the well-to-do was forming a class of men who shunned politics to pursue their own pleasures, or to avoid contact with cobblers, tanners, and hucksters, with the coarse manners and unreasoning will of the multitude.

We have to depend largely on Aeschylus, Pindar, and Bacchylides for knowledge of the best thought and sentiment of Athens and Greece in the age of Hiero, Themistocles, and Cimon. In the aristocratic philosophy of life a large place was inevitably held by natural endowment, as contrasted with acquired skill, yet nothing could be achieved without toil. These men of noble heritage and athletic training stood ready in need to fight for their country, and in time of peace employed their wealth for the public good, in patronage of the arts cultivated by their class, and in hospitality. They were constant, too, in their worship of the gods.

We catch interesting glimpses of their social life in the accounts of their banquets. Ion, a poet of Chios, tells of such a social gathering which he attended at Athens when a boy. After the libation of wine to the gods, the guests asked Cimon to sing, and he complied with such success as to win the warm applause of the company. Here was a man who had never studied music but who, to amuse his fellow-guests, was willing to sing—probably a rollicking sailor-song. Afterward he told the company the cleverest thing he had done in his life—how in the division of spoils he had outwitted the wily Ionians under his command. As a young man Cimon had acquired an unenviable reputation for disorderly habits and excesses in drink; handsome enough with his tall stature and thick curly locks, he displayed a dull wit and won no better nickname than simpleton; yet in later years he developed a noble character, able in command by land or sea, incorruptible, public-spirited, social, and generous. Any demesman was at liberty uninvited to pick his fruit or sit at his table; and whenever he went through the streets he was accompanied by servants who distributed clothes and money among the needy citizens.

Themistocles, on the other hand, a man of superior dignity and of vastly greater mental power, lacked the faculty of unbending at social gatherings. Delighting in hospitality, he gave sumptuous banquets; and though he did not venture to sing to his guests, he kept in his home a famous lyrist for their entertainment. His social field, however, was the market place and the Pnyx. There he met the citizens and saluted each one by name; and they, pleased with this individual attention, thought there was no man in the world like Themistocles. They readily brought him their disputes for arbitration; and in such cases he always showed himself a just judge.

In Athens thought and custom gravitated irresistibly toward democracy. The great representative of the tendency in literature was Aeschylus who, though a Eupatrid, glowed with a passion for freedom and gave his sympathy without reserve to the lowly. Against the aristocratic tradition which made the Eupatrid good and god-beloved and the poor base and vicious, Aeschylus upheld a more rational view of right and wrong and of their reward and punishment. He makes us understand, too, the feelings of a woman who has been taken captive in war, enslaved, and subjected to injustice and brutality. Such sentiments had their effect upon his audience, for no longer was there the same interest in women, whose traditional standing in society was now suffering impairment.

We have seen the great families of Athens connecting themselves closely with one another by intermarriage. It was still no uncommon thing for a noble to take a wife from abroad; in fact the number of great men descended from non-Athenian mothers in the period before and immediately after the Persian Wars is remarkable. They include Cleisthenes, Miltiades, Cimon, and Themistocles. The women who were thus taken and given in marriage were not mere pawns on the political chessboard. Whether at Athens or among her neighbors, high-born ladies were freer and wielded greater social influence in this aristocratic period than did those of the Periclean Age and after. The ideal woman was the mother of warriors and athletes, devoted to her husband, and the mistress of her household. This ideal may well have been realized in the life of Cimon and his wife Isodice, of whom he was passionately fond, and whose death left him inconsolable. An example of the "emancipated woman," strong of character and a power in politics, yet doubtless personally winsome, was Elpinice, sister of Cimon and wife of Callias, the wealthiest Athenian of his day. She charmed the famous painter Polygnotus, who placed her portrait among the Trojan matrons in one of his great mural scenes. As an example of her political influence we may cite the fact that she successfully intervened with Pericles in favor of her brother when he was prosecuted. It is significant, too, that there remained even in this age at least occasional lovemaking and courtship preliminary to marriage. But the honorable and relatively free place of woman in society was not assured. There were forces at work for her seclusion. At hand was the hard masculine age of Pericles, whose political intensity reduced woman and homelife to a minimum.

In spite of tendencies detrimental to woman the family remained a sacred institution, whose religious object was the worship of the dead and of the other household gods. Any disturbance of this harmony was monstrous. Most heinous was the shedding of kindred blood. But, Aeschylus tells us, the gods are merciful and have provided a way of escape from sin. The principle is illustrated in the house of Agamemnon. His father had committed an enormous crime, and he had inherited the curse. By it he was driven madly to more serious offenses. He sacrificed his own daughter Iphigeneia before sailing to Troy; and after capturing the city, he violated the temples and altars of its gods. When, therefore, he returned home, he reaped his reward—stabbed to death by his wife Clytemnestra, the strongest human character in the *Agamemnon,* possessing great intellectual strength and a "man's-way planning, hoping heart." In killing her husband she but served as a link in the resistless chain of blood-revenge. Next their son Orestes, as the avenger of his father, murdered his mother. The guilt he had inherited brought forth this monstrous fruit. Then the Furies of his mother pursued him, tormenting him with the most intense suffering. But this agonizing experience brought him knowledge of the law of righteousness and of his duty to it; suffering brought him obedience. Therefore he was purified by Apollo at Delphi, and acquitted by the Council of the Areopagus sitting under the presidency of Athena. In this way the family was ultimately saved from the consequences of its guilt. With God's aid, a family worked out its own redemption in suffering; but for future tranquility there was need of resignation.

This tempering of justice with mercy was in keeping with a growing spirit of kindliness, which expressed itself in diverse forms. Indeed, we are surprised to discover in this martial age so much humanity, such strong yearnings for peace. In the poets there is less of the glory of war than of its cruelty and suffering. The chafing of the people under miseries caused by needless wars, their hatred of the magistrates who were responsible for these sufferings, made for peace. Not only the growing kindliness of the age but also its religious spirit found their clearest expression in the poets, especially in Pindar and Aeschylus. The former was more conservative, the latter more progressive; yet both hold to the hereditary faith of their race, exalted and purified by splendid intelligence and brilliant imagination. In touch with the best thought of the age, they can only conceive of God as supreme above a host of celestial spirits. Pindar and Aeschylus combine, in the highest degree, power, splendor, and sublimity; both walk on a high plane of religious and moral purity. But the Pindaric glitter reflects the glory of earth and of the gods who live no higher than Olympus, whereas the words of Aeschylus spring from a loftier spiritual and moral inspiration. Yet mark the modesty of the one in contrast with the almost pompous pride of the other. Aeschylus, as his epitaph teaches, wished to be remembered not by his splendid dramas, but by his part in the battle of Marathon:

> This tomb the dust of Aeschylus doth hide—
> Euphorion's son and fruitful Gela's pride;
> How famed his valor Marathon may tell,—
> And long-haired Medes, who knew it all too well.

In Pindar's mind the glory of the games was equaled only by the poet's art. His own calling he esteemed above the sculptor's skill. His words are things of winged life and fleet motion: now honey bees flitting from tale to tale, now bronze-tipped spears hurled from the hand, or darts shot from the Muses' far-delivering bow, now rushing waves or a gale of glorious song. His finished poem he aptly compares to a majestic palace, whose marbles glitter in the sunlight. A minstrel of inborn genius, he is like the swift eagle, who loves the lone bosom of the cold ether, while far below flock his rivals, men of acquired cleverness merely.

ART

Grandeur was as typical of Greek art as of Greek literature and thought. The decades between 480 and 450 B.C. are generally spoken of as transitional, but all stages of growth are transitions, and actually the period was one of extraordinary achievement. The Persian invasion had destroyed Athens and other cities and consequently certain states were long in rebuilding their temples. Delphi and Olympia, however, had been spared and so had been the West (Figure 16). Thus, we are able to follow the development of Doric architecture, even

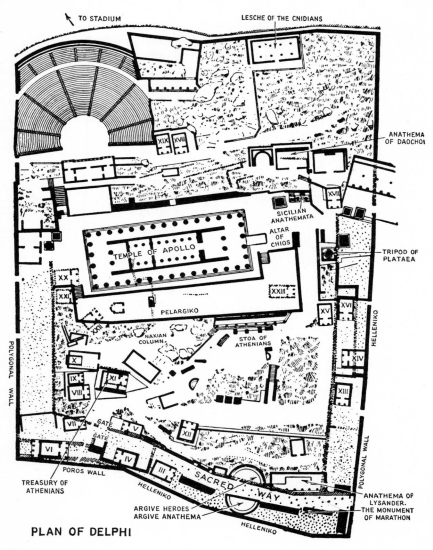

PLAN OF DELPHI

Map 26

though the remains of Ionic from Asia Minor and elsewhere are scant.

The Olympieum, or temple of the Giants, built by Theron at Acragas, is especially interesting, because the architect introduced unusual features in the hope of varying the normal Doric temple. High on the structure, whether on the inside or out is not known, colossal human figures were placed as supports. This experimentation is to be commended, for the Greek temple, although utterly beautiful, never succeeded in enclosing space, but simply in defining it. Experimentation along radical lines, however, was not continued, and the architects contented themselves with refining and perfecting what they had inherited from the past. We have already noticed the promise of a new day held out by the temple of Aphaia at Aegina. This promise was amply fulfilled at Acragas, Segesta, and Syracuse in Sicily and at Paestum in Italy, where the temple of Poseidon combines majestic dignity with grace and restrained ornamentation. Of signal importance, however, is Olympia, for in the Altis, or sanctuary, rose many buildings; not only temples, but also, as at Delphi, "treasuries," as the dedications of grateful states were called (Map 26; Map 28). The temple of Zeus, completed in 456 B.C., was the most beautiful. A normal Doric temple, having cella, *pronaos* and *opisthodomus* (each with two columns *in antis*), and six by thirteen columns along the peristyle, it was built of conglomerate blocks, covered with stucco. The cella was divided into a broad nave and two side aisles by two rows of six columns. Above these stood other columns, which supported the ceiling. Today the temple is in ruin, and its fame derives from the great marble sculptures (*ca.* 460 B.C.) excavated by the Germans in the last century.

These sculptures from the pediments of the temple of Zeus at Olympia, perhaps more than any others, suggest the grandeur of Aeschylus. Almost exact in their portrayal of the human form, they nevertheless contain the archaic striving for perfection. Strong and virile, with varying emotions freely expressed or suggested, they have a quiet simplicity and restraint, which make even the mortals appear superhuman. The sculptor or sculptors are quite unknown to us, although on the authority of Pausanias they were formerly thought to be Alcamenes and Paeonius. In planning their grand composition the sculptors were only slightly influenced by the art of bronze-casting, which had been discovered in the previous century. As a general guide they probably used a maquette, a rough sketch in clay or wax or stone from which a summary pointing was made. As a result, the Olympia sculptures represent the stone-carver's greatest achievement in ancient Greece. The eastern pediment contained the usual quiet scene, but a terrible foreboding seems to grip the figures as they gather round Zeus prior to the fateful chariot race between Pelops and King Oenomaus. In the western pediment was the conventional scene of violence, but it was no ordinary violence (Figure 49). We have a tremendous struggle between Lapiths and Centaurs representing the conflict between civilization and barbarism, but we are left with no doubt as to the outcome. In the center, undisturbed by the confusion around him, stands Apollo, the great Greek god of youth and Hellenism (Figure 50). The large figure looks symbolically along his extended right arm. Within the cella stood originally the chryselephantine statue of Zeus, by the Athenian Pheidias, but it has long since disappeared. Inside the colonnade, over the *pronaos* and *opisthodomus,* twelve sculptured metopes showed the labors of Heracles. Several of these are well preserved and have a rich charm.

The only statue from ancient Greece that can compare with the Apollo of Olympia in profound majesty is the large bronze Zeus, found in the sea near Cape Artemisium off Euboea (Figure 51). Here we have the greatest of the gods, the only God for many persons, in all his simple yet mighty grandeur. There is a wonderful balance to the figure as he hurls the thunderbolt. A marvelous bronze charioteer, dedicated by Polyzalus of Syracuse about 477 B.C. and discovered by the French at Delphi, was originally part of a chariot group (Figure 52). These figures, which are so often idealized, frequently have a quiet expression that contrasts strongly with their actions. This is particularly true of the discus-thrower by Myron, one of the great sculptors of the fifth century, though his statue is known to us only through Roman copies (Figure 53 and cf. Figure 54). We notice in these statues that Greek art has thrown off the old archaic stiffness, with its frontal pose, that the sculptors are rapidly becoming masters of their tools and material, and that the figures, at once simpler and more massive, have a beautiful nobility. This was true of the entire Greek world, though archaism lingered in Sicily and southern Italy, which were provincial.

Greek painting, unfortunately, is almost a closed book to us. That there were great painters, however, is certain, for ancient testimony is eloquent about the skill of some of the artists. Murals and easel pictures were common, but all have disappeared. Micon and Polygnotus adorned the Lesche (Hall) of the Cnidians at Delphi, where the Capture of Troy and the Descent of Odysseus to Hades were vigorously portrayed. Polygnotus' picture of the Battle of Marathon, in the Agora at Athens, included portraits of the polemarch Callimachus, of Miltiades and Aeschylus, and seems to have been at least partially successful in the use of perspective. Mural painting, of course, attracted the greatest artists, so that vase painting soon fell behind.

Athens, however, dominated the world's market in vases. Every kind of subject decorated the vases, especially scenes from daily life and from mythology. The technique was still the red-figured, and occasionally we find real masterpieces of drawing. A white-ground cylix in London, which shows Aphrodite on a swan, has rare delicacy and charm (Figure 55).

It is a great pity that we know so little of Greek music. Plato, Aristotle, and others wrote on the subject, and we know that music played an important part in education, the theater, and festivals. The chief instruments were the lyre, harp, and pipes, and of the various musicians Phrynis was especially popular.

The emphasis of these decades after Plataea was on moderation. This period has been called the end of the Hellenic moral experiment.

NOTE

As mentioned above, many animals were important to the Greek in his daily life, and it will be seen from Figures 56 to 59 that the artist was able to catch the essential traits of each. The development of animal sculpture was much the same as in the human figure, from archaic conventionalization and stylization to the naturalism of the fifth century and the marked realism of the Hellenistic Age. Many other objects have also survived, which, though not always beautiful, vividly illumine the public and private life of the Greeks; for example, Figures 60 and 61 suggest, as no words can, the actual setting in which much of the daily life of the Greeks was cast. For a further description of fifth-century life, see pp. 243 ff. and the Appendix on the Athenian Agora. As an example of the dramatic manner in which our knowledge can be suddenly increased, we may cite the discovery in the Agora excavations of a bronze shield captured by the Athenians from the Spartans in 424 B.C. at Sphacteria (pp. 216 ff.). This was originally placed in the *Stoa Poikile,* where the previously mentioned paintings of Polygnotus stood (cf. p. 444). Near the Stoa were the famous Hermae or herms (stone busts) celebrating Cimon's victories over the Persians at the Eurymedon and elsewhere (p. 159), which were mutilated on the eve of the Sicilian expedition (p. 225).

Chapter XII

THE ATHENIAN EMPIRE

N O GREAT contemporary historian has left a detailed history of the momentous half century between 478 and 431 B.C. (the so-called *Pentecontaetia*). Herodotus concluded his *History* with the Persian Wars, Thucydides' chief interest was in the Peloponnesian War, and the later writers, such as Ephorus, have survived only in fragments. Yet the period is one of extraordinary interest, especially for the years after the firm establishment of the Delian League. The growth of an Athenian land empire, the organization of the maritime empire, and the concomitant democratization of the constitution are the outstanding features. Athens was not able for long to maintain her empire on land, the pressures of war severely tested the constitution, and by the end of the century the maritime empire had also disappeared. A problem of the historian is properly to evaluate and weigh the successes and failures of Periclean policy. There is no question about the high enthusiasm of the Athenians, nor about their great achievements in art and literature; Athens became "the teacher of Greece," the meeting place of most of the leading minds of the time. All Greece, too, benefited by the suppression of piracy and by the elimination of the Persian danger. The existence of the Athenian Empire promoted commerce and prosperity, and seemed to promise future security and stability. Against this, however, we must balance the loss of life and liberty, the steady interference in the affairs of some states and the threats to others, which Athenian imperialism entailed. And we must remember, too, that Aeschylus and the Apollo of Olympia were possible without an Athenian Empire.

Sparta's abrupt dismissal of Cimon from Mt. Ithome paralyzed the Laconian faction within Athens and brought to the front Ephialtes and the democratic party, which was determined to make the city independent in Hellenic politics. Prosecutions of individual members of the Areopagus on various grounds had preceded Cimon's ostracism in 461 B.C., which was quickly followed by a reform of the Areopagus itself. Ephialtes' Reform left to the Areopagus jurisdiction in matters of homicide, but its other powers were divided among the Council of Five Hundred, the Assembly, and the *heliaea*. Precisely what these other powers were is difficult to say, for they are summed up in the phrase *the guardianship of the laws*. Apparently the Areopagus had been able to compel the magistrates to follow its own interpretation of the laws and thus had acquired an indirect control of the constitution. The Athenians were determined that this control should be in their own hands. They disliked, too, a body that had so long been associated with aristocracy and whose members held office for life. They also resented the power which the Areopagus had acquired over the citizenship rolls. It was not to be expected, however, that the aristocrats would not strike back, and shortly after the Reform Ephialtes was murdered by a member of one of the oligarchical clubs. His place as leader of the democratic party was taken by Pericles (Figure 62).

It was Pericles, of course, who brought his community to a summit of civilization never before reached by the human race and who incorporated and expressed in his own personality the highest ideals of his age. Born of a union of two illustrious families, he inherited the inspiring traditions of both. His father, Xanthippus, had been admiral at the battle of Mycale, whereas his mother, Agariste, was the niece of the great Alcmaeonid reformer, Cleisthenes. The thrilling events of his childhood and youth attending the struggle for freedom and the founding of empire were in Pericles transmuted into force and nobility of character directed to the political, intellectual, and moral elevation of his country. Pericles enjoyed the best education possible in that age. Music was taught him by the democrat Damonides, who became his chief political adviser. Among the teachers of his riper years was the philosopher Anaxagoras of Clazomenae, who freed his mind from superstition by directing it to a search for natural causes. Inherent tendency, under philosophic cultivation, developed into a serenity of temper, which no insult or abuse could ruffle. To the same combination of natural character and instruction is due his lofty, dignified eloquence, which earned for him the name Olympian. Though he had no instruction in rhetoric, which was introduced into Athens too late for his service, he took great pains with his language. His delivery was, as it were, statuesque. The weight of his words, the majesty of his person, his deep earnestness, and the confidence of the people in his patriotism, wisdom, and incorruptibility carried conviction.

In order to concentrate his whole energy upon public affairs, he gave over the management of his inherited estate to an able, trusty slave, Evangelus, who sold all the produce in a lump, and bought for the family the necessities of life as they were required. The method was far from economical, but Pericles was content with a mere subsistence from his estate, without increase or diminution of its value. Such was the ideal of his social class.

Pericles' wife was a kinswoman, Telesippe, the mother of his sons Xanthippus and Paralus. But as they could not live happily together, Pericles at her request found her another husband.[1] Afterward he was attracted to Aspasia, a highly accomplished woman from Miletus. As Athenian women had merely a domestic education and were now kept more strictly at home than they had been in the past, a class of non-Athenian women, termed *hetaerae,* or "companions," better educated and more attractive, usurped their place in the society of men. Under his own law of 451 B.C. Pericles could contract no more than an inferior marriage with Aspasia, which excluded the children from the citizenship. They had a son, Pericles, who was given the franchise by a special vote of the Assembly.

Except for two brief years following Cimon's return from exile, Pericles was the leading politician in Athens from the time of Ephial-

---

[1] Divorce at Athens was easy for a man. For women, however, it was made difficult, because the husband would have to repay his wife's dowry, and therefore women were compelled to appear before an archon. It may be added that Athenian parents not only had the power to name their sons, but could delete their names from the register and disinherit them, though the sons would not lose their political status. The first son was generally named after his grandfather.

tes' murder to his death in 429 B.C. A friend of Pheidias and other great artists and thinkers, he made Athens, as Thucydides has him say, the school of Hellas. Under him a thorough democracy was achieved.

His foreign policy, however, is more difficult to ascertain and to judge.

THE LAND EMPIRE

Cimon's dismissal from Ithome meant the end of the Lacedaemonian alliance. Athens now leagued herself with Argos, which had recently adopted a democratic constitution and was as usual hostile to Sparta. Thessaly, too, whose cities were generally governed by the old nobility, joined the new alliance. But if Athens were thus to challenge Sparta, it was necessary to seek peace with Persia. The Athenian embassy under Callias, however, met with no success, and Athens had to face the possibility of simultaneous war on land and at sea.

About 461 B.C. Megara, where the democratic party was now in control, sought Athens' protection from her neighbor Corinth, which was attempting forcibly to annex the little state. Athens welcomed the proposal and drove off the Corinthians. The alliance thus won for Megara independence and safety from spoliation by Corinth.

Nisaea, Megara's port, which was now connected with Megara itself by Long Walls, was occupied by Athenian troops. Of greater importance, however, was the fact that Athens gained control of the mountain passes leading to the Isthmus and of Pegae on the Corinthian Gulf. This gave her a convenient harbor from which to sail to the West. Most important of all, the possession of the Megarid secured Athens against invasion from the Peloponnese, if the expected clash with Sparta should come.

When, a few years later, the helots on Mt. Ithome surrendered, with the privilege of withdrawing from the Peloponnesus, and settled, with Athens' help, at Naupactus—a Gibraltar near the mouth of the Corinthian Gulf—it became clear that Athens intended not only to gain over this water the control which she already exercised over the Saronic Gulf but possibly to challenge Corinthian supremacy in the West as well. It is little wonder, as Thucydides remarks, that the Corinthians now conceived an "extreme hatred" for Athens.

The actions of Athens in these and in other quarters stirred her rivals Corinth and Aegina to war in 459 B.C. These two states, which had once enjoyed a commercial and naval superiority over Athens, now found their trade challenged by the rise of Piraeus and their power threatened by Athenian ambition. Although a large part of her fleet and armed forces was engaged in Egypt and Cyprus, Athens was able to overwhelm the combined navies of the enemy, to besiege Aegina, and to send the general Myronides to repel a Corinthian invasion of the Megarid. The resources of Athens at this time, apparently, were matched only by her vitality. Indeed, fearing a general war with the Peloponnesus, her next step was to construct Long Walls connecting the city with Piraeus (Map 37). They ran about four and a half miles in length and 550 feet apart, and thus enclosed a broad, strongly fortified road from Athens to her chief source of supplies. After their completion the city could never be effectively besieged so long as her fleet held the sea.

In the early summer of 457 B.C. Sparta was finally stirred to action. Thebes, by her Medism, had lost control of the Boeotian League and by now the League was hardly more than a name. But if Sparta were to find a new ally, strong enough to be effective in the coming struggle against Athens, Boeotia remained the one possibility. Accordingly Sparta sent an army into Boeotia to encourage the aristocrats in their resistance to Athens and especially to restore the Boeotian League under the supremacy of Thebes. The Athenians marched out to meet this army, and a fierce battle ensued at Tanagra, during which the Thessalian cavalry deserted to the enemy. Having won the victory, the Peloponnesians returned home through the Megarid, but without invading Attica. Two months later the Athenians, under Myronides, again took the field and overthrew a Boeotian army at Oenophyta. The Athenians made themselves masters of all Boeotia, except Thebes, and in most, if not all, of the towns set up democratic governments. Phocis became an ally of Athens, and the Locrians were coerced into the League and compelled to give hostages. Not long afterward Aegina fell and became a subject-ally in the Delian League, paying the heavy tribute of thirty talents a year. Troezen, on the opposite Peloponnesian coast, cast her lot with Athens, as did Achaea (Map 29).

The height of Athenian power on land was reached in 456 B.C. The Long Walls were now completed, and Athens was secure from every attack by land and sea. The imperial ambition of Pericles seemed to be wholly justified. In a period of five years Athens had built up a continental federation which included parts of the Peloponnesus and the entire territory from the Isthmus to Thermopylae, and embracing intermittently the inconstant Thessalians. Here truly was a threat to the Peloponnesian League. Could Athens hope to maintain both her land and sea empires? As if the control of the Saronic Gulf, through her possession of Megara, Aegina, and Troezen, were not enough, she

Map 27

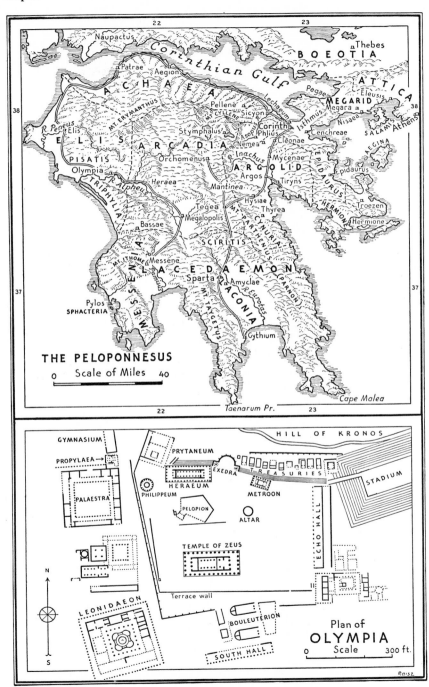

THE PELOPONNESUS

0   Scale of Miles   40

Plan of
OLYMPIA
Scale
0   300 ft.

Map 28

185

now became, thanks to Pegae, Achaea, and Naupactus, a power on the western seas. Could Athens, with impunity, offend the pride of the Peloponnesians by opposing to them a mightier empire than their own, and win their hatred by challenging their influence everywhere? And, above all, could she fight Persia at the same time? Even if she had the money, did Athens possess the manpower?

The ambition of Athens clearly exceeded her strength. Even in 459 B.C., when she was in need of all her forces at home for the struggle against Corinth and Aegina, Athens had dared to make war on Persia. The purpose of Pericles in sending two hundred ships against Cyprus was probably two-fold. It might be possible to add materially to the Delian League, or at the worst to deliver the Persian fleet (and this meant the Phoenician fleet) such a blow that it would cease to be a potential danger. The present king of Persia was Artaxerxes. In 465 B.C. Xerxes had closed his inglorious reign, murdered by his grand vizier, and had been suceeded by his son, who was too good-natured and too feeble to maintain peace throughout the Empire. In 459 B.C. Inaros, a prince of Libya, raised Egypt in revolt and appealed to Athens for support. In the hope of striking the Great King at the weakest point in his defense and perhaps of gaining control of the rich Nile valley, Athens diverted from Cyprus forty or fifty ships to support the rebellion. After several years of campaigning with various fortune in the neighborhood of Memphis, the armament was destroyed (453 B.C.), and few of the crews ever returned to their homes. Pericles, meanwhile, had taken steps to protect the Delian League. The maneuvers of the Persian fleet in 455 B.C. off Phoenicia were aimed ostensibly at Egypt, but might actually be directed to the Aegean, and in 454 B.C., therefore, Pericles transferred the treasury of the League from Delos to Athens for safe-keeping. The Egyptian disaster was a terrible, though not irreparable, blow. Rather unexpectedly, however, Athens managed to retrieve something, for an additional allied fleet, sent to Egypt to relieve the force already there, arrived too late, and on the way home the fleet stopped in Caria and compelled some of the towns to pay tribute.

The next years were quiet ones in Hellenic politics, but in 451 B.C. the period of Cimon's ostracism was over and he returned to his native city. Athens once more became the scene of party strife. Pericles had already further reduced the powers of the Areopagus, opened the highest offices in the state to the hoplite class, introduced pay for public service (especially for jury duty), and in many ways strengthened his position as a democratic leader. In 451 B.C. probably with the agreement of Cimon, Pericles restricted Athenian citizenship to those who could claim Athenian parentage on both sides. This must have been pleasing to the lower classes, for under Pericles citizenship had become a great prize and the state was hard-pressed to support a growing population. At the same time, the aristocrats and conservatives in general had always been opposed to the extension of the franchise.

By the time Cimon returned from exile in 451 B.C. the rules of the political game had been changed. No more could a political leader hope to keep the support of the masses by personal largess; people had grown accustomed to receive support from the government and to take a more direct role in politics than in the past. Cimon accepted the new conditions with his customary affability and patriotism. Already in 457 B.C., before the battle of Tanagra, he had proved that for him country came before party. Amid rumors of treason by his supporters, the ostracized Cimon had come to the Athenian camp to urge his friends to fight bravely and loyally, and many of them had died obeying his orders. Pericles had inherited the anti-Spartan policy from Ephialtes as part of the legacy of that leader of the democrats, but he carried it out without apparent enthusiasm. By 451 B.C., at any rate, he was ready for peace. It appears that the return of Cimon produced a coalition in which Pericles commanded the home front and Cimon resumed command of the old foreign policy of peace with Sparta and vigorous war against Persia. Cimon negotiated a five-year's truce with Sparta, and gave up the alliance with Argos, which now signed a thirty-year treaty with Sparta. In the summer of 450 B.C. Cimon set sail with two hundred ships against Cyprus. He died during the siege of Citium, but afterward his troops won a brilliant victory by land and sea at Cypriote Salamis. Though the victory was not followed up, it raised Athenian prestige immeasurably in the eastern Mediterranean.

Pericles, who was now supreme at Athens, recognized the limitations on the capacity of his city and the futility of war with Persia. It were far better to keep what Athens now had. He therefore sent an embassy, under Callias, to Susa to make peace. The proud king refused to acknowledge formally the cession of his former Greek provinces in Asia Minor to Athens. He consented, however, to leave them undisturbed by land and sea. Athens, on her part, agreed to cease her attacks upon the possessions of the Great King. The Peace of Callias, which was concluded early in 449 B.C., lasted almost forty years.

The Peace of Callias meant that the war was over. In March or early April of 449 B.C. Pericles suggested that the end of the war be celebrated by a panhellenic congress at Athens to discuss the rebuilding of the temples destroyed during the Persian invasions. Pericles probably knew that the invitation would not be accepted. It was a shrewd idea, calculated to win for Athens the implied moral leadership of the Greek

world, and was turned down by the Peloponnesian states. Pericles, however, proposed the motion to the Athenians, sometime before July 1,
449 B.C., that they at least should rebuild their own temples and should
use for the purpose the 5,000 talents of allied money that had accumulated. It was also voted that in the future any surplus money should
be handed over to Athena, until 3,000 talents had been collected.
Apparently there was no special purpose for this reserve fund, though
the ambition was realized by 434 B.C. The treasury of the Empire, however, had been turned over to Athena; her temple now became a state
bank, and the goddess (through her treasurers) could use the money as
she pleased. Here we have the change of the Delian League into the
Athenian Empire. As Plutarch remarks, Pericles now set about adorn-
ing Athens like a vain woman, draping around her neck precious stones
and statues and temples, for Pericles argued that, because the Athenians
protected the allies, they did not need to give them any reckoning.

The year 448 B.C. was chiefly marked by a quarrel over the control
of Delphi, and next year the Boeotian oligarchs, who were using Thebes
as a base for intrigue against Athens, openly revolted. Contrary to the
advice of Pericles, the Athenians sent a small force under the general
Tolmides against them. At Coronea Tolmides was slain and most of his
troops were captured. To secure their release, Athens agreed to evacuate
Boeotia. Locris and Phocis immediately deserted the alliance. In 446
B.C., just as the five-year truce expired, Euboea revolted, and while
Pericles was engaged in putting down this revolt, Megara rose and
massacred the Athenian garrison. Pericles returned to find the Spartan
king, Pleistoanax, in Attica, and only by energy, diplomacy, and probably a promise to conclude a reasonable peace did Pericles persuade him
to withdraw. Pericles returned to Euboea with a large force and
crushed the revolt. The landed aristocracy was exiled from Chalcis, and
Histiaea became an Athenian cleruchy.[2] Megara, however, returned to
the Peloponnesian League, and Thebes became the strong leader of the
oligarchic Boeotian League. The Athenian land empire had collapsed
almost overnight.

Pericles saw the exhaustion of the state. It had been impossible for
Athens to fight Sparta and Persia at the same time. The disaster in
Egypt, the substantial failure of the great expedition to Cyprus, the
heavy loss in men from the domestic wars which were often caused by a
yearning for autonomy, and the vast expense of all these undertakings

---

[2] A cleruchy, it will be recalled, was a special type of colony, peculiar to Athens.
Its members remained Athenian citizens. Cleruchies acted as garrisons and
stimulated Athenian trade. In addition to those in Euboea, cleruchies were established in various islands and in the Thracian Chersonese.

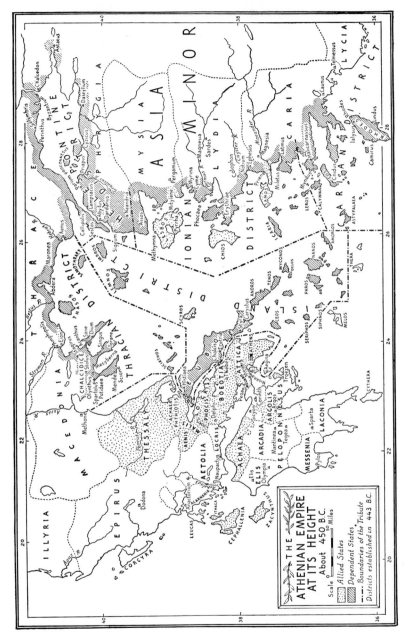

THE
ATHENIAN EMPIRE
AT ITS HEIGHT
About 450 B.C.

Scale _____ 50 Miles

░░░ Allied States
▨ Dependent States
–·–·– Boundaries of the Tribute
Districts established in 443 B.C.

Map 29

189

had overstrained the resources of Athens. In 445 B.C., accordingly, the Athenians agreed with the Peloponnesians to a Thirty Years' Peace. Athens surrendered her entire land empire, including Nisaea, Pegae, Troezen, and Achaea, retaining only Plataea, Aegina, and Naupactus, so that her situation differed little from that of 461 B.C. Sparta, on her part, acknowledged Athens' maritime empire. Neither party was to interfere with the allies of the other, but each remained free to make treaties with neutral states. It was agreed that disputes should be settled by arbitration. The lack of a clear understanding as to the means and method of arbitration rendered this provision less effective than it might have been. The treaty was realistic—considering the facts of Greek political life at that moment—and reflected rather accurately the power and interests of each side. Both parties to the treaty, freed from the heavy burden of the conflict which is sometimes known as the First Peloponnesian War, rejoiced in the advantages of mutual commerce, of internal recuperation and improvement promised them by the truce. The treaty, in effect, divided the Greek world into two spheres of influence and provided for peaceful coexistence between the two great powers. If each side were prudent, restrained its ambitions, kept to its own sphere, and ignored baseless fears, there was a chance that with reasonable luck a lasting peace might be obtained.

THE DEMOCRATIC CONSTITUTION

It was the growth of the power of the city masses at Piraeus and Athens, together with the possession of an empire, that determined the character of the Athenian constitution. The metics and slaves had, of course, no political rights, but within the citizen body the old issue of the few against the many persisted. In the new democratic world many of the old nobility, the Eupatrids, found themselves totally out of place. Their bitter complaints were given voice in a pamphlet issued by one of their number shortly after the death of Pericles—the earliest extant political treatise in any language. Unknown by name, the author has been aptly called the Old Oligarch. In his *Strictures on the Athenian Democracy* he laments the decline of those arts in which his class took chief pride, gymnastics and music, abolished by the masses not from disbelief in the beauty and honor of such training, but because their cultivation was beyond their powers. The mob can now enjoy luxuries, such as palaestras and baths built at public expense, which formerly were intended only for the rich. The rich man has to pay for the training of dramatic choruses, while the people reap the enjoyment.

He laments even more the growth of the naval power with its sailor crowd at the expense of the heavy infantry, composed of respectable middle-class citizens, the tyrannical treatment of the allies, the oppression of the wealthy throughout the Empire by the levy of taxes and by favoritism toward the poor—evils he has greatly exaggerated. "The fact that everywhere more consideration is shown to the base, the poor, and the common folk than to persons of good quality, far from being a matter of surprise, is evidently the keystone of the democracy. Within the ranks of the people will be found the utmost ignorance, disorderliness, and rascality, traceable chiefly to poverty. The people do not want the city to be well governed and themselves in slavery; they desire to be free and to be masters." These words reveal the existence of a class of men, strong in wealth, social standing, and intelligence, who were watching their opportunity to usurp the government and enslave the populace, who would hesitate at no violence or treason to gain their ends. Under Pericles they could only indulge in mutual grumblings or in indirect attacks upon the leading statesmen; later days were to see examples of their political methods.

Notwithstanding such men, the commons still cherished profound respect for the nobility. In fact Athenian culture thus far was chiefly their creation, and Eupatrids, not men from the masses, took the lead in democratizing the government. Although considerations of birth had long disappeared from the constitution, no one but a noble could actually command the votes necessary for an election to the generalship. The nobility formed a small minority of the population, but its sympathies were sometimes shared by the *zeugitae*. The majority of the *zeugitae* were freeholders of little farms, tilling their fields with the help of the family or, at best, of a slave or two. The increasing population of Athens and Piraeus, and the inflow of money from the Empire to its capital guaranteed rising prices of rural products, and brought the farming class to its highest reach of prosperity. The farms were well stocked and the dwellings and barns were better than in any other Greek state. These people of middle station, whose material happiness was now greater than in any earlier period, constituted the element of stability, the chief conservative force, in the state. They were generally content to support their families well above the condition of want and misery and to perform their military duties. Against all radicalism in politics and public economy, against wars with neighbors and peace with Persia, they were firmly set. Thus their sympathies were with the old landed aristocracy in opposition to the city population, industrialism, and absolute democracy. To the *zeugitae* were due the steadiness and the conservatism of Athens amid the forces that made powerfully for innovation. On the other hand, they were firmly against any return to an aristocratic state and any limitation on the democracy that Pericles had brought to completion. After the Peace of 445 B.C. they were among the firmest of the supporters of Periclean democracy.

The "poor," whom the Old Oligarch so despised, were not paupers, but the smallest land proprietors, shepherds, shopkeepers, artisans, day laborers, and sailors—in general, the *thetes*, the lowest class in the Solonian census. Most of the *thetes* were self-sustaining. The growing complexity of economic conditions, however, created by the development of commerce and industry, and making greater and greater demands upon the intelligence, produced an increasing number of persons who were incompetent to earn a living for themselves. Under an aristocracy they would have died of want or have fallen into slavery. The broader and more humane democracy, however, faced the problem of lifting this submerged class to the place of respectable citizenship. Thousands were placed in comfortable circumstances through colonization, and thousands more were engaged in the military and civil service. The great public works, too, furnished employment to a vast number of skilled and unskilled laborers. For a time these efforts of the government, re-enforced by unusual prosperity, eliminated poverty from Athens.

Payment for public service and for public works required a large state income. The Empire's tribute provided this. It is easy to understand, then, why the Athenian democracy was imperialistic. And because the maintenance of the Empire depended upon the navy, and the navy upon the rowers, the *thetes* held a position of special importance. The masses were determined to maintain and organize the Empire for their own benefit.

The first constitutional change after the Persian Wars was Ephialtes' reform of the Areopagus in 461 B.C. It will be recalled that the Areopagus retained jurisdiction in cases of homicide, but that its other powers were divided among the Assembly, Council, and *heliaea*. The people's sovereignty was vested in the popular Assembly (*ecclesia*), which embraced theoretically and potentially all male citizens over eighteen years of age, practically all with the leisure and inclination to attend.[3] The government did not as yet pay for attendance; hence the masses were present but rarely, on occasions of special interest or excitement. During the Peloponnesian War the number seldom reached 5,000 and must usually have been far smaller, though the patriot considered it his duty to be present and to take an interest in public affairs. The Assembly had forty regular meetings a year, passed the laws, and de-

---

[3] Men of nineteen and twenty, however, would generally be on military service.

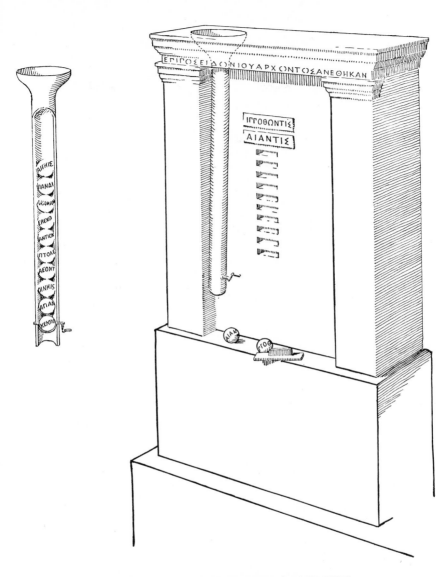

ATHENIAN ALLOTMENT MACHINE

Diagram 30

193

cided matters concerning foreign policy, war, food, and a multitude of details. The principle was accepted that not the people but the laws governed. The Assembly deliberated on a proposed question, and all had a right to speak, whether officers or private persons.

A measure was not initiated by the Assembly, but was brought to it, as a resolution (*probouleuma*), by the Council of Five Hundred (*boule*). The members of the Council were paid a drachma a day and were chosen by lot from citizens over thirty years of age. From it came the presiding officers of the Assembly. Much of the supervisory power, formerly wielded by the Areopagites, was transferred to this Council. It examined the fitness of candidates for office (*dokimasia*), as its own members had been examined, arranged for their election or sortition, and cooperated with them in most of their duties. It kept a strict watch over the magistrates—especially over those who handled money—and permitted no money to be received or disbursed apart from its supervision. For a time it had full power to punish for misuse of office. Furthermore the Council superintended the construction, repair, and preservation of triremes, or other vessels of war, and of public buildings, inspected the horses belonging to the state, revised the list of the cavalry, and attended to many other matters. It had the duty of prosecuting before the Assembly cases of treason (*eisangelia*). The Council had "the guardianship of the constitution," as Aristotle explains in his *Constitution of Athens,* and this involved the right of exercising in crises the power of life and death over both officials and private citizens. Far from giving rein to license and lawlessness, the Periclean democracy sternly enforced the moral discipline to which the people had grown accustomed under aristocratic rule.

The theory that, under the laws, the people themselves were sovereign could not be put into strict practice, for, as we have seen, the actual administration had to be entrusted mainly to a smaller, more wieldy body, the Council of Five Hundred. And, indeed, the Council itself was organized into ten smaller groups, known as prytanies, each consisting of the fifty members from a tribe and serving as a committee of the Council. Each prytany, in the period from 450 to 410 B.C., held office for thirty-six or thirty-seven days. To prevent bribery and improper pressure, it was not known till the very end of a prytany which tribe would succeed, and an allotment machine was devised to decide this secretly by lot (Diagram 30). A conciliar year, then, consisted of ten prytanies and approximated a solar year of about 365¼ days, the exact length being variable at the discretion of the government.[4]

[4] The conciliar year did not necessarily begin with the month of *Hecatombaeon* (July). It was, therefore, different from the ordinary civil year of twelve lunar

The Council, through its prytanies, was in continuous session and, because it formulated the measures to be considered by the people, served as a brake on the Assembly. The Assembly's action was also checked by the *heliaea* (popular court). The germ of this institution had existed from the time of Solon. Originally it was a court of appeal from the decisions of the archons, who were men of experience and ability, chosen for their special fitness from the two wealthiest classes in the Solonian census (the *pentacosiomedimni* and the knights). From a court of appeal the *heliaea* developed into a criminal court of the first instance. Athens outstripped other Greek states in the conception of its duties and powers in criminal law, although it had an undeveloped conception of public justice, much being left to private initiative.

It was probably in 487 B.C. that the economic growth of Athens necessitated dividing the *heliaea* into several juries (*dicasteries*). The 6,000 jurors (*dicasts*), 600 drawn annually by lot from each tribe, were normally divided into juries of five hundred and one, though we occasionally hear of smaller and larger panels. The decision was by majority vote. The jurors were citizens over thirty years of age, and at the beginning of their service were put under oath to give their decisions according to law, and in the absence of a statute covering the case, according to their best judgment and conscience. The chief reason for the large jury was to make bribery difficult, and in fact the Athenians devised a complicated system of choosing jurors and of assigning them to the several cases, with the result that a man did not know on what case he was to sit till he entered the courtroom (Figure 63). The large number, furthermore, was to provide against intimidation.[5]

Normally a case came first before a public arbitrator, for, because suits were private, they could be settled out of court and thus relieve pressure on the heliastic courts. The primary purpose of the arbitrator, however, was to sift the evidence before it reached the jury and to see to it that the evidence was put in writing and delivered, sealed, to the jury. The court was a jury without a judge—under an archon, a mere chairman who possessed neither the knowledge nor the right to inter-

---

months. Since the lunar calendar gave only 354 or 355 days to the year, intercalary months were added at irregular intervals. The Athenians also had a Panathenaic year, for the Treasurers of Athena took office at the time of the Panathenaea (August). In the fourth century it became the practice to date the years after the archons.

[5] In 453–452 B.C. the system of rural justices, established by Peisistratus, was restored. These judges, 30 in number, were also arbitrators. By the end of the fifth century they no longer went on circuit, on account of the Peloponnesian War and the consequent decline of agricultural life.

pret the law or to guide the proceedings. Under these circumstances there was no such thing as case law or precedent, for the Athenians had something they thought was better. Every heliastic decision was a fresh statement of the general sense of right. There was no fear of inconsistency, for it was assumed that every citizen was sufficiently acquainted with the code, and, besides, they were as likely to be right one time as another. It was fitting, too, so the Athenians thought, to confuse politics with justice. Because every man had to plead his own case, it was not uncommon for a person to pay some one to write his speech for him, and in this way developed a class of "lawyers," who were viewed with suspicion by plain men. The public prosecutors were private citizens, and those who specialized in the business were known as sycophants. The Athenians were, without question, a litigious people, a nation of lawyers, but they were also a nation of politicians, fighters, artists, and dramatists.

With the growth of the Empire Athens gradually obtained jurisdiction over the allies. As a general rule, the most important political, criminal, and commercial suits arising in the Empire were tried at Athens. This contributed greatly to the political education of the Athenian citizens, but the delays and the bias, which was often directed against the aristocrats, were resented. This extension of Athens' authority, coupled with the establishment of cleruchies in their midst, made many states feel that they were paying a high price for the suppression of piracy and the removal of the Persian danger.

Sometimes before 451–450 B.C. Pericles carried a measure for the payment of jurors, at the rate of two obols a day. This act completely democratized the institution, as it enabled the poorest to attend regularly and in large numbers. The introduction of pay, though made at a time of party strife, was in itself a sound idea, for the typical juror was an old man who drew his fee in lieu of an old-age pension. Many of the jurors had country homes near Athens, and in the *Wasps* of Aristophanes we see them before daybreak trudging, lantern in hand, along the road to the city, to be at court on time. We have already discussed Pericles' measure of limiting the franchise to those who could claim citizenship on both sides of the family. Apparently the law was not enforced at once, but when, in 445 B.C., Psammetichus, an Egyptian pretender, sent 45,000 bushels of grain as a gift to the citizens of Athens, the lists were revised and some 5,000 names struck off. In 457–456 B.C. the archonship, now an unimportant office, was thrown open to the *zeugitae,* and shortly afterward even the preliminary choice was determined by lot. It seems, too, that *thetes,* possibly through false pretenses, occasionally obtained the office.

In this virtual democracy there remained one safeguard to the constitution, the *graphe paranomon,* an indictment for bringing before the Assembly measures in conflict with the laws. Although it is true that the initiative lay with the Council and the decision with the Assembly, any citizen could propose a new law. In that event the bill went to the Council to be prepared as a new *probouleuma* for the Assembly. If the bill became law, any citizen could bring the proposer to trial before the Assembly, during which time the new law remained in abeyance. The prosecutor had to prove that unconstitutional procedure had been followed or that the law was inconsistent with some law other than the one to be amended or with the general body of law, the democratic constitution itself. In the trial, the prosecutor had to obtain at least a fifth of the votes; otherwise he was punishable with a fine of a thousand drachmas and disqualified from bringing further prosecutions. A person convicted under the *graphe paranomon* was liable to a heavy fine, to disfranchisement, or even to death. Politicians eventually found the *graphe paranomon* a convenient weapon for assailing one another. As a milder and less dangerous instrument of political warfare, it superseded ostracism. Indeed in the later years of the Peloponnesian War, the right of individual initiative became a real danger to the state. Unprincipled persons, from the lower classes and holding no office, were able to sway the masses and saddle upon the magistrates policies that they disapproved. The rise of demagogues, then, was partly due to the privilege citizens enjoyed of introducing legislation.

The number of officials at Athens was enormous. Aristotle reckons 700 at home and a number unknown to us, but doubtless large, for the Empire. They usually served in boards of ten. Most of these offices were filled annually by lot, without the privilege of reappointment, on the theory that all citizens above the *thetes* were competent to the ordinary duties of administration and were equally entitled to a share in it. The magistrates executed the decisions of the Assembly, and at the end of their year of office were required to give an accounting of their acts (*euthynae*). Except for the generals and other military officers, all the magistrates were paid. When we consider the jurors, soldiers, and sailors, we have at the very least 20,000 Athenians who were on the pay roll of their city. In addition, a citizen could draw from the Theoric Fund two obols a day during the Dionysiac festival, but this was not another way of giving him the price of admission, for he could spend the money as he pleased. In the fifth century the Empire made all this possible, but when, in the fourth century, the Empire had disappeared, payment for public service continued and even increased! In the fourth century payment was added for attendance at the Assembly and various religious festivals. Under Pericles, however, payment simply meant that every citizen of Athens had the rich opportunity of sharing in the actual government of the state.

The highest magistrates at Athens were the ten generals (*strategoi*), for the archonship had lost all imporance, except a sentimental one, after it had been thrown open to the lot in 487–486 B.C. The generals were elected annually, and re-election was allowed. It was through this position that Pericles governed during the greater part of his administration, being elected general fifteen times in succession. These generals not only commanded the army and navy but embraced most of the functions falling in a modern state to the Ministry or Cabinet. They kept informed on foreign affairs, conducted negotiations not otherwise provided for, and requested the prytanies to call special sessions of the Assembly in order to introduce foreign ambassadors. They attended to the defenses of the country and the preparations for war. The board had to keep in touch with the Assembly, and the member who excelled as orator and statesman inevitably took the lead of his colleagues.

An Athenian who undertook to guide the policy of his state had to bear a heavier weight of responsibility than has been necessary in any less democratic form of government. The masses who constituted the Assembly—fullers, cobblers, coppersmiths, stonemasons, hucksters, and farmers—could not be expected to have the same acquaintance with the details of policy, especially in foreign relations, that might be presupposed in a select body of public men, such for instance as the Roman Senate or a modern parliament. The democracy had to place greater trust in its advisers, and require of them expert knowledge. If a statesman succeeded, his glory was splendid, but if he failed, he was liable to severe punishment. Not infrequently he was embarrassed by the demagogue, for the Athenians did not fully appreciate that the right of private initiative in the Assembly might force a magistrate to execute a policy in which he had no confidence. The Periclean constitution, however, kept dread revolution (*stasis*) at a distance for many decades. The conservatives were practically powerless. Their leader, Thucydides, son of Melesias, in 444 B.C. opposed spending imperial funds for the construction of buildings at Athens and in the following year was ostracized.

THE THIRTY YEARS' PEACE

The agreement reached with Sparta under the Thirty Years' Peace (445 B.C.) freed Pericles' hands to complete the transformation of the

Delian League into an empire. This maritime confederacy, outlined by Aristeides and developed by Cimon, had enjoyed a leisurely expansion and depended in part on Athens' successes elsewhere. One by one the states of the League had been reduced to subjection, till only Lesbos, Chios, and Samos remained autonomous. They paid no tribute, but furnished naval forces, whereas the other states had been compelled to pay tribute and often to adopt democratic constitutions. The synod of the League no longer met, the treasury had been removed to Athens in 454 B.C. because of threatened danger from Persia, and the League's officials, the *Hellenotamiae,* were, of course, Athenian magistrates. Generally, new treaties were made with the individual states—imposed by the Athenian government and formally accepted by the allies. Certain decrees of about 450 B.C., for example those concerning Erythrae, Phaselis, and Sigeum, illustrate the organization and slow growth of the League.

In 454 B.C. there were about 140 contributing cities in the League, with a total tribute of about 350 talents. The number of tributaries was subsequently increased, but the peace which Callias secured with Persia in 449 B.C. removed the principal reason for the existence of the Delian League and resulted once more in the poor collection of the tribute. The resumption of payments on a large scale in 448 B.C. marks the death of the League and the firm establishment of the empire.

In the year 444 B.C., the year after the signing of the Thirty Years' Peace, Pericles proposed that imperial funds be used for public construction at Athens. The cost of the Parthenon, begun in 447 B.C., had been defrayed by the treasury of Athena, which in turn had been filled by the treasury of the old Delian League, but now these funds were exhausted. The Assembly therefore directed that the tribute be drawn upon. The great building program for the Athenian Acropolis was able to continue. Below the Acropolis a music hall, the Odeon, was built, work on the new Hall of the Mysteries at Eleusis was carried on, and a third Long Wall to Piraeus was laid down. The new wall made the communications with the harbor safer, and the wall to Phaleron was abandoned. Hippodamus, a philosopher and practical scientist of Miletus, was engaged to reconstruct Piraeus, with broad straight avenues crossing each other at right angles. About the same time the dockyards were substantially enlarged for the accommodation of the growing navy. These imperial aims roused the conservatives to action. Their leader, Thucydides, son of Melesias, charged that Pericles' negotiations with Persia had been traitorous, that Pericles was a real tyrant, another Peisistratus, and that he was using the money of the allies to bedeck Athens like a vain woman.

The ostracism of Thucydides in 443 B.C. left Pericles without serious opposition. He now brought more system into the administration of the Empire. The *Hellenotamiae*, for example, received a secretary and assistant secretary; collection of tribute became so efficient that they were able to obtain the expected sums. The assessment of 443 B.C. recognized by name for the first time the five tribute districts—Ionia, the Hellespont, the Thracian district, Caria, and the Islands—but it may be inferred from the quota lists for 446 B.C. that these same districts existed then, though unnamed.[6] In 438 B.C. Caria was merged with Ionia, and the four districts remained until the last assessment in Athens in 410 B.C. It is worth remarking that the man Pericles saw fit to appoint as chief treasurer for the reorganization of the Empire in 443 B.C. was the poet Sophocles, who produced his *Antigone* two years later and in the following year was general at Samos.

The tribute of the Empire was reassessed approximately every four years by Athenian officials. Pericles, however, exercised care in his dealings with the allies. "To maintain our rights against equals," he said, "to be politic with superiors and moderate toward inferiors is the way of safety." For commercial reasons, and quite as much through pride in their imperial rule, the Athenians forced their money, as well as their weights and measures, upon the allies, whose local mints were restricted to small denominations. There can be no question that all this made the Athenians unpopular in many quarters and among many people in her Empire. Freedom and autonomy were very precious to the Greeks and the Athenians had interfered with both. Few could be expected to realize that in a world in which two great powers had risen to eminence full freedom in foreign policy for small states was neither possible nor desirable. The Athenians exercised more and more control over their allies without giving them any participation in the great decisions. There was no thought in Athens of offering Athenian citizenship to the allies and it is unlikely that it would have been accepted had it been offered. A true federal government was even further from men's minds. In the conflict between the ideals of freedom and autonomy and the hard realities of world politics and Athenian control we may find the causes of increased resentment of Athens and the readiness of many to revolt.

Athens, however, brought to her subjects the blessings of peace and protection. Under the aegis of a powerful navy the ships of her humblest ally could safely plough the sea to Egypt and Tyre, to the Black Sea, or to the Pillars of Heracles. For many years the profound quiet

---

[6] Earlier assessments recognized but four districts, Caria being merged with Ionia.

was disturbed by no invader and, in most cases, by no domestic war. Skilled industry flourished; farms were well stocked and fields well tilled; in no period of the world's history has this region developed so great a prosperity. Under these circumstances the feelings of the allies toward Athens mingled good with ill. It was a grievance to carry their cases to Athens, and a hardship to pay the tribute. They resented, too, the Athenian cleruchies and cherished the genuine Hellenic love of sovereign independence for their cities. Yet positive antipathy was limited to the old families whom the Empire had robbed of their political ascendancy and to the scheming market-place politicians who saw in revolt their way to leadership in their states. The manufacturers and merchants, who paid the bulk of the tribute, must have been satisfied with the economic advantage assured them by Athenian rule; and the multitude in every state was loyal.

In 443 B.C. Pericles also turned his thought to southern Italy. A great colony, made up of Athenians and other Greeks, was planted at Thurii. Unlike other Athenian settlements it was publicly proclaimed as a pan-Hellenic colony. Pericles was probably glad to find another outlet for excess Athenian population, but his main purpose was to make clear to Sparta and Corinth that Athens had no designs on the West and was eager to live in peace under the terms of the treaty of 445 B.C. Even when the colony suffered defeat at the hands of the Spartan colony of Tarentum a few years later, and when it rejected its Athenian connection in 434 B.C., Pericles took no action and made no protest.

Two years later occurred the first serious revolt in the Empire. Samos had gone to war with Miletus over the possession of Priene, and when Miletus complained to Athens, Samos refused arbitration, but revolted under the instigation of the oligarchs. The Persians offered the aid of a Phoenician fleet; Byzantium revolted in sympathy; the continued existence of the Empire became questionable. But the Athenians met the crisis with extraordinary promptness. Pericles besieged the island and brought newly invented siege engines to bear upon the walls. Finally, in 439 B.C., after a great expenditure of men and money, Samos surrendered, and received the punishment formerly meted out to Naxos and Thasos. Byzantium in its turn submitted. While the revolt was still on and other Aegean allies were on the verge of joining the rebellion a meeting of the Peloponnesian League was called to consider aiding the rebels. If the vote had been favorable, Sparta and the Peloponnesians would have been allied with the rebellious allies of Athens and the Persian Empire in the same coalition which ultimately was to bring Athens to her knees in 404 B.C. At this crucial moment Corinth, the bitter enemy of Athens in the late war and the state which stood to lose the most by the prospect of Athenian imperialism in the West, argued against intervention and carried the day. It is plain that the Corinthians had received, understood, and approved the diplomatic signal which Pericles had sent by founding the pan-Hellenic colony at Thurii. The Corinthians, and with them the Peloponnesians, were prepared to accept the division of the Greek world into two discrete spheres of influence and to live in peace.

The Empire emerged from the crisis more strongly cemented than before. The slain were given a magnificent funeral; and as Pericles descended from the speaker's stand after delivering the eulogy on the dead, the women of Athens crowned him with wreaths and ribbons like a victorious athlete, so highly did they value his service in that momentous campaign.

The reassessment of the tribute in 438 B.C. reflected a change in Athenian policy. Henceforth various inland cities were allowed to go their own way, while Athens devoted herself to the maintenance of a thalassocracy. This explains why the seaboard of Caria was now merged with the Ionian tribute district. To compensate partially for this loss of income (some ten talents), the assessment of certain other states was raised; for example, in 434 B.C. that of Potidaea from six to fifteen talents. The Chalcidice, however, represented a special problem. Athens was not sure of its wholehearted loyalty, and, besides, the growing Macedonian and Thracian kingdoms were a menace. To block the Thracian kingdom and to control the important crossing of the Strymon river, as well as the approaches to the mines of Mt. Pangaeus, Athens founded the colony of Amphipolis in 437 B.C. This same year Pericles set out on an impressive voyage to the Black Sea His purpose was to extend the prestige and power of Athens among the native kingdoms, and to plant a few strategic colonies. Doubtless, however, the chief object of the trip was to promote closer relations with a region on which Athens depended more and more for supplies—for wheat and timber, metals, dyes, hides, slaves, and other commodities. Not merely the products of the sea and its coasts were thus brought to Athens and her neighbors, but also those of the distant interior; for from Olbia on the northern shore extended a great caravan route to the Ural mountains and thence east through Central Asia to the borders of China. From these regions were imported furs, drugs, gold, and silk. Close commercial ties with the Black Sea meant, too, that in case of a Peloponnesian War Athens would be independent of supplies from Dorian Sicily.

War with Sparta and Corinth was still a possibility, but Pericles no doubt felt that his diplomacy, if not the splendor of the Empire, would in the end prevent it. The grand success of his foreign policy naturally made Pericles' own position at Athens unassailable, though the opposition was strong enough to carry through, with the support of the ever fickle and ungrateful people, the exile of his instructors, Damonides and Anaxagoras, and, on the charge of embezzling gold and ivory for the statue of Athena, Pheidias. For a possible war Pericles had built up a financial reserve. In 434–431 B.C. the annual income of Athens from the Empire amounted to approximately 600 talents, the tribute alone accounting for 388 talents. This money was used for new buildings and for payments to magistrates and other officials. In 434 B.C. the reserve fund of 3,000 talents, voted fifteen years earlier, was paid to Athena, and a new financial board was organized, the Treasurers of the Other Gods. A decree of Callias for this year directed that repayment should be made from the funds of the *Hellenotamiae* to the gods for for loans during the Egyptian crisis (perhaps 200 talents) and that in the future any surplus should be deposited in the Opisthodomus, as the Old Temple of Athena on the Acropolis may have been called after it had been wrecked by the Persians. The financial boards in charge were to be the *Hellenotamiae,* the Treasurers of Athena, and the Treasurers of the Other Gods.

By 436 B.C. the prospects for peace among the Greek states were excellent. The First Peloponnesian War had taught both Athens and Sparta that each faced a formidable opponent with whom war was likely to be long and costly. The Peace of 445 B.C. was fair and realistic, and both sides had given evidence of a willingness to uphold it. This happy condition was rudely upset by the outbreak of a civil war in Epidamnus, an unimportant Corcyraean colony on the Adriatic coast, far from the center of Greek affairs. In a short time Corinth was embroiled with the neutral Corcyra, whose importance was heightened by her strategic position on the route to the West and by the fact that she possessed the second largest fleet in Greece. When Corcyra appealed to Athens for help the Athenians were torn between the desire to avoid trouble and the fear that if Corcyra lost to Corinth her fleet would fall into Peloponnesian hands and threaten the security of Athens. After long debate the Athenians decided on a moderate policy. They accepted a defensive alliance only and sent to Corcyra a token force of ten ships to warn off the Corinthians and to help defend Corcyra as a last resort. At the battle of Sybota in 433 B.C. the Athenian fleet was able to prevent the Corinthians from taking vengeance on Corcyra, but in so doing Athens earned the hatred of the Corinthians, who now set about to bring Sparta into the war to destroy the Athenian Empire.

A second "grievance" came from the north, for it still seemed impossible to rouse Sparta to war. Potidaea, though a colony of Corinth, was a member of the Athenian Empire. Vexed by the increase in her assessment and by the presence of near-by Amphipolis, and urged on by Perdiccas, the ambitious king of Macedon, Potidaea was ready for revolt in 432 B.C. The Corinthians, moreover, had obliquely threatened the Athenians with attempts to stir up rebellion in her Empire, and Potidaea was the likeliest candidate for such a revolt. Athens first made demands of Potidaea; when they were not met, she sent forces to besiege the city. Corinth replied by sending aid to her colony.

At about the same time, in the winter of 433–432 B.C., Pericles decided to punish Megara, one of the few Peloponnesian states to fight on the side of Corinth at Sybota, and so to discourage other Peloponnesian states from becoming involved. Pericles still hoped that Corinth might be persuaded to give up her attempt to humiliate Corcyra and so avoid war. If that should be impossible he hoped to keep the war local and to prevent Corinth from dragging other Peloponnesians, Sparta especially, into her own quarrel. He did not launch an attack on Megara, although its possession in a future war with the Peloponnesians would be the best possible guarantee of the safety of Attica. He knew that such an attack would be a breach of the peace and would compel Sparta to fight. Instead he passed a decree excluding Megara from the harbors and markets of Athens and her Empire. Such an action would punish Megara severely, but it was not a breach of the peace. Corinth, however, helped by Megara and Aegina, a subject member of the Athenian Empire which chafed under Athenian rule, persuaded the Spartans that Athens was a restlessly aggressive power with whom it was impossible to live in peace. The advocates of war in Sparta overcame the arguments of the peace party led by King Archidamus and the Spartans decided to go to war, "to liberate the Greeks." Pericles, using all his skill, offered to arbitrate. Thus the winter dragged on, without any formal declaration of war, when suddenly in March, 431 B.C., Thebes set the Greek world afire. In order to force Plataea, the ally of Athens, into the Boeotian League, Thebes laid siege to the city, after a secret attempt to capture it had failed. The Thirty Years' Peace had not run half its course.

Figure 1 An inscribed clay tablet, *ca.* 1200 B.C., from Pylos, recording vases with varying numbers of legs and handles—an aid to Ventris in deciphering this Linear B script of the Achaeans and proving the language to be an early form of Greek.

NATIONAL ARCHAEOLOGICAL MUSEUM, ATHENS.

PHOTOGRAPH: T.A.P.—ART REFERENCE BUREAU

(*Cf. pp. 11, 32, 36*)

Figure 2 Statuette of Snake Goddess, 16th century B.C. Minoan, ivory and gold.
COURTESY, MUSEUM OF FINE ARTS, BOSTON.
(*Cf. p. 25*)

Figure 3 Cup-bearer fresco, from Cnossus.
Late Minoan I.

CANDIA MUSEUM.

PHOTOGRAPH: T.A.P.—ART REFERENCE BUREAU

(*Cf. p. 26*)

Figure 4 A beautiful Late Minoan vase, from the American excavations at Gournia in Crete, showing an octopus amid seaweed and cuttlefish. A fine example of the relation of pattern to the shape of the vase.

HERAKLIAN MUSEUM.

PHOTOGRAPH: T.A.P.—ART REFERENCE BUREAU

(*Cf. p. 26*)

Figure 5 Prehellenic pottery jugs from prehistoric Zygouries, near Corinth. Early Helladic period (2200–2000 B.C.).

THE METROPOLITAN MUSEUM OF ART, GIFT OF THE GREEK GOVERNMENT, 1927.

Figure 6 Inlaid bronze daggers, from Mycenae. Late Helladic.
NATIONAL ARCHAEOLOGICAL MUSEUM, ATHENS.
PHOTOGRAPH: T.A.P.—ART REFERENCE BUREAU
(*Cf. p. 29*)

Figure 7 Treasury of Atreus. Mycenae.
(*Cf. pp. 29, 33*)

Figure 8 The Cyclopean wall of the Acropolis at Mycenae, with the famous Lion Gate. The Lion Relief indicates divine protection of the citadel.
PHOTOGRAPH: BRAUN
(*Cf. p. 33*)

Figure 9 One of the two Late Helladic gold cups found by the Greeks at Vaphio. A dramatic example of the skill of the Achaean metal workers.

NATIONAL ARCHAEOLOGICAL MUSEUM, ATHENS.

PHOTOGRAPH: T.A.P.—ART REFERENCE BUREAU

(*Cf. p. 34*)

Figure 10   Warrior Vase from Mycenae.
HIRMER FOTOARACHIV MUNCHEN.
(*Cf. p. 35*)

Figure 11 Megaron of the Bronze Age palace of Nestor, excavated by Americans at Homer's "sandy" Pylos. Beyond the portico and vestibule is the Great Hall with hearth and bases for columns.
(*Cf. p. 36*)

Figure 12 Geometric pottery, *ca.* 1000 B.C.
DEUTSCHES ARCHAOLOGISCHES INSTITUT, ATHENS.
(Cf. p. 41)

Figure 13   Idealized bust of Homer.
MUSEO NAZIONALE, NAPLES.
PHOTOGRAPH: ALINARI—ART REFERENCE BUREAU
(*Cf. p. 49*)

Figure 14 Geometric pottery.
DEUTSCHES ARCHAOLOGISCHES INSTITUT, ATHENS.
(*Cf. p. 50*)

Figure 15 Attic sepulchral amphora, from the Dipylon, 8th century B.C.
THE METROPOLITAN MUSEUM OF ART, FLETCHER FUND, 1934.
(*Cf. p. 50*)

Figure 16 The precinct of Apollo at Delphi. Foreground, the treasury of the Athenians, *ca.* 500 B.C.; rear, the Phaedriades (Shining) Cliffs of Parnassus, sacred to the Muses, below which lies the Castalian Spring.

PHOTOGRAPH: AGNES NEWHALL STILLWELL

(*Cf. p. 56*)

Figure 17 The "Basilica," *ca.* 540 B.C., and the Temple of Poseidon at Paestum, *ca.* 460 B.C.

PHOTOGRAPH: BRAUN

(Cf. pp. 67, 116)

Figure 18 King Arcesilas of Cyrene watching the weighing and packing of silphium. Laconian cylix, 1st half of 6th century B.C.

(*Cf. pp. 76, 111*)

Figure 19 In the wild uplands of Arcadia. The Temple of Apollo Epicurius at Bassae, *ca.* 450 B.C.

PHOTOGRAPH: SARAH ELIZABETH FREEMAN

(*Cf. pp. 82, 257*)

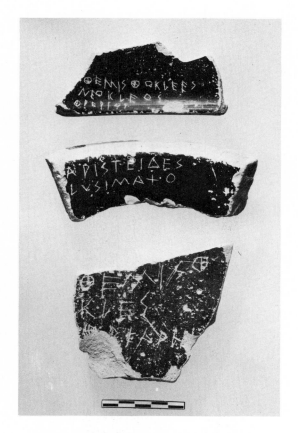

Figure 20 (A)   Ostraca from the Athenian Agora, inscribed with the names of Themistocles, son of Neocles, and Aristeides, son of Lysimachus.

(*Cf. p. 97n.*)

Figure 20 (B) Part of the list of Athenian tributaries in the first year of the Peloponnesian War (432–431 B.C.).

EPIGRAPHICAL MUSEUM, ATHENS.

PHOTOGRAPH: T.A.P.——ART REFERENCE BUREAU

(*Cf. p. 169*)

Figure 21   The great bronze Zeus, from the sea off Euboea. Probably by Ageladas of Argos, *ca.* 455 B.C.

NATIONAL MUSEUM, ATHENS.

PHOTOGRAPH: MARBURG—ART REFERENCE BUREAU

(*Cf. p. 100*)

Figure 22 West frieze of the Parthenon, 442–438 B.C.
(*Cf. p. 101*)

Figure 23 Corinthian stemmed lekanis and cover. Middle Corinthian, *ca.* 580 B.C.
COURTESY OF THE FOGG ART MUSEUM, CAMBRIDGE.
(*Cf. pp. 110, 254*)

Figure 24 The "François Vase." Wedding of Peleus and Thetis, and other subjects.
Attic crater, *ca.* 550 B.C., signed by the potter Ergotimos and the painter Klitias.
MUSEO ARCHEOLOGICO, FLORENCE.

PHOTOGRAPH: BROGI—ART REFERENCE BUREAU

(Cf. p. 111)

Figure 25   Dionysus in a ship. Cylix by the Attic master Exekias, 6th century B.C.
STAATLICHE ANTIKENSAMMLUNGEN UND GLYPTOTHEK, MUNCHEN.
(*Cf. p. 111*)

Figure 26 Achilles and Ajax playing at dice. Amphora by the Attic master Exekias, 3rd quarter of the 6th century B.C.

THE VATICAN, ROME.

PHOTOGRAPH: ALINARI—ART REFERENCE BUREAU

(*Cf. p. 111*)

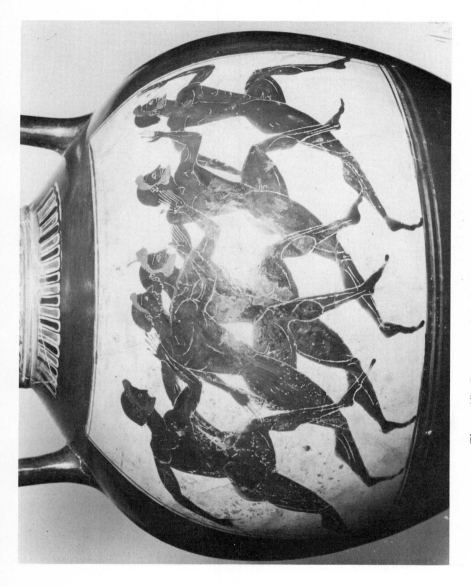

Figure 27 Runners on Panathenaic amphora, 6th century B.C.
STAATLICHE ANTIKENSAMMLUNGEN UND GLYPTOTHEK, MÜNCHEN.
(*Cf. p. 111*)

Figure 28   Theseus with Athena before Amphitrite. Cylix by the master Euphronios, *ca.* 500 B.C.

THE LOUVRE, PARIS.

PHOTOGRAPH: ALINARI—ART REFERENCE BUREAU

(*Cf. p. 111*)

Figure 29   Boy chasing a hare. Cylix, late 6th century B.C.
BRITISH MUSEUM, LONDON.
PHOTOGRAPH: FLEMING—ART REFERENCE BUREAU
(*Cf. p. 111*)

Figure 30 Attic black-figured plastic vase, 6th century B.C.
COURTESY, MUSEUM OF FINE ARTS, BOSTON.
(*Cf. p. 111*)

Figure 31 The Propylaea, from the east. Athens, *ca.* 437–432 B.C. (*Cf. pp. 112, 255*)

Figure 32 Capital and entablature of the North Porch of the Erechtheum. Athens. (*Cf. pp. 113, 256*)

Figure 33 The Temple of Aphaia at Aegina, *ca.* 489 B.C.
PHOTOGRAPH: BRAUN
(*Cf. p. 116*)

Figure 34 Bronze statuette of a girl running. Albania, 6th century, B.C.
BRITISH MUSEUM, LONDON.
PHOTOGRAPH: FLEMING—ART REFERENCE BUREAU
(*Cf. p. 117*)

Figure 35 Statue of a youth of the "Apollo type." Marble Athenian sculpture, 615–600 B.C.

(*Cf. p. 118*)

Figure 36 The Calf-bearer, dedicated by Rhombos on the Acropolis. Attic, *ca.* 560 B.C.

ACROPOLIS MUSEUM, ATHENS.

PHOTOGRAPH: ALINARI—ART REFERENCE BUREAU

(*Cf. p. 118*)

Figure 37 The Hera, from Samos, dedicated by Cheramyes, *ca.* 550 B.C.
THE LOUVRE, PARIS.
PHOTOGRAPH: ALINARI—ART REFERENCE BUREAU
(*Cf. p. 119*)

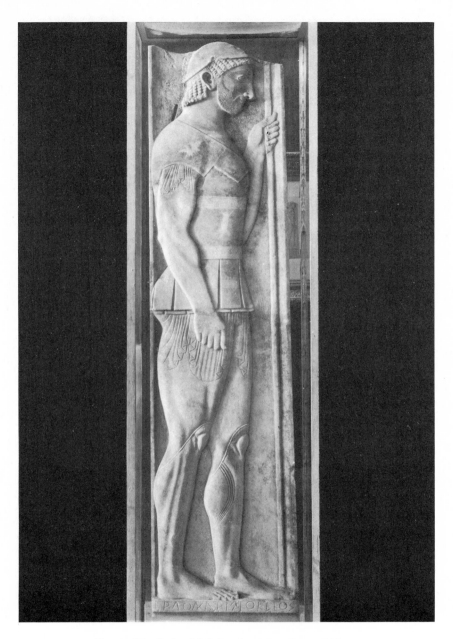

Figure 38   Stele of Aristion, by Aristocles, *ca.* 510 B.C.
NATIONAL MUSEUM, ATHENS.
PHOTOGRAPH: ALINARI—ART REFERENCE BUREAU
(*Cf. p. 120*)

Figure 39 Maiden with mantle, on the Acropolis, dedicated by Euthydikos, *ca.* 480 B.C.

ACROPOLIS MUSEUM, ATHENS.

PHOTOGRAPH: MARBURG—ART REFERENCE BUREAU

(*Cf. p. 120*)

Figure 40 Heracles, from the east pediment of the Temple of Aphaia at Aegina, *ca.* 480 B.C.

STAATLICHE ANTIKENSAMMLUNGEN UND GLYPTOTHEK, MUNCHEN.

(*Cf. p. 120*)

Figure 41 Striding warrior, from the east pediment of the Temple of Aphaia at Aegina, *ca.* 480 B.C.

THE GLYPTOTHEK, MUNICH.

PHOTOGRAPH: MARBURG—ART REFERENCE BUREAU

(*Cf. p. 120*)

Figure 42 (A)   Roman herm (bust), copied probably from a bronze statue of Themistocles, erected *ca.* 460 B.C. in the Theatre of Dionysus at Athens. An idealized conception of the hero of Salamis, with large features suggesting the barbarian (Thracian) origin of his mother.

OSTIA MUSEUM.

PHOTOGRAPH: GABINETTO FOTOGRAFICO NAZIONALE, ROME

(*Cf. p. 130*)

Figure 42 (B)   The bronze helmet of the hero of Marathon, inscribed, "Miltiades dedicated me to Zeus." Other recent discoveries by the Germans at Olympia—such as bronze battering rams of the 5th century B.C.—show that the Greeks had this kind of weapon at an earlier date than hitherto supposed.

OLYMPIA MUSEUM.

PHOTOGRAPH: T.A.P.—ART REFERENCE BUREAU

(*Cf. p. 133*)

Figure 43 Themistocles Decree, inscribed in the 3rd century B.C.
PHOTOGRAPH: ALISON FRANTZ

(*Cf. p. 147*)

Figure 44 Obverse and reverse of a Demareteion. Silver decadrachm of Syracuse struck in honor of the victory at Himera, 480 B.C.

(*Cf. p. 153n.*)

Figure 45 1. Croesus of Lydia; gold Stater; *ca.* 550 B.C.; 2. Aegina; Drachma; 550–480
B.C.; 3. Elis; Stater; *ca.* 421–385 B.C.; 4. Athens; Tetradrachm; 5th century B.C.; 5. Agrigentum (Acragas), Sicily; Tetradrachm; 472–415 B.C.; 6. Camarina, Sicily; Stater;
461–405 B.C.; 7. Metapontum; *ca.* 500 B.C. Coins of the sixth and fifth centuries B.C. The
coins are silver, except as noted.

AMERICAN NUMISMATIC SOCIETY, NEW YORK.

(*Cf. p. 166*)

Figure 46 1. Persia-Doric; gold; early 4th century B.C.; 2. Chalcidian League; 392–358 B.C.; 3. Corinth; 400–375 B.C.; 4. Ephesus; Drachma; 394–350 B.C.; 5. Thurii; Stater; 400–350 B.C.; 6. Thebes-Boetia; Didrachm; *ca.* 350 B.C.; 7. Syracuse; Decadrachm; *ca.* 395 B.C. Coins of the fifth and fourth centuries B.C. Coins are silver, except as noted.
AMERICAN NUMISMATIC SOCIETY, NEW YORK.
(*Cf. p. 166*)

Figure 47 1. Alexander the Great; gold Stater; *ca.* 315 B.C.; 2. Lysimachus, idealized portrait of Alexander; Tetradrachm; 290–280 B.C.; 3. Philip II; gold Tetradrachm; 4. Amphictyonic Council; Delphic Stater; 346–339 B.C.; 5. Demetrius Poliorcetes; 300–294 B.C.; 6. Arsinoe II; *ca.* 247 B.C.; 7. Perseus, Tetradrachm; 178–168 B.C.; 8. Demetrius of Bactria; 2nd century B.C. Coins of the fourth, third, and second centuries B.C. The coins are silver, except as noted.

AMERICAN NUMISMATIC SOCIETY, NEW YORK.

(*Cf. pp. 166, 206, 442*)

Figure 48 Herm of Herodotus, marble. Roman copy, probably 2nd century B.C., of a Greek original, late 5th century B.C. Found at Benha, Lower Egypt.

(*Cf. p. 268*)

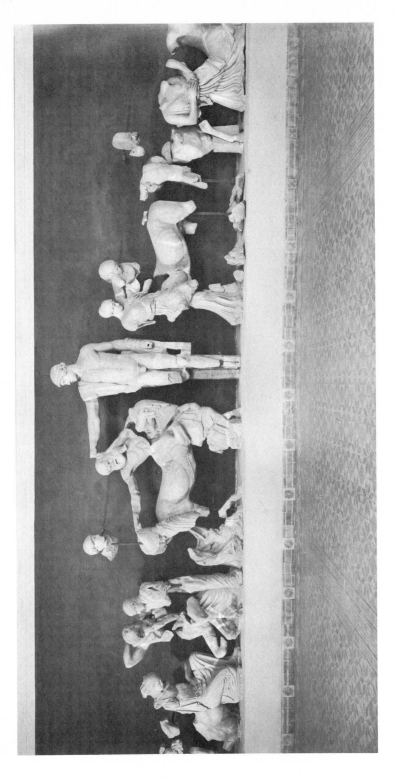

Figure 49 Battle between Lapiths and Centaurs. West pediment of the Temple of Zeus at Olympia,
ca. 460 B.C.

OLYMPIA MUSEUM.

PHOTOGRAPH: ALINARI—ART REFERENCE BUREAU

(*Cf. p. 178*)

Figure 50 Apollo, from the west pediment of the Temple of Zeus at Olympia, *ca.* 460 B.C.

OLYMPIA MUSEUM.

PHOTOGRAPH: MARBURG—ART REFERENCE BUREAU

(*Cf. p. 178*)

Figure 51 The great bronze Zeus, from the sea off Euboea. Probably by Ageladas of Argos, *ca.* 460 B.C.

NATIONAL MUSEUM, ATHENS.

PHOTOGRAPH: MARBURG—ART REFERENCE BUREAU

(*Cf. p. 178*)

Figure 52 Bronze Charioteer, from Delphi, *ca.* 477 B.C.
DELPHI MUSEUM.
PHOTOGRAPH: ALINARI—ART REFERENCE BUREAU
(*Cf. p. 178*)

Figure 53 The Discobolus. Roman copy of a bronze original by Myron, *ca.* 450 B.C.
PHOTOGRAPH: ALINARI—ART REFERENCE BUREAU
(*Cf. p. 178*)

Figure 54 Wounded Niobid, from Rome, *ca.* 445 B.C.
MUSEO NAZIONALE DELLE TERME, ROME.
PHOTOGRAPH: ALINARI—ART REFERENCE BUREAU
(*Cf. p. 178*)

Figure 55   Aphrodite on a swan. White-ground Attic cylix, *ca.* 465 B.C.
BRITISH MUSEUM, LONDON.
PHOTOGRAPH: ALINARI—ART REFERENCE BUREAU
(*Cf. p. 179*)

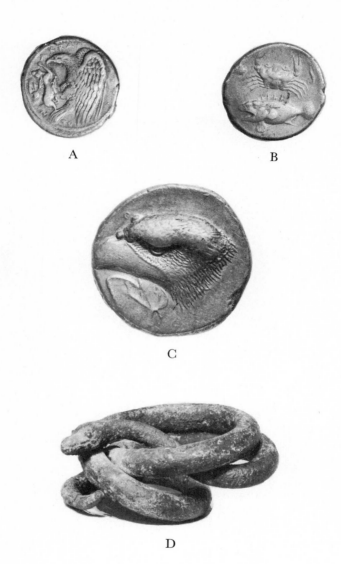

A   B

C

D

Figure 56 (A, B)   Eagle and hare, sea perch, and crab on silver tetradrachms of Acragas; (C) eagle on a silver didrachm of Elis; (D) bronze snake, 5th century B.C.
A, B, D, THE METROPOLITAN MUSEUM OF ART, ROGERS FUND, 1919.
C, COURTESY, MUSEUM OF FINE ARTS, BOSTON.
(*Cf. p. 179*)

Figure 57 Forgery of a Greek bronze horse, in the style of the 5th century B.C. (but kept on display because of its genuine beauty).

THE METROPOLITAN MUSEUM OF ART.

(*Cf. p. 179*)

Figure 58   Bronze statuette of a cow from Herculanum, late 5th century B.C.
BIBLIOTHEQUE NATIONALE, PARIS.
PHOTOGRAPH: GIRAUDON—ART REFERENCE BUREAU
(*Cf. p. 179*)

Figure 59 Bronze statuette of a deer, late 5th century B.C.
THE LOUVRE, PARIS.
PHOTOGRAPH: ALINARI—ART REFERENCE BUREAU
(*Cf. p. 179*)

Figure 60 Bronze objects illustrating Greek life. Left to right, top to bottom: Candelabrum, Ladle, Physician's probe, Stylus, Key, Ink wells, Mirror, Colander.
THE METROPOLITAN MUSEUM OF ART.
(*Cf. pp. 179, 244*)

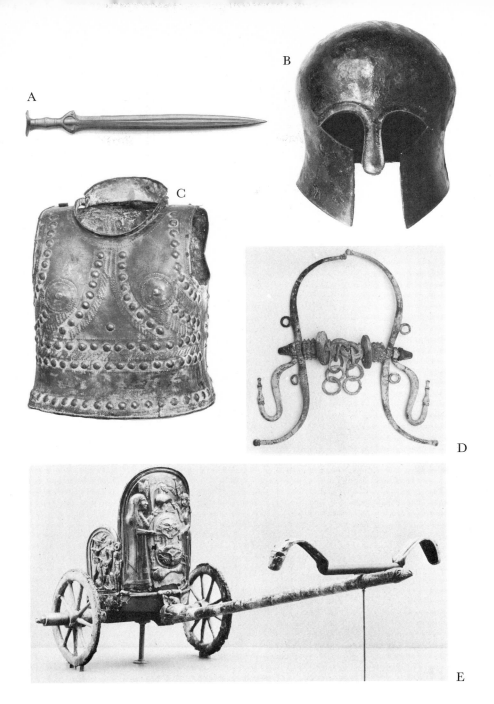

Figure 61 Bronze objects illustrating Greek life.
(A) Sword, bronze, Greek, Bronze Age; (B) Helmet of Corinthian type, bronze, 6th century B.C.; (C) Cuirass, bronze, Italic, *ca.* late 8th century B.C.; (D) Horse's bit, bronze, Roman, Imperial Period; (E) Biga (two-horse chariot), wood with bronze sheathing, Etruscan relief, from Monteleone, *ca.* 550–540 B.C.

(*Cf. pp. 179, 244*)

Figure 62 Herm of Pericles. Roman copy of the 5th century B.C. bronze original by Cresilas.

BRITISH MUSEUM, LONDON.

PHOTOGRAPH: FLEMING—ART REFERENCE BUREAU

(*Cf. pp. 181, 243*)

Figure 63 Bronze and terracotta objects illustrating Greek life.
(A) Statuette: Armorer working on helmet, bronze, Greek sculpture, 8th century B.C.
(Geometric Period);· (B) Statuette of an actor (caricature), inlaid with silver and
niello, Greek, *ca.* 300–100 B.C.; (C) Dicast's ticket; (D) Statuette of Standing draped
girl, terracotta, Tanagra type, Greek, 4th century B.C.; (E) Tragic mask; (F) Statuette:
Girl dancing, terracotta, from Tarentum, Greek, 3rd century B.C.
THE METROPOLITAN MUSEUM OF ART, (A) FLETCHER FUND; (B), (C), (D), (E), (F) ROGERS
FUND.
(*Cf. pp. 195, 244*)

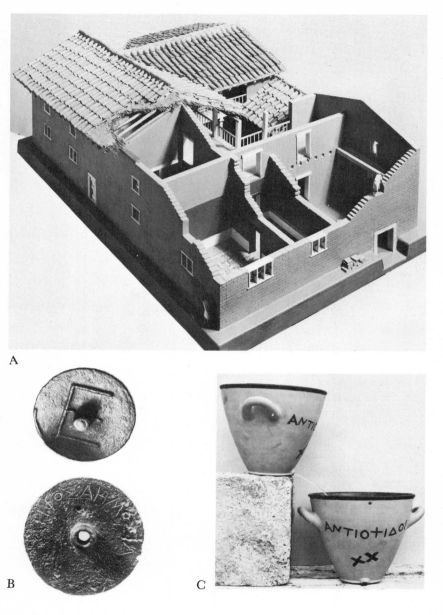

Figure 64 (A) Model of the "Villa of Good Fortune" at Olynthus, as seen from the northwest. Late 5th to first half of 4th century B.C. The American excavation at Olynthus revealed for the first time a large Greek city of the period before Alexander the Great; (B) Dicast's (juror's) ballots; (C) Dicast's water clock (See Appendix for detailed descriptions)

ROYAL ONTARIO MUSEUM, TORONTO.

PHOTOGRAPHS: AGORA EXCAVATIONS, AMERICAN SCHOOL OF CLASSICAL STUDIES AT ATHENS

Figure 65 The Temple of Hephaestus, from the southeast, overlooking the American excavations in the west end of the Athenian Agora; the circular Tholos is in the left foreground. The Eleusinian procession followed the Sacred Way from the city wall across Mt. Aegaleos (left background) to Eleusis. Mt. Parnes to the right.

(Cf. p. 246, Figure 66, and Appendix)

Figure 66 Plaster model of buildings along west side of the Athenian Agora: The Tholos (left), Metroön (directly behind, the Bouleuterion), Stoa of Zeus; rear, the Temple of Hephaestus. PHOTOGRAPH: AGORA EXCAVATIONS, AMERICAN SCHOOL OF CLASSICAL STUDIES AT ATHENS (*Cf. pp. 248, 252, 256, and Appendix*)

Figure 67   Aerial view of the Athenian Agora, from the southwest.
(*Cf. p. 248*)

Figure 68 Greek theatre.
(*Cf. p. 250*)

Figure 69 The choregic monument of Lysicrates at Athens, 334 B.C.
PHOTOGRAPH: ALINARI—ART REFERENCE BUREAU
(*Cf. pp. 252, 360*)

Figure 70 The Areopagus, Acropolis, and Mt. Hymettus, from the northwest. The Athenian Agora begins at the left of the photograph.

PHOTOGRAPH: ALISON FRANTZ

(Cf. p. 252, Figure 81, and Appendix)

Figure 71 The Parthenon, from the northwest. Athens, 447–432 B.C. (Cf. p. 252)

Figure 72   Procession of horsemen, from the Parthenon frieze, 442–438 B.C.

PHOTOGRAPH: BOISSONNAS

(*Cf. p. 254, and Appendix*)

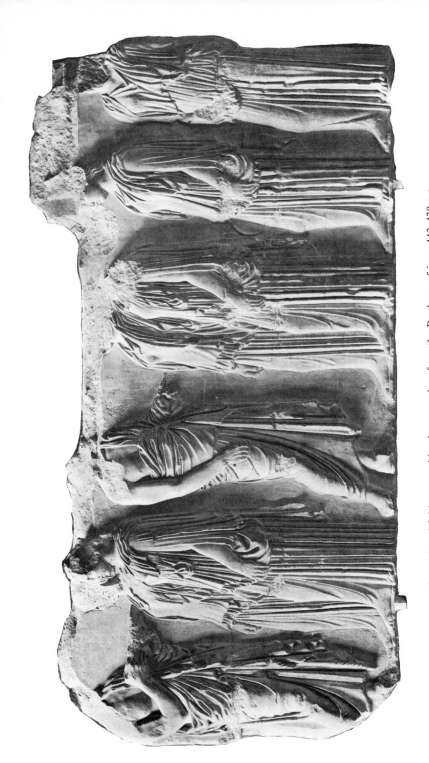

Figure 73 Maidens marching in procession, from the Parthenon frieze, 442–438 B.C.

THE LOUVRE, PARIS.

PHOTOGRAPH: ALINARI—ART REFERENCE BUREAU

(*Cf. p. 254, and Appendix*)

Figure 74 The "Three Fates," from the east pediment of the Parthenon, 438–432 B.C.
BRITISH MUSEUM, LONDON.

PHOTOGRAPH: FLEMING—ART REFERENCE BUREAU

(*Cf. p. 255*)

Figure 75 (A) "Theseus"; (B) Head of the horse of Selene. Both from the east pediment of the Parthenon, 438–432 B.C.

BRITISH MUSEUM, LONDON.

PHOTOGRAPH: FLEMING—ART REFERENCE BUREAU

(*Cf. p. 255*)

Figure 76 The Periclean entrance court of the Acropolis, perspective view. Drawn by G. P. Stevens.
(Cf. pp. 255, 256)

Figure 77   The Temple of Athena Nike, from the southeast. Athens, *ca.* 423 B.C. (*Cf. p. 255*)

Figure 78   Nike fastening her sandal, from the parapet of the Athena Nike Temple, *ca.* 410 B.C.

ACROPOLIS MUSEUM, ATHENS.

PHOTOGRAPH: ALINARI—ART REFERENCE BUREAU

(*Cf. p. 255*)

Figure 79 The Erechtheum, from the south. Athens, *ca.* 421–406 B.C.

PHOTOGRAPH: KENNEDY

(*Cf. p. 256*)

Figure 80 The Erechtheum. Porch of the Caryatids. *(Cf. p. 256)*

Figure 81 Plaster model of the Athenian Acropolis, from the west.

PHOTOGRAPH: AGORA EXCAVATIONS, AMERICAN SCHOOL OF CLASSICAL STUDIES AT ATHENS

(Cf. p. 256)

Figure 82 The temple of Poseidon at Sunium, *ca.* 425 B.C. (*Cf. p. 257*)

Figure 83 Stele (tombstone) of Hegeso, from the Cerameicus, *ca.* 400 B.C.
NATIONAL MUSEUM, ATHENS.
PHOTOGRAPH: ALINARI—ART REFERENCE BUREAU
(*Cf. p. 257*)

Figure 84   The Doryphorus, from Pompeii. Roman copy of a bronze original by the Argive Polycleitus, *ca.* 450 B.C.

MUSEO NAZIONALE, NAPLES.

PHOTOGRAPH: ALINARI—ART REFERENCE BUREAU

(*Cf. p. 257*)

Figure 85 (A)   The Nike, from Olympia, by Paeonius of Mende, *ca.* 420 B.C.
OLYMPIA MUSEUM.
PHOTOGRAPH: ALINARI—ART REFERENCE BUREAU
(*Cf. p.* 257)

Figure 85 (B)   Heron, chalcedony scaraboid (enlarged), Attributed to Dexamenus.
Greek, 5th century B.C.
COURTESY, MUSEUM OF FINE ARTS, BOSTON.
(*Cf. p. 257*)

Figure 86 Sophocles. Roman copy of Greek original of the 4th century B.C.
THE LATERAN, ROME.
PHOTOGRAPH: ALINARI—ART REFERENCE BUREAU
(*Cf. p. 260*)

Figure 87 Euripides. Roman copy of Greek original of the 4th century B.C.
THE VATICAN, ROME.
PHOTOGRAPH: ALINARI—ART REFERENCE BUREAU
(*Cf. p. 261*)

Figure 88 Statuette of Socrates. Hellenistic copy of 4th century B.C. original.
BRITISH MUSEUM, LONDON.
PHOTOGRAPH: FLEMING—ART REFERENCE BUREAU
(*Cf. p. 266*)

Figure 89 Demosthenes. Roman copy of an original by Polyeuctus, 280 B.C.
THE VATICAN, ROME.
PHOTOGRAPH: ALINARI—ART REFERENCE BUREAU
(*Cf. pp. 298, 368, 442*)

Figure 90 (A) Portrait of the deified Alexander on a silver tetradrachm of Lysimach-
us, 3rd century B.C. (above); (B) Silver tetradrachm of Heliocles of Bactria (left); and
(C) Silver tetradrachm of Antimachus I of Bactria, 2nd century, B.C. (right).
COURTESY, MUSEUM OF FINE ARTS, BOSTON.
(*Cf. pp. 306, 442*)

Figure 91 Aristotle. Roman copy of Greek original.
MUSEO NAZIONALE DELLE TERME, ROME.
PHOTOGRAPH: ALINARI—ART REFERENCE BUREAU
(*Cf. pp. 308, 372*)

Figure 92 Alexander the Great (on fragment of horse, left) at the battle of Darius and Alexander at Issus. Late Hellenistic mosaic from Pompeii, after a picture by Philoxenus of Eretria, *ca.* 300 B.C. MUSEO NAZIONALE, NAPLES.

PHOTOGRAPH: ALINARI—ART REFERENCE BUREAU

(*Cf. pp. 319n, 363*)

Figure 93 The rotunda, or Tholos, at Epidaurus. Designed by Polycleitus the Younger, *ca.* 350 B.C.

EPIDAURUS MUSEUM.

PHOTOGRAPH: BOISSONNAS

(*Cf. p. 360*)

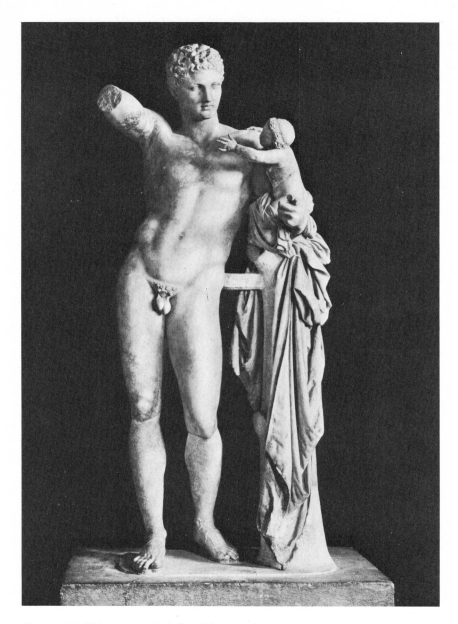

Figure 94 Hermes and the infant Dionysus, from Heraeum at Olympia, By Praxiteles of Athens, *ca.* 350 B.C.

OLYMPIA MUSEUM.

PHOTOGRAPH: ALINARI—ART REFERENCE BUREAU

(*Cf. p. 361*)

Figure 95 Bronze youth, from the sea off Marathon. School of Praxiteles, late 4th century B.C.

NATIONAL MUSEUM, ATHENS.

PHOTOGRAPH: MARBURG—ART REFERENCE BUREAU

(*Cf. p. 362*)

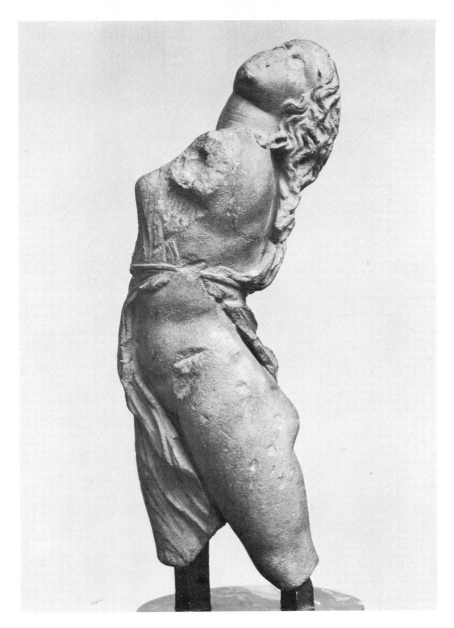

Figure 96   Statuette of a dancing Maenad. Roman copy after an original, probably
by Scopas of Paros, *ca.* 350 B.C.
STAATLICHE KUNSTSAMMLUNG, DRESDEN.
(*Cf. p. 362*)

Figure 97 Demeter, from Cnidus, *ca.* 350 B.C.
BRITISH MUSEUM, LONDON.
PHOTOGRAPH: FLEMING—ART REFERENCE BUREAU
(*Cf. p. 362*)

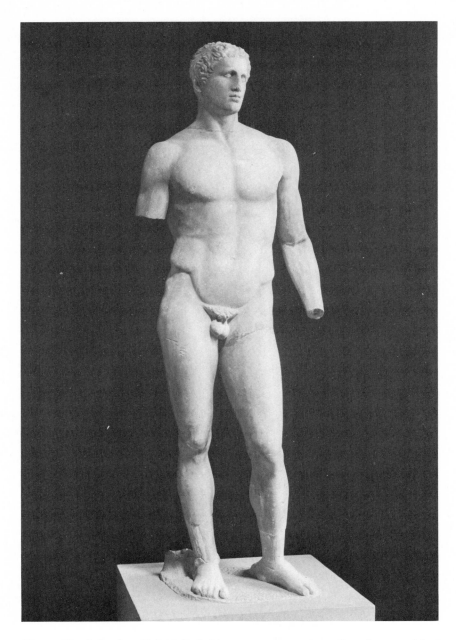

Figure 98 Agias, from Delphi. Probably a contemporary copy after a bronze original by Lysippus of Sicyon, *ca.* 337 B.C.

DELPHI MUSEUM.

PHOTOGRAPH: ALINARI—ART REFERENCE BUREAU

(*Cf. p. 362*)

Figure 99 (A) Ptolemy I; gold Stater; *ca.* 305 B.C. (left) ; (B) Antiochus I; portrait of Seleucus; *ca.* 280 B.C. (right). Coins of the fourth and third centuries B.C. AMERICAN NUMISMATIC SOCIETY, NEW YORK. (*Cf. p. 363*)

Figure 100 1. Demetrius Poliorcetes; 2. Seleucus I; 3. Antiochus I; Tetradrachm;
4. Antiochus II; Tetradrachm; 5. Philetaerus; 6. Ptolemy I; 7. Ptolemy II Philadelphus, and Arsinoe II (gold); 8. Arsinoe II; Decadrachm.

(*Cf. pp. 383, 415, 442*)

Figure 101   The Nike from Samothrace. By a Rhodian sculptor, mid-3rd century B.C.
THE LOUVRE, PARIS.
PHOTOGRAPH: ALINARI—ART REFERENCE BUREAU
(*Cf. p. 441*)

Figure 102 The Drinking Contest of Herakles and Dionysus. First century A.D. mosaic from Antioch, inspired by a Hellenistic painting.

Figure 103   Bronze head of a Berber. Hellenistic.
BRITISH MUSEUM, LONDON.
PHOTOGRAPH: FLEMING—ART REFERENCE BUREAU
(*Cf. p. 440*)

Figure 104 Dying Gaul. Roman copy of one of a group of originals dedicated by Attalus I in the court of the Temple of Athena at Pergamum, *ca.* 235–225 B.C. The Gauls, or Galatians, were among the fiercest fighters ever met by the Greeks.

CAPITOLINE MUSEUM, ROME.

PHOTOGRAPH: ALINARI—ART REFERENCE BUREAU

(*Cf. p. 441*)

Figure 105 Dying Persian. Roman copy of part of the dedication of Attalus I of Pergamum, *ca.* 235–225 B.C.

MUSEO NAZIONALE DELLE TERME, ROME.

PHOTOGRAPH: ALINARI—ART REFERENCE BUREAU

(*Cf. p. 441*)

Figure 106   A Gaul and his wife. Roman copy of part of the dedication in bronze by
Attalus I of Pergamum, *ca.* 235–225 B.C.
(*Cf. p. 441*)

Figure 107 The Aphrodite from Melos. Mid-2nd century B.C., by a sculptor of Antioch on the Maender, inspired by a late 4th century work.

THE LOUVRE, PARIS.

PHOTOGRAPH: ALINARI—ART REFERENCE BUREAU

(*Cf. p. 442*)

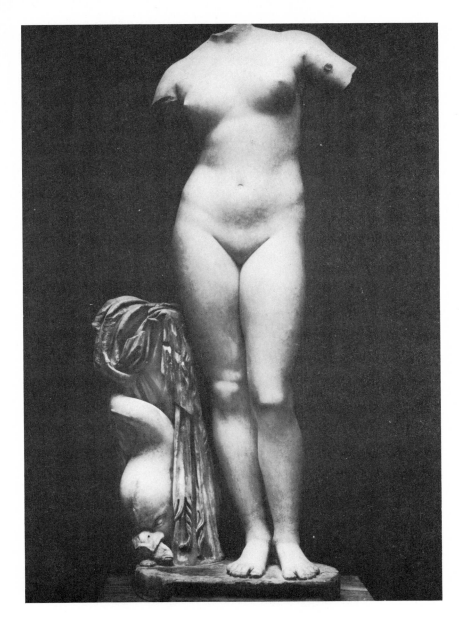

Figure 108   The Aphrodite from Cyrene. Roman copy of a late 4th century work.
MUSEO NAZIONALE DELLE TERME, ROME.
PHOTOGRAPH: ALINARI—ART REFERENCE BUREAU
(Cf. p. 442)

Figure 109 Drunken old woman. Roman copy after a bronze original, perhaps by Myron of Thebes, 2nd century B.C.

STAATLICHE ANTIKENSAMMLUNGEN UND GLYPTOTHEK, MUNCHEN.

(*Cf. p. 442*)

Figure 110 Old market woman, from Rome. 2nd century B.C.
THE METROPOLITAN MUSEUM OF ART.
(*Cf. p. 442*)

Figure 111 Bronze rider and horse, from the sea off Euboea, *ca.* 200 B.C.
NATIONAL MUSEUM, ATHENS.
PHOTOGRAPH: SEMNI KAROUZOU
(*Cf. p. 442*)

Figure 112   Bronze statue of a "Hellenistic Prince," from Rome. Probably by Apollonius, son of Nestor, *ca.* 50 B.C.

MUSEO NAZIONALE DELLE TERME, ROME.

PHOTOGRAPH: ALINARI—ART REFERENCE BUREAU

(*Cf. p. 442*)

Figure 113 Model of the north end of the Hellenistic Stoa of Attalus II. Two stories high (with outside stairs), 382 feet long and 64 feet wide, the Stoa stood at the east side of the Athenian Agora and has now been restored by the American excavators as the Agora Museum. The facade was of white and blue marble, with a terrace in front and a fountain house to the south. The 21 shops on each floor looked out on the principal square through a two-aisled colonnade. Portraits of distinguished citizens and of Hermes, God of Commerce, were set up within the Stoa.

AMERICAN SCHOOL OF CLASSICAL STUDIES AT ATHENS.

(*Cf. Appendix, p. 502*)

Chapter XIII THE PELOPONNESIAN WAR

THE ARCHIDAMIAN WAR, 431–421 B.C.

THE great historian,[1] whose genius it was to reduce the actualities of life to their generic and hence their lasting patterns, opens his *History of the Peloponnesian War* with these words:

Thucydides, an Athenian, wrote the history of the war in which the Peloponnesians and the Athenians fought against one another. He began to write when they first took up arms, believing that it would be great and memorable above any previous war. For he

[1] Thucydides, the son of Olorus, took part in the Peloponnesian War; see pp. 269 ff. for a fuller discussion. The translations here and elsewhere are those of B. Jowett (except as noted), with a few slight changes and much abbreviated. Thucydides' *History* comes to an end in the course of 411 B.C.; for the remainder of the War we are dependent on Xenophon's *Hellenica.* Also useful are Diodorus (who drew from Ephorus), various *Lives* of Plutarch, the comedies of Aristophanes, the tragedies of Sophocles and Euripides, Aristotle's *Constitution of Athens,* and inscriptions.

argued that both states were then at the full height of their military power, and he saw the rest of the Hellenes either siding or intending to side with one or other of them. No movement ever stirred Hellas more deeply than this; it was shared by many of the barbarians, and might be said even to affect the world at large. The character of the events which preceded, whether immediately or in more remote antiquity, owing to the lapse of time cannot be made out with certainty. But, judging from the evidence which I am able to trust after most careful inquiry, I should imagine that former ages were not great either in their wars or in anything else. And, though men will always judge any war in which they are actually fighting to be the greatest at the time, but, after it is over, revert to their admiration of some other which has preceded, still the Peloponnesian, if estimated by the actual facts, will certainly prove to have been the greatest ever known.

As to the speeches which were made either before or during the war, it was hard for me, and for others who reported them to me, to recollect the exact words. I have therefore put into the mouth of each speaker the sentiments proper to the occasion, expressed as I thought he would be likely to express them, while at the same time I endeavored, as nearly as I could, to give the general purport of what was actually said. Of the events of the war I have not ventured to speak from any chance information, nor according to any notion of my own; I have described nothing but what I either saw myself, or learned from others of whom I made the most careful and particular inquiry. The task was a laborious one, because eye-witnesses of the same occurrences gave different accounts of them, as they remembered or where interested in the actions of one side or the other. And very likely the strictly historical character of my narrative may be disappointing to the ear. But if he who desires to have before his eyes a true picture of the events which have happened, and of the like events which may be expected to happen hereafter in the order of human things, shall pronounce what I have written to be useful, then I shall be satisfied. My history is an everlasting possession, not a prize composition which is heard and forgotten.

The greatest achievement of former times was the Persian War; yet even this was speedily decided in two battles by sea and two by land. But the Peloponnesian War was a protracted struggle, and attended by calamities such as Hellas had never known within a like period of time. Never were so many cities captured and depopulated—some by barbarians, others by Hellenes themselves fighting against one another; and several of them after their capture were repeopled by strangers. Never were exile and slaughter more frequent, whether in the war or brought about by civil strife. And rumors, of which the like had often been current before, but rarely verified by fact, now appeared to be well grounded. There were earthquakes unparalleled in their extent and fury, and eclipses of the sun more numerous than are recorded to have happened in any former age; there were also in some places great droughts causing famines, and lastly the plague which did immense harm and destroyed numbers of the people. All these calamities fell upon Hellas simultaneously with the war, which began when the Athenians and Peloponnesians violated the thirty years' truce concluded by them after the recapture of Euboea. Why they broke it and what were the grounds of quarrel I will first set forth, that in time to come no man may be at a loss to know what was the origin of this great war. The real though unavowed cause I believe to have been the growth of the Athenian power, which terrified the Lacedaemonians and forced them into war; but the reasons publicly alleged on either side were as follows.[2]

Taken in a general way, Thucydides statement that the real reason for the Peloponnesian War was the Spartan fear of the Athenians and their increasing power seems fair. Not only had Athens' aggressions in the preceding half-century often been successful, but they had been aimed at many different quarters. Was there a limit to Athenian ambition, or must all states eventually bow before it? On the other hand, the dualism into which Greece had settled might have lasted, in spite of the growing antipathy between Sparta and Athens.

Among the causes of hostility was an Athenian claim to leadership generally considered incompatible with the liberties of individual states and with the long-established policy of Lacedaemon. The Athenians asserted that their hegemony had been forced upon them by Sparta's unwillingness to continue the war with Persia, that circumstances not under their control had converted the Delian League into an empire, and that, though they had been compelled thus to usurp an authority, they had made good their right to it by a justice and a moderation unparalleled in history. Against this claim their enemies, particularly the Corinthians, charged Athens with the enslavement of her allies and with the design of reducing other Hellenes to servitude, and called upon Sparta to take the lead in putting down the tyrant. The Spartans, in spite of their own constitution, considered themselves champions of the principle of city sovereignty, and were so regarded by their allies. Fear of Athens and the universal Greek love of liberty, then, were contributing factors to the Peloponnesian War.

Rivalry in trade was, of course, another irritant. For many decades Athenian pottery had enjoyed a virtual monopoly of the Italian market. Furthermore, the presence of Naupactus and the recent alliance with Corcyra proved that Athens wished to control the West as she did the East. The trade of Megara, Corinth, and Sicyon had been hurt. Finally, the difference in outlook between Sparta and Athens was immense. One, a Dorian state, was reactionary and narrow-minded, and in her splendid isolation headed a powerful land empire. The other, Ionian in blood and tradition, was democratic and progressive, the intellectual

---

[2] Thucydides, I, 1, 21–23.

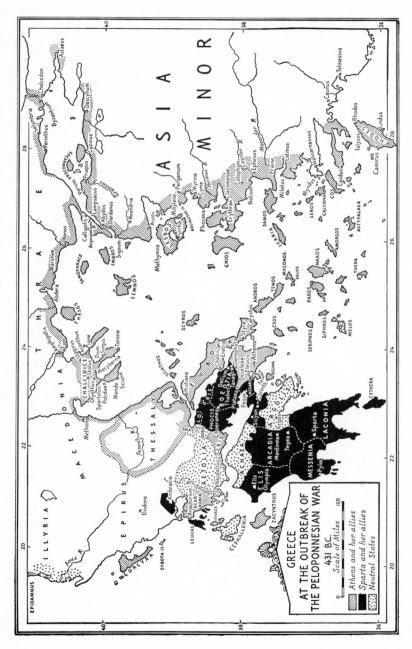

GREECE
AT THE OUTBREAK OF
THE PELOPONNESIAN WAR
431 B.C.
Scale of Miles

Athens and her allies
Sparta and her allies
Neutral States

Map 31

208

capital of Hellas and the possessor of a far-flung empire. These various factors, not one of which in itself was sufficient for war, charged the atmosphere of Greece with suspicion and hatred, so that any incident might force Sparta to lead the Peloponnesians against her rival. Even so, Greece might have survived the Megarian decree, the incidents at Corcyra and Potidaea, but the Theban attack on Plataea showed that it was futile to hope for peace any longer.

Pericles, now a man of sixty, not only was reconciled to war, but was convinced that it was better that it should come while he was still in the prime of life and Athens in excellent military condition. Hence he persuaded his countrymen to oppose every concession to the Peloponnesians. Knowing better than any contemporary the resources of Athens and her enemy, Pericles had ground for confidence. Arrayed against his state were the forces of nearly all the Peloponnesians—consisting of 24,000 hoplites and many light-armed troops—of the Boeotian confederacy under Theban leadership—with 10,000 hoplites and 1,000 cavalry—of lesser allies in the center and west of the peninsula. Obviously, the strategy of the Peloponnesians was to invade Attica and devastate the fields, hoping that the Athenians would be provoked into making a sally from their walls. But this was just what Athens must not do. The Athenian army consisted of 1,000 cavalry and 13,000 hoplites, but many of these were necessary to defend the Long Walls and the frontier forts, while others were absent at the siege of Potidaea. The strategy of Pericles, therefore, was to bring the entire population of the country, with their movable goods, into the city, although this meant the devastation of the fields. The enemy would not remain long in the country, because most of the Peloponnesians were small farmers, who personally tilled their lands, and because they had to bring their food supplies with them. However much they might ravage the fields, they could accomplish nothing against the strong fortifications of Athens and Piraeus. The Athenian fleet, manned by the *thetes* and allies, commanded the sea and would ensure the steady arrival at Athens of food supplies. In addition, the fleet would attack the coasts of the Peloponnesus and cut off its commerce; thus, while partially compensating the Athenians for damage to their fields, Pericles would gradually force the enemy to recognize Athens' right to her empire. Against the almost total lack of public funds among the enemy could be reckoned 6,000 talents stored in the treasuries on the Acropolis and an annual income from the tribute and other sources amounting to about 1,000 talents. The Peloponnesians conceived the idea of borrowing from the treasuries of Delphi and Olympia to enlarge their fleet, but it proved an idle dream.

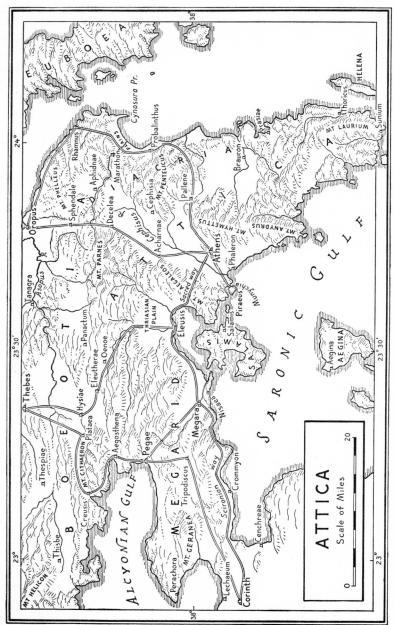

ATTICA

Scale of Miles

Map 32

210

In the spring of 431 B.C. the enemy entered Attica, under the able Spartan king, Archidamus, after whom the first ten years of the Peloponnesian War have been named. The orchards and the ripe grain in the fields were cut down. Pericles' cold calculating plan of removing the population into the city subjected Athenian nature to an excessive strain. The people were reluctant to leave their homes because of their long-continued life of independence in the country districts. They longed to go forth and fight the enemy. Gathering in knots on the streets, they complained bitterly of their plight, and laid the whole blame of the war and their losses upon Pericles. Tragic as was this first year in the struggle between two evenly balanced foes, it was as nothing compared to the years ahead. Two decades later, while the war still had several years to run, we can catch the pathos of it all in the *Lysistrata* of Aristophanes, for, in spite of the buffoonery of the comic poet, we see the ruin of family life at Athens, we see generation after generation of men swept away, leaving the women desolate, robbed of husbands, lovers, and children (Map 38).

Pericles, however, maintained his policy at home in spite of the grumblings, and sent a fleet to ravage the Peloponnesian coast. In the autumn he persuaded the people to decree a reserve of 1,000 talents, to be used only in case of an attack by sea, and to keep 100 triremes always at home in defense of Piraeus. In his naval operations and in diplomacy he had made real gains, and was undoubtedly pleased with the results. After the campaign the remains of those who had fallen in battle during the summer were solemnly conveyed to the cemetery in the Cerameicus— a beautiful spot outside the walls—and interred amid the lamentations of their kin, citizens and metics, women, and men. An empty bed, covered with a sheet, honored those whose bodies had not been recovered. After the burial Pericles addressed the people in a Funeral Oration, one of the most precious documents in the history of civilization. The Funeral Oration is much more than a defense of his own policy or a mere eulogy of Athens. It is a description of the ideal of Pericles in his best moments.

"Our constitution is named a democracy," said Pericles, "because it is in the hands not of the few but of the many. But our laws secure equal justice for all in their private disputes, and our public opinion welcomes and honors talent in every branch of achievement, not for any sectional reason but on grounds of excellence alone. And as we give free play to all in our public life, so we carry the same spirit into our daily relations with one another. We have no black looks or angry words for our neighbor if he enjoys himself in his own way, and we abstain from the little acts of churlishness which, though they leave no mark, yet cause annoyance to whoso notes them. Open and friendly in our private intercourse, in our public acts we keep strictly within the control of law. We acknowledge the restraint of reverence; we are obedient to whomsoever is set in authority, and to the laws, more especially to those which offer protection to the oppressed and those unwritten ordinances whose transgression brings admitted shame.

"Yet ours is no work-a-day city only. No other provides so many recreations for the spirit—contests and sacrifices all the year round, and beauty in our public buildings to cheer the heart and delight the eye day by day. We are lovers of beauty without extravagance, and we cultivate wisdom without weakness. Wealth to us is not mere material for vainglory but an opportunity for achievement; and poverty we think it no disgrace to acknowledge but a real degradation to make no effort to overcome. Our citizens attend both to public and private duties, and do not allow absorption in their own various affairs to interfere with their knowledge of the city's. We differ from other states in regarding the man who holds aloof from public life not as 'quiet' but as useless; we decide or debate, carefully and in person, all matters of policy, holding, not that words and deeds go ill together, but that acts are foredoomed to failure when undertaken undiscussed. For we are noted for being at once most adventurous in action and most reflective beforehand. Other men are bold in ignorance, while reflection will stop their onset. But the bravest are surely those who have the clearest vision of what is before them, glory and danger alike, and yet notwithstanding go out to meet it. In a word I claim that Athens is the school of Hellas, and that her members yield to none, man by man, for independence of spirit, many-sidedness of attainment, and complete self-reliance in limbs and brain.

"Such then is the city for whom, lest they should lose her, the men whom we celebrate died a soldier's death: and it is but natural that all of us, who survive them, should wish to spend ourselves in her service. That, indeed, is why I have spent many words upon the city. I wished to show that we have more at stake than men who have no such inheritance, and to support my praise of the dead by making clear to you what they have done.

"We survivors may pray to be spared their bitter hour, but must disdain to meet the foe with a spirit less triumphant. Let us draw strength, not merely from twice-told arguments—how fair and noble a thing it is to show courage in battle—but from the busy spectacle of our great city's life as we have it before us day by day, falling in love with her as we see her, and remembering that all this greatness she owes to men with the fighter's daring, the wise man's understanding of his duty, and the good man's self-discipline in its performance—to men who, if they failed in any ordeal, disdained to deprive the city of their services, but sacrificed their lives as the best offerings on her behalf. So they gave their bodies to the commonwealth and received, each for his own memory, praise that will never die, and with it the grandest of all sepulchres, not that in which their mortal bones are laid, but a home in the minds of men, where their glory remains fresh to stir to speech or action as the occasion comes by. For the whole earth is the sepulchre of famous men; and their story is not graven only on stone over their native earth, but lives on far away, without visible symbol, woven into the stuff of other men's lives. For you now it remains to rival what they have done and, knowing the secret of happiness to be freedom and the secret of freedom a brave heart, not idly to stand aside from the enemy's onset." [3]

In the second year of the war there was the usual invasion of Attica by the Peloponnesians and the Athenian voyage of desolation along the Peloponnesian coast. In fact, these operations were as a rule repeated during the early period of the war. The season had not far advanced, however, before a terrible plague, beginning in the East, reached Piraeus. Soon it passed up between the Long Walls to Athens.

As to the plague's probable origin [says Thucydides] or the causes which might or could have produced such a disturbance of nature, every man, whether a physician or not, will give his own opinion. But I shall describe its actual course, and the symptoms by which any one who knows them beforehand may recognize the disorder should it ever reappear. For I was myself attacked, and witnessed the sufferings of others.

The season was admitted to have been remarkably free from ordinary sickness; and if anybody was already ill of any other disease, it was absorbed in this. Many who were in perfect health, all in a moment, and without any apparent reason, were seized with violent heats in the head and with redness and inflammation of the eyes. Internally the throat and the tongue were quickly suffused with blood, and the breath became unnatural and fetid. There followed sneezing and hoarseness; in a short time the disorder, accompanied by a violent cough, reached the chest; then fastening lower down, it would move the stomach and bring on all the vomits of bile to which physicians have ever given names; and they were very distressing. An ineffectual retching producing violent convulsions attacked most of the sufferers; some as soon as the previous symptoms had abated, others not until long afterwards. The body externally was not so very hot to the touch, nor yet pale; it was of a livid color inclining to red, and breaking out in pustules and ulcers. But the internal fever was intense; the suffers could not bear to have on. them even the finest linen garment; they insisted on being naked, and there was nothing which they longed for more eagerly than to throw themselves into cold water. And many of those who had no one to look after them actually plunged into the cisterns, for they were tormented by unceasing thirst, which was not in the least assuaged whether they drank little or much. They could not sleep; a restlessness which was intolerable never left them. While the disease was at its height the body, instead of wasting away, held out amid these sufferings in a marvellous manner, and either they died on the seventh or ninth day, not of weakness, for their strength was not exhausted, but of internal fever, which was the end of most; or, if they survived, then the disease descended into the

[3] Thucydides, II, 37–43. A. Zimmern's translation, with a few slight changes and much abbreviated.

bowels and there produced violent ulceration; severe diarrhoea at the same time set in, and at a later stage caused exhaustion, which finally with few exceptions carried them off. For the disorder which had originally settled in the head passed gradually through the whole body, and, if a person got over the worst, would often seize the extremities and leaves its mark, attacking the genitals and the fingers and the toes; and some escaped with the loss of these, some with the loss of their eyes. Some again had no sooner recovered than they were seized with a forgetfulness of all things and knew neither themselves nor their friends.

The crowding of the people out of the country into the city aggravated the misery; and the newly arrived suffered most. For, having no houses of their own, but inhabiting in the height of summer stifling huts, the mortality among them was dreadful, and they perished in wild disorder. The dead lay as they had died, one upon another, while others hardly alive wallowed in the streets and crawled about every fountain craving for water. The temples in which they lodged were full of the corpses of those who died in them; for the violence of the calamity was such that men, not knowing where to turn, grew reckless of all law, human and divine. The customs which had hitherto been observed at funerals were universally violated, and they buried their dead each one as best he could. Many, having no proper appliances, because the deaths in their household had been so frequent, made no scruple of using the burial-place of others. When one man had raised a funeral pile, others would come, and throwing on their dead first, set fire to it; or when some other corpse was already burning, before they could be stopped would throw their own dead upon it and depart.

There were other and worse forms of lawlessness which the plague introduced at Athens. Men who had hitherto concealed their indulgence in pleasure now grew bolder. For, seeing the sudden change, how the rich died in a moment, and those who had nothing immediately inherited their property, they reflected that life and riches were alike transitory, and they resolved to enjoy themselves while they could, and to think only of pleasure. Who would be willing to sacrifice himself to the law of honor when he knew not whether he would ever live to be held in honor? The pleasure of the moment and any sort of thing which conduced to it took the place both of honor and of expediency. No fear of God or law of man deterred a criminal. Those who saw all perishing alike, thought that the worship or neglect of the gods made no difference. For offenses against human law no punishment was to be feared; no one would live long enough to be called to account. Already a far heavier sentence had been passed and was hanging over a man's head; before that fell, why should he not take a little pleasure? [4]

Fully a third of the population was swept away by the plague. The discouragement was all the greater because at the beginning of the war the Delphic Apollo had promised aid to the foe; and the people now

[4] Thucydides, II, 48–49, 52–53.

attributed the plague to his enmity. Humbly the Athenians sought peace of Sparta; but, repulsed by her, they turned against Pericles as the author of their woes. In spite of all he could say in defense of his policy, they suspended him from office and fined him. Having thus satisfied their resentment, they soon afterward re-elected him general with absolute power. In 429 B.C., however, Pericles himself fell a victim of the plague. Thus passed away the only man who stood sufficiently high above all individuals and parties to command universal respect. The leadership of the government now passed to men of the industrial class, demagogues such as Cleon the tanner, who, unable to win the powerful support of the old nobility and of the moderate class, had to resort to lower politics and cater to the baser and more brutal desires and instincts of the populace. The revolution, thus silently effected, was as great as the century-long conflict at Rome which opened the consulship to the plebians, and in its immediate consequences far more sweeping, for in her war with the Peloponnesus Athens lost through the death of Pericles centralization of leadership and continuity of policy.

The war, with its many expeditions, small defeats and victories, was a grievous affliction to the Athenians. No land could be tilled beyond the neighborhood of Athens and Piraeus; the work in the mines of Laurium nearly ceased; and in spite of the Athenian naval supremacy, commerce was hampered by pirates and by the enemy's fleet. As the revenues decreased, the expenses greatly increased. For a time the difference was met by loans from the funds of Athena and of the Other Gods. The desire for profit helped keep the war going. Merchants and mechanics expected to suffer little from it, and might hope to extend their business through conquests; the poor found a livelihood in naval service, or looked to the enlargement of the Empire for increased tribute and a lengthened pay roll. The intellectuals, the landed aristocracy, and most farmers of moderate wealth, however, longed for peace.

In spite of the plague and the hardships, the advantage lay with Athens in the first years of the war. Potidaea finally fell in 430 B.C., but the siege had cost Athens 2,000 talents and she was unable to follow up her success in the Chalcidice. Similarly, in the northwest, the admiral Phormio won naval victories and damaged Corinthian trade, but no permanent gain resulted. The Peloponnesian army avoided Attica in 429 B.C., on account of the plague, and after a siege of two years took Plataea. The Peloponnesians constantly hoped for aid from Persia and Sicily, but in vain. In 428 B.C., however, news arrived that Mytilene and most of the other towns of Lesbos had revolted. In the face of this new peril and of the huge cost of sieges, the Athenians for the first time resorted to a property tax (*eisphora*), which yielded 200 talents. The following year Mytilene fell, and the Athenians, exasperated by the revolt and wishing to strike terror into the hearts of all disaffected allies, voted to put to death all the men of Mytilene and to enslave the women and children. The advocate of this policy of terrorism was Cleon. Immediately repenting, the people met the next day, reversed the cruel sentence, and limited the punishment of death to the few most guilty, but the lands of the rebels were confiscated and divided among Athenian colonists.

In 427 B.C. and again in 425 B.C. Athens sent aid to her friends in Sicily, to Segesta, Rhegium, and Leontini, the purpose of which was to check the power of Dorian Syracuse. The expeditions, however, led to no permanent result, for the Sicilians ironed out their differences in a conference at Gela. But in May, 425 B.C., an Athenian fleet, which was supposed to bring aid to Corcyra, was driven by a storm into the harbor of Pylos, where one of the generals, Demosthenes, had hoped they might halt in any case, because it was an excellent spot from which to raid the Peloponnesian coast. The other generals, Eurymedon and Sophocles, dared not disobey orders and, at storm's end, proceeded on their journey, leaving Demosthenes with five triremes. Demosthenes set to work to fortify the peninsula of Pylos, both on the south and at the north, where a narrow neck of sand connected it with the mainland.

Alarmed by the news that an Athenian contingent was actually established in southwestern Peloponnesus, the Spartan government ordered its army home from Attica and told Brasidas, its courageous and extraordinarily able general at Corcyra, to return with the fleet. On his arrival at Pylos, attacks were launched by land and sea on Demosthenes, but Demosthenes held and Brasidas was wounded. The Spartans then landed 420 hoplites, with their helots, on the island of Sphacteria, separated from Pylos by a narrow strait, and prepared to blockade the Athenians by sea. At this point Eurymedon and Sophocles, who were no longer needed at Corcyra, returned and in a surprise attack overwhelmed the Spartan fleet.

The Peloponnesians on Sphacteria were now the besieged, and the Spartan government was so disturbed by their predicament that a truce was negotiated and envoys were dispatched to Athens to offer not only peace but alliance. Cleon, however, with all the arts and ambitions of the demagogue, destroyed all hope of a truly great Hellenic peace by demanding Nisaea and Pegae, Troezen and Achaea, which Athens, twenty years earlier, in the days of Pericles, had been too weak to hold. So the war continued (cf. p. 179, Note).

But Demosthenes could not take Sphacteria, and by August Cleon

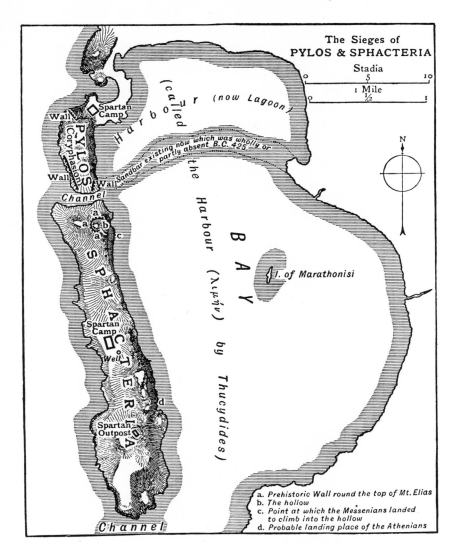

The Sieges of PYLOS & SPHACTERIA

Stadia
0   5   10

1 Mile
0   ½   1

Harbour (called (now Lagoon)

Sandbar existing now which was wholly or partly absent B.C. 425

the Harbour (Λιμήν) by Thucydides

B A Y

I. of Marathonisi

Spartan Camp

Wall

PYLOS (Coryphasion)

Wall   Wall

Channel

S P H A C T E R I A

a a
a b
c

Spartan Camp

Well

d

Spartan Outpost

Channel

N

a. *Prehistoric Wall round the top of Mt. Elias*
b. *The hollow*
c. *Point at which the Messenians landed to climb into the hollow*
d. *Probable landing place of the Athenians*

Map 33

was demanding in the Assembly that re-enforcements be sent. Nicias, the commander-in-chief, told Cleon that he might have his own powers as general, if he were so sure of himself; and Cleon, his bluff called, went off with overwhelming forces, saying that he would be victorious in twenty days. He relied, not without reason, on the generalship of Demosthenes. A surprise dawn attack on the island was successful, the

Spartans were driven behind some prehistoric walls, and then Cleon, realizing the value of capturing the enemy alive, offered quarter. The Spartans—their commander and 128 hoplites dead, no succor in sight, and being altogether in dire straits—asked their comrades on the mainland for advice and, when they were told to consult their own safety so long as it did not bring dishonor on them, surrendered. This act, so unusual for Spartans, astonished the Greek world, but Cleon, ready to reap the fruits of Demosthenes' victory, hurried back to Athens with his prisoners.

Cleon now stood without a rival at Athens, and in the flush of victory a reassessment of the Empire's tribute was carried through in 425 B.C. The allies were invited to send envoys to Athens to learn their fate, but they could hardly have guessed the cruel surprise in store for them, for the new assessment stood at more than 1,460 talents, three times the original assessment of Aristeides. The Athenians were now able to prosecute the war with greater energy and to raise the daily pay of the jurors from two obols to three. In vain the conservatives stood against Cleon; in vain Aristophanes sought in the *Knights* to crush him with ridicule and contempt. Although without military experience, Cleon was elected general in the spring of 424 B.C. and became more popular and dominant than ever.

The Athenians followed up their success at Pylos by seizing Cythera and other commanding positions along the Peloponnesian coast. But the tide began to turn. An attempt on Megara failed, though the harbor, Nisaea, and part of the Long Walls were captured. In an attempt to conquer Boeotia the Athenians were disastrously beaten at Delium. It was still more unfortunate for Athens that Brasidas, Sparta's ablest general, found the weak point in the Athenian Empire—the only part assailable by a land army, Chalcidice and its Thracian neighborhood. With a small force he stole northward, and appearing before Amphipolis persuaded that important city to revolt. These reverses induced the Athenian majority again to think of peace (423 B.C.). A truce of one year was followed by a renewal of the war, and then in a battle before Amphipolis both Brasidas and Cleon, the chief obstacles to peace, were killed.

Both sides were disappointed with the results of the war. The Peloponnesians had hoped to bring Athens to speedy terms by invading her territory, but had accomplished nothing in this direction, and they now saw their coast ravaged, their commerce cut off, and slaves and helots incited to desertion or rebellion by permanent Athenian garrisons on their border. In place of the naval supremacy they had hoped to win, they saw their triremes as well as their merchant ships swept from the seas. Athens, too, could balance her gains by as heavy losses in life and money; the reserves in the Acropolis were nearly exhausted; the main sources of prosperity had been choked by invasions; and the temper of the allies under their tribute was ominous. Under these circumstances the peace party, always strong, gained a majority in the Assembly. Their leader was Nicias, a man of great wealth and of respectable family. In the spring of 421 B.C. he negotiated the peace which bears his name. The Spartan king, Pleistoanax, who had been recalled from exile on the death of Archidamus, was equally anxious for peace. The Peace of Nicias was meant to endure for fifty years and in a general way provided for the exchange of prisoners and of captured cities. The subsequent alliance with Athens was necessary for Sparta, for she feared Corinth, which had been ruined by the war and stood to gain little by the Peace; and the Thirty Years' Truce with Argos would soon expire. The Athenian Empire, as Pericles had expected, came through the Archidamian War without great difficulty, but the present problem was to keep the Peace of Nicias.

THE PEACE OF NICIAS

Although the terms of peace were kept by neither side, the Lacedaemonians and the Athenians refrained from invading each other's territory for almost seven years. To most of the Athenians, apart from armorers and others whom war benefited, peace came as a boundless joy. Euripides, in the *Suppliants,* prays that war may never come again. The Agora overflowed with an unwonted happy life, as provisions grew more plentiful and prices dropped. The *Peace* of Aristophanes, presented at the City Dionysia of 421 B.C., represented the rural party as even more delighted with the new conditions. It was not merely to hard labor in the fields that the farmers trooped away, but also to rural pleasures, for the farmer was a Greek with the Greek view of life. In the midst of labors he found in homely festivals, in the gathering of friends to a simple meal in his house, rest from fatigues and an invigoration to future effort.

The outstanding feature of Athenian foreign policy in the next years was the dominating influence of Alcibiades, the nephew and ward of Pericles. Handsome, brilliant, vain, and daring, this young man had been petted and spoiled by his family and fellow citizens. Saturated in sophistic instruction, he recognized no principle but self-seeking, and deported himself in reckless violation of law and custom. Combining the arts of the demagogue with his own personal fascination, he won the generalship in 420 B.C., and at once began to rehabilitate the war party, in the hope of advancing his own interest.

Alcibiades' first moves were naturally directed toward the Peloponnesus. The Spartan alliance with Athens had been accompanied by a dissolution of the Peloponnesian League, for Sparta had been unable to persuade Corinth, Boeotia, and other states to accept the terms of peace. When the Thirty Years' Truce between Sparta and Argos came to an end in 421 B.C., Athens formed an alliance with Argos. Elis and Mantinea joined the alliance. Sparta, which meanwhile had placated Boeotia and Corinth, disastrously defeated the new allies at Mantinea in 418 B.C., restored her League, made a treaty with Argos, and left Athens isolated. A democratic revolution at Argos in 417 B.C. was followed in the next year by a new alliance with Athens (Map 43).

These actions were a serious blow to the cause of peace in Greece. The defeat at Mantinea robbed Athens of her advantageous position, and should have meant the downfall of Alcibiades. With this understanding of the situtaion Nicias, who had stood consistently for peace, now hoped to overthrow Alcibiades by a vote of ostracism. There was, however, a third party to the political struggle, Hyperbolus, the lamp maker, who with no knowledge of military affairs had risen from the industrial class to the leadership of those Athenians who looked to war for gain. Trained in oratory and successor to Cleon, though evidently inferior in ability, Hyperbolus dreamed of conquering Sicily and even of assailing Carthage. Alcibiades suggested to Nicias the advisability of joining forces to rid themselves of a man so hateful to both. The result was the ostracism of Hyperbolus in 417 B.C. It was the last time that ostracism was used at Athens, for the *graphe paranomon* was regarded as a sufficient safeguard for the state and a satisfactory weapon for assailing opponents. Hyperbolus' ostracism increased the importance of Alcibiades, whose war policy continually grew in favor with the Athenians.

Under Alcibiades' influence the Athenians sent an expedition in 416 B.C. against the island of Melos, a Dorian colony. In the famous Melian Dialogue that follows, Thucydides shows how the most humane state in the ancient world could be led to adopt the policy of might makes right, a resort to brutal force which aroused universal hatred and fear and gave to enemies a certain justification for the overthrow of Athens.

The Athenians made an expedition [says Thucydides] against the island of Melos with thirty ships of their own, six Chian, and two Lesbian, 1,200 hoplites and 300 archers besides twenty mounted archers of their own, and about 1,500 hoplites furnished by their allies in the islands. The Melians are colonists of the Lacedaemonians who would not submit to Athens like the other islanders. At first they were neutral and took no part. But when the Athenians tried to coerce them by ravaging their lands, they were driven into open hostilities. The generals, Cleomedes the son of Lycomedes and Tisias the son of Tisimachus, encamped with the Athenian forces on the island. But before they did the country any harm they sent envoys to negotiate with the Melians. Instead of bringing these envoys before the people, the Melians desired them to explain their errand to the magistrates and to the chief men.

Athenians: Well, then, we Athenians will use no fine words; we will not go out of our way to prove at length that we have a right to rule, because we overthrew the Persians; or that we attack you now because we are suffering any injury at your hands. We should not convince you if we did; nor must you expect to convince us by arguing that, although a colony of the Lacedaemonians, you have taken no part in their expeditions, or that you have never done us any wrong. But you and we should say what we really think, and aim only at what is possible, for we both alike know that into the discussion of human affairs the question of justice only enters where the pressure of necessity is equal, and that the powerful exact what they can, and the weak grant what they must.

Melians: Well, then, since you set aside justice and invite us to speak of expediency, in our judgment it is certainly expedient that you should respect a principle which is for the common good; and that to every man when in peril a reasonable claim should be accounted a claim of right, and any plea which he is disposed to urge, even if failing of the point a little, should help his cause. Your interest in this principle is quite as great as ours, inasmuch as you, if you fall, will incur the heaviest vengeance, and will be the most terrible example to mankind.

Athenians: The fall of our empire, if it should fall, is not an event to which we look forward with dismay; for ruling states such as Lacedaemon are not cruel to their vanquished enemies. And we are fighting not so much against the Lacedaemonians, as against our own subjects who may some day rise up and overcome their former masters. But this is a danger which you may leave to us. And we will now endeavor to show that we have come in the interests of our empire, and that in what we are about to say we are only seeking the preservation of your city. For we want to make you ours with the least trouble to ourselves, and it is for the interests of us both that you should not be destroyed.

Melians: It may be your interest to be our masters, but how can it be ours to be your slaves?

Athenians: To you the gain will be that by submission you will avert the worst; and we shall be all the richer for your preservation.

Melians: But must we be your enemies? Will you not receive us as friends if we are neutral and remain at peace with you?

Athenians: No, your enmity is not half so mischievous to us as your friendship; for the one is in the eyes of our subjects an argument of our power, the other of our weakness.

Melians: But are your subjects really unable to distinguish between states in which you have no concern, and those which are chiefly your own colonies, and in some cases have revolted and been subdued by you?

Athenians: Why, they do not doubt that both of them have a good deal to say for themselves on the score of justice, but they think that states like yours are left free because they are able to defend themselves, and that we do not attack them because we dare not. So that your subjection will give us an increase of security, as well as an extension of empire. For we are masters of the sea, and you who are islanders, and insignificant islanders too, must not be allowed to escape us.

Melians: Surely then, if you and your subjects will brave all this risk, you to preserve your empire and they to be quit of it, how base and cowardly would it be in us, who retain our freedom, not to do and suffer anything rather than be your slaves.

Athenians: Not so, if you calmly reflect: for you are not fighting against equals to whom you cannot yield without disgrace, but you are taking counsel whether or no you shall resist an overwhelming force. The question is not one of honor but of prudence.

Melians: But we know that the fortune of war is sometimes impartial, and not always on the side of numbers. If we yield now, all is over; but if we fight, there is yet a hope that we may stand upright.

Athenians: Hope is a good comforter in the hour of danger, and when men have something else to depend upon, although hurtful, she is not ruinous. But when her spendthrift nature has induced them to stake their all, they see her as she is in the moment of their fall, and not till then. While the knowledge of her might enable them to beware of her, she never fails. You are weak and a single turn of the scale might be your ruin. Do not you be thus deluded; avoid the error of which so many are guilty, who, although they might still be saved if they would take the natural means, when visible grounds of confidence forsake them, have recourse to the invisible, to prophecies and oracles and the like, which ruin men by the hopes which they inspire in them.

Melians: We know only too well how hard the struggle must be against your power, and against fortune, if she does not mean to be impartial. Nevertheless we do not despair of fortune; for we hope to stand as high as you in the favor of heaven, because we are righteous, and you against whom we contend are unrighteous; and we are satisfied that our deficiency in power will be compensated by the aid of our allies the Lacedaemonians; they cannot refuse to help us, if only because we are their kinsmen, and for the sake of their own honor. And therefore our confidence is not so utterly blind as you suppose.

Athenians: As for the gods, we expect to have quite as much of their favor as you: for we are not doing or claiming anything which goes beyond common opinion about divine or men's desires about human things. Of the gods we believe, and of men we know, that by a law of their nature wherever they can rule they will. This law was not made by us, and we are not the first who have acted upon it; we did but inherit it, and shall bequeath it to all time, and we know that you and all mankind, if you were as strong as we are, would do as we do. So much for the gods; we have told you why we expect to stand as high in their good opinion as you. And then as to the Lacedaemonians—when you imagine that out of very shame they will assist you, we admire the simplicity of your idea, but we do not envy you the folly of it. The Lacedaemonians are exceedingly virtuous among themselves, and according to their national standard of morality. But in respect of their dealings with others, although many things might be said, a word is enough to describe them, of all men whom we know they are the most notorious for identifying what is pleasant with what is honorable, and what is expedient with what is just. But how inconsistent is such a character with your present blind hope of deliverance!

Melians: That is the very reason we trust them; they will look to their interest, and therefore will not be willing to betray the Melians, who are their own colonists, lest they should be distrusted by their friends in Hellas and play into the hands of their enemies.

Athenians: Help may come from Lacedaemon to you as it has come to others, and should you ever have actual experience of it, then you will know that never once have the Athenians retired from a siege through fear of a foe elsewhere. You told us that the safety of your city would be your first care, but we remark that, in this long discussion, not a word has been uttered by you which would give a reasonable man expectation of deliverance. Your strongest grounds are hopes deferred, and what power you have is not to be compared with that which is already arrayed against you. Unless after we have withdrawn you mean to come, as even now you may, to a wiser conclusion, you are showing a great want of sense. For surely you cannot dream of flying to that false sense of honor which has been the ruin of so many when danger and dishonor were staring them in the face. Many men with their eyes still open to the consequences have found the word honor too much for them, and have suffered a mere name to lure them on, until it has drawn down upon them real and irretrievable calamities; through their own folly they have incurred a worse dishonor than fortune would have inflicted upon them. If you are wise you will not run this risk; you ought to see that there can be no disgrace in yielding to a great city which invites you to become her ally on reasonable terms, keeping your own land, and merely paying tribute; and that you will certainly gain no honor if, having to choose between two alternatives, safety and war, you obstinately prefer the worse. To maintain our rights against equals, to be politic with superiors, and to be moderate towards inferiors is the path of safety. Reflect once more when we have withdrawn, and say to yourselves over and over again that you are deliberating about your one and only country, which may be saved or may be destroyed by a single decision.

The Athenians left the conference: the Melians, after consulting among themselves, resolved to persevere in their refusal, and answered as follows, "Men of Athens, our resolution is unchanged; and we will not in a moment surrender that liberty which our city, founded 700 years ago, still enjoys; we will trust to the good fortune which, by the favor of the gods, has hitherto preserved us, and for human help to the Lacedaemonians, and endeavor to save ourselves. We are ready however to be your friends, and the enemies neither of you nor of the Lacedaemonians, and we ask you to leave our country when you have made such a peace as may appear to be in the interest of both parties."

Such was the answer of the Melians; the Athenians, as they quitted the conference, spoke as follows, "Well, we must say, judging from the decision at which you have arrived, that you are the only men who deem the future to be more certain than the present, and regard things unseen as already realized in your fond anticipation, and that the more you cast yourselves upon the Lacedaemonians and fortune, and hope, and trust them, the more complete will be your ruin."

The Athenian envoys returned to the army; and the generals, when they found that the Melians would not yield, immediately commenced hostilities. They surrounded the town of Melos with a wall, dividing the work among the several contingents. The place was now closely invested, and there was treachery among the citizens themselves. So the Melians were induced to surrender at discretion. The Athenians thereupon put to death all who were of military age, and made slaves of the women and children. They then colonized the island, sending thither 500 settlers of their own.[5]

The triumphant rise of Alcibiades meant a resumption of the policy of conquest, and nowhere opened so fair a field as Sicily. Increasing wealth brought comforts and luxuries to the citizens of Sicily, especially to those of the powerful Dorian state Syracuse, while across the straits, in southern Italy, the Lucanians, a branch of the Sabellians, were aggressively expanding. In 416 B.C. Segesta, a Sicilian ally, asked Athens for protection against Selinus, and promised to pay the expenses of an expedition. This was a pretext for an invasion of Sicily. Nicias strenuously opposed the undertaking. His contention was that Athens needed all her strength for restoring and maintaining her Empire, and for her own defense against Thebes and the Peloponnesus. Furthermore, even if Sicily could be conquered, it would be impossible to hold that great island in subjection. Alcibiades, of course, urged war, hoping that it would yield him the mastery of Athens. As a last resort, Nicias tried to dissuade the Athenians by magnifying the size of an expedition needed to conquer Sicily, but the Athenians replied by granting all that he asked.

[5] Thucydides, v, 86–116.

THE SICILIAN EXPEDITION

Finally, in 415 B.C., the great expedition was ready.

No armament so magnificent or costly, [says Thucydides,] had ever been sent out by any single Hellenic power. On the fleet the greatest pains and expense had been lavished by the captains and the state. Men were quite amazed at the boldness of the scheme and the magnificence of the spectacle, which were everywhere spoken of, no less than at the great disproportion of the force when compared with that of the enemy against whom it was intended. Never had a greater expedition been sent to a foreign land; never was there an enterprise in which the hope of future success seemed to be better justified by actual power.

All the financial reserves of Athens were devoted to the expedition. The fleet consisted of 134 triremes, with 130 supply boats. Over 5,000 hoplites, 1,300 light-armed troops, and 30 cavalry comprised the army. Counting the crews, at least 27,000 men made up this vast armada. The Athenians had placed three generals in charge, Alcibiades, Nicias, and Lamachus, a fighter of the old school. Shortly before the departure the Athenians were horrified one morning to find that the Hermae (Note, p. 179) in front of their doors had all been mutilated. The people were seized with terror lest, as a step toward overthrowing the democracy, a band of conspirators had attempted to deprive the city of her divine protectors. In a panic the citizens assembled on the Pnyx and voted immunity and rewards to any one who gave information against the perpetrators. No one came forward, however, for the deed had probably been committed by drunken youths; but it was revealed that certain persons, among them Alcibiades, had once profaned the Eleusinian mysteries by parodying them at private gatherings in the presence of the uninitiated. Democratic politicians, opposed to Alcibiades, schemed to prosecute him for the sacrilege, and he demanded an immediate trial. But, appreciating his popularity with the soldiers and sailors, they delayed till the expedition had sailed. An indictment for sacrilege was then voted against Alcibiades, and the *Salaminia,* the state trireme, sailed to Sicily to order his return. On the homeward voyage Alcibiades made his escape to the Peloponnesus, and finally took up his residence at Sparta. There his counsels proved dangerous to his country's welfare.

In Sicily, the Athenian commanders, disagreeing as to plan, frittered away nearly a year in petty undertakings, wasting their resources, discouraging their own men, and exciting contempt in the minds of the Sicilian Greeks. The following year, 414 B.C., they besieged Syracuse

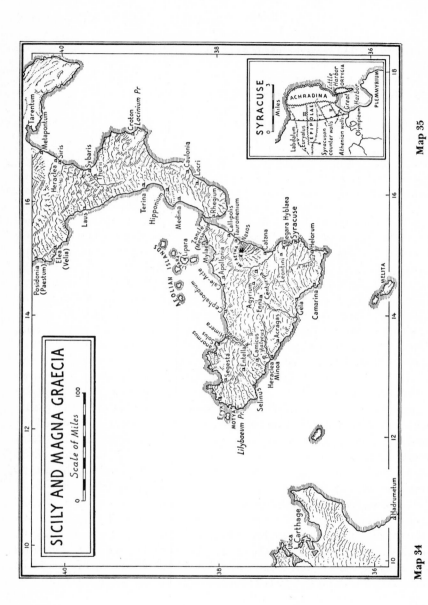

SICILY AND MAGNA GRAECIA

Scale of Miles

0   100

Map 34

SYRACUSE

Miles
0   3

Labdalum
Euryalus
EPIPOLAE
ACHRADINA
Syracuson
counter walls
Athenian walls
Olympieum
Little
Harbor
Great
Harbor
ORTYGIA
PLEMMYRIUM

Map 35

226

(Map 35). A strategic fort, Euryalus, and a commanding plateau, Epipolae, were captured, but in attempting to cut Syracuse off by a wall, Lamachus was killed, and this left Nicias, who had opposed the expedition from the beginning, in sole command. The Syracusans were further encouraged by the arrival of an able Spartan officer, Gylippus, with re-enforcements. Nicias proved wholly incompetent for a vigorous offensive. When autumn came, the besiegers were in a wretched plight; and Nicias, having made no appreciable headway, would gladly have abandoned the siege, but dared not face the Athenian Assembly. When, however, the Athenians received his report, which detailed the condition of the armament and asked that it be recalled or re-enforced, the Assembly, far from abandoning the enterprise, voted heavy re-enforcements. Eurymedon was sent off at once with a small force, and the next spring Demosthenes arrived with an armada of 15,000 men. The persistence of the Athenians in their plan of conquest, and their vitality in mustering all available resources, were extraordinary. The new fleet had been prepared in the midst of grave dangers at home, for in the spring of 413 B.C. the Peloponnesians, under King Agis, and the Boeotians resumed the war and invaded Attica. On the suggestion of Alcibiades they established a permanent garrison at Decelea in northern Attica, not far from Athens (Map 32). As a result, the Athenians were forced to give up their country houses and to withdraw permanently into the city. Thousands of slaves deserted to the enemy; industry and commerce shrank; and the people were soon cramped with want.

When Demosthenes arrived at Syracuse in 413 B.C., he found the besiegers in a miserable condition. They had lost a naval battle in the harbor, and this failure, together with sickness and want, had robbed them of all courage. The only hope was in immediate success. The strenuous offensive of Demosthenes, however, utterly failed, and when he proposed to embark the army and sail away, a total eclipse of the moon caused the superstitious Nicias to urge delay. The Syracusans, taking advantage of this, blocked the mouth of the harbor. Now robbed of the advantage of surprise, nothing remained for the Athenian fleet but to try to force its way into the open sea. The description of the ensuing sea battle, the retreat by land and the annihilation of practically all of the 45,000 Athenians and their allies, who had sailed in two glorious fleets against Syracuse with such high hopes, gains in the pages of Thucydides all the power of a great tragedy:

When Gylippus and the other Syracusan generals had, like Nicias, encouraged their troops, perceiving the Athenians to be manning their ships, they presently did the same. Nicias, overwhelmed by the situation, and seeing how great and how near the peril was (for the ships were on the very point of rowing out), feeling too, as men do on the eve of a great struggle, that all which he had done was nothing, and that he had not said half enough, again addressed the captains, and calling each of them by his father's name, and his own name, and the name of his tribe, he entreated those who had made any reputation for themselves not to be false to it, and those whose ancestors were eminent not to tarnish their hereditary fame. He reminded them that they were the inhabitants of the freest country in the world, and how in Athens there was no interference with the daily life of any man. He spoke to them of their wives and children and their fathers' Gods, as men will at such a time; for then they do not care whether their commonplace phrases seem to be out of date or not, but loudly reiterate the old appeals, believing that they may be of some service at the awful moment. When he thought that he had exhorted them, not enough, but as much as the scanty time allowed, he retired, and led the land-forces to the shore, extending the line as far as he could, so that they might be of the greatest use in encouraging the combatants on board ship. Demosthenes, Menander, and Euthydemus, who had gone on board the Athenian fleet to take the command, now quitted their own station, and proceeded straight to the closed mouth of the harbor, intending to force their way to the open sea where a passage was still left.

The Syracusans and their allies had already put out with nearly the same number of ships as before. A detachment of them guarded the entrance of the harbor; the remainder were disposed all round it in such a manner that they might fall on the Athenians from every side at once, and that their land-forces might at the same time be able to cooperate wherever the ships retreated to the shore. Sicanus and Agatharchus commanded the Syracusan fleet, each of them a wing; Pythen and the Corinthians occupied the center. When the Athenians approached the closed mouth of the harbor the violence of their onset overpowered the ships which were stationed there; they then attempted to loosen the fastenings. Whereupon from all sides the Syracusans and their allies came bearing down upon them, and the conflict was no longer confined to the entrance, but extended throughout the harbor. No previous engagement had been so fierce and obstinate. Great was the eagerness with which the rowers on both sides rushed upon their enemies whenever the word of command was given; and keen was the contest between the pilots as they manoeuvred one against another. The marines too were full of anxiety that, when ship struck ship, the service on deck should not fall short of the rest; every one in the place assigned to him was eager to be foremost among his fellows. Many vessels meeting—and never did so many fight in so small a space, for the two fleets together amounted to nearly 200—they were seldom able to strike in the regular manner, because they had no opportunity of first retiring or breaking the line; they generally fouled one another as ship dashed against ship in the hurry of flight or pursuit. All the time that another vessel was bearing down, the men on deck poured showers of javelins and arrows and stones upon the enemy; and when the two closed, the marines fought hand to hand, and endeavored to board. In many places, owing to the want of room, they who had struck another found that they were struck themselves; often two or even more vessels were unavoidably entangled about one, and the pilots had to make plans of attack and defense, not against one adversary only, but against several coming from different sides. The crash of so many ships dashing against one another took away the wits of the sailors, and made it impossible to hear the boatswains, whose voices in both fleets rose high, as they gave directions to the rowers, or cheered them on in the excitement of the struggle. On the Athenians side they were shouting to their men that they must force a passage and seize the opportunity now or never of returning in safety to their native land. To the Syracusans and their allies was represented the glory of preventing the escape of their enemies, and of a victory by which every man would exalt the honor of his own city. The commanders too, when they saw any ship backing water without necessity, would call the captain by his name, and ask, of the Athenians, whether they were retreating because they expected to be more at home upon the land of their bitterest foes than upon that sea which had been their own so long; on the Syracusan side, whether, when they knew perfectly well that the Athenians were only eager to find some means of flight, they would themselves fly from the fugitives.

While the naval engagement hung in the balance the two armies on shore had great trial and conflict of soul. The Sicilian soldier was animated by the hope of increasing the glory which he had already won, while the invader was tormented by the fear that his fortunes might sink lower still. The last chance of the Athenians lay in their ships, and their anxiety was dreadful. The fortune of the battle varied; and it was not possible that the spectators on the shore should all receive the same impression of it. Being quite close and having different points of view, they would some of them see their own ships victorious; their courage would then revive, and they would earnestly call upon the Gods not to take from them their hope of deliverance. But others, who saw their ships worsted, cried and shrieked aloud, and were by the sight alone more utterly unnerved than the defeated combatants themselves. Others again, who had fixed their gaze on some part of the struggle which was undecided, were in a state of excitement still more terrible; they kept swaying their bodies to and fro in an agony of hope and fear as the stubborn conflict went on and on; for at every instant they were all but saved or all but lost. And while the strife hung in the balance you might hear in the Athenian army at once lamentation, shouting, cries of victory or defeat, and all the various sounds which are wrung from a great host in extremity of danger. Not less agonizing were the feelings of those on board. At length the Syracusans and their allies, after a protracted struggle, put the Athenians to flight, and triumphantly bearing down upon them, and encouraging one another with loud cries and exhortations, drove them to land. Then that part of the navy which had not been taken in the deep water fell back in confusion to the shore, and the crews rushed out of the ships into the camp. And the land-forces, no longer now divided in feeling, but uttering one universal groan of intolerable anguish, ran, some of them to save the ships, others to defend what remained of the wall; but the greater number began to look to themselves and to their own safety. Never had there been a greater panic in an Athenian army than at that moment. They now suffered what they had done to others at Pylos. For at Pylos the Lacedaemonians, when they saw their ships destroyed, knew that their friends who had crossed over into the island of Sphacteria were lost with them. And so now the Athenians, after the rout of their fleet, knew that they had no hope of saving themselves by land unless events took some extraordinary turn.

Thus, after a fierce battle and a great destruction of ships and men on both sides, the Syracusans and their allies gained the victory. They gathered up the wrecks and bodies of the dead, and sailing back to the city, erected a trophy. The Athenians, overwhelmed by their misery, never so much as thought of recovering their wrecks or of asking leave to collect their dead. Their intention was to retreat that very night.

Hermocrates the Syracusan suspected their intention, and dreading what might happen if their vast army, retreating by land and settling somewhere in Sicily, should choose to renew the war, contrived the following plan: when it was growing dark he sent certain of his own acquaintances, accompanied by a few horsemen, to the Athenian camp. They rode up within earshot, and pretending to be friends (there were known to be men in the city who gave information to Nicias of what went on) called to some of the soldiers, and bade them tell him not to withdraw his army during the night, for the Syracusans were guarding the roads; he should make preparation at leisure and retire by day. Having delivered their message they departed, and those who had heard them informed the Athenian generals.

On receiving this message, which they supposed to be genuine, they remained during the night. And having once given up the intention of starting immediately, they decided to remain during the next day, that the soldiers might, as well as they could, put together their baggage in the most convenient form, and depart, taking with them the bare necessaries of life, but nothing else.

Meanwhile the Syracusans and Gylippus, going forth before them with their land-forces, blocked the roads in the country by which the Athenians were likely to pass, guarded the fords of the rivers and streams, and posted themselves at the best points for receiving and stopping them. Their sailors rowed up to the beach and dragged away the Athenian ships. The Athenians themselves burnt a few of them, as they had intended, but the rest the Syracusans towed away, unmolested and at their leisure, from the places where they had severally run aground, and conveyed them to the city.

On the third day after the sea-fight, when Nicias and Demosthenes thought that their preparations were complete, the army began to move. They were in a dreadful condition; not only was there the great fact that they had lost their whole fleet, and instead of their expected triumph had brought the utmost peril upon Athens as well as upon themselves, but also the sights which presented themselves as they quitted the camp were painful to every eye and mind. The dead were unburied, and when any one saw the body of a friend lying on the ground he was smitten with sorrow and dread, while the sick or wounded who still survived but had to be left were even a greater trial to the living, and more to be pitied than those who were gone. Their prayers and lamentations drove their companions to distraction; they would beg that they might be taken with them, and call by name any friend or relation whom they saw passing; they would hang upon their departing comrades and follow as far as they could, and when their limbs and strength failed them and they dropped behind many were the imprecations and cries which they uttered. So that the whole army was in tears, and such was their despair that they could hardly make up their minds to stir, although they were leaving an enemy's country, having suffered calamities too great for tears already, and dreading miseries yet greater in the unknown future. There was also a general feeling of shame and self-reproach,—indeed they seemed, not like an army, but like the fugitive population of a city captured after a siege; and of a great city too. For the whole multitude who were marching together numbered not less than 40,000. Each of them took with him anything he could carry which was likely to be of use. Even the heavy-armed and cavalry, contrary to their practice when under arms, conveyed about their persons their own food, some because they had no attendants, others because they could not trust them; for they had long been deserting, and most of them had gone off all at once. Nor was the food which they carried sufficient; for the supplies of the camp had failed. Their disgrace and the universality of the misery, although there might be some consolation in the very community of suffering, was nevertheless at that moment hard to bear, especially when they remembered from what pomp and splendor they had fallen into their present low estate. Never had an Hellenic army experienced such a reverse. They had come intending to enslave others, and they were going away in fear that they would be themselves enslaved. Instead of the prayers and hymns with which they had put to sea, they were now departing amid appeals to heaven of another sort. They were no longer sailors but landsmen, depending, not upon their fleet, but upon their infantry. Yet in face of the great danger which still threatened them all these things appeared endurable.

Exhorting his troops Nicias passed through the army, and wherever he saw gaps in the ranks or the men dropping out of line, he brought them back to their proper place. Demosthenes did the same for the troops under his command, and gave them similar exhortations. The army marched disposed in a hollow oblong: the division of Nicias leading, and that of Demosthenes following; the hoplites enclosed within their ranks the baggage-bearers and the rest of the army. When they arrived at the ford of the river Anapus they found a force of the Syracusans and of their allies drawn up to meet them; these they put to flight, and getting command of the ford, proceeded on their march. The Syracusans continually harassed them, the cavalry riding along-side, and the light-armed troops hurling darts at them. On this day the Athenians proceeded about four and a half miles and encamped at a hill. On the next day they started early, and, having advanced more than two miles, descended into a level plain, and encamped. The country was inhabited, and they were desirous of obtaining food from the houses, and also water which they might carry with them, as there was little to be had for many miles in the country which lay before them. Meanwhile the Syracusans had gone on before them, and at a point where the road ascends a steep hill called the Acraean height, and there is a precipitous ravine on either side, were blocking up the pass by a wall. On the next day the Athenians advanced, although again impeded by the numbers of the enemy's cavalry who rode along-side, and of their javelin-men who threw darts at them. For a long time the Athenians maintained the struggle, but at last retired to their own encampment. Their supplies were now cut off, because the horsemen circumscribed their movements.

The army was now in a miserable plight, being in want of every necessity, and by the continual assaults of the enemy great numbers of the soldiers had been wounded. Nicias and Demosthenes, perceiving their condition, resolved during the night to light as many watch-fires as possible and to lead off their forces. They intended to take another route and march towards the sea in the direction opposite to that from which the Syracusans were watching them. Now their whole line of march lay, not towards Catana, but towards the other side of Sicily, in the direction of Camarina and Gela, and the cities, Hellenic or barbarian, of that region. So they lighted numerous fires and departed in the night. And then, as constantly happens in armies, especially in very great ones, and as might be expected when they were marching by night in an enemy's country, and with the enemy from whom they were flying not far off, there arose a panic among them, and they fell into confusion. The army of Nicias, which led the way, kept together, and was considerably in advance, but that of Demosthenes, which was the larger half, got severed from the other division, and marched in less order.

When daylight broke and the Syracusans and their allies saw that the Athenians had departed, most of them thought that Gylippus had let them go on purpose, and were very angry with him. They easily found the line of their retreat, and quickly following, came up with them about the time of the midday meal. The troops of Demosthenes were last; they were marching slowly and in disorder, not having recovered from the panic of the previous night, when they were overtaken by the Syracusans, who immediately fell upon them and fought. Separated as they were from the others, they were easily hemmed in by the Syracusan cavalry and driven into a narrow space. The division of Nicias was as much as six miles in advance, for he marched faster, thinking that their safety depended at such a time, not in remaining and fighting, if they could avoid it, but in retreating as quickly as they could, and resisting only when they were positively compelled. Demosthenes, on the other hand, who had been more incessantly harassed throughout the retreat, because marching last he was first attacked by the enemy, now, when he saw the Syracusans pursuing him, instead of pressing onward, had ranged his army in order of battle. Thus lingering he was surrounded, and he and the Athenians under his command were in the greatest danger and confusion. For they were crushed into a walled enclosure, having a road on both sides and planted thickly with olive-trees, and missiles were hurled at them from all points. The Syracusans naturally preferred this mode of attack to a regular engagement. For to risk themselves against desperate men would have been only playing into the hands of the Athenians. Moreover, every one was sparing of his life; their good fortune was already assured, and they did not want to fall in the hour of victory. Even by this irregular mode of fighting they thought that they could overpower and capture the Athenians.

And so when they had gone on all day assailing them with missiles from every quarter, and saw that they were quite worn out with their wounds and all their other sufferings, Gylippus and the Syracusans made a proclamation, first of all to the islanders, that any of them who pleased might come over to them and have their freedom. But only a few cities accepted the offer. At length an agreement was made for the entire force under Demosthenes. Their arms were to be surrendered, but no one was to suffer death, either from violence or from imprisonment, or from want of the bare means of life. So they all surrendered, being in number 6,000, and gave up what money they had. This they threw into the hollows of shields and filled four. The captives were at once taken to the city. On the same day Nicias and his division reached the river Erineus, which he crossed, and halted his army on a rising ground.

When the day dawned Nicias led forward his army, and the Syracusans and the allies again assailed them on every side, hurling javelins and other missiles at them. The Athenians hurried on to the river Assinarus. They hoped to gain a little relief if they forded the river, for the mass of horsemen and other troops overwhelmed and crushed them; and they were worn out by fatigue and thirst. But no sooner did they reach the water than they lost all order and rushed in; every man was trying to cross first, and, the enemy pressing upon them at the same time, the passage of the river became hopeless. Being compelled to keep close together they fell one upon another, and trampled each other under foot: some at once perished, pierced by their own spears; others got entangled in the baggage and were carried down the stream. The Syracusans stood upon the further bank of the river, which was steep, and hurled missiles from above on the Athenians, who were huddled together in the deep bed of the stream and for the most part were drinking greedily. The Peloponnesians came down the bank and slaughtered them, falling chiefly upon those who were in the river. Whereupon the water at once became foul, but was drunk all the same, although muddy and dyed with blood, and the crowd fought for it.

At last, when the dead bodies were lying in heaps upon one another in the water and the army was utterly undone, some perishing in the river, and any who escaped being cut off by the cavalry, Nicias surrendered [6] to Gylippus, in whom he had more confidence than in the Syracusans. He entreated him and the Lacedaemonians to do what they pleased with himself, but not to go on killing the men. So Gylippus gave the word to make prisoners. Thereupon the survivors, not including however a large number whom the soldiers concealed, were brought in alive. The total of the public prisoners when collected

[6] September, 413 B.C.

was not great; for many were appropriated by the soldiers, and the whole of Sicily was full of them, they not having capitulated like the troops under Demosthenes. A large number also perished; the slaughter at the river being very great, quite as great as any which took place in the Sicilian war; and not a few had fallen in the frequent attacks which were made upon the Athenians during their march. Still many escaped, some at the time, others ran away after an interval of slavery, and all these found refuge at Catana.

The Syracusans and their allies collected their forces and returned with the spoil, and as many prisoners as they could take with them, into the city. The captive Athenians and allies they deposited in the quarries, which they thought would be the safest place of confinement. Nicias and Demosthenes they put to the sword, although against the will of Gylippus. For Gylippus thought that to carry home with him to Lacedaemon the generals of the enemy, over and above all his other successes, would be a brilliant triumph. One of them, Demosthenes, happened to be the greatest foe, and the other the greatest friend of the Lacedaemonians, both in the same matter of Pylos and Sphacteria. For Nicias had taken up their cause, and had persuaded the Athenians to make the peace which set at liberty the prisoners taken in the island. The Lacedaemonians were grateful to him for the service, and this was the main reason he trusted Gylippus and surrendered himself to him. But certain Syracusans, who had been in communication with him, were afraid (such was the report that on some suspicion of their guilt he might be put to the torture and bring trouble on them in the hour of their prosperity. Others, and especially the Corinthians, feared that, being rich, he might by bribery escape and do them further mischief. So the Syracusans gained the consent of the allies and had him executed. For these or the like reasons he suffered death. No one of the Hellenes in my time was less deserving of so miserable an end; for he lived in the practice of every customary virtue.

Those who were imprisoned in the quarries were at the beginning of their captivity harshly treated by the Syracusans. There were great numbers of them, and they were crowded in a deep and narrow place. At first the sun by day was still scorching and suffocating, for they had no roof over their heads, while the autumn nights were cold, and the extremes of temperaure engendered violent disorders. Being cramped for room they had to do everything on the same spot. The corpses of those who died from their wounds, exposure to the weather, and the like, lay heaped one upon another. The smells were intolerable; and they were at the same time afflicted by hunger and thirst. During eight months they were allowed only about half a pint of water and a pint of food a day. Every kind of misery which could befall man in such a place befell them. This was the condition of all the captives for about ten weeks. At length the Syracusans sold them, with the exception of the Athenians and of any Sicilian or Italian Greeks who had sided with them in the war. The whole number of the public prisoners is not accurately known, but they were not less than 7,000.

Of all the Hellenic actions which took place in this war, or indeed of all Hellenic actions which are on record, this was the greatest—the most glorious to the victors, the most ruinous to the vanquished; for they were utterly and at all points defeated, and their sufferings were prodigious. Fleet and army perished from the face of the earth; nothing was saved, and of the many who went forth few returned home.

Thus ended the Sicilian expedition.[7]

OLIGARCHICAL REVOLUTION IN ATHENS

For a time the Athenians at home could not believe that a disaster so great had befallen them. When, however, they came to appreciate the truth, they vented their rage upon the orators and the soothsayers who had persuaded them to the expedition. At first they were dejected by the utter hopelessness of the situation, their want of men, money, and ships; but soon their elastic spirits rose, and they determined to persist at all odds. Indeed, to increase their revenue to the uttermost without seeming to add new burdens to their allies, they had displaced the tribute in 414 B.C. by a 5 per cent tax on all imports and exports throughout the Empire. The new system was effective, though the tribute was revived in 410 B.C.

The Greeks now eagerly flocked to the Spartan standard in the hope of trampling upon the common foe. The Persian king, on condition of recovering the Greek cities of Asia Minor, gave money and promised the aid of a Phoenician fleet. The maritime allies, including Chios, began to revolt against Athens, and the victorious navy of Syracuse appeared in Aegean waters. But the persistence of the Athenians, stripped of resources, against these overwhelming odds during a period of eight more years is evidence of an almost indomitable will.

The Sicilian disaster had a serious effect on Athenian politics. There had always been a strong minority opposed to popular government. The recent misfortunes strengthened their hands by seemingly proving the worthlessness of democracy, and for the moment the majority recognized the need of a modification of the constitution. The most crying demand was for a responsible magistracy. The people accordingly instituted a board of ten commissioners (*probouloi*) to be filled by mature men annually elected. They were to take the place of the prytanies in initiating administrative measures, to control finance, and to attend to the building and the equipment of the navy. This wholesome reform was largely stultified by the choice of elderly men, like the poet Sophocles, who lacked resolution and energy.

The first decisive step toward abolishing the democracy, however,

[7] Thucydides, VII, 69–87.

was taken by an oligarchic club of officers in the army then encamped in Samos. Their leading motive was to secure for themselves the place in the government to which, in their opinion, their rank entitled them. At the same time they were receiving overtures from Alcibiades who, having fallen out with the Spartan king, Agis, had passed over to the Persians and was now plotting his return to Athens. With no hope of a recall through the democracy, Alcibiades promised the Athenians at Samos that if they should set up an oligarchy, Tissaphernes, satrap of Sardes, would transfer the Persian support from Sparta to Athens. Though groundless, the promise had its effect.

Peisander and other envoys from the oligarchs at Samos went to Athens, and against a storm of indignation proposed an oligarchy with a view chiefly to winning Persian favor. At the same time Peisander joined with Antiphon, a legal adviser and the brain of the impending revolution, in reorganizing the oligarchic clubs which had existed in Athens from immemorial time. It was their policy to intimidate the multitude by assassinating their leaders. Terrorized by political murders, the citizens permitted the institution in 411 B.C. of a Council of Four Hundred, who should appoint officials and conduct the administration with absolute power. As a sop to the moderates this form of government was termed provisional, and there was proposed a "definitive" constitution, under which the sovereignty was to be held by the 5,000 wealthiest citizens organized in four great councils rotating annually. The Council of the Four Hundred, as worked out by Theramenes, was modeled in part on the Boeotian League. A board of minor magistrates (*proedroi*) recruited the council by choosing one hundred citizens, each of whom co-opted three others. It is a noteworthy fact that the leaders of the oligarchic movement were neither Eupatrids nor experienced politicians. They were educated men who, having learned their politics in the schools of the sophists, were now engaged in political experimentation. Normally the Athenian constitution was an aggregate of traditional customs modified by written laws, but now for the first time, as could be expected of sophists, it was a document; both the provisional and definitive constitutions were written. The leading oligarchs intended by deferring the call for the Five Thousand to keep the Four Hundred permanently in power. A feature of the new system was the abolition of all pay for civil services, except to the nine archons and the councillors for the time being, and the devotion of the entire revenue to the war.

The Four Hundred proved unprincipled, unpatriotic, and incompetent. They could maintain themselves in no other way than by terrorism and secret murder; they offered to buy peace of Sparta at any price, and their weakness lost Euboea to the enemy. No sooner had their position grown insecure than they split into two factions. The extremists were led by Antiphon, Peisander, and Phrynichus. The moderates followed Theramenes, who had been largely instrumental in establishing the Four Hundred, but whose ideal was the limitation of the franchise to those who could equip themselves for service in the heavy infantry. His faction was supported by the troops at Samos. They overthrew their oligarchic leaders, elected Thrasybulus, an able patriot, and Thrasyllus to the generalship, and recalled Alcibiades, who was placed in chief command. A democrat once more, Alcibiades stood ready to devote his extraordinary talents to repairing the havoc he had wrought in his country's fortunes. These circumstances encouraged Theramenes and the moderates to overthrow the Four Hundred, after its rule of four months, and to establish in power nominally the Five Thousand, in reality all above the thetic census. The Five Thousand lasted eight months.

Under the weak rule of the Four Hundred the war had spread for the first time to the eastern Aegean, and even Byzantium, the key to the Black Sea trade, was lost. Alcibiades, however, gained a brilliant victory in 410 B.C. over the enemy at Cyzicus, capturing or destroying the entire fleet and killing the commander, Mindarus. The Spartans now offered peace on the basis of the *status quo*, but the Athenians, led by Cleophon, the lyre maker, rejected the terms. It was a terrible mistake, but they were unduly elated by the victory and by their hope in Alcibiades.

The victory led the Athenians to restore the complete democracy in 410 B.C. and to require of every citizen a solemn oath to support it. About the same time they appointed a commission to revise various public and criminal laws and to inscribe them on stone. As the revenues were increasing, the Athenians reintroduced pay for official service and celebrated the festivals with the old splendor. Cleophon, who had the demagogue's sharp eye for finance, began to build up the state's depleted reserves and in 409 B.C. started the conversion of temple properties into money. Work on the Erechtheum was resumed to provide jobs for the laborers. The extreme want of the poor in the city led to the distribution of two obols daily among the most needy.

In 408 B.C. Alcibiades brought Byzantium back into the Empire, and, returning home, was elected general for the next year. The temporary success of Athens was partly due to the vacillation and rivalry of the Persian satraps, Tissaphernes of Sardes and Pharnabazus of the Hellespontine region. In 408 B.C. Darius sent Cyrus, the younger of his two sons, to take the satrapy of Sardes with large powers, in order to give all possible aid to the Peloponnesians and end the war. The young man brought great ambition and unusual intelligence to the work. In the same year there came from Sparta to the seat of war Lysander, an able commander and crafty manager of men. His ultimate object was nothing less than a throne at Sparta. To reach the goal of his political hope, he needed military renown and an army devoted to himself. In brief, he was the Spartan counterpart of Alcibiades. Cyrus readily fell under his influence.

THE FALL OF ATHENS

In the following year (407 B.C.) Lysander defeated an Athenian fleet off Notium. During the absence of Alcibiades, his lieutenant Antiochus had ventured battle contrary to orders, and had lost fifteen ships of war. It was a mortal blow to the ascendancy of Alcibiades. Forgetting his uniform success against overwhelming foes during the past four years, the Athenians, misled by his enemies, defeated his candidacy for the following year. Fearing to return home, Alcibiades retired to the castles on the Hellespont and Propontis which he had prepared against such a contingency, and from which he quietly reviewed the further operations of the war.

Both sides now put forth herculean efforts in the hope of deciding the struggle in one more campaign. Callicratidas, supplaning Lysander, commanded 120 ships. The Athenians under eight generals met him with 150 triremes near the islands of Arginusae, between Lesbos and the Asia Minor coast (406 B.C.). In no other Greek naval battle were so many ships and men engaged. It was a complete victory for Athens. Seventy vessels of the Peloponnesians with their crews, amounting to 14,000 men and including their commander, were lost. The Athenians lost twenty-five ships, but, because of a sudden storm, it proved impossible to rescue some 2,000 sailors. Outraged at this, the Athenians at home deposed the commanders from office and brought to trial the six who dared to return. In violation of the constitution they condemned the accused to death by a single vote. Among these victims of popular fury was Pericles, the son of Pericles and Aspasia.

By 406 B.C. the financial strain on Athens was so great that there was a general melting down of the temple properties, gold coins were issued for the first time, and bronze coins were plated with silver. The two boards, the Treasurers of Athena and the Treasurers of the Other Gods, were amalgamated. Yet the Athenians could still refuse offers of peace. The obvious step for Sparta to take was to interrupt the transport of food supplies from the Black Sea to Athens. Consequently, Lysander was sent to the eastern Aegean. The Athenians dispatched against him their last possible fleet manned with their last available crews, 180 ships against the 200 of the Peloponnesians (405 B.C.). The Athenian fleet, stationed on the European side of the Hellespont at the mouth of the Aegospotami River, was taken by surprise while the crews were searching for provisions on shore. The Athenians were massacred. Conon, one of the generals, escaped to Cyprus with eight ships, having sent the state trireme *Paralus* to Piraeus with the sad news. The Athenian Xenophon has left a memorable description of its arrival and the last days (404 B.C.) of imperial Athens:

It was night when the *Paralus* reached Athens with her evil tidings, and a bitter wail of woe broke forth. From Piraeus, following the line of the Long Walls up to the heart of the city, it swept and swelled, as each man to his neighbor passed on the news. On that night no man slept. There was mourning and sorrow for those that were lost, but the lamentation for the dead was merged in even deeper sorrow for themselves, as they pictured the evils they were about to suffer, the like of which they had themselves inflicted upon the men of Melos, who were colonists of the Lacedaemonians, when they mastered them by siege. Or on the men of Histiaea; on Scione and Torone; on the Aeginetans, and many another Hellenic city. On the following day the public assembly met, and, after debate, it was resolved to block up all the harbors save one, to put the walls in a state of defense, to post guards at various points, and to make all other necessary preparation for a siege. Such were the concerns of the men of Athens.

Lysander presently left the Hellespont with two hundred ships and arrived at Lesbos, where he arranged things in Mytilene and the other cities of the island. Meanwhile he dispatched Eteonicus with a squadron of ten ships to the Thracian coast, where that officer brought the whole region into the hands of Lacedaemon. Indeed, in a moment of time, after the sea-fight, the whole of Hellas had revolted from Athens, with the exception of the Samians.[8] These, having massacred the nobles, held the state under their control. After a while Lysander sent messages to Agis at Decelea, and to Lacedaemon, announcing his approach with a squadron of two hundred ships.

In obedience to the command of Pausanias, the other king of Lacedaemon, a levy in force of the Lacedaemonians and all the rest of the Peloponnesus, except the Argives, was set in motion for a campaign. As soon as the several contingents had arrived, the king put himself at their head and marched against Athens, encamping in the Academy, as it is called. Lysander had now reached Aegina, where, having got together as many of the former inhabitants as possible, he formally reinstated them in their city; and what he

[8] In gratitude Athens granted the people of Samos citizenship; had this spirit of liberty been adopted at the beginning of the war, the result might have been far different.

did in behalf of the Aeginetans, he did also in behalf of the Melians, and of the rest who had been deprived of their countries. He then pillaged the island of Salamis, and anchored at Piraeus with 150 ships, and established a blockade against all merchant ships entering that harbor.

The Athenians, finding themselves besieged by land and sea, were at a loss what to do. Without ships, without allies, without provisions, the belief gained hold upon them that there was no way of escape. They must now, in their turn, suffer what they had themselves inflicted upon others; not in retaliation, indeed, for ills received, but out of sheer insolence, overriding the citizens of small states, and for no better reason than that these were allies of the very men now at their gates. In this frame of mind they enfranchised those who at any time had lost their civil rights, and schooled themselves to endurance; and, although many were dying of starvation, they refused to treat for peace. But when the stock of grain was absolutely insufficient,[9] they sent an embassy to Agis, proposing to become allies of the Lacedaemonians on the sole condition of keeping their fortification walls and Piraeus; and to draw up articles of treaty on these terms. Agis bade them betake themselves to Lacedaemon, seeing that he had no authority to act himself. With this answer the ambassadors returned to Athens, and were forthwith sent on to Lacedaemon. On reaching Sellasia, a town in Laconian territory, they waited till they got their answer from the ephors, who, having learnt their terms (which were identical with those already proposed to Agis), bade them instantly to be gone, and, if they really desired peace, to come with other proposals, the fruit of happier reflection. Thus the ambassadors returned home, and reported the result of their embassy, whereupon despondency fell upon all. It was a painful reflection that in the end they would be sold into slavery; and meanwhile, pending the return of a second embassy, many must fall victims to starvation. The razing of their fortifications was not a solution which any one cared to recommend. A member of the Council, Archestratus, had indeed put the question in the Council, whether it were not best to make peace with the Lacedaemonians on such terms as they were willing to propose; but he was thrown into prison. The Laconian proposals referred to involved the destruction of both Long Walls for a space of more than a mile. And a decree had been passed, making it illegal to submit any such proposition about the walls. Things having reached this pass, Theramenes made a proposal in the public assembly as follows: If they chose to send him as an ambassador to Lysander, he would go and find out why the Lacedaemonians were so unyielding about the walls; whether it was they really intended to enslave the city, or merely that they wanted a guarantee of good faith. Dispatched accordingly, he lingered on with Lysander for three whole months and more, watching for the time when the Athenians, at the last pinch of starvation, would be willing to accede to any terms that might be offered. At last, in the fourth month, he returned and reported to the public assembly that Lysander had detained

---

[9] So great was the want that the Treasurers of Athena and the Other Gods had to ration the grain.

him all this while, and had ended by bidding him betake himself to Lacedaemon, since he had no authority himself to answer his questions, which must be addressed directly to the ephors. After this Theramenes was chosen with nine others to go to Lacedaemon as ambassadors with full powers. Meanwhile Lysander had sent an Athenian exile, named Aristoteles, in company of certain Lacedaemonians, to Sparta to report to the board of ephors how he had answered Theramenes, that they, and they alone, had supreme authority in matters of peace and war.

Theramenes and his companions presently reached Sellasia, and being here questioned as to the reason of their visit, replied that they had full powers to treat of peace. After which the ephors ordered them to be summoned to their presence. On their arrival a general assembly was convened, in which the Corinthians and Thebans more particularly, though their views were shared by many other Hellenes also, urged the meeting not to come to terms with the Athenians, but to destroy them. The Lacedaemonians replied that they would never reduce to slavery a city which was itself an integral portion of Hellas, and had performed a great and noble service to Hellas in the most perilous of emergencies.[10] On the contrary, they were willing to offer peace on the terms now specified—namely, 'That the Long Walls and the fortifications of Piraeus should be destroyed; that the Athenian fleet, with the exception of twelve vessels, should be surrendered; that the exiles should be restored; and lastly, that the Athenians should acknowledge the headship of Sparta in peace and war, leaving to her the choice of friends and foes, and following her lead by land and sea.' Such were the terms which Theramenes and the rest who acted with him were able to report on their return to Athens. As they entered the city, a vast crowd met them, trembling lest their mission should have proved fruitless. For indeed delay was no longer possible, so long already was the list of victims daily perishing from starvation. On the day following, the ambassadors delivered their report, stating the terms upon which the Lacedaemonians were willing to make peace. Theramenes acted as spokesman, insisting that they ought to obey the Lacedaemonians and pull down the walls. A small minority raised their voice in opposition; but the majority were strongly in favor of the proposition, and the resolution was passed to accept the peace. After that, Lysander sailed into the Piraeus, and the exiles were readmitted. And so they fell to levelling the fortifications and walls with much enthusiasm, to the accompaniment of female flute players, deeming that day the beginning of liberty to Greece.[11]

In September, 404 B.C., the Thirty Tyrants began their rule at Athens. This board was instituted under intimidation from Lysander, ostensibly to draw up a new constitution for Athens, but in reality to govern with

---

[10] In addition to remembering Athens' noble services at the time of the Persian invasions, Sparta was probably also actuated by the desire to maintain in central Greece a balance to Thebes, whose self-aggrandizement had for some time been exciting her suspicion.

[11] Xenophon, *Hellenica*, II, 2. Translated by H. G. Dakyns.

absolute sway. One of the leaders was Critias, a Eupatrid writer—poet, rhetorician, political thinker, and atheist—a dilettante in literature, and in politics a heartless, calculating schemer. His colleague in the leadership was the shifty Theramenes who, while preferring a moderate oligarchy, had managed to emerge triumphant from every difficulty through which he had passed.

Beginning in moderation, the rule of the Thirty Tyrants rapidly degenerated to a selfish, bloody despotism. Supported by their Spartan *harmost* (garrison-commander), they proceeded to condemn and put to death their political enemies. Executions were always accompanied by confiscations of property. Still wanting funds for the payment of the garrison, they even proceeded against wealthy oligarchs and metics. There were wholesale banishments. Many fled, too, through fear, so that the surrounding states were full of fugitives from these monsters. Among their oppressive acts was an edict abolishing higher education in literature and philosophy, the effect of which, if long continued, would have been to wipe Athens from the history of civilization. More violent grew the reign of terror, till the number of dead mounted to 1,500 in eight months. Even Theramenes was compelled to drink the deadly hemlock.

In spite of orders from Sparta, the neighbors of Athens received the exiles with sympathy and aid. From Thebes Thrasybulus, one of these refugees, led a small band of patriots across the border to seize Phyle, a fortress on Mount Parnes. Thence, after increasing his force to 1,000, he occupied Piraeus and its hill Munychia. With so small a band it was a bold stroke, but this stronghold of democracy welcomed him and re-enforced his army. In the streets of Piraeus the patriots battled with a military force of the Thirty Tyrants, defeated it, and killed Critias (403 B.C.). Soon afterward the democracy was restored (Map 46).

The Peloponnesian War was a catastrophe for Athens and Greece. The Athenians had had it in their means with wise management to build up a lasting power, the strongest in Hellas, to win recognition of their political leadership from many or all the other Greeks, and to lift their race to a political destiny worthy of its civilization. All these possibilities were destroyed by the war. The Athenians' conduct of the war was filled with errors of undue ambition and miscalculation, yet even so they almost won it. It finally took a coalition of the Peloponnesians, their rebellious allies, and the Persian Empire to bring them to their knees. The Athenian Empire was destroyed, but if the subjects of Athens thought that the Spartan victory was a victory for freedom and autonomy they were soon disappointed.

Chapter XIV # THE PERICLEAN AGE

THE culture of the Periclean Age rested on belief in the all-comprehensive perfection of the state, to whose good the citizens were to subordinate their individual interests and devote their lives alike in war and peace. The whole spirit of the age glorified the greatness of Athens. It was Pericles' ambition that Athens should be the capital of Hellas, at once the strongest and the most beautiful city in the Greek world (Figure 62).

The ability of the Athenians, combined with the attraction which the city held for others, realized this ambition. In the busy city and its port labored citizens, metics, and slaves, while farmers, large and small, cultivated the olive, the vine, the wheat fields, and kitchen gardens. The marble quarries of Mt. Pentelicus, the silver mines of Laurium, the clay fields of the potter added to the natural wealth. The tribute of the allies made possible the construction of great public buildings, provided jobs for stone masons and other laborers, and at the same time, thanks to the payment for public service, gave the ordinary citizen enough leisure to attend actively to the affairs of state. As we noted earlier, in our discussion of the economic background of fifth-century Greece, the manufactures and commerce of this imperialist democracy spread far and wide.

Life, then, for the Athenian citizen was busy and serious. His chief concern was for his daily bread, but this was easily satisfied, because his needs were simple. Beside the narrow crooked streets of the city rose the houses of the people, one or two stories in height, and presenting a blank exterior. Life centered around the courtyard within. By the fourth century many Greek houses were sumptuous, with fine mosaics and fountains in the central court, which was surrounded by columns; behind the covered colonnade were located the various rooms. But it took the Greeks long to abandon the simpler house, a tradition that dated from the time when the city was small and the people huddled together for safety. This custom was re-enforced by Athenian public opinion, which was always coldly critical and quick to detect the unusual. The furniture of the house, the chairs, beds, tables, etc., though practical and beautiful, was neither varied nor numerous. (Map 36; Figures 60 and 61; Figures 63 and 64).

This simple abode was more a house than a home, for the warm climate and the democratic spirit invited out-of-door life. The ordinary Athenian citizen, on a day when work did not call, rose early, dressed in his short woollen chiton, had a small glass of wine, and then, attended perhaps by a slave or two, walked slowly to the center of town to do his shopping. The goods for sale—clothing, metal work, fish, oil, and so on —were concentrated in their own sections of the market place. Water clocks and sundials told the time, barber shops provided the gossip, and eventually the citizen returned home for lunch with his family. Unlike the Roman, the Athenian enjoyed neither a large meal nor a long siesta. Unless affairs of government demanded his attention, the Athenian, on an off-day, might spend his afternoon in a gymnasium. Here he not only wrestled, boxed, and ran, or, if older, played games with men of his own age, but also might listen to his fellow citizens as they discussed, perhaps with a sophist, some matter of moment. The evening would be spent quietly at home, unless friends had been invited to dinner. In that event, the men reclined on couches, reaching for the food which had been placed on tables in front of them, and at the conclusion of the meal the king of the symposium was elected. His function was to choose the topic of conversation and decide how much water should be mixed with the wine. An entire evening was often spent in this way. It will be observed that woman played but a

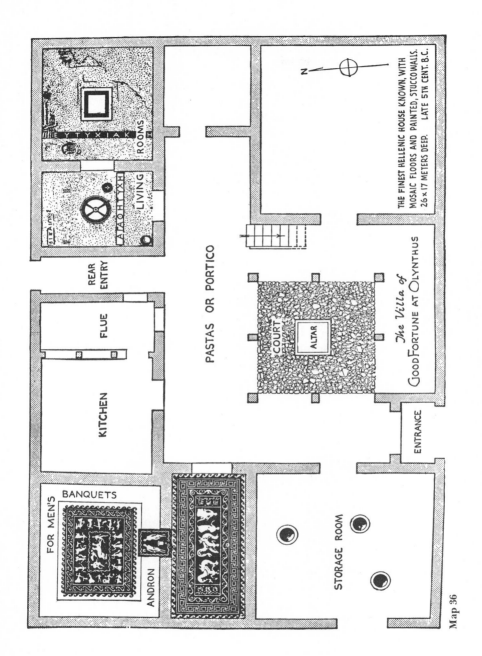

REAR ENTRY

LIVING ROOMS

ΕΥΤΥΧΙΑΚ

ΥΤΥΧΙ
ΑΓΑΘΗΤΥΧΗ

KITCHEN

FLUE

PASTAS OR PORTICO

FOR MEN'S BANQUETS

ANDRON

STORAGE ROOM

COURT

ALTAR

ENTRANCE

N

THE FINEST HELLENIC HOUSE KNOWN, WITH MOSAIC FLOORS AND PAINTED, STUCCO WALLS. 26 x 17 METERS DEEP. LATE 5TH CENT. B.C.

The Villa of Good Fortune at Olynthus

Map 36

245

small part in public life, being relegated to the home. Women of good families rarely appeared on the streets, though they were expected to attend funerals, weddings, the presentations of the tragic dramas, and had their own festival, the Thesmophorion, on the Pnyx.

Though life was a serious business for the citizens of Periclean Athens, it was also happy. Problems of government and Empire challenged their intellects and satisfied their pride; industry, commerce, and farming provided their livelihood; the traffic at Piraeus made them aware of a large world; a democratic constitution gave an outlet to their inventive minds. Certain of their strength and devoted to their state, the people were not oppressed by poverty. Within the city there was no housing problem, just as serfdom was unknown in the country. Extremes of wealth there were, though not as great nor as obvious as in a modern state, but an Athenian worth 100 talents was a rare individual. The state, it is true, demanded of each citizen his best, whether as architect or potter, but in return gave him ample opportunity to satisfy his ambition. Life was exuberant, throbbing with youth; optimism and a carefree lack of modesty filled the air. The many festivals gave the people the opportunity to gather in holiday mood and here, as elsewhere, complete freedom of speech was enjoyed; the Athenians endured all sorts of self-vituperation, until finally at the end of the fifth century, with the crises and disillusionment produced by the Peloponnesian War, comic license was restrained.

Much of Athenian life centered, of course, in the market place, or Agora. Here were located not only shops, but temples and buildings of the state. In the days before Solon the Agora had been located to the west of the Acropolis, between the Areopagus and the Pnyx, but the expansion of Athens in the sixth century, accompanied by the Peisistratids' construction of an aqueduct and various new buildings, necessitated a larger area. Thus the Agora of classical and post-classical times lay to the north of the Acropolis. It is now being uncovered by the great excavations of the American School of Classical Studies at Athens (Figure 65).[1] The plan as we have it shows buildings and monuments of various dates, for Athens was a growing city, subject, also, to foreign invasion and war. The Persian sack was followed by intense building activity under Pericles, and again in the fourth century. Hellenistic princes, in the period after Alexander, were happy to embellish the cultural capital of the world with buildings. The Roman Sulla destroyed some of Athens in 86 B.C., but it was not until the unsettled days of the third century A.D. that Athens suffered destruction on a large

[1] We are fortunate in possessing a fairly accurate description of the Agora from the hand of Pausanias, a traveler of the second century A.D.

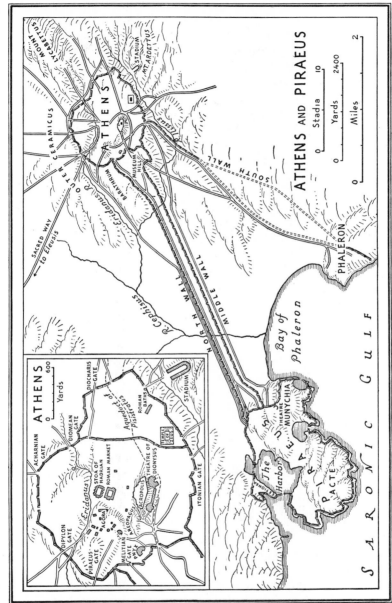

Map 38

Map 37

ATHENS and PIRAEUS

Stadia   10   2

Yards   2400

Miles

SARONIC GULF

Bay of Phaleron

PHALERON

MUNYCHIA

THEATRE

ACTE

The Harbor

IONIAN

SOUTH WALL

MIDDLE WALL

NORTH WALL

Cephisus

SACRED WAY to Eleusis

Outer Ceramicus

MOUNT LYCABETTUS

ATHENS

Ilissus

BARATHRUM

MUSEUM HILL

STADIUM

MT ARDETTUS

ATHENS

Yards   600

Eridanus

DIPYLON GATE

PIRAEUS GATE

MELITIAN GATE

PNYX

ACROPOLIS

AREOPAGUS

AGORA

STOA OF HADRIAN

ROMAN MARKET

THEATRE OF DIONYSUS

ACHARNIAN GATE

DIOMEAN GATE

Aqueduct of Pisistratus

ROMAN BATHS

DIOCHARIS GATE

TEMPLE OF ZEUS

STADIUM

ITONIAN GATE

247

scale. In the year 267 A.D. some Germanic barbarians, known as Herulians, sacked the city. The Athenians then abandoned the western
Agora, because it was too large to defend, and used materials from its
buildings for a new wall, named after the Roman emperor, Valerian.
The Stoa of Attalus became the western end of the Agora and business
centered in the area of the Roman oil market to the east of it (Map
57).

The Agora was dominated on the west by the hill of Colonus
Agoraeus. Further to the west lay the potters' quarter, or Cerameicus,
from which the Sacred Way led through the Dipylon, or double gate
in the city wall, past the cemetery to Eleusis. Around the hill of Colonus
congregated the metal workers, and on its top was placed, appropriately, the great Doric temple of Hephaestus, which was built soon after
450 B.C. and until recently was known as the Theseum. East of the
temple of Hephaestus, on lower ground, were various public buildings.
The Stoa of Zeus, or Royal Stoa, was a large covered colonnade, adorned
with mural paintings and affording protection from rain and sun.
Next to it was the temple of Apollo Patroös, and further to the south
the great Metroön, dedicated to the Mother of the Gods and used for
the housing of state archives. Behind the Metroön was the Bouleuterion, where the Council of Five Hundred met. The nearby circular
building, called the Tholos, was used by the *prytaneis*. Two great stoas
flanked the southern side of the Agora. Near the western end of one
was the nine-spouted fountain, Enneakrounos, while in front of the
other was the Odeon or music hall. The Hellenistic Stoa of Attalus, the
rear of which contained shops, extended along the eastern end of the
Agora. It is impossible to describe the northern side of the Agora,
because it has not been excavated, but just beside the tracks of the
Piraeus railway has been discovered the altar of the Twelve Gods,
whence points in Attica were measured. The famous Painted Stoa
(*Stoa Poikile*), with its murals by Polygnotus (p. 179), stood further
north. The Athenian Agora, then, was a great public square, crossed by
streets and filled with busy people. Certain stoas were mere gathering
places for conversation; others contained shops. Sanctuaries and temples
of the gods and buildings for the official use of governmental bodies
were placed here and there (Figure 66). (See further the Appendix pp.
498–499.)

South of the Acropolis, no less than to the north, were important
structures (Figure 67). At some distance, for example, were the
stadium, across the Ilissus, and the huge temple to Olympian Zeus. On
the southern slope of the Acropolis were located, at the eastern end, the
Odeon of Pericles, and at the western end the Odeon of Herodes

Interior of the temple of Hephaestus at Athens with superposed
rows of columns supporting the ceiling. Drawing by G. P. Stevens,
1947, showing at the end of the cella the bronze statues of Hephaestus
and Athena designed by Alcamenes in 421 B.C. Though begun earlier
than the Parthenon, the temple's interior arrangements reflect its influence. The metopes across the east front and those along the north
and south sides near the east end, were carved and showed exploits of
Heracles and Theseus. The sculptures of the east pediment represented
Heracles, in the presence of his patron Athena, presenting the apples
of the Hesperides to an enthroned Zeus. A formal garden was planted
beside the temple, which stands on the Hill of Colonus Agoraeus overlooking the Agora (Pl. 67)

Diagram 39

249

Atticus, the public-spirited philanthropist of the second century A.D. Of chief interest is the great theater of Dionysus, where the beautiful plays were produced in the days of Pericles.[2]

The Greek theater, as tragedy itself, had a long development. We may suppose that the dances in honor of Dionysus originally took place in a circular area, perhaps a threshing floor, and then were transferred to the foot of a hillside, where the spectators might sit. Beside the circular dancing floor was placed a hut (*skene*) for the storage of simple properties. In classical times these out-of-door theaters were very large, not infrequently seating 20,000 persons. The hillside, or auditorium, was now lined with stone seats and aisles and looked down upon the dancing floor, or orchestra, where all the action took place. In the middle of the orchestra was the *thymele,* an altar dedicated to Dionysus, beside which sat the musicians, for it must be remembered that there was much singing in a Greek play. Beyond the orchestra lay the *skene* (scene building), a long building for properties, from which the actors emerged. Immediately in front of the *skene,* and connected with it by a high roof, was the *proscenium*—a line of columns almost tangent with the orchestra—which served as a background for actors and chorus. At either end of the *proscenium* was a projection forward (*parascenium*), and between it and the auditorium was the entrance passage (*parodos*) for chorus and audience. The immense theater at Epidaurus best illustrates this plan, for the theater of Dionysus at Athens, like most Greek theaters, was remodeled in later days (Figure 68 and Diagram 40).[3]

The theater of Dionysus at Athens, we have said, was the scene of the great tragedies produced during the festival in March. Infinite care, naturally, was taken to insure its success. Well before the date of the City Dionysia authors submitted their manuscripts to a committee, which selected three tragedians and five comedians to compete. To each of the authors was assigned a *choregos,* a wealthy man who assumed the financial burden (liturgy) of supplying and training the chorus; to each author was also assigned the chief actor (protagonist), for this was to be a contest and it was only fair that an author should not obtain the

---

[2] In front of this theater were a stoa and two temples to Dionysus, while in Hellenistic times a prince, named Eumenes, built a long stoa to the west. Above this stoa lay the sanctuary of Asclepius, the god of healing, who became popular in the fourth century.

[3] The chief change was this: the roof, connecting *proscenium* and *skene,* which originally was used for isolated persons, such as the *deus ex machina,* was lowered and broadened in Hellenistic and Roman times to form a stage. The orchestra, no longer a circle, was reserved for privileged spectators.

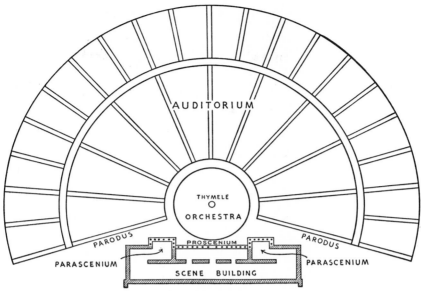

Plan of a Greek Theater.

Diagram 40

services of the three best actors.[4] At the time of the City Dionysia, then, the people of Athens, together with many foreigners, gathered in holiday mood to witness the best plays of the year, produced in a religious atmosphere and supported by the best talent of the state. The audience was a critical one, educated as it was by a succession of great dramatists; many in the audience, too, had actually taken part in performances. On each of three successive mornings three tragedies and a satyr-play were presented; on the first two afternoons, two comedies, and on the third afternoon, one.[5] At the conclusion, the judges, who had sat in the front row with the priest of Dionysus and other officials, rendered the verdict. The names of the winning dramatist, his plays and protagonist, were carved on stone, and the fortunate *choregos* was allowed to com-

----

[4] Until the days of Sophocles, the dramatist had also been protagonist, but Sophocles had a weak voice and abandoned the role, others following suit. It was Sophocles who raised the number of the chorus from the Aeschylean twelve to fifteen and the actors from two to three, although an actor might take more than one part. It was Sophocles, too, who introduced simple scenery, consisting chiefly of painted panels set between the columns of the *proscenium*.

[5] It will be recalled that comedies were also presented at the Lenaean festival in January.

memorate his service by building a small monument at his own expense. The Street of Tripods, winding around the eastern end of the Acropolis to the theater of Dionysus, was once lined with these choregic monuments (Figure 69).

ART

It was on the Acropolis itself, of course, that the most important and the most beautiful buildings of Athens, indeed of all Greece, were located (Figure 70 and Map 41). The Parthenon was erected in honor of Athena Parthenos, the serene Maiden who embodied all that is lovely in life, the patron of arts and labors, the protecting deity and symbol of the state (Figure 71). In this temple we have summed up the ideals and ambitions of the Athenians, a grand political spectacle in itself. It was dedicated during the great Panathenaic festival of 438 B.C., exactly fifty years after the basement of an earlier Parthenon had been laid. The Older Parthenon, though not completed, had been destroyed during the general burning of the Acropolis on the night of September 25–26, 480 B.C., two days before the battle of Salamis. For many years after the Persian sack the Acropolis lay in ruins, but its walls were rebuilt—on the southern side were constructed Cimon's handsome buttresses, and into the north wall were built columns and other fragments of the Older Parthenon, a permanent memorial to Athens' trial (Figure 66).

In 447 B.C. Pericles began a new and greater temple to Athena, on the site of the old one. The architects were Ictinus and Callicrates, the chief sculptor Pheidias. Except for the timber roof and the doors, the entire temple, including the tiles of the roof, was built of Pentelic marble. Through the genius of Ictinus the Parthenon achieved a noble majesty, to which the marvelous proportions and the delicate refinements, the curves and deviations from the normal, contributed mightily. The temple was Doric peripteral, with eight by seventeen columns, and measured approximately 100 by 230 feet. In addition to the usual *pronaos* and *opisthodomus,* before each of which stood six columns, the temple had two cellas. The smaller one, facing west, was called the Parthenon and was used as a treasury; its ceiling was supported by four tall Ionic columns. Facing the east was the main room, called the Hekatompedon, because it measured almost 100 feet and served as a sort of memorial to the former Hekatompedon, or Old Temple of Athena, lying immediately to the north, which had been damaged by the Persians. The interior of the Hekatompedon was divided into three aisles

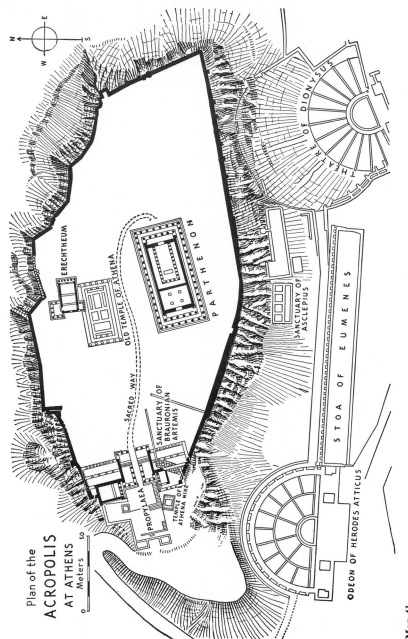

Plan of the
ACROPOLIS
AT ATHENS
Meters
0   50

ERECHTHEUM

OLD TEMPLE OF ATHENA

PARTHENON

SACRED WAY

SANCTUARY OF BRAURONIAN ARTEMIS

PROPYLAEA

TEMPLE OF ATHENA NIKE

SANCTUARY OF ASCLEPIUS

THEATRE OF DIONYSUS

STOA OF EUMENES

ODEON OF HERODES ATTICUS

Map 41

253

by two rows of superimposed Doric columns, ten on each side, with three at the back.

The charm of the Parthenon was greatly enhanced by the sculpture. Within the Hekatompedon stood Pheidias' statue of Athena, made of gold and ivory, as was also his statue of Zeus at Olympia. It has long since disappeared, but from copies made in later times and from ancient descriptions we can create in our imagination some of the overpowering beauty of the original. Athena stood erect, wearing the aegis, her left hand grasping a spear and shield, while a Victory alighted on her right hand. On either side of the shield were carved battles of giants and of amazons, on her sandals a struggle between Lapiths and Centaurs. Thus was suggested, as in the western pediment at Olympia, the triumph of civilization over barbarism. Athena, on her high pedestal, was the symbol of Hellenism and the greatness of Athens. The metopes, on the outside of the Parthenon, were carved in high relief and showed scenes of strife. They were executed by different sculptors and are therefore of varying quality, though some of them form grand compositions. An unusual feature of the Parthenon was the continuous Ionic frieze that ran around the outside of the cella, at the top—it was therefore intended to be viewed from a distance. This famous frieze commemorates the Panathenaic procession, celebrated with special magnificence every four years, when the best blood of Athens, young and old, youths and girls, brought a new robe or *peplos* for the old wooden statue of Athena on the Acropolis. We can watch them gallop along on horseback, full of life and pride, free citizens, each an individual and yet each deeply conscious that he is but a part of a great state. Others in the procession bear offerings for the gods, while still others bring animals for the sacrifice (Figure 23 and Figures 72, 73). At the eastern end, over the *pronaos,* await the gods of Olympus, giving their blessing the while to this outburst of civic pride and religious feeling.

It is obvious that no one artist could have carved all these sculptures. We think, rather, of Pheidias as the genius who designed the total composition and directed his assistants. The conception and execution of the sculptures, no less than their spirit, bespeak a new day and a great master. We saw at Olympia how a model might influence the composition; but in the Parthenon we detect the influence on technique as well. It was Pheidias who discovered how to use clay models and to reproduce faithfully, by pointing, all the details, giving to the drapery of figures, for example, a plastic quality dependent on clay. For five years after the dedication of the Parthenon in 438 B.C. the sculptors worked on the great figures in the round, which were to go in the pediments. The western gable showed the momentous struggle between Athena and Poseidon for the lordship of Attica (Diagram 42), and in the eastern gable was portrayed the birth of Athena, an event of significance for Athens and the world. The center of this group was occupied by the majestic figure of Zeus, nearby gods and goddesses marveling at Athena's wondrous birth, while other gods at a distance, not yet aware of the happy news, sat relaxed in thought. The rising Sun (Helios) with his chariot and the sinking Moon (Selene), in the corners of the gable, made the whole affair a matter of world importance (Figures 74 and 75). The wonderful sculptures of the Parthenon show great gods and idealized men—the work of artists who were masters of their tools and materials.

For many centuries the golden marble of the temple shone in all its splendor on the pink rock of the Acropolis. During the Middle Ages the Parthenon became a Christian church. In the fifteenth century, with the coming of the Turks, the church of the Virgin Mary was turned into a mosque, and in 1687 a Venetian bomb destroyed much of it. Early in the last century Lord Elgin brought many of the sculptures to London, where they form a part of the famous classical collection in the British Museum; but, for all that, the Parthenon can be really seen only in Athens, and then comes, swiftly, an insight into the imperial greatness of the ancient democracy.

No sooner had the Parthenon been dedicated than Pericles inaugurated the construction of a new and finer gateway to the Acropolis—at its western end, where the only entrance was possible. The great Propylaea were built between 437 and 432 B.C. from the designs of Mnesicles (Figure 31 and Figure 76). The original plans were changed somewhat, on account of the opposition of priests to encroachment on their land; and the outbreak of the Peloponnesian War necessitated a further curtailment. Thus the southwest wing was much abbreviated, and the east wings omitted altogether. The Propylaea were Doric, with Ionic features; for example, the columns along the broad central passageway were Ionic, for these were better suited to carry the high roof above the rising ground. The northwest wing was a picture gallery, the Pinacotheca. About 423 B.C. a graceful little temple, that of Athena Nike (Victory), was built by the architect Callicrates on the bastion in front of the Propylaea (Figure 77). This was a site of very great antiquity, now fittingly crowned by the delicate Ionic temple. At the end of the century a marble parapet was placed along the edge of the bastion, carved by six or seven sculptors with beautiful figures of Victories (Figure 78).

The Peace of Nicias (421 B.C.) enabled the Athenians to commence

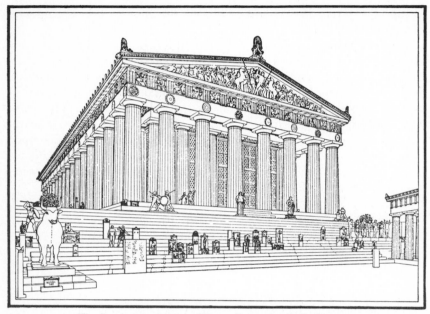

The Parthenon, from the West.   Drawn by G. P. Stevens.

Diagram 42

the Erechtheum, though work on it was soon abandoned and not begun again until 409 B.C. The Erechtheum is easily the most elaborate building on the Acropolis, a marvel of grace and delicacy, rich with the honeysuckle and other ornamentation that blend beautifully with the Ionic order (Figures 79, 80, 81; and Figure 32). It was built of Pentelic marble, but had nevertheless a frieze of black Eleusinian limestone, against which were pinned white marble sculptures. The Caryatid porch on the south side, where stately Maidens support the roof, is the temple's most striking feature; but the porch on the north, with its elaborately carved door, is perhaps even more beautiful. The Erechtheum was sacred to the guardian of the city, Athena Polias; to Erechtheus, the ancestral god of Attica; and to Poseidon. This fact, combined with the resistance of priests of other sanctuaries, probably accounts for its unusual shape. Every inch of the Acropolis was, of course, sacred ground, occupied by temples, sanctuaries, inscribed documents, and dedications; not least among the latter was Pheidias' colossal bronze statue of Athena Promachos, which could be seen from ships at sea (cf. Figures 66 and 76).

The extraordinary achievements of Athenian artists naturally attracted foreigners to the city; occasionally some of them were rewarded with important commissions, as when, for example, the Milesian Hippodamus was entrusted with laying out anew Piraeus. And, of course, Athenian artists were much in demand elsewhere. Pheidias, we have seen, worked at Olympia, and Ictinus designed the temple of Apollo Epicurius at Bassae (Figure 19), in wild Arcadia. Koroibos and Pausanias were the architects of the new Telesterion or Hall of the Mysteries at Eleusis, a great building 170 feet square. The inspiring temple of Nemesis at Rhamnus and that of Poseidon at Sunium (Figure 82) were other witnesses to the greatness of fifth-century Athens, but perhaps the simple tombstones (*stelae*) from the Athenian Cerameicus, made as they were by unknown sculptors, impress us more than anything else with the artistic genius of a gifted people (Figure 83). An artistic and economic depression hung over Asia Minor during this period, though the Nereid monument from Lycia has much charm; but all other parts of the Greek world—Olympia, Delphi, Sicily, and southern Italy—participated in the great artistic advance. One of the greatest Greek sculptors of the fifth century was the Argive Polycleitus, who was chiefly famous for his gold and ivory statue of Hera in the Argive Heraeum. No original work of Polycleitus has survived, but Roman copies give us an impression of his style, and particularly of his interest in anatomy, a subject on which he wrote a treatise. His Doryphorus shows a powerful youth carrying a spear, perhaps an Achilles; a wonderfully designed figure, full of life, where taut left arm and right leg are nicely balanced by the relaxed right arm and left leg (Figure 84). Polycleitus also made a famous and interesting statue of a youth binding his head (Diadumenus) and another of an Amazon; he worked chiefly in bronze, a medium popular not only in Argos, Corinth, and Sicyon, but in Athens and the West as well. The Nike at Olympia by Paeonius has the beautifully transparent drapery that is characteristic of the late fifth century B.C. (Figure 85A).

Of mural and easel pictures we unfortunately possess nothing, but we do know that Polygnotus and Micon were followed by Apollodorus of Athens, Zeuxis of Heraclea, Parrhasios of Ephesus, painters who understood how to handle light and shade. Greek vases, in particular the Attic and south Italian wares, often show fine drawing. Some of the sepulchral white lekythoi and red-figured vases have a strong appeal; among the minor arts the gems, especially those of Dexamenus (Figure 85B), and the coins have an exquisite and startling beauty (Figure 45). The minor arts and temples, the sculptures of men and animals, the vases and objects of daily life, all suggest that the Greeks throughout Hellas were an inspired people who loved the best in human experience.

LITERATURE

The culture of the Periclean Age, we have said, rested on belief in the all-comprehensive perfection of the state; it rested also on traditional belief purified by an expanding intelligence and humanism—belief in the power, wisdom, and goodness of the gods, in the superiority of the fathers, in the beneficence of the heroes of old. Into this culture, however, had been implanted the germ of individualism. Poets and sophists took the lead in questioning the problems of life and the old answers to them. During the second half of the fifth century the new progressive tendencies struggled with the old conservatism in a conflict fiercer and deadlier than was the strife of battle between Athenians and Peloponnesians.

Man's love of symbolism and his hope of future life went far to break the supremacy of the traditional faith. The old Olympian gods were too cold, and many people turned from them to the mystery religions and to the strange deities brought in by the swarms of foreign traders, metics, and slaves. Beside the official mysteries of Eleusis were introduced the more exciting mysteries from barbaric Samothrace. From Phrygia came Cybele, the Great Mother, during whose worship the processions, with beating drums and clashing cymbals, moved noisily through the streets. From Cyprus came the divine youth, Aphrodite's companion Adonis, whose untimely death sympathetic women lamented. Many were the new gods from Thrace, Phrygia, or the East, with their strange priests and curious rites, emotional and noisy, or secret and mystical. All alike were individualistic in contrast with the recognized civic cults. Scorned by the educated and the conservative, such innovations tended to loosen the hold of the community on its hereditary gods.

A far more active dissolvent was rationalism. While treating with forebearance the myths that formed the tragic poet's stock in trade and the background of his country's history, Euripides gives us to understand that many supernatural powers, traditionally assumed, have no real existence. The Furies that goad Orestes are but the creations of an excited mind. Homer had made the gods responsible for the good and evil acts of men; Euripides rejects the whole theory. He lays the responsibility for conduct upon the individual. The drama, then, spread advanced ideas over a large audience.

The Athenians needed the teachings and the inspiration of their great poets, for to meet the varied requirements of the citizen in this intense democracy, where life was civic duty, a man had to be well educated, not in books but in public affairs. During his education much attention was paid to manners and morals by parents, nurse, and teachers. He began his training on a small scale in the deme, where local matters were freely discussed in town meeting, and local offices gave a taste of communal management. Further experience he gained in one or more of the thousand administrative offices of the state and Empire, and in the Assembly and law courts. But this practical instruction was narrow. A broader, more idealistic education the Athenians received from the choral songs at festivals and particularly from the drama presented in the theater. More than sixty days, distributed throughout the year, were given to festivals, including dramatic exhibitions, to which must be added the holidays of the demes. Every year, too, from one to two thousand boys and men appeared before the public in choruses for the dramatic and other exhibitions which required them. These choral services, as well as others, generally rotated among the qualified citizens, thus giving all, or nearly all, a training in music and some study of literature.

Although it is true that the poets were the teachers of Athens, it is probable that they did not look upon themselves consciously as teachers, at least after Aeschylus. Certainly Sophocles (496–406 B.C.), of the suburb Colonus, did not regard himself as a teacher, nor, on the other hand, was he a skeptic, like Euripides; in religious matters he simply presented the better side of the gods as normal. The real concern of Sophocles was with the human fortunes of his characters. This inevitably grew out of his background, for as a man of wealth and education, who served the state in various capacities and mingled with all classes of people, Sophocles was chiefly interested in the effect of life upon a man's character and soul. The old legends were his vehicle, and his plays, which combine an exceptional harmony of beauty and reason, show him to be not only a great artist, but the most human of Greek tragedians.

Sophocles wrote more than 100 plays, but only seven survive entire. Of these the *Oedipus Rex* is probably the greatest. The house of Cadmus, founder of Thebes, is doomed to misfortune because it has offended the gods. Oedipus, heir to the power and the woes of this stock, is driven unwittingly to the commission of a dreadful sin, for he fulfills the dread prophecy that he will murder his father and marry his mother. He suffers unspeakable agony of mind, and his children inherit the curse. His daughter Antigone is buried alive; his two sons kill each other in civil war; the whole family sinks to ruin. The guilt, growing from generation to generation, brings its legitimate punishment. It is natural, however, that the scientific, inquiring spirit of the Periclean Age, involving rationalism and religious doubt, should reflect itself in the troubled life of the play. Oedipus, though by nature essentially religious, doubts the prophetic art of Teiresias, and seems to prove his point by irrefutable argument. His wife Jocasta rejects even the oracle of Apollo, and despising all moral law, advises a random, heedless life. But in the end all doubts are overwhelmed by the catastrophe of the drama (Figure 86).

The great exponent of the new spirit of individualism and the new humanism was the poet Euripides (*ca.* 480–406 B.C.). His life was contemporary with the manhood of Sophocles; his activity, beginning with the Age of Pericles, terminated shortly before the end of the Peloponnesian War; and yet an age seems to separate him from Sophocles. In the older poet beats the heart of Hellenism; his younger contemporary is distinctly the first of the moderns. A careful education in literature and athletics was followed by a brief career as painter, which gave him an appreciation of landscape and art noticeable in his plays. Particularly he studied the philosophers and sophists, and was among the first to collect a library. It is equally characteristic of Euripides that he held aloof from public life to apply his whole energy to the composition of plays—through no disparagement of politics, but in the consciousness that his own mission was superior to any civic achievement of the individual. The apostle of humanism, he issued his dramas as epistles to mankind. His message was the moral and spiritual interpretation of the utterance of Protagoras: Man is the measure of all things. The keen intellect and the sensitive conscience, developed by a marvelous civilization, are presented with all the artistic allurements of dramatic genius as the standards whereby to judge truth and right on earth and in heaven. Casting off from traditional moorings, he pilots mankind over the surging seas of thought and emotion; he bares the storm-tossed heart; but his ship reaches no haven, he finds no balm for the wounds he has opened. Euripides descends to the level of common folk, to sympathize with beggars and cripples, with women and slaves. The poet of the submerged majority of humanity found it no small part of his task to express the yearnings of Athenian women for a larger life and in a measure to create a sentiment in favor of their amelioration.

Skeptic and realist though he was, Euripides nevertheless wrote some magical and brilliant verse; he has not only violent invective, but tender pathos as well. The *Medea,* one of the nineteen plays that have survived from the original total of almost 100, is high tragedy, the story of a woman who is abandoned by the man she loves. Medea had helped Jason, against tremendous odds, to obtain the golden fleece and had then fled with him from her native country. At Corinth, however, Jason finds that he can marry the daughter of the king and dismisses Medea. Her love is turned to violent hatred and she murders their children. But, in Athenian eyes, Jason had not treated Medea badly, because it was not possible for a Greek and barbarian to marry. Euripides' target is not merely the Greek's attitude toward woman, but his innate smugness (Figure 87).

Boisterous comedy, rather than tragedy, was of course the usual medium by which a poet sought vigorously to impress his views upon the audience. Aristophanes (*ca.* 446–388 B.C.), the great poet of Old Comedy, was before all else a comedian, but he did not hesitate to ridicule his enemies and to advance the interests of his own conservative class. Much of the humor of Old Comedy derives from the fact that it violently attacked living persons, who as likely as not were seated in the theater. The plays of Aristophanes are full of fierce attacks upon prominent persons, cruel caricatures, gross indecencies, and, too, high flights of lyric genius. An especial object of his hatred was Cleon, but the *Knights* failed to crush the demagogue. It was different with the *Clouds,* for this made a lasting impression upon the Athenians and may have contributed eventually to the death of Socrates. As a conservative of the old school Aristophanes disliked the "new thought," and in his greatest play, the *Clouds,* tried to discredit it by attacking the leading intellectual of the day, Socrates. Similarly, in the *Frogs,* he attacked Euripides. As might be expected of a conservative landowner, Aristophanes opposed the Peloponnesian War and wrote several plays in favor of peace. It speaks well for Athenian tolerance and willingness to hear all points of view that this complete freedom of speech was allowed, but finally in the fourth century, with disillusionment and a new day, comedy forsook politics for social life. This change of subject marks the transformation from Old to Middle Comedy, which was tamer and more realistic and attempted, in quiet humor or good-natured satire, to set forth the manners and morals of the age, to picture scenes and characters from real life.

The scientific spirit of the Periclean Age was by no means limited to the dramatic poets, or to Athens itself, for ever since the intellectual awakening in sixth-century Ionia it had run swiftly through the length and breadth of Hellas, to incite in individuals a love of collecting facts and of systematizing them on a rational basis. Many literary products of this spirit served useful as well as theoretical purposes. Works on sculpture and architecture, music and literary criticism, were in part handbooks for learners of the respective arts. From the time of Pythagoras advances were made in arithmetic, geometry, and astronomy. His followers taught the rotundity of earth, sun, and moon. From a more careful study of the heavens the astronomer Meton of Athens devised a nineteen-year cycle for bringing the lunar and solar year into harmony. In this system the solar year was estimated at 365 5/19 days, about a half hour short of the truth.

From the time of Pythagoras, too, notable progress was made in medicine, so that not even the Egyptian physician could any longer compare with the Greek. Although cities were woefully backward in general sanitation, it may be set down to their credit that they supported from the public purse physicians who treated the citizens free of charge. While the masses still believed in expelling diseases by charms and prayer, or by visits to the shrines of Asclepius, the medical profession of the Periclean Age had eliminated magic and every form of superstition from theory and practice, and stood on the solid ground of scientific observation and experiment. Hippocrates of Cos (*ca.* 460–377 B.C.) was the most celebrated physician of the ancient world. In his family the profession had been hereditary, as was generally true of trades or other fields of technical skill. In view of the fact that medical knowledge had accumulated at the temples of Asclepius, where the sick and the maimed sought divine healing, it is significant of the scientific spirit of Hippocrates that in all his writings he never prescribes a visit to such a shrine. "Every illness," he declares, "has a natural cause; and without natural causes, nothing ever happens." He lays great stress on hygiene, especially diet, but he was ready to use drugs or, when necessary, cutting and cauterizing. It was his achievement to repel from his domain all assaults of sophists and speculative philosophers, and while maintaining and expanding the scientific method of his predecessors, to uphold for his profession the noblest ideals of devotion to duty and to right. Physicians today subscribe to the Hippocratic Oath.

Not only were special branches of knowledge being cultivated, but great progress was taking place in the philosophic attitude toward the world as a whole and its problems. In spite of the repudiation of Being by Heracleitus and his insistence on Becoming as the sole reality, the successors of Xenophanes the Eleatic continued more strongly than ever to deny motion and change, and to claim for Being alone a real existence. An attempt was made by Empedocles of Acragas (*ca.* 495–430 B.C.) to harmonize these views. With the Eleatics he denied absolute origin and decay; but unlike them, he believed in the plurality of Being; there are, he asserted, four elements—earth, water, air, and fire—of which all things are composed. The forces that combine and separate them are Love and Hate, the poetic antecedents of attraction and repulsion. In this way he was able to use both Being and Becoming in his theory of the formation of the world. He paid less attention to the character of his elements than to the processes of nature. In accounting for plant and animal forms he enunciated a principle crudely anticipative of the "survival of the fittest." At the same time he introduced into science the idea of "elements," which has survived to our own day. Unlike all his predecessors, Empedocles zealously courted popularity. He was a politician, a leader of the democracy of his city, a prophet, and a physician of miraculous power.

Every new philosopher, after learning what his predecessors had to teach, attempted to correct the faults of their suppositions or methods with a view of approaching nearer to the truth. Thus it was that Leucippus, a younger contemporary of Empedocles, began working out the problem of that thinker in a more scientific way. Seeing no reason why Being should be limited to precisely four elements, he assumed instead its division into an indefinite number of minute indivisible particles, termed atoms. By the side of Being, which he interpreted as matter, he assumed the exstence of Void—empty space—in which the atoms moved; in place of the mythical Love and Hate he substituted Gravitation, a strictly physical force. With Being, Void, and Gravitation, he proceeded to explain the formation of the world, the processes of nature, and even feeling and thought in a purely mechanical way. The atomic theory, developed into a system by his famous pupil Democritus in the fourth century, was generally denounced by the ancients as materialistic, hence as ethically demoralizing. Appreciating its value, however, the modern world has placed it in the foundation of science; and it still holds true, excepting that scientists have pushed the analysis of matter far beyond the atom.

More in accord with the general ethical direction of Greek thought, hence more influential, was Anaxagoras of Clazomenae (*ca.* 500–428 B.C.), the teacher of Pericles. His lasting contribution to philosophy was to substitute for gravitation an infinite and omniscient Intelligence, which orders all things. He did not consciously think of it as a person or as a deity, but regarded it merely as a directing force. If not immaterial, it was at least a substance unmixed and in quality unique. The religious and ethical consequences of his theory, however, were left mainly to future thinkers to draw.

The influence of these philosophers, or scientists, was limited to narrow circles of pupils. To the public the thinker seemed an odd, unnatural being, who in his search for the undiscoverable and the unpractical neglected everything that the Greek held dear—a subject for ridicule in comedy or for prosecution on the charge of atheism, of having substituted whirligig for Zeus. Those who, braving public opinion, became acquainted with the various systems of thought, were generally struck by their contradictions, the uncertain foundations on which they rested, and their utter uselessness in life. Thus far, in fact, Hellenic thinkers, while discovering the most fundamental principles of science and philosophy, had pursued the faulty method of generalization on the basis of too few facts. Little more could be accomplished without a careful and extensive study of nature, and for this scientific instruments were lacking.

Meanwhile with the rise of democracy, involving the theory of human equality, a demand was created for a technical education that would fit any man who wished for public life; statesmanship, once based on inborn gifts of speech and political wisdom, had to be democratized. This demand could not be met by the philosophers, and called into being the art of rhetoric, whose aim was to equip any man, however humble his talent, for public speaking. Shortly after the establishment of democracy in Syracuse (466 B.C.), Corax of that city developed the first method of juridical oratory. Rhetoric, however, concerned itself with nothing beyond the communication of thought and the persuasion to a belief or an action; it had to be supplemented by a working knowledge of government and society. Hence arose a class of men who professed to teach not only rhetoric, but all knowledge essential to the statesman. Such instructors in wisdom were termed sophists. They traveled from city to city, giving exhibitions of their knowledge and of their skill in argument, and imparting instruction to all who desired it, and who were able to pay the required fee.

The earliest of this class, and by far the most eminent, was Protagoras of Abdera (*ca.* 485–410 B.C.). The speculations of philosophers had led many to doubt the possibility of knowledge. Abandoning all hope of discovering the one true essence of the Universe, Protagoras boldly declared that "Man is the measure of all things"—in other words, everything is precisely what it seems to the individual. In two respects this declaration opened a new era. First, it directed attention to the mind and its relation to the outside world, and thus paved the way to a Mental Philosophy, or Psychology. Secondly, by shifting the center of attention from the world to man it gave, along with many co-operating forces, a tremendous impetus to the growth of individualism. Protagoras also had a theory to offer as to the basis of society and the state. The desire of self-preservation gathered mankind into cities, but fearing that men might destroy one another, Zeus sent Hermes to them all, bearing reverence and justice as the ordering principles of cities and the bonds of friendship and conciliation. Here was the beginning of a line of thought which led to the creation of sociology and political science.

Prodicus of Ceos, Hippias of Elis, and other sophists of the age borrowed from Protagoras his theory of knowledge and, with varying motive and ability, pursued the same methods. All laid stress on the distinction between nature, whose laws, observed by all nations, are morally binding, and convention—man-made customs and statutes, for which they cherished no reverence. The effect of this principle was to dissolve tradition, including the religion and the moral usages of the fathers. In their view the past was an age of ignorance and superstition; the present alone was worthy of consideration. The same principle tended equally to break down the barriers of social class and the boundaries of states. Though dissolvents of the established political, social, and religious order, the sophists were preparing the way to a world-wide humanism, to more friendly relations among states, to federations and empire. It is significant that one of the greater sophists, the Sicilian Gorgias of Leontini, seeing perhaps dimly the need of a universal language of culture, adopted for that purpose the Attic dialect.

Sophists without character or earnest purpose, however, pushed to ridiculous extremes the doctrine of Protagoras and asserted that everything is precisely as it appears to every individual. No affirmation can be false because it is impossible to state that which does not exist. If a thing is true, the opposite is equally true. Thus arose a class of disputants whose sole purpose was to confute their adversaries by quibbling with words, by fallacies of logic, and by sheer effrontery of manner. The effect was to fill the right-minded with disgust at sophistry. It is not surprising, therefore, that as an escape from the hopeless hubbub of skepticism a reaction should arise toward religious and philosophic faith. Here and there through the plays of Euripides may be found expressions of faith; and in his *Bacchae,* composed shortly before his death, the aged poet, renouncing radicalism, seeks comfort in the ancestral beliefs. The heaven he has learned to adore, however, is not the Homeric council of gods, but a moral and spiritual Power to whose guidance a man may wisely subject his soul.

A contemporary of Euripides, and a kindred spirit, was Socrates the philosopher (*ca.* 470–399 B.C.), wrongly regarded by the masses as a sophist. He was relatively poor; his estate barely enabled him to serve in the heavy infantry; and in youth he had trained as a sculptor in his father's shop. Little schooling fell to his lot; and his moderate acquaint-

ance with existing philosophers was but incidentally gained. From
early life, however, he neglected his worldly affairs to devote himself to
thought. He had the habit of standing for hours together, even for an
entire night, staring at vacancy, totally absorbed in reasoning out a
problem that chanced to interest him. Forsaking a trade which under
the circumstances could have afforded him but a meager sustenance,
he devoted his entire life to the pursuit of truth. In this vocation he was
encourged by an oracle of Apollo, which declared him to be the wisest
of men (Figure 88).

Through his whole life Socrates accepted and faithfully practised
the religion of the state, and was often seen sacrificing at the public
altars. His ideas of the gods, however, were enlightened. Whereas the
many still believed that their knowledge was limited, Socrates held
that the gods were present everywhere and knew all things. A divinity
or inner voice (*Daimonion*), accompanying him through life, gave him
warnings which he always heeded.

Socrates' belief in the greatness and the wisdom of God was strengthened by the argument of design. The world is made for man, and
every part of a human being is admirably adapted to a good purpose.
Existing things must, therefore, be the handiwork of a wise artificer,
full of love for all things living. As man is superior to animals, the
Deity has taken especial thought for him. He is pleased with those
things in us which conduce most to our well-being. Socrates drew, too,
from experience that the wisest and most enduring of human institutions are the most God-fearing, and that in the individual man the riper
his age and judgment, the deeper his religion. It was necessary for Socrates to make his sacrifices correspond with his small means, but he
believed that the joy of the Gods is great in proportion to the holi-
ness of the worshipper; and in the conviction that they well knew
his own interest, he used to pray simply, "Give me what is best
for me."

Socrates was not the mere prosaic teacher of Xenophon's memoirs;
but in addition to an ample fund of common sense he had within him
humor, imagination, intellectual power, and a love of truth so burning
as to become at times ecstatic. With such qualities he fascinated his
young companions, and some of them, especially Plato, he awakened to
a life of intense mental productivity. With Socrates true knowledge
was not simply the source but the substance of virtue; and he preferably sought that kind of truth which should determine the conduct of
men—for example, "What is piety and what impiety? What is the beautiful and what the ugly? What is the noble and what the base? What
are meant by just and unjust? What by sobriety and madness? What by

courage and cowardice? What is a state and what a statesman? What is a ruler over men and what a ruling character?"

The Socratic method of research was through conversation with one's fellows. Wherever the crowds were thickest, there Socrates could be found engaged in argument on his favorite subjects. It was easy for him to prove his opponent ignorant of the topic under discussion, as he was the most formidable reasoner of his age. Having thus cleared the ground, he proceeded by induction to establish precise definitions of general terms. "There are two things," declares Aristotle, "that one would rightly attribute to Socrates: inductive reasoning and universal definition. In fact these two things are the very foundation of knowledge." It was thus that, while professing ignorance on all subjects, he tried to build up a body of ethical science which might serve as a guide to himself and to others. In questioning all things, he stood on sophistic ground; but he made a vast advance in pointing to the reason, rather than the senses, as the universal and eternal element in man, the infallible criterion of truth, therefore, in the realm of conduct or of nature. As intellectual education, however, might increase a man's power for evil, he tried first of all to instruct his associates in self-control and to inspire them with a wise spirit in their relations with the Gods. Wisdom and Justice we should seek not only because of their use to us, but also because they are pleasing to the Gods. His teachings were quite as religious as philosophic.

Throughout his life Socrates gave evidence of loyalty and love for his fellow citizens and his country. Living with rare frugality on a small estate, he charged no fee for instruction, but lavished the wealth of his spirit on rich and poor alike. Many were his exhortations to brothers to love one another, to children to respect and obey their parents, and to citizens to be true to their country. Faithfully he performed his military duties, and as chairman of the Assembly he fearlessly adhered to law against popular clamor for injustice. He criticized the use of the lot for the appointment of officials on the ground that it brought incompetent men into public service, and with the general principles of democracy he had little sympathy. Rather than give his time to the holding of offices, he chose as a higher duty the task of preparing men to serve the state in war and peace with strong bodies, clear brains, and upright hearts.

It is true that most of his disciples were young aristocrats whose motives were less philosophical than practical. Many of them hated the democracy of Athens and were prepared to use any means to bring it down or to advance their own interests. The people of Athens could not overlook the fact that the traitor Alcibiades and Critias, the bloodiest of the Thirty Tyrants, had associated with Socrates. We should not be surprised that in 399 B.C. the enemies of Socrates were able to convince the Athenians to bring him to trial on a charge of introducing new deities and corrupting the youth and to condemn him to death.

The desire for serviceable knowledge, the interest in mankind, the absorption in the present, which characterized the intellectual movement of the Periclean Age, found notable expression in history. The spirit of scientific inquiry naturally involved an eagerness to know the past of the human race; and this desire created history. The first historian whose works have been preserved was Herodotus (*ca.* 484–425 B.C.). We are unable, therefore, to say definitely how great an advance he made beyond Hecataeus, his most distinguished predecessor, although we know that he borrowed extensively from him. Born in the period of the conflict with Persia, Herodotus lived through the earlier years of the Peloponnesian War. His native place was Halicarnassus, in Asia Minor. He spent much of his life at Athens, and traveled to Egypt, into Asia as far as Susa, to the countries about the Black Sea, to Italy—in brief, to most of the known world. Everywhere he gathered material which found its way into his work. His sources, accordingly, are of uneven value, but where he relied on his own observations Herodotus is, on the whole, thoroughly reliable (Figure 48).

As the genealogists were the literary descendants of Hesiod, Herodotus was a son of Homer, and his *History* might well be described as a great prose-epic, influenced to some extent by Sophocles and contemporary drama. A brief preface explains the object of his work: "This is a presentation of the *Inquiry—Historia—of Herodotus of Halicarnassus* to the end that time may not obliterate the great and marvelous deeds of Hellenes and barbarians, and especially that they may not forget the causes for which they waged war with one another." In his search for causes he narrates from earliest times the notable achievements of all the peoples who were involved in the Persian Wars, and thus his production may be described as a universal history. He used the Persian Wars as the unifying element of his work, and though he was ignorant of strategy and tactics, his *History* remains our chief source for the conflict. A fair-minded historian and a friend of Pericles, Herodotus described the glorious deeds of Athens, for it was Athens that had saved Greece.

So far as we know, Herodotus was the first to apply the word *history,* in its original sense of inquiry, to this field of literature. It aptly describes his method of gathering information by personal inquiry of those who were supposed to know. Often unsatisfied with an individual source, he pursued his investigation among various authorities, thus introducing the comparative method of research. We find him, accordingly, often expressing doubt as to what he hears, comparing the more with the less credible, or reasoning about the reliability of his source. Although his work abounds in myths and fictions—for no one loved a good story more than Herodotus—and though he was often at the mercy of untrustworthy informants, he was far from credulous. Even the fictitious tales are of value for illustrating the thought and life of the age.

Another great quality of Herodotus is his broad-mindedness, to which his cosmopolitan birthplace, on the borderland between Hellas and the Persian Empire, and his extensive travels contributed. He could understand that many foreign customs were at least as good as the Hellenic, that there were great and admirable characters among the barbarians, and that monarchy as well as democracy had its good features. A comparison of Egyptian with Hellenic tradition taught him the emptiness of the claim of certain Greeks to near descent from a god. His comparative study of religion convinced Herodotus that his countrymen entertained many false notions as to their own gods and as to the beginnings of the human race. Regarding the existence of the gods, however, and their providential dealings with men, the historian betrays no skepticism. With other enlightened men of his age he believes in a Divine Providence, who rules the world and in a kindly spirit watches over men, revealing his will through omens, dreams, and oracles. Like Aeschylus he seems to believe that the downfall of the great—for example of Xerxes—is in punishment for insolence (*hybris*) which unusual prosperity often induces.

In religion, therefore, though casting off much that is extraneous, Herodotus holds firmly to the enlightened orthodoxy of the time, whereas in moral character and purpose he stands on a level with the best men of his century. From the point of view of strict historical science, although advancing beyond Hecataeus, he is still crude and imperfect, whereas his broad sympathy and kindly interest in everything human, his high religious and moral principles, his inexhaustible fund of anecdotes illustrative of customs and character, his charming style and genial personality have entitled him to his place as the "father of history," as Cicero calls him, and have given his literary production a universal and eternal interest.

The greatest ancient historian, in some respects still without a rival, was the Athenian Thucydides, son of Olorus (*ca.* 471–399 B.C.). Thucydides resembled the men of the Periclean Age, not only in intensity and power of thought and style, but also in the fact that he was a man of action, as well as of words, a general in the Peloponnesian War, who could therefore season his writings with practical experience. His slowness in coming to the protection of Amphipolis led to his exile in 424 B.C. At the outbreak of the war, foreseeing that it would be memorable, he had begun to collect material for a history of it; and during the twenty years of his exile he traveled about, visiting the scenes of military operations and ascertaining facts from eyewitnesses. Doubtless he kept a record of events, which he corrected and expanded with the acquisition of new and more precise information. At the close of the war he undertook the final composition of his work, which described the great conflict between Athens and Sparta, although the first book contains a valuable sketch of the earlier years of Greece. The *History* comes to an end in the course of 411 B.C., doubtless cut short by his death.

The greatness of Thucydides as a historian rests on several kinds of excellence. One advance over his great predecessor was in the emphasis Thucydides put on the painstaking search for precision and accuracy. Thucydides' method in writing history, his desire for exact knowledge, can be found in this statement from the first book:

Of the events of the war I have not ventured to speak from any information, nor according to any notion of my own; I have described nothing but what I either saw myself or learned from others of whom I made the most careful and particular inquiry. The task was a laborious one, because eyewitnesses of the same occurrences gave different accounts of them, as they remembered or were interested in the actions of one side or the other.[6]

Another characteristic of Thucydides was his refusal to accept miraculous, mythical, or religious explanations for human events. On the other hand, he did not attempt to rationalize excessively, giving due weight to the importance of chance in human affairs. Nevertheless, he believed that a really talented statesman of the caliber of Themistocles or Pericles could significantly alter the course of events, and he hoped that his history might be useful to some such statesman in the future. Because Thucydides believed that human nature was essentially constant and that political situations often recur in similar forms, he expected his work, unlike that of Herodotus, which he took to be aimed merely at entertainment, to be of practical value and therefore "a possession forever."

The Peloponnesian War, Thucydides believed, was the most important event in the entire history of Greece—indeed, he was convinced that, as compared with the present, the past was insignificant. In study-

[6] I, 22 (Jowett's translation).

ing the war he was interested in the causes underlying the political actions of states. Some of these he connected with power, especially the peculiar sea power of the Athenian Empire. This power seemed to him to have a life of its own, to have a tendency to grow without limit unless checked. So objective is the style of Thucydides that we cannot know with certainty his attitude toward that power and empire. He seems to have taken some pride in its magnificence, but perhaps more basically he appears to have condemned its arrogance and the immoral and cruel actions to which it led. In domestic affairs Thucydides clearly disapproved of the radical democracy which followed the death of Pericles. At the same time he greatly admired Pericles and his governance of Athens, even though we consider it to have been thoroughly democratic. Thucydides reconciled this difficulty by calling Periclean Athens, "democracy in name, but the rule of the first citizen in fact." The clearest idea of Thucydides' own political opinion is given by his statement that the moderately oligarchic government of the Five Thousand instituted in 411 B.C. was the best government Athens had known up to that time.

The *History* is a literary masterpiece, influenced in part by the sophists. The speeches, which occupy a large part of the work, are, so to speak, its soul. Usually they are given in pairs, representing the opposing views of a situation or a question for decision before an assembly. The language of the speeches is Thucydides' the ideas, so far as they could be ascertained, are the orators', though even here, as the actual speeches were unwritten, the historian exercised large discretion in including what he considered appropriate to the occasion. Generally, therefore, the speeches embody the historian's conception of the situation which they present, and express most adequately his keen analytical intelligence.

Notwithstanding certain differences between ancient and modern conceptions of history, we may still look to Thucydides as a master, in important respects unrivaled. In his own personal reserve, in the determination with which he pursues his single aim, rejecting every extraneous matter, in the relentless analysis, which lays bare the souls of individuals, of factions, of communities, in the fairness and mental placidity with which he treats of personal enemies and opposing parties, in intellectual depth, keenness, and grasp, we may safely say that he has thus far no equal.

Greece in the fifth century produced a galaxy of brilliant men, many of whom were Athenians, or chose to live in the violet-crowned city. It was a crowded, complex century. While admiring the Parthenon and the Sophoclean drama, we recognize that they are so essentially

Hellenic as to defy imitation, whereas the sculpture of the Nike parapet, the plays of Euripides, and the reasoning of Socrates, however high their excellence, have an appreciable kinship with modern civilization. Needless to say, neither the private nor the public life was faultless. The blemishes of the civilization show themselves, for example, in the cramping of the lives of the women, in the existence of slavery, in the narrowness and exclusiveness of Athenian interests, as opposed to those of metics, allies, Hellenes, and the world. A part of this narrowness—at once the strength and the weakness of ancient Greece—was the self-sufficiency, the particularism, of each independent city-state. The morality of Hellas was essentially civic. The fundamental motive to right conduct, as Pericles himself asserts, is the good of the state.

I would have you day by day fix your eyes upon the greatness of Athens till you become filled with the love of her; and when you are impressed by the spectacle of her glory, reflect that this Empire she owes to men with the fighter's daring, the wise man's understanding of his duty, and the good man's self-discipline in its performance, to men who if they failed in any ordeal disdained to deprive the city of their services, but sacrificed their lives as the best offerings in her behalf.[7]

The patriotic devotion here required was too intense to be lasting. Not long after Pericles the gradual disintegration of the city-states resulted in depriving the citizen of his moral basis, and compelled him to fight out anew the whole battle of conduct on other, very different ground.

[7] Thucydides, II, 43 (Zimmern's translation).

Chapter XV

SPARTA AND THEBES

THE NEW DAY

THE Peloponnesian War closed an epoch in Greek history. Through waste of life and property and through the withdrawal of the energies of states from the productive works of peace it harmed the victors almost as much as the vanquished. The isolation of the Peloponnesus by the Athenian fleet during the early years of the struggle damaged its commerce. Toward the end of the conflict, when all fear of the Athenian naval supremacy had vanished, there began a concentration in cities and an industrial economy. These changes diminished the number of hoplites and farmers, and added to the number of day laborers and slaves. Hence, although the total population remained about the same in numbers, it underwent social deterioration. The military decline of the Peloponnesus during the fourth century may be traced to political disintegration more than to waste of war or to economic factors. But above all, the Spartan character had been sadly undermined.

Naturally Athens was among the chief sufferers in the Peloponnesian War. Her country was more systematically harried than any other in Hellas, the thin soil deteriorated from negligence in fertilizing and from the enemy's ravages. Country dwellings and barns had been burned or torn down and carried off by the Spartans and Thebans; the livestock had been killed and eaten by owners or driven off by the invaders. More than 20,000 slaves, many of them skilled workmen, had deserted to the enemy. Thus many citizens were deprived of their shop-hands and their livelihood. Merchant ships, as well as war galleys, had perished and industry shrank. The loss of property in the islands impoverished many citizens. Even more deplorable was the loss of life. In battle, plague, starvation, and executions under the Thirty Tyrants, the number of adult male citizens had appreciably sunk.

No people can live through so great a conflict and remain unchanged. The psychological effect of the collapse of the Athenian Empire was tremendous, for now the one institution which seemed to promise stability and some sort of union was gone. The significant point about fourth-century Greece is the apparent disintegration of society. Henceforth, wider group loyalties seem to be subordinated to narrower ones; and, indeed the individual, who through sophistic training had learned to question all authority, was in revolt against the group. It would be easy to overdo this. The general level of intelligence was now probably higher than ever before. Great thinkers, such as Plato and Aristotle, who were to influence thought in subsequent ages, lived in this century; so did important artists—though few poets of note. Athens, because she showed moderation in her restoration of the democracy and by her wise financial reforms, soon recovered some of her strength. Viewed in a certain light, fourth-century Greece, it is true, presents the picture of Panhellenic anarchy, of a race deliberately bent on suicide, but this was due in large measure to an economic depression. What was needed more than anything else was emigration, a resumption of the colonization of the archaic period. Thrown on their own insufficient resources, in a changing world, men inevitably considered their own good, not the state's. It is little wonder that some people advocated a return to the old Spartan discipline. The "spring had gone out of the year" long ago, but Greece remained, nevertheless, vital and interesting, virile and intelligent. The question that engaged many people, because Greece was clearly becoming cosmopolitan, was the possibility of union and the form it would take. Would the city-state be able to effect it?

The growth of individualism, as a matter of fact, fostered the development of monarchy as well as democracy. In the political disintegration of the fourth century, tyrannies sprang up in some of the smaller states; and in western Hellas the feebleness of the socialistic democracy of Syracuse, in the face of the Carthaginian peril, made possible the creation of a tyrannic empire, which in extent and power was thus far unrivaled in Hellas. At the same time, in the minds of the educated who, like Xenophon, had traveled and seen the advantages of monarchy or, like Isocrates and Plato, had brooded over the evils of the existing state system, there developed a sentiment in favor of one-man rule.

Notwithstanding these conditions, tyranny was less frequent in the fourth century than it had been in the seventh and sixth. The accumulation of knowledge, with its organization in departments, led to a corresponding specialization of activities. Statesman and general were clearly differentiated. The former was now a trained orator with a special knowledge of finance and of international administration, whereas the military leader had to acquire a knowledge of the science and art of war unknown in former periods. Hence, as a rule, it was no longer possible for a demagogue to command the means of making himself a tyrant, and the republican form of government thereby gained stability.

Aristocracy, in which a few good men ruled unselfishly and wisely for the general advantage of the community, was more a dream of the political theorist than a historical reality. Certainly in the fourth century little, if any, vestige of it existed, nor could a man of practical sense look upon it as among the possibilities of the future. The prevailing forms of government in the fourth century were oligarchy and democracy. With them the statesman, and any thinker above the mere visionary, had to deal as conditions too deeply seated to be cast aside, but capable of improvement.

The actual constitution hinged, of course, upon property and its distribution. The rich aimed not only to preserve their estates, but also to exploit the government and the masses for their own economic profit, whereas the poor were not content with protecting themselves from the aggressions of others, but strove to convert more or less of the property of the rich to the use of the state and of themselves. There existed, too, a middle class, chiefly farmers in comfortable circumstances, fairly satisfied with their condition and opposed to both oligarchic and democratic extremes. Political philosophers, such as Aristotle, and practical statesmen of broad intelligence concerned themselves with methods of preserving an equilibrium of these social forces, that neither extreme might gain the upper hand.

An unhappy aspect of the fourth century was the development of class consciousness, engendered by the growth of culture and luxury.

Priding themselves on their refinement, educated men of means despised those who in youth had been compelled to labor instead of attending school. Class feeling was increased not only by the widening differentiation of society into rich and poor, educated and ignorant, but also by the gathering of the people into the city. Never before in the history of the world were the masses so conscious of these economic-social contrasts or of their own power. Under these circumstances it was but natural that they, the controlling majority, should bring to the front a program more or less socialistic. Upon one thing at least they were determined: that the wealthy man in office should no longer exploit them for his own profit, that out of office the rich should not make an insolent display of their wealth. Lycurgus, for example, ordered that Athenian women should not ride in carriages to Eleusis at the time of the festival, "lest the poor appear more despicable than the rich." Another plank in the popular platform required the wealthy, willing or unwilling, to contribute liberally for naval and festival liturgies and to pay direct taxes in time of war according to their means. The amount of pressure thus brought upon the rich varied in different states and in the same state at different times. In Athens the ordinary revenues, added to the relative mildness of political feeling, generally assured to the wealthy an immunity from exactions. There as elsewhere, however, it was felt by many that inequality of property was the root of all evil, for which the only remedy was communism.

Another unhappy aspect of the fourth century was the withdrawal of many wealthy citizens from politics. Many young men of eupatrid rank now cared only for gambling and low company. A bourgeoisie, which had been recruited from the poorest class and nursed into prosperity by an expanding economy, could not neglect business for the service of the state in office or assembly. Duality of thought and action became more pronounced, as life grew more complex and specialized. In the degree, therefore, that a man devoted himself to philosophy or literature he unfitted himself for everything else. The thinker stood as far removed from the politician as the orator from the general. The pursuit of individualistic aims deprived the state of the service and guidance of its more intelligent and cultured citizens, leaving it to the mercy of professional politicians, who commanded the votes of the poorer and less enlightened minority. For the political evils of which fourth-century writers bitterly complain, they and their class were chiefly responsible, inasmuch as their own aloofness from public affairs left the democracy unbridled. The conditions lamented by conservatives, however, were a symptom and a cause of a vast political evolution slowly and silently underway throughout Hellas. The broadening humanity, the waning interest in local politics, and the aversion of cultured citizens from military life meant the decline of the *polis* and the development of a larger and more liberal state-system, the preparation of a transition from regional to world politics, from racial to cosmopolitan culture.

THE SPARTAN EMPIRE

As champions of particularism, of decentralization, and of the untrammeled sovereignty of the individual city-state, the Spartans had led their allies in the wearisome war with Athens. When, however, the Spartans found themselves masters of Greece and in their turn had an opportunity to unite the country, they could rise to no higher conception than that of holding what they had gained. Disregarding their promises, they thought merely to substitute their city for Athens as the head of an empire, no small part of which they had already sacrificed to Persia.

The change from Athenian to Spartan leadership was not an improvement for the subject states. The Lacedaemonians lacked the talents needed to govern an empire; they were totally without experience in imperial finance and in the administration of justice; nor did they have the necessary resources for governing an empire. The number of full Spartan citizens had so shrunk, to 2,000 perhaps, that they even had difficulty in keeping their own lower classes in subordination. It was a misfortune that no reform or revolution had succeeded in extending the citizenship at least to the perioeci and in emancipating the helots, for Sparta's rigid system was obsolete. And now the inflow of imperial funds and a widening horizon broke the old Spartan discipline and simplicity, so that even the women became ostentatious and arrogant. Dreamers like Plato, disregarding the facts, might in imagination transform the Spartans into ideal citizens, but Xenophon, though an enthusiastic admirer of Sparta, saw in the petty ambition and sordid greed of individuls a mark of decadence.

For a brief period after the conclusion of the Peloponnesian War the dominant figure in Greek politics was the victorious Spartan, Lysander. Unscrupulous and clever, with an astounding mastery of men and parties, Lysander hoped to make himself lord of Hellas. On him all eyes centered in fear or admiration; some persons even sacrificed to him as to a god. Throughout the Aegean world he organized oligarchies in the cities taken from Athens. These oligarchies of ten (*decarchies*) were his partisans and were generally supported by a Peloponnesian garrison and commander *(harmost)*. They reveled in the plunder, oppression, and murder of their fellow citizens, and in venting their hatred upon personal enemies. About the time of the restoration of the Athenian democracy many of the *decarchies* were abolished. The Spartans permitted this, because they disapproved of the insolence and the vaulting ambition of Lysander. Confronted by a menacing opposition at home, he retired into exile.

In spite of Lysander and the loss of the war, Athens slowly regained some of her strength. The violence of the Four Hundred and still more of the Thirty Tyrants had disgusted moderate Athenians with oligarchic methods and had assured the popular government a permanent lease of power. The democratic restoration in 403 B.C., therefore, was thoroughgoing. Against an effort, on the one hand, to limit the franchise to landowners and, on the other, to extend the citizenship to all, including even slaves who had aided the overthrow of the Thirty, conservative statesmen returned the government to its old democratic path. Their renewal of the Periclean law of 451 B.C., which limited the citizenship to those whose parents were both Athenians, was dictated largely by the poverty of the state. The democratic government proclaimed to those who had sided with the Thirty an amnesty, which was generally kept. All hatred gradually died out with the generation that had lived through the crisis.

An unhappy result of this disordered period was the increasing use of mercenaries. Greeks still continued to fight for their state; in fact, they fought so much that they were finally overcome by war-weariness. But the economic distress of small farmers was so great that many of them, especially in land-locked Arcadia, sought escape in a profession which, in spite of its precarious nature, promised a higher reward than some skilled workmen could hope for. His status being in an experimental stage, the fourth-century mercenary had considerable influence on contemporary politics. A notable example of this occurred in 401 B.C. when the young Cyrus set out at the head of some 13,000 Greek mercenaries and a much larger number of Asiatics against his brother Artaxerxes, who had succeeded to the kingship of Persia. The prize of battle was to be the throne. At the town of Cunaxa, not far from Babylon, the brothers met. The Greeks were victorious over a greatly superior force; but Cyrus was killed, and the expedition therefore failed. Though the Greek generals were trapped and slain by the enemy, the mercenary force elected new commanders, among them Xenophon. According to his account, vividly presented in the *Anabasis,* this young man, an Athenian of the school of Socrates, was the inspiring genius of the retreat. The homeward march of the Ten Thousand across rivers, over mountains, and through the deep snows of Armenia, ever harassed by the enemy and in want of food and clothing, was a heroic achievement. It proved that the Greeks had not lost their virility, and it laid bare the weakness of Persia.

A result of this expedition was war between Lacedaemon and Persia; for the Spartans had aided Cyrus. A Peloponnesian army, accordingly, invaded Asia Minor, and was re-enforced by the remnant of the Ten Thousand. Ultimately all, or nearly all, the Greek cities were liberated from Persia; and some native towns in the interior, including Pergamum, were taken. In 396 B.C. the Spartan king, Agesilaus, took command. Though far from brilliant, he was master of the art of war as taught in Sparta; and with an army of scarcely more than 20,000 men he made headway against the Persian forces. Encouraged by the expedition of Cyrus, he hoped to win a great part of Asia Minor.

To many Greeks, however, Sparta's policy seemed to be one of self-aggrandizement. Opposition in a weaker state she crushed with war and devastation. Her more important allies, such as Corinth and Thebes, were irritated by their exclusion from the advantages of victory over Athens. When Sparta interfered in their internal quarrels, the two states declared war. Argos, always at heart an enemy of Sparta, followed suit. The democrats at Athens, who controlled the government, were also hostile to Lacedaemon, and welcomed the opportunity to join with Thebes, Corinth, Argos, and a few lesser states in a coalition against Sparta. Thus arose the Corinthian War (395–387 B.C.).

Early in the war Sparta found it necessary to recall Agesilaus from Asia. Small victories were won by the Lacedaemonians, but the gains were more than offset by an overwhelming naval victory of Conon, off Cnidus, over a Spartan fleet (394 B.C.). Conon, an Athenian, was an admiral in the Persian fleet, and the fleet itself was now largely manned and commanded by Greeks. In the following year Conon sailed into the harbors of Piraeus. With the labor of his crews and with Persian money, increased by contributions from Thebes and other friendly states, he rebuilt the fortifications of the port town and the Long Walls. After the completion of these works Athens again counted as a power in Greece. She recovered Scyros, Imbros, and Lemnos, long occupied by her colonists, and renewed her alliance with various Aegean states. A graver misfortune, however, befell Lacedaemon by land. Recent years had seen a great development of light infantry. A master of this branch of warfare was the Athenian Iphicrates, who had trained his light troops to a high pitch of efficiency. With this force, in the neighborhood of Corinth, he attacked a heavy battalion (*mora*) of Lacedaemonians, 600 strong, and annihilated it (390 B.C.). Among the slain were 250

Spartans. It was a terrible calamity, for the whole Lacedaemonian force counted but six such battalions.

For some time Sparta had been treating with Persia for peace; and now as the tide of war turned decidedly against her, she urged on the negotiations. Her deputy Antalcidas rewon the Great King's support, which speedily restored to Sparta her dominance in the conflict. At the summons of the satrap Tiribazus, deputies from the Greek states met at Sardes to hear the terms of peace dictated by the King (387 B.C.). The King's Peace, as it was called, returned Asia Minor and Cyprus to Persia; the Athenians were required to give up their maritime league, Thebes to grant independence to her Boeotian allies, and Corinth and Argos to separate. All the more important enemies of Sparta disliked the terms, but all were constrained to accept them. It was unfortunate that the duty of enforcing the peace fell chiefly to the Spartans, who, having learned nothing by experience, exercised their renewed power with insolent brutality. But, above all, it was a disgrace to Greece that her Asiatic cities should be surrendered to the Great King, and that he should become the arbiter of her fate. Nevertheless, the King's Peace served as a beginning of the most important peace movement in Hellenic history.

To rid herself of possible enemies Sparta compelled the Mantineans to destroy their city and to scatter in villages (384 B.C.); and her general Phoebidas treacherously seized the Cadmeia, the citadel of Thebes, though the two states were officially at peace (382 B.C.). Sparta's influence steadily extended north, but not for long. By 374 B.C. Jason of Pherae succeeded in uniting all of Thessaly and contracted alliances with Macedon and the Boeotian League. Thessaly, always backward, was a pastoral and agricultural country, worked by serfs (*penestae*) and governed by the powerful barons of Pharsalus and other towns. The growth of towns had been accompanied by the development of a free Thessalian peasantry, so that the country, now united under Jason, was something of a power, until his assassination a few years later (Map 15).

Further to the north, and at a slightly earlier date, Sparta had another rival in the Chalcidice, where Olynthus, by absorbing adjacent communities, had become the leading city. She then made herself the center of a Chalcidian League of a type far more liberal and advanced than any other thus far known to Greece. The citizens of every city had rights of holding property, transacting business, and contracting marriage in every other city; one body of laws and one citizenship were the common possession of all. In a great degree the union had the character of a single state, in which the cities were municipalities. The Chalcidian

League was an aggressive power, ever intent on annexing new communities by persuasion or force, reaching out Thraceward toward the gold mines of Mt. Pangaeus and wresting from Amyntas, king of Macedon, his capital Pella. The Chalcidian League, perhaps, offered a solution of the peace problem of Greece; but at the request of some neighboring Greek states whose sovereignty was threatened by Olynthus, Sparta interfered, and in a four-year war destroyed the federation and forced Olynthus into alliance with herself (379 B.C.; Map 14).

By these measures and others of a like nature Sparta made herself supreme in Greece. She also formed a treaty of alliance with Dionysius, tyrant of Greek Sicily and Italy, so that Hellas now attained a higher degree of political unity than ever before. The man who had led his city to these achievements was the Spartan king, Agesilaus, the embodiment of the Lacedaemonian spirit, patriotic, ambitious, and efficient, but with stunted ideals, unprogressive alike in military art, in statesmanship, and in humanism—a man who tested the right or wrong of every action by the sole advantage of Sparta, whose vision, limited to brute power, took no account of the moral forces roused through Hellas by his policy of blood and iron. The catastrophe in the drama of Lacedaemonian supremacy began when a few patriots, who had fled to Athens, secretly returned to their native Thebes, destroyed the oligarchy, and expelled the Spartan garrison from the Cadmeia. Shortly afterward, when Sphodrias, the Spartan officer, tried to seize Piraeus, Athens sought an alliance with Thebes (378 B.C.).

After the battle of Cnidus (394 B.C.) the former allies of Athens, having had enough of Lacedaemonian tyranny, began returning to her. These alliances had been dissolved by the King's Peace of 387 B.C., but were almost immediately renewed. Now that she faced a new struggle with the Peloponnesus, Athens called upon all Hellenic states, and on all foreign states but Persia, to join in a league of protection from the comomn tyrant. Thus, in 377 B.C., the Second Athenian Confederacy was born. In reality, this new League was not an instrument of government, but an alliance designed to last as long as its principal members wished. It represents, nevertheless, an interesting attempt of certain Greek states to work out a federal system of government. All members of the confederacy were autonomous and were to send their representatives to a congress (*synedrion*) at Athens, in which the Athenians alone were to have no part. To be binding on the Confederacy, a resolution must pass the *synedrion* and the Athenian Assembly. Thus Athens was made equal to her collective allies, but was barred from tyranny over them. Other mistakes of the earlier Empire were avoided; the imposition of tribute and colonization were forbidden; the old system of handling commercial cases was continued, but there was no federal court for political and criminal cases: probably the jurisdiction of the allies was confined to offenders in their own states. Military and naval forces and money contributions were to be levied, by resolution, as needed. Athens, of course, encroached upon the autonomy of her allies, but gradually the Confederacy dissolved, without having made much impression upon contemporary life.

The war which had broken out in 377 B.C. between the Second Athenian Confederacy and Sparta continued for six years. Athens, supported by her admirals Chabrias and Timotheus, son of Conon, and guided by her statesman Callistratus, finally joined Sparta in an abortive Peace Convention. Thebes now abandoned the conflict with Sparta, and gave her attention to restoring the Boeotian League under her supremacy. Far from limiting her ambition to Boeotia, Thebes attempted the subjugation of Phocis—a movement that converted Athenian friendship into dislike and brought a Peloponnesian army into central Greece.

Under these circumstances Athens and Sparta were all the more ready to conclude peace. In 371 B.C. another Peace Convention assembled at Sparta. All the Greek governments sent their deputies, including even Dionysius of Sicily and Amyntas, king of Macedon. Envoys from the Persian king were present to take part in the deliberations, but not to dictate the terms. It was the most representative body that had thus far gathered in the history of the world, and was further notable for the fact that its purpose was not purely Hellenic but international. This "world peace congress" passed a scheme for general disarmament and the voluntary enforcement of sanctions. Sparta and Thebes, however, quickly brought it to nought, for when Epaminondas, the Theban representative, sought to sign the convention on behalf of all Boeotia, Agesilaus repudiated his claim and arbitrarily erased from the document the signature of Thebes. Epaminondas had acted on mature deliberation and in full confidence of the ability of his own state to maintain his principle. Boeotia had developed a body of heavy infantry unequaled in that generation, and her cavalry far surpassed that of the Peloponnesus. Epaminondas, a cultivated philosopher of the Pythagorean school, was a shrewd diplomatist and, as events proved, a great general and a patriotic, inspiring leader of youth as well.

The Peace Convention was dissolved, and the deputies returned to their homes, while Thebes prepared for the coming conflict with the Peloponnesus. The army sent by Sparta into Phocis, 10,000 strong, now received orders to invade Boeotia. King Cleombrotus, its general, obeyed. An army of 6,000 hoplites and 1,000 cavalry under the Boeotarchs, including Epaminondas, met him at Leuctra (371 B.C.). On his left wing Epaminondas massed his Thebans in a column fifty deep, and led them in an irresistible charge upon the Lacedaemonian force stationed opposite, while his Boeotian allies, in echelon formation, barely came to close quarters with the Peloponnesians. In other words, Epaminondas won by throwing a superior force upon the critical point in his enemy's line. Of the 700 Spartans present 400, including the king, were slain. Sparta acknowledged her defeat and withdrew her army. Her supremacy was forever ended.

THE ASCENDANCY OF THEBES

Xenophon, whose *Hellenica* is our chief source for the period between the end of Thucydides' *History* and the battle of Mantinea, relates in a vivid passage the manner in which the Spartans received the news of the disaster. The messenger arrived at the time of the *gymnopaedia,* but the ephors allowed the contest to run its natural course.

What the ephors did was to deliver the names of the slain to their friends and families, with a word of warning to the women not to make any loud lamentation, but to bear their sorrow in silence; and the next day it was a striking spectacle to see those who had relations among the fallen moving to and fro in public with bright and radiant looks, while of those whose friends were reported to be living barely a man was to be seen, and these persons flitted by with lowered heads and scowling brows as if in humiliation.[1]

Narrow and illiberal as were the Spartans, we cannot help admiring their resolution and their discipline. After the great loss at Leuctra there remained scarcely more than 1,000 Spartans, from the full citizens, capable of bearing arms, and what was far worse, their military prestige had vanished. No sooner did their allies become fully aware of the magnitude of the event at Leuctra than a democratic wave swept the Peloponnesus. Executions, banishments, revolutions, and massacres followed. The Peloponnesus seemed to be sinking into chaos.

In a desire to save for peace and order what they could from the general wreck, and doubtless too in their own interest, the Athenians summoned a Peace Convention to meet in their city. Through this Convention, which agreed to maintain the *status quo,* Athens attempted to usurp the place of Sparta as head of the Peloponnesian states. The first consequence of the Convention was the resolution of the Mantineans to rebuild their city. Next Mantinea, Tegea, and all the communities

---

[1] *Hellenica,* VI, 4, 16.

of southern and central Arcadia organized themselves in a league. As Sparta threatened the new federation, Thebes came to its assistance. Having recently gathered under her hegemony many states of central Greece, she was able to dispatch to the Peloponnesus an army which, increased on the way by the forces of allies, amounted to 40,000 men or more, under the command of Epaminondas. For the first time in recorded history Laconia was ravaged, but Sparta itself could not be taken (Map 27).

The permanent result of the expedition was the liberation of Messenia. While the perioecic towns of the south remained faithful to Sparta, the rest of the country was organized by Epaminondas into a new state. Thus, nearly a half of Lacedaemon, and that too the most fertile part, was wrested from Sparta. The helots, now emancipated, became its citizens, increased in number by the return of exiles. Messene was founded as the new capital on Mt. Ithome, the strongest military position south of Corinth. To hem Sparta in and to destroy her as a Peloponnesian power, Epaminondas founded another city, Megalopolis (369 B.C.), which became the capital of the Arcadian League. Here met the Council of Fifty (*damiorgoi*), representing the communities according to their population, and the Assembly of Ten Thousand, which included all the citizens of the League. Shortly afterward, through the campaigns of Pelopidas, a battle-thinker second to Epaminondas in generalship, Thebes forced her hegemony upon Thessaly and Macedon, but nowhere was she able to maintain peace or establish a firm control. Under these circumstances several more Peace Conventions were held. It is regrettable that seven Conventions, which had promised not only a Hellenic but an international peace, degenerated and died with little fruit.

The attempt of Pelopidas to establish through negotiation an empire for his city failed; nor were campaigns of Epaminondas north and south much more successful. The great impediment to Theban supremacy was the Athenian navy. Concluding, therefore, that he must by all means destroy it, Epaminondas built a fleet of 100 triremes, and in 364 B.C. sailed forth to dispute with Athens the control of the Aegean. Fortunately for Epaminondas the maritime states were resenting recent encroachments of Athens, and Byzantium passed over to him, while others wavered in their allegiance to Athens. His naval campaign was so great a success that the Thebans may well have hoped in another summer to drive Athens from the sea. The support of a navy, however, imposed upon the Thebans too great a strain to be long endurable, especially at a time when their interests in the peninsula demanded their whole attention. In the year of the naval campaign Pelopidas

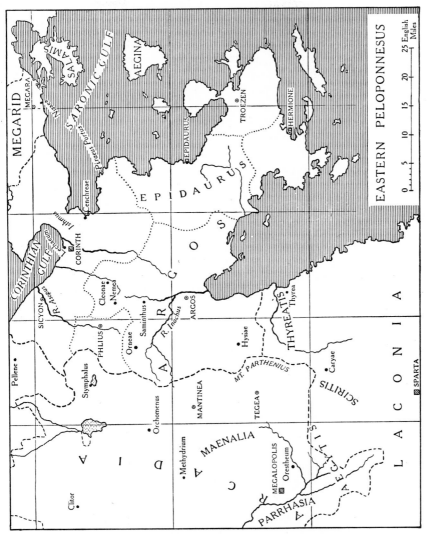

EASTERN PELOPONNESUS

Map 43

285

had to conduct a new expedition to Thessaly, during which he lost his life in battle. Although in the following year all Thessaly was reduced to obedience, the Thebans feared a disruption of their own League. They marched against Orchomenus, which they suspected of disloyalty, destroyed the city, executed the men as traitors, and enslaved the women and children. The horror aroused through Greece by this outrage foretold the catastrophe in the drama of Theban greatness.

The ground for this event was preparing in the Peloponnesus, which had long seethed in chaos. In Arcadia a strong party, too proud and too devoted to local interests to submit to Theban hegemony, had split the League in two and were building up a great anti-Theban coalition. Mantinea, with a majority of Arcadian cantons, joined with Elis, Achaea, Athens, Sparta, and one or two lesser states, on equal terms to prevent "the enslavement of the Peloponnesus." Epaminondas had at his command, in addition to Boeotians, troops from Euboea and Thessaly, and could count upon Argos, Tegea, and some other Arcadian communities. His hope was that his presence in the south might win him an overwhelming alliance, so that by peaceful means he could quiet the turmoil and restore the ascendancy of his state. He attempted, accordingly, in a night march to take Sparta by surprise; and failing in that effort, he hurriedly returned to Arcadia, where he tried to surprise the Mantinean population with their herds in the fields. When this strategy, too, proved fruitless, and no hostile state came over o his side, nothing remained but to give battle.

The battleground was the plain of Mantinea, surrounded by lofty peaks (362 B.C.). In spite of forced marches his men were in high spirits; they numbered about 33,000, whereas the enemy numbered about 22,000. Epaminondas gained the advantage, too, of taking the enemy by surprise. The main tactic movement of Leuctra was successfully repeated; but the great commander fell mortally wounded, in his last breath advising his countrymen to make peace. Though neither side won the battle, the death of Epaminondas amounted to a Theban defeat. Of the brilliant generalship of Epaminondas there can be no doubt. His private character, too, was lovable, and in public life he stood forth an unselfish patriot. It is impossible, however, to discover in him a sign of constructive statesmanship. As manifested by his conduct, his single idea was to substitute Thebes for Sparta as the head of Greece; and in working to that end he made use of the methods long in vogue. From the beginning the task was hopeless. The Thebans were as narrow as the Spartans, and had far less experience in dealing with other states; even in Boeotia they could maintain their control in no other way than by a policy of terrorism. More impotent were they to win the loyalty of other Greeks. Their sudden decline after the battle of Mantinea suggests that their ascendancy was largely due to one man.

The idea of institutional union of all the Hellenes on terms of equal participation in the central government, and with guarantees for the rights of the weaker states, probably no one as yet had conceived. The city-state supremacy had been essentially a tyranny, whether harsh or mild; and it was now at least proved that no Hellenic state was strong enough to force her rule upon the rest. The disintegration of Hellas resulting from the downfall of Sparta, the collapse of the Peloponnesian League, and the rise and decline of Thebes, were exceedingly discouraging to such men of broad vision and liberal mind as Isocrates. It was inevitable that the chaos should last long and injure the Greek world. For all that, it should not be hastily assumed that Greece was politically bankrupt, that her only salvation rested upon the interference of an outsider. The Greeks were still a great creative people. Their expanding intelligence and liberality, more capable than ever of solving the problem of unity, were equaled only by their superb physical vitality and by the martial energy stored up in the agricultural areas of Greece—a reservoir of military strength, which, if rightly applied, was capable not only of protecting Hellas, but of conquering and ruling an empire. Nor must it be assumed that these wars between Sparta and Thebes, the wars in Sicily, and the later wars with Macedon were contemptibly petty. The city-state is not the only institution which has sought to solve its problems through war. The antipathies and the rivalries of nations are of the same character as those among cities formerly, while the wars between groups of nations are incomparably more destructive to life and property and hence more prejudicial to civilization. The wars of the Greeks in the fourth century must be considered from the point of view of those engaged in them—and we may be sure that to them the wars were not only a matter of life and death, but often of high principle as well.

Chapter XVI SICILY AND MAGNA GRAECIA

THE fate of Hellas, her protection from foreign powers as well as from internecine warfare, depended upon a political unification prejudicial to the sovereignty of the *polis,* and was desired, therefore, neither by the masses nor by the great majority of statesmen. While in Greece proper the Spartans were engaged in a vain attempt to create and maintain an empire under the supremacy of the city, an experiment at empire making of a wholly different character was taking place in Sicily and southern Italy. It was but natural that this undertaking should proceed from Syracuse, by far the most powerful state of the West.

Ever since the removal of the tyrants in 466 B.C. the government of Syracuse had been the moderate form of democracy designated by Aristotle as a polity. It was inevitable that, after the victory over the Athenian besiegers in 413 B.C., the people should demand as a reward a fuller participation in the conduct and in the profits of government. At

288

Athens the failure of the siege created an oligarchy, in Syracuse the annihilation of the invader with equal logic changed the polity to an absolute democracy. Our knowledge for the next years of the city's history is not entirely satisfactory, resting as it does upon the uncritical work of Diodorus Siculus, a writer of the first century B.C., who drew from the Syracusan Philistus, Ephorus, and other fourth-century historians.

The removal of the Athenian peril gave the shortsighted Sicilians merely an opportunity for interstate warfare; they remained heedless of the overwhelming power of Carthage at their very doors. For seventy years the fear of the Athenian navy had held Persia and Carthage alike at bay; its collapse encouraged both to extend their power. A great fleet set sail from Carthage in 409 B.C. carrying to Sicily an army much greater than Athens had brought to Syracuse. It was made up of a Carthaginian nucleus, enlarged by Libyan, Iberian, Campanian, and even Greek mercenaries. This force captured Selinus after a fierce nine days' siege. Whereas among the Greeks, through their regard for the lives of their own soldiers, the besieging of cities was notably mild, it was far different with Carthage, to whom a few thousand mercenaries counted as nothing. The city was taken by storm and the scene of butchery that followed passes the imagination. It was the first Sicilian city to be taken by foreigners, having enjoyed two and a half centuries of freedom. A few days later Himera suffered a like fate. An attempt of Syracuse to rescue the city failed. Content with his conquest, Hannibal, the Carthaginian general, returned home with his armament.

The great disaster awakened western Hellas to a sense of its peril. When Hannibal returned in 406 B.C. to lay siege to Acragas, 30,000 soldiers from the states of Sicily and southern Italy swarmed into Syracuse to defend what remained of Hellenic soil. Even this considerable force, under the command of the Syracusan Daphnaeus, accomplished nothing more than the removal of the people of Acragas before that city, too, fell into the invaders' hands.

The people of Syracuse were convinced that their generals had failed through incompetence or treason. A young officer named Dionysius, taking advantage of this feeling, persuaded the Assembly to depose the generals and to elect a new board, which included himself. His next step was to depose his colleagues, so that he became sole general. The citizens readily voted him a personal guard, with which he usurped the tyranny (405 B.C.). In the face of the advancing Carthaginians, however, Dionysius could for the moment accomplish nothing better than his democratic predecessors had achieved; the people of Gela and Camarina were withdrawn from their cities, and the entire southern coast was yielded to the enemy. Dionysius, who had his eye fixed upon a more distant goal, relentlessly overrode all discontent. To secure his own hold on the government and to save the city a siege, he came to terms with the enemy. The freedom of Syracuse and a few other Greek cities in the east end of the island was purchased by the cession of the remainder of Sicily to the Carthaginians.

In order to entrench himself in power, Dionysius first built on the island of Ortygia a strongly fortified castle and surrounded himself with mercenaries. Country estates were confiscated, divided into small farms, and assigned to newly made citizens, who were either mercenaries or emancipated slaves. To such means tyrants had often resorted, but none had equaled the ruthlessness of Dionysius. The civic body, thus reconstituted, found its only safety in upholding the despot. In extending his power by annexing the territory of neighboring communities, he did not hesitate to sell into slavery the population of Hellenic towns, that his Campanian mercenaries might possess their estates. Dionysius' use of Sicel and Italian mercenaries was based on the belief that they were more amenable to military discipline and physically more virile than the Greeks.

Having thus enlarged and consolidated his power, Dionysius began military preparations on a gigantic scale. He surrounded Syracuse and its suburbs with a great wall, so that it became the largest and most strongly fortified city in Europe. He built a navy of more than 300 warships, including many quinqueremes. His engineers invented catapults, which could throw large stones several hundred yards. His army of perhaps 80,000 men was splendidly organized and equipped. It included heavy and light infantry, artillery, and cavalry—the largest, the most complex in organization and equipment, and the most efficient body of troops that Hellas had thus far created. In fact, Dionysius introduced an epoch in the history of warfare.

With these magnificent forces Dionysius began war against the Carthaginians with the object of expelling them wholly from Sicily (397–392 B.C.). But the enemy had boundless resources in money and therefore in mercenaries. Syracusan victory in the west was followed by a Punic success which destroyed Messene and came near overwhelming Syracuse. Only the mighty walls saved Syracuse from the enemy. After years of hard fighting Dionysius contented himself with a peace that assured him the greater part of the island, with the extreme west remaining in Carthaginian hands.

Dionysius was now in a position to interfere in the affairs of Italy. Here, as in Sicily, he displayed no scruple in accomplishing his ends. With the barbarous Lucanians of the interior, who were conquering

Hellenic cities, he gladly cooperated. His share of the conquest extended from the strait to Croton. Many inhabitants of the region he sold into slavery; others he removed to Syracuse, and others were won to his cause by unexpected clemency. The empire that he built up in Sicily and Italy was the strongest military power in Europe to that day.

To his conquests Dionysius added an extensive colonial policy. Founding settlements on both shores of the Adriatic, he brought that sea into his sphere of influence. His object was partly to facilitate communications with the Greek peninsula, on which he entertained political designs, and more immediately to capture the trade that poured into the Adriatic from central Europe. Allying himself with the Gauls, he ravaged the coast of Etruria, established a naval base on Corsica, and occupied Elba, where doubtless he worked the iron mines. By such means the tyrant of Syracuse encircled Italy, possibly in the hope of dominating the entire peninsula. At all events, the power of his realm overawed the central Mediterranean region and came near monopolizing its commerce. Meanwhile, as we have seen, he entered into close alliance with Sparta and took an active part in the wars and diplomacy of old Greece.

The form of government at Syracuse was still republican, for the Council and the popular Assembly continued to meet; and the tyrant, avoiding every unrepublican title, held the office of general with absolute command of the army, although at least in foreign relations he was called archon of Sicily. His wars, extensive buildings, and splendid court consumed enormous sums of money, which he supplied by confiscations, temple robberies, sale of whole communities into slavery, debasement of the coinage, and oppressive taxes and arbitrary exactions upon his subjects.

As to the character of this extraordinary person we have few though telling hints. Dionysius' life was free from the vices that had brought many a tyrant to ruin. He had, however, two wives simultaneously, with both of whom he lived happily. With an artistic temperament his conduct was swayed not only by a Napoleonic ambition, but by friendship, fear, jealousy, and hatred. In hours of relaxation he composed dramas. So far as we can judge, Dionysius was totally devoid of moral principle and of reverence for things sacred. Although he consorted with men of ability in various fields, he followed his own counsels. The Athenian philosopher Plato came to Syracuse in the hope of realizing his ideal state through the power of the despot; but in response to his arguments the princely host is said to have had him sold as a slave. In brief, Dionysius, like Alcibiades and Lysander, was a product of his age —a nonmoral, nonreligious but otherwise splendidly gifted egoist.

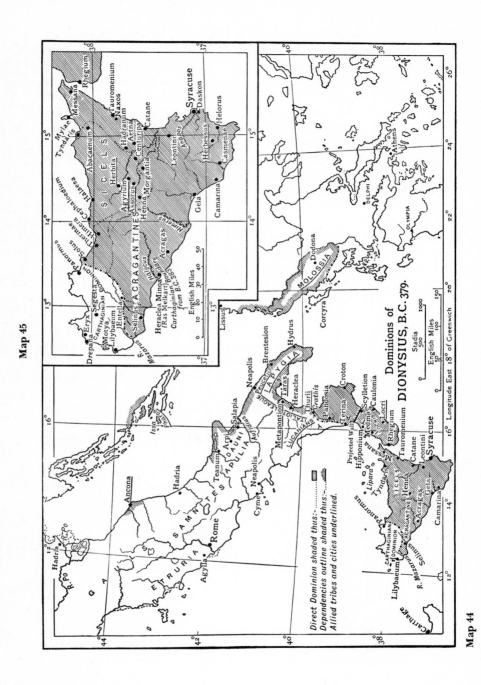

Map 45

Rhegium
Mylae
Tyndaris
Messana
Tauromenium
Naxos
Halaesa
Hadranum
Aetna
Centuripe
Catane
Cephaloedium
S I C E L S
Abacaenum
Herbita
Herbessus
Lasmenae
Agyrium
Assorus
Enna
Morgantia
Leontini
Kyamosorus
Syracuse
Daskon
Helorus
Panormus
Solus
Himera
Tisiatae
A C R A G A N T I N E S
Halycus
Acragas
Gela
Camarina
Eryx
Segesta
Drepana
Morya
Lilybaeum
Entella
Selinus
Heraclea Minoa
(Ras Melkart)
Carthaginian Dominion
from B.C. 383
Lissus

English Miles
10 20 30 40 50

Dominions of
DIONYSIUS, B.C. 379.

MOLOSSIA
Dodona
Corcyra

DELPHI
OLYMPIA
Athens

Ancona
Hadria
Agylla
Rome
ETRURIA
SAMNITES
Teanum
Neapolis
Cymē
APULIA
DAUNI
Arpi
Salapia
Luceria
Aufidus
Neapolis
Brentesion
Hydrus
I A P Y G I A
Taras
Metapontion
Heraclea
LUCANIANS
ITALIOTES
Thurii
Crathis
Siris
Pandosia
Croton
Terina
Scylletion
Caulonia
Hipponium
Medma
Locri
Projected Wall
Lipara
Rhegium
Messana
Tyndaris
Tauromenium
Catane
Leontini
Syracuse
Panormus
S I C E L S
ACRAGANTINES
Henna
Acragas
Gela
Camarina
CARTHAGINIAN
DOMINION
Lilybaeum
Mozya
Selinus
R.
Carthage

Direct Dominion shaded thus:- ......
Dependencies outline shaded thus:- ------
Allied tribes and cities underlined.

Stadia
500 1000

English Miles
50 100 150

16° Longitude East 18° of Greenwich

Map 44

292

As the modern historian reviews the destruction of Hellenic cities, the enslavement of entire populations, the grinding financial exactions, and most of all, the political and moral degradation of the free citizens under this despotism, he is inclined to look upon Dionysius as a curse to humanity. On the other side of the picture is the strong man who builds up a realm of civilized people capable of defending themselves against the assaults of the barbarians in one direction and of Orientals in the other, when both these enemies of European civilization were growing continually mightier. Appreciating the political weaknesses of the Greek character, he tried to supplement it by an introduction of native Italian and Sicel blood. Thus Dionysius was a champion of Europeanism rather than of Hellenism; and in his blending of foreigners with Greeks he stood forth as the first Hellenistic prince. Had he been followed by a line of able successors, his realm would have expanded, and might have taken the place of Rome as the civilizer of the West. As matters stood, his only service was to check the progress of Carthage till Rome grew sufficiently strong to protect Europe from the encroachment of Oriental civilization.

Dionysius died in 367 B.C. and was succeeded by his son, Dionysius II, an incapable person. The realm fell to pieces, the cities came under the rule of petty tyrants, and the power of Carthage threatened to overwhelm the entire island. Under these circumstances Corinth listened to the plea of its colony and sent Timoleon with a few hundred mercenaries to Sicily in 344 B.C. Within a few years Timoleon expelled the tyrants, and in a great victory by the Crimisus river, near Segesta, drove the Carthaginians into their strongholds on the western coast. All the cities were reorganized as moderate democracies, in which the people exercised the franchise while leaving the executive strong. A federation of the Hellenic cities provided for defense against internal and foreign enemies. Colonies from old Greece made good the depopulation caused by war, and an era of material prosperity began.

The incompetence of Dionysius II was a setback for western Hellenism; despotic, dissolute, and unenterprising, his chief desire had been to enjoy his inheritance. The fruits of his rule—civil anarchy and murder—were mitigated, temporarily at least, by the sound policy of Timoleon, the aristocratic, wise, and courageous Corinthian, but when Timoleon died in 336 B.C., clouds had once more gathered over Sicily.

Chapter XVII

THE RISE OF MACEDON

W E HAVE already remarked that a transition from regional to world politics was being prepared in fourth-century Greece. The idea, apparently, first occurred to people like Isocrates, who bemoaned the civil strife of the Greeks and thought it a pity that their country-men did not war against a common foe instead. Other Greeks, however, did not go so far in their thinking, and believed simply that the cure of all their troubles lay in monarchy. These two ideas appealed to many persons, and were fused by them, so that there developed in the Greek world a conviction that the Greeks should unite under a king and make war against a common enemy. The common enemy, of course, would be Persia, and the Macedonian monarchy seemed the ideal instrument of union.

There was no inherent reason why the city-state should not have brought about this union, for, as a matter of fact, it involved little more than the resolution of the old dilemma of Greek politics, the apparent incompatibility of autonomy and federation. Panhellenism had its difficulties, but they were not insuperable. The only real question was whether the Greeks might effect their union before it was forced on them by an outsider; and this is precisely where the city-state failed. The Macedonian monarchy was not fitted constitutionally to unite the Greeks, as later centuries were to prove, but it did produce at exactly the right moment an extraordinary individual who was able to do so. Demosthenes, who led the Athenian opposition to Macedon, and who sometimes spoke as if he were living in Periclean Athens instead of the troubled days of the fourth century, did not realize that the true enemy was Philip and not Macedon. Demosthenes viewed the struggle between Greece and Macedon as a war between free states and a primitive country under an autocratic king. His ideal, then, in opposing union under Macedon, was not a narrow one, for the issue seemed to him to be no less than one between civilization and barbarism.

We now know that the Macedonians were Greeks, but in ancient times they were regarded as barbarians with a slight veneer of Hellenism who spoke a Greek dialect. For that reason they desired all the more to be accepted as Greeks by Greeks. There was, however, this great difference between them and the Greeks; the Macedonians looked upon themselves as one people, not as citizens of this city or that. In other words, they formed the first nation in European history. Their country, Macedonia, consisted of a narrow plain bordering the northwestern Aegean and a rough hill district in the interior. The people lived a simple life in villages. The Athenians had taken possession of the coast, and had cut the country off from maritime communications with the world. The earlier history of Macedon hinged on the conflict between plain and highland. The uplands comprised several broad river valleys separated by high ridges. Each valley was the home of a tribe under its chief. Similarly, the long, narrow plain, which lay between the highland and the coast possessions of Athens, had its king. The chiefs of the interior owed an unwilling allegiance to the king of the plain, and were often in open revolt. It was King Archelaus (413–399 B.C.) who first gained a real mastery over the upland, thanks largely to his careful organization of the army and to his construction of roads. Archelaus also fostered Hellenic civilization among his people, and entertained Euripides at his court. The work of reducing Macedon to unity, however, belonged chiefly to King Amyntas III (390–369 B.C.). His reign was full of strife and anarchy, intrigue, and murder. At one time the Illyrians drove him from his kingdom; and at another the Chalcidian League robbed him of his possessions near the sea; but after its fall, in 379 B.C., the Macedonian king for the first time could reasonably hope to acquire a seaboard. Death at an advanced age snatched this opportunity from him. With a talent for governmental business and accomplished as a general, Amyntas had spent his life, sword in hand, interminably battling with Olynthians, or with the savage Illyrians and Paeonians of the northwest, repressing rebellions in his upper feudatories, or stamping out disaffection in his own household. Three lawful sons were left—Alexander, Perdiccas, and Philip—all destined to royalty and to violent deaths. After his two elder brothers had fulfilled their brief careers, Philip II, now twenty-three years of age, mounted a throne overshadowed by internal dissension and foreign war (359 B.C.). A remarkable man, his reign was to prove one of the most momentous in history (Map 14).

At the age of fifteen Philip had been sent as a hostage to Thebes, where he remained three years. This sojourn may well be compared with that of Peter the Great in Holland and England. In spite of the infiltration of Hellenic culture, the Macedonians were still uncivilized, and Philip had inherited the savage appetites and passions of his royal ancestors. His long stay in Thebes, at that time the military and political center of Hellas, was an education of the highest type. The schools and gymnasia, the armories and arsenals, the splendid Boeotian phalanx, Epaminondas and his brilliant associates, all served him as models and as an inspiration to make his own country a state of the Hellenic type and to win for himself a place among these men of superior breeding and intelligence (Figure 47, No. 3).

With a quick mind and strong hand Philip put an end to anarchy within his borders, and inspired unruly neighbors with respect for his power. Aside from his own inborn ability, perhaps the greatest element of his success was his seizure of Amphipolis in 357 B.C. and the gold mines of Mt. Pangaeus, just across the Thracian border. The mines, according to report, brought him 1,000 talents a year and constituted the foundation of his power, for their proceeds enabled him to unite his country by roads and to create, for the first time in history, a standing army of professional soldiers, superior to anything heretofore known to the world. From the peasants and shepherds, who were excellent fighting material, Philip selected the best, and formed them in a relatively shallow phalanx. These "foot companions," as they were honorably named, he armed more lightly than was customary, but he increased the length of their spears (*sarissa*). To achieve mobility, the space between man and man was increased. Philip added archers, slingers, and mercenaries as auxiliaries to the phalanx. The cavalry were equipped as light and heavy; and in the latter the nobles served as "companions" of the king. From Thebes he borrowed the idea of combined cavalry and infantry tactics, and of the tactical distinction between the two wings; one to be offensive, the other defensive. Philip not only drilled these troops, but exercised them in long rapid marches, carrying their arms and provisions. They were kept under rigid discipline, and encouraged to take part in athletic competitions. To this fighting machine he was able, when occasion demanded, to attach an efficient siege train. Thus Philip developed a military system even more complex and more efficient than that of Dionysius I of Syracuse. Its superiority consisted mainly in the soldierly qualities of the men, the professional efficiency which they acquired through long service, and the ability of the commander and his generals.

The gold of Mt. Pangaeus formed an essential element of the diplomacy in which Philip developed a masterful skill. Through ability to buy friends and reward his faithful henchmen, as well as through urbanity, good fellowship, and general adroitness in the management of men, he created in every Hellenic state a party devoted to his cause. States whose interests were threatened by his aggressions he could usually lull to a sense of security till the time was ripe for striking the fatal blow. No scruple—no lying or truce breaking—stood in the way of his seizing an advantage. Philip's ambitions were, actually, personal and dynastic rather than national. He was more than a national king of Macedon, and probably viewed Greeks and Macedonians in much the same light; the Greeks would be useful to him as soldiers and administrators, and their city life and culture should be copied by the Macedonians. Philip's aim was to increase his personal power, and in doing so he developed a consistent policy. As he conquered a new district, he always incorporated it in the body of his growing state.

The determination of Philip to win the coast region adjoining his country conflicted with the interests of the Chalcidian League and of Athens. His characteristic diplomacy kept the Chalcidice quiet, while he proceeded to annex Amphipolis and other possessions of Athens. To check his aggressions, Athens began a war upon him in 357 B.C., which, though involving only occasional hostilities, nominally continued eleven years. Meanwhile Philip made himself master of Thessaly and the greater part of Thrace. His occupation of a long line of coast added rich port customs to his revenue and enabled him to build ships to prey upon Athenian commerce. Athens was further weakened by the Social War (357–355 B.C.), during which Byzantium, Chios, and other states revolted from her Confederacy. At the end of the Social War only Euboea, some of the Cyclades and northern islands, and a part of Thrace remained to Athens. The Athenian policy of devoting a large share of the public revenues to the feeding and entertainment of the populace was also a severe strain on her resources. The control of the Theoric Fund, which received all surplus money, meant in reality the control of the state's finances; and it was fortunate for Athens that her chief statesman after the Social War, Eubulus, was a wise financial administrator.

The preoccupation of Athens with her Social War prevented her from playing a significant role in the Sacred War, which broke out in 356 B.C. Thebes had seized control of the Delphic Amphictyony during her supremacy, and used this power against her enemies. Because Phocis seemed disinclined to bear the Theban supremacy, the Council proceeded to fine some leading Phocians for alleged trespassing upon the oracle of Apollo. On the refusal of the accused to pay the fines, the Council declared a Sacred War upon their country. The Phocian commander, Onomarchus, seized the treasury at Delphi, with which he hired a great force of mercenaries. Thus provided, he was able to make headway against the Boeotians, to carry the war into Thessaly, and to contend with Philip. Hellenic sentiment disapproved of the seizure of the Delphic treasury; and though both Athenians and Spartans were allied to Phocis, neither gave material aid. Ultimately Philip expelled the Phocians from Thessaly, but for the moment, at least, he was prevented from passing beyond Thermopylae.

It was Demosthenes who roused the Athenians to their danger. Eubulus stood for peace, as most rich men at Athens did, but opposed to the peace party was the military party, consisting of persons who looked back to the old days of Athenian greatness. Proclaiming anew the civil ideals of Themistocles and Pericles, Demosthenes urged his countrymen to sacrifice and suffer for their country. In his *First Philippic,* delivered in 351 B.C., he told the Athenians that Philip had grown great through their own inaction, and that if they were to check his further aggrandizement they should keep a fleet in the northern Aegean, large numbers of men should enlist, and the wealthy should contribute to the cost. But Demosthenes was still young, and his words carried little weight. Nothing was done on that occasion, and Philip continued to gain ground (Figure 89).

Two years later, after demoralizing the Chalcidic cities with bribes, Philip entered openly upon their conquest. Appeals to Athens for help were supported by the eloquence of Demosthenes in his three *Olynthiac Orations.* In the spirit of the *First Philippic* Demosthenes urged his countrymen to join with the Olynthians in putting down the common enemy, while he was still at a distance. Far from losing himself in eloquent generalities, the young statesman had a definite plan to propose,

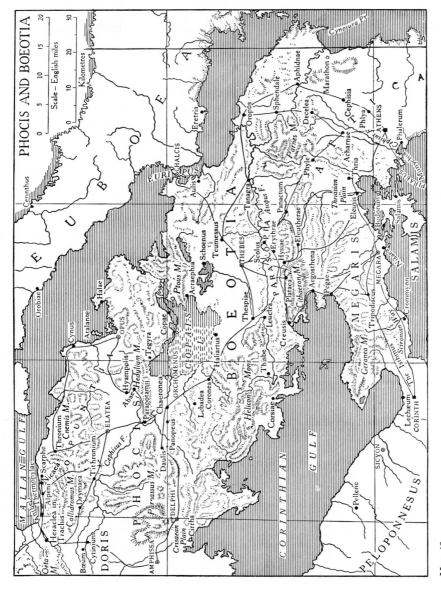

PHOCIS AND BEOTIA

Map 46

299

as on other occasions, worked out in minute detail. If the citizens were to receive money from the state, he maintained, they should earn it by labor—the young men by military duty, the elders by service at home. The appeal fell on deaf ears, for only inadequate and tardy help was sent. The Chalcidian League fell (348 B.C.). Of the cities which composed it a few only were spared and were admitted to the Macedonian state on an equality with the neighboring towns. The rest, including Olynthus, were destroyed, and the inhabitants enslaved.

It was now clear even to the average statesman that Hellas had a master, whose policy toward the Greeks was not only intrigue, insinuation, and bribery, but likewise blood and iron. His direct sway extended from the Hellespont to Thermopylae; and many a city farther south was controlled by his paid henchmen. Athens had lost all of Euboea, except Carystus, and was anxious for peace. In 346 B.C. the leading Athenian statesman, Philocrates, negotiated a treaty which established not only peace, but also a defensive alliance. It was acknowledged that the *status quo* extended to the allies of both parties with the exception of the Phocians. Accepting the inevitable, Demonsthenes had worked for the peace. The Athenians voted for it, however, under the strange delusion that Philip intended to spare Phocis and to attack the Thebans. Philip, however, had other plans, and when the amphictyonic Council invited him to put an end to the Sacred War, he hastened to accept. He defeated the Phocians at Thermopylae, and then destroyed their towns and scattered the people in villages. The helpless Phocians were further compelled to replace the plundered treasure by an annual tribute of sixty talents. To see that these measures were carried out, the king quartered troops in the country. The Phocians were excluded from the Delphic Amphictyony and their two votes were transferred to Philip and his descendants. Thus it came about that the man whom patriot Greeks had scoffed at as a barbarian and drunkard was now publicly acknowledged as a Hellene and was given the presidency of the Pythian games held that autumn. Philip was now the arbiter of Greek affairs, and his name was on every man's lips (Map 46).

About this time Philip began to think of making war upon the Persian Empire. We have no way of knowing whether his ambition ranged as far as Persia itself or was limited to Asia Minor. Probably his plan was indefinite beyond the fact that the expedition was to be Panhellenic in character, under his command. It was typical of Philip's policy—a policy, it will be recalled, that incorporated newly won districts in the body of his state by persuasion; or failing that, by force—that he should have tried to bring this about by peaceful means. His entry into Greece after the Peace of Philocrates had been ostensibly as the champion of

Delphi. He now courted the friendship of the Greeks, hoping that they would accepted him as overlord. The good will of Athens he particularly desired, not simply because it was the cultural center of Hellas, but because its navy would be indispensable in an attack upon Persia. Philip, therefore, avoided force, until the speeches of Demosthenes made it impossible. The strength of the anti-Macedonian party at Athens was growing from day to day. Shocked at the ruin of the Phocians, and considering the treaty of Philocrates a disgrace to themselves, the Athenians drove Philocrates into exile. Demosthenes brought his rival, Aeschines, to trial on the charge of having bartered to Philip the interests of Athens; he alleged that this misconduct was on the occasion of the embassies to Philip, in which they had both taken part, in connection with the Peace of Philocrates. The speeches of these adversaries at the trial of 343 B.C. are a hopeless maze of contradictions; neither antagonist seems to have hesitated at falsehood. Aeschines was acquitted by only thirty votes. Against him it must at least be said that from the bitterest opponent of Philip he was suddenly converted, in the embassy preceding the Peace, into an ardent champion, and it is not improbable that he and Philocrates had received from Philip estates in the conquered territory of Olynthus. Be that as it may, Philip's friends at Athens were now in disrepute; and the popularity of Demosthenes, Lycurgus, Hypereides, and the other leaders of the anti-Macedonian party was greatly increased. These men looked upon the Peace merely as a breathing time, during which they should seize every opportunity to hamper the further extension of Macedon.

Athens now won for herself a considerable federation, including Euboea, Megara, Corinth, Achaea, Acarnania, Leucas, Phocis, and, shortly before the battle of Chaeronea, Thebes, still the most powerful city-state on the peninsula. Because the battle of Mantinea (362 B.C.) had put an end to city supremacy, its place was filled by the principle of the balance of power. In the new political system the object of the statesman was to prevent any one of the greater city-states—Thebes, Athens, Sparta, and Argos—from growing so powerful as to menace the liberties of the rest. From the beginning of his public career Demosthenes consistently upheld this principle. In his judgment Athens should protect the weaker states and should refrain from exercising compulsion toward any of them. She should make herself an efficient military power, so as to be ready to accept the leadership when voluntarily tendered by Hellas. The new federation was largely his work; and the union between Athens and Thebes, the leading city-states of Greece, who had long cherished toward each other the bitterest hatred, was an achievement of statesmanship, as it formed a step toward Hellenic unity. It must be confessed, however, that the new federation was in-spired more by fear of Macedon than by a desire for permanent union. The Greeks were still unable to reconcile autonomy and hegemony.

Seeing, then, that he could not win the leading states by persuasion, Philip accepted the alternative. He placed Alexander, his brother-in-law, on the throne of Epirus, strengthened his hold upon Thrace and Thessaly, and by characteristic methods gained an ascendancy in the Peloponnesus. In 342 B.C. he marched to the Thracian Chersonese, planning to cut off Athens' grain supply from the Black Sea. When Byzantium and Perinthus, his nominal allies, refused to aid him in an attack on the Athenians in the Chersonese, Philip suddenly laid siege to Perinthus (340 B.C.). Athens had been roused to its danger by Demos-thenes in a great oration, the *Third Philippic,* and now, with Byzantium and Persia, sent aid to Perinthus. After a few fruitless months before Perinthus, Philip quickly turned against Byzantium, but here, too, he failed. Philip, consequently, withdrew from the Chersonese; but he delayed his return to Pella, his capital, long enough to undertake a punitive expedition against the Scythians and to fight the Triballi, wild mountaineers of the northwest.

A situation now arose in Greece which was precisely to Philip's lik-ing. The Council of the Delphic Amphictyony declared a Sacred War on the little town of Amphissa, in Locris, for alleged trespassing upon the property of Apollo, and invited Philip to assume the leadership of the war. Philip quickly passed Thermopylae and stopped at Elatea in Phocis. Here he could control the highway to Thebes and Athens, and he hoped that his delay might bring the enemy to their senses. The Athenians, however, paid no heed to the advice of their general, Pho-cion, but, on the insistence of Demosthenes, entered into a close alli-ance with Thebes and diverted the money from the Theoric Fund to war purposes. In the summer of 338 B.C. the two hostile armies, each more than 30,000 strong, met at Chaeronea, on the plains of Boeotia. Philip's young son, Alexander, commanded the left wing and annihi-lated the famous "Sacred Band" of the Thebans; Philip, on the right, feigned retreat and then routed the Athenians opposed to him. Demos-thenes and some others escaped. The great lion, which today rises from the lonely sweep of Boeotia, does more than honor the fallen; essen-tially it marks the end of the city-state.

Philip was now free to organize Greece. The Peloponnesian states submitted to him, except Sparta, whose country he ravaged; and, though he trimmed off a large part of its territory, he was unable to conquer the state. In meting out punishment Philip was most severe upon Thebes, which had deserted him at the last hour. Thebes lost her hegemony over Boeotia; those leaders of the revolt who had failed to escape were put to death; and a Macedonian garrison was placed in the Cadmeia. Philip also found it advisable to garrison Chalcis and Corinth. Athens, on the other hand, which had opposed him most consistently, received unexpected favors. The city still commanded the sea, and Philip could not risk a long and uncertain siege, especially as Athens might be able to bring Persia and many Greek states to her support. Hoping for her future cooperation and respecting her past glory, Philip freed the Athenian prisoners without ransom and left the city her constitution and her territory, including Samos, Lemnos, Delos, and some other islands settled by her colonists. But Athens had to ally herself with Philip and forego her Confederacy. She also had to abandon the Thracian Chersonese, but received in exchange the Boeotian Oropus. No Macedonian troops crossed her border, and none of her statesmen was touched.

Having arranged the affairs of the individual states, Philip next proceeded to the organization of Greece. On his invitation the various states of central and southern Greece, except Sparta, and those of the Aegean islands sent deputies to a congress at Corinth in 338 B.C. The states were represented according to population. The constitution of the Corinthian League, as the new union was called, was incorporated in a treaty between it and Philip. It was agreed that the states should be independent and self-governing, illegal executions or banishments were forbidden, no state was to harbor militant exiles, and all were free to navigate the sea; in brief, all were to keep the peace. Between Philip and the Corinthian League there was to be an offensive and defensive alliance, with Philip as commander-in-chief. This arrangement of uniting the Greeks, instead of dividing them, as one would expect of an imperialist, clearly meant that the partnership was more than nominal. The next year it was further decided that Macedon and the League should wage jointly a war against Persia under Philip's command. Early in 336 B.C. the distinguished Macedonian general, Parmenio, crossed the Hellespont with an advance force. Philip planned to follow later, but lingered now to divide his time between state business and carousals. Throughout his life this extraordinary man, a great general and shrewd diplomat, had enjoyed violent debaucheries, as his mountaineer ancestors had done. The various women that he married enmeshed him in the web of their intrigues. One of them, Olympias, the mother of Alexander, having been repudiated in favor of another woman, plotted Philip's death, or so unfounded rumor had it. In any case, at the time of his daughter's marriage to king Alexander of Epirus, and in the presence of a notable gathering, Philip was murdered.

The old problem of the city-state—the institution which had produced great men, but loved autonomy so much that it brought Greece
to the verge of anarchy—had been solved by an outsider. Philip brought
unification to Greece. The freedom of the people, however, was not
destroyed, but merely abridged, by the battle of Chaeronea. But the
centrifugal tendencies of the cities were still strong; and, furthermore,
the Greeks had no guarantee that their present degree of freedom
would be continued. The supremacy of Philip was resented because, in
the first place, it meant the rule of a semi-civilized people over a highly
cultured race, and, in the second place, because it centralized military
power in the hands of a man who, in spite of his benevolence to Hellas
and his admiration for her culture, was essentially an egoist. The question now before the civilized world was what Philip's successor would
do with his inheritance.

Chapter XVIII

ALEXANDER THE GREAT

THE EARLY YEARS

I T WAS commonly believed in antiquity that the temple of Artemis at Ephesus burned to the ground on the night of Alexander's birth. Hegesias of Magnesia, we are told, made a remark frigid enough to extinguish the flames, to the effect that it was little wonder that the temple had burned, because the goddess was busy bringing Alexander into the world. The Magi at Ephesus, looking upon the temple's disaster as a sign of further disaster, ran about, beating their faces and crying that the calamity of Asia had that day been born. The ancient Greeks, moreover, loving coincidences as they did, probably moved the month of Alexander's birth back to mid-summer (356 B.C.), in order that Philip, who had just taken Potidaea, might receive three messages simultaneously: that Parmenio had conquered the Illyrians in a great battle; that his race horse had won a vic-

305

tory at the Olympic games; and that Alexander III, as he was later called, had been born at Pella, his capital. The seers added to Philip's delight by saying that the son whose birth coincided with three victories would always be victorious.

Alexander was average in height and had the build of an athlete. His outward appearance, Plutarch tells us,[1] was best represented by his favorite sculptor, Lysippus, who was able to catch the liquid and melting glance of the eyes and the peculiarities imitated afterward by many of his friends and successors, especially the poise of the neck, bent slightly to the left. Apelles, Plutarch continues, painted Alexander as wielder of the thunderbolt, but made his complexion too dark and swarthy, whereas his color actually was fair and the fairness passed into ruddiness, particularly on his breast and face. Apelles' picture, nevertheless, was so highly regarded for its vivid and natural expression that people used to say that of the two Alexanders, Alexander, son of Philip, was invincible, but the Alexander of Apelles was inimitable. His hair is reputed to have stood above his forehead like a lion's, and for centuries men followed his habit of shaving clean (Figure 90A).

Alexander was influenced to a preeminent degree by his background. Sprung, according to tradition, from Heracles and Achilles, he was of Greek descent, but from both parents he had some Illyrian (Albanian) blood. His military skill and cold rationalism were inherited from his father, but his own inner being, his mysticism and romanticism and impetuousness, came from his mother, Olympias, a fiery, passionate princess of Epirus. Perhaps from her, too, came the ability to kindle the imagination of multitudes by a single act; as when, for example, at the outset of his expedition and desiring to rally the Greeks wholeheartedly to his cause, he visited Troy and stirred in the breast of every Greek glorious memories and the picture of a new Trojan War against the Asiatic foe. And again, realizing that unimportant gestures can win great ends, his eventual adoption of a modified form of Persian dress led to the cliché that Alexander conquered the bodies of the Asiatics by his army, but won over their souls by his apparel, though his own particular comment was that people should consider as akin to themselves all good men and as foreigners only the wicked. The distinguishing mark of the Greek, he said, should be seen in virtue and that of the foreigner in iniquity; clothing and food, marriage and manner of life they should regard as common to all, being blended into one by ties of blood and children.

At the age of thirteen Alexander had Aristotle as a teacher, and dur-

[1] The adaptations from Plutarch are based on the translation of B. Perrin (*Loeb Classical Library*).

ing three impressionable years his keen mind became thoroughly Greek in character, and his romantic imagination developed a love for Homer and the heroic age of Greece. His admiration for Greek culture, however, was tempered by the simple, vital, active life of Macedonia.

Even as a youth Alexander exercised self-restraint. Though he was impetuous and violent in other matters, says Plutarch, the pleasures of the body had little hold on him and he indulged in them with great moderation, thinking it more kingly to conquer himself than others. Throughout his life he rarely drank, and then it was generally a deliberate action, enabling him to associate freely with old comrades, from whom his new position was slowly isolating him. So far as the record goes, he had no mistress. He was married twice, for reasons of policy; to Roxane, the daughter of a powerful Iranian baron, and to a daughter of Darius, the Persian king. By Roxane only did he have a child, born after his death, who with its mother was killed a dozen years later.

Ambition kept Alexander's boyish spirit serious and lofty in advance of his years. He did not court every kind of fame, as Philip did, who like a sophist plumed himself on the power of his oratory and engraved on his coins the victories of his chariots at Olympia. When people asked Alexander if he would contend in the foot race at Olympia, because he was swift of foot, "Yes," he replied, "if I could have kings as my contestants." [2] In general, he was averse to the whole race of athletes, but nevertheless he understood the value of contests as a means of pleasure and relaxation for his men, and instituted many in Asia, gymnastic, literary, and musical. He never showed any interest, however, in offering prizes for boxing.

At the age of sixteen, while his father was besieging Byzantium, Alexander crushed a Thracian rebellion and founded in the land a city which he named after himself, Alexandropolis, the first in a long line. During Philip's absence he also entertained envoys from Persia and associated with them freely. It is said that he won them by his friendliness and astonished them by asking no childish or trivial questions about the Hanging Gardens or the dress of the Great King, but rather about the roads, the size of the Persian army, the position of the king in battle, and similar matters, so that the envoys exclaimed, "This boy is a great king; ours is only wealthy."

Philip provided many persons as Alexander's tutors and teachers, but when he saw that his son's nature was unyielding and resisted compulsion, though he was easily led by reasoning into the path of duty, Philip tried to persuade rather than to command him; and because he would not wholly entrust the direction and training of the boy to the

[2] The Philippeum at Olympia (p. 185) was the gift of Philip.

ordinary teachers of poetry and the formal studies, feeling that it was a matter of too great importance, and in the words of Sophocles, "A task for many bits and rudder-sweeps as well," he sent for the famous and learned philosopher Aristotle, and paid him a noble and appropriate fee. He also peopled again Aristotle's native city, Stageira, which he had himself destroyed, and restored to it those of its citizens who were in exile or slavery (Figure 91).

As a place where master and pupil could labor and study, Philip assigned them the precinct of the nymphs near Mieza, where four centuries later, in Plutarch's day, the visitor was still shown the stone seats and shady walks of Aristotle. Alexander not only received from his master ethical and political doctrines, but also participated in those more profound teachings which philosophers were wont to communicate to the select few. He learned, for example, that moderation is necessary in government—a virtue he was not likely to get from Olympias—and he also learned, or rather was taught, that all barbarians (non-Greeks) were slaves by nature, especially those of Asia.

It seems clear that Aristotle implanted in the youth a love of learning, of the encyclopaedic sort, with a special interest in scientific investigation and medicine. The study of geography, zoology, botany, and ethnology was to benefit directly from this, and also the health of his men, for he was not only fond of the theory of medicine, but actually came to the aid of sick friends and prescribed treatments. Aristotle also instilled in Alexander a love of the *Iliad* and its hero Achilles, his supposed ancestor, though his favorite line was the one that says of Agamemnon, "Both things is he: both a goodly king and a warrior mighty." On his expedition to Asia Alexander brought with him a recension of the *Iliad,* which Aristotle had made for him, and kept it with his dagger under his pillow at night. For his other reading during the expedition he ordered quantities of books from home, especially the tragedies of Aeschylus, Sophocles and Euripides.

Alexander admired Aristotle at first and loved him (he used to say) more than his father, for the one had given him life, but the other had taught him a noble life. Later on, however, he held the philosopher more or less in suspicion, and the two became estranged. In fact, it is surprising how little either of the two men really influenced the other.

At the time of Philip's murder Alexander, whose legitimacy hostile gossip had doubted, found himself surrounded by powerful generals and other possible successors. With the rapidity that always characterized him, though he was but twenty years old, he won the allegiance of the army and hence of Macedonia. He put to death the conspirators, and later in the year marched to Corinth, where the Greeks (except

Sparta) swore allegiance to him, as they had to Philip, and elected him commander-in-chief of the war of revenge against Persia.

Alexander was anxious to be off. His whole life had been spent in the atmosphere of a Panhellenic war of revenge. Isocrates had preached it, and Philip had planned it. Before he could start, however, it was necessary to instill into the tribes of the north and west respect for his authority, lest his lines of communication be cut. In 335 B.C., therefore, Alexander marched against the Triballi through the northern forests and swamps as far as the Danube, and crossed against the Getae—a feat rendered possible by the simultaneous arrival of his fleet from Byzantium. His next activities were in the northwest, during which a report spread to Greece that he was dead. Covering 250 miles in a fortnight, Alexander appeared before revolting Thebes. He hoped that the city would repent of its action, but when it did not, he took it by storm. Thousands of Thebans were killed, the remainder enslaved, and the city razed to the ground. The fate of Thebes was not unusual in the history of Greek warfare, but Alexander's remorse was great, and Arrian's remark may be recalled that Alexander was the only one of the ancient kings who, from nobility of character, repented of the errors which he had committed. Alexander, however, made it clear to the Greeks that there was a difference between himself and the Persian invader of 480 B.C., for he spared the city's temples and the house of the famous poet Pindar; and doubtless he also felt that he would be able to set off for Persia without fear of the Greeks rising in his rear.

ALEXANDER'S ARMY

That autumn Alexander returned to Macedonia and summoned Parmenio from Asia. Parmenio had secured the bridgeheads of the Hellespont and was now to help Alexander in preparing the army—Philip's army, essentially—for the invasion of Persia. The core of the army was the Macedonian farmer and noble, who had spent years of professional service in infantry and cavalry and enjoyed a better training and discipline than any body of men elsewhere. It is not necessary, even if it were possible, to list precisely all of Alexander's troops and to give an exact description of his regular order of battle, because death, re-enforcements and garrisons were constantly changing the numbers, and because he always varied his tactics to suit the particular situation. We can, however, attempt a generalization for the first years at least.

The close union of light troops and cavalry with the phalanx largely explains the invincibility of the Macedonian military machine. Perhaps this represents an advance by Alexander over Philip's ideas, and sprang from a desire to develop Persian cavalry tactics, which had been tested in the wide spaces of Asia. Aside from that, Alexander's success was in large part due to his handling of the magnificent cavalry, which now became for the first time in Greek history the real striking arm; its most important section was the so-called Companion cavalry, 2,000 strong. Drawn from the influential families of Macedonia, they were divided into eight territorial squadrons under the general command of Philotas, son of Parmenio. They were heavily armed, with helmet, breastplate, greaves, a short sword, a short thrusting-spear, and a small round shield, and, as was the custom, they rode without stirrups. These men received a special share of prize money, and were destined, the best of them, to become officers and administrators. The first squadron, under "Black" Cleitus, was called the Royal and was generally led by Alexander himself, though if the occasion required it, he did not hesitate to lead the phalanx, the hypaspists, or the archers, for, in the days before reserves were extensively used, sound tactics and good morale demanded the presence of the general in or near the front line. The Companion cavalry, consisting of small units of 250 men massed against a single point, had a terrific impetus.

The famous Macedonian phalanx was mobile and flexible. The heavy-armed foot soldier (hoplite or phalangite) wore a helmet, breastplate, greaves, shield, short sword, and a spear (*sarissa*) perhaps 13 feet in length. The butt of the spear was weighted, so that the hoplite could seize it several feet from the end. The spears of the front ranks were couched, projecting several feet in front of the line, and thus the phalanx began its deadly work long before the enemy with his short sword, though Persian and Macedonian were quick to learn from one another. As a rule, the phalanx fought in open order, with 3 feet between the men. This requires soldiers who are highly trained and disciplined, but it also means that rough ground or momentary shocks from the enemy will not disarrange the mass. If necessary, the hoplites could lock shields or go through a variety of formations; indeed, the mere arranging and rearranging of the phalanx could terrify an enemy. The phalanx advanced as a slow moving mass, and by the time the paean had passed into the battle cry it was a brave opponent who stood his ground.

The phalanx generally formed as a rectangle, but its exact disposition depended on the situation. It might be square, or elongated, or narrowed for a thrust against the enemy; it could be divided and made to face left and right, to ward off flank attacks; and it could take the shape of a wedge or pincers. It was usually eight, ten or sixteen men in depth. The arrangement toward the end of the expedition was the file of sixteen men—with the file leader and extra-pay men front and rear —and when these formed sixteen men square, we have the tactical unit of 256 men. The phalanx, subordinate though it was to the cavalry, consisted of 9,000 Macedonians, called foot companions. They were divided into six territorial battalions which were known by the names of their commanders—Craterus, Perdiccas, Amyntas, Meleager, Philip, and Parmenio's son-in-law, Coenus.

If Alexander's success was due in large part to his masterly handling of the Companion cavalry, some of it at least resulted from comparable skill in the management of the hypaspists. These shield-bearing guards, as they were called, were fully armed, and their chief distinction from the phalangites lay apparently in their recruitment from a higher level of society. The hypaspists were Macedonians, 3,000 strong, in three battalions under Nicanor, Parmenio's son. One of these battalions, the so-called *agema,* was Alexander's guard.

Alexander also had 12,000 heavy-armed Greeks. Seven thousand of these were Greek allies, the contingents of the Corinthian League, under the future king, Antigonus—perhaps Alexander looked upon them as hostages for the good behavior of Greece during his absence. The remaining 5,000 Greeks were mercenaries, over a third of whom were peltasts, light infantry with more than the usual armor, a small round shield, sword and short spear; unreliable, as mercenaries are wont to be, they were never employed for important duty. Alexander had other light-armed infantry: 4,000 Thracians; 1,000 Agrianian javelin men, under Attalus, fine warriors who were especially valuable as mountaineers and skirmishers; some slingers; and 1,000 Cretan archers, who were among his best and fiercest fighters.

This army of more than 30,000 infantry and 5,000 cavalry rarely fought as a body, but even when only small contingents were engaged, Alexander combined the various arms, a practice that was to prove one of his major keys of success, and he invariably pursued the enemy with the aim of destroying him utterly, a policy which von Clausewitz has termed "the strategy of defeat." In a pitched battle, however, the army lined up somewhat as follows. In the center was the phalanx (intended as a firm anchor), with the hypaspists to the right. Then came Alexander and the Companion cavalry, with the Macedonian lancers and other light cavalry, Agrianian javelin men and Cretan archers thrown out to their right as flankers and skirmishers. To the left of the phalanx were Thracian light cavalry, unless they had already been detailed to guard the camp; then came the Thessalian cavalry, with light troops to their left. Parmenio, the second in command, was in charge of the left wing;

as an able and cautious tactician he was especially suited for this post, since in the oblique order of battle (the favorite of generals from Epaminondas to Frederick the Great) it was the duty of the left wing to hold firm, while Alexander, choosing the decisive moment, charged from the right.

Alexander's great organizing ability also manifested itself in the siege train, which was far superior to anything of its kind elsewhere. There were siege towers, placed on rollers or wheels and covered with hides to protect them from fire, which might be over 150 feet high (two are known at Tyre), with many stories, so that any part of the enemy's wall could be reached by the artillery; boarding bridges were used at Tyre for the first time in history. It was possible to undermine the enemy's walls by tunneling or to knock them down with battering rams, which had huge beams over 100 feet long, with a metallic head. The besiegers themselves were protected by movable sheds, known in later days as tortoises. But the greatest military invention of antiquity, used for the first time at Tyre by Alexander, was the torsion catapult. It was not superseded until the invention of gunpowder, though at the beginning of the last century a musket could not be aimed with precision for a distance of more than 100 yards, whereas the torsion catapult could fire huge arrows accurately for 200 yards, as well as stones weighing 50 to 60 pounds. Alexander never employed catapults as field artillery in a pitched battle, but he used them in irregular warfare, in sieges, mounted on merchant ships, as at Tyre, and to clear a river's bank of the enemy.

Over this professional army, infused with a proud professional spirit, stood Alexander, commander-in-chief of Macedonia and the League of Corinth, and as king of Macedon responsible to no one but himself in military matters and, subject to the role of the army assembly, in civil as well. By his side he had seven Bodyguards, a staff of general officers as we might describe them, and also a group of eighty or one hundred influential officers, known simply as Companions. These men—Parmenio, Philotas, Cleitus, the future kings Ptolemy, Seleucus, and Lysimachus, and his personal friends Hephaestion and Nearchus—formed his council, as it were, and provided military and civil officers as needed. The royal pages were officers in the making; young boys from the upper classes, their responsibilities included the duty of guarding Alexander in his sleep and of accompanying him on the chase.

Alexander's strategy was to fight on land, for his fleet of 160 triremes (from the Corinthian League) was far inferior to the Cypriot and Phoenician contingents which the Great King had at his disposal. Precisely how many men Persia might put in the field depended on the seriousness with which it viewed Alexander's continuing advance, for the new king, Darius III, was to reveal himself as an incompetent despot as well as a coward. The Persian Empire, however, had seemingly recovered from its recent internal weaknesses, and the lands from the Hellespont to the frontiers of India, some 2,700 miles in extent, bristled with its armed men. Tribesmen from the hills, nomads from the desert, serfs, splendid warriors from eastern Iran, especially the remarkable Bactrians—in short, a variety of races and fighters—could be called upon, but the backbone of the army was the superb Persian cavalry (20,000 of whom were in Asia Minor alone), the subordinate, but famous, Persian archers, an Oriental body of professional heavy infantry, called Cardaces, who were armed like Greek hoplites, and 20,000 obstinate Greek mercenaries, the Empire's chief hope as heavy infantry.

Speaking generally, the Persian command is probably to be criticized primarily for deciding to meet the Macedonians in formal *batailles rangées* where the superior quality of Alexander's army had every advantage. Given the great traditions of the Achaemenid Empire it is understandable that this mistake should have been made, but had Persia adopted "Parthian" tactics and the scorched earth policy advocated by Memnon of Rhodes, avoiding decisive encounters, harassing Alexander's lines of communication with their ample and excellent cavalry and subsidizing disturbances in Greece, the issue might well have been different.

The Grand Army was destined to march under Alexander many thousands of miles, often at terrific speed, during eleven long years. Events frequently proved his personal bravery and self-discipline and humanity, and more than once he was wounded—on the neck and head at the Granicus, in the thigh at Issus, on the shoulder at Gaza; the fibula of his leg was broken in Turkestan, thrice he was wounded in Afghanistan, and in India an arrow pierced his lung, while there were in addition other wounds and attacks of fever and dysentery. Every inch of the march was new, and yet, throughout this period, his reenforcements reached him regularly, over 60,000 in the first eight years alone. And every inch of the way he met opposition (save in Egypt); he fought four pitched battles—three with Persia and another with an Indian rajah in the Punjab, where he encountered for the first time large numbers of terrifying elephants who barred his passage of a great river. These were not armies of degenerate Oriental masses that he defeated, but disciplined, able forces that greatly outnumbered his own. But there were also fierce mountain tribes to conquer and deserts to overcome; a long guerrilla warfare with its utterly strange tactics awaited him in eastern Iran; and he had strong cities to besiege, the capture of the island-city of Tyre alone requiring seven months and all his tenacity.

If Alexander's plan was to conquer as large a part of the Persian Empire as possible and hold on to it, his every success opened up further vistas until the possession of the entire Empire was in sight. To him and to everyone else of that day this was equivalent to world conquest, for the Persian Empire was essentially the civilized world. As it happened, Alexander did not set foot in all the border districts of that Empire—those, with the uncivilized patches behind them, could be ignored or attended to later—but in India he went beyond its frontiers and was stopped just short, so he thought, of reaching Ocean and the limits of the world by a mutiny of his worn-out troops. Several years before his death his incredible successes led him to consider the possibility of a western expedition, one that would bring him from Babylon round Arabia and Africa (concerning whose size he was as ignorant as he was of Asia's) to Europe.

The conquests confronted Alexander with two chief problems. In the first place, he had to decide the general character of administration as well as the precise position of himself within the state. His solution essentially was to take over the existing forms of government and to assume a different relation to the various sections of the Empire, much in the manner of the British monarch of a later day. In one part of the world, that is to say, he became king, in another a general elected for life or a suzerain or a god or the adopted son of a native ruler. The second problem was far more difficult, for it involved giving a sense of unity to a world state. World brotherhood might be the answer, but how to achieve it? Alexander believed that mixed marriages would be an instrument, though no more than that, and ultimately he may have conceived the remarkable idea of a common culture for the world. Because he entertained no doubts about the superiority of Greek culture, he determined that the Greek language, Greek customs and Greek law should unite the many different races. It would all take time, and it did take time, but the Hellenization of the East was the most important result of Alexander's life.

The Panhellenic campaign of revenge had an air of permanency about it from the beginning. Artists, poets, philosophers, and historians accompanied the expedition; geographers, hydrographers, geologists, botanists, and other scientists came along to study the phenomena of Asia and perhaps to send back to Aristotle specimens for further observation. Aristotle's nephew, Callisthenes of Olynthus, came as self-appointed historian, a pompous individual who remarked that Alexander's fame depended not on what he did, but on what he, Callisthenes, chose to record; Alexander bemoaned the better fate of his ancestor, Achilles, who had had a Homer. Another historian was Aristobulus. Eumenes of Cardia had the chief task of writing the *Ephemerides* or Royal Journal, which in the dry fashion of a diary recorded the "official" truth concerning each day's events. The best history of the expedition, however, was written by a general, Ptolemy, son of Lagus, who in his later years as king of Egypt composed his memoirs, based on his own recollections as well as on Callisthenes and the Royal Journal. With Aristobulus, Ptolemy was the chief source of Arrian, whose history is the best consecutive account we possess of the expedition.

In the early spring of 334 B.C. Alexander was ready to start. Antipater, an austere and reliable sexagenarian, was ordered to remain in Macedonia, with a body of 12,000 foot and 1,500 horse soldiers, as regent to keep an eye on the restive Greeks. As they were about to start, many portents from heaven were reported. It was said, for example, that the statue of Orpheus, which was made of cypress wood, sweated profusely. Most people feared the sign, but Aristander, the famous seer of Telmessus, bade Alexander be of good cheer, assured that he was to perform deeds worthy of song and story, which would cost poets and musicians much toil and sweat to celebrate. Thus, amid great excitement, more than 30,000 infantry and 5,000 cavalry set out for Asia under a leader who was destined never to return.

ASIA MINOR

Alexander crossed the Hellespont to Asia in 334 B.C., in a dual capacity, as king of Macedon and as general of the allied Greeks. One of his first acts in Asia was a side trip to Troy, where he and Hephaestion paid homage to the memory of Achilles and other heroes. This illustrates the romantic strain in Alexander's temperament—it was, too, his way of emphasizing the Panhellenic character of the enterprise, of substituting for the smouldering Greek opposition the enthusiasm of a national war.

Darius had not thought it worth his while to meet Alexander in Asia Minor, but the Persian satraps were ready for him with a large body of cavalry, four times his own, re-enforced by Memnon and Greek mercenaries. With Parmenio commanding the left and himself the right, Alexander charged the Persians drawn up on the opposite bank of the river Granicus. The battle was desperately fought, and had it not been for "Black" Cleitus, Alexander might have been killed. After his victory, Alexander proceeded along the Asia Minor coast, freeing the Greek cities from the Persian rule. Some surrendered on his approach; others, such as Miletus and Halicarnassus, he had to storm. At Miletus he dismissed his fleet, not wishing to run the risk of defeat on sea and realizing that a decisive victory over Darius would mean the capitulation of the enemy's navy, anyway. Everywhere Alexander won great popularity by restoring democratic government in the Greek cities, which now became his allies; for the rest, he was prone to leave the organization pretty much as he found it. The Persian system of satrapies was adopted, with the important difference that finance was placed in the hands of a separate official. The officials he appointed in Asia Minor were chiefly Macedonian (or Greek), but already we note barbarians among them—either Alexander was too intent to find Darius to trouble much about his provincial arrangements, or he was discovering by actual contact with barbarians that Aristotle was wrong. In any case, on his entrance into Caria he allowed the queen, Ada, to adopt him, and thus showed the barbarians of the region that he had a personal interest in them and was not come as a mere conqueror.

Alexander spent the winter in campaigning against the hill tribes of Lycia and Pisidia. He did not continue along the coast in the spring, however, but turned inland, to make sure that the center of Asia Minor owed him at least nominal allegiance, before he proceeded further east. At Gordium the famous chariot, with its curious knot of cornel bark, was shown him. According to legend, the man who could untie the knot would rule Asia, and Alexander drew his sword and cut it. At Gordium he was met by Athenian envoys—embassies from various states were to become a common occurrence—but to ensure the fidelity of Athens he refused to surrender the men captured at the Granicus. His fear of the Persian fleet raising Greece in revolt was, however, soon dissipated, with the death of the admiral Memnon. Alexander, with his customary care of his men and an understanding of their psychology, had permitted those who had been recently married to spend the winter of 334–333 B.C. in Macedonia. These men, together with re-enforcements, now joined him. As we view his years in Asia, perhaps nothing strikes us more than the perfection of his commissariat and his intelligence service, and the regularity with which his re-enforcements reached him.

The task now before Alexander was to pass the Cilician Gates before the enemy blocked them. This he did, by forced marches, and arrived at Tarsus in time to prevent the Persians from firing the city. But Alexander was hot and tired, and a swim in the Cydnus river gave him a fever. Perhaps he deliberately delayed his convalescence, for he had heard that Darius was awaiting him with a great force on the plains of

Syria—how much better it would be if Darius could be enticed into the narrow plain of Cilicia? An invader, however, must ever be on the move, and at last Alexander marched to Issus, where he left his sick and wounded beside the Pinarus river. Then, by the Jonah pass, he crossed to Myriandrus on the Syrian coast. His intelligence service, this time, had broken down, for Darius had left Sochi on the Syrian plains and had crossed into Cilicia by the Amanic Gates. The Persian army was at Alexander's back; the Empire ahead of him. He quickly turned toward Issus, where meanwhile Darius had butchered the sick and wounded.

At the approach of dawn, late in October, 333 B.C., Alexander began to descend from the pass along the road; and as long as the space was narrow he led his army in column, but when the mountains parted to leave a plain between them, he kept opening out the column into the phalanx, marching one detachment of heavy-armed infantry after another up into line toward the mountain on the right and the sea on the left. He had with him as many cavalry, 5,000, as at the Granicus, but probably his infantry no longer numbered 30,000, for—in spite of re-enforcements—death and garrison duty had claimed thousands. As he advanced toward the Pinarus, he found that the ground widened a little, and posted most of the cavalry with himself on the right wing; the rest he sent to Parmenio on the left, with orders not to abandon the sea under any circumstances. Various light troops held the extreme wings.

Arrian tells us that Darius' army amounted to 600,000 fighting men, but the Persian Empire could not produce an army this size, nor was the plain of Issus large enough to contain it. Because, however, the Pinarus ran for about three miles from mountain to sea, and because Darius had more men than he could use, it seems likely that the number of his troops exceeded 100,000, including perhaps 15,000 Greek mercenaries, who were famous as fierce fighters. As soon as he learned of Alexander's approach, Darius sent some of his superb cavalry and light infantry across the river, in order that he might draw up the rest of his forces with ease. Of the heavy infantry he placed the Greek mercenaries in the center opposite the Macedonian phalanx, and on both sides of these the native infantry, called Cardaces; in front of the Cardaces, at the left, were placed the splendid archers in expectation of Alexander's charge from his right.

The remaining thousands of light and heavy infantry were marshalled by nations to an unserviceable depth in the rear. Darius then recalled his cavalry from across the river and placed most of them on the right wing under Nabarzanes, facing Parmenio, because here the ground was more suitable for the evolutions of cavalry. According to the custom of the Persian kings, Darius occupied the center of the whole army, but behind the Greek mercenaries.

Meantime, when Alexander perceived that the Persian cavalry had changed their ground and gone to his left toward the sea, and that on his side only a few horsemen were posted there, he sent the Thessalian cavalry thither with speed, ordering them to ride behind the phalanx so as not to be seen. Having thus marshalled his men, he caused them to rest for some time and then led them forward slowly. Darius remained in his position upon the bank of the river, which was in many parts precipitous; and in certain places where it seemed more easy to ascend, he had extended a stockade along it. But when at length the armies were close to each other, Alexander rode about in every direction and exhorted his troops to show their valor, mentioning with befitting epithets the names, not only of the generals, but also those of the captains of the cavalry and infantry, and of his Greek mercenaries as many as were more distinguished either by reputation or by any deed of bravery. From all sides there arose a shout not to delay but to attack Darius and wrest his empire from him. At first he still led them on in close array with measured step, lest by a too hasty march any part of the phalanx should fluctuate from the line and get separated from the rest.

But when they came within range of the arrows, Alexander himself and those around him on the right wing, following the tactics of the oblique formation, dashed into the river with a run, in order to alarm the Persians by the rapidity of their onset, and by coming sooner to close conflict to avoid being too greatly injured by the archers. Crushing the Persian left, Alexander turned against the center, where, in the rhetoric of Curtius,[3] he did

the work of a soldier no less than that of a leader. For there stood Darius towering aloft in his chariot, a sight that prompted alike friends to shield him and foes to assail him. So then his brother Oxathres, when he saw Alexander rushing toward him, gathered the horsemen of his command and threw them in the very front of the chariot of the king. Conspicuous above all the rest, with his armor and giant frame, fighting now the battle of his life, he laid low those who recklessly surged against him; others he turned to flight. But the Macedonians grouped about Alexander, heartened by one another's exhortations, burst in upon the line. Then came the desolation of ruin. Around the chariot of Darius you'd see lying leaders of highest rank, perished in a glorious death, all prone upon their faces, just as they had fallen in their struggle, wounds all in the front. Among them you would find Atizyes and Rheomithres and Sabaces, the satrap of Egypt, all generals of great armies;

[3] Wheeler's translation.

piled up around them a mass of footmen and horsemen of meaner fame. Of the Macedonians, too, many were slain, good men and true. Alexander himself was wounded in the right thigh with a sword. And now the horses attached to Darius' chariot, pricked with spears and infuriated with pain, tossed the yoke on their necks, and threatened to throw Darius from the car. Then he, in fear lest he should fall alive into the hands of the enemy [turned and fled (Figure 92)].

The Macedonian phalanx, meanwhile, had broken its line in climbing the steep bank of the river and was being desperately attacked by Darius' Greek mercenaries, for the intensity of feeling that existed between Greek and Macedonian only added to the fury of their struggle. Alexander now wheeled against the mercenaries and, rolling them back from the river, began to cut them up. The Persian cavalry, opposite Parmenio, had not been inactive, but had crossed the river and made a vigorous attack; nor did they give way until they saw that Darius had fled and the Greek mercenaries were being defeated. Then at last there ensued a decided flight and on all sides.

So great was the slaughter that Ptolemy, who accompanied Alexander, says that the men who were with them pursuing Darius passed over a ravine upon the corpses. But Darius made good his escape. As long as the ground was level he continued in his chariot, but when he came to rough ground, he abandoned it, leaving in it his shield and mantle and even his bow, and fled on horseback. Night alone rescued him, for Alexander had delayed the pursuit until the Greek mercenaries and the Persian cavalry had been driven away from the river; he returned to camp, however, with Darius' chariot and its contents.

Alexander found his Macedonians carrying off the wealth from the camp of the barbarians, and the wealth was of surpassing abundance, although its owners had come to the battle in light marching order and had left most of their baggage in Damascus; he found, too, that his men had picked out for him the tent of Darius, which was full to overflowing with gorgeous servitors and furniture, and many treasures. Straightway, then, according to Plutarch, Alexander put off his armor and went to the bath, saying, "Let us go and wash off the sweat of the battle in the bath of Darius." "No, indeed," said a Companion, "but rather in that of Alexander." And when he saw the basins and pitchers and tubs and caskets, all of gold and curiously wrought, while the apartment was marvellously fragrant with spices and unguents, and when he passed from this into a tent which was worthy of admiration for its size and height, and for the adornment of the couch and tables and banquet prepared for him, he turned his eyes upon his Companions and said, "This, as it would seem, is to be a king."

As he was betaking himself to supper, someone told him that among the prisoners were the mother and wife and two unmarried daughters of Darius, and that at the sight of his chariot and bow they beat their breasts and lamented, believing that he was dead. Accordingly, after a considerable pause, more affected by their affliction than by his own success, he sent Leonnatus, a Companion, with orders to tell them that Darius was not dead, and that they need have no fear of Alexander; for it was Darius upon whom he was waging war for supremacy, but they should have everything which they used to think their due when Darius was undisputed king. Such are the statements of Ptolemy and Aristobulus. But there is another report to the effect that on the following day Alexander himself went into the tent, accompanied only by Hephaestion. The mother of Darius, being in doubt which of them was the king (for they were both dressed in the same way), went up to Hephaestion, because he appeared to her the taller of the two, and prostrated herself before him. But when he drew back, and one of her attendants pointed out Alexander, saying he was the king, she was ashamed of her mistake and was going to retire. But Alexander told her she had made no mistake, for Hephaestion was also Alexander.

Alexander never laid eyes on the wife of Darius, who was reputedly the most beautiful woman in Asia, though years later he married one of the daughters. As for the other captive women, seeing that they were surpassingly stately and beautiful, he merely said jestingly that Persian women were torments to the eyes. He expected his men to maintain the same high standards, and when he learned, for example, that two Macedonian soldiers under Parmenio's command had raped the wives of certain mercenaries, he wrote to Parmenio ordering him, in case the men were convicted, to punish them and put them to death as wild beasts born for the destruction of mankind.

On the day following the battle Alexander, still suffering from the dagger wound in his thigh, visited the wounded, and after collecting the bodies of the slain (apparently only 450 in number) he gave them a splendid burial, with all his forces brilliantly marshalled in order of battle. He also praised those who had performed any gallant deed and gave to each a gift of money in proportion to his desert. Then, as all looked on, he erected by the bank of the Pinarus altars to Zeus, Heracles, and Athena, memorials of his great victory which were still standing three centuries later in Cicero's day.

The enemy's losses in battle must have been immense, and yet we know of only five dignitaries who were killed. Of those who escaped some 2,000 Greek mercenaries and several thousand Persians joined Darius, who was fleeing as rapidly as he could, hoping to put the

Euphrates between himself and Alexander. There was not even time to gather up the wealth left behind at Damascus, and this was ultimately secured by Parmenio.

The battle of Issus is one of the great battles of history, for in essence it meant the end of Asiatic power in the Mediterranean. It also left its mark on Alexander, for obviously Darius was finished or soon would be. Who was to take his place, another Persian or his conqueror? It would be rash to suppose that this fervently ambitious young man did not determine to become Lord of Asia at least from the time of his victory at Issus. The fact that he continued along the coast to Egypt might indicate that he was simply resolved to drive Darius entirely from the Mediterranean, but from Egypt he turned automatically to Mesopotamia. His every action after Issus reveals a determination to sit on the throne of the Achaemenids and become the Great King of Persia. This does not mean that he planned to abandon his kingship in Europe and merge it in an Oriental despotism, but rather that he would hold different positions simultaneously in the different portions of his realm.

The Panhellenic character of the expedition had begun to yield even before Issus to Alexander's personal power. In this connection it is of fundamental importance to note that, whereas after the Granicus Alexander sent the Greek mercenaries of Darius to Macedonia in chains as traitors to the Corinthian League, at Miletus he took other Greek mercenaries into his service. This implies, at an early stage, a disregard of the League itself. He further weakened Panhellenism by not adding the Greek cities of Asia Minor to the League, but by uniting them to himself by treaty "as free and independent allies"; and, indeed, as he advanced through the non-Greek districts of Asia Minor he claimed the tribute which they had previously paid the Great King. Alexander's conception of his own position, it is clear, developed constantly, so that by Issus he was not only king of Macedon, commander-in-chief of the Corinthian League, and the adopted son of the native Ada, but also the "ally" of the Greek cities of Asia Minor and the Great King of the native districts.

It must be emphasized, however, that Alexander never set foot in whole sections of Asia Minor. He did not go within a hundred miles of the Black Sea, and even places near his line of march did not owe him allegiance. Nevertheless he had brought a large area over from one régime to another with a minimum of disturbance, and with changes for the better. The Greek cities had been freed of the tyrants set up by the Persians, an event that was likely to release their creative genius and, with renewed facilities for trade and the support of public works, restore their economic prosperity. Democratic government had been established in most places, and everywhere there was an insistence on internal peace. As Alexander's free and independent allies, they were required to furnish ships, but not troops. Their tribute was smaller than previously and was called a "voluntary contribution," paid directly to Alexander, and they were wholly free of the satraps and their subordinates. For the non-Greek districts Alexander took over the Persian system of satrapies. His satraps were Macedonian generals, chiefly, but he also used natives—a fact that is generally overlooked by those who maintain that Alexander's settled policy, later on, of including barbarians among his appointees to office was motivated by a scarcity of Greeks and Macedonians—and at Sardes a division had been made of military and civil functions, though it is not till later that we find the great advance on Persian administration through the strict separation of military, civil and financial powers.

This impressive record had been made in a year and a half. Furthermore, Alexander had won two pitched battles, and Darius was in flight. If he was to realize his other ambitions, he must now capture Darius.

TYRE AND EGYPT

Though Darius had escaped from Issus and might re-form his army at any moment, Alexander's best plan was first to strike along the coast, secure his communications, and bring about the collapse of the enemy's fleet. On his way down the Phoenician coast Alexander received the surrender of one city after another and finally met envoys from Tyre who promised formal submission. He thanked them and said that he merely wished to enter their island-city and sacrifice to his ancestor Heracles (Melkart), but the Tyrians caught the point and, remembering how they had withstood Nebuchadrezzar's siege for thirteen years, replied that they were not admitting any Persians or Macedonians into their city; however, they added, there was an even older shrine to Heracles on the mainland where he might sacrifice to his ancestor if he wished.

The island of Tyre was protected by high, heavy walls of solid stone, two miles in circumference, and lay a half mile offshore; near the coast the water was shallow, but it reached a depth of eighteen feet at the island. The mole, which Alexander finally succeeded in building, ultimately became covered with silt, so that today island and mainland are joined by an isthmus. The Tyrians had a strong navy and two fine harbors, the Sidonian to the north and the Egyptian to the south.

Clearly this powerful naval base could not be left behind in hostile hands, and Alexander instantly resolved on attack, even though he had no fleet of his own. When he learned that many Macedonians considered it well-nigh hopeless to besiege the city, he called together his officers and encouraged them by saying that the capture of Tyre would give them the entire Persian fleet and permit them to continue safely to Egypt and Mesopotamia. They were further cheered by the report that Alexander had dreamed that as he was approaching the walls of Tyre Heracles had taken him by the right hand and led him into the city, a dream that Aristander, the seer, interpreted as meaning that Tyre would be taken, though by labor, because the deeds of Heracles were accomplished by labor (Map 17).

And many of the Tyrians themselves dreamed that Apollo told them he was going away to Alexander, because he was displeased at what was happening in the city. Whereupon, as if the god had been a common deserter caught in the act of going over to the enemy, they encircled his colossal statue with cords and nailed it down to its pedestal, calling him an Alexandrist. In another dream, too, Alexander thought he saw a satyr who mocked him at a distance, and eluded his grasp when he tried to catch him, but finally, after much coaxing and chasing, surrendered. The seers, dividing the word *satyros* into two parts, said to him, plausibly enough, "Tyre is to be yours."

Amid hopes and fears the task was begun of building a mole, some 200 feet broad, from the mainland to the island. Alexander added to the zeal of his men by his own hard work, as well as by speeches and presents of money. In order to keep the Tyrian ships at a distance, the Macedonians erected two towers upon the mole and placed within them engines of war. But the Tyrians filled a large ship with dry twigs and other combustible wood, together with pitch and brimstone, and hung from the yard arms of the two masts caldrons full of inflammable matter. Then they set the vessel on fire and ran it on to the mole. As the towers burned, the caldrons on the yard arms added fuel to the flames, while men in triremes kept shooting arrows at the Macedonians, and other Tyrians sailed to the mole and completed its destruction.

Alexander now began to construct a wider mole from the mainland, capable of containing more towers, and ordered his engineers to prepare fresh engines. While this was being done, he took the heavy infantry known as hypaspists and the Agrianian skirmishers and set out for Sidon to collect all the triremes he could, because it was clear to him that he must try to seize the sovereignty of the sea. About this time, too, the kings of Aradus and Byblus, ascertaining that their cities were in Alexander's possession, deserted and surrendered their own fleet and some Sidonian vessels, so that about eighty Phoenician triremes now joined Alexander; and then the kings of Cyprus, terrified by the news of Issus, put into Sidon with 120 ships. Not long afterward Cleander arrived from the Peloponnesus with 4,000 Greek mercenaries.

While his fleet was being fitted up, Alexander marched into the Antilebanon to subdue the mountaineers and obtain much-needed timber, and it was during this expedition that he risked his life to save his old pedagogue, Lysimachus. When, however, the fleet was finally ready, Alexander embarked on it some hypaspists and set sail for Tyre with his ships arranged in order, but the Tyrians were so amazed at the sight that they refused battle. Except for scattered engagements on sea, the siege of Tyre now resolved itself into an attempt on the part of the Macedonians to bring their engines against the walls of the city, either by ships or along the new mole which was being fast completed. The Tyrians, on their side, replied with clever and desperate measures of defense, for it was in Phoenicia and the neighboring lands that the art of military machinery had been born. They hurled into the sea, for example, great boulders which prevented the enemy's ships from approaching too near the walls, and when Alexander tried to drag them away, they sent divers to cut the cables of his anchors. He then fastened chains to his anchors, and with the help of cranes dropped the bounders into deep water.

And as the Macedonians erected bridges against this or that section of the wall, the Tyrians threw nets over them and pulled them to the ground, or actually plucked them off with iron instruments called crows. They fastened sharp hooks to long poles and cut the cords of the battering rams, and shot large pieces of red hot iron at the Macedonians. They also filled their shields with sand and heated them in the fire until the sand was scorching hot and then hurled it upon the Macedonians; it got inside their breastplates and cruelly burned their flesh.

Eventually, however, a part of the wall was knocked down, and Alexander, according to Arrian:

ordered the ships with the engines to retire, and brought up two others with bridges, which he intended to throw upon the breach in the wall. He also ordered some triremes to sail against the two harbors and others to sail right round the wall and to run aground wherever practicable and begin shooting, so that the Tyrians, being shot at from all quarters, might become distracted and not know where to turn in their distress. When Alexander's ships drew close to the city and the bridges were thrown upon the wall, the hypaspists mounted valiantly, led by Admetus, and Alexander accompanied them, both as a courageous participant in the action itself and as a witness of brilliant and dangerous feats of valor performed by others. Admetus was the first to mount the wall but, while cheering on his men, was struck by a spear and died on the spot. After a struggle, Alexander and his troops took the wall and advanced into the city against the main body of the Tyrians, who had rallied at the sanctuary of Agenor, and routed them. Great was the slaughter also made by those who had forced the harbors, for the Macedonians were full of rage, not only on account of the length of the siege, but also because the Tyrians, having captured some of their men, had brought them to the top of the wall, where the deed might be visible from the camp, and after slaughtering them, had cast their bodies into the sea. About 8,000 Tyrians were now killed; and of the Macedonians, besides Admetus, twenty died in the initial assault that day, and about four hundred in the entire siege.[4]

Alexander gave an amnesty to all those who had fled for refuge into the temple of Melkart, including the king and magistrates of Tyre and envoys from Carthage, who had come to their mother city to attend certain religious ceremonies. The rest of the Tyrians, to the number of many thousands, were sold into slavery. Thus Tyre fell in July, 332 B.C., after a siege of seven months. Alexander sacrificed to Heracles and dedicated in the temple the engine which had battered down the wall, and held military, religious, and athletic processions. Nothing, however, could hide the fact that the Phoenician coast had been won by the commission of an enormous crime. But we can point to one thing that has recently been proved; that, though Greek warfare often produced ruined cities and many slaves, Alexander's expedition did not affect appreciably the world's slave markets.

While Alexander was still occupied with the siege of Tyre, ambassadors once again came to him from Darius offering 10,000 talents for his family, all the territory west of the Euphrates, a daughter in marriage, and friendship and alliance. When these proposals were announced in a conference of the Companions, Parmenio is said to have remarked, "If I were Alexander, I would accept these terms and put an end to the war." "And so indeed would I," replied Alexander, "were I Parmenio." But as he was Alexander he told Darius that he already had practically everything that he offered. When Darius heard this, he despaired of coming to terms with Alexander and frantically began to make fresh preparations for war. The story of the conference of the Companions illustrates the sharp difference between the Macedonian point of view and Alexander's. The Greeks and Macedonians were ready to organize the eastern Mediterranean for their own profit, but by overstepping Asia Minor Alexander had already gone beyond their first intentions. To Alexander, on the other hand, opened the possibility of a new system —a larger, perhaps a world, society—but he kept his thoughts pretty much to himself, for few persons, then or later, could understand him.

[4] Chinnock's translation.

He merely told them what they could comprehend, that one more battle with Darius was necessary and that then peace would come.

Pure logic might have told Alexander that it would be easier to administer an empire that rested on the Euphrates rather than on the Indus, but it would be a mistake always to conceive him in too rational or cool a way. He could be intensely practical—for example, in a military campaign—but in other matters he could also be a great dreamer. He was realist enough to know that an arrangement which left Persia with a large empire held the possibility of continued warfare and in any case reduced his own expedition to the stature of another one of those interminable wars where brute force determines boundaries. His decision to fight Darius meant that he proposed to have the entire Persian Empire; and it is fair to add, in the light of his actions in Asia Minor, that he planned for mankind a new society or a new type of imperialism, call it what one will.

Alexander hastened from Tyre to Egypt late in 332 B.C., storming Gaza on the way. Egypt fell without a blow, for it was glad to be rid of the Persian misrule. In Egypt we catch important glimpses of Alexander's character and policy. He now had a large empire, far larger than any Greek had ever dreamed of. If this empire was to be organized and governed, it must have great satrapal seats, centers of administration, defense, and trade. The destruction of Tyre made it necessary to find another center for the trade of the eastern Mediterranean. In the days of the Pharaohs the Nile had been connected with the Red Sea by a canal, and now, undoubtedly, reports of the eastern seas came to Alexander. Egypt, then, seemed the ideal place, not only as the mart of the eastern Mediterranean, but also as a possible link between East and West. Alexander proceeded to lay out on the westernmost mouth of the Nile a great city, to be named Alexandria after him. While the army was engaged with the new city, Alexander took a few friends and went along the coast to Paraetonium, where envoys from Cyrene offered submission. He then struck across the desert on his famous and hazardous trip to the oracle of Ammon (the oasis of Siwah). The oracle of Zeus Ammon was, after Delphi and Dodona, the most important in the Greek world—and here was his chance to see it. The wily priests proclaimed him, as they would any king of Egypt, the son of God— or so it was reported, but Alexander had too much good sense to take it seriously. His real motive in going to the oracle was to confirm that the Libyan desert was in fact a natural frontier and to subsidize the priests to police the area for him. On his return to Memphis Alexander made his arrangements for Egypt, following his usual scheme of divided responsibility. He appointed Egyptians as governors of the land, but the financial affairs were placed in the hands of a Greek, and the military entrusted to two generals and an admiral, all Greeks.[5]

GAUGAMELA AND PERSIA

It was high time, now, to seek Darius. Marching up the Phoenician coast, Alexander cut over to Thapsacus and crossed the Euphrates. The two armies met at Gaugamela, some sixty miles from Arbela; their fierce struggle can be fairly acclaimed as the greatest battle in antiquity, since it decided the course of all subsequent history. First, Alexander ordered the soldiers to take dinner and rest themselves. While his Macedonians slept, he himself passed the night in front of his tent with his seer Aristander, celebrating certain mysterious sacred rites and sacrificing to the god Fear. And it is said that the older of his Companions, and particularly Parmenio, when they saw the plain and mountains all lighted up with the barbarian fires, with a sound of voices arising from their camp as if from a vast ocean, were astonished at their multitude and argued that it would be difficult to repel such a tide of war in broad daylight. They therefore came to Alexander's tent, when he had finished his sacrifices, and on their behalf Parmenio urged him to make a night attack upon the Persians. But Alexander, realizing the hazards of a battle in the dark, gave them the celebrated reply, "I will not steal my victory."

Next morning, after he had dressed, Alexander came out from his tent. He was fully armed, with a vest of Sicilian make girt about him, and over this a breastplate of two-ply linen from the spoils taken at Issus. His helmet was of iron, but gleamed like polished silver, a work of Theophilus; and there was fitted to this a throat-piece, likewise of iron, set with precious stones. He had a sword, too, of astonishing temper and lightness, a gift from the king of the Citieans, and he had trained himself to use a sword for the most part in his battles. He wore a belt also, which was too elaborate for the rest of his armor, for it was a work of Helicon the ancient, and a mark of honor from the city of Rhodes, which had given it to him; this also he was wont to wear in his battles.

Darius, for his part, had kept his men under arms the entire night, suspecting a surprise attack, a fact that not only lowered their vitality, but added to their natural fear. The Persian army, however, was very large, representing as it did the levy of the Empire. Though it did not even approach the million infantry and 40,000 cavalry of legend, it was

---

[5] For the sake of convenience Greeks and Macedonians are here regarded as one.

larger than the army at Issus, so much larger than Alexander's, indeed, that it extended well beyond his flanks. On his left wing Darius posted his splendid Bactrian cavalry, under his cousin Bessus, a remarkable prince, and at the point exactly opposite Alexander's right he placed some scythe-bearing chariots, the total number of which was considerably less than the reported 200. The broad battlefield had been carefully leveled for these chariots, and much was expected of them, especially because little was hoped for from the infantry. The right wing, under Mazaeus, was held by men of various races, including 1,000 mailed Saca horse, and in front were the excellent Armenian and Cappadocian cavalry and more scythe-bearing chariots.

In the center was Darius, towering conspicuous, a fine-looking man and tall, standing on a lofty chariot, and surrounded by the King's Kinsmen and the Persian guards carrying spears with golden apples at the butt end, Indians, Carians and Mardian archers. In front of Darius' royal squadron of cavalry stood some scythe-bearing chariots and fifteen elephants, which, had they not been handled badly, could have struck terror into a Western army. The Greek mercenaries, of whom Darius now had but 2,000, were alone considered capable of coping with the Macedonians and were stationed right opposite their phalanx. This, in brief, was the Persian order of battle, as captured after the conflict. Special reliance was placed on the scythe-bearing chariots and the cavalry of the two wings, who were armed better than previously; the line between consisted of both cavalry and infantry, but the forces that counted most here were the Persian cavalry and Greek mercenaries.

Alexander's infantry is reported to have numbered 40,000 men, but it is likely that his re-enforcements to date had only been sufficient to make good the losses caused by death and garrison duty and that he had approximately the same number of foot, 30,000, as at the Granicus; it is possible, however, that the number of his cavalry had grown to 7,000. Alexander commanded the right wing. Here were the Companion cavalry under Philotas, son of Parmenio; in front of them, as a protection against the scythe-bearing chariots, were Agrianian skirmishers, Macedonian archers and javelin men. Toward the center were the hypaspists under Nicanor, another son of Parmenio, and the phalanx. The left wing was commanded by Parmenio himself, who had the superb Thessalian cavalry.

Behind the phalanx Alexander placed another line of troops, made up of mercenaries, with orders to wheel round and face the enemy, should they attack from the rear; this was perhaps the second time in Greek history that reserves were employed in battle. Alexander was afraid that he might be surrounded, and therefore set to work to complete the other two sides of his square. The men on the sides were ranged in deep columns, at an angle with the center, and were instructed to attack the Persians in the flank, if they should ride round their wing.

It was October 1, 331 B.C. As long as Alexander rode about, marshalling his men and exhorting them, he spared Bucephalas, his famous horse, who was now past his prime, and used another, but when he was ready to go into action, Bucephalas was led up, and he mounted him. Shifting his lance to his left hand, as Callisthenes tells us, with his right hand he appealed to the gods, praying them to defend and strengthen the Greeks. Aristander, wearing a white mantle and having a crown of gold upon his head, rode along the ranks pointing out an eagle which soared above the head of Alexander and directed its flight straight against the enemy, at which sight great courage filled the beholders.

Alexander then led his army to the right, and the Persians marched along parallel with him, far outflanking him upon their left. In spite of skirmishes with the Scythian cavalry, Alexander calmly persisted in his rightward march and got almost entirely beyond the ground which had been cleared and leveled by the Persians. Darius, fearing that his chariots would become useless if the enemy advanced into the uneven ground, launched them against Alexander, but as soon as they approached, the Agrianians and javelin men, who were in front of the Companion cavalry, hurled their weapons at some of the horses; others they seized by the reins and pulled their drivers off, and standing round the horses killed them.

A decisive moment in the battle occurred when the Persians allowed a gap to open on the left of their line. Instantly Alexander, who had kept his main forces intact until it was certain that Bessus could be held on his flank, wheeled toward the opening and, forming a wedge of the Companion cavalry and part of the phalanx, led them with a quick charge and loud battle cry straight toward Darius himself. For a short time there ensued a hand-to-hand fight; but when the Macedonian cavalry, commanded by Alexander, pressed on vigorously, thrusting themselves against the Persians and striking their faces with their spears, and when the Macedonian phalanx in dense array and bristling with long pikes had also attacked them, Darius was seized with terror and was the first to turn and flee.

After a brief halt to support Parmenio, who was badly in need of help, Alexander wheeled round and started off in pursuit of Darius, keeping up the chase as long as there was daylight. Resting his horsemen until midnight, he again advanced by a forced march toward Arbela (Erbil), which he reached the next day, a distance of more than sixty miles from the battlefield of Gaugamela. But Darius was gone. As after Issus, Alexander captured his chariot and spear and bow, together with his money and other property. Parmenio, meanwhile, had seized the baggage, elephants and camels in the Persian camp. When Arrian tells us that Alexander lost 100 men and Darius 300,000, we see that it is impossible to form an opinion of the number killed in the battle.

In the course of his flight Darius gathered together remnants of his troops—the Bactrian cavalry, the King's Kinsmen, some of the so-called Apple-bearers, and the 2,000 Greek mercenaries—and hastened toward Media, for he conjectured that Alexander would take the direct and easy road to Babylon and Susa, which after all were the prizes of war. Though it was clear that Darius would never fight again, Alexander must have realized that new and even more difficult problems now lay before him. As the first step toward organizing and administering his state, it would be necessary to examine the vast area of the former Persian Empire and to establish order, but this could not be quickly done, for there were already large districts beyond his actual line of march which did not yet owe him allegiance. Thus the purpose of the two cities which he founded after the battle was to control his communications and police the neighborhood; the general intention of his foundations (which more often than not consisted of garrisons added to existing towns) was to provide the countryside with a gendarmerie. As he proceeded east, into a land that boasted few cities, the new foundations resembled rather administrative seats, but no matter what their character these settlements of unfit soldiers became in time centers for the spread of Hellenism.

Alexander now had before him the glorious capitals of the ancient East. At Babylon the people greeted him as a deliverer; he reappointed Mazaeus satrap, though the garrison was given to a Macedonian; and he won popularity by permitting the people their ancestral customs. Alexander next went to Susa, and then, after some hard fighting at the Persian Gates, entered Persis, the ancient home of the Persians.

It is not difficult to imagine Alexander's thoughts as he strolled among the great palaces of Persepolis, which even today are magnificent in their ruin. The hereditary foe of Greece had been utterly defeated; he was master of the capitals and lands of the ancient East, of Macedon and Greece as well, the ruler of the largest empire the world had ever seen. On beholding a statue of Xerxes which had been overthrown by a throng that forced its way into the palace, Alexander stopped before it, and accosting it as if it had been alive, said, "Shall I pass on and leave you lying there, because of your expedition against the Greeks, or, because of your magnanimity and virtue in other ways, shall I set you up again?" But finally, after communing with himself a long time in silence, he passed on. And we are told that when he took his seat for the first time under the golden canopy on the royal throne, his old friend, Demaratus of Corinth, burst into tears and declared that those Greeks were deprived of great pleasure who had died before seeing Alexander seated on the throne of Darius. Acting against Parmenio's advice, Alexander deliberately set fire to Xerxes' palace, in order that the world might clearly understand that one regime had given way to another. Legend created from this the fanciful story of Thais, the Athenian courtesan, who incited the banqueters to the act and thus punished Xerxes for his evil deeds. But the cold fact was that the rule of the Achaemenids had come to an end; so, too, had the war of revenge and with it, perhaps, Alexander's dependence upon the Greeks.

EASTERN IRAN

During the halt at Persepolis news reached Alexander that the Spartans had finally been defeated in battle—welcome as it was, he remarked that "while we were conquering Darius, a battle of mice seems to have been fought in Greece"—but the Persian days were spent in a routine way, without revealing any imaginative plans for his great dominion. Probably he wished first to become the undisputed master of the former Persian Empire, in theory as well as in fact and without a rival, but this entailed the capture of Darius, who was biding his time in Ecbatana (Hamadan), the famous capital of the Medes. Suddenly a report reached Alexander that Darius had sent his women and baggage to the so-called Caspian Gates and was planning, in case Alexander moved, to flee eastward to Bactria, laying waste all the land as he did so. Alexander immediately set out from Persepolis (late March, 330 B.C.) and advanced toward Media, but on the way he was told that Darius had already fled.

Alexander could hardly afford to delay the pursuit, but each step from now on would bring him into lands wholly unfamiliar to the Greek world, and it was altogether unwise to continue into the East without an explanation of his future plans. He therefore resolved to halt at Ecbatana and put into effect some of the ideas he had been considering, perhaps, during his stay at Persepolis; it is probable, too, that the arrival of 6,000 Greek mercenaries at this moment made his decision easier. In spite of the fact that the four years since his departure from Greece had been crowded with battles and marches and the details of administration, Alexander had grown enough to alter or abandon many of his original aims. Brought up in Plato's theory that all barbarians were enemies of the Greeks by nature, and in that of Aristotle that all barbarians were slaves by nature, especially those of Asia, Alexander had been able to test the smugness of the Greek by actual contact with barbarians, on the battlefield and off, and experience had apparently convinced him of the essential sameness of all people. It was back in Egypt, according to Plutarch, that Alexander had accepted the teaching of Psammon, the philosopher, that all mankind are under the kingship of God, since in every case that which gets the mastery and rules is divine. Still more philosophical, continues Plutarch, was Alexander's own opinion that although God is indeed a common father of all mankind, still, He makes peculiarly His own the noblest and best of them.

The fundamental question before Alexander, then, was whether this new and vast empire of many races was to be governed in the old familiar fashion, with Hellenic despotism substituted for Oriental, or whether a new world state could be formed along very different lines. He had already given partial expression to his ideas by the appointment of barbarians, as well as Greeks and Macedonians, to important administrative posts, and yet his sincerity was open to question since there were clearly not enough Greeks and Macedonians to go around. We have noticed, however, that no sooner had the expedition set out than Alexander began to assert his independence of the Corinthian League. He had every intention of maintaining the League, and of dealing with it legally wherever he could, because it was a convenient instrument for governing the Greeks, but he now decided to make absolutely clear that Panhellenism had died with the war of revenge. He would remain king of Macedon and commander-in-chief of the Corinthian League, but in addition he must somehow convince the barbarians that he was their king, too, for it was not enough simply to proclaim himself the Lord of Asia and the Great King of the former Persian Empire.

Thus, in a dramatic gesture designed to prove that the special partnership with the Greeks had come to an end, Alexander dismissed the Thessalian cavalry and his other Greek allies. They were given generous presents; and many availed themselves of the opportunity to re-enlist, but henceforth, while they might be marshalled according to nationality, they marched as a part of the imperial army and not as allies. Alexander's adoption not long afterward of a modified form of Persian dress, which was far simpler than the Median, was interpreted by hostile gossip as a surrender to Oriental luxury, but actually it was part of his plan to convince the barbarians of their equality within the Empire, and it also served notice upon the Greeks and Macedonians that they were not to occupy a privileged position. But none of this, Alexander saw, went far enough. Daring as was his conception of equality for different peoples, united by various means to himself as ruler, nevertheless some additional bond was needed, the idea of a common fate, or perhaps the ideal of the brotherhood of man. To supply this bond was his hardest task. Because, however, he was convinced of the superiority of Greek culture, Hellenism might in time serve as the vehicle; its own spread would be facilitated by those very settlements whose primary purpose was to garrison the countryside.

Alexander now promoted his friend, Harpalus, to the newly created post of Imperial Treasurer and placed in his charge the 180,000 talents which had been brought from Persepolis; and, breaking significantly with the past, he left Parmenio behind at Ecbatana to guard the lines of communication. Then he marched against Darius, who was fleeing eastward across the desert. In the forced march that followed, many of the soldiers were left behind, worn out with fatigue, and many of the horses died, but nevertheless he pressed on to Rhagae (near Teheran), and thence a one day's march of fifty miles through the Caspian Gates as far as the desert.

Word now reached Alexander that the Bactrian prince Bessus had arrested Darius. Hearing this, Alexander pursued with all his might and covered 200 miles in five days from Rhagae. In a dreary desert spot not far from Hecatompylos (Damghan) he came upon the murdered body of Darius. Alexander was manifestly distressed at what had happened, but he must have realized, too, how much easier his own position had become, with Darius dead rather than alive.

At the Caspian Sea, not much later, Alexander, the student of Aristotle, was fascinated by an ancient question. Was the Caspian an inland sea, or a stagnant overflow of the Sea of Azov, or could it by any chance be a gulf of Ocean, that Outer Sea which rings the inhabited world? Had he, in fact, reached the earth's northern limits? He did not know, but he proposed to find out, particularly because everything from now on would be strange, and constant study was necessary if he was to know even the simplest facts concerning his whereabouts. An exploring expedition was organized, but since it was already mid-June he could not wait for a report. The immediate task was to seize Bessus.

Alexander's thought had been to follow the great caravan route direct to Bactria, but rebellion on his flank forced him to make a wide sweep southward through Aria and into Seistan, where the conspiracy of Philotas occurred. No doubt Philotas, the distinguished son of the great Parmenio, had many grievances, real and imaginary, against Alexander. Alexander's endless marches, for one thing, prevented the conquerors from settling down to the enjoyment of their labors, but probably most important of all was the fact that in Macedonia the king was little better than the nobles, and yet here was Alexander grown powerful and aloof, acting and thinking strangely. Had not the time come for the Macedonian nobles to take things into their own hands?

Near the Lake of Seistan the "plot of Philotas" was discovered. The evidence against Philotas was far from clear. It appears that there may indeed have been a plot, but Philotas was not involved. At worst he may have withheld knowledge of the scheme in the realization that it was not dangerous and with the desire of not implicating his friends.

He was tried, nevertheless, in Macedonian fashion, by the army, convicted, and executed. Immediately, orders were sent to the commanders in Media to put Parmenio to death. Judicial though the executions were, it is difficult to believe that Alexander, had he wished, could not have persuaded the army to different action, but his main purpose probably was to break the Macedonian opposition to him. It is even possible that Alexander took advantage of the opportunity afforded by the discovery of a plot to implicate Philotas and through him Parmenio. In this way he may have continued the purge of the old nobility who owed their loyalty more to Phillip than to Alexander.

Alexander had created several great satrapal seats since leaving the Caspian Sea, for this part of the world boasted few towns in the western sense of the word; and he spent the winter by the Hindu Kush founding yet another, Alexandria of the Caucasus as it was called. Its curious name arose from the fact that the Hindu Kush was believed to be an extension of the Caucasus range in the west. Alexander might not be in doubt about the immediate terrain, but obviously there were large geographical problems still demanding solution.

Because of the early season (spring, 329 B.C.), Alexander decided to cross the Hindu Kush by the low, though long, Khawak pass (11,600 feet high), but the soldiers suffered keenly nonetheless from the intense cold and lack of provisions. In the rapid pursuit that followed, Bessus was captured and sent to Bactra (Balkh), the capital of Bactria and the traditional home of Zoroastrianism, to await trial; but his redoubtable ally, Spitamenes, escaped across the Oxus river (Amu Daria) into Sogdiana (Turkestan). Alexander pressed on to Maracanda (Samarcand), the summer capital of Sogdiana, and thence into Ferghana as far as the Jaxartes (Syr Daria). This river, the northern limit of the Persian Empire, Alexander took to be the Tanais (Don), which flows into the Sea of Azov, and the land beyond it, therefore, he thought was Europe and its people "Scythians." He founded a city beside the river, Alexandria the Farthest (Alexandreschate), and to ensure order along his frontier he crossed the river against the "Scythians," as he had once crossed the

Danube and on another occasion had marched to the oracle of Ammon in the Libyan desert.

Two years of guerrilla warfare were necessary to put down the national resistance of eastern Iran. The years—hard years of incessant fighting, marching and treachery—also saw Alexander's murder of Cleitus in a drunken brawl, the same "Black" Cleitus who had saved his life at the Granicus. But events were forcing Alexander to dramatic decisions as well. He saw that if he were really to be king of the barbarians, no less than of the Macedonians, he must give them a stake in his success, and accordingly he added Asiatics to his army who, as it turned out, were the ones to capture Spitamenes. Not much later he married Roxane, the beautiful daughter of a Bactrian baron, but it was a political alliance designed to reward eastern Iran, as it surely deserved, for cooperation. Long ago he had adopted Oriental dress and by his appointment of barbarians to responsible posts had further shown his desire to place Greeks, Macedonians, and Persians on one plane. Recently, to, he had revealed his plans, in simple but real terms, for world conquest, which ultimately took shape in his mind as a Western expedition. Now he ordered that 30,000 native youths should be trained in Macedonian fashion. These were not merely epochal, visionary ideas of collaboration between peoples, for they had already been translated, in the large, into reality. Because, moreover, he had achieved a legal relation to the barbarian world as successor to Darius, there remained only one great problem, that of his relation to Greece. How was he to ensure the efficient administration of a divided land, if normal methods failed?

Deification was the natural answer, because the Hellenic world was accustomed to it in one form or another, and even in this century had raised living men to the ranks of the gods. It was a political device, and no one, least of all Alexander, considered him a god. Callisthenes thwarted his proposal at this time, and Alexander abandoned the idea, temporarily for the Greeks, permanently for the Macedonians. Not much later Callisthenes was implicated in a conspiracy of the pages and, whether justly or not, was arrested and executed.

INDIA

The conquest of Bactria-Sogdiana left India as the only part of the old Persian Empire that Alexander had not yet visited, and he turned to it as a matter of course, though the land of fable, where even Dionysus and Heracles had gone in days of old, must have excited his imagination. In the spring of 327 B.C., with many Asiatics in his army, he re-crossed the Hindu Kush. The route to the Indus—roughly, down the Cabul valley and the Khyber pass—was marked by hard fighting, and in particular by the well-nigh impossible capture of Aornos, a famous "rock" which has now been identified with the precipitous ridge of Pir-sar.

When Alexander reached the Indus in 326 B.C., he was greeted by Taxiles, the reigning prince of the district. He was entertained at the capital Taxila, received elephants and other presents from Taxiles, and an alliance was concluded between them. India, with its ancient civilization, its curious customs, and its ascetics, made a great impression upon the Greeks and Macedonians. The Brahmans explained to Alexander that his invasion was much like a man standing on a skin filled with water: where he stood, all was quiet; but roundabout everything swelled up, in revolt. And that was about true, so far as India was concerned, for Alexander's expedition left no impression on the country, and on his death India returned to its native state—unless we are to count the invasion of the Bactrian Greeks a century and a half later, their long rule, and the still later economic penetration by Rome. For the moment, however, Alexander had other ideas. The old Persian Empire had extended further east, and there Alexander must go; somewhere, not very far off, lay Ocean, too. Clearly he was utterly ignorant of the Indian peninsula and of China.

Though the wonders of Taxila filled the Macedonians with awe, Alexander remained in the city but a brief time, for it was necessary to reach the Hydaspes river, over 100 miles to the east, before the melting snows of the Himalayas and the tropical rains made it impassable. Beyond the Hydaspes, he was told, was Taxiles' enemy, Porus, a magnificent man almost 7 feet tall, who in addition to the resources of his own kingdom was now receiving aid from the deceitful Abisares, rajah of the country to the north. Alexander, therefore, sent Coenus back to the Indus, with instructions to cut in pieces the triakonters (warships with fifteen oars to a side) and other vessels which he had prepared for the passage of that river, and to bring them to the Hydaspes on wagons. Enlarging the kingdom of Taxiles, who was reduced to the status of a vassal prince, Alexander appointed Philip, son of Machatas, satrap, and left a garrison in Taxila, as well as the soldiers who were invalided by sickness. He also added 5,000 Indians to his army. Perhaps his lengthening lines of communication made this necessary, though the thought that Ocean was not far off must have relieved his mind of any special worry concerning personnel; no doubt, too, he was determined that the army should continue, in a sense, as an imperial "melting pot," for his experiment during the past years of employing barbarian troops had been fully justified.

Alexander met little opposition on his march through the Punjab as far as the Hydaspes (Jhelum); he held to a southerly route, in order to draw Porus as far away as possible from the territory of Abisares, crossed the Salt Range by the Nandana pass, continued through a much broken table-land and in early June struck the Hydaspes at Haranpur. On the opposite bank, half a mile away, could be seen the great Paurava king, an extraordinarily able and powerful ruler of a rich and populous land, who was to give Alexander the greatest fight of his life and extend to the limit his versatility and genius. Porus had considerably more infantry than Alexander, as well as several hundred scythe-bearing chariots and over 200 elephants. Alexander's sole superiority was in his cavalry, but it was doubtful if the horses would face the unfamiliar and terrifying elephants, with their strange odor and trumpeting, and, indeed, it was highly problematical whether he would be able to cross the river at all, for the rains had already begun, and each day the Hydaspes was rising; at the few possible fords Porus had stationed guards.

As soon as he had surveyed the situation, Alexander decided to move his army in various directions, in order to distract the attention of Porus and confuse him. Dividing his army into many sections, he himself led some of his troops now into one part of the land and now into another, at one time ravaging the country, at another looking out for a place where the river might appear easier to ford. The rest of his troops he entrusted to his different generals, and sent them about in many directions. Because his vessels were sailing up and down the river, and skins were being filled with hay, and the whole bank appeared to be covered in one place with cavalry and in another with infantry, Porus was not allowed to keep at rest. But when Porus found that all the noise and marching led to nothing, he no longer continued to move about to meet the imaginary crossing, but posted scouts along the bank and withdrew to his camp. Alexander then devised the following stratagem.

In his marching back and forth, Alexander had discovered eighteen miles above Porus' camp a projecting point, at Jalalpur, where the river makes a bend. The promontory was wooded, as was the island opposite it, which would serve to screen an attempt to cross. He had most of his ships from the Indus secretly put together at this place, and all along the bank of the river posted sentries, close enough together to hear any order that might be passed along. He then openly prepared his measures for crossing from his camp at Haranpur. Craterus was left here with some cavalry and infantry, including the 5,000 Indians. "If Porus should march against me with part of his army and leave some of the elephants in camp," Alexander ordered Craterus, "remain where you are. But if he takes all the elephants, and leaves a part of the army in camp, or if he is defeated, then cross the river with all speed, for it is the elephants alone that make it impossible for the horses to land on the opposite bank."

Alexander then took 15,000 men—heavy and light infantry and cavalry—and made a secret march, keeping far away from the river, to the promontory where he had resolved to cross. During the night—it was just after the summer solstice—a furious storm occurred, which helped to hide his preparations, because the claps of thunder drowned the clatter of the weapons and the orders given by the officers. At the approach of dawn both the wind and rain calmed down, and the men crossed to the island in boats and on skins. Alexander himself embarked in a triakonter with Ptolemy, who later became king of Egypt; Perdiccas, the future regent; Lysimachus, the future king of Thrace, and Seleucus, the new commander of the hypaspists, who inherited his Asiatic empire. They were not seen by the sentinels of Porus until they had begun to cross from the island to the farther bank. Through ignorance of the topography, however, Alexander and his men landed not on the opposite bank, but on another island, which was ordinarily cut off from it by shallow water, but the recent rain had turned the stream into a torrent. It was one of the most critical moments in his life, and might have been disastrous, if the ford had not been found, or if too much time had been wasted in locating it. When at last the ford was discovered, he led his men through it with difficulty, for the water reached to the breasts of the infantry and the heads of the horses.

When it was reported to Porus that Alexander had crossed and routed a detachment sent against him—that his whole strategical advantage had, in short, been cancelled—he still could not make up his mind what course to take, because Craterus was seen to be attempting to cross the river from the camp directly opposite his position. At last, however, he decided to leave a small force of elephants to frighten the cavalry under Craterus from the bank of the river, and with the rest of his army marched against Alexander. When he found a place where there was no clay, but which was sandy and reasonably satisfactory for his cavalry and bowmen, he drew up his forces. In the center, for a space of four miles, he placed 200 elephants, each separated from the next by not less than 100 feet; in the intervals between the elephants, but behind them and extending beyond their flanks, was the infantry, greatly outnumbering the troops Alexander had been able to transport across the river; on each wing were 2,000 cavalry (somewhat less than Alexander's), with 150 chariots stationed in front of each.

When Alexander came near the enemy, he told his men to rest while he examined the situation. His chief task was to match somehow, without any elephants of his own, the elephants of Porus. This, he decided, was best done by attacking some other section of the enemy and rolling it back upon the beasts. He therefore posted all his cavalry under himself on the right wing, in the hope that he might throw the enemy's left into utter confusion. In the center he placed the phalanx, with the light-armed on either side, and ordered them not to engage in the action until they observed the enemy's cavalry and infantry thrown into disorder by his own attack.

The fact that the Hydaspes bends westward in this neighborhood prevented Porus from resting his cavalry on the river, and therefore he drew it up in columns, which offered a better defense than a line, but at the last moment he made the fatal mistake of rearranging and massing all his cavalry on his left wing, to meet Alexander's threat. Alexander acted in a flash. First he sent his Asiatic horse-archers against the enemy's left wing to attack that section of the infantry which extended beyond the elephants, and to rain upon it an incessant storm of arrows. Then he ordered Coenus to take half the cavalry, sweep around his own left wing, continue behind the enemy and attack Porus' cavalry in the rear. The Indians, observing this maneuver, were compelled to make their cavalry face both ways. While they were rearranging their horse again, Coenus took them in the rear, and Alexander charged with such vigor that they were forced back to the elephants. Upon this, the drivers of the elephants urged the animals forward against Alexander, but now the Macedonian phalanx was advancing against them, the men (keeping a wide open order, as they had been instructed) casting javelins at riders and beasts. The wounded elephants, frantic with pain, rushed at friends and foes alike, until, worn out, "they began to retire slowly, facing the enemy like ships backing water, and merely uttering a shrill, piping sound."

Alexander then surrounded the whole line with his cavalry and gave the signal that the infantry should link their shields together and attack. Accordingly there ensued a great slaughter of the Indian cavalry and infantry, and those who could turned and fled through the intervals between Alexander's cavalry.

At the same time Craterus and his men, who had been left behind on the bank of the Hydaspes, crossed the river, when they perceived that Alexander was winning a brilliant victory. These men, being fresh, followed up the pursuit instead of Alexander's exhausted troops, and continued the slaughter of the Indians in their retreat. As long as any group of Indians remained compact, Porus continued the fight, exhibiting great bravery and skill; but after he received a wound in his right shoulder, which was the only part of his body not encased in his remarkable coat of mail, he wheeled round his huge elephant and began to retire, convinced that surrender was the only was to prevent a general massacre. Alexander hoped to save his life and sent Meroes, an Indian friend, to him. Porus by this time was overcome with thirst, and when he heard Meroes' message, he stopped his elephant and dismounted. After he had drunk some water and felt refreshed, he ordered Meroes to lead him to Alexander.

When Alexander learned that Meroes was bringing Porus to him, as the ancient writers describe the scene:

he rode in front of the line with a few Companions to meet him; and stopping his horse, he admired his handsome figure and great stature, for he was almost seven feet tall. He was also surprised that Porus did not seem to be cowed in spirit, but advanced to meet him as one brave man would meet another, after having gallantly struggled in defense of his own kingdom. Then indeed Alexander was the first to speak, bidding him say how he would be treated. The story goes that Porus replied, "Like a king"; and to another question whether he had anything else to say, replied that everything was included in that.

The battle of the Hydaspes, Alexander's fourth and last pitched battle, had raged eight hours. Porus' losses were immense, though we cannot recover the exact figure. Nor shall we ever know the extent of Alexander's losses, for the army was so shaken by the struggle that it seemed wise to minimize them. We do know, however, that when the army refused to follow Alexander beyond the Hyphasis not long afterward, a contributory factor was the knowledge that still more elephants were to be met.

After the battle Alexander paid all due honors to the slain, offered the customary sacrifices and celebrated various contests. He also founded two cities, Nicaea (Victory) at Jalalpur and, on the east bank where the battle had been fought, Bucephala. Bucephala was named in memory of his horse and became eventually an important city. Craterus was left behind with part of the army to erect and fortify the cities and build a fleet, for in his conviction that his march eastward would soon bring him to Ocean, Alexander was already planning to return to the Hydaspes and sail down it to the Indian Ocean, the southern limit of the world.

But Alexander's ideas of empire were changing no less than his plans.

He was beginning to sense the size of India and the immensity of its population. For the Punjab, therefore, the system of satrapies was abandoned in favor of a less centralized and more flexible type of government; the new scheme might perhaps be best described as an association of allied powers, with Alexander, of course, the dominant member. In any case, Porus was left wholly free within his kingdom, which was greatly enlarged and extended ultimately from the Hydaspes to the Hyphasis. Taxiles was reconciled to his old enemy and sent back to Taxila to rule the broad land from the Indus to the Hydaspes; no longer was he to be subject to the satrap, Philip, son of Machatas.

The victorious march continued until Gurdaspur on the Hyphasis (Beas) was reached. Then the troops mutinied, not against Alexander, for he alone could bring them home, and it was home that his veterans insisted on going. They had seen enough; in fact, during the past eight and a half years they had marched over 11,000 miles. Like his ancestor Achilles, Alexander withdrew to his tent and sulked for three days, but when the army refused to changed its mind, he yielded.

Alexander's disappointment was keen, for he had been unnecessarily prevented, so he thought, from continuing those last few miles to Ocean, the eastern and natural limit of his empire, where great cities and harbors of his creation would produce a wonderful prosperity and serve to tie together in an economic whole the various sections of the state. To mark the farthest point of his advance he erected twelve tremendous altars to the Olympian gods and offered sacrifice upon them, and celebrated gymnastic and cavalry contests. The tendency of the rivers of the Punjab to shift westward has long since obliterated the altars, but we are told by Plutarch that Chandragupta used to offer sacrifices upon them. Alexander also prepared armor that was larger than usual, and mangers for horses that were higher, and bits that were heavier than those in common use, and left them scattered up and down to impress later generations with the manner of men who had come that way—this in a land whose literature does not even mention his name, though it is probably true that his life inspired the subsequent unification of India under Chandragupta and Asoka and of China under the Han dynasty.

THE RETURN

Alexander did not return, however, by the route his men expected, for he had already determined, back at the Hydaspes, that some day he would sail down it to the Indian Ocean on the south. He had, therefore, left men behind to build a fleet of 800 ships, and this he now found nearly completed. Nearchus was made admiral. Alexander went on board (November, 326 B.C.) with a large body of troops, while the rest of the army followed on shore, in three divisions. During the descent of the rivers he met many tribes and in storming one of their cities, that of the Malli, he nearly lost his life. Alexander had been wounded in battle several times before, but this was a dangerous wound. His soldiers were tired, and to urge them on, Alexander hurried up a scaling-ladder, which broke almost as soon as he reached the top of the wall. With a handful of men he jumped down into the city. A desperate fight followed—Alexander was shot in the chest by an arrow, he fainted, and Peucestas held over him the sacred shield which had been taken from Troy. When the Macedonians finally broke into the city, they massacred the population.

Patala, in the delta, was reached in the summer of 325 B.C. Now Alexander made vigorous plans for his return. Craterus had already been sent back by the Mulla pass with some of the men. The first task was to found cities here beside Ocean, the southern limit of his empire, to build docks, in general to create an economic link in his empire. The next task was to explore the route to Babylon—Nearchus going with the fleet up the Persian Gulf, Alexander supporting him on land. By September they were ready to start.

The return across Gedrosia was full of difficulties—unexpected mountains forced Alexander from the sea, so that he could not keep in touch with Nearchus and provision him; the guides lost the way; the desert heat necessitated marching by night; food and water were scarce; many died. But it was a triumph to get an army of 15,000 or more across. Nearchus, too, had his experiences. Savages, who lived on fish, were encountered; so was a school of whales, which the Greeks frightened off with trumpets. In Carmania Alexander, Nearchus, and Craterus met, and legend has turned the natural celebration of this reunion into a Dionysiac revel.

When he reached Susa in the spring of 324 B.C., Alexander found that some of his provincial officials had governed unjustly during his absence. He put them to death, and made various new appointments. Harpalus, the chief financial officer of the empire and an old friend, had embezzled much money and fled to Greece. Alexander, nevertheless, undertook important financial reforms. The gold standard of Persia was abolished, and in its place was substituted a uniform currency on the Attic standard. The problems of Greece also lay heavily on Alexander's mind. To bring order to the country he decreed that the Greek states should take back their exiles and that he should be deified. Other ideas were taking shape, too. The 30,000 native youths, who, back in Bactria, had been trained in Macedonian fashion, now arrived and were incorporated in the army. At a great wedding feast Alexander married Barsine, daughter of Darius, while Hephaestion married her sister Drypetis; in all, eighty of his officers married daughters of noble Medes and Persians; during the entire expedition 10,000 Greeks and Macedonians had taken barbarian wives.

By his own marriage and those of his friends Alexander wished to place his stamp of approval on the fusion of races, a natural counterpart, as it were, of his belief in the fatherhood of God. He hoped that this might be accomplished by example and persuasion, for he planned neither a deliberate Hellenization of the East nor a barbarization of the Greeks and Macedonians. Those who wished were free to pursue their own national life—and they would inevitably represent the overwhelming majority—but beside this there was to develop a new life based on an interchange and mixture of customs and blood. Here was to be the driving force of the empire—a new nationality, if such it may be called, new hopes and new opportunities, a new attitude toward the world. As Plutarch so passionately expressed it: "At the sight of these marriages I should have cried out for joy, 'O dullard Xerxes, stupid fool that spent so much fruitless toil to bridge the Hellespont! This is the way that wise kings join Asia with Europe; it is not by beams nor rafts, nor by lifeless and unfeeling bonds, but by the ties of lawful love and chaste nuptials and mutual joy in children that they join the nations together.' "

Mixed marriages, however, were not the only means at Alexander's hand for the amalgamation of his empire, for even greater faith was placed on the possibilities of a common Greek culture and law. The cities which he founded, seventy in number according to tradition and more often than not old setlements which he enlarged, were intended primarily, to be sure, to police the countryside and guard his communications, but because they were placed along the great trade routes they became, together with the uniform currency, powerful stimulants of trade and unification, a policy which his successors followed.

Not all of these ideas were popular with all of his men, and when at Opis on the Tigris Alexander decided to send home 10,000 veterans, the army was convinced that he no longer cared for it and mutinied. Alexander, enraged, discharged them all and told them to go home and say how they had abandoned their leader in the heart of Asia. He then began to create a Persian army. His old soldiers, with tears rolling down their cheeks, repented and begged to be taken back.

Alexander sealed the reconciliation between himself and the army by a banquet for 9,000 persons. At his own table sat Macedonians, Persians, Greek seers, Median Magi, and distinguished representatives of the other peoples of the empire and, after dinner, they all drew wine from a great crater, or mixing bowl, the Greek seers and the Magi commencing the ceremony, and then the whole 9,000 together made one libation at the sound of a trumpet. It was this crater that Alexander had in mind when he said that he had a kingly mission from the deity to be the harmonizer and reconciler of the world, uniting and mixing men's lives and customs and marriages as in a loving cup. Then Alexander prayed for partnership in the empire and for unity and concord (in the Greek, *Homonoia,* a union of hearts) in a joint commonwealth where all peoples were to be partners rather than subjects—a prayer that marks a revolution in human thought. Alexander's dream of the brotherhood of man, a dream of peace and union between Greek and barbarian, was a clear and ennobling restatement of his considered policy these many years, that mankind should contemplate not exclusive, "national" societies, but universalism, the idea of the *oecumene* or "inhabited world," where all men are indeed sons of one Father.

Alexander's devotion to his friends was matched by the love his men bore him. With rare exceptions he called forth their full and hearty support, and on the few occasions that they disagreed, he generally had his way. The short-lived mutiny at Opis, itself the result of hard marches and of misunderstandings as to Alexander's intentions, is a case in point, for he sent back to Greece the men he had originally decided upon, 10,000 veterans who were no longer physically fit or young enough for military service.

Later that year at Ecbatana Hephaestion died, Alexander's dear friend who had been almost the only one to catch and share his vision of the new world. In the spring of 323 B.C. Alexander returned to Babylon and set at once to his plans, plans of colonization, of exploration around Arabia and the Caspian. We are struck by the detailed care which Alexander gave so many different matters. On the one hand, he supported artists and scientists—Aristotle alone received 800 talents —and on the other hand, he planned the draining of Lake Copais in Greece and the exploitation of the mineral wealth of India; but it all took money, too, and when to the lavish presents he made to friends and strangers we add the ordinary expenses of government, the maintenance of the army, the building of dockyards and cities and temples, we are not surprised at the report that only 50,000 talents were left in the treasury on his death.

It is Alexander's early death that makes us regret so keenly his absorption with conquest and exploration, for it robbed him of the opportunity of developing his ideas of world government. No doubt he intended that the peoples of the empire should assume their share in working out the pattern; the measure of freedom and the details of government would vary from area to area and depend in part upon the condition of civilization of the individual peoples. This variety would have been but the reflection of his own position in the state, for he was at once the king of Macedon and commander-in-chief of the League of Corinth, the suzerain of Indian rajahs and the adopted son of a Carian queen, the Great King of the former Persian Empire and the "ally" of the Greek cities of Asia Minor, a god in Greece and Egypt.

Still, the outline of Alexander's chief thoughts was there. There could be little doubt about his ideas on world conquest and his own relation to a world state, the use of barbarians in administration and army, universal brotherhood, the fusion of races, and personal deification. His aim clearly was to unify the empire and bind it together as a social, political, and economic whole—or, as he expressed it, he bade all men to consider as their fatherland the whole inhabited earth, where they would have concord and peace and community of interests, and he further pledged himself to render all upon earth subject to one law of reason and one form of government, that of justice. But if government was to be on this high level, it was a task requiring all his time, and this Alexander was unwilling to give.

ALEXANDER'S DEATH

Envoys now arrived from Greece, with crowns upon their heads, as though they had been deputed to pay Alexander divine honors. Their requests, and other problems of empire, commanded his attention, but nevertheless the Arabian expedition never left his mind; he often reviewed the fleet, organized sham battles in the river, and awarded prizes to the best rowers and pilots. But it was too much. The ceaseless mental and physical activity, the tremendous responsibilities of empire, the long marches and dangerous wounds had so lowered his vitality that he was not able to throw off a fever. Thus ended Alexander's life at Babylon on June 13, 323 B.C.; he was not yet thirty-three years of age, and had reigned twelve years and eight months.

For four days and four nights, we are told, a terrible silence fell on Babylon. People could not believe the news, and at Athens an opponent cried, "It cannot be true; if Alexander were dead, the whole habitable world would have smelt of his carcass." Alexander had left his empire simply "to the best," and before long the inevitable disputes began. It was finally decided to make Perdiccas regent and to proclaim Arrhidaeus, the feeble-minded bastard son of Philip, king, and if Roxane's child should be a boy, to call him king, too. A month later the little Alexander was born, but within a dozen years mother and son were put to death, while in the interim Olympias had murdered Arrhidaeus, and herself met a violent end.

A year was to pass before the funeral train commenced its long journey from Babylon to Damascus, Memphis and Alexandria, where today the holiest spot is reputedly the Conqueror's grave. Indeed, the true personality of the man who moved the imagination of posterity as few have done was ultimately lost in legend, buried under an extraordinary body of literature that has nothing to do with history. The Alexander Romance, as it is called, began to form not long after his death and, passing under the name of Callisthenes, its eighty versions in twenty-four languages circulated from Iceland to Malaya. To mediaeval Europe and to the Orient at all periods the Alexander of Romance has been the Alexander of reality. Today, for example, the Parsees curse him for having destroyed their sacred books, and throughout Central Asia he is worshipped as Iskander, founder of ancient cities, while his red silk banner is still displayed in Ferghana. In remote parts of Turkestan the chiefs claim descent from Alexander, the ordinary folk are sprung from his soldiers and the very horses from Bucephalas. The Bedouin thought that Napoleon was Iskander, whereas the Russians regarded Napoleon and his army as Gog and Magog under the leadership of the Antichrist.

A Christian saint in Ethiopia and a knight in France, Alexander appears in the Koran as Dulcarnain, the Lord of the Two Horns, and according to the Moslem poets he prayed in the Kaaba of Mecca. The Egyptians considered him the son of their last pharaoh, the magician Nectanebo, who in the guise of a dragon deceived the childless Olympias; their son was small and deformed, yet cunning and brave. The early Christians portrayed Jesus in Alexander's likeness, and the Jews looked upon him as a propagandist of the Most High. He was supposed to have built a gate to exclude Gog and Magog, who were later equated with the Ten Tribes of Israel and then with barbarism itself; with expanding geographical knowledge the gate was moved from the pass of Derbend in the Caucasus to the Great Wall of China and to the Arctic Circle. Still other stories brought this world-conqueror to the Ganges and cannibal kingdoms, to the Blue Nile and Britain—indeed, to the four corners of the earth—and then, as if that were not enough, to the heavens and on to the Land of Darkness and even further to the end of the world, where one finds the Well of Life. Thence he descended to the bottom of the sea in a diving bell and then, after the fish had paid him homage, he returned to Babylon, where he died by poison.

But how much greater is Alexander the man! Though it would be idle to speculate on what he might have achieved, had he lived his full term and come to grips with the problems of governing his vast empire, this much we do know: his meteoric career was sufficient to introduce a new epoch in human history. It took a supreme force to bring it into being. Gone was the small democratic city-state; gone, too, the homogeneous civilization concentrated around the Aegean Sea. The high standards of taste, the freedom, responsibility, and intensity of Periclean life become things of the past. But it was the new culture of the succeeding Hellenistic Age—the only Greek culture the world ever really knew, until modern scholarship resurrected that of Periclean Athens—that civilized Rome and facilitated her creation of a world state and Christianity's conquest of that state. As such, it is Alexander's monument, while his dreams have been, and still are, a challenge to humanity to substitute the idea of the solidarity of the world, and with it the dignity of the individual and his labor, for narrowness and strife.

Chapter XIX

GREECE DURING ALEXANDER'S ABSENCE

WHEN Alexander set out for Asia in 334 B.C., the Greek peninsula, outwardly at least, was united behind him, though the Theban revolt had shown how close to the surface disaffection really was. Many states seemed merely to be biding their time, except that Sparta was openly hostile. The Spartan king, Agis III, hoped to shake off the Macedonian yoke, but his efforts were in vain and he was killed in battle at Megalopolis in 331 B.C. Sparta was now compelled to join the Corinthian League. Alexander's regent in Europe, Antipater, kept the Greeks in order by working through the Corinthian League, but he favored, wherever he could, oligarchies and not democracies within the individual cities. Many states considered this a violation of the League's constitution, which prohibited any interference with their internal affairs, and they resented, too, the Macedonian garrisons in the Theban Cadmeia, at Chalcis, and Corinth. As a result of the new peace, however, prosperity began to return to Greece.

Most states, of course, had pro-Macedonian and anti-Macedonian factions. At Athens, for example, the radicals under Hypereides were violently anti-Macedonian, but their influence was balanced by that of the people of means, who followed Phocion and Demades in a conciliatory attitude toward Macedon. The real power at Athens lay with Lycurgus, who had replaced Demosthenes as the leader of the democrats. During the dozen years after Chaeronea Lycurgus devoted his entire energies to building up Athens, so that, when the time came, she might return to her rightful place as leader of Greece. Lycurgus' regime was one of the most important in Athenian history. The great theater of Dionysus was reconstructed in stone, the stadium was built, the famous arsenal of Philon at Piraeus was finished. These building operations were made possible by a rigorous administration of finance. Careful economy, combined with increased income, enabled Athens to reorganize her war resources. Lycurgus not only added to the fleet, but changed the ephebate. The ephebi, Athenian youths of nineteen and twenty, were now compelled to spend one year in military training, to be followed by a second year in garrison duty along the frontier. The number of their recruits annually was about 450. The strength of the Athenian state was returning, and returning rapidly, and the people seemed satisfied with the policy of Lycurgus. Until shortly before his death in 324 B.C., indeed, there were only two major crises at Athens. The first was the prosecution of Demosthenes. After the battle of Chaeronea Ctesiphon had proposed that Demosthenes be given a golden crown for his great services against Macedon, even though he had been unsuccessful in his efforts to preserve Greek freedom. The suggestion was soon forgotten, but in 330 B.C. Aeschines reopened the case by prosecuting Ctesiphon for having made an illegal proposal. Demosthenes hastened to the defense, for the attack was really aimed at the policies he had advocated throughout his life. His great oration *On the Crown* completely won the jury, and Aeschines was forced into exile, from which he never returned. The second crisis was of a more serious nature. Beginning in 330 B.C., and continuing for several years, Athens suffered from a wheat shortage. This illustrated how closely knit the world had become, for Egyptian wheat was being held for high prices, and Athenian officials were taxed to the uttermost to provide the populace with cheap grain.

Alexander's return to Susa in 324 B.C. precipitated another crisis in Greece, for many people had expected that he would be killed in India. Harpalus, the Empire's treasurer, had squandered a fortune in riotous living during Alexander's absence and now fled to Greece on his approach. He was finally admitted to Athens with a few men, but he had an enormous sum of money and set about bribing various people. On Demosthenes' suggestion Harpalus was jailed, though he soon escaped and was murdered. His money, however, was placed in the Parthenon, and a check of it showed that a good deal was missing. Demosthenes was tried and convicted of having taken a bribe and was forced into exile at Aegina. His prosecution was due to a resurgence of Hypereides and the anti-Macedonian party at Athens, so that it is now impossible to pass judgment on the guilt or innocence of Demosthenes. Anti-Macedonian feeling was increasing all over Greece on account of Alexander's two decrees, those concerning his deification and the return of the exiles. What right had Alexander to give orders to Greece—was it not a violation of the constitution of the Corinthian League? The Greeks were ready enough to grant him divine honors—Demosthenes had said that he might be the son of Zeus and of Poseidon, too, if he liked—but how could 20,000 exiles be suddenly taken back by their cities, and on what principle was their property to be restored to them?

Alexander's desire, of course, was to put an end to the confusion which 20,000 homeless and desperate men inevitably caused in a small country, but it is easy to sympathize, nevertheless, with the states which had settled down to the new order of things and had relieved their own problems by wholesale confiscation of property. This was particularly true of the Athenians, who had recolonized Samos, and of the Aetolians. Alexander's sudden death in 323 B.C. greatly confused the picture, for many Greeks at once began thinking in the old terms of autonomy, without realizing that the new day, which had irrevocably come, demanded their cooperation in Hellenizing, under Macedonian dominion, a new world—a course which promised real opportunity and perhaps salvation. Instead of that, Athens took the lead in abolishing the Corinthian League and substituting in its place what came to be known as the Hellenic League. Thanks to Demosthenes' and Lycurgus' patient policy of building up the state, and with the huge sum of money, possibly 6,000 talents, which had been seized from Harpalus, Athens found herself in a favorable position to wage war against Antipater. Hypereides and the radicals overrode the moderates under Phocion and Demades, and persuaded the people to vote for war. This was the beginning of the so-called Lamian War (Map 15).

Leosthenes was appointed general and was ordered to proceed to Taenarum, in Laconia, where large numbers of mercenaries were generally available. At the same time Athens entered into alliance with many states of central and southern Greece, especially with the Aetolians, and with the Thessalians, who had now deserted Antipater. Antipater, for his part, could count on Boeotia and Corinth, but he was pressed for troops, because so many men had been sent to Alexander, and, besides, he had only 110 ships against Athens' 240. The excitement at Athens during her frantic preparations to win freedom and leadership can be easily imagined. Aristotle found it impossible to live in the city and withdrew to Chalcis, where he died the next year (322 B.C.). On the other hand, Demosthenes was recalled from exile and given every opportunity to devote his services to the state. Leosthenes, meanwhile, marched north with his troops, re-enforced by the Aetolians, passed Thermopylae, and shut Antipater up in Lamia. The siege lasted throughout the winter, during which the Aetolians withdrew, leaving the Athenians and the Thessalians to carry on. Antipater was in a very difficult position, and sent a hurry call to Asia Minor for help. When Leonnatus, the Phrygian satrap, arrived early in 322 B.C., he found that Leosthenes had been killed during the winter, but that the enemy, nevertheless, was determined and had superior forces. In the battle that followed Leonnatus fell, but Antipater succeeded in evacuating Lamia and withdrawing to Macedonia. Here he awaited Craterus, who was on his way back from Asia with the veterans discharged by Alexander. The situation now began to change rapidly. The Athenian fleet was destroyed by Alexander's admiral Cleitus, who appeared on the scene, in two naval engagements, at Abydos and Amorgos; and Antipater and Craterus, joining forces, marched into Thessaly, where they defeated the allies at Crannon (322 B.C.).

The independence of the Greek city-state was now dead. Athens had lost forever her strength at sea. Antipater disbanded the Hellenic League, and, not recognizing the Corinthian League as being in existence, insisted on making his arrangements with each state individually. Thus he won dominion over Greece, excepting Aetolia, which lay too far to the west to be conquered in a short time. A Macedonian garrison was placed in Munychia, the hill of Piraeus, and in 321 B.C. a new constitution was given Athens. It was spoken of as a return to the laws of Solon, but actually it made possible the rule of an oligarchy, which was Antipater's favorite way of controlling the Greeks. The franchise was limited to citizens worth 2,000 drachmas or more, and while it is difficult to believe that in this period of rising prices there should be so few persons worth that amount, nevertheless our figures seem to indicate that the new limitation deprived 22,000 of the 31,000 citizens of their civic rights. Sortition, in general, was abolished in favor of straight election, while the number of offices and payments for public service were reduced. Antipater's victory and the reorganization of Athens and other states were not unaccompanied by blood-letting. Hypereides was murdered, but Demosthenes escaped to Argolis, where he committed suicide by taking poison. The civilized world was now ready to settle down to a new order—an order where the political units were large, and the civilization a common one, the so-called Hellenistic Age.

Chapter XX GREEK CIVILIZATION IN THE FOURTH CENTURY

G REEK civilization in the fourth century before Christ is of immense interest, for we see how a country, recovering from the shock of the Peloponnesian War, was able to forge ahead along the old paths, even if the tempo was at times somewhat slower. This recovery was particularly true in states such as Athens, where people agreed to accept the *status quo* and to try to settle their differences peacefully; although in certain other parts of Greece an economic depression, combined with political restlessness, resulted in constant warfare. In spite of the wars, many states enjoyed a vigorous economic life and produced significant art and profound thought. We have already remarked that the fourth century witnessed a growing cosmopolitanism. This was noticeable not only in federations, such as the Boeotian, Chalcidian, and Arcadian Leagues, where a citizen of a state within the federation could move to another state and enjoy the same rights, but it was to be seen, too, in the way that non-Greeks began to copy Greek life. Furthermore, Athens was now the showplace of Greece and all educated persons spoke and wrote the Attic dialect.

The economic recovery of Athens was the more remarkable in view of the competition of new centers of manufacture, such as Asia Minor, Syracuse, and Tarentum. The reason for the greatness of Tarentum lay in the fact that her port was the first reached by ships sailing westward from Greece or southward from the Adriatic coasts, which poured a considerable trade into southern Italy and Sicily. The fertile soil of the Tarentines, their fisheries, handicrafts, and extensive trade with the interior, as well as with foreign lands, brought them extraordinary wealth. Men wore delicately fringed gowns, such as only the most luxurious women elsewhere could afford, and they multiplied the festivals till, it was said, their number exceeded the days of the year. Despite the commerce and industry of Tarentum, Syracuse, and lesser cities, the economy of Sicily and Magna Graecia was chiefly agricultural. The Greeks of Asia first suffered through lack of respect in the Persian government for the personality of its subjects, but in time there came an era of quiet in which, so far as material gains can atone for loss of freedom, they were repaid by an extraordinary increase of wealth and prosperity, chiefly due to freedom of commerce with the interior. Under these favorable circumstances, Ephesus assumed a splendor unknown to her past, and Halicarnassus revived as the capital of Caria. At the same time the Asiatic Greeks gradually adapted themselves to Oriental ideas and conditions of life. There was no marked recovery, however, among the Aegean islands until the opening of the East by Alexander, when the center of commerce shifted from Piraeus to Rhodes.

The Athenians, too, achieved recovery, in spite of the loss of their Empire and the destruction of much of their wealth. The urban masses, who comprised a majority of the voters, nevertheless refused to cut down the expenditures, and, to insure their own dominance, made the magistrates and Council subservient to the Assembly. A chief reason for the revival of Athens was a healthful country economy. Although many holdings were dwelling lots in the city or Piraeus, there is abundant evidence that through the fourth century Attica remained a country of small farms. A study, for example, of rural mortgages, ranging from 500 to 8,000 drachmas, shows that one half of them were within the limit of 1,000 drachmas. A similar study of rural inheritances, ranging from 2,000 to 15,000 drachmas and representing therefore the better class of landed properties, reveals that the average value was 7,500 drachmas. Far from any tendency toward latifundia, the process of dividing larger estates among several owners was under way in this period; so that, when a relatively great farm came upon the market, often it was divided into small plots in order to attract purchasers with restricted means. An estate of forty-five acres, one half for cultivation, the rest for woodland and pasture, was considered very comfortable, whereas one of sixty-five acres was opulent. Conditions elsewhere in Hellas were similar.

The restoration of the ruined Attic farms after the Peloponnesian War, involving the planting of trees, the rebuilding of houses, the purchase of tools and stock, was heroically accomplished in the face of enormous difficulties and discouragements; of that fact the great number of mortgage inscriptions of the fourth century give evidence. The farmers also had to compete with imported grain kept cheap by governmental regulation; at the time of the wheat shortage in 330 B.C., for example, the government actually bought wheat at the prevailing high prices and sold it at a low price. There can be no doubt, however, that it was not only possible to make a living by agriculture, but also to accumulate property. A man who wished to acquire a knowledge of agriculture could read scientific books on the subject by specialists— Xenophon's *Oeconomicus,* for example—so that scientific farming came into being. Farmers of the fourth century paid great attention to the enrichment of the soil; evidently they were acquainted even with mineral fertilizers. Ordinarily they allowed their land to lie fallow in alternate years, as had been the custom for ages, but they also took the first step toward the rotation of crops by planting a field two successive summers for different products and leaving it fallow the third.

Another important factor in the revival of Athens was the great growth of her commerce, which consisted largely of importations and of the transit of merchandise through Piraeus to other countries. In the first place, Attica produced only a third of the grain consumed by its inhabitants, so that the remainder had to be imported from the Black Sea, Egypt, Sicily, and elsewhere. The trade with the Black Sea was particularly active and was cultivated by the Athenians to make good their partial exclusion from the West. In the Tauric Chersonese (Crimea) the native dynasty of Spartocids, having built up a considerable kingdom, entered into close commercial relations with Athens. King Leucon (389–349 B.C.) granted the Athenians exemption from export duties. So anxious were the Athenians to provide for a grain supply that they made it a capital crime for a citizen or a metic to carry grain to any non-Attic port; still, they only required that two thirds of the grain had to be sold in the country itself, thus permitting the traders to profit by reexport elsewhere. Among other imports were salt, fish, hides, timber for ship-building, slaves, fine wines, drugs, paints and dyes, iron, copper, ivory, papyrus, linen, and innumerable other articles of use and luxury for home consumption or for reshipment to neighboring states; in fact, Piraeus was the chief distributing center of the Hellenic world. Commerce yielded ample profits to merchants and shipowners, although it should be emphasized that the state had no commercial policy and entered into commercial treaties only where essentials were concerned.

In exchange for all these products the Athenians could export wine and oil in their vases, although these were now not so artistically made and were therefore less eagerly sought, especially in the West. They also sent abroad honey and the products of their shops, arms, cutlery, and household furniture. A considerable trade in books was growing up. With papyrus brought from Egypt books were made in the form of rolls, which were packed in chests and shipped to all parts of the Mediterranean world and even to the Black Sea. There was an increasing demand for Attic marble; another natural resource of great importance lay in the silver mines of Laurium, whose output had greatly shrunk during the Peloponnesian War. Toward the middle of the fourth century, however, as new veins were discovered and the silver-bearing area widened, the yield became so abundant as to attract an increasing number of contractors and to encourage the false idea that the field was inexhaustible. The right to mine was sold for a lump sum to contractors, who paid annually, in addition to the purchase money, a twenty-fourth of the product. The annual income of the state from this source must have varied greatly and is unknown. Free labor, however, profited little from it, for the manual work was done by slaves. Although contractors sometimes lost money, we hear of one individual who amassed 160, another 200, talents, which were vast fortunes for that age.

Industry was a safe and profitable enterprise at Athens, but it was conducted on a very small scale and seems to have been scarcely more capitalized than agriculture. The shop of Cephalus, employing 120 slaves in the manufacture of shields, was exceptional. The two shops of Demosthenes, father of the orator, manned by twenty and thirty-two slaves, respectively, appear to be typical. Often, in fact, an individual with one or two slaves, or with only his sons, as in the fifth century, managed his diminutive industry, whether shoe making, stone cutting, or some other enterprise. During the fourth century the cost of living nearly doubled. The normal price of wheat per *medimnus* rose from three to five or six drachmas; and there was perhaps an even greater advance in the cost of meat, a sheep costing thirty drachmas and an ox 400. At the same time, however, wages doubled or trebled. The daily pay of an ordinary freeman rose from three obols to one and a half drachmas; that of a mechanic from one to two or two and a half drachmas. So great was the demand for laborers that unemployment presented a small problem, though it must be added that the workers were not protected by any legislation. Small farms were still cultivated, as in the fifth century, mainly by free hands, but slavery had encroached upon free labor somewhat beyond the condition of the Periclean Age. The growth of slavery, however, was retarded by the humane spirit of the day, which expressed itself, for example, in the law of Lycurgus making it illegal to enslave a freeman captured in war.

Increasing commerce led to a demand for money, which in turn promoted the growth of banking. The temples had long been accustomed to receive from states and individuals deposits for safe-keeping; and in time it was found more and more practicable to let out such sums on interest. Private banks of deposit were a development from the money-changer's trade, which lay in the hands of slaves and freedmen. The great bankers of the fourth century were freedmen, with the customary metic status, Phormion, Hermias, and notably Pasion. Beginning with nothing, Pasion amassed during his lifetime a fortune of thirty talents. His public benefactions were rewarded with citizenship, and the soundness of his business character gave him credit throughout the Hellenic world. The method of business was to receive deposits on interest, to make loans at a higher rate on the security of land or capital, to issue letters of credit, to grant loans on bottomry, and to engage in various enterprises. In a business of this kind it was especially advantageous to have an extensive capital and security. With this end in view partnerships were sometimes formed, or banking stock was sold. The growth of partnerships and companies was a sign of the increased specialization of the day, which, we have seen, extended to the various departments of government. The taxes were, for a time, collected by companies, though this function was taken over later by the Council. The total property of the citizens and metics at Athens, it has been estimated, was worth about 5,750 talents. Naturally the wealthy were called upon to shoulder many burdens, though the task of supplying warships (*trierarchy*) was now so expensive that it had to be assumed by groups of individuals. An immense amount of money was spent on festivals, and it will be recalled how Eubulus diverted into the Theoric Fund all surplus revenue, until Lycurgus finally called a halt.

The resources of Greece were, of course, limited. The land itself was poor, and, in addition, the Greeks found their field of activity narrowly restricted—on the east by the Persian Empire, on the west by the Carthaginian sphere of influence. From the richest portions of the known world, therefore, they were cut off, and thus from the possibility of amassing gigantic fortunes. Among other contributory causes to the moderate wealth of Greece were the smallness and instability of the states, the rarity and temporary character of partnerships and of business corporations, the love of respectability surpassing the desire for wealth, and the spirit of self-restraint which fixed a limit to material desires and ambitions. Hence it was that in fourth-century Athens, the commercial center and money market of Hellas, there was no overgrowth of capitalism with its attendant laboring proletariat, in fact no serious disturbance in the proportion of rich and poor.

A potent reason for the slow growth of specialized industries lay in the economic organization of the household, which made it in a high degree self-sufficing. Although day laborers and shopkeepers had to buy their subsistence, the majority of Athenians derived from their farms all or nearly all the vegetable and animal products which they needed for their own use. Within the household these raw materials were converted into flour, bread, yarn, cloth and clothes, leather, and other necessary articles. A few wares only, such as wheat, metals, dyes, and medicine, had to be bought; and the well-to-do purchased in the market fine cloths, shoes, jewelry, wines, and other luxuries, whereas for slaves home-made articles were good enough. The management of such a household was divided between husband and wife. The husband supervised the out-of-door labors, which were mainly concerned with the production of raw materials; he left to his wife their conversion into useful goods. Although Athenian women were still legally incapacitated for business, and were often spoken of as inferior, the intelligent man willingly admitted that his wife was equal to himself in worth and might even be his superior. Some, like Plato, were of the opinion that women were by nature like men and should for that reason engage in political and military life; others, like Xenophon, held that, though equal, they were different by nature and adapted therefore to a different set of functions. As the Athenians were not essentially a money-making people, they attached great importance to keeping the paternal estate within the family. In this spirit they preferred to give a daughter or sister in marriage to a kinsman that the dowry might not fall into alien hands. Property was divided equally among sons, and girls received dowries roughly proportioned to the value of the estate. If there were daughters only, they inherited; but in that case the nearest male kinsmen had a right to claim them in marriage. To clear the way for such unions it often happened that divorces were brought about.

Our most intimate knowledge of Athenian life and social thought is reached through the medium of the orators—through the pleadings of plaintiff and defendant in the courts of law. It is the nature of such sources to bring to the light of day the most sordid and petty side of a people's character; and yet the modern reader of these speeches is forced to the conviction that the Athenian litigants and their relatives had normal ideas of right and wrong, that they possessed approximately the same failings and the same virtues as the people of today, that there was among them no widespread want or misery, that, in brief, the average life of the plain Athenians was wholesome and happy.

ART

Probably no field of activity was hit so hard by the aftermath of the Peloponnesian War as architecture. To undertake the construction of many temples proved a financial impossibility, and, it must be confessed, there were two other factors at work. For one thing, the Greeks were turning from the old religion, and, for another, there was little more that could be done with the Greek temple—unless, indeed, architects were to strike out along new lines and try, for example, to enclose space and not simply define it. The Greeks, however, contented themselves with the elaboration of old principles and left daring innovations to the architects of Rome and Byzantium. We have already noticed a tendency in the fifth century to combine the orders; for example, the Parthenon had an Ionic frieze, the central colonnade of the Propylaea was Ionic, and the temple of Apollo Epicurius at Bassae, another Doric structure, had interior Ionic semicolumns with Corinthian columns at the rear, separating the two cellas. This idea, in keeping with the growing cosmopolitanism, was continued during the fourth century. The temple of Athena Alea at Tegea (360 B.C.), for example, combined all three orders. The temple of Zeus at Nemea (330 B.C.) has very tall Doric columns, another characteristic of the fourth century. These two temples, and those of Asclepius at Epidaurus, Apollo at Delphi, and Zeus at Stratos, represent, as a matter of fact, practically the entire religious architecture of the Greek mainland during the fourth century.

The first half of the fourth century saw very little construction in Asia Minor, but as the Greeks grew accustomed to Persian rule and as trade and prosperity returned, there began a great revival, which Alexander later supported. The Ionian temperament had always loved grandeur and it now expressed itself in elaborate ornamentation, in the multiplication of columns, in magnificence, and in sheer size. The results are always interesting and not infrequently impressive, even though the decline in taste is obvious. The archaic temple of Artemis at Ephesus, according to report, burned to the ground the night Alexander was born, but the Ephesians immediately set to work to build another (356 B.C.). This great Ionic temple had at least 117 columns, sixteen or more of the lower drums being sculptured (as had been the case in the old temple). Even larger was the Ionic temple of Apollo at Didyma (334 B.C.), with its 120 columns: there was a double row of columns around the temple (that is, it was dipteral), as many as ten columns being extended along the façades. From the volutes of the capitals projected busts of gods and other figures, which the spectators no doubt admired. The temple was so immense that the cella was never roofed over, but was left open to the sky (*hypaethral*); just beyond the *pronaos* was an awe-inspiring chamber where oracles were delivered. There were other important temples at Sardes (Cybele) and at Priene (Athena Polias) (Diagram 54).

The tholos (a circular building) was popular during the fourth century. The one at Epidaurus, for example, has beautiful Corinthian capitals (Figure 93), whereas that of Lysicrates at Athens is our best preserved choregic monument (Figure 69). The fourth century was particularly noteworthy for its civic architecture. We have already seen that the economy (and war preparations) of Lycurgus made possible spirited building activity at Athens. The stadium was built and the theater was reconstructed in stone, as were those at Epidaurus and elsewhere. Temples of Isis and other foreign gods were built, either in deference to the resident alien population or because the Athenians were finding some comfort in foreign gods. Philon added a fine portico to the Hall of the Mysteries at Eleusis, and his arsenal at Piraeus was for the use of the navy. At Megalopolis the Arcadians built for their new League a great assembly hall (Thersilion), which covered 35,000 square feet.

If a declining interest in religion is discernible in the architecture of fourth-century Greece, it is even more so in the sculpture. Some beautiful grave monuments, it is true, were made. The frieze of the Mausoleum at Halicarnassus depicts struggling Greeks and Amazons, whose furious movements are in keeping with their tense expressions. The Mausoleum was erected by Queen Artemisia for her husband, Mausolus, the semi-Hellenized king of Caria, who died in 353 B.C. It was a large structure, measuring 108 by 127 feet, and 140 feet in height. On a high foundation, around the top of which ran the frieze, rose a building with an Ionic peristyle, and above this was a pyramidal roof crowned by statues of Mausolus and Artemisia, with a quadriga. The frieze was the work of four sculptors, Scopas, Timotheus, Bryaxis, and Leochares. The so-called Alexander sarcophagus (*ca.* 325 B.C.), made of marble and still retaining much of the color, delicate blues, yellows, and reds, shows Alexander in battle and hunting. Attic gravestones still have much of their old simplicity; particularly touching are the tender scenes and farewells between the dead and loved ones (Figure 83). As the fourth century wears on, however, the figures, now in very high relief and enclosed by frames, become stereotyped and self-conscious, so that we are almost glad that Demetrius of Phaleron decreed in 317 B.C. that no more should be made. His decree, it must be added, had nothing to do with artistic feeling, but probably reflected the envy of the populace, which resented the fact that the front lots of the Cerameicus were beyond their reach.

Though sculpture had always been the handmaiden of architecture, the comparative lack of temples in the fourth century had little to do with the absence of religious feeling in the sculpture. This was due to the new humanism and is admirably illustrated by the Hermes of Praxiteles (350 B.C.), one of the most famous and provocative statues of antiquity (Figure 94). The youthful god Hermes stands gazing lazily into the distance; on his left arm rests the infant Dionysus, whereas the arm itself leans on a tree-trunk; the prop is necessary for a marble statue, though not for one in bronze, and is here covered with drapery, which is treated as a separate entity. Hermes does not look at Dionysus, but in his musing dangles before the child a bunch of grapes held in his right hand (now lost). Dionysus is not sculptured as well as Hermes, for all our attention must be directed at the god. The individualism of the fourth century can be seen in the personal stamp which the sculptor has placed on the statue; the day of "schools" has passed, and Praxiteles, like his contemporaries, has his own definite style. Praxiteles has a way of throwing the weight of the lower part of the body on one leg and the weight of the upper part on the opposite arm, which gives to the body a wonderful sweep and curve. The figure is, of course, marvelously modeled; the tufts of hair are more realistic than the wavy lines and curls of an earlier period; the areas of the face form a natural whole; the body is slender and has muscles, real flesh, and blood. The statue, though of a god ostensibly and though found in the Heraeum at Olympia, is, nevertheless, of a young man, slightly idealized. The statue has a high polish, which adds to its charm in a photograph, though actually it detracts from it and heightens its unquestioned softness. For, in spite of the fame of the statue, and when everything is considered, the Hermes of Praxiteles is not a great Greek statue. We see this as soon as we place it beside the great bronze Zeus from the sea off Euboea (Figures 21 and 51), or the stirring Apollo from the temple of Zeus at Olympia (Figure 50), and we miss at once the simple vigor and restraint of the earlier work. Religion and faith were lacking in the fourth century; empires, and with them the promise of security and stability, had gone; the individual, being thrown back on himself, often thought more of himself than of the state. Sculptors tended to become personal and to carve statues of men rather than of Man. While admiring an original artist who knew how to handle his tools and materials, and while applauding his humanism, we nevertheless find that the Hermes, for all its technical skill, lacks the ennobling qualities which we like most to associate with mankind.

Other statues of Praxiteles—his lizard-slayer, his famous Eros of Thespiae, and his even more famous statue of the Cnidian Aphrodite, which boldly shows a goddess in the nude—have come down to us, if at all, in Roman copies; indeed, even the Hermes has been thought to be a Roman copy, though without sufficient evidence. Praxiteles was an Athenian and had a profound influence on other sculptors, one of whom made the charming bronze boy, recently recovered from the sea near Marathon (Figure 95).

According to Pliny and other ancient writers, Scopas of Paros was a sculptor of great power and originality (Figure 96). We have already seen that he was one of the sculptors engaged at the Mausoleum, and as architect of the temple of Athena Alea at Tegea he probably had something to do with its sculptures, several heads of which have survived. It is customary to speak of the fire and passion of his figures, the half-opened mouths and deeply undercut eyes, but we have so little that is definitely from the hand of Scopas that it is dangerous to generalize. The Eirene and Plutus (Peace and Wealth, ca. 375 B.C.) of Cephisodotus commemorates an abortive peace of the fourth century; due to the realism of the day the drapery is no longer transparent, but heavy, which is also true of the noble and stately Demeter from Cnidus (Figure 97).

Lysippus of Sicyon instilled new life and new ideas into sculpture. Like Polycleitus, he was interested in anatomy and in proportions, but his figures have more latent motion and seem taller than do those of Polycleitus. Lysippus made the heads of his statues smaller in relation to the total height of the body and the legs longer. In the Delphi museum there is a marble copy of his Agias, made soon after the original bronze was set up (340 B.C.), a fine athletic type (Figure 98). His Apoxyomenus (325 B.C.), which is a Roman copy, shows an athlete scraping oil from his body and is remarkable for the realism of its contours. Lysippus was famous for his portraits of Alexander. Portraiture flourished throughout the fourth century. Statues were made of Socrates, Plato, Euripides, and others—it was another sign of the individualism of the day. The fifth century thought little about such matters, and even the famous herm of Pericles by Cresilas is more a type than an individual. Realistic portraiture reached its height in the period after Alexander.

Of the minor arts in the fourth century, the coins are decidedly the most beautiful and interesting (Figure 99). Beginning with Alexander it became customary to stamp on coins the heads of rulers. Vase painting, however, loses all its interest in the fourth century, and of course the famous paintings by Apelles of Colophon and others have long since disappeared. The wall-paintings of Pompeii give us faint echoes, but of more importance is the famous picture, a Pompeian copy in mosaic, of Alexander and Darius in battle (Figure 92).

LITERATURE

As the central idea in Hellenism declined—the idea of the city-state with all its traditional associations, religious, social, and civic—there emerged two others, the individual and the human race, which were now in conflict, now in sympathy. These new developments, we have seen, affected every human activity. In literature the most obvious change was from poetry to prose. Poetry had devoted itself extensively to the state; the choral songs were chiefly for public occasions, and the drama appealed to the entire community. Drama was still immensely enjoyed—Lycurgus had "official" copies made of the plays of the fifth-century playwrights—but the production of new tragedies, for example, fell off. The decline of these forms of literature meant a changing relation between the individual and the state, a shifting of interest to private and social affairs, and from the emotional life maintained by tradition to the life of reason, which was sufficient unto itself and an enemy of all control.

Almost nothing has survived of the lyric and tragic poetry composed in the fourth century. The transformation from Old to Middle Comedy, we have remarked, occurred at this time. Comedy, instead of attacking prominent persons and indulging in politics, now humorously portrayed the life of the day. The literature of the fourth century, however, was mainly prose, and comprised three great departments, history, oratory, and philosophy. A noticeable feature is the narrow specialization of the authors, involving a strict separation of the fields. To us it is surprising, for example, how little the orator or the philosopher knew of his country's past. Before Aristotle authors were not learned men, but creative artists. The most liberal field was that of the historian, whose search for the truth made him akin to the scientist and whose rhetoric brought him into touch with the orator; at the same time his study of motive and his analysis of government gave him points of contact with the ethical and political philosopher. The historian of broad vision composed the annals of Hellas, or of a great part of Hellas, for a definite period. By thus combining in treatment a multitude of city-states, he contributed to the mental preparation for a unified Hellenic nation. At the same time the growing interest in prominent individuals produced biography. Thus it was that Isocrates, writing to King Nicocles of Cyprus, presented a eulogistic account of the achievements and character of Evagoras, the father and predecessor of Nicocles. The *Evagoras,* for all its extravagant praise, is the first Greek biography of any length consciously written as such.

Undoubtedly this particular work, as well as the general development of individualism, greatly influenced the intellectual attitude of Xenophon, the fourth-century historian with whom we have most to do. Xenophon (*ca.* 434–354 B.C.) was born in a well-to-do family of pronounced conservative inclinations. From his social environment he absorbed the sentiments that distinguished his rank, including a punctilious regard for the externals of religion, ethical reflection, refinement of feeling and speech, an interest in military training and in out-of-door sports, courage, a dislike of the multitude, and fidelity to his class—in a word, Hellenic chivalry. His attachment to Socrates brought out the best that was in him, and in fact illuminated his entire life. His *Memorabilia* of Socrates faithfully photographs the exterior of the great master and of his teachings, though it fails to penetrate to the depths. In fact, Xenophon is in everything superficial. This work and the *Agesilaus* illustrate his interest in individuals, though we find the same love of biography in all his historical writings. The *Anabasis,* for example, is chiefly valuable for the insight it affords us into the composition and psychology of a mercenary army, drawn from many parts of Hellas and passing through various phases of success and peril. The *Hellenica,* his chief historical work, is a continuation of Thucydides, from 411 to 362 B.C. Xenophon, banished for treason from his native Athens, wrote under Lacedaemonian patronage. His *Constitution of the Lacedaemonians, Oeconomicus,* and *Ways and Means* are other important sources for the history of ancient Greece. The *Cyropaedeia*—education of Cyrus—is a historical romance, in which the author sets forth a model education of the child and youth, whence emerges the ideal man and sovereign. The preservation of Xenophon's works is due to the interest of later ages in Socrates and to a questionable standard of judgment as to style and general worth. In mentioning his shortcomings, however, we should not lose sight of his positive merits. His interest in personal traits, which is wanting in Thucydides, but which marks Xenophon as a true child of his age, especially appeals to the modern student of Hellenic life and culture. He had traveled much, had acquired a wide knowledge of the world; and in his breadth of mind, his liberal education and his ethical and religious principles he represents the best features of the educated class of his generation.

Xenophon's literary style betrays almost no influence of the rhetoric which flourished in his day. Akin to rhetoric, however, were the chronicles, whose interest lay in the collection and the systematizing of facts. Such chronicles of Athens were termed *Atthides*. They began with the earliest mythical kings; and for the regal period they seem to have grouped events and institutions according to reigns. For the historical period they arranged the material annalistically under the appropriate archons. Far from limiting himself to political and military happenings, the atthidographer included all kinds of institutional, personal, and cultural material. Except for a few brief fragments, all the *Atthides* have been lost. To us the chronicler of greatest interest was Androtion, a prominent statesman of Athens, whose *Atthis* appeared in 330 B.C. It was the chief source for Aristotle's *Constitution of Athens,* published a few years aferward. The latter work is one of a collection of 158 constitutional histories of states, mostly Hellenic, composed by Aristotle with the collaboration of his pupils. Each history consisted of the narrative of constitutional growth to the philosopher's own time and a contemporary survey of the constitution. The treatise on the Athenian constitution, the greater part of which was recovered in Egypt in 1890, is the only one we have of the vast collection, though its value can hardly be overestimated.

The growth of rhetoric influenced not simply the content but also the artistic form of literature, especially that of oratory, which came more and more to be composed by set rule and principle. The extant orations of Lysias, however, belonging mainly to the first two decades of the fourth century, show a freshness, vigor, and independence unfettered by rhetorical bonds. Having taken his lessons of the rhetorician, Lysias nevertheless preserves his own mastery of style. In appearance his language is that of everyday life, in fact it is highly idealized. Lysias is a model of simple narrative, of dramatic skill in adapting speech to the character of the speaker for whom he professionally writes, of *ethos,* the gentle current of feeling that wins the sympathy of the hearers. These qualities render his speeches most valuable, not only as pictures

of common life, but as psychological views both of the individual litigants and of the multitudinous jury. A Syracusan resident in Athens,
Lysias gained a livelihood by writing speeches for persons whose property had been confiscated by the Thirty Tyrants. Another orator was
Isaeus, perhaps also a metic, whose extant productions range from 390
to 353 B.C. They have to do with family law, with cases of adoption
and inheritance. Isaeus is more argumentative and militant than Lysias,
and, while clinging to the simple Lysian style, reveals the beginnings
of the mature, powerful oratory of the Demosthenic age.

It was in Isocrates of Athens that rhetoric came to full maturity.
His life (436–338 B.C.) was contemporary with the whole development
of prose literature, and with the culmination and incipient decay of
the city-state. It was his achievement to mould the oration into a formal
work of art, comparable to a Pindaric ode or to a piece of sculpture.
With a delicate taste for literary form he gave the most minute and
prolonged attention to the elaboration of a nicely adjusted periodology,
and to the exquisite choice and arrangement of words with a view to
euphony and rhythm. Although a few of his orations are judicial, the
greater number are in fact essays, for reading rather than for delivery.
Isocrates also conducted a school of statesmanship. The young man
who went forth from his school was to possess a largeness of view which
considered the interest, not of his native city alone, but of the entire
Hellenic nation. The *Panegyricus,* on which he is said to have labored
ten years, advocated Hellenic union. It has sentiments that might be
interpreted as cosmopolitan, though the meaning of one of its most
famous sentences seems to be simply that culture has become a more
notable characteristic of Hellas than blood: "So far has our city left
the rest of mankind behind her in thought and expression that her
citizens have become the teachers of others, and have made the name
Hellenes a mark no longer of birth but of intellect, and have caused
those to be called Hellenes who share in our culture rather than in our
descent." Isocrates' leading political principle of Hellas against Persia,
however, shows him to be an exponent of nationalism rather than of
humanism. In home politics he was a conservative who preferred the
constitution of Solonian and Cleisthenic times, and wrote the *Areo-
pagiticus* to prove his point, without realizing that reform by such
reaction is neither wise nor practicable. Isocrates moulded public opinion chiefly through his school. In a three- or four-year course he trained
his pupils in oratory and supplied them with the information essential
to public careers. They came from all parts of Hellas, from regions as
distant as the Black Sea, Cyprus, and Sicily—highly endowed youths
from prominent families. Having completed this education, a goodly

number became philosophers, rhetoricians, and historians, generals, statesmen, and even kings.

Through the efforts of two of these pupils, Ephorus of Cumae, in Aeolis, and Theopompus of Chios, both born about 380 B.C., rhetoric entered the historical field. The principal work of Ephorus was a universal history in thirty books from the Return of the Heracleidae (Dorian invasion) to the siege of Perinthus in 340 B.C. He probably outlived Philip, but death cut his narrative short. His *History* has been lost with the exception of a few fragments, and yet it is of great interest to us as the chief source on that period for Diodorus and for the historical parts of Strabo the geographer. Ephorus laid claim to critical discrimination and aimed to gain a personal knowledge of the geography and topography of the events narrated; but in fact he has often marred his pages with bias or puerility in the treatment of motive, with exaggerations of numbers in military affairs, and similar defects. His rhetorical style ran in a smooth but languid current, agreeable to the ear though monotonous.

Theopompus, his schoolmate, was, like Isocrates, a writer of speeches on matters of public interest. In the historical field he composed a *Hellenica* in twelve books, which continued the work of Thucydides, and a *Philippica* in fifty-eight books, a detailed history of his own time. In keeping with the thought of his age Theopompus did not advocate war against Asia, but rather the extension and consolidation of conquest in Europe. He conceived a great European state, under Philip, as opposed to Asiatic Persia. The extant fragments of Theopompus are preserved especially in Athenaeus and show an interest in society, culture, and character with a disproportionate love of exhibiting the luxuries and vices of mankind. In spite of the shortcomings of Ephorus and Theopompus the finding of the works of either author would greatly enlarge our knowledge of Greek history and civilization. This loss has been brought home to us by the discovery of papyrus fragments of a history known as the *Oxyrhynchus Hellenica,* from the place of its finding in Egypt. It gives a detailed account of the events of 396 B.C. and includes a surprisingly interesting digression on the Boeotian federal constitution. The work is composed in a smooth flowing style that reveals the influence of Isocrates and has been variously assigned to Cratippus, Ephorus, and Theopompus.

The growth of the Macedonian power, which divided men into two parties, Macedonian and anti-Macedonian, brought the oratory of Athens to a height of perfection. In Athens, we have seen, the most conspicuous defender of Philip was Aeschines, the most brilliant opponent Demosthenes. The orator of this period learned not only to appeal to reason, but to play upon all the keys of human emotion. To the winsome *ethos* of Lysias, and to the argumentative skill of Isaeus, he added a vehemence that overwhelmed his hearers. Demosthenes, the greatest orator of antiquity, was the son of a well-to-do manufacturer, but he was left fatherless in childhood and cheated of his inheritance by his guardians. He grew up in poor health, unsocial, seemingly unfitted for active life, and cherishing the desire for vengeance on those who had wronged him. To accomplish this, and in order to serve his country as a statesman, Demosthenes overcame a weak voice by prolonged training and prepared himself for the life of an orator. He steeped his mind in Thucydides, whence he drew his knowledge of the past and his militant ideal of the state. From Isaeus, Isocrates, and others he learned useful lessons, and for delivery he studied under a successful actor. Behind this external equipment we discover a literary genius unsurpassed, and a burning patriotism combined with the religious zeal of a prophet, the practical statesman, who in the sweep of his eloquence never fails to point out the concrete way to success, the moral idealist, the champion of local freedom against encroaching despotism, of a high culture against the advance of an inferior civilization. If Demosthenes opposed the events that contributed to the universalization of Hellenism, at least he enriched Hellenism by his supreme oratory, and still more by his defense of human freedom, the greatest gift of Hellas to mankind (Figure 89).

The third great department of literature in the fourth century was philosophy. Plato, the great creative philosopher of the age, was born at Athens in 427 B.C. of highly aristocratic parents. A kinsman was Critias, the violent leader of the Thirty Tyrants. On the overthrow of this oligarchy Plato thought of entering public life; but the condemnation of Socrates, his revered master, awakened in him an undying hatred of democracy. He could do nothing, therefore, but remain in private life and satisfy his political longings with the creation of ideal constitutions or appeal to a tyrant, such as Dionysius of Syracuse, for the realization of his vision of the perfect state. It was probably in the year 387 B.C. that Plato opened in his private house a school called the Academy from its nearness to the public garden of that name.

His literary works are *Dialogues*. We know, however, that he considered these writings a popular presentation of such views as in his opinion the laity could understand. In his school he lectured more learnedly on mathematics, astronomy, harmonics, and ethics. In this work he leaned upon the Pythagoreans, while giving his pupils an impetus to further mathematical and physical researches. Though holding to the end that the earth is the center of the universe, he finally accepted the doctrine of the earth's rotation on its axis. Following his suggestion, a Pythagorean friend, Eudoxus, attempted to explain the seemingly irregular movements of sun, moon, and planets, by a theory of homocentric hollow spheres revolving around the earth at different velocities. The heavenly bodies, he assumes, are fastened to these spheres. To the sun and moon he assigns three spheres each; to the five known planets four spheres each, whereas a single sphere suffices for all the fixed stars. Although these spheres are a pure fiction, mathematically they serve their purpose.

Concerning the lectures of Plato, however, we have only mere hints. It is upon the *Dialogues,* in addition to the little that can be gathered from his pupil Aristotle, that we must chiefly rely for our knowledge of his views. The *Dialogue,* which had long been a favorite instrument of the philosopher, received from Plato an artistic form. It shows him not a dry reasoner, but a highly imaginative poet. Though prose in form, his language, brilliantly versatile, sparkles with poetic gems. He is gifted, too, with rare dramatic power. The speakers of the *Dialogues* are living persons, who everywhere retain their psychological identity.

We should not look to his writings for a consistent system of knowledge, for through an active life of eighty-one years his mind continually developed. During this time he came into contact, or renewed his acquaintance, with existing philosophies, one after another, from each of which he received an enlargement of his mental horizon and a new impetus to creative work. At the basis of his thought lies his doctrine of ideas. Socrates had taught him that the only objects of knowledge are concepts, universal truths established by induction. With Plato the concept becomes an idea, a word derived from the Pythagoreans and signifying form. Ideas are not forms in the geometrical sense, but are colorless, shapeless, intangible realities, which the mind alone can perceive. In distinction from our ideas, which have their being in the mind alone, those of Plato are objective realities, in fact the only things that exist. The objects of sense are real insofar only as they "partake of" these pure realities.

Plato's chief concern was with ethics. The greatest of all ideas, he taught, is God, who created the world and gave to it a soul, through which reason and order and life came into all things. At His command the lesser gods fashioned the body of man, and He Himself prepared the soul, making it of the same substance as the world soul, though less pure. Each human soul is given a star to which it will return after having completed a good life on earth; but the soul that has lived badly will at the next birth enter an inferior creature. This theory of creation and of human life is presented not as a dogma, but as a mere approximation of the truth, a metaphor continually varied throughout his writings. By means of education man advances toward the highest Good, which is neither knowledge nor happiness, but the utmost likeness to God. Happiness, altogether different from bodily pleasure, is the possession of the good. In Plato's doctrine, taken from the Orphists, the body is merely the dungeon or the tomb of the soul. From the body the soul must purify itself in order to attain to the good and to virtue, which is the fitness of the soul for its proper work.

An important division of ethics is politics. In the view of Plato the state is not the all-in-all of the citizen, as it had been in former time. The calm existence of the philosopher, the solving of the problems of the essential and the eternal, is a nobler being than that of the politician. The body only of the philosopher lives in the state, while his soul dwells elsewhere, untouched by political ambition. This is true of a community like Athens, he asserts, governed by the ignorant majority, whose greatest statesmen, Pericles, Cimon, Miltiades, and Themistocles, utterly have failed in the function of improving the character of the citizens. It would be quite otherwise with a state philosophically organized, like that set forth in his *Republic*. As any state is an individual "writ large," the ideal state is constituted like a perfect individual with the baser parts subordinate to the nobler. In this ideal community there are to be three social classes, the laborers, the soldiers, and the rulers, the last two constituting the guardians. These elements are borrowed from the actual Hellenic world. Evidently the laborers on the farm and in the trades are helots and perioeci; the soldiers are the Spartan warriors, whereas the philosophic rulers look to the Pythagoreans as their prototype. The lowest class is intellectually least endowed, and fit for nothing but manual labor. Their virtue, like that of the soul's lowest faculty, is obedience to the higher powers. The middle class are the warriors, whose virtue is courage. They do no manual work, but devote their lives to their special function. It is upon them and the ruling class that Plato bestows his chief attention. These gradations, however, are not castes, but each is formed by a careful selection from the class just below; so that men are constantly rising from the lower to the higher grades of society. Praiseworthy are the assignment of rank according to capacity, the division of labor which makes for efficiency, and the abolition of slavery.

The education of the guardians is to begin at birth. All who have infants in charge are to see that every act performed and every word spoken in the child's presence shall be such as will contribute to the right growth of character. From seven to seventeen the child pursues elementary studies, reading, writing, the lower mathematics, gymnastics, and music, including literature. Most of the poets, along with Homer, are rejected because they suggest immoral or irreligious views; nothing but the strengthening and the ennobling is acceptable. From seventeen to twenty the youth has his preliminary training in arms. At this period it is determied who are to be warriors, and who are to continue the intellectual education essential to statesmen. From twenty to thirty the latter class are to devote themselves to the thorough study of the sciences. If incapable of advancing farther, they enter public life as minor officials, whereas the few who are better gifted devote five additional years to the study of ideas. From thirty-five to fifty these intellectuals govern the state, after which they retire to a life of higher philosophic thought. In planning for an advanced intellectual education carefully regulated, Plato made one of his greatest contributions to civilization. That the guardians, both warriors and statesmen, may devote themselves unselfishly and untrammeled to their functions, individual wealth and the family itself are abolished. Property is held in common, and the mating of men and women is managed by the state with a single eye to the birth of strong, healthful children. Eugenics is pushed to extremes. Women, relieved of the care of children, are to have the same training as men and perform the same military and political services.

Such a state is too unnatural to be capable of realization. From the first Plato saw that no community would voluntarily adopt it, and in his old age substituted a more workable political system in one of his latest writings, the *Laws*. The chief value of the *Republic* lies in its individual suggestions as to educational, social, and political reforms, and in the powerful impetus it gives to the intellectual life of the reader. In brief, it is not the knowledge discovered by Plato, but his belief in spiritual realities, his aspiration to the beautiful, the good, and the true, his conception of the vast heights attainable by man that place him among the most powerful intellectual and moral forces that operate upon the human race.

After the death of its founder the Academy continued under other masters and gradually degenerated. Meanwhile the creative and organizing activities within the philosophic field were carried on with greater success by others. The real heir to Plato was his most brilliant pupil, Aristotle (384–322 B.C.), from Stagirus in the Chalcidice. He studied twenty years under Plato. Three years (343–340 B.C.) he was a teacher of Alexander. Still later he returned to Athens and established a school of his own named the Lyceum, after the famous gymnasium in which he taught. His system of thought is also described as peripatetic, from the circumstance that he walked with his pupils while giving instruction. His *Dialogues,* which were popular like those of Plato, have been lost; but most of his technical works, corresponding to Plato's lectures, are extant. Among them, however, are studies either finished or wholly composed by his pupils, which we cannot, with certainty in every case, distinguish from writings exclusively his own.

In Aristotle we discover a new type of mind, that of the scholar as distinguished from the essentially creative intelligence. It is true that he was himself a discoverer, but his great achievement was to systematize and reduce to writing the knowledge which the Greeks had thus far accumulated. Accepting in the main the method and system of Plato, he made corrections in detail; and with his more logical mind and a greater command of facts, he was able to render the method more precise and to widen the field of scientific thought. In this task he discovered that the most insignificant fact of nature is worthy of attention as the potential source of valuable knowledge. In general, Aristotle was less concerned with abstract reasoning than Plato and more with observation and experience. The work of scientific experimentation, however, was then in its infancy, and the observer was hampered by a lack of instruments. The remarkable thing is that with his limitations he was able to accomplish so much.

The main divisions of knowledge in his classification are logic, metaphysics, natural history, and ethics. Under the head of metaphysics he places his First Philosophy, universal principles on which everything else is based. Natural history includes physics and astronomy as well as psychology and physiology, zoology, botany, and other studies of nature. Rhetoric and politics are branches of ethics. A fifth department of knowledge may be described as a philosophy of art, represented by his *Poetics.* Aristotle did not cultivate mathematics as an independent study. In logic he completed a system of proof begun by Socrates. From particulars he rises to universals by induction, as the earlier philosopher taught; from principles he reasons back to particulars by the process of deduction through the syllogism, a formula of reasoning first clearly set forth by himself (Figure 91).

Despite his considerable study of nature the least valuable parts of Aristotle's system are those which depend upon observation rather than upon abstract thought. This fact is illustrated by his astronomy, a system of the universe cruder perhaps than that of Eudoxus mentioned above. The collection of material for his study of plants and animals was probably facilitated by Alexander. That Aristotle made many mistakes in describing animals he had never seen was inevitable; and we need not be surprised to find him in error as to the functions of some of the most vital organs. Flesh, he supposed, is the medium of sensation. Chief of all organs is the heart, which prepares the blood and aids in motion and sensation. The blood, purified by the heart, flows from thence to the various parts of the body, whereas the brain serves to cool the blood and moderate the heat arising from the heart. The study of plants begun by him was carried farther and ultimately published by Theophrastus, his successor. Most interesting is Aristotle's theory as to progress made by the creative power of nature. Beginning with the lowest forms of life, nature gradually passes to the higher; having fashioned the plants, she proceeds to the invention of animals and thence to men. This process is an evolution, not of organic nature itself, but of the creative power.

Whereas Plato gives inspiration, Aristotle conveys knowledge. The one soars above the clouds, the other keeps his feet firmly on earth. In his *Ethics,* as elsewhere, Aristotle appeals more strongly to the average man. Casting aside the dictum of Socrates and Plato that knowledge is virtue, he recognizes that a man may know the right, but have too weak a will to do it. Only those thoughts that lead to useful actions are useful; and happiness, the supreme good, is nothing more than good and efficient life regulated by right rules of conduct. It is the function of ethics to supply these rules. Pleasures which involve mere self-indulgence are wholly bad; others, arising from the normal exercise of any faculty, though not ends in themselves, are desirable. Although well-being, including health, wealth, friends, and family, are helpful to the cultivation of virtue, they are not essential, and a philosopher may draw strength from illness and poverty.

"No man liveth unto himself" is one of the strongest tenets of Aristotle. Personal affections within and outside the family constitute friendship. True friendship, involving a love of the good qualities discoverable in the friend and an unselfish desire to benefit, is one of the most powerful moral forces in society. A broadening of friendship brings us to the common life of the community. Man is a political animal, and his highest existence is in the state. The aim of the state is not simply the protection of the life and property of the citizens, but their education to the highest reach of moral and spiritual fitness. In the *Politics* the author does not seek the ideal state; his aim rather is to determine the nature of the state in all the varieties furnished by the Hellenic world; to discover the constitution best adapted to every typical community; to ascertain defects of various political systems and remedies for them. His task in brief is to create a political science on the basis of induction from actual conditions furnished by a multitude of city-states, chiefly Hellenic but including a few foreign cities like Carthage. Despite incompleteness and an imperfect text the *Politics* is the greatest contribution to political and social science made by the ancient world.

Chapter XXI

THE
NEW ERA

THE extraordinary centuries after the death of Alexander the Great are known as the Hellenistic Age, for in this period Hellenism, Greek culture, became widespread. It would be as great a mistake to assume that the new order came into being at once as it would be to suggest that the old way of life suddenly disappeared. But Alexander's meteoric career had cut so deeply that it was perfectly clear that there could be no return to the old order. Alexander left neither a will nor an heir, and though the generals at Babylon might disagree on details, there was no thought in any one's mind of giving up the territory which had been conquered. The main question before the generals was whether the Empire could be held together—the vital question for humanity was the direction the new rule might take.

Some of Alexander's ideas took root slowly—indeed, it is fair to say that some of them have not yet fully matured—

but if his idea of the brotherhood of man did not find immediate acceptance, nevertheless that of the *oecumene,* the inhabited world, did. In the Hellenistic Age man thought of himself more and more as a member of a world society, a society in which there might be (and were) striking differences, but in which a common culture nonetheless acted as a natural bond. This common culture was different in many ways from that of the fifth century, for it was affected both by the rapid rise of the ordinary man and by close contact with Orientalism. It was this new culture, in certain respects diluted and in others vitalized, which Hellenized Rome and served as the vehicle of Christianity. Alexander's policy of founding settlements was carried on by the Successors and here, in the urban centers, Hellenism was strongest. In the villages and countryside of the East the Hellenic veneer was thin, and after the first great creative push of the Hellenistic Age had spent itself and after the energy of Rome had weakened, the Oriental background once more came to the surface. The externals of life, however, were Greek. The non-Greek considered it essential to have some Greek culture, and for business reasons, if for no other, a common dialect, the Greek *koine,* was adopted.

The most striking difference between the Hellenistic Age and the preceding centuries was the size of the political unit. Large kingdoms, modeled on the Macedonian monarchy, were the rule, though the Greek cities within the kingdoms often had a large measure of freedom, and some proudly considered themselves city-states. In Greece the love of liberty, and with it the idea of the city-state, persisted; or, where it proved impossible to maintain the freedom of individual cities, leagues were formed. The true role of the Greeks, however, was to Hellenize the East under Macedonian dominion, and, partly because of their need of the Greeks and partly because Greek opposition could be stiff, the rulers of the new world sought the cooperation of Greece. Greek mercenaries and Greek settlers were in constant demand, to say nothing of the artists, writers, and scientists who were to adorn the various courts. The new cities and capitals of the Hellenistic Age— Alexandria, Antioch on the Orontes, Seleuceia on the Tigris, Pergamum, Rhodes,—were busy centers of trade and industry. A cosmopolitan population gathered in them, intent chiefly on money making and pleasure, and inevitably the ideas and customs of the diverse peoples reacted on one another and tended to merge. At the top of the system stood the king, now far removed from his subjects, and considered, officially, as a god—that is to say, his deification was a sort of symbol of his right to rule and made it easier to unite under him different races. The king was surrounded by a vast bureaucracy, for the task of governing was complex and, like other activities, required specialists. It was natural, too, for the kings to wish to attract the intellectuals of the day to their court, but the patronage of the arts, together with constant warfare, made necessary an exacting taxation.

Warfare in the Hellenistic Age was well-nigh continuous; mercenaries were a common sight in every army of the third century; multitudes of people were killed; and yet, with it all, warfare grew more humane, as the practice slowly developed, for example, of sparing the population of a captured city. Nor was it uncommon to resort first to arbitration. It is especially important, however, to see beyond the wars and to grasp the meaning of the new day. The large state, the birth of a common culture do not tell the whole story. We are particularly struck by the complexities and contradictions, in fact by the very modernity, of the Hellenistic Age. The scientific spirit and a keen desire to understand the universe blossomed wonderfully at this time; much labor was spent on editing the writers of the past; but superstition and ignorance remained, and the literature and art, while often interesting and sometimes pleasing, frequently strove for mere effect. Side by side with luxury and sophistication existed poverty and slavery. Mass production and far-flung trade routes meant wealth, a widening horizon, and social revolution. The forces of the day let loose a rampant individualism, for the ordinary citizen, cut off from political life— from the life, that is, which had absorbed his every energy in the past— was thrown back on his own insufficient resources and felt lost in the changing world. It is hardly strange, then, that in his effort to understand life and to enjoy it he should have turned to new philosophic systems, to foreign religions, to social clubs, and to business partnerships. Viewed in the large and compared with previous periods, the Hellenistic Age, materially at least, represented a great improvement for the common man. Now a citizen of the world, he might travel anywhere; the products of the world came to his door; but high standards of taste, freedom, responsibility, and the intensity of Periclean life were definitely things of the past. Is it significant that the one great genius of the Age, Archimedes, came from Syracuse, a city-state? We must, however, return to Babylon.

Alexander's men were stunned by his death. No plans had been made for this contingency, but on his death bed Alexander had given his ring to Perdiccas. Perdiccas now summoned the chief officers to deliberate on the changed situation. Inspired by loyalty to the Macedonian royal house, they had no idea of dividing the Empire and suggested that they should await the birth of Roxane's child, shortly expected, and, if a boy, make him king. This plan, however, was unacceptable to the Macedonian army which, from early days, had had the right of passing upon each new king. The army declared for Alexander's half-brother, Arrhidaeus, and illegitimate, weak-minded son of Philip II. The difference of opinion produced a crisis which might have been serious, but a compromise was made and it was decided to crown Arrhidaeus as Philip III and to make Roxane's hoped-for son joint king. The next task was to assign satrapies to the various generals. Antipater, who had been Alexander's regent in Europe, was confirmed in his post, and Asia was given to Perdiccas and Craterus. In reality this was a victory for Perdiccas, because Craterus was already on his way to Europe with Alexander's discharged veterans, and Perdiccas foresaw that affairs in Greece would keep him busy and out of his way. Alexander's officers were men of extraordinary ability and ambition, none more so than Ptolemy, who won Egypt as his prize. Ptolemy had the vision to see that Egypt, somewhat removed from the center of action and rich in resources, held great possibilities. Most of Asia Minor was given to the satrap of Phrygia, Antigonus the One-eyed. Hellespontine Phrygia went to Leonnatus, Thrace to Lysimachus, whereas Eumenes of Cardia,[1] Alexander's secretary and one of the few Greeks to receive an important political assignment, won Paphlagonia and Cappadocia. To Atropates was given northern Media, where he later founded the state of Atropatene. The idea, then, was to hold and govern Alexander's Empire. His other plans, such as the exploration of Arabia, were perforce abandoned. Perdiccas remained in Babylon as regent of Asia, with the prestige and advantage of possessing the kings, Philip Arrhidaeus and Roxane's child, Alexander IV.

Alexander's death produced rebellion on the edges of the Empire. The Greeks left behind in Bactria had long fretted over their unhappy lot. Stationed in a far-off and wild country, they wanted nothing so much as to return to their homeland. Now, joined by natives, they mutinied and began the homeward march, 23,000 strong. Perdiccas sent Peithon, the satrap of Media, against them; by treachery and with savagery he put them down, and Bactria was then added to Aria and Drangiana and given to the satrap Stasanor. At the same time, and perhaps in cooperation, the Lamian War broke out in Greece. It will be recalled that Hypereides and the war party got the upper hand at Athens and that Antipater, supported by Craterus, finally defeated the Greeks and converted them into subjects.

It was impossible that these ambitious generals should remain at peace with one another. It took forty years of fighting among Alex-

---

[1] His fellow townsman, Hieronymus, is our chief source for this period, through Diodorus.

ander's Successors (Diadochi) before the new order assumed final shape. These wars were due to various causes; the desire of personal aggrandizement was certainly one; the need for secure frontiers was another; but it was also necessary to protect trade routes, to control the sources of war materials, and to be able to draw from Greece an uninterrupted supply of mercenaries. The art of war was correspondingly developed, too. Stronger city walls had to be built to withstand the new artillery, repeating catapults, flame carriers, and immense movable towers. Quinqueremes and other large warships, with catapults, were built, though their superiority over the trireme is doubtful. Another feature of Hellenistic warfare was the use of large numbers of elephants; their proper function was to serve as a screen against cavalry attacks. The cavalry was the chief arm of offense, even the phalanx being subordinated to it. Diplomacy, intrigue, propaganda, and the emergence of women in political life were natural developments. Even though the people of Macedonia would never have a woman as ruler, the Successors wished, above all else, to marry into the royal family of Philip II. Most of the Hellenistic queens were simply wives and mothers, and when they exerted influence at all, it was in statesmanship and not in battles. Some, it is true, were adventurous and daring, but their reputation for cruelty is, on the whole, unjustified. The Hellenistic queens present a striking picture of the growth of woman's power and ability, and in Egypt they eventually won a *de facto* equality with the men.

We have already seen that Olympias, Alexander's mother, did not hesitate to meddle in affairs during her son's absence in Asia. Naturally, Antipater hated her. In various ways Olympias now succeeded in creating a rift between Perdiccas and Antipater. At the same time Cynane, daughter of Philip II, crossed to Asia and gave her daughter Eurydice to Philip Arrhidaeus. Perdiccas was becoming isolated and was forced into alliance with Eumenes, and the growth of his power was alarming the other generals. Antigonus fled to Antipater and Craterus with the news that Perdiccas wished to be king. They immediately negotiated with Ptolemy for an alliance. Ptolemy had been quietly consolidating his power in Egypt, and had sent an officer, Ophellas, against Thibron, the Spartan governor of Cyrene. The prestige resulting from the annexation of Cyrene, however, was nothing compared to the possession of Alexander's body. Perdiccas had sent the royal corpse with an escort on its journey from Babylon to Europe, but at Damascus Ptolemy persuaded them to turn toward Egypt. Alexander's body was temporarily laid away at Memphis, awaiting final burial in the heart of his own city, Alexandria. This enraged Perdiccas and when, next year (321 B.C.), Antigonus, Antipater, and Ptolemy entered into an alliance against him, he decided to strike. Ordering Eumenes to keep Antipater and Craterus from marching through Asia Minor into Syria, Perdiccas hurried to the Nile, where, failing to cross, he was murdered by his own men. Eumenes, who was to prove himself one of the ablest generals of the day, found that Antipater and Craterus had divided their troops; therefore he forced Craterus into battle and killed him. Craterus' men, however, succeeded in rejoining Antipater. Meanwhile Antigonus had defeated Perdiccas' fleet off Cyprus.

The victorious generals met at Triparadeisus in Syria. The Macedonian army, exercising its prerogatives, made Antipater regent. This was a natural choice, for Antipater, a grand old man of almost eighty, had been especially close to Alexander. Antigonus was appointed general for Asia, and Seleucus, a man of capacity, who had married Apama, the daughter of the great Sogdian prince Spitamenes, was made satrap of Babylon. The eastern satrapies were assigned to Peithon, and Ptolemy was confirmed in his possession of Egypt and Cyrene. Antipater returned to Europe with the king, Philip Arrhidaeus and Alexander IV, and gave his daughter Phila, the widow of Craterus, in marriage to Antigonus' son Demetrius, later known as the Besieger. Antipater's death in 319 B.C. meant in reality the end of individual supremacy within the Empire, for never again could the army be gathered together to elect a regent or king, never again was any one powerful enough to establish his supremacy over the others. Just before his death Antipater designated an officer, Polyperchon, as regent, a choice confirmed by the army in Macedonia, though naturally the sections of the army elsewhere would not consider it valid. Polyperchon, hoping for the support of the Greeks, reversed Antipater's policy and proclaimed Greece free. He ordered that democracies should be established and the exiles recalled, and then entered into an alliance with Eumenes. The election of Polyperchon, however, was a blow to Antipater's son Cassander, who thought he had been unjustly treated and was determined to right the wrong.

The two powerful personalities at the moment were Antigonus, who had secured Hellespontine Phrygia and the command of the sea, and Ptolemy, who had taken Syria and Phoenicia from Laomedon, creating thereby a frontier question. Cassander, Ptolemy, and Antigonus now formed a coalition against Polyperchon. In 317 B.C. Cassander gained control of Athens, which he ruled for ten years through an agent, Demetrius of Phaleron. Demetrius, an educated Athenian citizen and peripatetic, was in reality a tyrant, who cloaked his rule under the title of *strategos* or archon and kept himself in power through the Macedonian garrison in Munychia, the citadel of Piraeus. Although he excluded

only the poorest from the citizenship—a man needed but 1,000 drachmas to be a citizen—nevertheless Demetrius ruled in the interests of the
rich, abolished the liturgies, and allotted to the Areopagus the punitive
powers of the Board of Eleven. He codified the law and established a
board of seven *Nomophylakes,* who were to act as guardians of the laws
and had the right of veto over any legislation. In spite of his own loose
life and his sumptuary legislation, prosperity returned to Athens under
Demetrius of Phaleron.

After his successful coup at Athens Cassander marched to Macedonia,
where the queen, Eurydice, wife of Philip Arrhidaeus, declared for him.
He was elected regent and then hurried to the Peloponnesus. On Cassander's approach to Macedonia Polyperchon had fled to Epirus and
persuaded Olympias that the time had finally come for her return.
When the Macedonian troops saw the old mother of Alexander, they
went over to her, although they were soon sickened by the savage
nature which could kill Philip Arrhidaeus and cause Eurydice to commit suicide. Cassander immediately abandoned his siege of Tegea and
hastened north. He had to ferry his troops across the Malian Gulf, for
the Aetolians held Thermopylae, but he finally reached Macedonia
and shut Olympias up in Pydna. In 316 B.C., reduced by famine, Olympias surrendered and was executed. Cassander now began to act like a
king. He had possession of Roxane and Alexander IV, but kept them
closely guarded in Amphipolis and six years later put them to death
when the young man approached the age for ascending the throne.
Cassander married Thessalonice, daughter of Philip II, after whom he
named a new city, Thessalonica, and founded his capital, Cassandreia,
on the site of Potidaea. His policy toward the Greeks was the opposite
of Alexander's, for he relied upon oligarchies in the various cities and
gained some popularity by rebuilding Thebes.

Polyperchon's ally, Eumenes, at first had great success in Asia Minor.
The opposition to him, as a Greek, he partly overcame by attaching
himself loyally to Alexander's house and by erecting in his tent a sort
of shrine as a memorial to and reminder of Alexander. After some
minor victories over Antigonus, Eumenes marched east, to raise a revolt, but was killed finally by Antigonus, in 316 B.C., in the district of
Gabiene (Media). For the next decade and a half Antigonus was the
dominating figure of the Hellenistic world. Possessing most of Asia and
a strong army, and fortunate in his devoted and able son Demetrius,
he aimed at nothing short of the entire Empire. A coalition was formed
against him. The Hellenistic world in 315 B.C., then, saw Antigonus in
Asia opposed to a coalition consisting of Ptolemy in Egypt, Seleucus

(who had recently fled from Babylon to Ptolemy), Lysimachus in Thrace, and Cassander in Macedonia.

Antigonus first invaded Syria, with Ptolemy cautiously retiring before him, and after a 13 months' siege captured Tyre. He was then in a position to acquire a large Phoenician fleet, although he could not prevent Ptolemy from taking Cyprus. Because it was impossible for him to leave for Europe at the moment, Antigonus tried to undermine Cassander's position by intrigue and propaganda. In 314 B.C. he proclaimed Greece free and announced a return to Alexander's policy of democratic government, as opposed to Cassander's oligarchies and garrisons. Naturally, the new policy was immensely popular in Greece, and it looked as if it might succeed. Greece and the Aegean were still the most important area in the world, and their control meant not only prestige, but an access to the best mercenaries of the day. Antigonus' fleet sailed to the Aegean, where Lemnos, Imbros, and Delos had already revolted from Athens and the Cyclades from Cassander. Antigonus, apparently, was sincere in his desire to free the Greeks, whom he formed, wherever he could, into leagues. The League of the Islanders, with its capital at Delos, and the Ionian League were revived at this time. A Council, consisting of representatives from the cities within the League, was the normal method of government. Antigonus also followed Alexander's policy of founding new settlements—Dura-Europos was founded on the Euphrates at this time—and prepared to move his capital from Celaenae in Phrygia to a new one in northern Syria, Antigoneia on the Orontes (Diagram 51).

In 312 B.C. Ptolemy, who had lost Cyrene in a revolt of Ophellas, inflicted a heavy defeat on Demetrius at Gaza and won back Syria and Phoenicia, although once again he withdrew on the approach of Antigonus. Seleucus, however, seized this moment to dash across the desert to Babylon and reinstate himself in his old satrapy. The Seleucids dated their Era from this event (October, 312 B.C.). Seleucus made himself master of the land east of Babylon, but about 308 B.C. he had to cede the Indus country, Gedrosia, and Arachosia to the great Mauryan king, Chandragupta. He received 500 war elephants in return, kept Bactria, and founded his capital, Seleuceia on the Tigris (Figure 99, Nos. 2, 8).

By 311 B.C. it was clear that neither Antigonus nor the coalition could win, and a peace was arranged on the basis of the *status quo*. The peace could not last long because, for one thing, it left Antigonus in a superior position, and, for another, Cassander ended Alexander's dynasty the next year by the murder of Roxane and Alexander IV. The scales slowly turned, however, against Antigonus. Ptolemy actually crossed to Greece and, playing Antigonus' game, posed as a friend of Greek freedom and tried to recreate the Corinthian League. The best plan, so Antigonus thought despite his eighty years, was to aim once more for the entire Empire.

In 307 B.C. Antigonus' son Demetrius, one of the ablest of Alexander's Successors, took Athens. Thus ended the regime of Demetrius of Phaleron, who retired to Alexandria, where he helped found the Museum. Demetrius, the Antigonid, razed Munychia and proclaimed the Athenians free. With the restoration of the democracy, Lemnos and Imbros returned to Athenian rule. The new policy let loose a flood of adulation. Led by the demagogue Stratocles, the Athenians called Antigonus and Demetrius their kings and added in their honor two new tribes, Antigonis and Demetrias, thereby increasing the number of the Council from 500 to 600. A sumptuary law, which would have restricted the teaching of philosophy, fortunately lasted but one year, for the role of Athens henceforth, whatever her other ambitions, was that of the intellectual center of the world. Not long before, Zeno, the great Semite from Cyprus, had arrived. Theophrastus and Epicurus were already there.

Antigonus, still intent on the destruction of Ptolemy, recalled his son and dispatched him to Cyprus. In a bitter battle off Salamis Demetrius overwhelmingly defeated Ptolemy (306 B.C.). Antigonus and Demetrius now took the title of king and were followed the next year by Ptolemy, Cassander, Lysimachus, and Seleucus, who formed a coalition against them. There was now no idea of trying to hold the Empire together; indeed, as a sign of their right to rule the kings issued their own money; that of Demetrius is the first example in the history of European Greece of a portrait of a living man on coins.

Rhodes was an important source of supplies to Ptolemy, and Antigonus sent his son against it. For one year Demetrius besieged the city, using 100-foot towers and powerful artillery, which won for him the title of Besieger (Poliorcetes), in spite of his failure to take it. The Aetolians, acting as arbitrators, arranged a truce, which stipulated that Rhodes should be the ally of Antigonus in all affairs except those touching its good customer Ptolemy (304 B.C.). Meanwhile, Athens had been engaged in a four-year war with Cassander. Demochares, a nephew of Demosthenes, was in charge of the army, while Olympiodorus, operating from Aetolia in Cassander's rear, had gained a victory at Elatea in Phocis. Demetrius arrived in time to raise Cassander's siege of Athens. This sojourn in Greece revealed the evil side of Demetrius' nature. He led a loose life, even carrying on his debaucheries in the Parthenon, and caused his mistress Lamia to be worshipped as Aphrodite. However, he revived the Corinthian League and became its president. The constitution followed closely Philip's lines and granted a considerable degree of initiative to the Greeks.

In 302 B.C. Antigonus recalled Demetrius, for the enemy coalition was on the move. Lysimachus, who now had consolidated his position against the Thracian tribes and had created a capital, Lysimacheia, crossed the Hellespont with re-enforcement received from Cassander. Seleucus crossed the Taurus and wintered in Cappadocia. Demetrius was at Ephesus, and Antigonus was on the march from Antigoneia. The next year the kings met at Ipsus in Phrygia. Antigonus and Demetrius had 70,000 foot soldiers, 10,000 cavalry, and seventy-five elephants. Lysimachus and Seleucus were slightly inferior in infantry, had approximately the same number of cavalry, and in addition had 120 war chariots and 480 elephants. In the course of the battle Demetrius pursued his opponents too far and Antigonus was killed. His death meant the end of any chance of recreating a unified Empire; it meant the division of the world into separate states. Ipsus marked a turning in the world's affairs. The kingdom of Antigonus was split up. Lysimachus added Asia Minor to his Thracian dominions. To Seleucus went Mesopotamia and, in theory, Syria, but Ptolemy, who had befriended Seleucus, was in actual possession of Syria. Cilicia was treated as a buffer state and was handed over to Pleistarchus, the brother of Cassander. Demetrius, who had fled to Ephesus after the battle, ruled the sea and held Tyre and Sidon and a few cities in Asia Minor and Greece. Cassander was declared king of Macedon. A new order was clearly in the making (301 B.C.), although it was to take another twenty years before it assumed final form. (For portraits of Alexander's Successors, see Figure 100.)

CHAPTER XXII

THE THIRD CENTURY

THE WEST

ALTHOUGH the Greeks had little difficulty in maintaining their civilization among more numerous Orientals, the cause of Hellenic freedom in Sicily and southern Italy became critical during the third century B.C. The fine work of Timoleon did not long outlast his death in 336 B.C., for Syracuse was soon divided by factional strife and Sicily was again exposed to Carthaginian aggression. Affairs grew continually more hopeless until Agathocles, an adventurous soldier of fortune, set himself up as tyrant of Syracuse in 317 B.C. By clever diplomacy, sheer luck, and a show of force, by a combination of harshness and mildness, he entrenched himsef in power and gained the hegemony over the Greek cities of the island.

The rapid rise to power of Agathocles naturally alarmed the Carthaginians, who feared that they might be driven from their own western half of Sicily. The Sicilian Greeks had not yet developed a political consciousness of their nationality, but vacillated between Agathocles and the Carthaginians as the considerations of the moment dictated. It was not difficult, therefore, for Hamilcar to drive Agathocles back into Syracuse in 311 B.C. and to besiege him there. The next year, though he had only a few allies and a small fleet, Agathocles conceived the amazing scheme of running the blockade and of transferring the war to Africa. Ophellas, the governor of Cyrene, came to his aid, only to be treacherously murdered; but Agathocles now added Ophellas' troops to his own and, re-enforced by a few Libyans, took Utica and other towns. The whole enterprise laid bare the weakness of Carthage, for her towns were unfortified and disloyal, and the general reliance on mercenaries threatened the safety of even Carthage herself. Notwithstanding some victories, Agathocles was finally forced to flee from Africa and in 306 B.C. signed a treaty with the enemy. Carthage retained the western half of Sicily, and Agathocles became master of the rest.

Until these events Agathocles had been satisfied to preserve the externals of constitutional government, styling himself merely general, but in 304 B.C. he assumed the title of king of the Sicilians, in imitation of Alexander's Successors; he entered into close relations with these sovereigns through diplomatic marriages. He also aided the Greek cities of Italy against the native Lucanians and gained for his realm a strip of Italian coast. The chief aim of his life, however, was the expulsion of the Carthaginians from Sicily; and in his old age he resumed preparations for a gigantic struggle with the national enemy. To this end he negotiated a treaty of alliance with Macedon. At last there dawned the hope that the Greeks were so organized in east and west as to maintain themselves and gain new ground. The realization of the dream of Agathocles would have given the western Mediterranean to Hellenism and have changed the course of the world's history. In the midst of his preparations, however, he died (289 B.C.). With his death went a great champion of Hellenism, a statesman and warrior scarcely excelled in administrative ability and in boldness combined with prudence. In his dying moments Agathocles had restored the republic (with its fatal weaknesses) to the Syracusans. The next years, consequently, saw the rise of tyrants in various cities, class struggle, and in particular a general desire to be rid of the Italian mercenaries, who had been brought to the island. Some of the mercenaries, instead of returning to Italy, seized Messene, and, under the name of Mamertines, set up a robber state.

The western Greeks were confronted by enemies so powerful and aggressive that the only opportunity for national independence lay in centralization under a military monarch. This truth they were unable to appreciate; and accordingly the death of Agathocles made their situation desperate. Although in Italy the Sabellians had spent their energy, what they failed to conquer became the prey of Rome. Rome, situated on the lower Tiber, began appreciably to extend her power about 400 B.C. with the conquest of Veii, an Etruscan city in the neighborhood. Rome either annexed conquered territory—settling it with her own people and incorporating the acquired population as citizens—or subjected it to her military command by treaties of alliance. Her just treatment of dependents and friends, no less than the severity with which she punished revolting allies, contributed to the growth and the solidity of her power. In a series of Latin and Samnite wars (343–290 B.C.), involving conflicts also with Etruscans, Umbrians, and Gauls, she extended her supremacy over the peninsula from the Rubicon river to the Greek settlements in the extreme south. In 326 B.C. Neapolis (Naples) entered into the Roman alliance. Like most allies of Rome she retained self-government in local affairs, but gave military aid in war. As a maritime state her chief military obligations lay in furnishing ships of war together with their crews.

The Greek cities of Italy, which were still free, made little concerted effort, however, to preserve their liberty. There was a union among them, but it counted for little. The democracy of Tarentum, the most populous and wealthy, had built up a considerable dominion, which stretched from the Ionian Sea into Apulia, and had made a treaty with Rome, which prohibited Roman warships from passing the Lacinian promontory. In the course of her varied struggles Tarentum sought and obtained aid from her mother city, Sparta, and from Alexander, king of Epirus; but the luxurious inhabitants, unwilling to submit to discipline or military authority and fearing for their liberties, nullified all such assistance by the reluctance of their cooperation. After Rome had extended her supremacy into southern Italy, Thurii, Rhegium, and Locri entered her alliance on substantially the same terms as Neapolis. Tarentum alone, with a few unimportant allies, remained independent.

When Roman aggressions forced Tarentum into war, she appealed once more to Greece for aid, this time to Pyrrhus, king of Epirus (281 B.C.). Pyrrhus had formed the Molossians, Thesprotians, and Chaonians into a strong Epirote state, with its capital at Ambracia, and he now crossed to Italy with elephants and an army of 25,000 men organized in the Macedonian system. Pyrrhus won victories over the Romans at Heraclea and Asculum, and in 278 B.C. answered an appeal for aid from Syracuse. In Sicily he also won striking victories over the Carthaginians, but he received little support from the Greeks and retired to

Italy and thence, after a defeat at the hands of the Romans, to Epirus (275 B.C.). Had he been well supported by the Greeks, Pyrrhus might have secured their national freedom and have organized them in a kingdom for himself; but, though a brilliant general, he lacked statesmanlike tact, and the Greeks were unwilling to sustain his absolute command and to fill the gaps in his ranks. Three years later Tarentum surrendered to the Romans, who in this way completed their supremacy over Italy. In Sicily the Carthaginians granted a peace, which greatly circumscribed the influence of Syracuse. A new leader of Syracuse, however, quickly arose. In 264 B.C., having meanwhile defeated the Mamertines, he was proclaimed king, as Hiero II. In this year the First Punic War broke out, and, as an ally of Rome, Hiero gave valuable aid. His reign was long and memorable, for he did not die till 215 B.C.; and when Rome shortly afterward annexed Syracuse, she found that she had really acquired a city-state learned in the ways of the Hellenistic East. From it Rome gained much knowledge, both culturally and in the field of finance.

It was inevitable that Rome and Carthage, the two great powers of the West, should clash. In the long, severe war Rome achieved the task that had proved too great for Dionysius, Agathocles, and Pyrrhus, the expulsion of the Carthaginians from Sicily. Instead of the emergence of a Greek nation, however, there resulted ultimately a deadening bondage, loss of political freedom, economic retrogression, depopulation, and a rapid decline of culture. Despite obvious advantages, the Roman conquest proved in the end an irremediable calamity.

THE SITUATION AFTER IPSUS

For the twenty years that divide the battles of Ipsus and Corupedium it is possible to treat the history of the East as a unit. The passing of the Successors of Alexander (the Diadochi), however, meant the end of rapidly changing frontiers and personalities; under the Epigoni (Afterborn)[1] Alexander's Empire assumed its final shape of three large, independent kingdoms, whose history can be followed separately until the Roman conquest, when they became integral parts of a world state.

We have already seen that after the battle of Ipsus (301 B.C.) Cassander was king in Macedonia; Seleucus I Nicator was master of a huge state, including northern Syria, Mesopotamia, and Asia as far as Bactria-Sogdiana; Lysimachus held Thrace and much of Asia Minor;

---

[1] It is more convenient, however, to speak of the Diadochi and Epigoni, together, as the Successors.

Ptolemy ruled Egypt and southern Syria. Syria was long a bone of contention between Seleucus and Ptolemy, and to bolster his position Ptolemy gave Arsinoe in marriage to Lysimachus. She was the daughter by his second queen, Berenice, and was to prove an extraordinary queen herself. Demetrius Poliorcetes, the son of Antigonus I, was, however, without a kingdom. His command of the sea and his possession of Tyre, Sidon, and some cities in Asia Minor and Greece made him a dangerous rival, and the next years were a witness to his disturbing influence.

Demetrius was an able, versatile individual, but he was also vain and fond of luxury, and was capable neither of pursuing a settled policy nor of governing well what he happened to hold. First he seized Cilicia from Pleistarchus, but the death of Cassander in 298 B.C. gave him his real opportunity. Demetrius hastened to Greece, only to find that his coming did not awaken the expected enthusiasm. Although Greeks of wealth were pro-Macedonian in their sympathies, most states were trying to preserve neutrality in the sea of strife. This was especially true of the democracies, of Athens, for example, under Phaedrus and Lachares. Lachares had made himself tyrant of the city some time before Cassander's death, and, to stifle opposition, had not only limited the franchise and abolished election by lot, but had abandoned Lycurgus' system of compulsory military training. The number of ephebi, consequently, dropped to a mere thirty. The Athenians, however, fought desperately for their independence, even melting down the gold of the Pheidian Athena, but in March, 295 B.C., Demetrius captured the city. Demetrius treated Athens with surprising leniency, permitting the people their own laws, but he did garrison Munychia, Piraeus, and the Hill of the Muses. Meanwhile, wild disorder had broken out in Macedonia, where the sons of Cassander were quarreling over the succession. Taking advantage of this, Demetrius marched to Macedonia, and without much difficulty had himself proclaimed king in the spring of 294 B.C. As befitted his new position, he now married Lanassa, the daughter of Agathocles, founded a capital, Demetrius, strategically situated on the Gulf of Pagasae, and caused himself to be worshipped as a god in certain localities. In addition to Macedonia and Thessaly, his state included central Greece, Athens, Corinth, and the League of the Islanders. His chief opponents were Sparta, Pyrrhus, and the new Aetolian League, which in 292 B.C. was powerful enough to seize Delphi. Demetrius controlled his cities mainly through oligarchies and, in spite of his unpopularity, planned an expedition to Asia.

The ambitions of Demetrius naturally disturbed the other sovereigns. Ptolemy had recently added Cyprus to his rule; Lysimachus had increased his realm in Asia Minor; and Seleucus had not only taken east-

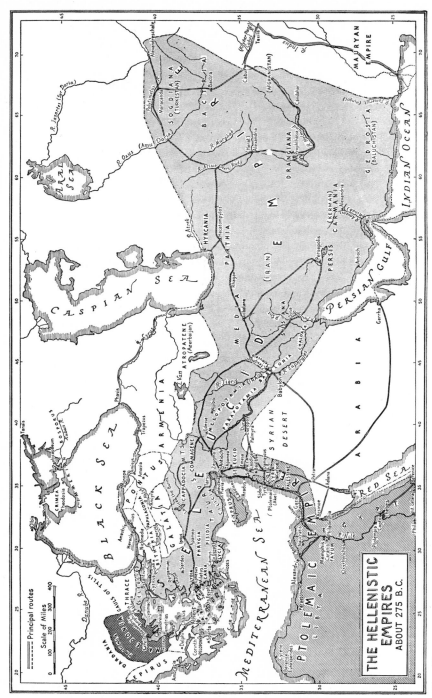

THE HELLENISTIC EMPIRES
ABOUT 275 B.C.

Map 47

Principal routes
Scale of Miles
0   100   200   300   400

389

ern Cilicia, but had built a great capital for himself, Antioch on the Orontes. The three kings formed a coalition against Demetrius (289 B.C.). Lysimachus also entered into negotiations with Pyrrhus, with the result that in the following year Demetrius found himself attacked simultaneously from the east and west. Macedonia was divided between Lysimachus and Pyrrhus, but this was not Demetrius' only loss. On the approach of Ptolemy's fleet, the democrats at Athens, under Olympiodorus, revolted and drove the adherents of Demetrius from the city, except for those at Piraeus. The administration of the city, which had previously been in the hands of an individual, was placed under a board, and election by lot was restored. The end of Demetrius was now in sight. Crossing to Asia Minor, he was captured by Seleucus in Cilicia (285 B.C.), and two years later died.

The death of Demetrius relieved the tension of the Greek world but momentarily. He had left behind a son, Antigonus II Gonatas, whose mother, Phila, was the daughter of Antipater, Alexander's old regent. It was the ambition of Antigonus Gonatas to restore his father's kingdom, though the prospect did not seem very promising, for he soon lost Piraeus to Olympiodorus and was left with little except central Greece and the Peloponnesus. Demetrius' death, however, did increase the strength of two of his opponents. Oddly enough his captor, Seleucus, profited little by it, territorially, for Seleucus was busy consolidating his power. His son (Antiochus I), by the Sogdian Apama, he made joint king with himself and gave him for a capital Seleuceia on the Tigris. The special task of Antiochus was to govern the eastern satrapies. Lysimachus and Ptolemy, on the other hand, gained greatly by Demetrius' death. Lysimachus quickly drove Pyrrhus from his share of Macedonia, had himself proclaimed king of Macedon, and annexed Thessaly. His kingdom now stretched from Thessaly and Macedonia through Thrace to the Black Sea and included the coast of Asia Minor and Heraclea and other towns on the Black Sea. In spite of his rather arbitrary rule and heavy taxation, Lysimachus was an able king and brought prosperity to his state. Ptolemy, for his part, obtained much of Demetrius' fleet, Sidon and Tyre, Caunus in Asia Minor, and the League of the Islanders. Ptolemy had also put his household in order. His wife Eurydice, the daughter of Antipater, he repudiated and in 287 B.C. married his mistress Berenice. Two years later he made his son by this union joint king, Ptolemy II Philadelphus.

Ptolemy I, Alexander's historian and one of his ablest generals, died in 283 B.C. after a notable reign. The arrangements which he had made for the succession naturally displeased his son by Eurydice, Ptolemy Ceraunus, the Thunderbolt. Ceraunus, therefore, fled to Lysimachus, who was desperately in need of help, for Seleucus had his eye on Asia Minor. In 281 B.C. at Corupedium, in Lydia, Seleucus and Lysimachus met in battle. Lysimachus was killed. Seleucus continued his victorious march to Europe, but soon after crossing the Hellespont this last of Alexander's companions was murdered by Ceraunus (281 B.C.). Ceraunus maintained himself in Macedonia and Thrace for a short while and rendered Pyrrhus help in his expedition to Italy. Seleucus' son, Antiochus, was now master of most of Alexander's Empire (excepting Egypt and the Indus country), but his connections with Europe and the Black Sea were hampered by the rise of the Northern League—consisting of Byzantium, Chalcedon, Heraclea, and other cities on the Black Sea—and by Mithridates, king of Pontus, and Nicomedes, king of Bithynia.

Danger now arose in an entirely unsuspected quarter. In 279 B.C. three different bands of Celts, known as Galatians, burst upon Thrace and Macedonia. One group, under Bolgius, killed Ceraunus and, after two years of depredations, finally withdrew. Another group, under Brennus, forced its way into Thessaly. The cities of Greece were hardly prepared to defend their country, for most of them were once more free and were consequently not willing to act in unison. An army of Boeotians and Aetolians, however, defended Thermopylae, but the pass was turned, and the Galatians continued to Delphi. At last they were beaten back by the Aetolians, and Brennus committed suicide; but the Galatians had spread fear everywhere. Though not disciplined and lacking the machinery to take cities, they were wildly courageous in battle. To commemorate the salvation of Grece, the Delphic Amphictyons instituted the festival of the Soteria in 278 B.C.; twenty-four years later the festival was reorganized on an even more impressive scale. The fear of the Galatians led Antigonus Gonatas and Antiochus to conclude an important treaty; Gonatas agreed not to interfere in Asia, and Antiochus undertook to give Gonatas a free hand in Europe. This treaty contributed greatly to stable relations between the two. But in 278 B.C. the third group of Galatians crossed to Asia Minor, producing the same extreme fear. Three years later they were beaten by Antiochus and his son Seleucus, and Antiochus assumed the title Soter (the Savior). As a protection against Antiochus, Nicomedes and Mithridates settled the Galatians on the Phrygian plateau, known after them as Galatia. Still other Galatians formed the kingdom of Tylis, stretching from the Danube to the Propontis, and thus cut Macedon off from Thrace and the Black Sea. One notable result of the invasions was the fame Antigonus Gonatas won by defeating some Galatians in 277 B.C. It promptly won him the throne of Macedon. Macedonia had finally acquired an enduring dynasty. The two other great states of the Hellenistic world were the Seleucid Empire in Asia, under Antiochus I, and the Ptolemaic Empire in Egypt, under Ptolemy II. Frontiers might change, but the Antigonid, Seleucid, and Ptolemaic kingdoms remained until the coming of Rome.

GREECE

Antigonus Gonatas devised a new policy toward Greece, for he abandoned the old system of garrisons and in its place adopted the scheme of holding the cities by means of tyrants, who were favorable to him. The garrisons at Piraeus and Corinth were necessary exceptions, because they formed vital links in his line of communications. Nor did Antigonus Gonatas try to bring the Greeks together in a federation or league, but, on the contrary, kept them isolated. His regime had the advantage of promising stability for Greece, although it was opposed from the beginning.

In the first place, Areus, king of Sparta, hoped to re-create the Peloponnesian League, and, though he was doomed to failure, he did succeed in so damaging Macedon that by 275 B.C. Antigonus Gonatas held little outside of Macedonia, except Demetrias, Piraeus, and Corinth. The real enemy of Antigonus Gonatas, however, was Egypt. Ptolemy II was a man chiefly interested in conserving his own realm, but he had repudiated his first wife, Arsinoe I, the daughter of Lysimachus, in favor of Lysimachus' widow, Arsinoe II, his own sister. Arsinoe II was a woman of extraordinary ability and ambition, and perhaps it was she who saw that the best method of preventing a strong Macedon was by supporting its enemies. A strong Macedon, of course, would be a threat to the Egyptian thalassocracy, and if the Egyptian fleet was not preponderant in the Aegean, Egypt might not only be cut off from the source of the much-needed mercenaries, but she would also lose the prestige which attached to a close connection with Greece. The Hellenistic kings hoped, above all else, for the favor of Greece. Accordingly, when Pyrrhus returned from Italy to Greece in 275 B.C., Ptolemy promised him aid against Macedon. It will be noted that Ptolemy neither came himself nor offered strong assistance; his policy was to remain in Egypt, if he could, and to harm his enemies by halfheartedly supporting their neighbors. Pyrrhus began by overrunning Macedonia and Thessaly, but he lacked, as always, the ability to organize his victories, and during a triumphant tour of the Peloponnesus, to which he had come as the champioin of Greek freedom, he was finally cornered in

Argos and slain during a street fight (272 B.C.). The death of Pyrrhus left Antigonus Gonatas supreme in the Peloponnesus, with the chief exception of Sparta, which still obstinately maintained its freedom in the Eurotas valley. Antigonus Gonatas set up friendly tyrants in Argos, Sicyon, and other cities, and cemented his contacts with the Aetolian League.

After the death of Pyrrhus, Ptolemy turned his eyes to Greece proper for a possible ally. At Athens Chremonides had learned the love of country from Zeno and now, in a passionate speech on freedom, he persuaded his fellow citizens to vote for a war, which is known after him as the Chremonidean War (267 B.C.). Areus, the king of Sparta, allied himself with the good cause, but it was impossible for him to render effective help, for the troops of Antigonus Gonatas held the Corinthian Isthmus and Areus was slain trying to force his passage. Ptolemy's admiral, Patroclus, instead of cutting Gonatas' line at the Isthmus, contented himself with lying off Sunium and smuggling food past the Macedonian garrison in Piraeus to the beleaguered Athenians. Late in 262 B.C. Athens surrendered and in the following year Antigonus Gonatas made peace with Egypt. Athens received harsh treatment for her actions, as might have been expected. In addition to the garrison at Piraeus, Antigonus Gonatas placed soldiers on the Hill of the Muses in Athens itself, and shut the country in by a series of forts along the borders of Attica. The magistracies were abolished, and the administration of the city was placed in the hands of a single superintendent (*epistates*). In 255 B.C., however, Antigonus Gonatas relented, withdrew his troops from the Hill of the Muses, and permitted an Athenian to command the garrison at Piraeus. The constitution was restored, with the sovereignty vested in the Council of Six Hundred and the Assembly; election by lot was retained, but payment for public service was abandoned. Athens never again counted as a political power. She settled down to a course of peaceful neutrality and the enjoyment of her constitution. She remained, of course, the cultural center of the world, a city whose favor kings courted and which they loved to honor with buildings and other gifts.

After the Chremonidean War Antigonus Gonatas built a fleet and resolved to end Ptolemy's supremacy in the Aegean. In a battle off Cos, he defeated the Egyptian navy (258 B.C.) and three years later won the Cyclades. The famous Victory of Samothrace is a beautiful memorial of his extraordinary prowess (Figure 101 and cf. Figure 47, No. 6). The opposition to Gonatas, however, was now in the Peloponnesus, where in 251 B.C. the eleven cities of Achaea began to expand their League. This expansion started with Aratus, a native of Sicyon, who drove out the local tyrant and joined his city to the Achaean League. Aratus was a practical politician who addressed himself to the main problem of Greek politics, the creation of a United States of Greece. High-minded though he was, and consumed by a bitter hatred of Antigonus Gonatas and all tyrants, he could be unscrupulous and did not hesitate to break the peace, which most Greeks now favored, if he thought the expansion of the Achaean League could be brought about in that way. Beginning in 245 B.C., and for almost thirty years thereafter, Aratus was elected general of the League in alternate years. Though Athens remained faithful to Antigonus Gonatas and refused the advances of Aratus, the Achaean League quickly absorbed Corinth, Megara, Epidaurus, and other communities, and entered into an alliance with Sparta (Map 55).

The internal situation at Sparta was well-nigh desperate. Wars and the lure of the East had so reduced the population that scarcely 700 Spartiates were left. Many of the old customs had disappeared, a money economy had been introduced, the division between rich and poor was sharp, and almost two fifths of the land belonged to the women. The cry, so familiar to Greece, for the redistribution of land and the abolition of debts was now heard in Sparta. The young king, Agis IV, hoped to lead this social revolution and advocated a return to the constitution of Lycurgus, but he was soon put to death. The alliance with Sparta, then, held a double disadvantage for the Achaean League. In the first place, because the ruling Achaeans were moderately wealthy landowners, it was dangerous to have for an ally a state that advocated, in reality, communism; and in the second place, it was doubtful whether Sparta would ever willingly accept as a neighbor a league that was based on sympolity.

In 245 B.C. Antigonus Gonatas had again defeated an Egyptian fleet, that of Ptolemy III off Andros, and, with his control of the Cyclades, he put an end to the League of the Islanders. He now cast about for an ally against the new combination of Sparta and the Achaean League. The Aetolian League was just what he needed. The Aetolians, in spite of their general backwardness, enjoyed considerable prestige through their possession of Delphi and their defeat of the Galatians in 279 B.C. Their League was also expending rapidly. After a defeat of the Boeotians at Chaeronea in 245 B.C., the League won Phocis and Locris, and even some places in the Peloponnesus, such as Tegea, Mantinea, and Elis. The Aetolians were a rough mountain people, a distinctly disturbing influence on Greece, and their piratical raids extended even to the islands of the Ionian and Aegean Seas. In 240 B.C. the Achaean League made peace with the Aetolians and Antigonus Gonatas; but when he died, in the following year, the two Leagues turned on his son and successor, Demetrius II. The War of Demetrius (238–229 B.C.), as it is called, accomplished little. Demetrius won back some of central Greece, and fared perhaps even better in the Peloponnesus, though Megalopolis, Argos, and other cities joined the Achaean League; and the Macedonian garrison was finally persuaded to withdraw from Athens. But the real danger to Demetrius lay on his northern frontier, where Dardanians were trying to invade Macedonia. Demetrius fell in an expedition against them in 229 B.C.

The two Leagues were now at their height. The Aetolian League stretched across central Greece from sea to sea and into the Peloponnesus. The Achaean League included much of the Peloponnesus—not only Achaea itself, Sicyon, Corinth, and Megara, but also Argos, Megalopolis, and other Arcadian cities—indeed, Aratus had finally succeeded in ridding the Peloponnesus of the hated Macedonian influence. The strength and solidarity of the two Leagues lay in the fact that a tribe (*ethnos*) was the basis of each. They were able to grow because they held out the promise of municipal autonomy combined with cooperation, and because the power was vested in the common Assembly and not delegated to a board, which would have been regarded as an aristocratic sign. The government of the two Leagues was in many ways similar. The Aetolian League had its federal center at the temple of Apollo at Thermon. Politically, the League was a sympolity, since the citizens of a city incorporated in the League became Aetolians; all the arms-bearing citizens formed the Assembly, which met twice a year and controlled the military and foreign policy, and minted the money. The individual towns, which often were not much more than a fort and its countryside, retained their own government; however, distant towns that joined the League in the course of its expansion were not incorporated in the League, but enjoyed isopolity; that is to say, an exchange of citizenship was granted, but the citizen of the distant town could not exercise his rights as an Aetolian citizen unless he chose to live in Aetolia. The Council of the League consisted of deputies from the constituent units, in proportion to their military levy, but it possessed little power. An undemocratic feature of the Aetolian League was the inner committee of the Council, known as the *Apocletoi*. This committee, together with the general, who was elected annually and was ineligible for re-election in successive years, became the executive power of the Aetolian League.

The Achaean League was also a sympolity, with its center at the temple of Zeus Amarios at Aegion. The League controlled the weights and measures of the federation, but permitted the locally autonomous cities to mint their own money on a specified standard. Vital questions, such as those concerning peace and war, were referred to all arms-bearing citizens over thirty years of age; and on those occasions the votes were cast by cities. The Achaean League of Aratus' day, strictly speaking, did not have an Assembly (except the general gathering just referred to), but the Council (*synodos*), which met twice a year, was so very large that it amounted to the same thing. The *synodos* was made up of representatives from the constituent cities in proportion to their military strength and here, too, the voting was by cities. The chief office was that of general, an annually elected official, with reëlection in successive years forbidden. The general and a small committee of ten *demiourgoi* were the executive. The Aetolian and Achaean Leagues were wonderfully adapted to the Greek character and marked a new advance in the field of government; the Achaean League, it will have been noted, practically achieved representative government. Had they not been menaced by the superior powers of the Hellenistic kingdoms and the Roman Republic, the two Leagues might have solved the most difficult of Hellenic problems, the apparent incompatibility of autonomy and federation.

The Aetolian and Achaean Leagues were often at war with each other, but Sparta soon became the chief danger to the Achaean League. Cleomenes III, the new king of Sparta, entertained ideas of social revolution, as had Agis IV, but it seemed to him the wiser policy to build up his state first. In 228 B.C., with the support of Ptolemy III, he entered on a career of conquest, defeated Aratus in battle, and won Tegea and other cities. He then returned to Sparta and established, as he claimed, the constitution of Lycurgus. The ephors were removed, debts abolished, land redistributed, and 4,000 perioeci admitted to citizenship. Cleomenes was practically tyrant of Sparta. At Hecatombaeum, in Achaea, he again defeated Aratus, and with the adherence of Mantinea became the virtual master of the Peloponnesus. In 226 B.C. Cleomenes demanded the presidency of the much restricted Achaean League. Aratus, who had spent his life fighting Macedonian tyrants, was faced with the dilemma of appealing to his old enemy or seeing his League fall to pieces. He decided to ask Macedon for help, for Cleomenes was the new tyrant of the Peloponnesus and his support of the poor party at Sparta was a danger to the land-owning Achaeans.

When Demetrius II was killed by the Dardanians in 229 B.C., Philip, his son by his mistress Chryseis, was a child. The general conditions were so unsettled that the boy's guardian, Antigonus Doson, took the kingship two years later with the understanding that Philip would succeed him—an arrangement that an Antigonid could be trusted to keep.

First Antigonus Doson drove out the Dardanians and gained the neutrality of the Aetolians; but when Aratus asked him for aid, he replied that he must have Acrocorinth, the citadel of Corinth. Acrocorinth was being besieged by Cleomenes at that very moment (224 B.C.), and after some hesitation Aratus decided to yield the key of the Peloponnesus to the Macedonian. Antigonus Doson was something of a statesman and, using the old Corinthian League of Philip II as a model, he created a Hellenic League of Leagues. Many states, such as Athens, Sparta, Elis, and the Aetolian League, were not members of the new League, to be sure, but still it represented one more attempt at federation. The characteristic feature of the union was that the decisions of the federal congress had to be ratified by the individual states. The next year Antigonus Doson took Mantinea, and to repay it for its conduct toward the Achaean League, razed the city to the ground and sold its inhabitants as slaves. In 222 B.C. Antigonus Doson and the Achaeans, with a force of 28,000 men, met Cleomenes at Sellasia, near Sparta. It was a crushing defeat for Cleomenes, who made his way to Alexandria, where he later died trying to stir up a revolt in the name of freedom, a word not understood by the Alexandrians. For the first time in its history Sparta was taken. The ephors and the old constitution were restored. Antigonus Doson was master of Greece, but he did not live to enjoy his hegemony long. In 221 B.C. he died and was succeeded by Philip V, now a youth of seventeen. In the following year a Social War broke out between Sparta, Elis, and the Aetolian League, which once more was indulging in its piratical raids, and Philip V and the Hellenic League. Philip took Thermon, the federal center of Aetolia, but the Greeks were war-weary and desired peace; besides, the Second Punic War between Rome and Carthage had recently begun, and a new danger might at any moment arise. At the peace conference at Naupactus in 217 B.C. Agelaus, an Aetolian, spoke of the need of Greek unity against the "cloud in the West."

EGYPT AND ASIA

The hostility between Egypt and Macedon was largely limited, we have seen, to Ptolemaic support of Macedon's enemies. It was otherwise in the case of Egypt's relations with Seleucid Asia, for the Egyptian army and navy had perforce to assume an active rôle. The warfare between the two Hellenistic kingdoms was the greater pity, for, because they did not even have the advantage of being national states, the wars actually hindered the spread and firm establishment of

Hellenism. The necessity of remaining supreme in the Aegean explained Egypt's hostility to Macedon; supremacy in that area gave Egypt not only prestige, but a steady supply of mercenaries. Egypt's interest in Asia Minor can be explained on similar grounds. In the case of Syria, however, the motives were slightly different. The forests of Mt. Lebanon provided timber for the Egyptian navy, but of greater importance was the fact that several trade routes from the East ended on the Syrian coast. Ptolemy II, ruling a compact wealthy kingdom, pursued a mercantile policy. Nubia and Ethiopia, to the south, were the sources of elephants and gold; the Red Sea coasts were developed for the Arabian and Indian trade; and it was proposed that the benefits of the Syrian trade should also accrue to Egypt. All these factors, however, operated more strongly in the interests of the Seleucids, who had a large, unwieldy empire and whose eastern provinces constantly threatened revolt. If the Seleucids should lose Asia Minor, they might cease to count in the Hellenic world, and if at the same time they should lose Syria, they would be practically excluded from the Mediterranean. The desire for power, then, was behind the struggle between the Ptolemies and Seleucids.

The Syrian question, it will be recalled, dated from the battle of Ipsus, which awarded Syria to Seleucus, though his friend Ptolemy I was in actual possession. The question did not concern northern Syria, which was Seleucid, but southern Syria and Palestine, which can be roughly described as Coele Syria. About 275 B.C. Ptolemy II Philadelphus began the First Syrian War by invading Seleucid Syria. Antiochus I drove him back and then turned to the problems caused by the Galatian invasion of Asia Minor. He was able, also, to weaken Ptolemy by an alliance with Ptolemy's half-brother Magas, the governor of Cyrene, a district important to Egypt as a protecting western neighbor and for its Mediterranean trade. In spite of his ambitions Ptolemy was no general, as he had come to realize some years before. In 276 B.C., therefore, he had married his full sister, Arsinoe II, and it was she, no doubt, who had conceived the plan of weakening Macedon by supporting its enemies. Unfortunately for Egypt, Arsinoe died in 270 B.C., but not before she had carried the Syrian War through to a successful conclusion. Though Ptolemy did not gain as much as he had hoped, the peace of 271 B.C. left him with Phoenicia, much of Asia Minor, and the Cyclades. The Ptolemaic policy of allying with the neighbors of enemies can also be seen in Asia Minor, where Eumenes had succeeded Philetaerus as governor of Pergamum. In 263 B.C. Ptolemy and Eumenes became allies. Eumenes defeated Antiochus in battle near Sardes, and proceeded to build up a semi-independent power in the valley of the

Caïcus river. Seleucid authority in Asia Minor was further weakened by the Persian Ariarathes, who declared himself king of Cappadocia.

Early in 261 B.C. Antiochus I died and was succeeded by Antiochus II Theos (the God), who opened the Second Syrian War within two years of his accession. Most of the war was carried on in Asia Minor, and in 253 B.C., probably, peace was finally signed. Ptolemy, who no longer enjoyed the help of Arsinoe, had lost the Syrian coast north of Sidon and much of Asia Minor to Antiochus. During the war, too, Antiochus had been aided by Antigonus Gonatas, who defeated the Egyptian fleet off Cos and took over the League of the Islanders. Ptolemy was now left with only Thera as a base in the Aegean. Antigonus Gonatus also sent his half-brother Demetrius the Fair (father of Antigonus Doson) to Cyrene, where Magas had recently died. Demetrius the Fair was, however, assassinated, whereupon two tyrant-slayers from Megalopolis, Ecdemus and Demophanes, created a short-lived federation in the Cyrenaica, but the district soon returned to Egypt. The activities of Antigonus Gonatas made Ptolemy particularly anxious to be free of commitments in Asia, so that he might be able to turn his entire attention on the Macedonian. He therefore persuaded Antiochus, in 253 B.C., to put away his wife Laodice in favor of Ptolemy's daughter Berenice, with the understanding that Berenice's son should succeed to the throne. Berenice brought with her an immense dowry, but it was idle to hope that peace might be won by repudiating a Macedonian queen.

In 246 B.C. Ptolemy died and was succeeded by Ptolemy III Euergetes (the Benefactor). About the same time Antiochus died at Ephesus, having named as his successor Seleucus II, the son of Laodice, who was now domiciled in Asia Minor. After some hesitation, Ptolemy decided to enforce the arrangements which his predecessor had made and thereupon declared himself for Berenice. He captured Seleucia in Pieria, Antioch's great harbor, and continued to Antioch itself. In actual fact, however, Berenice and her son had been murdered in Antioch, but this was kept secret, so that Ptolemy might appear not as an invader, but as one who had come on behalf of the legitimate heir to the throne. Though the details are by no means clear, Ptolemy seems to have enjoyed something of a triumphant tour of Asia. He occupied Seleuceia on the Tigris and sent orders to the governors of Bactria and the other eastern provinces; indeed, his authority extended along the Asia Minor coast into Thrace. And then, quite mysteriously, he hurried back to Egypt, where disorders had broken out, and settled down to his habitual caution.

The struggle of Seleucus II to establish his authority is known as the Third Syrian or Laodicean War. His successes began in Asia Minor, although to improve his position he had to surrender some of Asia Minor to Mithridates, king of Pontus, and to Ariarathes, king of Cappadocia, to each of whom he gave a sister in marriage. Seleucus gained Cilicia and his central provinces, but he could not take Seleuceia in Pieria, nor the Phoenician coast, from Ptolemy. Ptolemy's fleet, however, was badly defeated by Antigonus Gonatas off Andros in 245 B.C., and with the defeat disappeared the Egyptian thalassocracy. In 241 B.C. Ptolemy and Seleucus made peace. Their kingdoms were still strong, but the war had unfortunately and needlessly weakened them. Ptolemy had lost control of the sea, and Seleucus had lost his eastern provinces. Not only did Bactria break away, but Arsaces, the chief of the nomad Parni, killed the Seleucid governor of Parthia, Andragoras. Not much later his brother, Tiridates, founded the strong state of Parthia, and declared himself king, as Arsaces II.

Seleucus fared even worse in Asia Minor. During his war with Ptolemy his brother Antiochus Hierax, the Hawk, had forced him to acknowledge him as joint king. Now that there was peace, Seleucus asked Hierax for the return of Asia Minor, and in the War of the Brothers, as it is called, he was badly defeated at Ancyra and had to surrender Asia Minor to Hierax (236 B.C.). Hierax had been aided by the Galatians, who were still far from civilized and who now set off on another of their raids. This, incidentally, led to the birth of the small, but important, Hellenistic kingdom of Pergamum. Eumenes had gradually asserted his independence of the Seleucids, and on his death in 241 B.C. was succeeded by his nephew, Attalus I. Attalus took the apparently unusual step of refusing tribute to the Galatians and defeated them in battle at Pergamum. Hierax was driven from Asia Minor and subsequently died in Thrace. Attalus, who now stood in the role of the great defender of civilization, held most of the Seleucid territory north of Taurus and took the title of king.

The Greek cities northward, along the south coast of the Black Sea, had of course never belonged to the Seleucids, except perhaps momentarily. Some of these cities, such as Heraclea, it will be recalled, had joined with Byzantium and Chalcedon to form a Northern League. The general purpose of the Northern League was to defend its members against all enemies. Nearby were the barbarian kingdom of Pontus, founded in the third century by the Persian Mithridates, and the Hellenized kingdom of Bithynia, whose King Nicomedes had created a capital at Nicomedia. The Byzantines, however, had another enemy in the Gauls of Tylis in Thrace, who levied tribute from them. To pay for this tribute Byzantium decided to place a toll on ships passing through the Bosporus, but in 219 B.C. the great commercial city of

Rhodes, aided by Prusias of Bithynia, secured by force of arms the freedom of the Bosporus. The Greeks still further to the north, in the Crimea, were, however, completely beyond the orbit of Hellenistic politics. Nevertheless, they were intermediaries in the trade with central Asia, spread civilization among the Scythians, and sent much-needed grain to the Greek world. Under the protection of the local Spartocids there grew up a small Bosporan kingdom, with its capital at Panticapaeum on the Cimmerian Bosporus.

Seleucus II died during a Parthian campaign in 226 B.C. and was succeeded by his son, Seleucus III, who ruled but three years. With the accession of Antiochus III, a younger son of Seleucus II, our information becomes more satisfactory, thanks to the pages of Polybius, and the history of the Seleucid Empire more happy; indeed, Antiochus so rehabilitated his realm that he won the titles of "the Great" and "Restitutor Orbis." In 221 B.C. Antiochus set about the task of restoring his Empire by an attack on Egypt, where a new ruler, Ptolemy IV Philopator, an indolent voluptuary, had become king. Ptolemy left the conduct of government to his minister Sosibius and gave himself up to the pleasures of art and the mysteries of religion, eventually becoming dominated by his mistress Agathoclea and her brother Agathocles. The attack on Egypt, however, failed, for Antiochus himself was under the influence of a strong-minded minister, Hermias, and divided counsels caused the plan to miscarry; but in Asia Minor a cousin of Antiochus, Achaeus, regained Seleucid Asia Minor from Attalus. Having failed in his attempt on the Egyptian frontier, Antiochus next turned to Mesopotamia, where a rebel governor, Molon, had declared himself. Molon was crushed, and Antiochus, who was shocked by the cruelties of Hermias, seized the occasion to have his minister murdered. Artabazanes, the king of Atropatene, the state to the north which had long been independent, was compelled to acknowledge Antiochus as his master. At the same time (220 B.C.) Achaeus proclaimed himself king of Asia Minor, but his troops refused to march on Antioch against their true king, so that Antiochus felt safe in devoting his attention to other matters; when, a half dozen years later, he defeated and killed Achaeus at Sardes, he had completely established his authority within his kingdom.

The Fourth Syrian War broke out in 219 B.C. Antiochus was at first successful, capturing Seleuceia in Pieria and Tyre, but he made the fatal mistake of not marching quickly against Egypt itself. Egypt not only had ceased to count on the sea, but the army had become demoralized, and actually the country was an easy victim for any invader. But Sosibius, Ptolemy's minister, frantically set to work to rebuild the army, and kept Antiochus off by promises of negotiations. Ptolemy bestirred himself, too, and before many months a well-drilled and well-equipped force had been got together, but unhappily for him 20,000 native Egyptians were included in the army. For practically the first time in a century native Egyptians were called upon to defend their country, and once they discovered their value to the state, it was inevitable that they should make demands. In 217 B.C. the Egyptian army crossed to Palestine and took up its position at Raphia, south of Gaza. Ptolemy was in command and had 55,000 men and 73 African elephants. Antiochus opposed him with 68,000 men and 102 Indian elephants. The battle was fought on June 22nd and ended with Ptolemy victorious and Antiochus in flight. The peace treaty awarded Seleuceia in Pieria to Antiochus, but Ptolemy won southern Syria and Palestine; native revolts, however, were already taking place in Egypt.

Chapter XXIII THE SOCIAL AND ECONOMIC CONDITIONS OF THE HELLENISTIC AGE

ERHAPS the most striking fact about the Hellenistic Age is the unity of the large world which had been opened by Alexander's expedition. In spite of the warfare of the various states, trade between East and West was now easier. New lands—Egypt, India, Bactria-Sogdiana, Iran, China, Arabia, Central Africa, Western Africa, Western Europe—now came, in one way or another, within the orbit of the Greeks. Alexander gave a new impetus to the economy, and indeed to every aspect of the life, of the ancient world. With the political domination of new lands, with the diffusion of Hellenism and city life came new opportunities and new markets. The Greeks were responsible for the spectacular growth of the wealth and population of Asia and Egypt and were quick to take advantage of it. The sense of unity was heightened by the breaking down of barriers between cities; in fact, we have already seen that many cities ceased to exist as separate political entities. The new order of the day was the large state; people were conscious of ths *oecumene,* the inhabited world, and some individuals were actually thinking about the brotherhood of man.

The large state had been bought at a price, for it meant the triumph of monarchy, which was anathema to most Greeks. In Greece proper, to be sure, many cities retained their liberty, and where the Antigonids held sway, it was generally through alliance, although they occasionally made use of tyrants and garrisons. But for the new large states, such as that of the Seleucids, monarchy was especially suited. It was almost necessary in states of wide areas, with slow communications and different populations. The problem was further aggravated by the crowds of Greeks, who settled in Asia and Egypt and stood apart from the natives. The kings did all they could to attract Greeks, for they were necessary for the development and the defense of the state. Consequently, we find concessions to the Greek love of autonomy —a new type of democracy and without much real meaning, but the Successors did grant a large measure of self-government to the Greeks in their new cities. The status of the new foundations varied, but as a rule they had their own Assembly and Council and owned much land. The new cities were nominally the allies of the king, but in reality the king owned all the land round about and subjected the population to taxation and conscription; in Egypt Ptolemy owned the entire valley of the Nile, which made possible a despotic control of the individual's life (Map 48).

The Successors of Alexander took as their model the old Macedonian monarchy, with a certain outward simplicity to the court life, but actually they were autocratic rulers, who made the laws and appointed the officials, and upon their death were deified, if this had not already been done during their life. Deification was unknown to Macedonia, however, where all of life was far simpler and more democratic, but it was developed by the Ptolemies into an official imperial cult.

The native peasants formed the mass of the population in the new Hellenistic kingdoms. They lived in villages, without much self-government, and interference with their ancestral ways was rare. Hellenism touched them little, as events, proved, but the ambitious native would learn Greek and Greek ways and try for a minor post in the bureaucracy. It was inevitable that there should be some fusion between Greek and Oriental, but this had always been the case. The Greek never had any racial prejudice, of a physical sort, although he

Map 49

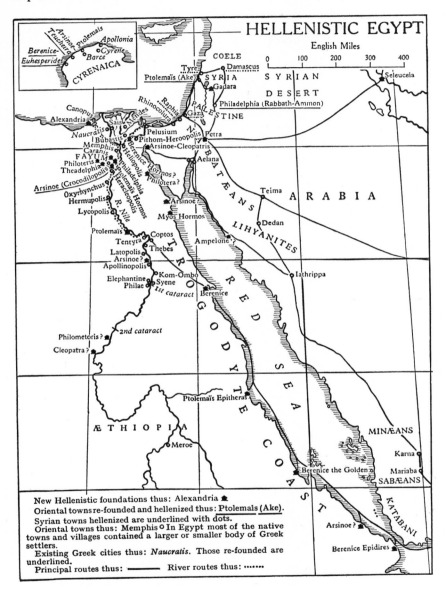

HELLENISTIC EGYPT

New Hellenistic foundations thus: Alexandria ♠
Oriental towns re-founded and hellenized thus: Ptolemaïs (Ake).
Syrian towns hellenized are underlined with dots.
Oriental towns thus: Memphis ○ In Egypt most of the native
towns and villages contained a larger or smaller body of Greek
settlers.
Existing Greek cities thus: *Naucratis*. Those re-founded are
underlined.
Principal routes thus: ———— River routes thus: ·······

Map 48

405

disliked the confusion which resulted, for example, from a mixture of customs, and considered his own political institutions and his culture superior. In the Hellenistic Age culture, and not race, became the important thing, but it must be emphasized that, so far as actual race mixture in Asia was concerned, there was no great increase during the Hellenistic Age. The Hellenistic world did, however, constitute a single culture sphere.

In this vast new world man emerged as an individual. He could live anywhere; in fact, the Cynics said, "make the world your city." This meant that a substitute had to be found for the city-state of old, with all its obligations and privileges; clubs and associations might be a poor substitute, but they satisfied man's longing in part. The clubs were generally of a social and religious nature and were usually small, though the associations of Dionysiac artists were as large as they were popular. Similarly, we can understand the growth of astrology, mystery cults, and other strange religions. The Hellenistic Age was a period of experiment, novelties, and individualism. A feature of the time, along with the greater humanity in warfare, was the growth of arbitration between cities, a disinterested city being invited to appoint a commission for the task. In like manner the disputes between individuals were often settled by judicial commissions from another city, but the irregularity of their visits made them a not wholly satisfactory substitute for the old-time juries and their political activities. The desire for arbitration was promoted by trade and by the consciousness of a common nationality and led in time to a certain standardization of laws and customs. The solidarity and friendliness of the Hellenistic Age is illustrated, for example, by the way in which kings and cities rushed aid to Rhodes at the time of her disastrous earthquake in 225 B.C. It is also illustrated by the numerous grants of citizenship by one city to individuals in another city and indeed to entire cities (isopolity).

The provision of a steady and adequate supply of grain was a pressing problem for most Greek cities, the possibility of hunger being the chief cause, no doubt, for the marked limitation of the size of families (by infanticide). Some cities had regular grain funds and regulated the wheat trade by law, but in time of famine it was often necessary to appeal to the rich. The rich could generally be counted upon in any crisis, though their gifts would be intended for the entire population and not for the poor as such. Another pressing problem for most Greek cities was the perpetually bad state of finances. The Greeks raised much of their revenue by indirect taxation, but they had no reserves and no budget. The cities, however, did take a greater interest in education, which was centered in the gymnasia under the charge of officials called gymnasiarchs; a settlement without its gymnasium could not hope to be regarded as a city. Emancipation was possible for women, because girls as well as boys now received an education. At nineteen a boy went on to the ephebate, a system that was universal, though no longer compulsory. The training was athletic and intellectual, the military features having been dropped, and at the end of the year the youth who desired a higher education sought his own teacher.

The Hellenistic Age was also a period of contradictions. In the midst of all the festivals and luxury, with a spirit of *homonoia,* Concord, abroad, the condition of the laboring man was very low. Alexander's capture of the Persian hoard had put an enormous amount of money into circulation, so that the value of the drachma grew less. Prices inevitably rose (wheat doubling in price) and though these later fell, the wages of the worker rarely rose above the fourth-century level. This led, of course, to social unrest, and the familiar cry for the cancellation of debts and the redistribution of property was heard.

The desire for wealth was largely responsible for exploration during the Hellenistic Age, though when one considers the profound effects of Alexander's expedition, it is surprising how little exploration was done. Much was learned of India from Megasthenes, who as Seleucus' envoy to Chandragupta lived at Pataliputra (Patna) on the Ganges, but warfare and other problems prevented much active exploration. The Seleucids colonized along the Persian Gulf for purposes of trade, although they abandoned Alexander's plan for the circumnavigation of Arabia, which would have diverted trade up the Red Sea to the benefit of the Ptolemies. The Ptolemies, however, did what they could to develop the Red Sea traffic and explored further down the African coast. Patrocles did some exploring of the Caspian, while Pytheas set out from Massilia for the North Atlantic; he managed to elude the Carthaginians at Gades and to sail to Jutland. A result of his journey was more active traffic along the rivers of Gaul, bringing especially the tin of Cornwall. During the late Hellenistic period, or early in the days of the Roman Empire, Hippalus discovered the monsoons, which made possible a quick direct sail to India. On the whole, however, exploration played a small role in Hellenistic life, and the world settled down to develop its resources as it found them.

Agriculture, of course, was the basis of the Hellenistic world. It will be recalled that in Greece property was private and belonged to the individual, but in the East, owing to the divine or semidivine position of the ruler, the king theoretically owned the land, except for the land of the new Greek cities. Consequently, the Greeks found themselves competing in the East with royal and temple estates, worked by slaves, but nevertheless their initiative and ability won them a livelihood. Technical works were written on agriculture, and in Egypt especially experimentation was carried on. Vine growing was introduced to western Asia; the Greeks for their part had to learn methods of irrigation. Many sections of the world were famous for their special products. Fertile Asia Minor was famous for its olives, wine, sheep, and grain; Syria and Mesopotamia for their barley, wheat, and vegetables. Because of the annual overflow of the Nile, Egypt was extraordinarily fertile and produced large quantities of grain, flax, vegetables, papyrus, sesame and other plants. From the Black Sea came salt fish, from Athens oil and honey, from Bithynia cheese, from Pontus fruits and, later, medical drugs. The nuts of Babylonia, the prunes of Damascus, the raisins of Berytus were prized and show that relatively small products competed in the international markets; of greater importance were the timber of Macedon, the cedars of Lebanon, and the pitch of Mt. Ida in the Troad.

All these products, and many more, were exchanged, as well as used locally; indeed, it was commerce that tied the Hellenistic world together. Each king tried to attract trade to his own state, the Seleucids looking especially toward India and the Far East, the Ptolemies toward India, Arabia, Nubia, and Central Africa; both states competed with Macedon in the Aegean. Ships sailed the Mediterranean and other seas, going as far as Arabia Felix and the Deccan and to the cinnamon country of east Africa. The rivers of Europe, Asia, and Africa were laden with traffic. Everything was done to make travel safe; desert routes were policed and provided with wells; harbors were improved; breakwaters built. The excellent road system of the Persian Empire was expanded, and great caravans wound their way across Central Asia. Men traveled from the Adriatic and the Balkans to Ethiopia, from Arabia and India to the Jaxartes and southern Russia. There were three main routes connecting the East with the Mediterranean (Maps 47 and 50). The northern one, from Bactra across the Caspian to the Black Sea, was little used. The central route was the most important. It ran by sea from India to the Persian Gulf and up the Tigris to Seleuceia, the commercial capital of Asia. Cross-continental caravans also ended their journey at Seleuceia. Thence the goods were sent overland to Antioch and Ephesus. The southern route also came from India by sea, but it rounded Arabia and continued up the Red Sea. Much traffic eventually reached Petra in this manner, but the Ptolemies, who were most interested in the traffic, developed Berenice as a port on the Red Sea; goods were sent thence across the desert to Coptos on the Nile. There was a lively traffic, of course, between the various ports of the Mediterranean, and as Italy increased in importance, we note the rise of two new ports, Puteoli, near Naples and Pompeii, and Ostia, at the mouth of the Tiber. The boats were generally small, of about 250 tons, although the world saw several pretentious and unmanageable ships, such as Hiero's *Syracosia* of 4,200 tons and Philopator's house boat, which was really a floating villa.

Agricultural produce, timber, wool, raw materials, and manufactured articles were sought and traded. Gold came from Nubia, Spain, and India; silver from Spain and Mt. Pangaeus, though no longer from Laurium; copper came from Cyprus; tin from Cornwall and Brittany; iron from various sections, but especially from the land of the Chalybes in northern Armenia. Parian and Pentelic marble were exported. Lake Tatta in Asia Minor produced salt, Cappadocia talc for windows, Lydia natron for bleaching cloth. The balsam of Jericho and the aromatic plants of Syria were necessary for perfumery. Tyre and Aradus grew rich on the purple dye industry, while the Dead Sea produced bitumen, which was used in Egypt for embalming the dead. Ebony from India, ivory from India and Africa, gems from India and Arabia constituted a luxury trade, though in this category first place was held by the trade in spices, the cinnamon of India, and especially the frankincense of Arabia, which was used by every religion. The greatest trade was in grain. Though most sections produced enough grain for their ordinary needs, certain places, such as Athens, Corinth, Delos, and Ionia, were compelled to import. The great exporting areas were Egypt and Cyrene, Sicily, Numidia, and the Crimea until invasions from the hinterland, after the third century, destroyed its importance. Regular depôts for the international grain trade were established at Rhodes and Delos.

Certain cities grew rich on trade. Athens and Piraeus declined in importance, but not Corinth, which was famous for its bronzes and had a great transit trade. New importance attached to Ephesus, the terminus for trade from the East; to Petra, the capital of the Nabataeans, whose trade was enormously increased after Parthia's rise interfered with traffic across Central Asia; to Seleuceia on the Tigris; to Alexandria, Tyre and Sidon, Antioch, Seleuceia in Pieria, Byzantium, and Tanais. The wealth of these cities was in large part, and in certain instances exclusively, due to the transit trade. Rhodes and Delos are special cases in point. Rhodes is famous for its prestige in antiquity, for its love of learning, the beauty of its city, the great docks, the temples, and its Colossus—Apollo as the Sun god astride the harbor. It was also a great commercial city, with a busy carrying-trade, the meeting point of East and West. The chief trade was in grain, and we can form an idea of the importance of the total trade when we consider that the customs revenue of Rhodes in 170 B.C. was a million drachmas as against the 200,000 drachmas of Athens in 401 B.C. (the rate of duty in each case being 2 per cent). Rhodes had a cosmopolitan population, with many merchants and bankers. It was the policy of the state to suppress piracy, to enforce the freedom of the seas, and to maintain the independence of the Greek cities. The Rhodian sea law was so famous that it was eventually adopted by the Mediterranean states.

To destroy the dominance of Rhodes, Rome declared Delos a free port in 167 B.C. Delos had always been something of a banking center, because the sanctity of the island made it a safe place for deposits, but after 167 B.C. its importance greatly increased. The island became an Athenian cleruchy in name, with Athenian magistrates in charge, but actually the merchants and bankers were in control. The merchants had their own associations, the Italians, with their large meeting hall, being particularly well organized. Delos owed much of its prosperity to the slave trade and could handle, so it was said, 10,000 slaves in a day; but there was no real reason for its wealth, and in the first century it declined before the attacks of Mithridates.

The prevalence of slavery probably prevented the invention of machinery in antiquity, and consequently industry did not develop as rapidly as trade and commerce. Old Greece maintained its prosperity as compared with its own past—certainly there was little poverty or depopulation before the Roman Sulla in the first century—but it did not share the great increase in prosperity of the rest of the world. In fact, during the Hellenistic Age the center of industry shifted eastward to Asia Minor, Rhodes, and Egypt. Alexandria was easily the busiest industrial center, with factories for paper, textiles, oil, perfumery, beer, linen weaving, metal work, and so on. Alexandria, like Sidon, was famous for its glass, and, like Pergamum, had factories in which the workers were slaves and serfs. Pergamum had a monopoly of parchment, and its textiles, particularly its gold-woven cloth, enjoyed a great reputation. The demand for textiles was large; indeed, Greek textiles have been found in Mongolia. Miletus was the center of the wool industry, as Alexandria was of the linen. Cos spun silk from the thread of the wild silkworm of Asia Minor, though beginning in the first century Chinese silk was imported. In the West, Tarentum was noted for its textiles and its pottery, but fine ceramics were driven from the market by the demand for silver plate; ordinary pots came from Samos, Rhodes, and other places.

The spread of the Greek language and the gradual development of common principles and of a common law greatly helped trade. Trade was also promoted by the growth of a money economy, which was rare in the Near East before Alexander. There had always been money changers, but now the world saw regular banks—private, city, and state—which received money on deposit and made loans. Commerce, of course, needed credit, and the business in mercantile loans, as well as the investment business, was large. Cheques and letters of credit were in use. We have already said that Alexander's capture of the Persian bullion put an enormous amount of money into circulation, and the fact that there were fewer mints during the Hellenistic Age and that two main currencies became widely adopted served further to break down the barriers to trade. The Alexander-drachma was based on the Attic and was in use in Macedonia, Athens, Asia Minor, and the Seleucid Empire generally. The Ptolemies adopted the Phoenician standard, which was used at Carthage, Syracuse, and Massilia.

It is clear that the upper and middle classes were well off during the Hellenistic Age and that their higher standard of living stimulated trade. Wealth, however, was unevenly distributed, and the lot of the worker, as already stated, was bad, though nothing could equal the condition of the convicts in the mines and quarries. The free craftsman generally followed in his father's steps and was the victim of extreme specialization; for example, the stone mason did not sharpen his own tools. The free craftsman, too, had to compete with the serf and slave workshops of kings and priests in Egypt and Asia. There was a slow development of trade guilds, particularly in Egypt, but strikes were rare, passive resistance being adopted instead. As wages failed to rise, however, or actually fell, unemployment and social unrest followed. Some people began to advocate communism, especially as developed by the Stoics. There was a regular crop of Utopias, the most famous of which was Iambulus' Sun-State, situated on an island in the Indian Ocean. By the third century Delos and other cities were issuing free corn—Rome did not invent bread and circuses as an antidote to revolution—and by the second century revolts of slaves had broken out in Sicily, Greece, and Pergamum. In the midst of the great trade in slaves it is refreshing to note that Delphi steadily preached the necessity of manumission; it became common for a slave to purchase his freedom, generally by a "sale" to a god, and thereupon he acquired the status, essentially, of a metic. But the Cilician pirates, who throve on the slave trade, war, and the threat of domestic revolution retarded trade in the Hellenistic Age. To understand that period better, we must consider Egypt and Asia under Alexander's Successors in somewhat greater detail.

Chapter XXIV

EGYPT AND ASIA UNDER THE SUCCESSORS

PTOLEMAIC EGYPT

A STUDY of Egypt under the Ptolemies is doubly fascinating. In the first place the vast quantities of papyri that have been discovered in recent years give us an extraordinarily detailed picture of certain aspects of contemporary life. The papyri, which are chiefly official documents, come from outside Alexandria, so that unfortunately we cannot follow events closely in the capital itself, but must draw the main outline from provincial papers; how detailed this can be, however, can be seen from the fact that we are able to watch the progress of a single lawsuit over a period of ten years. And, in the second place, Ptolemaic Egypt is fascinating because it represents a vast experiment in state nationalization. Egypt stood apart from the Hellenistic world, for special reasons, and in some ways is practically unique in history. Because the king actually owned the valley of the Nile, because he was, in other words, the state, it was possible to regulate every private activity, so that a man who wished to go fishing, for example, not only had to obtain a license, but was accompanied by an official to make sure that 25 per cent of the catch went to the king.

The general lines of administration were laid down by Ptolemy II, and it can be said at the outset that the main purpose was to exploit the country to the uttermost. The task was made easier for Ptolemy, because over the centuries the Pharoahs had developed an intricate bureaucracy, which had, however, been allowed to decay during the Persian rule. The Ptolemies, of course, were aliens, and their chief problem was to reconcile the Egyptians to the new régime and to make it work. Egypt was a compact state, with seven or eight million people living beside the Nile, a people with long traditions, a great art, and an awe-inspiring religion. How was a new king to govern them? Obviously, Alexander's policy, which the Seleucids were following in Asia, of Hellenizing by means of new foundations would not succeed in this old settled society—and perhaps it suited the best interests of the Ptolemies, too, not to foster the idea of freedom within their kingdom. Greeks were necessary,[1] for in the last analysis the power of the Ptolemies rested on force, and this meant the importation of large numbers of Greek mercenaries. Greek initiative and industry, and Greek capital, were also needed to develop the country, and consequently the Ptolemies had to offer special inducements to persuade Greeks to settle in the land. The result was that the Greeks poured into Egypt, bent on making money and determined to maintain their old ways of life. Though they were impressed with the antiquity of Egypt and stood in some awe of the religion, the Greeks, on the whole, looked down upon the natives, kept to themselves, refused to learn the Egyptian language, and, for a time, would not intermarry. They brought with them their own life, their gymnasia and schools, and formed clubs under the protection of some deity. But they were divorced from political life, and although some of them might live in cities, they did not live in city-states, so that they were destined to lose the spirit of Greece and to keep only the external forms.

The great mass of Egyptian peasants (fellahin) was Hellenized, if at all, only superficially. The Machimoi, or old warrior class, eventually assumed some importance in the state, but the power of the priests, who formed the only native aristocracy in Egypt, was restricted. As time went on, an ambitious Egyptian, wishing to rise in the bureaucracy, would learn Greek and perhaps take a Greek name; and the Greeks outside the cities, where Greek women would not be numerous,

---

[1] The distinction between Greeks and Macedonians ceased to exist.

took Egyptian wives, so that distinction of race yielded to culture in importance. The Asiatics in Egypt, on the other hand, became Hellenized, at least superficially, and the Jews found it necessary to translate their scriptures, now renamed *Septuagint*, into Greek. Egypt, then, consisted of a conglomeration of new-comers from many lands, overlaid on a compact native foundation, and ruled by Graeco-Macedonian kings in their own interest, though the earlier kings, at least, considered the welfare of their subjects and brought some happiness to them.

The Greeks spread throughout all of Egypt, though they were most numerous in the three Greek cities of the land; in Naucratis, an old city where Greeks had lived for many centuries; in Alexandria, the capital, founded by Alexander the Great; and in Ptolemais, founded in Upper Egypt by Ptolemy I. These three cities were the only concessions to the Greek love of autonomy to be found in Egypt, and Alexandria was by far the most important; indeed, it was the metropolis of the civilized world. Deinocrates had laid out the city, with broad streets crossing each other at right angles, interrupted now and then by squares and parks (Map 56). The principal thoroughfare, known as Canopic Street, was 100 feet wide and ran from east to west. At its point of intersection with another street of equal width were located some of the chief buildings of the city, though the houses of ordinary men were impressive, being several stories in height. The landmark of Alexandria was the lighthouse by Sostratus of Cnidus, 400 feet high, on the island of Pharos, which was connected with the mainland by a mole, called the Heptastadion. Here were the busy harbors and docks. Alexandria, however, will be chiefly remembered for its Museum and Library, which Demetrius of Phaleron had helped Ptolemy I to found. Here we see the bid of the Ptolemies to create a sort of university center, rivaling Athens and giving some glamor and substance to a rule which, at heart, was sordid. The best scholars, scientists, poets, and artists of the day were invited to live in Alexandria, exempt from taxation, and it is interesting to observe how little real influence the city had on them; their work is chiefly Hellenic, international, not Alexandrian. The Library contained almost half a million rolls of papyri, and was presided over by a succession of great scholars; by Zenodotus of Ephesus, a Homeric scholar; Apollonius of Rhodes; Eratosthenes of Cyrene, perhaps the greatest librarian, a learned geographer; Aristophanes of Byzantium, another Homeric scholar.

Royal and civic buildings dominated the city. In the very center was the tomb of Alexander; near the Museum and Library were the palace, with its gardens, and the barracks for the Royal Guards. These Guards were Macedonians and were supplemented by heavy and light infantry, cavalry, mercenaries, elephants—the basis of Ptolemaic rule. In the harbor, nearby, rode the navy, a great expense to the Ptolemies and the wealthy citizens, who had to assume part of its cost as a liturgy. The vast bureaucracy had its offices in the city, but equally busy centers were the state bank for taxes paid in money and the granaries, where the corn, paid as taxes, was stored. Theaters, gymnasia, hippodromes, the Serapeum and other temples dotted the city, and the luxurious villas of the rich stretched to Canopus, the playground of the city masses. The population of Alexandria grew to about a million, and of these more than a third were "Alexandrians," as the free Greek citizens were called. In addition to the Greeks and Egyptians, however, were crowds of Persians, Jews, Syrians, Anatolians, and, indeed, Arabs, Indians, Negroes, and Italians—a motley conglomeration, ever ready to riot in the streets.

Alexandria was divided into five quarters, named after the letters of the alphabet, and the various nationalities tended to congregate in groups (*politeumata*). The most important group consisted of the Greeks, for they were the citizens. Their constitution was not unlike that of a *polis;* the people were divided into tribes and demes, chose their own magistrates, and passed laws through their Assembly and Council. The Jews also enjoyed special rights, for they were valued by the Ptolemies as good soldiers. Ptolemy could interfere with municipal administration, if he wished, and in time the authority of the autonomous Greek city of Ptolemais was circumscribed by the governor (*epistrategos*) of the Thebaid. The court of the Ptolemies was essentially Macedonian, though it revealed the influence of the Egyptian and Persian courts, with the extraordinary number of officials and titles, ministers, courtiers, eunuchs, and slaves. The pomp was un-Greek, but the language, dress, and externals remained Greek—the rulers, like the Alexandrians, did not marry natives, though the Egyptian custom of brother-and-sister marriage grew apace (for example, Ptolemy II and Arsinoe II, Figure 100).

At the top of the entire administration was the king, who always took the name Ptolemy, but the dynasty is also termed Lagid, after Lagus, the father of the first Ptolemy. Though the Ptolemies claimed to be descended from Dionysus and Heracles, and though the old cults of Zeus and other Greek gods still persisted, it was the mystical religions, such as the Eleusinian mysteries and the cult of Adonis, which appealed chiefly to the Greeks. The Ptolemies had to reconcile the Greeks, as well as the Egyptians, to their absolute rule. This they did, in the case of the Greeks, by the encouragement of essays upon the theory of kingship and the proposition that the rule of one man, the best, was the ideal form of government. It was not difficult for the Greeks to accept their rulers as divine, for it seemed natural that a man of great merit should be counted as a god. Ptolemy I had created a state cult of Alexander, thus giving the dynasty a certain legitimacy, and Ptolemy II further legitimatized it by declaring his parents gods. Temples were erected for Ptolemy I and Berenice, the Savior Gods, and every four years a festival of great magnificence was celebrated in their honor. Ptolemy II and Arsinoe shared a temple with Alexander, where they were worshipped as the Brother-and-Sister Gods. The Egyptian religion, especially the cult of Serapis, was partially taken over by the Greeks, who were also prone to worship Egyptian gods under Greek names, but the Ptolemies, to strengthen their rule, completely accepted the Egyptian religion. They appeared on the walls of temples with the dress and titles of the ancient Pharaohs, but they cut down the privileges of the priests as much as they dared; for example, though the temples were allowed the special privilege of continuing the manufacture of linen, the linen could be used only in the temples and some of it had to be given to the king; or, again, the peasants on temple land were compelled to pay rent to the king, instead of to the temple, and thus lost their feeling of dependence on the priests.

As the head of the religion and army, as the embodiment of the state itself, the king was surrounded by a multitude of officials, many of whom had their own courts. The chief personage after the king, as might be expected in a mercantile state, was the Minister of Finance (*Dioecetes,* manager). If Ptolemy II was the richest of all Hellenistic monarchs, his *Dioecetes* Apollonius must have been a close second, for he maintained an elaborate court in the capital and owned thousands of acres, including Philadelphia and several other villages, and even found time to engage in overseas trade on his own account. A voluminous correspondence with Zeno, his steward in the Fayum, has come down to us. Ptolemy II, who, we have said, laid down the general lines of administration, treated Egypt like a conquered country. He kept the old Pharaonic division of Egypt into nomes, about forty; the nomes of Upper Egypt, the Thebaid, were separate, but all the nomes were divided into districts (toparchies) and these were divided again into villages. The titular head of a nome was the nomarch, or governor, an office to which a native might aspire, but it lost much of its importance. The real head was the Greek general, *strategos,* who was responsible for maintaining order in his nome and perhaps was the chief judge in criminal suits; he had no control, however, over financial affairs, which were left to the *economus.* Though the Ptolemies could issue a law at any time they wished, they were content to let the Egyptians live under their old laws. Egypt, then, had two legal systems, for the Greeks, we have seen, passed their own laws. Accordingly, it was necessary to have two different methods for the administration of justice. Civil suits between natives were tried before the Laocritae, native judges, while Greek judges, called Chrematistae, went on circuit to hear the suits of the Greeks. Justice was not always speedy nor sure, but Ptolemy tried to make himself accessible to his subjects by keeping a window through which any one might throw a petition. A mixed court tried suits between Greeks and natives, but by the second century, when race tended to be more a matter of culture, the language in which the documents were written decided the appropriate court. An army of minor officials was also necessary for the postal service, for the up-keep of roads, canals, and dams, and for the collection and storage of produce paid as rent and taxes. These minor officials received a small salary which was supplemented by graft (though they were carefully supervised), and planned to make their work a life career, hoping meanwhile to rise in the complex bureaucracy. To keep a strict account of the people and land of Egypt minute statistics were gathered in each village, in each nome, and in the capital itself.

The Greeks lived not only in the three Greek cities, but also in Memphis, Egypt's ancient capital, and in other native towns, and in villages scattered along the countryside. They came as traders and soldiers, and to secure more room for them, to say nothing of increasing the possibilities for wealth, Ptolemy II drained Lake Moeris, to the west of the Nile, and thus won a large district for cultivation, known as the Fayum. Except for Naucratis, Alexandria, and Ptolemais, the king owned all the land, which can be divided into two classes. The King's Land he occupied himself, theoretically. It was worked by the King's Peasants, in reality serfs, who were not allowed to leave it and who had to pay the king a large rent, in money or kind. The other class of land may be described as semiprivate; it consisted of estates given to favorites, the sacred land of temples, and the lots (*kleroi*) given to soldiers. The Greek soldiers, of course, received the largest lots. The idea was to make life in Egypt attractive, to give the soldiers something to do during periods of peace, and incidentally to increase the productivity of the land. Every occupant of land paid rent to the king, but in practice the king allowed a cleruch—a soldier who had received a lot—to will his lot to his son, for this would insure a permanent military class. The land of Egypt was strictly supervised to make certain that every drachma was wrung from it. It was forbidden to cut a tree without permission, garden produce was taxed, the king owned all the pasture land and charged a fee for its use, in addition to the tax placed on the animals themselves, on the horses, donkeys, camels, sheep, goats, and geese. The state decided what the land should be used for; whether for cereals, flax, vegetables, orchards, or vineyards; the actual amount to be raised was determined in advance; and the King's Peasants were given the seed to sow. Irrigation received the closest attention, since life in Egypt depended on the regulation of the Nile's flood; forced labor on the canals was a regular part of life. Crops were rotated, excellent manures were used, new breeds of sheep were imported, the bee industry was studied, and, in short, everything was done to improve Egyptian agriculture.

It is clear, then, that the Ptolemies received an enormous income, in money and in kind, from the land. The chief staple was wheat, and the tax on this land was always paid directly to the king in kind. We can watch the wretched fellahin bringing their grain to the threshing floor; thence it was brought to the granaries of village and nome on donkeys, which had been pressed into service, and then finally it was borne down the Nile, on barges belonging to the king, to be placed in the great storage houses of Alexandria. Of particular interest is the oil industry, which was one of several state monopolies. Because olive trees were scarce in Egypt, oil was secured from sesame, linseed, and other plants. The quantity to be planted in each nome was strictly fixed by the king, for he was to buy the entire output. The grower sold the crop to the state at a fixed price, the oil was made in state factories, and the retail price was fixed by the state. A 50 per cent tax was placed on imported oil, so that Ptolemy's immense profit might not be affected adversely. Ptolemy II sold his oil at fifty-two drachmas the *metretes,* almost three times the cost of real olive oil at Delos, for example. Imported wine and wool paid customs taxes of 33½ and 20 per cent, respectively.

Customs dues were collected at the ports and even on the borders of the nomes. They effectively swelled Ptolemy's treasury, or prevented competition with his monopolies. In addition to his oil monopoly, the kind had a monopoly in textiles, in papyrus, the ancient writing paper, in various mines, including salt, and in banking; and either licensed or owned outright many types of business—dyeing, leather, perfumery, cosmetics, glass, pottery, the brewing of beer, and so on. Industry flourished in Alexandria because of the large local demand and because many raw materials were turned into finished articles for export to the Mediterranean world. The chief exports were grain, paper, linen, blown glass, and various luxuries, such as cosmetics; the chief imports from the Mediterranean were metals, timber, marble, and purple dyes, whereas from southern Arabia and India came frankincense, myrrh, spices, and silk. The trade with the Aegean promoted money as a medium of exchange, but the Ptolemies, unlike Alexander's other Successors, did not follow the Attic standard, but the Phoenician. The currency was bimetallic, with the ratio of gold to silver in the early third century standing at 13 to 1, though debasement and inflation brought on by wars caused the silver later to lose much of its value; in the country districts copper was used extensively and, indeed, barter was never entirely abandoned. To encourage the trade with the East Ptolemy II reopened the old canal between the Nile and the Red Sea; it soon fell into disuse, however, and goods from the East were landed at Red Sea ports instead and brought overland. The main route crossed the desert between Berenice and Coptos, and was policed and provided with wells. Elephants were a familiar sight, being brought from further Africa by special barges, then overland to Coptos, where they were floated down the Nile to be used in warfare. Tracks also ran into the desert to the porphyry, granite, alabaster, and limestone quarries, which were another royal monopoly. Wages for the ordinary workman, a drachma a day or less, were so small that slaves were little used, except in households, but conditions were so bad that the workers often rioted or went on strike; that is to say, they sought sanctuary in a temple and refused to return to work until their demands, generally very moderate, were met, though some workers, such as sailors, were well enough organized in guilds to be able to force a raise in their pay.

It would be impossible to list the many taxes, over 200 in number, some of them incredibly petty and annoying, but it is clear that Ptolemy reaped a profit almost every time a man moved in Egypt. A large revenue was necessary to keep up the bureaucracy and the splendor of the courts, to pay for the army and the navy, and to construct various public buildings. Ptolemy's chief revenue, we have seen, was the land, with industry next, but everyone, except the priests, the soldiers, and officials, paid a poll tax; trades and professions were licensed; men and animals were requisitioned to move the harvest and to repair the dykes (a service from which the Greeks were exempt, thanks to a special tax); the wealthy were burdened with liturgies and with the obligation to give "crowns" to the rulers on special occasions. There was a 10 per cent sales tax, a tax of 5 per cent on the rent of a house, an inheritance tax, a tax on slaves. We have also seen that one army of officials kept a strict account of every item of wealth in the country, whereas another army was necessary to collect the taxes. The rent of the King's Land and the tax in kind on the cornland were collected directly by the state; most taxes, except those on cornland, were paid in money, and it was customary to farm them out, often to corporations.

The Ptolemies had possessions outside Egypt, in Asia Minor, Syria, the Cyclades, Cyprus, and other islands, and even in the Argolid, at Methana. They showed little respect for their Greek cities, subjecting them to heavy taxation, and ruling them through garrisons commanded by a general.

The Egyptians never accepted the Greeks, who not only were their political masters, but had appropriated the best land and grown rich at their expense. After the battle of Raphia (217 B.C.), when Egyptian troops were used, native revolts broke out and continued intermittently for a century. The Ptolemies were unable to crush these revolts at one fell swoop by importing mercenaries, for the supply of the Greek home-land was fast drying up, and, besides, the Ptolemies now had less land to hold out as inducements for newcomers. The Ptolemies, therefore, were forced to rely more and more upon the Machimoi, the native sol-dier class, and to make various concessions to Egyptian sentiment; for example, more temples were granted the right of sanctuary. In spite of all this, the fusion of races continued, and, had not Rome stepped in to stop the process, would have probably ended with the submer-gence of the Greeks. As it was, the Greeks lost their spirit, keeping up only their language and the externals of their civilization, and becom-ing Egyptianized in blood, religion, and customs; in return, the Egyp-tians received a veneer of Greek civilization. Terrible as life was for the Egyptian peasants under the Ptolemies, it could be much worse and was under the Romans.

SELEUCID ASIA

If our information for Ptolemaic Egypt is fairly abundant, the pre-cise opposite is true of Seleucid Asia. This is greatly to be regretted, for the Seleucid Empire was so vast and the policy of Hellenization so intensive that in many ways we are confronted with the most interest-ing of the Hellenistic states. The extent of the Seleucid Empire varied from time to time, depending on the outcome of foreign struggles, but at its greatest it reached from the Hellespont to the Indus. The prob-lems of government were tremendous. Not only did many races inhabit this Empire—Greek, Semitic, Iranian—not only did the customs differ sharply from one section to another, some of them dating from pre-Aryan days, but each area had its own traditions of life and govern-ment, which no ruler could afford to overlook. The center of the Seleu-cid Empire was Syria, which, with Palestine, Babylonia, and Assyria, formed a compact Semitic mass. The land to the east was essentially

Iranian, and to the west lay Asia Minor, a conglomeration of civilizations. Along the Asia Minor coast were old established Greek cities, but the population of the interior was heterogeneous.

To administer a state of such size and complexity was no easy task. One course open to the Seleucids was to rest content with a sort of overlordship, allowing each area wide latitude in local matters; another course would have been to attempt rigid control from the center; in actual fact, however, Seleucid policy fell somewhere between the two. The old Persian system of decentralization was adopted, a wise plan for the heirs of a successful Empire to follow, but in addition Alexander's scheme of Hellenization was carried on in the hope of bringing unity to the realm. Unfortunately we do not know how many scores of settlements were founded by the Seleucids, but we do know that the great founders were Seleucus I, Antiochus I, and Antiochus IV. These settlements were islands of Hellenism, destined to bring Greek ideas, Greek law, and Greek life to numberless Asiatics—they were also designed to promote trade and to be the chief prop of the state, for naturally the Greek and Macedonian inhabitants vigorously supported their king. Because the Seleucid Empire consisted essentially of king, army, and bureaucracy, held together by the personality of the quasidivine monarch standing above the clash of nationalities, the main object of the Seleucids in filling Asia with Greek settlements was to make of the unwieldy Empire a strong state—in short, to give to the framework of the Empire substance and living tissue. Cities and military colonies were founded along trade routes, especially along the great route that ran from Mesopotamia to the Asia Minor coast; beyond the Taurus, the Seleucids rarely held much except the actual route, until Ionia was reached. East of Mesopotamia Alexander's foundations were maintained, and new settlements were created, but we do not know whether they were founded in groups or not. Northern Syria was in a special category, for so many Greeks and Macedonians settled there that the entire district became a second Greece.

The basis of the Seleucid settlement of Asia was the military colony and not the Greek city, the *polis*. It would have been too much for any one king to found many *poleis,* for this meant that the king must find land for the city, build a wall, supply food, seed corn, cattle, and tools to give the people a start; he must also remit taxation until the city was on its feet, give it a constitution, and settle the city law, probably by the adoption of some well-known city code. The founding of a military colony, on the other hand, could be delegated to a subordinate. The idea went back to Alexander. The military colony was located near a native village and was settled with time-expired troops, who were generally Greeks west of the Euphrates and who received from the king the land and money required. Each settler was given a *kleros,* an allotment of land that carried with it the obligation to serve in the army, if needed. The military colony was walled, because it existed primarily for defense. It was a planned foundation, with its own officials and with some control of its internal affairs. The official language was Greek. Every military colony hoped in time to become a full *polis;* that is to say, the inhabitants, whether Greeks or not, hoped to achieve Greek organization and civic forms. The *poleis,* many of which were founded with the help of the old Ionian cities, had of course greater autonomy, with their own Council and Assembly; the Greek population was divided into tribes and elected the magistrates. The king's represenative (*epistates*) within the city stood above the clash of nationalities. These new cities were tied to the king by any terms he wished to impose; in fact, the rights of the various cities within the Empire constituted almost the sole limitation to the king's power. The evolution of the military colonies in *poleis* was one of the great achievements of the Seleucids, for it was this which really affected Asia, because it caused many Asiatics to desire the form of the Greek *polis.*

The problem of the Seleucids was not simply to govern Greeks and natives, for the Greeks themselves formed two classes, those of the old cities in Asia Minor and those of the new foundations. The Asiatics, we have already said, had their own age-old traditions of life. The picture was further complicated by the existence in western Asia and Asia Minor of a large number of temple-states. These temple-states, which were of great antiquity, had generally succeeded in maintaining their separate existence, no matter who happened to rule Asia. The territory of a temple-state varied in size, but its center was a town, with priests, temple, and female sacred slaves, sometimes several thousand in number, who for a period prostituted themselves to the Great Mother of Asia. The district roundabout was cultivated by the peasants, who were serfs, and each year a colorful fair was held in the town. The Empire inherited by the Seleucids also contained great estates owned by grandees, who lived in fortified castles and looked upon themselves as independent; and, indeed, within the Empire, or on its very borders, were independent native dynasts, such as those of Armenia, Phrygia, Pontus, and Cappadocia.

The only practicable plan for the Seleucids was to stand in a different relation to the various peoples, cities, and states within the Empire, enforcing their will where they could and yielding where it was politic. The general scheme of administration can be recovered, though our sources fail us at many points. At the head of the state was the king, descended from Apollo and worshipped, by some Greeks at least, as a Benefactor; the cult of the king served as a bond for the entire Empire. The king's court was essentially Macedonian, with oriental features. In addition to the Chief Minister, Council, and Secretariat, there were Friends, Kinsmen, tutors, physicians, and so on. The court was not unlike the Egyptian, except that it was not nearly so elaborate, and the entire government was far less bureaucratic. This was due primarily to the fact that the Seleucids did not rule a compact state, like Egypt, and secondarily to the great cost of war, foreign and domestic. The Persian system of government through satrapies was taken over. The country was divided into twenty-five or more satrapies, and these were broken up into some seventy-two eparchies, with a further subdivision into hyparchies. The governor of each satrapy was a general, but the financial administration was under a separate official, called the *economus,* who was responsible to the *Dioecetes* at Antioch. The famous royal roads and postal service united various parts of the Empire.

If the policy of intensive Hellenization differentiated the Seleucids from the Ptolemies, so too did their treatment of the land. The Seleucids had inherited what was called King's Land, and this was very extensive. Some of it they occupied themselves, theoretically, and it was worked by the King's Peasants, who paid taxes in kind or money to officials of the state. The rest of the King's Land was held in grant by wealthy landowners; for example, by the grandees mentioned above; the workers on these lands were serfs. The Seleucids broke the independent power of these grandees where they could, and not infrequently sold the land to the workers, on the condition that the land should be attached to a city. The sale netted the king much needed money and diminished serfdom, for the workers on city land were peasants and not serfs. The Seleucids also deprived many temple-states of their political power, and consequently of much of their wealth, but they allowed them religious freedom. The old Greek cities of Asia Minor were intermittently free and subject, depending on the strength of the individual king; speaking generally, they were tied to the Seleucids by an alliance. At times they were taxed, at times not; but on the whole they were allowed internal autonomy, and each had its city land. Ephesus, at the end of a great trade route, was the largest city on the coast of Asia Minor, but Miletus, which had a thriving wool industry, had at least 100,000 souls, and so too, probably, did Smyrna. Nearby, in the Aegean, were Delos, a center of brokers rather than a city, and Rhodes, a great social and cultural capital, which believed in free trade and tried to maintain a balance of power in the world. Greek and Macedonian soldiers, as already stated, were placed on the land by the thousand. The king probably retained title to the land, which was not regained for cultivation. In the new foundations Greeks predominated, of course, since one of the primary purposes was the Hellenization of the Empire, but many other races congregated in them, each race generally forming its own *politeuma,* or quarter. Different types of land—King's Land, temple land, and the city land of the Greek cities—no less than the diverse races in the Empire contributed to the problems of the Seleucids.

The capital of this great Empire was in northern Syria, at Antioch on the Orontes. Antioch was a Greek city of about half a million inhabitants, but it included many Jews, Syrians, and other races. Josephus, the distinguished historian of the Jews, tells us that the Jews enjoyed the same rights as the Greeks. The Greeks were divided into tribes and eighteen demes, and had their own Assembly, Council, and magistrates. Antioch was not a center of learning in the sense that Alexandria was, but it did produce some good art and later became the capital of Christianity. Antioch was primarily a city of trade and pleasure—its suburb Daphne was famous for its luxury, as most of the Greek towns of northern Syria were, and this tradition is being confirmed today by the quantities of house mosaics, some of them very fine, which the highly successful excavations are uncovering (Figure 102). Circumstances, however, forced the Seleucids to spend little upon artists and officials, though, as the capital city, Antioch was naturally the center of the land registry bureau and other offices. Near Antioch was Apamea, the arsenal of the Empire, where weapons, war elephants, 300 stallions, and 30,000 mares were kept; and not far from the mouth of the Orontes lay Antioch's port, Seleuceia in Pieria. Further down the coast was the commercial city of Laodicea. The capital of the eastern part of the Empire was Seleuceia on the Tigris, where the heir apparent generally lived. This great city, with its 600,000 inhabitants, was larger than Antioch itself; many different peoples lived in it, with the Greeks, who were formed in a *polis,* predominating.

The life blood of the Seleucid Empire was trade. A glance at the maps on pp. 389, 405, and 425 will show that Seleuceia on the Tigris was the terminus for the overland trade from the Eastern provinces and for the trade coming up the Persian Gulf, which, it was hoped, would damage the Red Sea traffic of the Ptolemies. From Seleuceia on the Tigris the caravans went north along the Tigris or Euphrates to Zeugma and Antioch, and thence over the Taurus to Ionia. At Dura-Europos, on the Euphrates, an alternate route later crossed the Syrian desert to the oasis of Palmyra and continued to the great highway running north from Petra through Damascus to Antioch; this "highway," it will

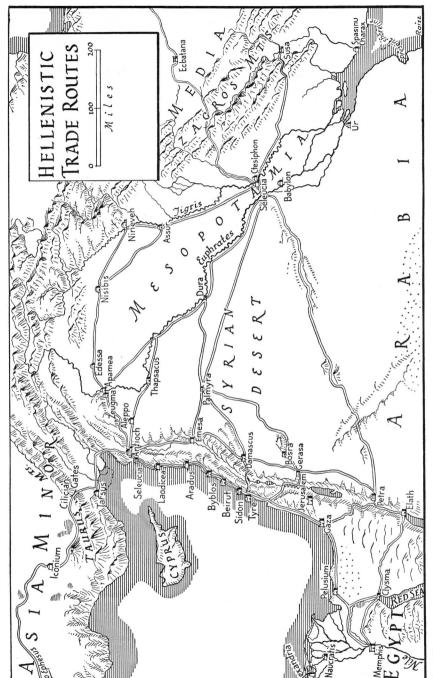

HELLENISTIC
TRADE ROUTES

Miles

0   100   200

ASIA MINOR

to Ephesus

Iconium

Cilician
Gates

TAURUS MTS.

Tarsus

Seleucia

Laodicea

CYPRUS

Aradus

Byblos

Beirut

Sidon

Tyre

Pelusium

Gaza

Jerusalem

Gerasa

Bosra

Damascus

Emesa

Palmyra

Antioch

Aleppo

Zeugma

Apamea

Edessa

Thapsacus

Dura

Nisibis

Assur

Nineveh

MESOPOTAMIA

Tigris

Euphrates

MEDIA

ZAGROS MTS.

Ecbatana

Ctesiphon

Seleucia

Babylon

Susa

Ur

Spasinu
Charax

Sbore

Raisz

ARABIA

SYRIAN   DESERT

Petra

Elath

Clysma

RED SEA

EGYPT

Memphis

Naucratis

Alexandria

Nile

Map 50

425

be seen, also joined at various points the paralled coast road from Pelusium and Tyre to Antioch. Fleets stationed in the Persian Gulf and Mediterranean, together with the army of regular soldiers and mercenaries, protected this trade and commerce; but of equal importance were the military colonies and cities, especially those in the interior of Asia Minor, at river crossings, oases, and other strategic points. The Seleucids placed a tax on commerce, but unfortunately our knowledge of the entire subject is very slight. We do know, however, that Seleucid taxes were relatively light, much less than the Egyptian. The Seleucids derived a large income from the famous tithe on King's Land, which took a fixed percentage from a peasant and not a fixed amount—the hated Ptolemaic system might ruin a peasant in a poor year. The sums paid by cities as taxes or tribute constituted another source of income, as did harbor dues and the mines, one of the few state monopolies. Various industries flourished in the Empire, and an inscription from Sardes, the capital of Lydia and the center for the manufacture of beautiful carpets, reveals how the temples, through their wealth and corporate permanence, fulfilled many of the functions of modern banks. The Attic standard was adopted for the coinage, with mints at Antioch and in the provinces. (For a plan of a caravan city, see Map 51).

The Greek cities with their ephebes, gymnasia, and theaters, spread Hellenism throughout the Empire, but the Asiatic remained, at bottom, unaffected by Greek civilization. In the Greek cities of Asia Minor Hellenism remained fairly pure, and elsewhere in Asia the Greeks maintained their political organization, their names and language, and, above all, their laws, though their life and religion were greatly modified by the Asiatics. The native elements in Iran successfully resisted Hellenism, especially in religious matters, partly because the Seleucids followed a policy of peaceful fusion, without trying to suppress the Asiatic element, and partly because Greek culture was of the city, whereas Zoroastrianism was the religion of the cultivated land. The Seleucids never won the confidence of the Iranian landowners, which Alexander had recognized as vital; in fact, the Iranian civilization, like the Babylonian, was too strong for the Greeks to affect. Perhaps, however, the chief reason why the Seleucids failed to Hellenize Asia was because the area was too vast. Greek eventually yielded in the Tigris-Euphrates valley to Aramaic, but not for several centuries; some parchments from Avroman, in Assyria, which record deeds of sale in the first century A.D., are written in Greek, though the persons mentioned in the documents have Iranian names. Eastern Hellenism did not receive its death blow until 164 A.D., when the Romans destroyed Seleuceia on the Tigris.

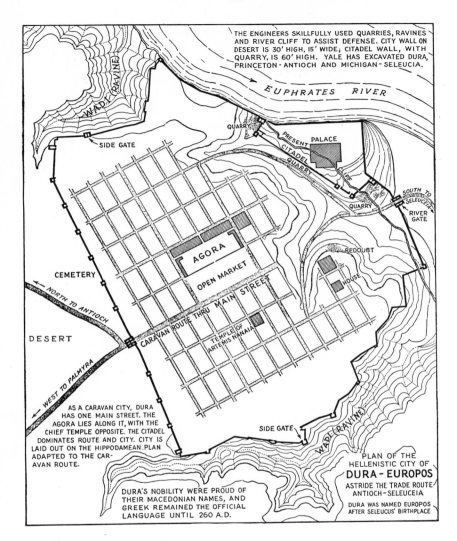

THE ENGINEERS SKILLFULLY USED QUARRIES, RAVINES AND RIVER CLIFF TO ASSIST DEFENSE. CITY WALL ON DESERT IS 30' HIGH, 15' WIDE; CITADEL WALL, WITH QUARRY, IS 60' HIGH. YALE HAS EXCAVATED DURA, PRINCETON - ANTIOCH AND MICHIGAN - SELEUCIA.

EUPHRATES RIVER

WADI (RAVINE)

SIDE GATE

QUARRY

PRESENT CITADEL QUARRY

PALACE

SOUTH TO SELEUCIA

QUARRY

RIVER GATE

CEMETERY

NORTH TO ANTIOCH

AGORA

OPEN MARKET

REDOUBT

HOUSE

CARAVAN ROUTE THRU MAIN STREET

DESERT

WEST TO PALMYRA

TEMPLE OF ARTEMIS NANAIA

AS A CARAVAN CITY, DURA HAS ONE MAIN STREET. THE AGORA LIES ALONG IT, WITH THE CHIEF TEMPLE OPPOSITE. THE CITADEL DOMINATES ROUTE AND CITY. CITY IS LAID OUT ON THE HIPPODAMEAN PLAN ADAPTED TO THE CARAVAN ROUTE.

SIDE GATE

WADI (RAVINE)

PLAN OF THE HELLENISTIC CITY OF DURA - EUROPOS
ASTRIDE THE TRADE ROUTE ANTIOCH - SELEUCEIA
DURA WAS NAMED EUROPOS AFTER SELEUCUS' BIRTHPLACE

DURA'S NOBILITY WERE PROUD OF THEIR MACEDONIAN NAMES, AND GREEK REMAINED THE OFFICIAL LANGUAGE UNTIL 260 A.D.

Map 51

The Seleucids had many enemies. They stabilized their relations with the native dynasts of Asia Minor by treaties, but the Galatians and Ptolemies and ultimately the Romans opposed them. The greatest enemy of the Seleucid Empire, however, was Pergamum. For a brief period in the third century, and again from 188–133 B.C., Pergamum ruled much of Asia Minor and hence deprived the Seleucids of one of their most important areas. The Attalids were looked upon as intruders in the Hellenistic world, upstarts who finally betrayed Hellenism by willing their state to Rome. Because of their opposition to the Galatians, however, the Attalids liked to look upon themselves as the defenders of Hellenism. They made their capital, Pergamum, a center of the Greek world, where a few literary persons and some excellent artists gathered. The great altar to Zeus Soter, the library, temples, theaters, and gymnasia made the city something of a showplace. The Attalids themselves lived simply, as far as appearances went at least, their palace being little more than a private house, and they further proclaimed their devotion to Hellenism by ostentatious gifts to Greece.

Eumenes II adopted the Seleucid system of government, though in foreign policy Pergamum was hostile to the Seleucids and friendly to the Ptolemies. The kings and queens of Pergamum were worshipped during their life-time, and upon death became gods. The Attalids founded few cities, but they allowed the King's Land to grow, especially in the native districts, where the workers were serfs. The satrapies were ruled by generals. Of the old Greek cities some were free, while others were subject and paid taxes. In the capital itself the people were divided into tribes and demes, with their own Assembly, Council, and magistrates; but in reality the king held the power, for he appointed the five generals, who alone presided at the meetings of the Assembly and proposed motions. The Attalids will be chiefly remembered as money makers. Their serfs and slaves worked on the farms and in the factories. Trade from the East and the populous cities of the coast added to their wealth. The royal factories at Pergamum were famous for their fine parchment and textiles, while the abundant pitch from Mt. Ida was in demand for the ships of the day. The kingdom of Pergamum will also be remembered as the power which weakened the Seleucids. Some day, no doubt, excavations will make clearer the details of the great Empire which embraced so much of Asia.

BACTRIA AND INDIA

The Hellenistic kingdoms, as we have seen, knew three state-forms: Antigonid Macedonia, with a monarchy limited by the rights of the people under arms; Seleucid Asia, with a monarchy limited by the rights of many more or less autonomous cities; and Ptolemaic Egypt, with an unfettered monarchy. (The Attalids of Pergamum, who were successivly the protegés of Egypt and of Rome, were of secondary importance.) These three state forms, though each went back to some aspect of Alexander's monarchy, were not voluntarily limited by the rights of the native subjects, except in religious matters. The significance of the Greek kingdom of Bactria and India is that it tried to put into practice Alexander's dream of cooperation between peoples. Until recently the story of the Bactrian Greeks has been relegated to Indian history, where it has no meaning, but now, thanks to the labors of a distinguished British scholar,[2] our very fragmentary evidence—brief notices in Oriental and Western literature, and coins [3]—has been sorted and arranged, so that we now have not four, but five Hellenistic dynasties.

About the middle of the third century before Christ, when the Seleucid grip on the East was weakening and the Parni were creating their kingdom of Parthia, Bactria (today northern Afghanistan) became the shield of the Graeco-Iranian world against the nomads, just as previously Macedonia had protected the Greeks from the barbarians of the North. Bactria, then, was a march state. History abundantly proves that such a state, under the stimulus of external pressure, can develop such strength that it will not only master the pressure, but have plenty of energy over for other purposes.

The period of Bactrian history which chiefly concerns us is covered by three reigns, those of Euthydemus, his son Demetrius, and Demetrius' son-in-law Meander; roughly the first half of the second century B.C. In 246 B.C., or thereabouts, when Ptolemy III made his parade through the Seleucid Empire as far as Seleuceia, Seleucus II gave his sister, a daughter of Antiochus II, to Diodotus, the satrap of Bactria-Sogdiana. Seleucus hoped thus to keep his hold on the eastern provinces, but apparently the satrapy slowly broke away, and about 228 B.C. Diodotus' successor took the royal title. The successor, Diodotus II, was not of Seleucid blood, being a son by a former marriage, and immediately reversed his father's foreign policy by allying himself with the enemies of the Seleucids, the Parthians. The new policy was distasteful, no doubt, to the Bactrian Greeks and particularly to the queen mother, the Seleucid widow of Diodotus I. She now gave a daughter in marriage to Euthydemus, a Greek from Magnesia on the Maeander, probably a Bactrian satrap at the time, who conspired to kill Diodotus II and took the crown.

So long as the Seleucids were strong, Euthydemus confined himself to what had been the Bactrian satrapy; that is, to Bactria and Sogdiana. Indeed, in 208 B.C., he had to stand a siege of two years from Antiochus

[2] W. W. Tarn (*The Greeks in Bactria and India,* Cambridge University Press, 1938), whose kind permission has made possible this sketch.

[3] The Bactrian coins, with their wonderful portraiture, are purely Greek and show the vitality of Hellenism in the East (Figs. 90 b, c and 47, No. 10).

III, which was only terminated when it was brought home to Antiochus what would happen to the Hellenic world, if the Sacas and other nomads should be called in. Antiochus raised the siege and made an alliance with Euthydemus, and then, after a brief glimpse of India, as if he were Alexander, returned home. Soon after 206 B.C. Euthydemus crossed the Arius and captured a small district, Margiane and its center Merv, from the Parthians, which he left under his son Antimachus, as subking. The institution of subkings, quite distinct from that of joint kings, was peculiar to the Euthydemid dynasty. Euthydemus also struck out in another direction, to Ferghana, on the route to Chinese Turkestan. He hoped that he might reopen the old gold route to China, which the shifting of populations had closed, and that he might reach the Seres, who were the middlemen in the gold trade, around Lake Issyk Kul. Though he failed to obtain gold, Euthydemus did procure nickel, which originated in China; and he was responsible for Hellenic influences and products traveling far to the East. Bactria's most important trade, however, was with India; the capital Bactra, the modern Balkh, was a clearing house for the Indian trade with the West.

The kernel of Euthydemus' kingdom was Bactria and southern Sogdiana, an enormously fertile country. Bactria was famous as "the land of a thousand cities," and Bactra as "the paradise of the earth." Bactra, the traditional home of Zoroastrianism, was a great fortress, with a striking temple to its native goddess Anaïtis. The first business of the Greek king of Bactria was to protect this land, the gateway of Iran, from the semi-barbarism of the north, and in particular to guard against the strong confederacy of the Massagetae, who were massed across the Oxus and Jaxartes rivers. For purposes of administration and defense Bactria-Sogdiana was divided into a number of satrapies, which corresponded roughly to the old Seleucid eparchies. The governors were generals, and on the whole the administrative system was based on that of the Seleucids. No doubt many thousands of Greek settlers had come to Bactria from the West during the third century, and these had made their homes in cities and military colonies. The country itself possessed the ordinary Iranian feudal system; the land, other than the King's Land with its serfs, was in the hands of Iranian barons, who had their own strongholds.

But how are we to explain "the thousand cities" of Bactria? The only explanation possible is that the Euthydemids so raised the general level of the serf population, and therefore of the villages, that the serf village evolved into an organized and quasi-autonomous township. This was one of the most important things done by the Greeks in Asia, for it was this which really touched the native mass. In some way the

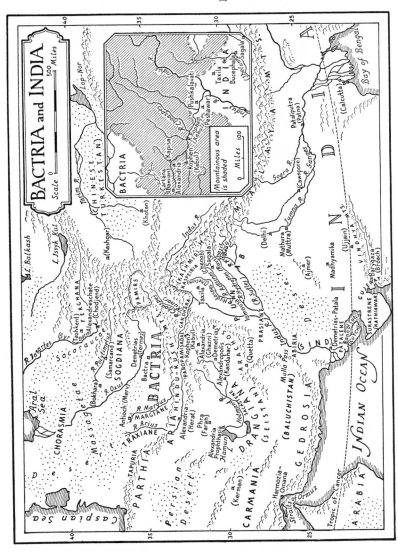

Map 53

Map 52

431

Euthydemids won the loyalty of the Bactrian aristocracy. We must imagine something like a double state, with the Bactrian landowners managing their estates and yet coming to court and sharing in the administration. Unlike any of the other Successors, the Euthydemids gained the support of Iran, because they took it into partnership.

Euthydemus probably died about 189 B.C., not long after the battle of Magnesia, a battle which, owing to Rome's power, shook the foundations of the Seleucid Empire. He was succeeded by his son Demetrius, who, by 184 B.C., annexed the three Seleucid provinces of Aria, Arachosia, and Seistan, and thus gained control of the trade routes between India and the West. He also captured eastern Gedrosia for its spices. In Arachosia Demetrius founded an important city, Demetrias, and he also controlled the land of the Paropamisadae, below the Hindu Kush, where many Greeks lived. Demetrius' thoughts now turned to India. He intended to copy Alexander, and to sit on the throne of the Mauryas as Alexander had sat on the throne of the Persian Achaemenids. His idea of an empire, which was to be a kind of partnership between Greek and Indian, was inspired by the Alexander who had dreamt of a human brotherhood. Demetrius was not guided by sentiment any more than Euthydemus had been; but, desiring a great empire, they believed that in the world of their day cooperation between Greek and Asiatic, such as Alexander had envisaged, offered the best chance of making one.

Profound changes had taken place in India since Alexander's day. Then it had been a land of disconnected states, but soon after his death much of the country, including most of the peninsula, was welded into a strong empire by the great Maurya Chandragupta and his grandson, Asoka. The capital was at Pataliputra (Patna) on the Ganges. The Greeks knew something of Chandragupta from the Seleucid envoy Megasthenes. It is important for what follows to note that Asoka was converted to Buddhism, though Brahmanism remained strong.

It was the death of Asoka and the decline of the Mauryan Empire that gave Demetrius his opportunity. In 183 B.C. Demetrius crossed the Hindu Kush, having appointed his eldest son, Euthydemus II, as joint king of Bactria-Sogdiana. At Alexandria-Kapisa, the capital of the Paropamisadae, he left his son Demetrius II as subking. The task of Demetrius II was to govern the Paropamisadae and Gandhara—everything, that is, between the Hindu Kush and the Indus—and to keep open the line of communications with Bactria. Demetrius, however, came to India as no ordinary conqueror, for, as we have said, he took Alexander as his model. He wore the elephant scalp, the symbol of Alexander's power, and, after crossing the Indus, assumed the title "Invincible," a title which had been conferred on Alexander by the Delphic Apollo. From Taxila he sent his general Menander, a Greek commoner who had been born in the Paropamisadae, across the Punjab to the Ganges. We are not able to follow Menander's journey in detail, but we know that he occupied Sagala (Sialkot), which he later made his capital, and captured the Mauryan capital, Pataliputra on the Ganges (*ca.* 175 B.C.). Meanwhile, Demetrius and his brother, Apollodotus, marched down the Indus and conquered Sind, where Patala was refounded as Demetrias. Threatening danger from the northern nomads and the death of Euthydemus II, however, forced Demetrius to return to Bactria. Apollodotus continued with his conquests, taking the coastal provinces east of the Indus delta and Barygaza. This was his realm, as subking, for several years. Barygaza was a good port for trade with the West and was also the terminus of the road across India from Pataliputra. It seems likely that Apollodotus took Madhyamika, in southern Rajputana, and Ujjain, a commercial center and seat of learning.

Demetrius' strategy now becomes clear. The Mauryan Empire had pivoted upon three great cities: Pataliputra, the capital and seat of the emperor; Taxila, the seat of the viceroy of the Northwest; and Ujjain, the seat of the viceroy of the West. With these cities in his possession, the rest of the Empire would come as a matter of course. The new capital, however, was at Taxila, because this ensured close connections with Bactria. For a few years Demetrius governed a state that stretched from the Jaxartes to Barygaza, from the Persian desert to the middle Ganges. On his return to Bactria, however, Demetrius was compelled to make certain changes in his appointments. Because of the death of Euthydemus II he transferred Demetrius II from the Paropamisadae to Bactria as joint king, which makes it appear as if Demetrius intended to return to India. As the new subking of the Paropamisadae, Seistan, and Arachosia he appointed his son Pantaleon, and, on his death, another son, Agathocles. Except for Menander's sphere, everything in India was turned over to Apollodotus as subking. Apollodotus, therefore, ruled the broad land from Pushkalavati, the capital of Gandhara, to Barygaza. He probably made Taxila his seat, holding the southern provinces through generals, though Ujjain and other places in the interior were soon lost.

It is important to discover the reason for Demetrius' success. How could he conquer India and traverse such extraordinary distances? Clearly it would have been impossible, had he met consistently hostile peoples as Alexander had. This brings us back to Asoka's conversion to Buddhism, which had become the official religion of the Empire. During the second century, however, there was a resurgence of Brahmanism. A Brahman, Pushyamitra, murdered the last Maurya, seized the crown, and tried to restore the Brahman religion as the religion of India, an action which naturally offended the Buddhists. The Greeks made use of these feelings and fought Pushyamitra, not because he was a Brahman—a Greek rarely troubled about the next man's religion—but because they both wanted the same thing, the huge derelict Empire. In the struggle the Greeks found the Buddhists useful political allies, and that is why the conquest was so easy. We can imagine Demetrius coming to India and proclaiming the "freedom" of the people; indeed, we catch an echo of his proclamations on the coinage of Apollodotus and Menander, which bear the legend "Soter" (Savior). In Demetrius' brain, too, was conceived the plan of organization. The new realm was to be a partnership of Greek and Indian, with himself as the head of both races. He was to be an Indian king no less than a Greek one. In this spirit he rebult Taxila, his capital, as an Indian rather than a Greek city; and, contrary to the Seleucid practice with regard to Greek cities with dynastic names, he admitted Indians as citizens of Demetrias in Sind. He caused Demetrius II, when he was governor west of the Indus, to issue a bilingual coinage, with a Greek legend on the obverse, and a Prakrit legend written in Kharoshthi on the reverse; every Greek king in India copied this. It is not surprising, then, that some Indians saw in Demetrius the traditional King of Justice.

The fall of Demetrius and the consequent weakening of Hellenism in the East were due to Antiochus IV Epiphanes. For two decades after the battle of Magnesia the Seleucid Empire had refrained from war in the hope of recovering its strength. Asia Minor seemed permanently lost, the Eastern provinces had been taken by Demetrius, and, above all, Antiochus feared Rome. If the West were lost forever, the East remained, and Antiochus conceived the idea of restoring Alexander's Empire, with the capital at Babylon. He set about Hellenizing his Empire—which led to difficulties with the Jews—in order that it might be a strong organic whole, an effective counterpoise to the centralization of Rome. The unifying force in the state was to be his divine monarchy. In 169 B.C., therefore, as part of his new program, he remodeled the Seleucid coinage and substituted for the old Apollo type the Olympian Zeus, and changed the legend "Of King Antiochus" to "Of King Antiochus the god manifest." Shortly afterward a Roman envoy brusquely ordered him from Egypt—an insult that Antiochus was willing to swallow, for he had made up his mind about the East. Late in 169 B.C. Antiochus sent his first cousin, Eucratides, to recover the eastern provinces. Eucratides was the son of Heliocles and Laodice, the sister of Antiochus III, and probably had already proved himself a competent general. His route from Babylonia to Bactria went by way of Herat and Merv, so that the two subkings, Antimachus and Agathocles, had to bear the first shock of his invasion. By 167 B.C., however, he had killed Demetrius and conquered Bactria-Sogdiana.

At first glance it seems a little difficult to understand how Eucratides, with a very small force, should be able to carry through such a conquest so quickly. The answer is to be found in the abiding loyalty of the Graeco-Macedonian settlers to the person of the reigning Seleucid. In other words, Eucratides led a rebellion. A Seleucid himself, he held a commission from Antiochus as subking; that is to say, Antiochus' action meant that in the future there were to be two Seleucid realms, with himself as ruler of one and suzerain of the other. We must imagine Eucratides coming to the East and calling upon the Greeks to rise against the pretender and return to their rightful ruler, the reigning Seleucid. Once again the coins give an echo to the manifestoes and proclamations. As propaganda against Eucratides, Antimachus and Agathocles issued their famous "memorial" coins, which gave their pedigree and showed that they, too, were Seleucids and, as they claimed, were descended from Alexander. Eucratides answered this by issuing coins which figured his mother as a Seleucid princess. The rebellion was a success, helped, perhaps, by the preference of many Bactrian Greeks for the Hellenizing policy of Antiochus rather than for the pro-native policy of Demetrius—a difficulty that Alexander had encountered with his Macedonians long before.

Antiochus celebrated his great success by a magnificent festival at Daphne, the suburb of Antioch, in 166 B.C. His mighty army marched by in review, and in every way the occasion was made the Greek counterpart of a Roman triumph. He then went to Babylon, where he was greeted as the "Savior of Asia" and celebrated the Charisteria, a thanksgiving. His new coins exhibited Zeus occasionally with his features and carried a revised legend, "Of King Antiochus the god manifest, the Victorious." He was, indeed, becoming a counterpoise to Rome. His next step was to attack Parthia and thus consolidate his realm, but at Gabae he died.

Eucratides, who could now consider himself an independent king, left Bactria for India in 165 B.C., where he killed Apollodotus. It seems probable that Menander checked his advance somewhere in the Indus district. In any case, he soon returned hurriedly to Bactria, for Mithridates of Parthia had recovered the Bactrian conquests west of the Arius, and now, with the help of the surviving Euthydemids, was overrunning Bactria. In the battle that followed Eucratides was killed (*ca.* 159 B.C.). The real results of Eucratides' extraordinary expedition and his exhausting wars were the failure of the Euthydemid attempt to revive the Mauryan Empire, the acquisition by the Parthians of much of the Euthydemid realm in Iran, and a great weakening of the Greek position in Bactria and eventually in India.

Menander was now left master of the situation in India. He was the most famous of the "Yavana" kings; indeed, he became, as Milinda, the chief character of the *Milindapanha* or *Questions of Milinda,* the one extant work professedly dealing with any of the Greek monarchs in the Far East. Menander legitimatized his rule by marrying Agathoclea, the daughter of Demetrius, and until his death held all the territory remaining to the Greeks in India. His Empire extended in a horseshoe from Mathura in the east to Barygaza in the west; his capital was at Sagala, for he had abandoned Pataliputra on Demetrius' return to Bactria. Barygaza was his great port for the sea trade between India and the West. From India were exported ebony and other woods, peacocks, spices, ivory, dogs, cattle, precious stones, pepper. The goods left India in Indian bottoms, but were brought to their ultimate destination by middlemen; by the southern Arabs to Egypt, by the Gerrhaeans and people living about the Straits of Ormuz to Babylonia. The Indian trade accounts for the outburst of prosperity of Seleuceia in the middle of the second century B.C. Menander's Empire, in spite of its Greek satrapal organization, was in reality a collection of vassal states and "free" peoples, much as Asoka's had been, but with some attempt at founding settlements in the north. Sagala, however, was a great Indian city; there were few Greek *poleis* in India, and none east of Bucephala. Each satrapy probably had a small nucleus of Greek officials for administration, with a Greek general and some soldiers, but Menander could not, like the Seleucids, rely on Greeks in cities. Menander's Council was composed of men of different races, for the Empire was not Greek, as the Seleucid was meant to be; it was essentially an Indian Empire with a small Greek ruling caste, a partnership between the races, in the spirit of Demetrius. Menander was famous for his rule of equity, which has led to the unfounded belief that he became a Buddhist. He did, however, acquire a legend and therefore must have struck the imagination of his contemporaries.

Menander's Empire began to break up on his death (*ca.* 150 B.C.), though Greek rule survived for more than a century in some places of India. The Saca invasion (*ca.* 120 B.C.) marked the beginning of the end; in fact, by 30 B.C. everything that the Greeks had once ruled east of the Euphrates belonged to peoples from the northern steppes. Greek rule did not last so long in Bactria, but here, as in India, the primary reason for the weakening of the Greek position was not some external force, but, as might be expected, the internecine quarrelling of the

Greeks themselves. Heliocles, the son of Eucratides, was probably the last Greek king of Bactria. The people apparently rallied to him against the Parthians, who by 141 B.C., under Mithridates I, had conquered most of Iran, except Bactria, from the Caspian to the Persian Gulf. In this year, too, the curtain falls on the Greeks of Bactria, to rise again in 128 B.C. upon new peoples and new names. In 128 B.C. the Chinese general and diplomat, Chang-k'ien, was in Bactria, and his Report to his emperor, the Han Wu-ti, supplies us with our knowledge of Bactria after its conquest by a nomad horde, the Yueh-chi from northwest China. Chang-k'ien opened up to China a new world in the West, and enabled regular trade communication to be started between China and Iran along the subsequently famous Silk Route. In 106 B.C. the first through caravan reached Parthia from China, by way of Bactra.

Nothing that might be called Greek remained in India after 50 A.D. What, then, did the Greeks accomplish in India? We have seen that the Indians of one Greek city, Demetrias in Sind, and probably of the other Greek cities, were admitted as citizens and held office as a matter of policy. Taxila and Sagala, the capitals of Demetrius and Menander, were Indian, not Greek, cities. The satrapies were managed by the retention of much of the existing Indian arrangements; the Euthydemid provincial administration was essentially Graeco-Indian, under Greek generals. The Greeks introduced a calendar, that of the Seleucid Era, and produced some literature, as an assertion of their continuing Greekhood. The two peoples lived side by side on good terms, but the Indians took little from the Greeks; Indians did not become "culture-Greeks." It was otherwise with the Greeks. In western Asia the Greeks influenced the native population, but, except for religion, the only people who really affected them in turn were the Babylonians. In India, however, many Greeks knew an Indian language, and by 100 B.C. most Greeks were becoming Indianized, which does not mean at all that they became Eurasians. The Indianization of the Greeks led to the one great mark which they set upon India: the idea of representing Buddha as a man. The content of Gandhara sculpture is purely Buddhist, but the form at the start is largely Hellenistic, with commonplace Greek motifs used freely as decoration. In the West a Greek might make a statue of Isis, for example, because he wanted it—he did not do it for the benefit of the Egyptian religion—but in Gandhara the Greeks worked for the Buddhist world, because it was their world, with the result that Buddha ceased to be an abstraction in art and became a man. But all the other works of the Greeks have long since vanished from India; indeed, India would be exactly the same today had the Greeks never existed.

Chapter XXV

THE ART AND LITERATURE OF THE HELLENISTIC AGE

ART

THE spirit of the Hellenistic Age revealed itself as surely in art as in other aspects of life. We might be certain, for example, that the growth and rivalry of the new states, the creation of new capitals and many new foundations, would lead to the science of town-planning. We have already seen that Hippodamus of Miletus was commissioned in the fifth century to lay out Piraeus, but now it became the ordinary practice to build a city on a preconceived plan. It was customary for the Hellenistic architects to take advantage of the general lay of the land, but, when possible, they preferred a rectangular plan. The streets crossed each other at right angles but, except for the main thoroughfares, were still narrow. Roman engineers of a later day were masters in this field, but we must not be blind to the fact that most of the new tendencies were already present in the Hellenistic

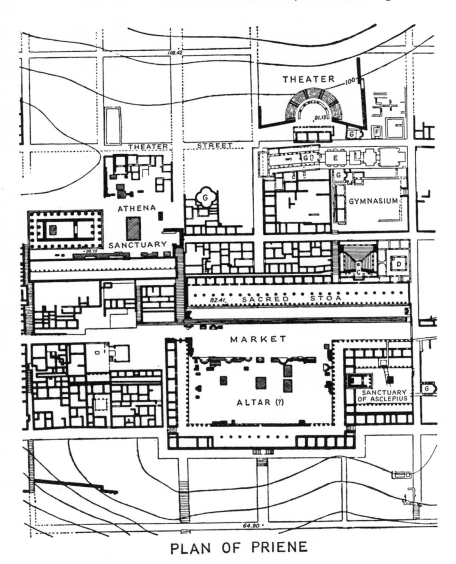

PLAN OF PRIENE

Map 54

Age and that some of them were carried to a high peak. For example, great care was taken with the water supply, though it was not yet common to pipe the water directly to private houses; paved streets and covered drains were still the exception (Map 51, 54, and 56).

The new big cities of the Hellenistic Age were divided into quarters.

Palaces and temples there might be—though unfortunately practically all the palaces have long since disappeared—but in any case a Hellenistic city would surely have its gymnasia, theaters, baths, and Agora. The fortification walls were very strong, to withstand the new siege engines, and not infrequently were many miles in circuit, enclosing farm land against a siege. The best examples of private houses can today be seen at Delos and Priene; they are more luxurious than those of earlier centuries (Diagram 36), are several stories high, and are built around the familiar colonnaded court. Because love of gods and city was not the primary driving force of the Hellenistic Age, we note a marked decrease in the number of temples. Hermogenes was the architect of the Ionic temple of Artemis Leucophryene at Magnesia on the Meander (150 B.C.). The Roman architect Cossutius was commissioned by Antiochus IV Epiphanes in 174 B.C. to finish the great temple of Olympian Zeus at Athens. This had been begun as an Ionic building under the Peisistratids, but the more ornate Corinthian order became popular during the Hellenistic Age, and the Olympieum was reconstituted as a Corinthian structure 135 by 354 feet, standing in a peribolus of 424 by 680 feet. The temple had two rows of twenty columns each along the flanks, with eight columns, three rows deep, across the front and rear. In the first century B.C. Sulla removed some of the columns to Rome, where they were an inspiration to Roman architects, and finally in the second century A.D. Hadrian completed the building.

The patronage of kings and wealthy citizens extended also to sculpture. In fact, in the sculpture particularly do we catch the spirit of the Hellenistic Age. Here we have all the conflicts of the day, the love of beauty and of the commonplace, realism and romanticism, adventure and reaction. Some sculptors struck out along new paths, whereas others clung closely to the past. There were not necessarily any restraints in this day of rampant individualism. Genre figures, grotesques, realistic portraiture were in greater demand than were statues of the Olympian gods. The output of statues was very large, and, though many of those that are preserved are mediocre, some are truly great, and practically all reveal high technical skill. For some of the sculpture, too, we are dependent on inferior Roman copies. (See, however, Figure 103.)

Hellenistic sculptors were handicapped by the fact that subjects had been exhausted. Some tremendous new force was needed to carry sculpture to a different and great level, and this was only partially provided by the invasion of the Gauls. Interest in everyday life also filled this lack in part. But the old themes, of gods and battles, had been adequately treated in the past, and it was not enough now to render drapery in new ways, or to combine, in a curious eclecticism, old ideas with new methods of execution.

Hellenistic sculptors traveled from city to city, borrowing ideas from one another and from the past. When we speak of schools, therefore, we must think primarily of cities that patronized art and not imagine that the artists were necessarily native sons. The Rhodian School is an illustration. Here worked pupils of Lysippus of Sicyon, artists interested in athletes. They produced a strong and virile art. We have already spoken of the bronze Colossus of Rhodès—one of the wonders of the ancient world—by Chares of Lindus. It commemorated the resistance of the city to Demetrius in 304 B.C. and showed Apollo, so we are told, astride the harbor as the Sun-god. Eutychides, another pupil of Lysippus, made the famous statue of the Tyche of Antioch. Tyche (Fortune) is the personification of the city; she sits on a rock, a turreted crown (the city walls) resting on her head; at the base of the rock the river Orontes, as a youth, rushes along. Another Rhodian sculptor made the magnificent Nike of Samothrace (Figure 101). This statue was probably set up by Antigonus Gonatas to celebrate the naval victory over Ptolemy II at Cos (about 258 B.C.) and shows Victory alighting on the prow of a warship. The great wings, the strong, beautiful body beneath the whirling drapery, the majestic dignity tempered by restless motion, mark this statue as one of the superb creations of the Hellenistic Age. The Rhodian School was important throughout the entire period, for as late as 25 B.C. it produced the famous group of Laocoön and his sons —unrestrained, moving figures, without, however, much real feeling.

Alexandria loved luxury and art, but, except for a certain interest in pictorial reliefs and in the minor arts, it produced little significant sculpture. It was far otherwise with Pergamum. The havoc wrought by the Gauls in Asia Minor will be recalled; when victory finally came to the Greeks, dread fear yielded to rejoicing, and artists were called upon in the third quarter of the third century B.C. to commemorate the deliverance of the Greeks. The artists of the First Pergamene School rose to their new opportunity. Though we must study them through Roman copies, it is abundantly clear that these artists were thinking along new lines, that they had not only a high technical skill, but that they could show rest and motion and inner feeling as few have ever done. Their enemies had been great fighters and they carved them, therefore, as great men. This we see in the Dying Gaul (Figure 104), the Dying Persian (Figure 105), and the Gaul who has killed his wife, rather than let her fall into the hands of the barbarous Greeks, and is defiantly stabbing himself (Figure 106). Early in the second century Eumenes II celebrated the battle of Magnesia with a monument which is now the pride of Berlin. Artists of the Second Pergamene School decorated the great altar of Zeus Soter with a frieze depicting the struggle of gods and giants. Really, it is symbolic of the victory of civilization over barbarism; the writhing figures themselves bespeak the contradictions and inner conflicts of the Hellenistic Age.

The Aphrodite of Melos, now in the Louvre in Paris, is a fine example of the mid-second-century conception of the gods (Figure 107, and cf. Figure 108). It is a statue of a serene and physically beautiful woman—technically perfect; it is inspired by the past, but lacks nobility. People were also interested in more ordinary matters, in drunken women (Figure 109), in old market women (Figure 110), in children at play, and so on (Figure 111). The realistic temper of the day also called forth great portraits. The best examples, by far, are on the coins: the wonderfully idealized heads of Alexander on the coins of Lysimachus, and the brutally frank heads of the Graeco-Bactrian kings, which possess, as well, a spiritual quality (Figures 90, 100, 47). Of the many superb portrait statues, few can be identified, but among the best are a statue of Demosthenes by Polyeuctus and the so-called Hellenistic Prince (Figures 89, 112).

On the Greek mainland Damophon of Messene carved statues at Lycosura in Arcadia, in the second century, which recalled some of the splendor and majesty of an earlier day, but most artists, it will have been noted, worked elsewhere. Hellenistic princes, however, delighted to make gifts to the Greek homeland, and at Athens, Olympia, Delphi, and Delos are to be found many of their dedications. When we count the memorial statues—most of which, incidentally, were paid for by the individuals honored—we see that thousands of statues were made during the Hellenistic Age. After the sack of Corinth in 146 B.C. statues by the thousand were sent to Rome, the new Mediterranean power, which was determined to have some sort of Hellenic culture.

Our knowledge of Hellenistic painting is slight, for vase painting had ceased to count, and the other pictures have disappeared. Delos and Dura-Europos shed some light on the subject, however, and the murals at Pompeii and Herculaneum are often inspired by great Hellenistic paintings and occasionally are more or less exact copies of them (Figure 102). We see, furthermore, that the Hellenistic painters successfully handled problems of composition, perspective, and color. For subject-matter they still clung to mythology, though they could paint fine portraits and lovely scenes from still life. Landscape, unfortunately, was used only as a background for people. Except for two hymns to the Delphic Apollo, dating from the second century B.C., our knowledge of music is practically a blank. This is regrettable, for music was very popular during the Hellenistic Age.

LITERATURE

It was but natural that the revolution in Hellenic government and society since the fourth century should be accompanied by a corresponding change in literature. The Hellenistic Age was marked by a great interest in research and science, though the lack of scientific instruments and the Greek dislike of applied knowledge prevented the full development of scientific studies. The Greek found the study of philosophy more congenial. The interest in philosophy was also due in part to the fact that the old gods of Olympus no longer satisfied intellectuals. Any generalization, however, would be dangerous, for Fortune was worshipped by many persons of modest education, and the masses still clung to their ancestral religion. Kings and cities paid at least lip-service to the old religion, and it is fair to say that all Greeks, in one way or another, associated themselves with it, for it served to set them apart from the barbarian world. But the new forces of the day were weakening the traditional religion, as is amply proved by the growth of king worship and the increasing appeal of mystery cults, the cult of Eleusis, Orphic cults, astrology, and magic. The Eastern religions, too, made some progress among the Greeks, especially among the offspring of mixed marriages, and in particular two Egyptian cults appealed to many Greeks: that of Serapis, the guardian of sailors as he became, whose worship was carried far and wide; and that of Isis, who was very popular because of her promises of future bliss. Among Orientals, however, the Olympic religion made no headway—except among those who, hoping for personal advancement, took over the externals of Hellenism —for the Eastern religions were of great antiquity and as a rule were given complete tolerance by the Successors.

During the Hellenistic Age philosophy, we have intimated, underwent a change. Philosophic thought had previously rested on two principles: first, the complete trust reposed in abstract thinking for the discovery of truth and, second, the perfect correspondence assumed between the inner man and the world without. This correspondence was supported by a religion which peopled nature with souls like those of men. It was partly this relation between the world and man which led the philosophers to believe that by mere thinking they could discover the principles of nature, and partly the circumstance that philosophic thought was as yet in its infancy with its limitations unknown and the value of its products untested. With the breaking down of the city-state and of traditional religion and the concomitant growth of individualism and humanism, philosophy, abandoning her original foundation, attempted to lay a new basis in the changed conditions of life. The ground had been prepared by Antisthenes of Athens, a disciple of Socrates, and an older contemporary of Plato. From his teaching in the gymnasium of the Cynosarges his school was called Cynic. In his doctrine virtue is the only good, vice the sole evil. Wealth, social position, honor, and country are nothing. A tattered mantle, a piece of barley bread, and water are all that a man needs. The Cynics taught that we should renounce every bodily pleasure and comfort for the spiritual contentment derived from the exercise of virtue. Through the contempt of this school for convention, for nearly everything mankind holds dear, the word *cynic* has degenerated to its present meaning.

In the Hellenistic Age, although the members of the Cynic school degenerated to boorish and brutal tramp philosophers, the better elements of their philosophy were adopted by the Stoics. The founder of this school was Zeno, a Semite of Citium in Cyprus, who had come to Athens in 311 B.C. There for a time he studied with the Cynics, but ten years later he began to teach independently in the Painted Porch—*Stoa Poikile*—which gave its name to his school. His Semitic nationality shows itself, not in the content of his teaching, which is Hellenic, but in its utterance. Stoicism is less rational, more dogmatic, than any previous philosophy. Zeno's object was the moulding of man's character to meet the difficulties of the world, and regardless of consistency he presented the doctrines suited to this end, implanting them in the minds of others less by reason than as the utterance of a prophet. It seemed to him, amid the wreck of religious and moral ideas formerly sustained by the city state, that mankind needed a higher degree of individual self-sufficiency. To reach this end it is necessary, he taught, to train the will into conformity with nature, to desire only those things that are certain of realization independently of ourselves. In order to prove that this central doctrine is rational and that it will assure happiness Zeno developed a whole system of philosophy. It consists of three branches, logic, physics, and ethics. Logic includes a theory of knowledge. While the skeptics of his age were denying the possibility of knowing, Zeno insisted that we could accept as the truth all "grasping impressions," the sense perceptions that come to us with irresistible strength. Whereas to the acute thinker this dictum was childish folly, it sufficed for a commonsense philosophy. Logic included also everything connected with the expression of thought and feeling from grammar to rhetoric and music, as well as the forms of reasoning. In this department the Stoics contributed little to existing knowledge. In physics, the study of nature, their most startling dogma is that everything is material, even God and the human soul. The qualities of objects, emotions, virtues, and vices are all corporeal. In fact, the purely practical object of Zeno's system seemed to him to demand that it be grounded upon ordinary experience, which has to do primarily with material things. It is our common experience, too, that matter cannot move itself or take on living forms; nothing but a soul can bring about such changes. The world, therefore, has a soul; this is God, the reason, and motive power of the universe. He is a Providence who in loving care watches over the world and every part of it, who maintains it in physical and moral perfection. Everything in nature therefore is rational and good. Thus from physics we pass imperceptibly to ethics. The soul of man is a part of the divine soul, and a virtuous life is conformity to nature. Everything that exists is advantageous to man, even sickness, noxious animals, earthquakes and the like; they are intended for our education. Thus we are gradually led back to the central idea of Stoicism that happiness, the supreme good, is reached by making our will conform to the laws of nature, which are absolutely rational and just.

Under Zeno and his successors—notably, Cleanthes, Chrysippus, and Panaetius of Rhodes—Stoicism became a religion. The only motive to right conduct, conformity to nature, is nothing more than submission to the will of God. It is a pure monotheism, the worship of one Supreme Being. As He wishes only well for us, and blesses but never harms, we, who are parts of Him, have no reason to fear Him, but should only revere and love. For this worship there is no need of altars or temples or images or even of prayer, but only of purity in life and thought. The gods of popular belief with their foibles and vices are creatures of the imagination, and the many myths are worthy only of contempt. To a certain extent, however, the Stoics compromised with popular faith. Just as the Christians grant the existence of angels and devils, the Stoics assume the activity of superhuman beings, called gods, but subject to the Supreme Being. In like manner, while repeating the literal content of myths, the Stoics were able to save them for a useful purpose by giving them an allegorical interpretation. In this activity they were but extending an invention of earlier philosophies. Necessarily their interpretations were fantastical. For example, Heracles was not merely a strong man, but a great philosopher. His slaying of monsters signifies his conquest of human vices; and when he leads the three-headed dog from the nether world to earth's surface, he is merely bringing to light the three heads of philosophy—logic, physics, and ethics. The effect of such teaching was to purify myth of all immoralities, and to preserve the traditional religion while endowing it with a wholly new meaning.

Zeno took over Alexander's vision of a world-state and of *homonoia*, Concord, but under the Stoics the idea of the brotherhood of man became more the business of individuals than of kings. The trend of Stoicism, while strengthening religious faith, was to make the individual self-sufficient, independent of all externals, human and material, and to give him an absolute mastery of himself. He is lord of his own life, and may put an end to it when he judges best. Though he may have been suddenly converted to Stoicism, it is possible to grow in character throughout life; but only a few men of old, such as Socrates, have attained to a perfection of virtue. Society, too, exists, and the individual has social instincts, which are natural, and therefore good. All are members of one body; all are parts of one God, bound together in a common sympathy. In striving to benefit our fellows we do but obey a law of nature. While working out the problem of virtue many Stoics were driven into seclusion or lived in a commonwealth of their own imagining, out of space and time, where no sordid ambitions or passions or human weaknesses found entrance, but all dwelt in perfect harmony and content. Others in the hope of impressing their fellow men mingled in society or became statesmen and rulers. Their creed, though appealing to the intellectuals rather than the mass, has served us as a positive force in the history of thought and conduct. It moulded Roman law; it contributed to the humanism of Roman imperial times; at various points it proved akin to Christianity; and much of it, remaining in the ethics of today, still makes for strength and stability of character.

In opposition to the Stoics there were powerful forces of disintegration. There were Skeptics, who, while accepting appearances as such, denied the possibility of real knowledge. Thoroughly typical of these disturbed intellectual conditions is the work of Euhemerus of Messene. In a book entitled *Sacred Inscription,* composed early in the third century, he pretended that on a visit to a distant island he found in a temple of Zeus an ancient inscription which detailed the origin and doings of the gods. It was there set forth that Zeus was once a man who had distinguished himself as king and conqueror and had received divine worship in reward for his benefits, and similarly that all the deities, Apollo, Aphrodite, and the rest, were once human beings who had attained to fame and had been raised to the rank of gods in human opinion, whereas in fact they died like all other mortals and are no more. While undermining what remained of the traditional faith, this book supported the deification of kings.

The philosophic system, however, which is rightly set down as the opponent of Stoicism was that of Epicurus of Samos, who founded his school at Athens in 306 B.C. His school, like the Stoa, was materialistic; he accepted substantially the atomic theory of Democritus. Even the soul, he asserted, is material and dissolves at death. As it is mortal, we have nothing to fear from a future life. Gods exist, but not those of popular faith. The real deities live apart from the world in unalloyed happiness, caring nothing for the human race. In the Epicurean system, as among the Stoics, the whole superstructure is occupied by ethics. The supreme Good is apparently the same in both philosophies, happiness. With Epicurus, however, happiness is freedom from pain, or from fear, which is mental suffering. The aim was not hedonism, but quietism. Pleasures and pains differ in degrees; and in making choice the wise man will aim to avoid the severest and the most lasting pains and to seek the highest and the most permanent pleasures. The delights of sensation are coarse and transitory, those of mind exalted and lasting. Hence the wise man will choose poverty and bodily suffering if necessary to secure the highest pleasures. The intelligent Epicurean will be as virtuous as the Stoic, because through virtue he secures the utmost happiness. The founder of the school was himself an admirable character; and his object was undoubtedly to benefit his fellow men. His system, though it has many points of likeness to Stoicism, has been condemned by the tribunal of history. The reason is that it is essentially selfish. Individual man is his own all-in-all. Different from the Stoic, the Epicurean is subject to no spiritual ideal toward which he should strive. It is true that the system as originally taught produced a few eminently worthy characters; but its general effect has been demoralizing. The doctrine of happiness was too readily perverted; and Epicureanism became synonymous with a love of eating and drinking, with gluttony and the coarsest pleasures.

The mental attitude of the Hellenistic Age, however, was essentially an appreciation of the past and an effort to master its vast intellectual treasures. The originality of the age, the achievement of adding to the accumulated store of knowledge is seen in its scientific discoveries and mechanical inventions. Fortunately for the progress of science the task which Aristotle set for himself was not only the collection of facts and the organization of knowledge, but also the direction of his pupils to individual fields of research. His work continued therefore after his death. An added impetus to the study of geography and astronomy, of plants and animals, to discovery and invention in general, was given by the marches of Alexander. And the interest of the Ptolemies in art and science devoted a goodly share of Egyptian wealth to collections and institutions for the furtherance of scholarly and scientific progress.

One of the necessary requisites to this work was the founding of a library. Under the earlier Ptolemies a search for valuable manuscripts was made throughout the Hellenic world; and within a few years a collection was made of 500,000 volumes (rolls), which in time was further increased. This was the royal library, the greatest in the ancient world. Callimachus, a peripatetic of Cyrene (*ca.* 310–240 B.C.), one of the chief librarians, compiled a catalogue, said to have filled 120 volumes, comprising the authors and their works in order. It included, too, short biographies of the authors and a few critical data for the evaluation of the books. Briefer aids to the choice and use of books were added by various scholars. Other Hellenistic kings established libraries in their respective capitals, notably in Pergamum and Antioch, none of which, however, equaled that of Alexandria. The Museum, connected with the Library of Alexandria, was an association of scholars and investigators, like the Academy and the Lyceum, formed nominally for the worship of the Muses. Their president was a priest appointed by the king, who assigned them quarters in his palace, a large hall, in which they took their meals in common, a garden with seats and an agreeable place for walking. The members received money for support from the king's treasury.

Members of this association and other learned men in the Aristotelian spirit mapped out the fields of knowledge, which they vigorously cultivated according to their several tastes. Under grammar, nearly equivalent to our philology, may be included everything relating to the study of language and of literature. Scholars, of whom we know scarcely more than the names, wrote histories of the various departments of literature, as the drama, poetry, and philosophy, and biographies of famous authors. A most valuable service was the comparison and criticism of manuscripts with a view to purifying the texts of errors and interpolations. This textual criticism centered in the poems of Homer. It had begun as early as the sixth century, but the first scholarly edition of Homer was prepared by Zenodotus, the first librarian at Alexandria (285–260 B.C.). It put the text substantially in the form in which we read it today. The division of the *Iliad* and the *Odyssey* into books was made either by this scholar or by his immediate successors. In his judgment these were the only works of Homer, whereas others, the Separatists, assigned the two poems to different authors. The texts of the classic poets and many prose writers were similarly treated; and minute commentaries on the language and the subject matter were prepared. Philology included also technical grammar, which had a relatively slow growth, prosody, and lexicons. The scientific spirit of Alexandria was Aristotelian, whereas that of the rival Pergamene school was Stoic. The famous master at Pergamum was Crates of Mallos, an opponent of the Alexandrian librarian, Aristarchus. The Stoic love of allegory, prominent in this school's interpretation of the poets, blurred their scientific perception. This shortcoming is counterbalanced by great attention to the subject matter of literature, rather than to textual criticism, and in general to the collection and organization of facts.

For the progress of physical science a careful foundation in pure mathematics had to be laid. This service was performed by Euclid of Alexandria (*ca.* 300 B.C.), who continued the mathematical studies of Plato and the Academy. His chief work, named *Elements,* still extant, is a textbook on geometry, so precise, clear, and logical that little improvement has since been made upon it.

More inventive was Archimedes of Syracuse (*ca.* 287–212 B.C.), one of the geniuses of antiquity. His main interest was in pure mathematics, in the exact measurement of the circle, the sphere, the cone, conoids, spheroids, and the cylinder. In some of his operations he has anticipated the principle of integral calculus; and in his applied mathematics he reveals a command of the principles of higher algebra. His work in applied science, though in his own judgment distinctly subsidiary, was in fact epoch making. The founder of mechanics and hydrostatics, Archimedes invented a planetarium, the compound pulley, and the so-called Archimedean drill—an endless screw used to pump water from ships and to drain Egyptian fields after the flood of the Nile. He discovered a means of determining the center of gravity of complex forms and of computing the specific gravity of objects; the latter discovery was the result of his observation of the water he displaced in his bath, whereupon he rushed home naked, crying, *"Eureka,* I have found it." He invented engines for hurling great missiles with which his fellow citizens long kept at bay the besieging Romans, the helix for launching great ships and conveying other heavy weights, and other useful machines. In the application of power Archimedes and other ancient mechanics made use of water, compressed air (pneumatics), with levers, screws, and cogged wheels. Some inventions added to the conveniences of life, such as water mills, automatic door openers, washing machines; others were for entertainment, including fountains adorned with automatically moving figurines, and an automatic theater in which the figures performed their parts through five complicated acts.

The advance of mathematical and mechanical study inevitably led to a development of astronomy and of mathematical geography. The first Hellenistic master of this field was Eratosthenes of Cyrene (*ca.* 275–195 B.C.), the successor of Callimachus as chief librarian at Alexandria. There he was able to study the heavens in an observatory patterned after those of ancient Babylon. His most celebrated achievement was the computation of the circumference of the earth. By means of sun-dials placed at Syene and Alexandria, he determined the positions of the sun from these two points; and with the angle thus formed he computed the earth's circumference at 252,000 stadia, or 24,662 miles. He wrote a *History of Geography* from Homer to his own day, in which he recognized the limitations of earlier authors. It included his own map of the world with an explanation of it, in which he expressed the possibility of reaching India by sailing west across the Atlantic, though, he added, the intervening space might be divided longitudinally by land. The similarity in the tides of the Atlantic and Indian Oceans led Eratosthenes to the conclusion that one could sail from Spain around Africa to India. His achievements were vast and so accurate that until the beginning of modern times no improvements were made upon them except in minor details (see inset, Maps 59 and 60).

Astronomy had always been the special province of the Babylonians, from whom the Greeks learned much; indeed, in this field we find real cooperation between people of different race. In the third century, however, Aristarchus of Samos (*ca.* 310–230 B.C.) brought astronomy to the highest reach attained by the ancients. He discovered that the volume of the sun is many times greater than that of the earth. It was this fact that led him ultimately to the conclusion that "the earth annually revolves round the sun in the circumference of a circle, in the center of which the sun remains fixed." The heliocentric theory seemed too radical for popular acceptance, and in the second century the world reverted to the geocentric theory with Hipparchus of Nicea, the discoverer of the precession of the equinoxes—if, indeed, this discovery had not already been made by Kidenas, the distinguished Babylonian, whose calculation of the length of the year was but seven minutes and sixteen seconds too short for the year 300 B.C. The theory of the spheres now continued with an important modification. Instead of assigning a plurality of spheres to the planet, it was found more practicable to assume that each planet moved in a little circle whose center lay in a larger circle surrounding the earth. This theory of epicycles—circles upon circles—prevailed, and was accepted by the Egyptian Claudius Ptolemy, an encylopaedic compiler of sciences who flourished in the second century A.D. After him it came to be known as the Ptolemaic system, and held its place till overthrown by Copernicus.

The permeation of Egypt and western Asia by the Greeks brought to their knowledge a vast number of animals and plants, hitherto unknown to them; and the Ptolemies maintained a zoological garden at Alexandria. In spite of these opportunities, however, zoology and botany failed to make an appreciable advance beyond the works of Aristotle and Theophrastus. People had but a curious interest in animals, whereas botany was more vigorously studied as an auxiliary to medicine. A limited number of plants and animals had to be taken into account in scientific agriculture, horticulture, bee keeping, and stock breeding, all of which were diligently cultivated. The loss of all the books in these fields with the exception of a few fragments has left us ignorant of Hellenic intelligence in one of its most useful departments.

The growth of civilization and the urbanization of mankind makes an ever-increasing demand upon the physician for hygienic regulations and for the cure of new diseases. Acqaintance with the Egyptian custom of embalming expelled from the minds of Greek physicians their last scruples against the dissection of the human body. For the first time in history vivisection was practiced on condemned criminals furnished to the physicians by the Egyptian king. The result was an advance in anatomy and physiology which made an epoch in the history of medical science.

The leading physician of the early third century was Herophilus of Chalcedon, whose achievement was to bring medical science to a height never exceeded by the ancients. He discovered that the brain is the seat of the mind, and that the nerves, branching out from the brain and spine, are the medium for the conveyance of sensation and will power respectively. His study of the eye is noteworthy. In his diagnosis of ailments, for which he was especially famous, he discovered the value of pulsation, which became the chief criterion of the patient's condition. Whereas other physicians believed that the arteries were normally filled with air, Herophilus discovered that they contain blood, which they convey from the heart to all parts of the body. In other words, he discovered substantially the circulation of the blood. Without neglecting diet and exercise for the cure of illness, he laid great stress on drugs, especially vegetable medicines, as the "hands of God."

Unfortunately Herophilus was too far in advance of his age to find complete acceptance. The most eminent physician after him, Erasistratus of Ceos, insisted that the arteries were normally filled with air and that the presence of blood in the arteries is a symptom of illness. In other respects he made actual improvements upon Herophilus, as in his greater stress on hygiene and his clearer distinction between sensory and motor nerves. Opposed to the teachings of these eminent scientists were the Empiricists, who, rejecting all reason, depended wholly on experimentation. There were charlatans, too, as at present; and despite all intellectual progress incubation and magical cures persisted, and sanctuaries of Asclepius still grew in popularity.

For an appreciation of the artistic literature of the Hellenistic Age it is necessary to take account of the general environment, especially the intense urbanization of the Greeks, the growth of libraries, the keen interest in science and erudition. Since the mind of the Hellenistic Greek was so largely concentrated upon the riches of the past and upon scientific discoveries, we shall find in literature analogous efforts manifested in imitations of the past and in the working out of new problems suggested by the greatly changed environment. It was inevitable that the polite literature should taste of erudition, that it should be labored and pedantic. The generality of men, however, who lived in a highly artificial atmosphere, longed for diversion and rest, the freshness of nature; and at the same time the spirit of science was experimenting with emotions hitherto but little used. The period, therefore, saw the beginning of a new literary treatment of nature and man. The novel element in nature is the environment of common people, of shepherds, ploughmen, and charcoal burners, refreshed with the dew and clear in the sunlight of morning. The new force in human kind is romantic love between man and woman.

These are prominent features in the Sicilian Theocritus (*ca.* 315–250 B.C.), the last Greek classic and the first and greatest of Hellenistic poets. His creation, the idyll, is a short poem exquisitely wrought. It possesses a wide range of character, epic, lyric, and dramatic. Preferably his idylls treat of common persons in rural scenes, and hence have been described as pastoral. Though he lived his later years at the court of the Ptolemies, he drew his inspiration from the lovely air and the beautiful landscapes of Sicily, which wafted through his sweet poems refreshing breezes, with delicious memories of cool shade of green fields and radiant flowers, into the dusty streets and arid studios of Alexandria.

Whereas Theocritus stands at the threshold of Alexandrian life, Callimachus occupies its inmost shrine, though he belongs to neither Europe nor Asia. In him the Hellenistic spirit found its purest expression. The chief librarian and a man of vast learning, he is equally conspicuous as a poet of stupendous productivity. His own writings are said to have filled 800 volumes (rolls). Of all these works there remain a few hymns and epigrams. The hymns are courtly, composed for royal occasions. With great talent the author creates brilliant effects for their own sake. Doubtless there is feeling in the poet, but it is hidden in the elaborate apparatus of his song. At the same time Callimachus was proclaimed the greatest master of elegy. This form of poetry was used for the expression of sentiment on all subjects and, in this age particularly, for mythical tales of love. The epigrams show him to better advantage. They are in the elegiac meter, but are short and highly polished. Usually the epigram expresses an occasional sentiment of the author on any subject that attracted his attention.

In didactic verse the spirit of scholarship prevailed. The aim was to teach, and the lines were without imagination or charm. This kind of poem remained dead till the Roman Lucretius endowed it with life and power. Quite different was the romantic epic, represented by the *Argonautica* of Apollonius, an emigrant from Alexandria to Rhodes. This work is a long narrative of a popular myth, the quest for the Golden Fleece. In this respect it is an imitation of the past, an echo from Homer. In his presentation of Medea's love for Jason, the analysis of its origin and growth and conflict with duty, the author has created a new theme, but one oft-treated from that day to this. Although the poet lacked the genius for making it a success, the work has a value in illustrating the intellectual efforts of the period and in the suggestion it offered to Vergil for his *Aeneid,* an incomparably superior work.

Hellenistic poetry appealed only to the selected few, which helps to explain the popularity of the mimes of Herondas, dealing lightly, as they did, with everyday matters. But Hellenistic poetry lost its spiritual relation to religion and no longer was the manifestation of the Greek nation. Speaking generally, it is self-conscious, the child of the society of poets who gathered in cosmopolitan Alexandria, where the despotism of the court caused it to lose its Hellenic spirit. Elaboration and criticism took the place of creation in the Hellenistic Age, and the poets, undertaking researches themselves, consciously went back to forms which were no longer current, to epic, iambic, and elegiac poetry.

Prosperity, as we have seen, enabled Alexandria to seize the leadership of the world of letters, though the schools of philosophy gave Athens a certain pre-eminence. Athens was also the center for comedy. This was the New Comedy, so-called, the comedy of manners, typically Athenian and yet immensely popular throughout the Greek world. Of the many comedians, Diphilus, Philemon, and others, by far the greatest was Menander (*ca.* 342–291 B.C.). The sands of Egypt have recently yielded extended fragments of his plays. Menander has a tremendous appeal, because he depicts sympathetic characters in trouble and gives a lively and varied portrayal of daily life, a realistic picture of domestic difficulties with happy endings. The plots of *The Arbitration* and his other plays deal with separated families that are reunited in the end after a recognition scene, but the atmosphere, incidents, and principal characters are different. Menander had a great influence on succeeding centuries, from Terence to Shakespeare. After the third century comedy lost its vigor, a fate that had befallen tragedy even earlier. Interest in rhetoric, however, continued, but the new order of the day, which permitted so little real liberty, was responsible for the decline of oratory.

It was far otherwise with history. Many histories were written during the Hellenistic Age. Their emphasis, characteristically, was on contemporary events, a trend which had received impetus from Callisthenes, Ptolemy, Aristobulus and others who had accompanied Alexander on his expedition. The new humanism and the great stress placed on research led many into the field of biography, and, indeed, Aratus of Sicyon wrote his autobiography, an important source, through Plutarch, for the Achaean League. Most of the Hellenistic historians, unfortunately, are lost to us, but judging from the extant fragments it is clear that, though many of the works were plain straight-forward accounts, many more were spoiled by too great attention to style.

One of the most important Hellenistic historians was Hieronymus of Cardia, whose *History of the Successors* covered the period from 323 to 266 B.C. His work, for the first two decades, is preserved in Diodorus of Sicily (*ca.* 27 B.C.) and shows him to have been a sound writer, chiefly interested in political and military history. His *History* was continued by the florid pro-Spartan Phylarchus, whom Plutarch used occasionally. Timaeus of Tauromenium wrote for a wider public, filling his work with strange tales, but, for all that, his *History* of the western Greeks from the earliest times to 264 B.C. would be a valuable addition to our knowledge. It was Timaeus who began the system of dating by Olympiads. By far the greatest of Hellenistic historians was Polybius of Megalopolis in Arcadia, who ranks second only to Thucydides among all Greek historians. Polybius came from a prominent family and played an active role in the affairs of the Achaean League. In 167 B.C., after the Third Macedonian War, he was carried off as a hostage to Rome, where he became the friend of Scipio Aemilianus and other important Romans. He soon grew to admire Rome tremendously, and was inspired with the ambition to tell the moving story of the new world power. His *History* covered the period from 221 to 146 B.C., and of the forty books the first five and various extracts remain. Polybius believed that contemporary politicians could learn much from the past and he therefore addressed himself to them and not to the general public. As a result, he does not make exciting reading. He makes many digressions and is verbose; he is unfair to Carthage, and allots too much space to the Achaean League. Nevertheless, Polybius was a scientific historian, who diligently studied his sources and often traveled to various sites to verify his data. Though he lacked detachment, Polybius was industrious and, with his own experience in political affairs, succeeded to a large degree in writing a critical and immensely valuable account of the Mediterranean world. Posidonius, of Apamea on the Orontes, continued the work of Polybius to the time of Sulla, the Roman general.

Chapter XXVI

THE ENCROACHMENT OF ROME

A T THE peace conference of Naupactus in 217 B.C., it will be recalled, the Aetolian Agelaus had spoken of the need of Greek unity against the "cloud in the West." Two years later, however, Philip V of Macedon entered the momentous struggle between Rome and Carthage by sending envoys to Hannibal and by attacking the Romans in Illyria. Rome countered by an alliance with the Aetolian League (211 B.C.) and with Attalus I of Pergamum. This led to an inconclusive war, known as the First Macedonian War, during which Philip's allies, Carthage and Prusias I of Bithynia, failed him. The peace of Phoenice finally brought the war to an end in 205 B.C.

It will also be recalled that after the battle of Raphia (217 B.C.) Antiochus III, in spite of his defeat, had driven Achaeus from Asia Minor and then, having re-established his authority, undertook his grand tour which carried him as far as India. Antiochus the Great, as he became known, now cast his eye on Egypt. The death of Ptolemy IV in 203 B.C. brought to the throne an infant, Ptolemy V Epiphanes. The guardian of the child was the cruel minister Agathocles, who spent his days in debauchery and executions. The motley population of Alexandria, which was always ready to riot, resolved to be rid of Agathocles and his sister, and after several days of wild rioting accomplished their purpose. The time, therefore, seemed propitious to Antiochus and Philip to combine in an attack on Egypt's foreign possessions. In 202 B.C. Antiochus opened the Fifth Syrian War by an invasion of southern Syria; after the capture of Gaza, he defeated Scopas, an Aetolian commanding the Egyptian army, at Panion near the Jordan (200 B.C.). Egypt lost Syria and Phoenicia forever.

The Fifth Syrian War led indirectly to the establishment of the independent kingdom of Judaea. At first the new administration made little difference to the Jews, but somewhat later, as we have already explained, Antiochus IV decided that a strong Hellenic state was his best safeguard against Rome. He therefore abandoned the tolerant attitude of the Successors, and tried deliberately to Hellenize the Jews, among others. A garrison was established in Jerusalem, and the Temple was consecrated to Zeus Olympius. Naturally, there were many who were anxious to do Antiochus' bidding; but a strong opposition developed, first around the priest Mattathiah in 166 B.C., and then around his son Judas Maccabaeus. A guerrilla warfare continued for many years, but in 142 B.C. Judaea won its freedom. Simon became the hereditary High Priest and was recognized by Rome. Under his son, John Hyrcanus, the dynasty of the Maccabees flourished, only to fall upon evil days. Ten years after the reign of the able but cruel client-king Herod, Judaea became a Roman province (6 A.D.). In Judaea Graeco-Roman civilization made no conquests.

At the time of the Fifth Syrian War, and counting on his understanding with Antiochus III, Philip captured Lysimacheia, Chalcedon, and Samos, and laid siege to Chios. Thoroughly alarmed, Rhodes, Pergamum, Egypt, and Athens appealed to Rome, who had just emerged victorious from her great struggle with Carthage and was now the arbiter of world affairs. The Roman Republic, at this time, had no thought of annexing territory in the East; but not many years were to pass, however, before success weakened her character, and, introducing the world once more to inhumane warfare, she sacked cities, filled the world with slaves, and treated her allies with contempt. In 200 B.C. Rome merely feared the coalition of Philip and Antiochus, and, hoping to divide them, posed as the champion of Greek liberty. In the Second Macedonian War, as it is called, Rome was helped by the Aetolian

League and by the fleets of Rhodes and Pergamum. The first two years were indecisive, though Philip's fleet was defeated off Chios, but in 197 B.C. an energetic Roman commander appeared on the scene, the proconsul T. Quinctius Flamininus. At Cynoscephalae, in Thessaly, the legion proved its superiority over the phalanx, and Philip was forced to pay an indemnity of 1,000 talents, to become the ally of Rome, and to surrender his foreign possessions and the so-called fetters of Greece, Corinth, Chalcis, and Demetrias. The next year, at the Isthmian games, Flamininus proclaimed the freedom of Greece.

Antiochus had rendered Philip no help, but instead had conquered most of the coast of Asia Minor, thereby incurring the hatred of Eumenes II of Pergamum. The exile Hannibal had recently joined him, and, feeling strong in his victories, Antiochus was in no mood to obey the Roman envoys when they met him at Lysimacheia and ordered him from Europe. Instead, he encouraged the Aetolian League against Rome, for the Aetolians had been angered by Rome's relatively light punishment of Philip. In 192 B.C. Antiochus crossed to Greece with 10,000 troops, to free the Greeks from the Roman tyrant, as he said, but neither Philip nor Achaea deserted to him. The Achaean League had now grown strong because of the energy of Philopoemen of Megalopolis; upon the death of Nabis, tyrant of Sparta, Philopoemen forced Sparta and many other communities into the League, so that it now included the entire Peloponnesus. Antiochus managed to escape to Asia after a bad defeat at Thermopylae (191 B.C.), and in the following year L. Cornelius Scipio and his famous brother Africanus, with the help of Eumenes, decisively beat him at Magnesia. By the peace of Apamea (188 B.C.) Antiochus was compelled to pay an indemnity and to limit his frontier at the Taurus. The great Seleucid died in 187 B.C. and was succeeded, after the brief reign of Seleucus IV, by Antiochus IV Epiphanes.

The peace of Apamea greatly augmented the territory of Rome's friends, Pergamum and Rhodes, the latter now queen of the seas. In 179 B.C. Philip died, having spent the last years of his life in building up his state with an eye to a war of revenge on Rome. He was succeeded by his son Perseus, who had the same ambition. Throughout Greece there was popular enthusiasm for Perseus; on the whole, the democracies were for independence, whereas the aristocrats and the rich favored Rome. By 172 B.C. Perseus' activities so alarmed Eumenes that he went to Rome to report on him. This led, in the next year, to the Third Macedonian War. In June, 168 B.C., the Roman commander, L. Aemilius Paullus, defeated Perseus at Pydna in southern Macedonia and carried him off to Rome, where he later died. Macedon had been a danger to Rome long enough. Rome, therefore, divided the country into four republics and—following a familiar custom—forbade inter-marriage and commercial relations between them.

Greece presented a confused picture after Pydna. The country was full of exiles; and to insure loyalty, Rome took many hostages, including a thousand, with Polybius, from the Achaean League alone. With the passing of the Macedonian danger, however, Rome no longer felt the need of her former friends. She accused Rhodes of trying to arbitrate the dispute with Perseus, and irreparably harmed her by the creation of Delos as a free port (167 B.C.). Indeed, Rome made known her hostile feelings even to Pergamum.

In 169 B.C. Antiochus IV invaded Egypt. He was an extraordinary man, who had lived for many years in Rome and admired both it and Greece; a patron of Athens, he had also cultivated the resources of his own state. Egypt seemed an easy prey. Ever since the use of native troops in the battle of Raphia the Egyptian natives had been a problem to the Ptolemies; and now the death of Ptolemy V produced a complicated struggle for the throne, between Ptolemy VI Philometor and Ptolemy VII Euergetes II. But at Alexandria Antiochus was met by a Roman envoy, who dramatically drew a circle around him in the sand and told him not to step out until he had chosen whether to leave Egypt. Antiochus decided to leave, for, it will be recalled, he had his eye on a greater prize, Bactria and the East. After his death in 163 B.C. the Empire had only one more Seleucid of ability, Antiochus VII Sidetes, who was killed in 129 B.C. by the Parthian king Phraates.

The confusion of Greece after Pydna was made worse by one Andriscus, who claimed to be the son of Perseus and gained much popular support. In 148 B.C. Rome put him down and chose the occasion to punish the four Macedonian republics and to make Macedonia a Roman province. In the same year Sparta seceded from the Achaean League, which led to border warfare. Rome held a congress at Corinth and ordered the League to give up Sparta and other cities, an action which brought the anti-Roman feeling in Greece to fever heat. The opposition collapsed, however, in 146 B.C. when the Roman L. Mummius captured Corinth, razed the city to the ground, and enslaved the population. The Greek leagues were disbanded, and although Rome did not yet formally make Greece a province, she exercised a sort of suzerainty over the country.

The enforced peace brought prosperity to Greece; the pity of it was that the Hellenistic East had to be caught up in the ambitions and wars of individual Romans, who strove in the next century for personal dominion. Not only did Greece revive toward the end of the second century, however, but Pergamum reached the height of its prosperity under Attalus II, who had succeeded in 159 B.C. on the death of Eumenes. Attalus III (138–133 B.C.) is famous because, on his death, he willed the kingdom of Pergamum to Rome—this was not the last time that Rome was to receive a sate by testament. Naturally, Attalus' heir, Aristonicus, was displeased, but the uprising of the slaves which he caused proved ineffective. In 129 B.C. Pergamum was organized as the Roman province of Asia.

The bitter hatred of Rome in the Hellenistic East was due in part to the publicani, who bought the right of collecting the taxes—themselves reasonable enough—and then proceeded to bleed the provincials. There was great popular support, therefore, for Mithridates, king of Pontus, the new enemy of Rome (88 B.C.). Revolutions flared up in many cities; Roman traders were massacred by the thousand. But Sulla captured Athens, and, in one way or another, Rome acquired all of Asia Minor —either by conquest or by making native kings her clients. It was the Roman civil wars, however, that ruined Greece. The warring generals stripped the country of much of its wealth, and large sections, notably the Peloponnesus, were depouplated. Asia lost her wealth, too, though not her people, and needed only peace for a revival. In 64 B.C. Pompey made northern Syria—all that was left now of the former Seleucid Empire—a Roman province. Ptolemy XI Auletes, the flute player, managed to keep Rome off for some years, though the popular party at Rome was anxious to annex Egypt for its grain. Ptolemaic Egypt came to an end during the reign of Ptolemy XII and his sister Cleopatra VII. The story of Cleopatra's career is famous—how she fascinated Julius Caesar and Antony, and almost made herself empress of the civilized world. But Antony lost the throne of Rome to Augustus at the battle of Actium (31 B.C.), and thenceforth Egypt belonged to the Roman emperors. In 27 B.C. the Peloponnesus was organized as the Roman province of Achaea.

The Roman Empire brought peace to the civilized world for two centuries. Nothing like it has been seen since. From England to the Euphrates people paid taxes into the same treasury, were protected by the same army, and were governed by the same law. Greece, to be sure, was stagnant, but Athens remained a university town. Speaking generally, the mighty Roman Empire meant prosperity for the world; and within it, peoples of different race and religion and custom learned to live happily with one another. With the passage of time, however, the imperial administration robbed the people of their freedom of thought and speech, and grew continually more oppressive and grinding. Perhaps, after all, it was unfortunate that it was not given to the Greeks, with their greater imagination, rather than to the Romans, to rule a world state.

Map 55

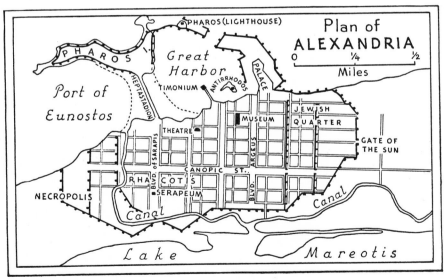

Map 56

461

CHRONOLOGICAL TABLE

ALL DATES ARE B.C.

Bronze Age civilization	3rd and 2nd millennia
Height of Minoan civilization	1600
Height of Mycenaean civilization	1400
Fall of Troy	*ca.* 1184
Dorian Invasion	*ca.* 1100
The Greek Middle Age	*ca.* 1100–750
Homer	*ca.* 800
First Olympic Games (traditional)	776
Hesiod	*ca.* 750
Colonization	*ca.* 750–550
Archaic Greek civilization	*ca.* 750–479
Spartan conquest of Messenia	*ca.* 730
Synoikismos at Athens	*before* 700
Tyranny	7th and 6th cents.
Draco	*ca.* 621
Reform of Lycurgus at Sparta	*ca.* 600

GLOSSARY

As a rule, terms which appear but one in the text, and are there defined, are omitted, since they can be readily located in the Index.

Abacus. The uppermost member of the capital of a column.

Abrasive. A substance, such as emery, used for grinding or polishing.

Acropolis. The upper city or citadel, notably the one at Athens.

Acroterion (pl. *acroteria*). The ornament or figure at the corner or apex of a pediment.

Agora. A market place or public square of a Greek city.

Alabaster. A hard translucent variety of gypsum or calcite, usually white and sometimes banded.

Amber. A yellowish translucent resin, capable of a good polish.

Amphictyony. A union of neighbors ostensibly for a religious object.

Amphiprostyle. A temple with portico of columns in front and rear.

Amphora. A two-handled vase, commonly used for holding water.

Aniconic. Without idols or statues.

Anta (pl. *antae*). A slightly projecting pilaster that terminates the side wall of a cella; columns standing between antae are spoken of as "in antis."

Antefix. A decorative termination of the cover tiles of a roof, placed sometimes also along the top of the ridge.

Apaturia. An Athenian festival, in celebration of all Ionians, when grown sons were enrolled as citizens.

Apella. The Assembly of citizens at Sparta.

Architrave. The lowest member of the entablature: a lintel carried from the top of one column to another.

Archon. One of the nine chief magistrates at Athens. See *Thesmothetae.*

Areopagus. A hill near the Athenian Acropolis; the aristocratic Council which met there and took its name was a development of the Homeric Council of elders.

Aristocracy. Government by the best; that is, usually by a small privileged class.

Arris. A sharp edge formed by the meeting of two flutes of a Doric column.

Ashlar masonry. Regular masonry of squared stone, with horizontal courses and vertical joints.

Boeotarch. A chief magistrate of the Boeotian League.

Boule. The Council; at Athens, the Council of Five Hundred.

Bouleuterion. The building in which a Greek Council met.

Breccia. A rock of larger than sand grains, cemented together, usually of varied colors.

Carnelian. A reddish variety of chalcedony, capable of a fine polish, hard, and often used for seals.

Caryatid. The figure of a maiden which, in lieu of a column, supports an entablature, as in the South Porch of the Erechtheum at Athens.

Cella. A temple's main chamber or sanctuary, called *naos* in Greek.

Chalcedony. A translucent variety of quartz, pale blue or gray in color.

Chiton. An oblong garment or tunic (woolen in the Doric, linen in the Ionic) worn long or short next to the skin by both sexes, with openings for the arms along the upper edge.

Choregos. A wealthy man who was assigned the liturgy of supplying and training a chorus.

Chryselephantine. A statue generally with a wooden core, whose drapery and ornaments are of gold and the flesh of ivory.

Cleruchy. A colony, peculiar to Athens, planted in foreign soil and in which all the people (cleruchs) remained Athenian citizens.

Colacretae. The chief financial officials at Athens.

Colonnade. A range of columns.

Conglomerate. A consolidated rock of gravel embedded in sand.

Corbel. Courses of stones, set in a wall, each projecting slightly beyond the course below; when continued, the top courses can be joined by a capstone (corbel arch).

Cornice. The crowning member of the entablature: a projection designed to throw rain water from the face of a building; the diagonal cornices of a pediment are spoken of as "raking."

Corona. A cornice's projecting member, with a vertical face.

Crater. A bowl, primarily used for mixing wine at banquets.

Crepidoma. The stepped platform of a Greek temple.

Cyclopean masonry. Rough, massive masonry employed in the Bronze Age for the walls of cities and citadels.

Cylix. A drinking cup.

Dactyl. A poetical foot of three syllables, one long followed by two short.

Dado. The lower portion of a wall when treated as a continuous wainscot.

Dais. A raised bench or platform on which a person of prominence sits, as the king's dais in the megaron at Tiryns.

Decarchy. An oligarchy of ten officials set up by Lysander after the Peloponnesian War.

Deme. A township of Attica or a section of Athens. The demes' elected officials were known as demarchs.

Demiourgoi. A board of ten magistrates, especially of the Achaean League.

Dentils. Rectangular blocks in a cornice's bed-mould, which represented originally the ends of roof beams.

Deus ex machina. The interference of a god to solve superhuman difficulties.

Diadochi. The immediate successors of Alexander the Great.

Diadumenus. Specifically, Polycleitus' statue of a youth tying a fillet around his head.

Dicasts. The 6,000 jurors who formed the juries (dicasteries) at Athens.

Dioecetes. The Minister of Finance in Ptolemaic Egypt or Seleucid Asia.

Discobolus. Specifically, Myron's statue of a youth throwing the discus.

Doryphorus. Specifically, Polycleitus' statue of a youth carrying a spear.

Drachma. Six obols. Didrachm, two drachmas; tetradrachm, four drachmas; decadrachm, ten drachmas.

Dromos. The entrance passage of a Mycenaean tomb.

Drum. One of the cylindrical blocks of which the shaft of a column is composed.

Ecclesia. The Assembly of citizens at Athens.
Echinus. The convex moulding which supports the abacus of a capital.
Economus. A financial official in the Hellenistic Age, responsible to the Dioecetes.
Eisphora. An Athenian property tax.
Electrum. An alloy of gold and silver.
Emery. A very hard mineral (corundum) useful for polishing.
Entablature. The superstructure carried by the columns, consisting of architrave, frieze (often omitted in the Asiatic Ionic order), and cornice.
Entasis. The slight convex curve of a column.
Eparchy. One of seventy-two administrative districts which formed the twenty-five satrapies of the Seleucid Empire.
Ephebi. Athenian youths of nineteen and twenty engaged in military training.
Ephor. One of the five chief magistrates at Sparta.
Epic. Narrative poetry treating a theme of action in heroic proportions and style.
Epinician. An ode in honor of a victor.
Epistates. A single administrative superintendent of a city; in Seleucid Asia, the king's representative.
Ethnos. A tribe, or tribal group, such as formed the basis of the Aetolian and Achaean Leagues.
Eupatrids. The landed nobility at Athens.
Exedra. A semicircular stone seat or recess.

Faïence. A colorful glazed earthenware.
Fascia. One of the three planes into which the architrave of the Ionic and Corinthian orders is subdivided.
Fillet. A flat band or moulding.
Flutes. The vertical channels in the shafts of columns, separated from each other by an arris in the Doric order and by a fillet in the Ionic and Corinthian orders.
Foot. The Greek foot measured 11.65 inches.
Frieze. The middle member of the entablature, or any sculptured horizontal band.

Gable. See *Pediment.*
Genos (pl. *gene*). A clan, the memebrs of which traced their ancestry to a common hero or god; at Athens, limited to the nobility.

Gerousia. The Spartan Council, consisting of twenty-eight elders and the two kings.

Graphe paranomon. A constitutional safeguard at Athens, under which an indictment was possible for bringing before the Assembly measures in conflict with the laws.

Guttae. Small peglike cylinders under Doric regulae and mutules.

Gymnasium. A training school for physical education, where exercises, such as running, required considerable space.

Gymnopaedia. An annual Spartan festival, in honor of those who fell at Thyrea, at which naked boys danced and went through gymnastic exercises.

Gypsum. A mineral, notable for its crystals, that easily splits into thin layers.

Harmost. A Spartan garrison commander.

Hegemony. Leadership, or the preponderant influence of one state on another.

Hektemoroi. Athenian tenant-farmers who had to pay one sixth of their produce to the great landowners.

Heliaea. The law courts at Athens, eventually divided into several juries (dicasteries).

Hellenotamiae. The chief financial officials at Athens in charge of the imperial funds.

Helot. Term given particularly to the non-Dorian inhabitants of Laconia and Messenia reduced to a state of serfdom by the Spartans.

Hexameter. A verse of six measures or feet; in Homer the first four feet may be dactyls or spondees, the fifth is regularly a dactyl, the sixth a spondee.

Himation. A rectangular cloth mantle, about 7 feet long and as wide as the wearer's height, wrapped around the body in any way that delighted the wearer; worn by both sexes.

Hippeis. Knights; the second wealthiest class in the Solonian census.

Homonoia. Unity and Concord.

Hoopoe. A bird of cinnamon-colored, black and white plumage, with a slender decurved bill and erectile crest, about the size of a thrush.

Hoplite. A heavy-armed foot soldier.

Intercalary. Days or months that are added to the ordinary year.

Isopolity. A grant of citizenship by one city to individuals in another city and to entire cities.

Kleros. An allotment of land, common in the Hellenistic Age, and requiring military obligations of the settler.

Kore (pl. *korai*). A maiden or an archaic statue of a maiden.
Kouros (pl. *kouroi*). A youth or an archaic statue of a youth.

Latifundia. Large estates, notably at Rome.
Lintel. A horizontal member spanning an opening.
Liturgy. A capital tax on wealthy citizens, whereby they assumed the burden, for example, of supplying and training a dramatic chorus.
Lustral. Pertaining to purification.
Lyric poetry. Expressive of the poet's feeling, whether actually sung or not.

Medimnus. About 9 gallons, or 1½ bushels dry measure.
Megaron. The main or men's hall in a Mycenaean palace.
Metic. An alien domiciled in Athens, subject to a special tax and military service, but without political rights.
Metope. The sunk panel (often sculptured) between the triglyphs of the Doric frieze course.
Mina. 100 drachmas.
Monolith. A single block of stone.
Mutule. A projecting slab on the soffit of a Doric cornice.

Naos. The cella of the Greek temple.
Nauarch. A subordinate naval officer.
Naucraries. Administrative districts in Attica.
Niello. A dark metallic alloy of sulphur with silver or copper.
Nike. Victory.
Nome. An administrative district in Egypt.

Obol. The smallest monetary unit; often referred to loosely as "equivalent" to three American cents. It has been estimated that a single man could live on two obols a day in late fifth-century Athens.
Obsidian. Dark volcanic glass, translucent in thin splinters, which are sharp-edged and therefore useful in, for example, the manufacture of knives.
Odeon. A roofed building for musical performances.
Oligarchy. Government by the few.
Olympiad. A period of four years from one Olympian festival to the next.
Opisthodomus. The porch in the rear of a temple.
Orchestra. The circular dancing floor of a Greek theater, where all the action took place.

Ossuary. A depository for the bones of the dead.

Paean. A battle song.

Palaestra. A training school for physical exercises, such as wrestling and boxing, but smaller than the gymnasium.

Panoply. A full complement of armor.

Papyrus. The ancient writing material, derived from a tall Egyptian plant (sedge), cut into strips, arranged crosswise and pressed into a smooth surface.

Paralus. One of the two Athenian state triremes, used for sacred embassies and official business.

Parascenium. One of the symmetrical wings of the *skene* which project toward the orchestra of a Greek theater.

Parodos. The entrance passage, between auditorium and *skene,* into the theater, used by chorus and audience.

Pediment. The triangular frame, above the entablature at either end of the temple, formed by raking and horizontal cornices; within this area often stood sculpture in the round.

Peltast. A light-armed foot soldier.

Pentacosiomedimni. The wealthiest class in the Solonian census, consisting of persons whose estates produced annually 500 measures of produce or whose annual income in drachmas was of approximately the same value.

Peplos. A shawl-like garment worn by women.

Perioeci ("dwellers around"). Term given particularly to the non-Dorian inhabitants of Laconia who, though personally free, were dependent on Sparta.

Peripteral. Term given to a temple, whose cella is surrounded by a peristyle.

Peristyle. A covered colonnade surrounding a building; or an inner court lined with a colonnade.

Phalanx. A compact mass of heavy infantry, often eight deep, but greatly developed by Philip and Alexander of Macedon.

Phratry. An association ("brotherhood") originally of close kinsmen; in early Athens birth into a phratry was necessary for citizenship.

Phyle. A tribe, though usually not in the "racial" sense of *ethnos,* but denoting rather a large political division, as at Athens.

Polemarch. A general. At Athens, the archon originally in command of the army.

Polis (pl. *poleis*). City-state.

Poros. Tufa; a kind of marble, but lighter.

Porphyry. A dark red or purple rock of feldspar crystals.

Portico. A porch or entrance to a building.

Probouleuma. At Athens, a resolution prepared by the *boule* for the consideration of the *ecclesia*.

Pronaos. The porch or vestibule at the front of a temple.

Propylaeum (pl. *propylaea*). The monumental entrance gate to a *temenos*. A simple building of this type is known as a *propylon*.

Proscenium. The colonnade between *skene* and orchestra of a theater.

Prostyle. A temple with portico of columns in front.

Prytany. One of ten committees of the Athenian *boule,* each consisting of fifty councillors (*prytaneis*) and presiding for a tenth of the year.

Regula. A narrow strip under the Doric taenia, beneath which are carved the guttae.

Rhapsode. A professional reciter of epic poems.

Salaminia. One of the two Athenian state triremes, used for sacred embassies and official business.

Sarcophagus. A coffin, usually of stone.

Satrapy. The province of a Persian governor (satrap).

Silphium. A plant, growing especially in the region of Cyrene, which the Greeks considered to have medicinal value.

Sima. The gutter on the gables and flanks of a building.

Skene. The scene building of a Greek theater.

Socle. A projecting member at the foot of a wall; for example, in the Bronze Age, the courses of field stones laid on the ground to raise the sun-dried bricks of a house wall as far as possible above potentially damaging rain water.

Spartiates. Citizens of Sparta.

Spondee. A poetical foot of two long syllables.

Stade. Six hundred Greek feet; a racecourse (stadium) was of that length.

Steatite. A soft mineral (talc) of a grayish green color.

Stele. A tombstone, or any stone slab used for sculptured reliefs or inscriptions.

Stereobate. The substructure of a temple.

Stoa. A building whose roof is supported by one or more rows of columns parallel to the rear wall.

Stylobate. A pavement on which columns stand, such as the upper step of a temple.

Sympolity. A common citizenship, enjoyed, for example, by all the members of the Aetolian and Achaean Leagues.

Synoikismos. The transference by the people of an area, such as Attica, of their political sovereignty in favor of one city (Athens).

Syssition (pl. *syssitia*). The common mess at Sparta.

Taenia. The projecting fillet of the Doric architrave.

Talent. Sixty minas; often referred to loosely as "equivalent" to 1,080 American dollars.

Temenos. The sacred enclosure in which one or more Greek temples stand.

Thalassocracy. Maritime supremacy.

Theoric Fund. At Athens, from the time of Pericles, for the purpose of giving money from the treasury to poor citizens to pay for their seats at the theater (two obols), but also for other purposes.

Thesmothetae. Athenian officials, six in number and originally charged with guarding public documents and recording legal decisions, who formed the board of nine archons with the *archon eponymos* (who gave his name to the year), *archon basileus* (king archon, in charge of religion) and *polemarch* (commander-in-chief).

Thetes. The fourth and lowest class in the Solonian census.

Tholos. A circular Mycenaean tomb; a circular Greek temple.

Timocracy. A state in which political honors are dependent on a property rating.

Triglyph. A projecting member, with vertical channels and chamfers, that separates the metopes of the Doric frieze course.

Triology. Three dramas, devoted to a general theme.

Trireme. The regular Greek warship, widely and erroneously regarded as consisting of three banks of rowers. A trireme had three *squads* of about sixty oarsmen each, seated respectively in the bow, amidships, and in the stern; each man had one .oar and no oar was pulled by more than one man. The prow was armed under water—it projected well out in front—with a bronze ram weighing about 170 pounds. The craft was long and low and narrow, being about 120 feet in length and about 20 feet broad. Rigidity and seaworthiness were strengthened by at least one heavy cable passed all the way around the hull, drawn taut, and secured in place against the hull. The mast was demountable. The oarsmen were protected from the sun by awnings, and possibly from missiles by leather curtains hung beside them in battle. It may have been partly due to the awnings and the curtains that entire crews often perished when the ship went down: they were trapped.

Trittys (pl. *trittyes*). A "Third," three of which formed the Cleisthenic tribe; it consisted of one or more demes and constituted the link between deme and tribe.

Tympanum. The rear, triangular wall of the pediment, enclosed by the raking and horizontal cornices.

Volute. The spiral scroll of an Ionic capital.

Zeugitae. The solid middle class at Athens, being the third class in the Solonian census.

SELECTED
BIBLIOGRAPHY

This bibliography, consisting chiefly of English titles, does not aim at completeness, though it is intended to put the reader on the track of a full bibliography. It does not necessarily include all the works utilized in the writing of the chapters; reviews, reports, and, except in rare instances, articles are omitted altogether. Special attention is called to the monumental *Cambridge Ancient History* and *Histoire Grecque*, and their bibliographies, where there will also be found a good summary of the ancient sources. *The Year's Work in Classical Studies* (London), Bursian's *Jahresbericht* (Leipzig), and Marouzeeau's *L'Année philologique* (Paris) ordinarily report current publications. Specialized articles, reviews, and abstracts of journals may be found in the more important periodicals in the English language (American Journal of Philology, Classical Philology, Classical Weekly, Classical Journal, American Historical Review, Journal of Hellenic Studies, Classical Review, American Journal of Archaeology, which includes notices of various excavations, and Hesperia, which reports the excavations in the Athenian Agora).

The importance of art and archaeology for the study of Greek history cannot be overemphasized. In addition to the monumental *Inscriptiones Graecae,* the *Corpus Vasorum Antiquorum,* the *British Museum Catalogue of Greek Coins,* and the publications of excavations, good "picture-books" have their own special value. The following works, of particular significance, are recommended: *The Architecture of Ancient Greece,* by W. J. Anderson, R. P. Spiers and W. B. Dinsmoor (New York, 1927); *The Sculpture and Sculptors of the Greeks,* by G. M. A. Richter (2nd ed., New Haven, 1930); *The Acropolis,* by W. Hege and G. Rodenwaldt (Oxford, 1930); *A Selection of Greek Historical Inscriptions,* by M. N. Tod (Oxford, 1946); *Olympia,* by W. Hege and G. Rodenwaldt (London, 1936); *Hellas and Rome,* by H. T. Bossert and W. Zschietzschmann (London, 1936); *Epigraphica Attica,* by B. D. Meritt (Cambridge, Mass., 1940); *Delphes,* by P. de La Coste-Messelière (Paris, 1943); *Hellas,* by H. Chisholm, G. Hoyningen-Huene, and A. Koiransky (New York, 1943); *Baalbek-Palmyra,* by G. Hoyningen-Huene and D. M. Robinson (New York, 1946).

GENERAL HISTORIES AND REFERENCE WORKS

Andrewes, A. *The Greeks.* New York, 1967.

Beloch, K. J. *Griechische Geschichte.* 2nd ed. 4 vols. Berlin, 1912–1927.

Bengtson, H. *Einführung in die alte Geschichte.* Munich, 1959.

———. *Griechische Geschichte.* 3rd ed. Munich, 1965.

Berve, H. *Griechische Geschichte.* 3 vols. Freiburg, 1959–1960.

Botsford, G. W., and Sihler, E. G. *Hellenic Civilization.* New York, 1920.

Bowra, C. M. *The Greek Experience.* London, 1957.

Bury, J. B. *History of Greece.* 3rd ed. London, 1952.

———, Cook, S. A., Adcock, F. E., and Charlesworth, M. P. (eds.). *Cambridge Ancient History.* 12 vols., 5 vols. of plates. New York, 1923–1939.

Busolt, G. *Griechische Geschichte.* 3 vols. Gotha, 1893–1904.

Daremberg, C. V., and Saglio, E. *Dictionnaire des antiquités grecques et romaines.* 5 vols. Paris, 1877–1919.

De Sanctis, G. *Storia dei Greci.* 2 vols. Florence, 1963.

Finley, M. I. *The Ancient Greeks.* New York, 1963.

Glotz, G. *et al. Histoire grecque.* 4 vols. Paris, 1925–1938.

Grote, G. *A History of Greece.* 12 vols. London, 1884.

Hammond, N. G. L. *History of Greece to 322 B.C.* 2nd ed. New York, 1967.

Harvey, P. *The Oxford Companion to Classical Literature.* Oxford, 1937.

Kagan, D. *Problems in Ancient History.* Vol. 1: *The Ancient Orient and Greece.* New York, 1966.

Kitto, H. D. F. *The Greeks.* Baltimore, 1951.

Laistner, M. L. W. *A History of the Greek World from 479 to 323 B.C.* London, 1936.

Lloyd-Jones, H. (ed.). *The Greek World.* Baltimore, 1965.

Meyer, E. *Geschichte des Altertums.* 5th ed. 5 vols. Stuttgart, 1925–1931.

Müller, I. *Handbuch der Klassischen Altertumswissenschaft.* Munich, various dates.

Pauly, A. F., Wissowa, G., and Kroll, W. *Real-Encyclopädie der Klassischen Altertumswissenschaft.* Stuttgart, in progress.

Sandys, J. E. *History of Classical Scholarship.* 3rd ed. 2 vols. New York, 1921.

Whibley, L. (ed.). *A Companion to Greek Studies.* 4th ed. Cambridge, 1931.

GEOGRAPHY AND REGIONAL HISTORY

Ball, J. *Egypt in the Classical Geographers.* Cairo, 1942.

Berve, H. *Sparta.* Leipzig, 1937.

Boardman, J. *The Greeks Overseas.* Baltimore, 1964.

Carpenter, R. *The Greeks in Spain.* New York, 1925.

Cary, M. *The Geographical Background of Greek and Roman History.* London, 1949.

——, and Warmington, E. H. *The Ancient Explorers.* New York, 1929.

Casson, S. *Macedonia, Thrace, and Illyria.* Oxford, 1926.

Ciaceri, E. *Storia della Magna Grecia.* Rome, 1927–1932.

Cloché, P. *Thèbes de Béotie.* Namur, Louvain, and Paris (n.d).

Cook, J. M. *The Greeks in Ionia and the East.* New York, 1962.

Cross, G. N. *Epirus.* Cambridge, 1932.

Dunbabin, T. J. *The Western Greeks.* London, 1948.

——. *The Greeks and their Near Eastern Neighbors.* London, 1957.

Freeman, E. A. *History of Sicily.* Oxford, 1891–1894.

Freeman, K. *Greek City-States.* London, 1950.

Hammond, N. G. L. *Epirus.* Oxford, 1967.

Huxley, G. L. *The Early Ionians.* London, 1906.

Jones, A. H. M. *Sparta.* Cambridge, Mass., 1967.

Laidlaw, W. A. *A History of Delos.* Oxford, 1933.

Michell, H. *Sparta.* New York, 1952.

Roebuck, C. *Ionian Trade and Colonization*. New York, 1959.

Roussel, P. *Sparte*. 2nd ed. Paris, 1962.

Scullard, H. H. *Atlas of the Classical World*. London, 1969.

Warmington, E. H., (ed.). *Greek Geography*. London, 1934.

West, A. B. *The History of the Chalcidic League*. Madison, 1919.

Westlake H. D. *Thessaly in the Fourth Century*. London 1935.

Will, E. *Korinthiaka*. Paris, 1955.

Willetts, R. F. *Ancient Crete*. London, 1965.

Woodhead, A. G. *The Greeks in the West*. New York, 1962.

ANCILLARY DISCIPLINES: ARCHAEOLOGY, EPIGRAPHY, NUMISMATICS

GENERAL

Head, B. V. *Historia Numorum*. London, 1911.

Klaffenbach, G. *Griechische Epigraphik*. Göttingen, 1957.

Kraay, C. M., and Hirmer, M. *Greek Coins*. New York, 1966.

MacKendrick, P. *The Greek Stones Speak*. New York, 1962.

Seltman, C. *Greek Coins*. 2nd ed. London, 1955.

Tod, M. B. *A Selection of Greek Historical Inscriptions*. 2 vols. London, 1946–1948.

Woodhead, A. G. *The Study of Greek Inscriptions*. Cambridge, 1959.

THE BRONZE AGE

Blegen, C. W. *Troy*. 3 vols. Princeton, 1950–1953.

———. *The Mycenaean Age*. Cincinnati, 1962.

———. *Troy and the Trojans*. London, 1963.

Chadwick, J. *The Decipherment of Linear B*. Cambridge, 1959.

Desborough, V. R. d'A. *The Last Mycenaeans and Their Successors*. New York, 1964.

Evans, A. J. *Scripta Minoa*. Oxford, 1909.

———. *The Palace of Minos at Knossos*. 4 vols. London, 1921–1935.

Forsdyke, J. *Greece before Homer*. London, 1956.

Furumark, A. *The Mycenaean Pottery*. Stockholm, 1941.

Graham, J. *The Palaces of Crete*. Princeton, 1962.

Hutchinson, R. *Prehistoric Crete*. Baltimore, 1962.

Kantor, H. J. *The Aegean and the Orient in the Second Millennium B.C.* Bloomington, 1947.

Marinatos, S. N., and Hirmer, M. *Crete and Mycenae*. London, 1960.

Matz, F. *Crete and Early Greece*. London, 1962.

McDonald, W. A. *Progress into the Past.* New York, 1967.

Mylonas, G. *Ancient Mycenae.* Princeton, 1957.

Myres, J. L. *Who Were the Greeks?* Berkeley, 1930.

Nilsson, M. P. *The Mycenaean Origin of Greek Mythology.* Berkeley, 1932.

Palmer, L. R. *Mycenaeans and Minoans.* 2nd ed. New York, 1965.

Pendlebury, J. D. S. *The Archaeology of Crete.* London, 1939.

Schachermeyer, F. *Die ältesten Kulturen Griechenlands.* Stuttgart, 1955.

Taylour, W. *The Mycenaeans.* London, 1964.

Ventris, M., and Chadwick, J. *Documents in Mycenaean Greek.* New York, 1956.

Vermeule, E. *Greece in the Bronze Age.* Chicago, 1964.

Wace, A. J. B. *Mycenae.* Princeton, 1949.

Webster, T. B. L. *From Mycenae to Homer.* London, 1958.

HOMER AND THE MIDDLE AGES

Bowra, C. M. *Heroic Poetry.* London, 1952.

———. *Homer and his Forerunners.* Edinburgh, 1955.

Burn, A. R. *The World of Hesiod.* London, 1936.

Carpenter, R. *Folk Tale, Fiction and Saga in the Homeric Epic.* Berkeley, 1946.

Finley, M. I. *The World of Odysseus.* New York, 1954.

Kirk, G. S. *The Songs of Homer.* New York, 1962.

——— (ed.). *The Language and Background of Homer.* New York, 1964.

Lord, A. B. *Serbo-Crotian Heroic Songs.* Cambridge, Mass., 1954.

———. *The Singer of Tales.* Cambridge, Mass., 1960.

Lorimer, H. L. *Homer and the Monuments.* London, 1950.

Murray, G. *The Rise of the Greek Epic.* 3rd ed. Oxford, 1924.

Nilsson, M. *Homer and Mycenae.* London, 1933.

Page, D. *The Homeric Odyssey.* Oxford, 1955.

———. *History and the Homeric Iliad.* Berkeley, 1959.

Parry, M. *L'Epithète traditionelle dans Homère.* Paris, 1928.

———. *Les Formules et la Métrique d'Homère.* Paris, 1928.

Scott, J. A. *The Unity of Homer.* Berkeley, 1921.

Starr, C. G. *The Origins of Greek Civilization, 1100–650 B.C.* New York, 1901.

Wace, A. J. B., and Stubbings, F. H. *A Companion to Homer.* London, 1962.

Wade-Gery, H. T. *The Poet of the Iliad.* Cambridge, 1952.

Whitman, C. H. *Homer and the Heroic Tradition.* Cambridge, Mass., 1958.

THE ARCHAIC PERIOD

Andrewes, A. *The Greek Tyrants.* New York, 1956.

Bérard, J. *La Colonisation grecque de l'Italie méridionale et de la Sicile dans l'antiquité: L'Histoir de la légende.* 2nd ed. Paris, 1957.

Burn, A. R. *The Lyric Age of Greece.* New York, 1961.

Cornelius, F. *Die Tyrannis in Athen.* Munich, 1929.

Huxley, G. L. *Early Sparta.* Cambridge, Mass., 1962.

Linforth, I. M. *Solon, the Athenian.* Berkeley, 1919.

Masaracchia, A. *Solone.* Florence, 1958.

Seltman, C. T. *Athens, Its History and Coinage Before the Persian Invasion.* Cambridge, 1924.

Ure, P. N. *The Origin of Tyranny.* Cambridge, 1922.

Woodhouse, W. J. *Solon the Liberator.* Oxford, 1938.

Zimmern, A. *Solon and Croesus.* London, 1928.

THE FIFTH CENTURY

Abbott, E. *Pericles and the Golden Age of Athens.* 2nd ed. New York, 1925.

Beloch, K. J. *Die Attische Politik seit Perikles.* Leipzig, 1884.

Burn, A. R. *Pericles and Athens.* New York, 1949.

Cloché, P. *La Restauration démocratique à Athènes en 403 avant J. C.* Paris, 1915.

Croiset, M. *Aristophanes and the Political Parties at Athens.* London, 1909.

Delbrück, H. *Die Strategie des Perikles.* Berlin, 1890.

De Sanctis, G. *Pericle.* Milan and Messina, 1944.

Ehrenberg, V. *Sophocles and Pericles.* Oxford, 1954.

Gomme, A. W. *A Historical Commentary on Thucydides.* 3 vols. Oxford, 1950–1956.

Grundy, G. B. *The Great Persian War.* London, 1901.

———. *Thucydides and the History of his Age.* 2nd ed., 2 vols. Oxford, 1948.

Hatzfeld, J. *Alcibiade.* Paris, 1951.

Henderson, B. W. *The Great War Between Athens and Sparta.* London, 1927.

Hignett, C. *Xerxes' Invasion of Greece.* Oxford, 1963.

Homo, L. P. *Périclès.* Paris, 1954.

Meritt, B. D. *The Athenian Calendar in the Fifth Century*. Cambridge, Mass., 1928.

——, and West, A. B. *The Athenian Assessment of 425 B.C.* Ann Arbor, 1934.

——, Wade-Gery, H. T., and McGregor, M. F. *The Athenian Tribute Lists*. 4 vols. Princeton, 1939–1953.

Murray, G. *Aristophanes and the War Party*. London, 1919.

Olmstead, A. T. E. *History of the Persian Empire*. Chicago, 1948.

Pflugk-Hartung, J. von. *Perikles als Feldherr*. Stuttgart, 1884.

Robertson, H. G. *The Administration of Justice in the Athenian Empire*. Toronto, 1924.

Woodhouse, W. J. *King Agis of Sparta and His Campaign in Arkadia in 418 B.C.* Oxford, 1933.

Zimmern, A. *The Greek Commonwealth*. 5th ed. New York, 1931.

THE FOURTH CENTURY

Accame, S. *La lega ateniese del Sec. IV A.C.* Rome, 1941.

——. *Ricerche intorno alla guerra corinzia*. Naples, n.d.

Cloché, P. *La Politique extérieure d'Athènes de 404 à 338*. Paris, 1934.

——. *Demosthènes et la fin de la démocratie athénienne*. Paris, 1937.

Drerup, E. *Demosthenes im Urteile des Altertums*. Wurzburg, 1923.

Glover, T. R. *From Pericles to Philip*. London, 1919.

Jaeger, W. *Demosthenes: The Origin and Growth of His Policy*. Berkeley, 1938.

Marshall, F. H. *The Second Athenian Confederacy*. Cambridge, 1905.

Momigliano, A. *Filippo il Macedone*. Florence, 1934.

Mossé, C. *La Fin de la démocratie athénienne*. Paris, 1962.

Pickard-Cambridge, A. W. *Demosthenes and the Last Days of Greek Freedom*. New York, 1914.

Ryder, T. T. B. *Koine Eirene*. London, 1965.

Wuest, F. R. *Philipp II von Makedonien und Griechenland in den Jahren von 346 bis 338*. Munich, 1938.

ALEXANDER THE GREAT

Berve, H. *Das Alexanderreich auf prosopographischer Grundlage*. Munich, 1926.

Ehrenberg, V. *Alexander and the Greeks*. Oxford, 1938.

Griffith, G. T. (ed.). *Alexander the Great: The Main Problems*. New York, 1966.

Hogarth, D. G. *Philip and Alexander of Macedon*. London, 1897.

Pearson, L. *The Lost Histories of Alexander the Great*. London, 1960.

Radet, G. *Alexandre le Grand*. Paris, 1931.

Robinson, C. A., Jr. *The Ephemerides of Alexander's Expedition*. Providence, 1932.

———. *Alexander the Great*. New York, 1947.

———. *The History of Alexander the Great*. 2 vols. Providence, 1953–1963.

Stein, A. *On Alexander's Track to the Indus*. London, 1929.

Tarn, W. W. *Alexander the Great*. 2 vols. London, 1948.

Wheeler, B. I. *Alexander the Great*. New York, 1900.

Wilcken, U. *Alexander the Great*. New York, 1932.

THE HELLENISTIC AGE

Barker, E. *From Alexander to Constantine*. Oxford, 1956.

Bevan, E. R. *The House of Seleucus*. London, 1902.

———. *Jerusalem under the High Priests*. London, 1912.

———. *A History of Egypt under the Ptolemaic Dynasty*. London, 1927.

Bikerman, E. *Institutions des Séleucides*. Paris, 1938.

Bouché-Leclerq, A. *Histoire des Séleucides*. Paris, 1938.

Bury, J. B. *et al. The Hellenistic Age*. Cambridge, 1925.

Cardinali, G. *Il regno di Pergamo*. Rome, 1906.

Cary, M. *A History of the Greek World from 323 to 146 B.C.* London, 1963.

Debevoise, N. C. *A Political History of Parthia*. Chicago, 1938.

Dinsmoor, W. B. *The Athenian Archon List in the Light of Recent Discoveries*. New York, 1930.

———. *The Archons of Athens in the Hellenistic Age*. Cambridge, Mass., 1931.

Droysen, J. G. *Geschichte des Hellenismus*. 3 vols. Gotha, 1877–1878.

Ferguson, W. S. *Hellenistic Athens*. London, 1911.

———. *Athenian Tribal Cycles in the Hellenistic Age*. Cambridge, Mass., 1932.

Ferrabino, O. *Arato di Sicione e l'idea federale*. Florence, 1921.

Feyel, M. *Polybe et l'histoire de Béotie au III ème siècle avant notre ère*. Paris, 1942.

Frank, T. *Roman Imperialism*. New York, 1925.

Freeman, E. A. *History of Federal Government in Greece and Italy*. New York, 1893.

Hadas, M. *Hellenistic Culture*. New York, 1959.

Hansen, E. V. *The Attalids of Pergamon*. Ithaca, 1947.

Holleaux, M. *Rome, la Grèce, et les monarchies héllénistiques au III ème siècle avant J. C.* Paris, 1921.

Jouguet, P. *Macedonian Imperialism and the Hellenization of the East*. New York, 1928.

Kaerst, J. *Geschichte des Hellenismus*. Leipzig, 1926.

Lévèque, P. *Pyrrhos*. Paris, 1957.

McEwan, C. W. *The Oriental Origin of Hellenistic Kingship*. Chicago, 1934.

Macurdy, G. H. *Hellenistic Queens*. Baltimore, 1932.

Meyer, E. *Blute und Niedgergang des Hellenismus in Asien*. Berlin, 1925.

Otto, W., and Bengtson, H. *Zur Geschichte des Niederganges des Ptolemäerreiches*. Munich, 1938.

Pritchett, W. K., and Meritt, B. D. *The Chronology of Hellenistic Athens*. Cambridge, Mass., 1940.

Rawlinson, H. G. *Bactria*. London, 1912.

———. *Intercourse of India and the Western World*. Cambridge, 1916.

Rostovtzeff, M. *A Large Estate in Egypt in the Third Century*. Madison, 1922.

———. *Caravan Cities*. Oxford, 1932.

———. *The Social and Economic History of the Hellenistic World*. 3 vols. Oxford, 1941.

Tarn, W. W. *Antigonus Gonatas*. Oxford, 1913.

———. *The Greeks in Bactria and India*. Cambridge, 1938.

———, and Griffith, G. T. *Hellenistic Civilization*. 3rd ed. New York, 1952.

Tcherikover, V. *Hellenistic Civilization and the Jews*. Philadelphia, 1959.

Tillyard, H. J. W. *Agathocles*. Cambridge, 1908.

Walbank, F. W. *Aratus of Sicyon*. Cambridge, 1933.

———. *Philip V of Macedon*. Cambridge, 1940.

———. *A Historical Commentary on Polybius*. Vol. 1. Oxford, 1957.

Welles, C. B. *Royal Correspondence in the Hellenistic Period*. New Haven, 1934.

ARCHAEOLOGY, ART AND ARCHITECTURE

GENERAL

Beazley, J. D., and Ashmole, B. *Greek Sculpture and Painting*. Cambridge, 1932.
Boardman, J. *Greek Art*. New York, 1964.
Carpenter, R. *The Esthetic Basis of Greek Art*. Bloomington, 1959.
Richter, G. M. A. *The Development of Pictorial Representation from Archaic to Graeco-Roman Times*. New York, 1944.
Webster, T. B. L. *Art and Literature in Fourth Century Athens*. London, 1956.

ARCHAEOLOGY

Hill, I. T. *Ancient City of Athens*. Cambridge, Mass., 1953.
Hege, W., and Rodenwaldt, G. *The Acropolis*. Oxford, 1930.
——————. *Olympia*. London, 1936.
Judeich, W. *Topographie von Athen*. Munich, 1931.
Poulsen, F. *Delphi*. London, 1920.
Richter, G. M. A. *Ancient Furniture*. Oxford, 1926.
——. *Archaic Attic Gravestones*. Cambridge, Mass., 1944.
Weller, C. H. *Athens and Its Monuments*. New York, 1913.
Wycherley, R. E. *How the Greeks Built Cities*. 2nd ed. New York, 1962.

ARCHITECTURE

Dinsmoor, W. B. *Architecture of Ancient Greece*. 3rd ed. London, 1950.
Grinnell, I. H. *Greek Temples*. New York, 1943.
Lawrence, A. W. *Greek Architecture*. Baltimore, 1957.
Robertson, D. S. *A Handbook of Greek and Roman Architecture*. Cambridge, 1943.
Stevens, G. P., and Paton, J. M. *The Erechtheum*. Cambridge, Mass., 1927.

PAINTING

Davambez, P. *Greek Painting*. New York, 1962.
Robertson, C. M. *Greek Painting*. New York, 1959.
Swindler, M. H. *Ancient Painting*. New Haven, 1929.

SCULPTURE

Carpenter, R. *Greek Sculpture.* Chicago, 1960.

Casson, S. *The Technique of Early Greek Sculpture.* Oxford, 1933.

Corbett, P. E. *The Sculpture of the Parthenon.* Baltimore, 1959.

Hinks, R. P. *Greek and Roman Portrait-Sculpture.* London, 1935.

Johnson, F. P. *Lysippos.* Durham, 1927.

Lawrence, A. W. *Classical Sculpture.* London, 1944.

Lullies, R., and Hirmer, M. *Greek Sculpture.* New York, 1957.

Payne H., and Young, G. M. *Archaic Marble Sculpture from the Acropolis.* London, n.d.

Richter, G. M. A. *Animals in Greek Sculpture.* New York, 1930.

———. *The Sculpture and Sculptors of the Greeks.* New Haven, 1930.

———. *Kouroi.* New York, 1942.

Smith, A. H. *The Sculptures of the Parthenon.* London, 1910.

Wace, A. J. B. *An Approach to Greek Sculpture.* Cambridge, 1935.

POTTERY

Beazley, J. D. *Attic Black-Figure.* London, 1928.

———. *Attic White Lekythoi.* Oxford, 1938.

———. *Attic Red-Figure Vase-Painters.* Oxford, 1942.

———. *Potter and Painter in Ancient Athens.* London, 1946.

Cook, R. M. *Grek Painted Pottery.* London, 1960.

Lane, A. *Greek Pottery.* New York, 1949.

Richter, G. M. A. *Red-Figured Athenian Vases.* New Haven, 1936.

POLITICAL THOUGHT AND CONSTITUTIONAL HISTORY

GENERAL

Barker, E. *Greek Political Theory.* London, 1908.

Bengtson, H. *Die Staatsveträge der griechischrömischen Welt von 700 bis 338 v. Chr.* 2 vols. Munich and Berlin, 1962.

Bloom, A. *Plato's Republic.* New York, 1968.

Bonner, R. J. *Aspects of Athenian Democracy.* Berkeley, 1934.

Busolt, G., and Swoboda, H. *Griechische Staatskunde.* 2 vols. Munich, 1920, 1926.

Calhoun, G. M. *Athenian Clubs in Politics and Litigation.* Austin, 1913.

Day, J., and Chambers, M. *Aristotle's History of Athenian Democracy.* Berkeley and Los Angeles, 1962.

De Sanctis, G. *Atthis: Storia della republica ateniese.* Turin, 1912.

Ehrenberg, V. *The Greek State.* New York, 1960.

Ferguson, W. S. *Greek Imperialism.* New York, 1913.

Forrest, W. G. *The Emergence of Greek Democracy.* London, 1966.

Fritz, K. von. *Pythagorean Politics in Southern Italy.* New York, 1940.

Fuks, A. *The Ancestral Constitution.* London, 1953.

Glotz, G. *The Greek City.* New York, 1965.

Graham, A. J. *Colony and Mother City in Ancient Greece.* Manchester, 1964.

Greenidge, A. H. J. *Handbook of Greek Constitutional History.* London, 1911.

Grene, P. *Man in His Pride.* Chicago, 1950.

Havelock, E. A. *The Liberal Temper in Greek Politics.* New Haven, 1957.

Headlam, J. W. *Election by Lot at Athens.* 2nd ed. Cambridge, 1933.

Hignett, C. *History of the Athenian Constitution.* Oxford, 1952.

Hugill, W. M. *Panhellenism in Aristophanes.* Chicago, 1936.

Jones, A. H. M. *Athenian Democracy.* New York, 1957.

Kagan, D. *The Great Dialogue: A History of Greek Political Thought from Homer to Polybius.* New York, 1965.

———. *Sources in Greek Political Thought.* New York, 1965.

Kahrstedt, U. *Griechische Staatsrecht.* Gottingen, 1922.

Larsen, J. A. O. *Representative Government in Greek and Roman History.* Berkeley and Los Angeles, 1955.

McDonald, W. A. *The Political Meeting Places of the Greeks.* Baltimore, 1943.

Myres, J. L. *The Political Ideas of the Greeks.* London, 1927.

Oliver, J. H. *Demokratia, the Gods, and the Free World.* Baltimore, 1960.

Sinclair, T. A. *History of Greek Political Thought.* London, 1952.

Strauss, L. *On Tyranny.* Ithaca, 1968.

———. *The City and Man.* Chicago, 1964.

———. *Socrates and Aristophanes.* New York, 1966.

Wade-Gery, H. T. *Essays in Greek History.* London, 1958.

Whibley, L. *Greek Oligarchies.* Cambridge, 1896.

PHILOSOPHY

Adkins, A. W. H. *Merit and Responsibility: A Study in Greek Values.* New York, 1960.

Allan, D. *The Philosophy of Aristotle.* London, 1952.

Bailey, C. *Epicurus.* Oxford, 1926.

———. *The Greek Atomists and Epicurus.* Oxford, 1928.

Baldry, H. C. *The Unity of Mankind in Greek Thought.* New York, 1965.

Bevan, E. R. *Stoics and Sceptics.* New York, 1959.

Brumbaugh, R. S. *The Philosophers of Greece.* New York, 1964.

Burnet, J. *Platonism.* Berkeley, 1928.

———. *Early Greek Philosophy.* 4th ed. London, 1930.

Cherniss, H. F. *Aristotle's Criticism of the Pre-Socratics.* Baltimore, 1935.

———. *Aristotle's Criticism of Plato and the Academy.* Baltimore, 1944.

———. *The Riddle of the Early Academy.* Stanford, 1954.

Chroust, A. H. *Socrates, Man and Myth.* London, 1957.

Cornford, F. M. *From Religion to Philosophy.* New York, 1912.

———. *Before and After Socrates.* London, 1950.

Dudley, D. R. *A History of Cynicism from Diogenes to the Sixth Century A.D.* London, 1937.

Friedländer, P. *Plato I. An Introduction.* New York, 1958.

Gomperz, T. *The Greek Thinkers.* 4 vols. London, 1912–20.

Green, W. C. *Moira, Fate, Good, and Evil in Greek Thought.* Cambridge, Mass., 1944.

Grube, R. M. A. *Plato's Thought.* London, 1935.

Guthrie, W. K. C. *A History of Greek Philosophy.* Vols. 1–2. Cambridge, 1962–1965.

Havelock, E. A. *Preface to Plato.* Cambridge, Mass., 1963.

Hicks, R. D. *Stoic and Epicurean.* London, 1910.

Jaeger, W. *Aristotle: Fundamentals of the History of his Development.* Oxford, 1934.

———. *Early Christianity and Greek Paideia.* Cambridge, Mass., 1962.

Kahn, C. H. *Anaximander and the Origins of Greek Cosmology.* New York, 1960.

Kirk, G. S. *Heraclitus: the Cosmic Fragments.* Cambridge, 1954.

———, and Raven, J. E. *The Presocratic Philosophers.* Cambridge, 1960.

Levinson, R. B. *In Defense of Plato.* Cambridge, 1954.

More, P. E. *Hellenistic Philosophies.* Princeton, 1923.

Morrow, G. R. *Plato's Cretan City.* Princeton, 1960.

Randall, J. H., Jr. *Aristotle.* New York, 1962.

Raven, J. E. *Pythagoreans and Eleatics.* Cambridge, 1948.

Robinson, R. *Plato's Earlier Dialectic.* 2nd ed. Oxford, 1953.

Ross, W. D. *Aristotle.* London, 1955.

Shorey, P. *What Plato Said.* Chicago, 1933.

———. *Platonism, Ancient and Modern.* Berkeley, 1938.

Snell, B. *The Discovery of the Mind.* New York, 1960.

Solmsen, F. *Aristotle's Natural World.* Ithaca, 1963.

Taylor, A. E. *Plato: The Man and His Work.* New York, 1927.

———. *Socrates.* New York, 1933.

———. *Plato, The Man and his Work,* 6th ed. New York, 1952.

Untersteiner, M. *The Sophists.* New York, 1954.

Wenley, R. M. *Stoicism and Its Influence.* New York, 1925.

Wheelwright, P. *Heraclitus.* Princeton, 1959.

Wilamowitz-Moellendorff, U. von. *Aristoteles und Athen.* Berlin, 1893.

———. *Der Glaube der Hellenen.* Berlin, 1931–32.

Zeller, E. *The Stoics, Epicureans, and Sceptics.* London, 1880.

LITERATURE

General

Bowra, C. M. *Ancient Greek Literature.* New York, 1960.

Christ, W. von, Schmid, W., and Stählin, O. *Geschichte der griechischen Literatur.* Munich, 1912–1924.

Croiset, A., and Croiset, M. *Histoire de la littérature grecque.* Paris, 1910–1921.

Finley, J. H., Jr. *Pindar and Aeschylus.* Cambridge, Mass., 1955.

Gomme, A. W. *Essays in Greek Literature and History.* Oxford, 1937.

Hadas, M. *History of Greek Literature.* New York, 1950.

Kenyon, F. G. *Books and Readers in Ancient Greece and Rome.* London, 1951.

Lesky, A. *A History of Greek Literature.* 2nd ed. New York, 1963.

Solmsen, F. *Hesiod and Aeschylus.* Ithaca, 1949.

Thompson, J. W. *Ancient Libraries.* Berkeley, 1940.

Lyric Poetry, etc.

Bowra, C. M. *Early Greek Elegists.* Cambridge, Mass., 1938.

———. *Greek Lyric Poetry from Alcman to Simonides.* 2nd ed. London, 1961.

———. *Pindar.* New York, 1964.

Carrière, J. *Théognis de Mégare.* Paris, 1949.

Couat, A. *Alexandrian Poetry under the First Three Ptolemies.* New York, 1931.

Farnell, L. R. *The Works of Pindar.* 3 vols. London, 1930.

Harrison, E. *Studies in Theognis.* Cambridge, 1902.

Korte, A. *Hellenistic Poetry.* New York, 1929.

Norwood, G. *Pindar*. Berkeley, 1945.
Page, D. L. *Alcman: The Partheneion*. London, 1951.
——. *Sappho and Alcaeus*. New York, 1955.
Van Groningen, B. A. *Pindare au Banquet*. Leiden, 1960.
Wilamowitz-Moellendorff, U. von. *Hellenistische Dichtung in der Zeit des Kallimachos*. Berlin, 1924.

Tragedy

Bieber, M. *The History of the Greek and Roman Theatre*. 2nd ed. Princeton, 1961.
Flickinger, R. C. *The Greek Theater and Its Drama*. Chicago, 1936.
Grube, G. M. A. *The Drama of Euripides*. London, 1941.
Jones, J. *On Aristotle and Greek Tragedy*. London, 1962.
Kirkwood, G. M. *A Study of Sophoclean Drama*. Ithaca, 1958.
Kitto, H. D. F. *Greek Tragedy*. New York, 1954.
——. *Form and Meaning in Drama*. New York, 1957.
——. *Sophocles: Dramatist and Philosopher*. London, 1958.
Knox, B. M. W. *Oedipus at Thebes*. New Haven, 1957.
——. *The Heroic Temper: Studies In Sophoclean Tragedy*. Berkeley, 1964.
Murray, G. *Euripides and His Age*. New York, 1913.
——. *Aeschylus, the Creator of Tragedy*. New York, 1940.
Norwood, G. *Greek Tragedy*. London, 1920.
Pickard-Cambridge, W. W. *Dithyramb, Tragedy and Comedy*. 2nd ed. Rev. by T. B. L. Webster. New York, 1962.
Reinhardt, K. *Sophokles*. Frankfurt, 1947.
Thomson, G. *Aeschylus and Athens*. London, 1941.
Verrall, A. W. *Euripides the Rationalist*. Cambridge, 1913.
Waldock, A. J. A. *Sophocles the Dramatist*. Cambridge, 1951.
Webster, T. B. L. *Greek Theatre Production*. New York, 1956.
Whitman, Cedric H. *Sophocles: A Study of Heroic Humanism*. Cambridge, Mass., 1951.

Comedy

Cornford, F. M. *The Origin of Attic Comedy*. New York, 1961.
Murray, G. *Aristophanes*. Oxford, 1933.
Norwood, G. *Greek Comedy*. London, 1931.
Webster, T. B. L. *Studies in Menander*. Manchester, 1950.
Whitman, C. H. *Aristophanes and the Comic Hero*. Cambridge, Mass., 1964.

History

Abbott, G. F. *Thucydides: A Study in Historical Reality*. London, 1925.
Adcock, F. E. *Thucydides and his History*. Cambridge, 1963.
Barber, G. L. *The Historian Ephorus*. Cambridge, 1935.
Bury, J. B. *Ancient Greek Historians*. New York, 1957.
Cochrane, C. N. *Thucydides and the Science of History*. Oxford, 1929.
Cornford, F. M. *Thucydides Mythistoricus*. New York, 1907.
Delebecque, F. *Essai sur la vie de Xénophon*. Paris, 1957.
De Selincourt, A. *The World of Herodotus*. Boston, 1962.
Finley, J. H., Jr. *Thucydides*. Cambridge, Mass., 1942.
Glover, R. R. *Herodotus*. Berkeley, 1924.
How, W. W., and Wells, J. *Commentary on Herodotus*. 2 vols. Oxford, 1912.
Immerwahr, H. R. *Form and Thought in Herodotus*. Cleveland, 1966.
Jacoby, F. *Atthis*. Oxford, 1949.
Macan, R. W. *Herodotus, The Fourth, Fifth and Sixth Books*. 2 vols. London, 1895.
———. *Herodotus, The Seventh, Eighth and Ninth Books*. 2 vols. London, 1908.
Momigliano, A. *Studies in Historiography*. London, 1966.
Pearson, L. *Early Ionian Historians*. Oxford, 1939.
Powell, J. E. *The History of Herodotus*. Cambridge, 1939.
Romilly, H. de. *Thucydides and Athenian Imperialism*. English Translation. Oxford, 1963.
Stahl, H. P. *Thukydides*. Munich, 1966.
Wells, J. *Studies in Herodotus*. Oxford, 1923.

Rhetoric

Adams, C. D. *Demosthenes and His Influence*. New York, 1927.
Jebb, R. C. *The Attic Orators*. London, 1893.
Kennedy, G. *The Art of Persuasion in Greece*. Princeton, 1963.
Roberts, W. R. *Greek Rhetoric and Literary Criticism*. New York, 1928.

Science

Brock, A. J. *Greek Medicine*. New York, 1929.
Cohen, M. R., and Drabkin, I. E. *Source Book in Greek Science*. Cambridge, Mass., 1958.
Edelstein, L. *The Hippocratic Oath. Text, Translation and Interpretation*. Baltimore, 1943.

Farrington, B. *Science and Politics in the Ancient World*. London, 1939.
———. *Greek Science*. Baltimore, 1953.
Clagett, M. *Greek Science in Antiquity*. New York, 1963.
Heath, T. L. *Archimedes*. London, 1920.
———. *Aristarchus of Samos*. Oxford, 1920.
———. *A History of Greek Mathematics*. Oxford, 1921.
———. *Manual of Greek Mathematics*. Oxford, 1931.
Hort, A. *Theophrastus, Enquiry into Plants*. London, 1916.
Neugebauer, O. *The Exact Sciences of Antiquity*. Copenhagen, 1951.
Sambursky, S. *The Physical World of the Greeks*. New York, 1956.
Singer, C. *Greek Biology and Greek Medicine*. New York, 1922.

Religion

Bevan, E. R. *Later Greek Religion*. New York, 1927.
Cook, A. B. *Zeus*. 3 vols. Cambridge, 1914–1940.
Cornford, F. M. *Greek Religious Thought from Homer to the Age of Alexander*. New York, 1923.
Deubner, L. A. *Attische Feste*. Berlin, 1932.
Dodds, E. R. *The Greeks and the Irrational*. Berkeley, 1951.
Farnell, L. R. *The Cults of the Greek States*. 5 vols. Oxford, 1896–1909.
———. *Greek Hero Cults and Ideas of Immortality*. Oxford, 1921.
Festugière, A. J. *Personal Religion among the Greeks*. Berkeley, 1960.
Goodenough, E. R. *By Light, Light: The Mystic Gospel of Hellenistic Judaism*. New Haven, 1935.
Guthrie, W. K. C. *Orpheus and Greek Religion*. London, 1935.
———. *The Greeks and Their Gods*. Boston, 1965.
Murray, G. *Five Stages of Greek Religion*. New York, 1955.
Nilsson, M. P. *The Minoan-Mycenaean Religion and Its Survival in Greek Religion*. Oxford, 1927.
———. *Greek Popular Religion*. New York, 1940.
———. *History of Greek Religion*. 2nd ed. Oxford, 1949.
Parke, H. W. *The Oracles of Zeus*. London, 1967.
———, and Wormell, D. E. W. *The Delphic Oracle*. New York, 1956.
Rose, H. J. *Gods and Heroes of the Greeks*. London, 1957.
———. *Handbook of Greek Mythology*. 6th ed. New York, 1960.

Society and Economics

Andreades, A. *A History of Greek Public Finance*. Cambridge, Mass., 1933.
Calhoun, G. M. *The Business Life of Ancient Athens*. Chicago, 1926.
Cavaignac, E. *L'Économie grecque*. Paris, 1951.

Diller, A. *Race Mixture among the Greeks Before Alexander*. Urbana, 1937.

Ehrenberg, V. *The People of Aristophanes. A Sociology of Old Attic Comedy*. Oxford, 1943.

Fine, J. V. A. *Horoi, Studies in Mortgages, Real Security and Land Tenure in Ancient Athens*. Princeton, 1951.

Finley, M. I. (ed.). *Slavery in Antiquity*. Cambridge, 1960.

Francotte, H. *Les Finances des cités grecques*. Paris, 1909.

Freeman, K. J. *Schools of Hellas*. 3rd ed. London, 1922.

French, A. *The Growth of the Athenian Economy*. London, 1964.

Gardiner, E. N. *Athletics of the Ancient World*. Oxford, 1930.

Glotz, G. *Ancient Greece at Work*. New York, 1926.

Gomme, A. W. *The Population of Athens in the Fifth and Fourth Centuries*. Oxford, 1933.

Guiraud, P. *La Propriété foncière en Grèce jusqu'à la conquête romaine*. Paris, 1893.

Hasebroek, J. *Trade and Politics in Ancient Greece*. London, 1933.

Heichelheim, F. W. *An Economic History of the Ancient World*. Leiden, 1958, 1964.

Hill, D. K. *Ancient Greek Dress*. Baltimore, 1945.

Jaeger, W. *Paideia*. 3 vols. New York, 1939–1944.

Licht, H. *Sexual Life in Ancient Greece*. New York, 1932.

Marrou, H. I. *History of Education in Antiquity*. New York, 1956.

Michell, H. *The Economics of Ancient Greece*. 2nd ed. New York, 1963.

Ormerod, H. A. *Piracy in the Ancient World*. London, 1924.

Poehlman, R. von. *Geschichte der sozialen Frage und des Sozialismus in der antiken Welt*. Munich, 1925.

Quennell, M., and C. H. B. *Everyday Things in Classical Greece*. London, 1932.

Rider, B. C. *The Greek House*. Cambridge, 1916.

Robinson, C. E. *Everyday life in Ancient Greece*. Oxford, 1933.

Sachs, C. *The Size of the Slave Population at Athens during the Fifth and Fourth Centuries B.C.* Urbana, 1924.

Stow, H. H. *Greek Athletics and Festivals in the Fifth Century*. Boston, 1939.

Toutain, J. *The Economic Life of the Ancient World*. New York, 1930.

Trever, A. A. *A History of Greek Economic Thought*. Chicago, 1916.

Westermann, W. C. *The Slave System of Greek and Roman Antiquity*. Philadelphia, 1955.

Will, E. *Doriens et Ioniens*. Paris, 1956.

Law

Bonner, R. J. *Lawyers and Litigants in Ancient Athens.* Chicago, 1927.
————, and Smith, G. *The Administration of Justice from Homer to Aristotle.* 2 vols. Chicago, 1930–38.
Calabi, I. *Ricerche sui rapporti tra le poleis.* Florence, 1952.
Calhoun, G. M. *The Growth of Criminal Law in Ancient Greece.* Berkeley, 1927.
Jones, J. W. *Law and Legal Theory of the Greeks.* Oxford, 1952.
Martin, V. *La Vie internationale dans la Grèce des cités.* Paris, 1940.
Tenekides, R. *La notion juridique d'independance et la tradition héllénique d'autonomie et fédéralisme aux Ve et IVe siècles av. J. C.* Athens, 1954.
Tod, M. N. *International Arbitration Amongst the Greeks.* Oxford, 1913.
Vinogradoff, P. *Outlines of Historical Jurisprudence. Vol. II, The Jurisprudence of the Greek City.* Oxford, 1922.

Military and Naval Affairs

Adcock, F. E. *The Greek and Macedonian Art of War.* Berkeley, 1957.
Casson, L. *The Ancient Mariners, Seafarers and Sea Fighters of the Mediterranean in Ancient Times.* New York, 1959.
Delbrück, H. *Geschichte der Kriegskunst.* Berlin, 1920.
Griffith, G. T. *The Mercenaries of the Hellenistic World.* Cambridge, 1935.
Köster, A. *Das Antike Seewesen.* Berlin, 1923.
Kromayer, J., and Veith, G. *Antike Schlachtfelder in Griechenland.* Berlin, 1903–1929.
Parke, H. W. *Greek Mercenary Soldiers from the Earliest Times to the Battle of Ipsus.* Oxford, 1933.
Rodgers, W. L. *Greek and Roman Naval Warfare.* Annapolis, 1937.
Snodgrass, A. E. *Early Greek Armour and Weapons.* Edinburgh, 1964.
Tarn, W. W. *Hellenistic Military and Naval Developments.* Cambridge, 1930.

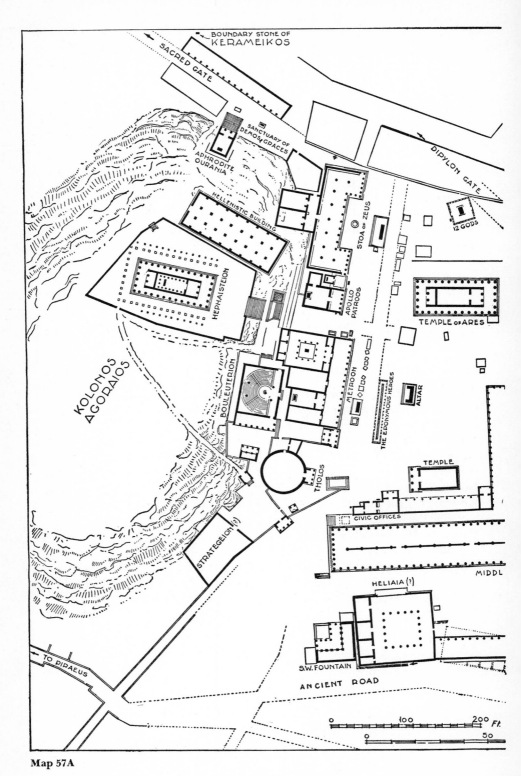

Map 57A

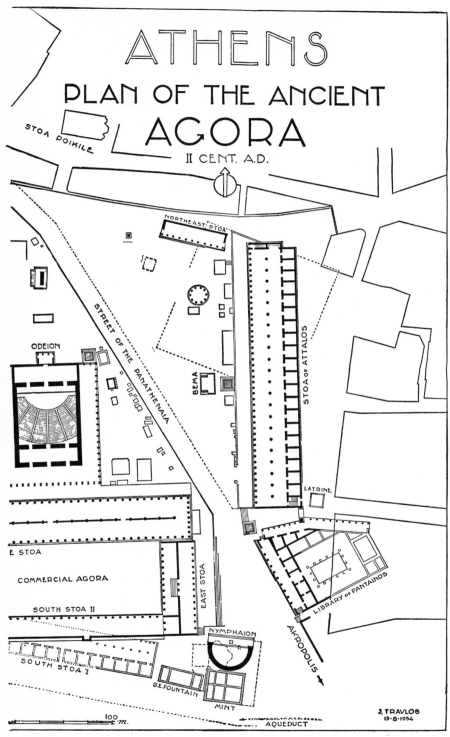

ATHENS
PLAN OF THE ANCIENT
AGORA
II CENT. A.D.

STOA POIKILE

NORTHEAST STOA

STREET OF THE PANATHENAIA

ODEION

BEMA

STOA OF ATTALOS

LATRINE

E STOA

COMMERCIAL AGORA

SOUTH STOA II

EAST STOA

LIBRARY OF PANTAINOS

NYMPHAION

AKROPOLIS

SOUTH STOA I

S.E. FOUNTAIN

MINT

100 m.

AQUEDUCT

J. TRAVLOS
13·8·1954

Map 57B

497

APPENDIX

THE ATHENIAN AGORA

Scholars have long known that the Agora, or market place—the center of the political, commercial, and social life of ancient Athens—lay in the broad hollow north of the Acropolis and Areopagus and east of the Hill of Colonus Agoraeus, where the marble temple of Hephaestus stands (Map 38, p. 247, Diagram 39, p. 249; and Figures 65, 66, and 70). It was not until 1931, however, that extensive and sustained excavation of the site was undertaken, at which time the American School of Classical Studies at Athens bought twenty-six acres in the middle of the busy city with the help of Mr. John D. Rockefeller, Jr. and the Rockefeller Foundation. Modern houses, occupying 350 pieces of property, were torn down, and 300,000 tons of earth were then removed. When the excavation, going down in places through an accumulation of 40 feet (including cemeteries antedating the fifth century B.C.) and 5,000 years of history (to the Neolithic Age), was completed on a large scale in 1954, the civic center of the cultural capital of antiquity had been laid bare. The work of the American School of Classical Studies represents a triumph of scholarship, and further detailed study of the site, together with its publication, will take many more years. The civic and religious buildings, the coins, sculpture, pottery (Figure 20), and other antiquities (Figure 64) that have been found give lifeblood to our understanding of Athens. Over 60,000 catalogued objects alone have been recovered, among them valuable inscriptions. The Stoa of Attalus has been restored as a museum for these objects.

The Agora was a precinct marked out by boundary stones and provided with basins of holy water whereby one purified himself on entering; criminals were barred. Bearing in mind our preliminary remarks on p. 246 f., and map 57 on pp. 496–497, let us first note the important governmental buildings on the west side of the square. Most fortunately, we now possess the Bouleuterion, or Council House, where the Council of Five Hundred (*boule*) held its meetings and prepared the legislation for the Assembly (*ecclesia*). It will be recalled (pp. 96, 194 f.) that the *boule* consisted of fifty men from each of the ten tribes, chosen by allotment (cf. p. 194) each year. These tribal groups of fifty served in monthly succession as group Chairmen (*prytaneis*) of the *boule;* they ate in the Tholos, the circular building next door, and arranged the meetings of the *boule* and *ecclesia.* Indeed, one third of the *prytaneis* slept at night in the Tholos, so that responsible officials were always on hand. The Tholos was thus the headquarters of the Athenian government; it was also the seat of various cults connected with civic life and contained, among other things, the official standards of weights and measures. In front of the Bouleuterion stands the Metroön, which accommodated both the sanctuary of the Mother of the Gods and the state archives, written on papyrus and parchment. Public notices were posted on the base of the Peribolos of the Eponymous Heroes, a sanctuary just east of the Metroön and containing statues of the traditional patrons of the ten tribes. Legend says that the common father of the entire Ionian race, to which the Athenians belonged, was Ion, and *his* father, Apollo, was celebrated by the neighboring temple of Apollo Patroös. To the north is the Stoa of Zeus, which honored Zeus in his role as savior of the Athenians from the Persians; a place of business, it was also famous for its paintings and as the spot where Socrates (Figure 88) discussed philosophy with his friends. Public documents, such as the law codes of Draco and Solon, were set up here.

Altars, temples and government buildings, a speaker's platform (bema), shady stoas (p. 179, Note), a multitude of statues and monuments dotted the Agora, as did more ordinary reminders of everyday

Reference map of

ANCIENT GREECE

Scale of Miles

0   100

Map 59

500

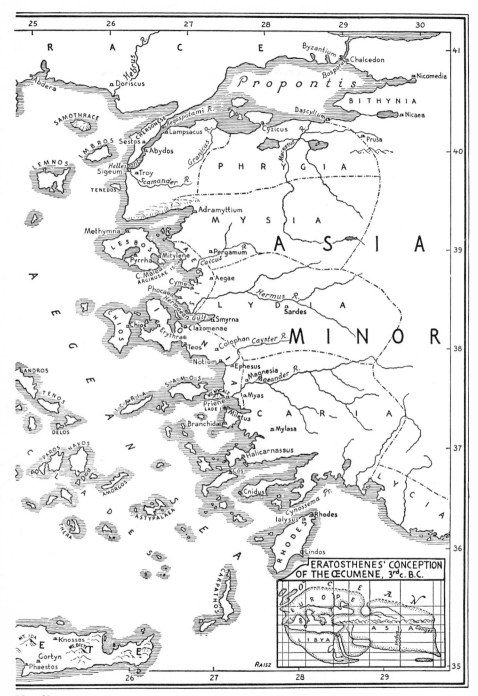

Map 60

life, such as markets and water clocks and the humble homes of artisans and their workshops. Toward the south side have been uncovered two important buildings, which round out our picture of the functioning of Athenian government. One of these is apparently the Strategeion, the headquarters of the ten annually elected *strategoi* (generals), the highest officials in the state. The second is the Heliaea, the largest Athenian law court. Figure 64 shows a dicast's (juror's) ticket and ballots—a solid hub for acquittal (marked with E to denote the number of the dicastic section), a pierced hub for conviction (inscribed with the official designation "State Ballot")—together with a dicast's water clock (*klepsydra*) in action. The klepsydra was used to time speeches in the law courts. The XX indicates that the contents measure 2 choes (6.4 litres), the time (six minutes) allotted for the rebuttal speech in suits involving sums up to 5,000 drachmas. The name Antiochis refers to the tribe of the *prytaneis* in office at the time of use.

The strictly commercial life of the Agora was concentrated in the area south of the Middle Stoa and was controlled from the Civic Offices. Other significant buildings in this neighborhood include the Mint, the Arsenal, and the Library of Pantainos (with its inscription, "No book may be taken out. The Library will be open from morning to midday"). Dramatic competitions and athletic festivals were held in the open and well-drained square—the central part of the Agora, just north of the Middle Stoa—until Augustus' famous lieutenant, Agrippa, erected an Odeon there, a roofed structure for theatrical performances seating 1,000 persons; later, the University of Athens was built over the site, to be closed eventually, with all Schools of Philosophy, by the Emperor Justinian in 529 A.D. The east side of the square—across from the Tholos and other governmental buildings—was graced by yet another gift to the city, the Stoa of Attalus, King of Pergamum (159–138 B.C.); as a young prince, he had studied in Athens under Carneades, the head of the New Academy, and was an honorary citizen. The rental of the Stoa's shops (twenty-one on each of two floors) produced income for the city (Figure 113). As the fountain houses, wells, and cisterns attest, the Agora had a good supply of water. Willows and plane trees shaded the Street of the Panathenaia. The annual Panathenaic procession in honor of Athena, immortalized on the Parthenon frieze (Figures 72, 73), assembled near the Dipylon Gate and followed this Street across the Agora and up to the Acropolis. After the sack of the Agora by the Herulians in 267 A.D., silt from the adjacent hills buried the area, and, except for brief revivals, habitation was not really resumed until the tenth century. We have modern scholarship to thank for this dramatic recovery of the community center of a great imperial democracy.

INDEX

A

Abdera, 126

Abydos, naval engagement at, 351

Academy of Plato, 368, 371, 448

Acarnania, Acarnanians, 57, 301

Achaea, 40; under Athenian Empire, 184, 186; under Thirty Years' Peace, 190; under Thebes, 286; alliance with Athens, 301; as a Roman province, 460

Achaean League, 393–6; and Sparta, 458, 459

Achaeans, ch. II, 48; as colonists, 67

Achaeus, king of Asia Minor, 401, 456

Achilles, 47; and Alexander, 306, 308, 315, 341

Achradina, 164

Acragas (Agrigentum), 68, 170, 289; under Theron, 164; Olympieum, 177

Acrocorinth, 61; besieged by Cleomenes III, 397

Acropolis of Athens, early settlements on, 36, 85; Opisthodomus (Old Temple of Athena?), 203; buildings of the fifth century on, 252–6

Actium, battle of, 460

Ada, queen of Caria, 316

Adonis, cult of, 258, 415

Adrastus, cult of, 73

Aegina, 28, 82, 170; industries and commerce, 61, 70; Aeginetan standard, 71, 90; during Persian Wars, 131, 138; under Athenian Empire, 183–6, 204; under Thirty Years' Peace, 190; temple at, 116, 170, 177

ALEXANDER'S EMPIRE

MILES 0 50 100   200   300   400

Allied Territory   Independent States

Subject Territory   • • • Route of Alexander

Borysthenes R.

Don R.

Olbia

Lake Maeotis

BLACK SEA

Phanagoria

Danube R.

THRACE

MACEDON

Byzantium

Calchedon

BITHYNIA

Sinope

Phasis

Thessalonica

Pella

Pydna

Amphipolis

Abdera

Lysimachia

Heraclea

Nicomedia

PAPHLAGONIA

Amasia

Trapezus

EPIRUS

THESSALY

AEGEAN SEA

LEMNOS

Pergamum

LESBOS

Cyzicus

Ancyra

Gordium

CAPPADOCIA

Halys R.

ARMENIA

CORCYRA

PELOPONNESUS

Delphi

Thebes

Athens

Corinth

CHIOS

Sardes

Ipsus

PHRYGIA

Iconium

Megalopolis

Sparta

Smyrna

Magnesia

Ephesus

Miletus

CARIA

PISIDIA

LYCAONIA

Tarsus

CILICIA

Issus

Zeugma

Nisibis

Gaugamela

Arbela

Halicarnassus

Gortyn

RHODES

LYCIA

Antioch

ASSYRIA

CRETE

Euphrates R.

Tigris R.

MEDITERRANEAN

SEA

Paphos

Salamis

Citium

Apamea

Palmyra

Dura

MESOPOTAMIA

Ctesiphon

CYPRUS

SYRIA

Ptolemais

Cyrene

Byblos

Sidon

Damascus

Seleucia

CYRENAICA

PHOENICIA

Tyre

Babylon

BABYLON

Naucratis

Alexandria

Gaza

Samaria

Pelusium

Jerusalem

PALESTINE

Oasis of Siwah

Memphis

Arsinoe

Oxyrhynchus

SINAI

EGYPT

Nile R.

Ptolemais

Myos Hormos

ARABIA

LIBYA

Thebes

RED SEA

Syene

Berenice